Microsoft

Windows Server Inside Out

Updated for Windows Server 2025

Orin Thomas

Windows Server Inside Out: Updated for Windows Server 2025
Published with the authorization of Microsoft Corporation by:
Pearson Education, Inc.

Copyright © 2026 by Orin Thomas

Hoboken, New Jersey

All rights reserved. This publication is protected by copyright, and permission must be obtained from the publisher prior to any prohibited reproduction, storage in a retrieval system, or transmission in any form or by any means, electronic, mechanical, photocopying, recording, or likewise. For information regarding permissions, request forms, and the appropriate contacts within the Pearson Education Global Rights & Permissions Department, please visit *www.pearson.com/global-permission-granting.html*.

No patent liability is assumed with respect to the use of the information contained herein. Although every precaution has been taken in the preparation of this book, the publisher and author assume no responsibility for errors or omissions. Nor is any liability assumed for damages resulting from the use of the information contained herein.

ISBN-13: 978-0-13-534589-4
ISBN-10: 0-13-534589-8

Library of Congress Control Number: 2025949234
1 2025

Trademarks
Microsoft and the trademarks listed at *http://www.microsoft.com* on the "Trademarks" webpage are trademarks of the Microsoft group of companies. All other marks are property of their respective owners.

Warning and Disclaimer
Every effort has been made to make this book as complete and as accurate as possible, but no warranty or fitness is implied. The information provided is on an "as is" basis. The author, the publisher, and Microsoft Corporation shall have neither liability nor responsibility to any person or entity with respect to any loss or damages arising from the information contained in this book or from the use of the programs accompanying it.

Program Manager: Loretta Yates
Acquisitions Editor: Shourav Bose
Development Editor: Rick Kughen
Managing Editor: Sandra Schroeder
Senior Project Editor: Charlotte Kughen
Copy Editor: Charlotte Kughen
Indexer: Cheryl Lenser
Technical Editor: Vince Averello
Cover Designer: Twist Creative, Seattle
Compositor: Bronkella Publishing, Inc.

Figure Credits
Figure 26-1: © 2025 Ollama
Figure 26-2: BrainDrive LLC
Figure 26-4 to 26-6: Copyright © 2025 Open WebUI

Contents at a Glance

Table of Contents

About the Author

Orin Thomas is a Principal Cloud Advocate at Microsoft. A recognized cloud and data center subject matter expert, he has written more than 40 books for Microsoft Press and has been writing books on Windows Server for more than 20 years. He works with the Windows Server product group at Microsoft to create product documentation and training materials. He is the architect of the Windows Server Hybrid Administrator Associate certification.

Acknowledgments

I'd like to thank Shourav Bose, Rick and Charlotte Kughen, Vince Averello, and Loretta Yates for the assistance they provided in bringing this text to print. For the last seven years, I've been working with the Windows Server product team and other people at Microsoft and can't express how useful it has been to seek the advice of Ned Pyle, Jeff Woolsey, Robin Harwood, Dan Cuomo, Rob Hindman, Ben Armstrong, James Seymour, Tony Jamieson, Rob Barefoot, Elden Christiensen, Theo Tran, Yash Shekar, Rick Claus, and too many others to note. Their help has been invaluable for helping me understand and know how to explain Windows Server and other Microsoft technologies.

Finally my endless and eternal gratitude and love to my beautiful partner, Lynette.

Introduction

This book is primarily written for IT professionals who work with Windows Server operating systems on a regular basis. As such, it's likely that Windows Server 2025 isn't the first version of Windows Server that you've been responsible for managing. This is because the majority of Windows Server administrators have been working with some version of the operating system for more than a decade, with a good percentage having experience going back to the days of Windows NT 4.

This book is also written under the assumption that as an experienced IT professional, you know how to use a search engine or LLM chatbot to find relevant technical information. This leads to an obvious question: "Why would I buy a book if I can find relevant technical information by asking an LLM to explain this to me?" The answer is that even though you may be good at tracking down technical information and have experience filtering useful knowledge from wildly inaccurate guesses, you can only ask an AI for information about something if you have an idea about it in the first place. In Douglas Adam's *Hitchhiker's Guide to the Galaxy*, Deep Thought—the ultimate AI mega-computer—after eons of cogitation, provided the famous answer 42. When asked to provide some context as to what 42 actually meant, Deep Thought had to design an even bigger computer to be built by the planet engineers of Magrathea to calculate the nature of the actual question. This all is a roundabout way of saying if you don't know about a role, feature, or bit of functionality, how can you ask an LLM to explain it to you? Just by flipping through the pages of this book, you're likely to encounter things you weren't aware of and wouldn't have thought to ask about.

When presenting at conferences and user groups on Windows Server topics, I regularly encounter IT professionals who have worked with Windows Server for many years who are unaware of specific functionality or techniques related to the product, even if that functionality or technique has been available for many years. This can even be true with people I work with on the Windows Server product team who are deeply knowledgeable about their specific role or service but might not know much about other functionality they haven't worked on. This is because Windows Server includes so many roles, features, and moving parts that you're unlikely to know everything about the operating system.

My aim with this book is to give you comprehensive coverage so that you'll learn things that you didn't know or simply missed, possibly because when you've been solving a critical problem, you've been focused on the specifics of that problem and haven't had time to explore every facet of what the Windows Server operating system is capable of. I'm constantly adding new things to my notes as I learn them, and even though I've been writing Windows Server books for more than 20 years and published several million words on the subject, there are still interesting facets of Windows Server that I and members of the product team discover on a regular basis.

Notes on mature roles and features

Windows Server includes a large number of roles and features that no longer receive substantive updates but are still supported for the lifetime of the server. Sometimes these features are listed as deprecated. Deprecated features are still in the operating system but may be removed at some point in the future. It's important to note that if the operating system ships with a feature, it will be supported for the lifetime of the operating system.

Although a role or feature may be deprecated, it doesn't mean it's going away. WINS is still in the operating system, and it's fair to say that few organizations have needed that functionality for more than 20 years.

Other features have reached a level of maturity where there really isn't much more that needs to be added. We're more likely to see improvements in Hyper-V and Active Directory in future releases of Windows Server than we are to see any changes in services like DHCP, basic file shares, and DNS. Over the coming years and decades, we'll see incremental, rather than revolutionary, improvements to Windows Server.

Conventions

The following conventions are used in this book:

- **Boldface** type is used to indicate text that you type.

- *Italic* type is used to indicate new terms, measures, calculated columns, tables, and database names.

- The first letters of the names of dialogs, dialog elements, and commands are capitalized. For example, the Save As dialog.

- The names of ribbon tabs are given in ALL CAPS.

- Keyboard shortcuts are indicated by a plus sign (+) separating the key names. For example, Ctrl+Alt+Delete means that you press the Ctrl, Alt, and Delete keys at the same time.

Errata, updates, and book support

We have made every effort to ensure the accuracy of this book and of its companion content. If you find an error, please submit it to us at

MicrosoftPressStore.com/windowsinsideout/errata

If you discover an error that is not already listed, please submit it to us at the same page.

For additional book support and information, please visit

MicrosoftPressStore.com/Support

Please note that product support for Microsoft software and hardware is not offered through the previous addresses. For help with Microsoft software or hardware, go to

support.microsoft.com.

Administration tools

Windows Server includes a variety of administration tools built into the operating system or available through tools like WinGet. A challenge for administrators is that no one set of administration tools is complete and does everything. To get your job done, you'll find yourself switching from tools like Windows Admin Center to perform tasks on more recently released features like storage migration services and having to go back to the old school Microsoft Management Consoles if you want to manage roles like Active Directory Certificate Services. With Windows Server, there is no "one size fits all," and you will always need to look for the tool that does the task you need to do, and to understand that that tool might not be the one that is the most recently released.

If there were such a thing, Microsoft's general systems administration philosophy might be characterized as that while you can do almost everything with a graphical console such as Windows Admin Center, Active Directory Administrative Center, or the Server Manager console, any task that you do repeatedly should be automated using PowerShell. While getting automation right could be time-consuming in the past, with the rise of generative AI tools, including various copilots and LLM chatbots, automating most Windows Server tasks with PowerShell is a lot less time-intensive today.

Another Microsoft recommended practice is that you should perform almost all administration tasks remotely using "fan out administration" rather than performing tasks locally on each server.

This chapter looks at how you can perform administration tasks remotely, what to consider when putting together your remote administration toolkit, and the various tools that you can use to remotely administer the Windows Server operating system.

CHAPTER 1

Remote not local

You can perform most Windows Server administration tasks remotely. You should avoid signing in to each server individually using Remote Desktop and firing up the console that is relevant to the role or feature that you want to manage. You should also avoid using Remote Desktop to connect to a server just to run a PowerShell script.

The main reason you should avoid Remote Desktop is that it only allows you to interact with one server at a time. Consider the amount of time that it takes to perform a task, such as configuring a service to use a group-managed service account across 100 different servers. If you were doing it using remote desktop, you'd have to connect to each server individually, change the password, sign off, and move on to the next server. If you were doing it using a tool, such as leveraging PowerShell's remote functionality, you might be able to accomplish the same goal with a single script that you could write and execute in a fraction of the time.

Inside OUT

Automate where possible

Automate your tasks where possible and when it makes sense. Understand that you won't be able to automate everything. Concentrate on automating what you can. In the long run, automation will reduce the amount of time that you spend on tasks that you know how to do. Generative AI is exceptionally useful at creating first drafts of automation scripts, so once you decide to automate a process, try using generative AI to create a first draft and then test and iterate from there. Automating as much as possible will also allow you to spend more time figuring out how to perform those complex tasks that resist automation.

Principle of least privilege

The principle of least privilege is that you should only grant the minimum necessary privileges to a security principal that are needed to perform required tasks. A very bad habit of many IT professionals is to simply add accounts to the local Administrators group on the computer where the access is required to ensure that whatever account they use can perform any task they might need to perform.

Rather than using the default built-in Administrator account or having everyone in the IT team's accounts be members of the Domain Admins group, least privilege is the practice of assigning only the minimum required privileges to an account for the account to perform its assigned tasks.

The benefit of using least privilege is that in the event that an attacker manages to compromise an account, that attacker is limited to acting with the privileges assigned to that account. Least-privilege also reduces the chance that damage might inadvertently be done to a system. For example, an account used for backup and recovery can't be used to add or remove software from the server if that account doesn't have permission to do anything beyond backup and recovery.

Inside OUT

Day-to-day accounts

IT operations staff and developers in your organization should have separate accounts for performing day-to-day activities, such as reading email, browsing the Internet, and filling in TPS reports. The day-to-day accounts of IT operations staff and developers should not have local administrative privileges. Should a change in the configuration of IT staff workstations need to occur, a specific privileged account that exists to perform that task should be used. In highly secure and well-resourced organizations, privileged accounts can only be used on special privileged-access workstations (PAWs). These workstations are locked down using technologies such as Device Guard and Credential Guard, which make them especially resistant to malware, credential theft, and reuse attacks.

More Info

Least privilege

You can learn more about the principle of least privilege at: *https://learn.micro-soft.com/en-us/windows-server/identity/ad-ds/plan/security-best-practices/implementing-least-privilege-administrative-models.*

Privileged Access Workstations

Servers are only as secure as the computers that you use to manage them. An increasing number of security incidents have occurred because a privileged user's computer was infected with malware, and that computer was then used to perform server administration tasks. Privileged Access Workstations (PAWs) are specially configured computers that you use to perform remote administration tasks. The idea of a PAW is that you have a computer with a locked-down configuration that you only use to perform server administration tasks. You don't use this computer to read your email or browse the Internet; you just use it to perform server administration tasks.

Consider configuring a PAW in the following way:

- Configure Windows Defender Application Control (Device Guard) to allow only specifically authorized and digitally signed software to run on the computer.

- Configure Credential Guard to protect credentials stored on the computer.

- Use BitLocker to encrypt the computer's storage and protect the boot environment.

- The computer should not be used to browse the Internet or to check email. Server administrators should have completely separate computers to perform their other daily job tasks. Block Internet browsing on the PAW both locally and on the perimeter network firewall.

- Block the PAW from accessing the Internet. Software updates should be obtained from a dedicated secure update server on the local network. External tools should be obtained from another computer and transferred to the PAW.

- Server administrators should not sign in to the PAW using an account that has administrative privileges on the PAW.

- Only specific user accounts used by server administrators should be able to sign on to the PAW. Consider additional restrictions such as sign-in hours. Block privileged accounts from signing in to computers that are not PAWs or servers to be managed, such as the IT staff's everyday work computers.

- Configure servers to only accept administrator connections from PAWs. This can be done through Windows Defender Firewall with Advanced Security with isolation policies.

- Use configuration-management tools to monitor the configuration of the PAW. Some organizations rebuild PAWs entirely every 24 hours to ensure that configurations are not altered. Use these tools to restrict local group membership and ensure that the PAW has all appropriate recent software updates applied.

- Ensure that audit logs from PAWs are forwarded to a separate secure location.

- Disable the use of unauthorized storage devices. For example, you can configure policies so that only USB storage devices that have a specific BitLocker organizational ID can be used with the computer.

- Block unsolicited inbound network traffic to the PAW using Windows Defender Firewall.

Many of the technologies that you can use to harden Windows Server are discussed in more detail in Chapter 12, "Hardening Windows Server," and Chapter 14, "Security systems and services."

Inside OUT

Jump servers

Jump servers are another security procedure that can be used in conjunction with privileged-access workstations. Jump servers only allow servers to accept administrative connections from specific hosts. For example, you only allow domain controllers to be administered from computers that have a specific IP address and a computer certificate issued by a specific certification authority. You can configure jump servers to accept connections only from PAWs, and servers to be administered to accept connections only from jump servers. Some organizations that use jump servers have them rebuilt and redeployed every 24 hours to ensure that their configuration does not drift from the approved configuration.

Windows Admin Center

Windows Admin Center is a web-based console that allows you to remotely manage Windows Server through a web browser. You can connect to and use Windows Admin Center using Edge, Firefox, and Chrome.

You can install Windows Admin Center on computers running Windows 10 and later and Windows Server 2016 and later. Windows Admin Center can be installed on Windows Server, deployed using the Server Core installation option.

You can use Windows Admin Center, shown in Figure 1-1, to manage computers running Windows Server 2012 and later.

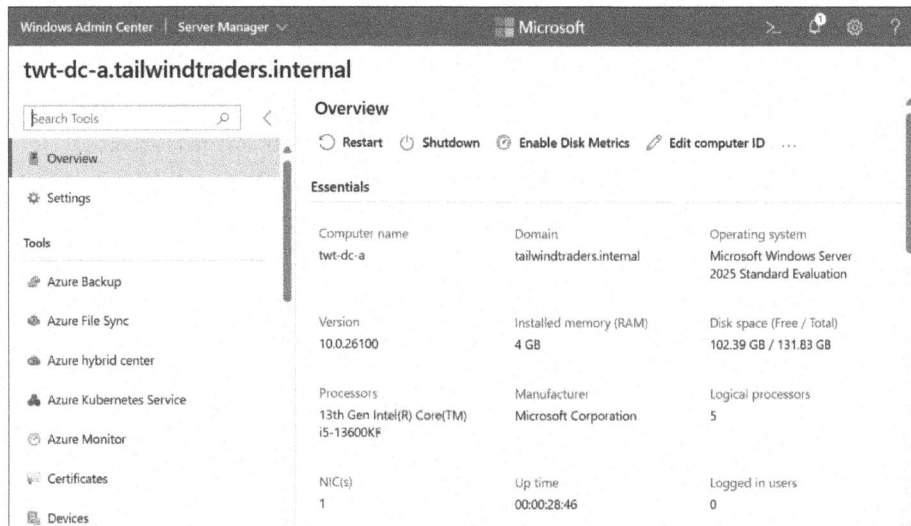

Figure 1-1   Windows Admin Center

CHAPTER 1

When connected to a gateway server, click Add on the All Connections page, shown in Figure 1-2, to add additional servers that you want to manage. A dialog will prompt you to enter the credentials of an account that has local Administrative privileges on the server that you want to add.

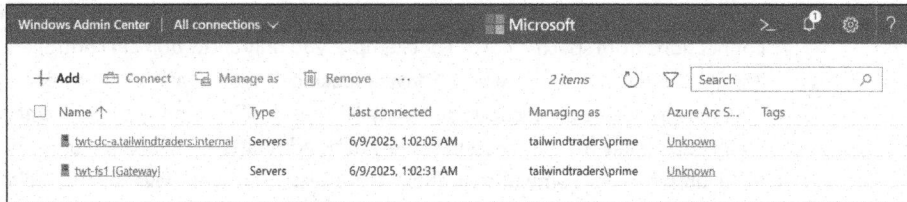

Windows Admin Center	All connections ∨				Microsoft			⟩_ △❶ ⚙ ?
+ Add	🖳 Connect	🖳 Manage as	🗑 Remove	⋯		2 items	↻ ▽	Search ρ
☐ Name ↑		Type	Last connected		Managing as		Azure Arc S...	Tags
🖳 twt-dc-a.tailwindtraders.internal		Servers	6/9/2025, 1:02:05 AM		tailwindtraders\prime		Unknown	
🖳 twt-fs1 [Gateway]		Servers	6/9/2025, 1:02:31 AM		tailwindtraders\prime		Unknown	

Figure 1-2   Windows Admin Center All Connections

You can use Windows Admin Center to perform the on-premises server management tasks listed in Table 1-1.

Table 1-1   Default WAC tools and functionality

WAC Tool	Function
Overview	Server details and control the server state.
Azure Backup	Manage Azure Backup.
Azure File Sync	Manage Azure File Sync.
Azure hybrid center	Manage Azure hybrid services.
Azure Kubernetes Service	Manage the Kubernetes management cluster and services.
Azure Monitor	Configure events and performance counter data to be forwarded to Azure for analysis.
Certificates	View and modify certificates, including certificate expiration.
Devices	Manage devices (similar to the Device Manager console).
Events	View events. Similar to the Event Viewer console.
Files and file sharing	Browse files and folders and manage file shares.
Firewall	Manage firewall rules.
Installed Apps	Add and remove programs.
Local Users and Groups	Manage local users and groups.
Networks	Manage network devices and Azure Network Adapter.
Packet monitoring	Allows you to perform packet capture and analysis. Will install Wireshark Dissector and PayloadParser on the computer.
Performance Monitor	Monitor the performance of the server.
PowerShell	Interact with the server through a web-based PowerShell session.

WAC Tool	Function
Processes	Manage running processes.
Registry	Remotely manage the registry.
Remote Desktop	Connect to the server using a web-based remote desktop client.
Roles and Features	Manage server roles and features.
Scheduled Tasks	Manage scheduled tasks.
Security	Manage virus and threat protection, secure-core server, and OSConfig baselines.
Services	Manage services.
Storage	Manage server storage devices.
Storage Replica	Manage storage replication.
Updates	Manage software updates.
Virtual Machines	Manage Hyper-V virtual machines.
Virtual Switches	View and manage virtual switches.

CHAPTER 1

Inside OUT

The future is WAC?

When it was released, WAC was meant to supplant existing GUI tools. The reality is that WAC will generally do well with features added since Windows Server 2019, but the functionality isn't there for traditional roles and features such as Active Directory Domain Services and Internet Information Services.

Installing Windows Admin Center

You can install Windows Admin Center (WAC) by downloading it from Microsoft's website at the address *https://aka.ms/WACDownload*. This will ensure you have the most recent version (the current version on WinGet is not the most recent at the time of writing). If you want to only allow WAC to be accessible from the local computer and not available to other hosts on the network, perform a custom installation. The Express setup option will configure the server as a WAC Gateway, which allows other hosts to access WAC as long as they have appropriate credentials. When you use the express option, WAC will default to being available on Port 443. If you need to change the WAC port, you can do it by modifying the program in the list of installed applications in Settings.

When you install on Windows Server configured with the desktop experience GUI installation option, you can choose between using a self-signed SSL (TLS) certificate or an SSL (TLS) certificate that is already installed on the computer.

Inside OUT

WAC and Enterprise CA

If you're deploying a gateway server, things will be a lot simpler if you deploy an SSL (TLS) certificate from a trusted CA because it won't be necessary to go through the hassle of responding to dialogs about whether to trust the certificate. When you deploy WAC for the first time, the self-signed SSL certificate will expire after a short amount of time. Having an Enterprise CA and configuring autoenrollment and certificate renewal for servers allows you to circumvent the problems of certificate trust and expiring certificates.

You can install Windows Admin Center on a Server Core instance of Windows Server using `msiexec` and by specifying the management port and SSL certificate option. The syntax of the command-line installation where a trusted certificate is used is

```
msiexec /i <WindowsAdminCenterInstallerName>.msi /qn /L*v log.txt SME_PORT=<port> SME_
THUMBPRINT=<thumbprint> SSL_CERTIFICATE_OPTION=installed
```

The `SME_PORT` is the port you want to use, and the `SME_THUMBPRINT` is the thumbprint of the installed SSL (TLS) certificate.

By default, installing WAC updates the computer's trusted host files. When you deploy WAC, you can configure it to update automatically or manually. When you configure Windows Admin Center to update automatically, new versions will be installed as they become available through Microsoft Update. If you don't configure this option, you'll need to manually install newer versions of Windows Admin Center as they become available.

More Info

Installing Windows Admin Center

You can learn more installing Windows Admin Center at *https://learn.microsoft.com/windows-server/manage/windows-admin-center/plan/installation-options*.

Inside OUT

WAC web server

Windows Admin Center doesn't use Internet Information Services; instead, it uses its own web server. While it's possible to deploy Windows Admin Center on a computer that has IIS installed, generally, you'll be better off deploying WAC in a gateway configuration and using the gateway server to remotely manage a computer that has IIS installed on it.

Windows Admin Center extensions

Windows Admin Center extensions allow for the extension of Windows Admin Center functionality. Windows Admin Center includes extensions for roles built into Windows Server, such as Storage Migration Services and third-party extensions. Microsoft is encouraging third parties to add extensions to Windows Admin Center as an alternative to requiring systems administrators to use product-specific consoles.

By default, Windows Admin Center will display extensions published to Microsoft's official NuGet feed. This feed includes extensions published and updated by Microsoft as well as those published by trusted third-party vendors. Also, you can configure Windows Admin Center to display extensions or installations from any NuGet feed that supports the NuGet V2 APIs or a specially configured file share accessible to the computer hosting Windows Admin Center.

Extensions are available in Windows Admin Center by selecting the settings icon and then selecting Extensions. The Available Extension pane, shown in Figure 1-3, displays all extensions that are available but not installed from the currently configured feed. You can update currently installed extensions if new versions of those extensions are available through the Installed Extensions pane.

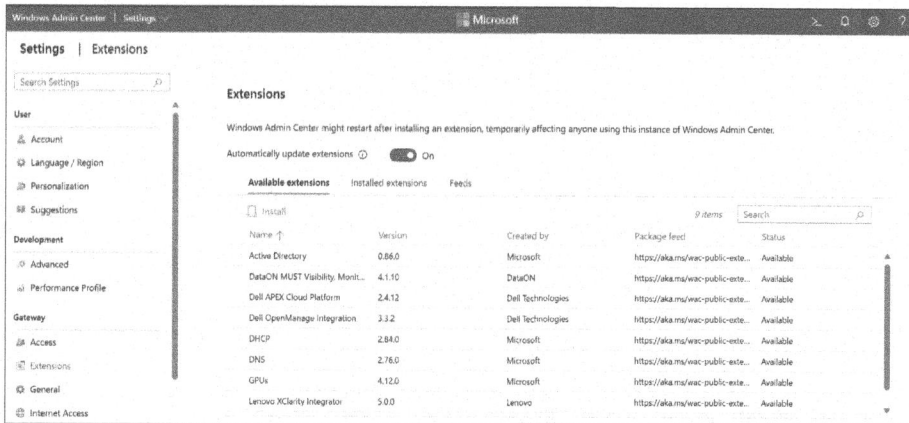

Figure 1-3 Windows Admin Center Extensions

More Info

WAC extensions

You can learn more about WAC extensions at *https://learn.microsoft.com/ windows-server/manage/windows-admin-center/configure/using-extensions*.

Show script

When you perform a task in Windows Admin Center, you can click the PowerShell icon in the Windows Admin Center title bar to view PowerShell source code relevant to the tasks, as shown in Figure 1-4. This allows you to copy and save useful PowerShell code for reuse later.

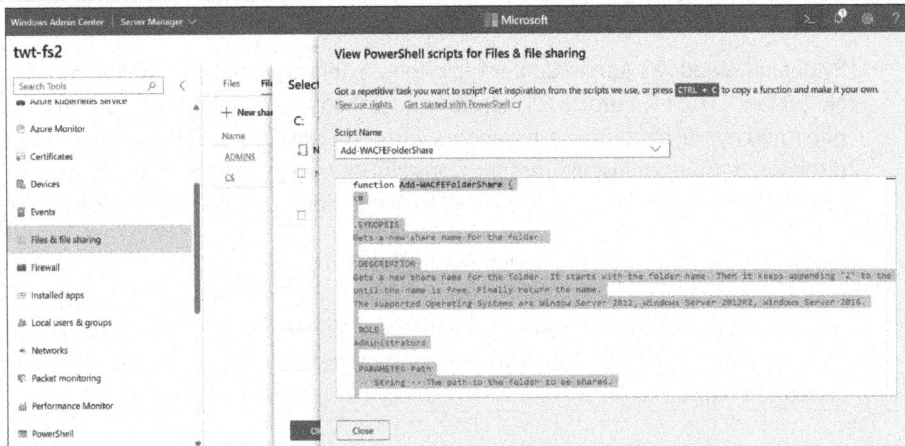

Figure 1-4   Displayed script

Remote Server Administration Tools

The Remote Server Administration Tools (RSAT) are a set of consoles that you can install on a computer running Windows 11 that allow you to manage computers running Windows Server. The RSAT consoles can also be installed on a computer running Windows Server by running this command:

```
Install-WindowsFeature -IncludeAllSubFeature RSAT
```

Running this command will install all RSAT consoles. You can be selective and install specific consoles using `Install-WindowsFeature` and specifying the appropriate management tool.

Installing the RSAT tools on a computer running Windows client involves running the command

```
Get-WindowsCapability -Name RSAT* -Online | Add-WindowsCapability -Online
```

RSAT consoles

Table 1-2 provides a list of the RSAT tools that are available on Windows Server. Most of these tools are available from the Tools menu of the Server Manager console. Included is the command you can use from a command prompt or PowerShell prompt to directly open the tool.

Even though some of these tools are included as remote management tools, they will only function if the role or feature they manage is installed on the local server.

Table 1-2 RSAT consoles

Console	Function
Active Directory Administrative Center (`dsac.exe`)	This is an advanced console for managing Active Directory users, computers, domains, and forests, as well as Dynamic Access Control and Authentication policies. It performs most of the functions from the traditional Active Directory management consoles available on earlier versions of the Windows Server operating system.
Active Directory Domains and Trust (`domain.msc`)	This is a console for configuring and managing trust relationships between domains and forests.
Active Directory Rights Management Services (`adrms.msc`)	This allows you to manage and configure Active Directory Rights Management Services.
Active Directory Sites and Services (`dssite.msc`)	This allows you to manage Active Directory Site configuration, including Global Catalog servers and universal group membership caching.
ADSI Edit (`adsiedit.msc`)	ADSI Edit is an Active Directory object and attribute editor.
Certification Authority (`certsrv.msc`)	A CA is used to manage Active Directory Certificate Services.
Cluster-Aware Updating (`ClusterUpdateUI.exe`)	This is used to manage cluster-aware updating.
Component Services (`dcomcnfg.exe`)	This allows you to manage component services, view the event log, and manage services.
Computer Management (`compmgmt.msc`)	The Computer Management console allows you to manage Tasks, Event Viewer, Shared Folders, Local Users and Groups, Performance, Device Manager, Disk Management, and Services.
Defragment and Optimize Drives (`dfrgui.exe`)	This allows you to manage the defragmentation and optimization of drives.
DFS Management (`dfsmgmt.msc`)	This allows you to manage the Distributed File System.
DHCP (`dhcpmgmt.msc`)	This allows you to manage Dynamic Host Configuration Protocol servers.

CHAPTER 1

Console	Function
Disk Cleanup (`cleanmgr.exe`)	This console allows you to remove files and folders that are no longer necessary, such as old updates and temporary files.
DNS (`dmsmgmt.msc`)	This console is where you configure and manage DNS servers.
Event Viewer (`eventvwr.msc`)	This console allows you to view and manage event logs.
Failover Cluster Manager (`cluadmin.msc`)	This allows you to configure and manage failover clusters.
Fax Service Manager (`fxsadmin.msc`)	This allows you to configure and manage the fax service. Yes, this is still in Windows Server 2025.
File Server Resource Manager (`fsrm.msc`)	This console is for managing file servers, including file classification, storage reports, and quotas.
Group Policy Management (`gpmc.msc`)	Use this console for management of group policies, including running the resultant set of policy reports.
Hyper-V Manager (`virtmgmt.msc`)	Use this console to configure and manage Hyper-V virtualization.
Internet Information Services (IIS) Manager (`inetmgr.exe`)	This is where you configure and manage IIS, version 7 and later.
iSCSI Initiator (`iscsicpl.exe`)	This console allows you to configure iSCSI initiator settings.
Local Security Policy (`secpol.msc`)	Here is where you configure and manage local security policy settings.
Network Load Balancing Manager (`nlbmgr.exe`)	This is where you can configure and manage network load balancing.
Network Policy Server (`nps.msc`)	Use this console to configure Network Policies.
ODBC Data Sources (32-bit) (`C:\Windows\SysWOW64\odbcad32.exe`)	This is where you manage 32-bit ODBC data sources. Note that the command for the 32-bit version is in SysWOW64.
ODBC Data Sources (64-bit) (`C:\Windows\System32\odbcad32.exe`)	Use this console to manage 64-bit ODBC data sources.
Online Responder Management	Online Responder Management is where you configure and manage Online Certificate Status Protocol arrays.
Performance Monitor (`perfmon.exe`)	This console allows you to view performance information.
Print Management (`printmanagement.msc`)	You can configure and manage print servers from this console.

Console	Function
Remote Access Management (`ramgmtui.msc`)	You can configure and manage remote access from this console.
Remote Desktop Services (`rdms.msc`, `tsadmin.msc`)	Use this console to configure and manage Remote Desktop Services.
Resource Monitor (`resmon.exe`)	The Resource Monitor provides real-time monitoring of RAM, CPU, disk, and network utilization.
Routing and Remote Access (`rras.msc`)	This allows you to configure and manage routing and remote access, including DirectAccess.
Services (`services.msc`)	This console is where you configure and manage services.
Shielding Data File Wizard (`ShieldingDataFileWizard.exe`)	This console is where you manage shielded data files and policies for shielded VMs.
System Configuration (`msconfig.exe`)	System Configuration allows you to manage the system configuration, including boot and startup information.
System Information (`msinfo32.exe`)	Use this console to view system information.
Task Scheduler (`taskschd.msc`)	Use the Task Scheduler to configure and manage scheduled tasks.
Template Disk Wizard (`TemplateDiskWizard.exe`)	Use this wizard to configure and manage virtual hard disk templates for shielded VMs.
Volume Activation Tools (`VolumeActivationTools.exe`)	Use this console to configure and manage volume licensing.
Windows Deployment Services (`wdsmgmt.msc`)	Use this console to configure and manage Windows Deployment Services.
Windows Firewall with Advanced Security (`wf.msc`)	This console allows you to configure and manage Windows Firewall with Advanced Security.
Windows Memory Diagnostics (`mdsched.exe`)	The Windows Memory Diagnostics console is where you perform memory diagnostics to check whether the server's memory is corrupted. A reboot may be required.
Windows Server Backup (`wbadmin.msc`)	This is where you configure and manage Windows Server Backup.
Windows Server Update Services (`wsus.msc`)	This allows you to configure and manage the Windows Server Update Services server.
WINS (`winsmgmt.msc`)	The WINS console allows you to configure and manage the Windows Internet Naming Services server.

CHAPTER 1

Server Manager console

Perhaps the most important RSAT console is the Server Manager console. This console opens automatically on a computer running Windows Server if you install the server with the Desktop Experience option. You can also run it by executing the `ServerManager.exe` command from the command prompt or PowerShell.

A number of roles that had separate consoles in previous versions of Windows Server have that functionality included in the Server Manager console. For example, many storage-management tasks and IPAM tasks are completed in Server Manager rather than in individual role-related consoles. Many of these tasks are available to a greater or lesser degree in Windows Admin Center.

When you launch the Server Manager console, it will query the servers that you have added to the All Servers group to determine which roles are installed on those servers. Then it will provide a list of categories based on the roles detected on the servers.

To add servers to the All Servers group, right-click the All Servers node of the Server Manager console and click Add Servers. In the Add Servers dialog, select the servers using one of three methods: by querying Active Directory, by searching on the basis of DNS name, or by importing servers from a list.

Once you have a list of roles in Server Manager, you can perform role-specific administration on each server by right-clicking that server. When you do this, the appropriate RSAT console will be launched with the target server in focus. Figure 1-5 shows MEL-DC selected in the list of DNS servers, which includes an option to launch the DNS Manager console. You can also use the context menu—available by right-clicking—to do the following (where supported):

- Add roles and features to the target server

- Restart the target server

- Open the Computer Management console

- Open a Remote Desktop Connection session to the target server

- Open a Windows PowerShell session on the target server

- Configure NIC Teaming on the target server

- Manage the server using an alternate set of credentials

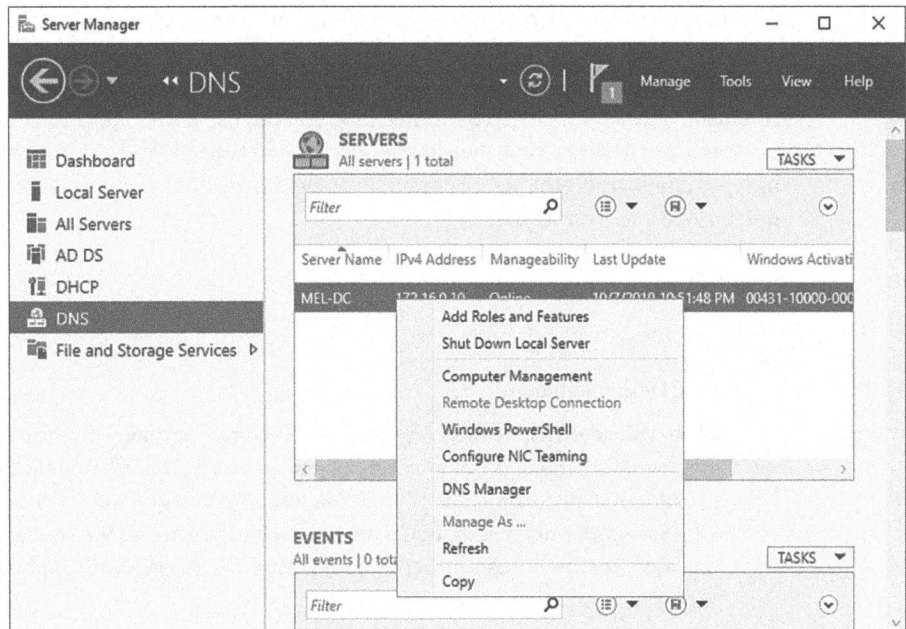

Figure 1-5   Server Manager individual server context menu

PowerShell

PowerShell is Microsoft's primary scripting, automation, and management tool. It's not hyperbole to suggest that the most important skill for Windows Server administrators going forward is using PowerShell. In almost all cases, you can access greater functionality and settings through PowerShell than you can through Windows Admin Center or the RSAT consoles.

Windows Server ships with a default version of Windows PowerShell 5.1 built on the full .NET Framework version 4.5, which is behind the most current version, Microsoft PowerShell. Microsoft PowerShell is built on .NET Core and is currently releasing stable versions in the 7.x series.

You can install the most recent version of PowerShell side by side with version 5.1 by running the following WinGet command:

```
WinGet install Microsoft.PowerShell
```

For offline server scenarios, you can obtain the PowerShell binaries from the PowerShell GitHub repository at *https://github.com/PowerShell/PowerShell*.

You can run version 5.1 of PowerShell by running the command powershell.exe, and the updated version of PowerShell by running the command pwsh.exe. You can determine what version of PowerShell you are using by running the command:

```
$PSVersionTable.PSVersion
```

PowerShell includes a substantial amount of documentation explaining what each cmdlet can do and how you can do it. While you'll learn the names of the PowerShell cmdlets that are relevant to each role covered by each chapter of this book, once you know the name of the command you want to use to perform a task, you can use PowerShell's built-in help to learn the precise details of how to use that cmdlet to perform that task. You can get help for each cmdlet by typing **help cmdletname**. For example, to get help with the get-service cmdlet, type **Help get-service** into a PowerShell session.

Inside OUT

Latest documentation

When you need help with a PowerShell cmdlet, the first thing you should do is run the update-help cmdlet on an Internet-connected server. This will pull the most up-to-date PowerShell documentation from Microsoft's servers on the Internet down to your local server. This documentation is almost always the same as the cmdlet's documentation available on Microsoft's website, so it saves you a search with your favorite search engine.

Some important basic commands to get you started with PowerShell are listed in Table 1-3.

Table 1-3 PowerShell help commands

Cmdlet or command	Functionality
Update-Help	This command updates the help documentation for each cmdlet to the most recent version available from Microsoft.
Get-Command	This lists all the PowerShell commands available on the computer.
Get-Command -Module <ModuleName>	This command allows you to get all cmdlets in a specific PowerShell module. For example, to view all the DNS server cmdlets, run the command Get-Command -Module DNSServer.
Get-Command -Noun <NounName>	Each PowerShell cmdlet is made up of a verb-noun combination. You can use this command to view all cmdlets associated with a particular noun. For example, to view all the cmdlets associated with the DNSServer noun, run this command: Get-command -noun DNSserver.
Help <cmdletname>	This command allows you to view the summary help documentation for a specific PowerShell cmdlet.

Cmdlet or command	Functionality
`Help -detailed <cmdletname>`	Use this command to view the detailed help documentation for a specific PowerShell cmdlet.
`Help -examples <cmdletname>`	This command allows you to view examples of how to use a specific PowerShell cmdlet to perform tasks.

Modules

Modules are collections of PowerShell cmdlets. In older versions of PowerShell, you needed to manually load a module each time you want to use one of its associated cmdlets. In Windows Server 2016 and later, any module that is installed will load automatically when you try to run an associated cmdlet. Viewing cmdlets by module using the `Get-Command -Module <modulename>` cmdlet allows you to view just those cmdlets associated with a specific role or feature.

PowerShell Gallery

The PowerShell Gallery is a collection of modules published by the community that extend the functionality of PowerShell beyond what is available with a default installation of Windows Server. Table 1-4 lists the commands that you can use to get started with the PowerShell Gallery.

Table 1-4   PowerShell Gallery basics

Command	Functionality
`Find-Module -Repository PSGallery | out-host -paging`	This will list the available modules in the PowerShell Gallery in a paged format. You'll be prompted to install the NuGetProvider to interact with the PowerShell Gallery.
`Find-Module -Repository PSGallery -Name <ModuleName>`	This will list the modules with a specific name. You can use wildcards. For example, to view all modules that start with the name *AzureRM*, run the command `Find-Module -Repository PSGallery -Name AzureRM*`.
`Install-Module -Repository PSGallery -Name <ModuleName>`	This will install the *Modulename* module. For example, to install the *AzureRM* module, run the command `Install-Module -Repository PSGallery -Name AzureRM`.
`Update-Module`	This will update any module that you've installed using `Install-Module`.
`Get-InstalledModule`	Use this command to view all modules installed from the PowerShell Gallery.

Remoting

By default, PowerShell remoting is enabled on Windows Server, but also by default, it requires a connection from a private network and an account that is a member of the local Administrators group. A remote session allows you to run commands on a remote computer in a manner similar to how you'd remotely enact commands when connected using an SSH session.

You can enter a remote session to a Windows Server computer that is a member of the same Active Directory forest by using the following commands, which will prompt you for the credentials that you will use to connect to the remote computer, as shown in Figure 1-6.

```
$cred = Get-Credential
Enter-PSSession -computername <computername> -Credential $cred
```

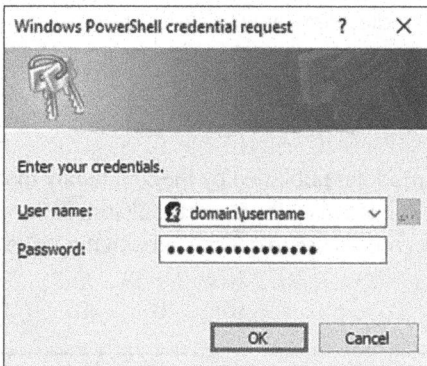

Figure 1-6   Get-Credential

Inside OUT

Get-Credential

The PowerShell command $variablename = Get-Credential will open a dialog, which allows you to enter a username and password that will then be stored in an encrypted variable that you can use in future PowerShell commands within the same session.

You can enable PowerShell remoting using the Enable-PSRemoting cmdlet if it has been disabled. PowerShell remoting relies on WSMan (Web Server Management). WSMan uses port 5985 and can be configured to support TLS over port 5986.

Remote PowerShell connections are made to a defined endpoint, usually the default endpoint. The account used to make a connection to this remote endpoint needs to have local Administrator privileges on the target computer. With Just Enough Administration, which you'll learn about in Chapter 12, you'll learn about creating additional endpoints that allow connections to limited privilege restricted sessions.

To enable PowerShell remoting to computers that are not domain-joined, you need to configure the trusted hosts list on the client computer from which you want to establish the remote session. You do this on the client computer using the `set-item` cmdlet. For example, to trust the computer at IP address 192.168.3.200, you'll need to run this command:

```
Set-Item wsman:\localhost\Client\TrustedHosts -Value 192.168.3.200 -Concatenate
```

Once you've run the command to configure the client, you'll be able to establish a PowerShell remote session using the `Enter-PSSession` cmdlet. If you want more information about remoting, you can run the following command to bring up help text on the subject:

```
Help about_Remote_faq -ShowWindow
```

One-to-many remoting

PowerShell allows you to run one command against many machines, which is known as one-to-many remoting or fan-out administration. You can use one-to-many remoting to run the same command against any number of computers. Rather than signing in to each computer to check whether a particular service is running, you can use PowerShell remoting to run the same command that checks the status of the service against each computer within the scope of the command.

For example, you could use the following command to read a list of computers from a text file named `computers.txt`:

```
$Computers = Get-Content c:\Computers.txt
```

You could then use the following command to get the properties of the Windows Update service:

```
Invoke-Command -ScriptBlock { get-service wuauserv } -computername $Computers
```

You can also use the `Invoke-Command` cmdlet to run a script from the local computer against a number of remote computers. For example, to run the script `FixStuff.ps1` against the computers in the file `computers.txt`, run this command:

```
$Computers = Get-Content c:\Computers.txt
Invoke-Command -FilePath c:\FixStuff.ps1
```

PowerShell ISE

PowerShell ISE (Integrated Scripting Environment) is a tool that is built into the operating system that you can use to create, manage, and run PowerShell scripts and commands. You can use the Windows Server App Compatibility Features on Demand feature to deploy PowerShell ISE on a Server Core deployment.

PowerShell ISE includes a script pane and a command window, and it also provides you with the option to list the available cmdlets sorted by module, as shown in Figure 1-7.

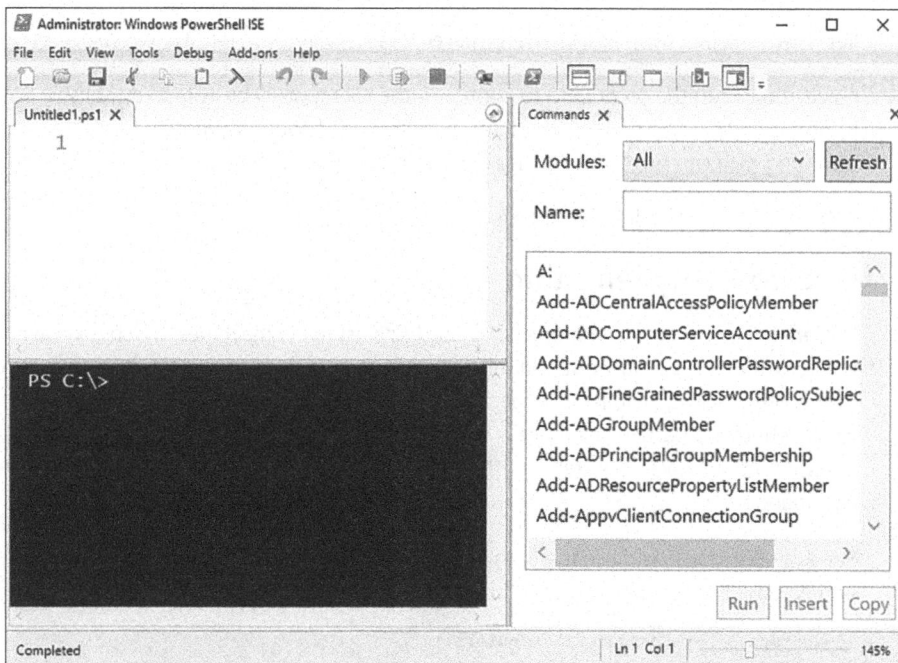

Figure 1-7   PowerShell ISE

PowerShell ISE includes the following functionality:

- **IntelliSense**   IntelliSense provides code completion and displays possible cmdlets, parameters, parameter values, files, and folders. Code completion functionality extends to the command window.

- **Color coding**   PowerShell code is color-coded to assist code readability. This color coding extends to the command window.

- **Visual debugging**   Visual debugging allows you to step through PowerShell code and configure and manage breakpoints.

- **Brace Matching**   Brace matching allows you to locate matching braces to ensure that closing braces match all opened braces.

- **Context-sensitive help**   Context-sensitive help allows you to view information about cmdlets, parameters, and values.

- **Run all code or just a selection**   Rather than running all the PowerShell code in the script pane, you can instead just highlight and run discrete lines of PowerShell code.

Remote tabs

Remote tabs allow you to establish remote PowerShell sessions using PowerShell ISE rather than using the `Enter-PSSession` PowerShell cmdlet. To initiate a remote session, click the New Remote PowerShell Tab item in the PowerShell ISE's File menu. You'll be prompted for the address of the computer to which you want to connect, as well as the name of the user account with which you want to make the connection, as shown in Figure 1-8.

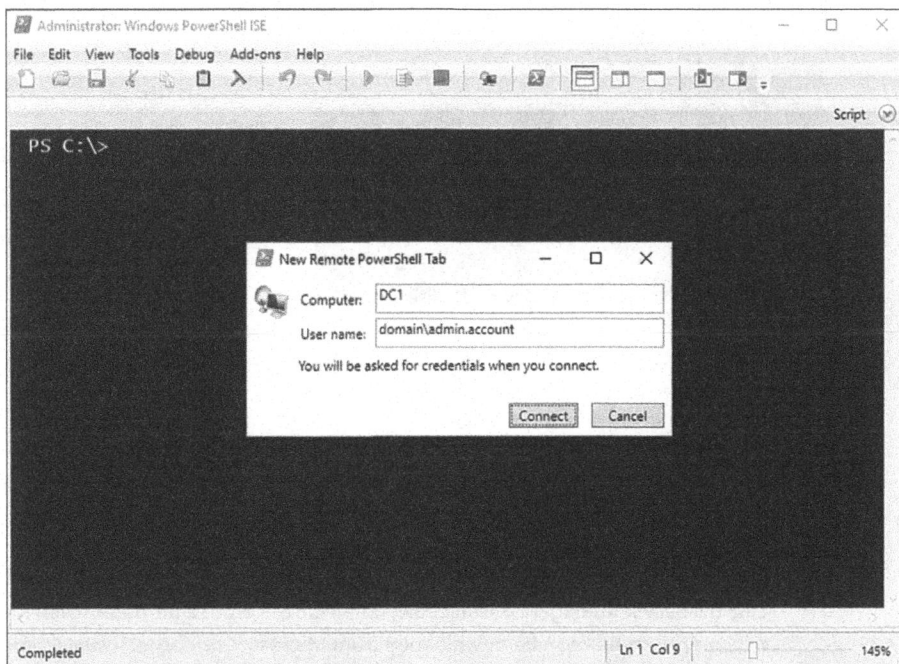

Figure 1-8   New Remote PowerShell Tab

Once a session is established, you can use the PowerShell ISE script pane to run scripts or sections of PowerShell code in the same manner that you would use if you were using PowerShell ISE on the local computer.

Snippets

Snippets are commonly used small sections of code that you can insert into your PowerShell scripts. Figure 1-9 shows an `If-Else` snippet already in the script pane, with the properties of a `do-while` snippet displayed. You can add snippets to the PowerShell ISE using the `New-Snippet` cmdlet.

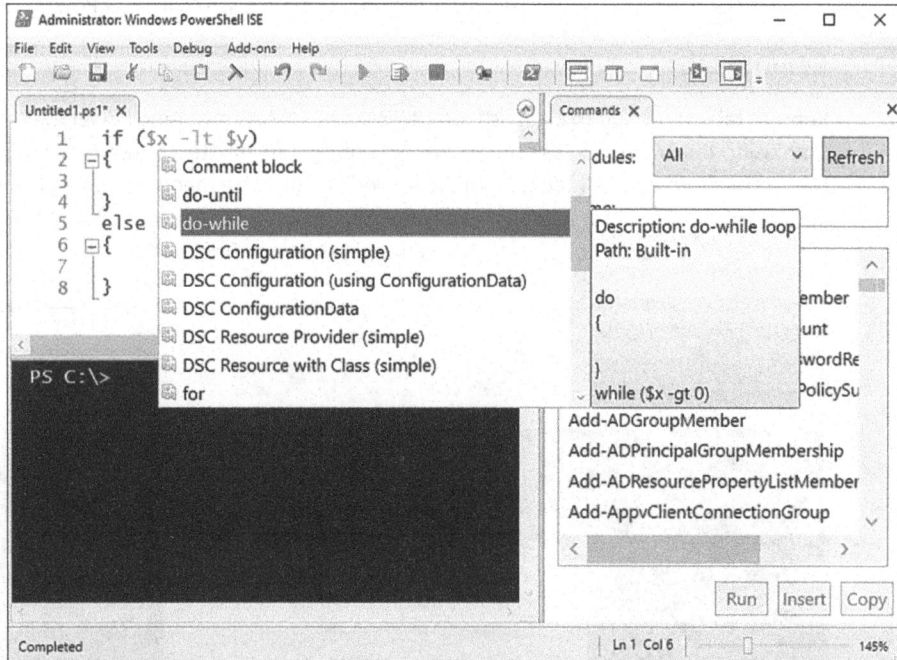

Figure 1-9   Snippets

Inside OUT

VSCode

Like the Server Manager console, PowerShell ISE is a bit of a dinosaur when it comes to newer options that can be downloaded from Microsoft's website. Visual Studio Code (VSCode) is a free Integrated Development Environment (IDE) that has extensions that can greatly assist in the creation and debugging of PowerShell scripts. Like Windows Admin Center, VSCode enjoys a rapid update cycle, which is one of the reasons it isn't included with the operating system. Generally speaking, you should write your PowerShell scripts on your workstation using a tool like VSCode with all its cool PowerShell extensions and add-ins like GitHub Copilot. If you have to debug a PowerShell script on the server on which the script is running, then you should use PowerShell ISE.

PowerShell Direct

PowerShell Direct allows you to create a connection from a virtualization host to a VM running on that host. To use PowerShell Direct, you must have Hyper-V administrator privileges on the Hyper-V host computer and administrator credentials on the virtual machine to which you want to connect. PowerShell Direct can allow you to make a connection to a virtual machine that may not otherwise be configured to support remote connections. It can also be used to make a connection to the VM when there is a network disruption.

PowerShell direct only works with Hyper-V hosts and guests running Windows Server 2016 and later. To get a list of the virtual machines on the host Hyper-V server, use the command Get-VM. To connect to the virtual machine using PowerShell Direct, use the Enter-PSSession cmdlet with the -VMName parameter.

To create a direct connection from the Hyper-V virtualization host to a computer running a supported version of Linux, ensure that the distribution's virtualization extensions are installed and that an SSH server is installed. Once these steps have been taken, you can use the hvc.exe command to connect. For example, the following command allows you to make an SSH connection using the prime user account to a VM named Ubuntu-Server from an elevated PowerShell prompt on the virtualization host:

```
Hvc.exe ssh prime@ubuntu-server -v
```

Remote Desktop

Remote Desktop is the way that many administrators are likely to remotely perform one-off tasks on servers running the GUI version of Windows Server. While best practice is to use PowerShell or Windows Admin Center for remote administration, sometimes it's quicker to just establish a Remote Desktop session because using Remote Desktop allows you to perform tasks on the remote server in a manner that appears similar to being directly signed in at the console.

By default, Remote Desktop is disabled on computers running Windows Server. You enable it either through the Remote tab of the System Properties dialog or by running the following PowerShell command:

```
Set-ItemProperty -Path "HKLM:\System\CurrentControlSet\Control\Terminal Server" -Name
"fDenyTSConnections" -Value 0
```

You can make Remote Desktop connections to computers running the Server Core installation option if Remote Desktop is enabled.

By default, Remote Desktop Connection connects to Remote Desktop services on port 3389. When you enable Remote Desktop using the GUI, a remote desktop–related firewall is automatically enabled. If you enable Remote Desktop using PowerShell, you'll also need to manually enable a firewall rule to allow connections. You can do this using the following PowerShell command:

```
Enable-NetFirewallRule -DisplayGroup "Remote Desktop"
```

By default, the Allow Connections Only From Computers Running Remote Desktop With Network Level Authentication option is selected, as shown in Figure 1-10. Network Level Authentication requires that a user be authenticated prior to the remote desktop session being established. Network Level Authentication is supported by the Remote Desktop Connection client, which is available on all Windows operating systems, but it might not be supported by third-party Remote Desktop clients.

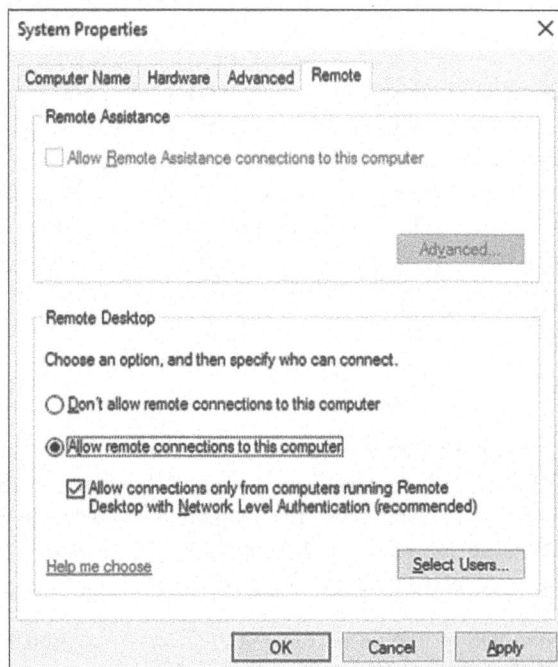

Figure 1-10   Allow Remote Desktop Connections To This Computer option

Only users who are members of the local Administrators group and members of the local Remote Desktop Users group can make connections via Remote Desktop. If you want to grant someone permission to access the server without granting them full administrative privileges, add the user to the local Remote Desktop Users group.

You can map local volumes to a remote host in an active Remote Desktop Connection session by configuring the Local Resources And Devices setting on the Local Resources tab of the Remote Desktop Connection dialog, as shown in Figure 1-11. While it's less effective over low-bandwidth connections, it can provide a simple way to transfer files from your client computer to a remote server instead of setting up FTP or another file transfer method.

Figure 1-11   Remote Desktop Connection dialog

Copilots and agents

Copilot add-ons to Windows Server allow you to have an LLM running locally on the Windows Server instance that provides you with assistance in managing that server using conversational queries. For example, a copilot add-on will allow you to query the event log using natural language queries rather than remembering the appropriate filters or PowerShell syntax. Local LLMs will also likely be able to generate scripts for you that you can run separately and perform basic configuration options based on queries such as "how do I deploy storage spaces direct given my current configuration?"

Small LLMs will run on Windows Server directly using tools such as Foundry Local. Because of their size, these LLMs are unlikely to be as functional as AI services that run in the cloud. You'll have to find a balance between what you can accomplish with AI that runs locally, given the resource constraints of your deployment, and how much access you want to grant those tools to your production environment.

There are also likely to be AI operations products that run in the cloud. For example, you can use AI operations tools running in Azure to manage Azure Arc–enabled computers running on-premises. The trick with these new tools is to determine where they can save you time and where you're better off using your existing tried and trusted techniques. You should keep an eye on what capabilities become available while remembering that these tools tend to spend more time on new features and functionality, while ignoring many of the more mature roles and services.

SSH

SSH is a cryptographic network protocol that enables secure communication, generally using a command-line interface, between a client and a remote server over an unsecured network. SSH has been used as a way of managing Linux and UNIX servers for decades, and it has been possible to add SSH server software to allow remote connections for the administration of Windows Server.

Windows Server 2025

SSH Server is included in Windows Server 2025 and later. To enable SSH server, perform the following steps:

1.   In Server Manager, select the Local Server node.

2.   Next to Remote SSH Access, click the blue text (which is Disabled by default).

3.   A script will run to enable the SSH server. When prompted, type **yes** to allow the script to execute and complete the setup.

You can also enable SSH Server on Windows Server 2025 by running the following PowerShell commands, which enable the sshd service and start the service.

```
Set-Service -Name sshd -StartupType Automatic
Start-Service sshd
```

Once the script has run, you may need to configure Windows Firewall with Advanced Security to allow inbound SSH traffic. By default, the rule only allows traffic in the Private Profile. You can do this by editing the OpenSSH Server (sshd) firewall rule in Windows Firewall with Advanced Security or using the Set-NetFirewallRule command. For example, to allow the OpenSSH server to accept traffic when set to the Domain and Private profiles, use this command:

```
Set-NetFirewallRule -Name 'OpenSSH-Server-In-TCP' -Profile Domain,Private
```

The other element to managing SSH server connections is the configuration of the local OpenSSH Users group. By default, this group has no members, so you'll need to add accounts to grant access to the server via SSH.

To initiate a connection, use the following syntax in a terminal or PowerShell window:

```
ssh DOMAIN\username@server_name
```

Replace DOMAIN with your domain name, username with your user account, and server_name with the name of the Windows Server you enabled SSH on.

1.   The first time you connect, you'll see a prompt about the server's key fingerprint. Type **yes** to continue.

2. Enter your password when prompted.

3. You should now have a remote SSH session into your Windows Server 2025 computer.

SSH Server Key Management

To generate key files by using the ECDSA algorithm, run the following command in a PowerShell or Command Prompt window on your client:

```
ssh-keygen -t ecdsa
```

You will be asked for a location to save the file and to provide a passphrase to protect the key, as shown in Figure 1-12.

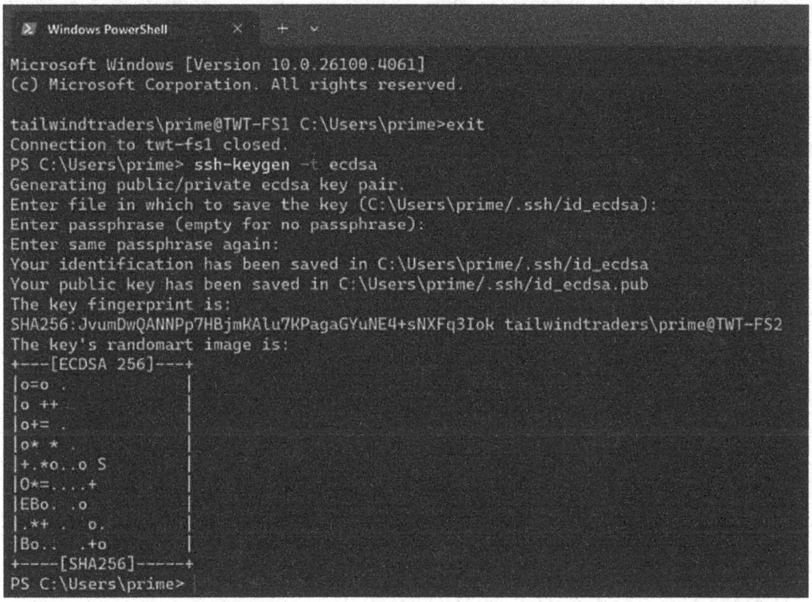

Figure 1-12 Create SSH key pair

Two files will be created in the C:\users\username\.ssh folder, id_ecdsa and id_ecdsa.pub. The id_ecdsa.pub file is the public key file, and the file without the filename extension is the private key. You should back up the private key to a secure location.

If you want to store the private key within Windows, you can enable the ssh-agent service and add the key. Once you do this, the ssh-agent automatically retrieves the local private key and passes it to the client when you initiate an SSH connection. To enable this functionality, run the following commands:

```
Get-Service ssh-agent | Set-Service -StartupType Automatic
Start-Service ssh-agent
ssh-add $env:USERPROFILE\.ssh\id_ecdsa
```

To deploy the key to a target server in the standard user context, run the following commands, substituting the username, server name, and domain name as appropriate:

```
$authorizedKey = Get-Content -Path $env:USERPROFILE\.ssh\id_ecdsa.pub
$remotePowershell = "powershell New-Item -Force -ItemType Directory -Path
$env:USERPROFILE\.ssh; Add-Content -Force -Path $env:USERPROFILE\.ssh\authorized_keys
-Value '$authorizedKey'"
ssh username@domain1@contoso.com $remotePowershell
```

To deploy the key to a target server in the administrator user context, run the following commands, substituting the username, server name, and domain name as appropriate:

```
$authorizedKey = Get-Content -Path $env:USERPROFILE\.ssh\id_ecdsa.pub
$remotePowershell = "powershell Add-Content -Force -Path $env:ProgramData\
ssh\administrators_authorized_keys -Value '''$authorizedKey''';icacls.exe
""$env:ProgramData\ssh\administrators_authorized_keys"" /inheritance:r /grant
""Administrators:F"" /grant ""SYSTEM:F"""
ssh username@domain1@contoso.com $remotePowershell
```

You will also need to edit the SSH server config file at C:\ProgramData\ssh\sshd_config and uncomment this line:

```
PubkeyAuthentication yes
```

More Info

OpenSSH on Windows Server

You can learn more about key-based authentication for OpenSSH at *https://learn.microsoft.com/en-us/windows-server/administration/openssh/openssh_keymanagement.*

Windows Server 2022 and earlier

Windows Server 2022 and earlier don't include SSH Server out of the box, and you need to install it manually.

To add an SSH client and SSH server to Windows Server 2022 and earlier, use the following PowerShell commands:

```
Add-WindowsCapability -Online -Name OpenSSH.Server~~~~0.0.1.0
Add-WindowsCapability -Online -Name OpenSSH.Client~~~~0.0.1.0
```

Even though the version appears to be version 0.0.1.0 from the command, the most recent supported version will be installed. You can check which version of SSH is installed using the command SSH -V from the command prompt.

Once you've added the capability, you need to do a few things to get the SSH server working before you're ready to go.

Once you have run these commands, it's necessary to configure the disabled `ssh-agent` service to automatically start, and you also need to configure the `sshd` service to automatically start. You can do this by running the following PowerShell commands:

```
Set-Service -Name ssh-agent -StartupType 'Automatic'
Set-Service -Name sshd -StartupType 'Automatic'
```

The final step to get SSH running on Windows Server 2022 and earlier is to run the following commands to start the relevant services:

```
Start-Service ssh-agent
Start-Service sshd
```

If you do all this, you'll be able to connect using password-based authentication from an SSH client using this syntax:

```
ssh username@hostname_or_IP_address
```

If you're connecting to a domain account, use this format:

```
ssh username@domain@hostname_or_IP_address
```

More Info

OpenSSH on Windows Server

You can learn more about OpenSSH on Windows Server at *https://learn.microsoft.com/windows-server/administration/OpenSSH/openssh-server-configuration*.

Services console

The Services console, show in Figure 1-13, allows you to view and edit the status of services running on the Windows Server computer.

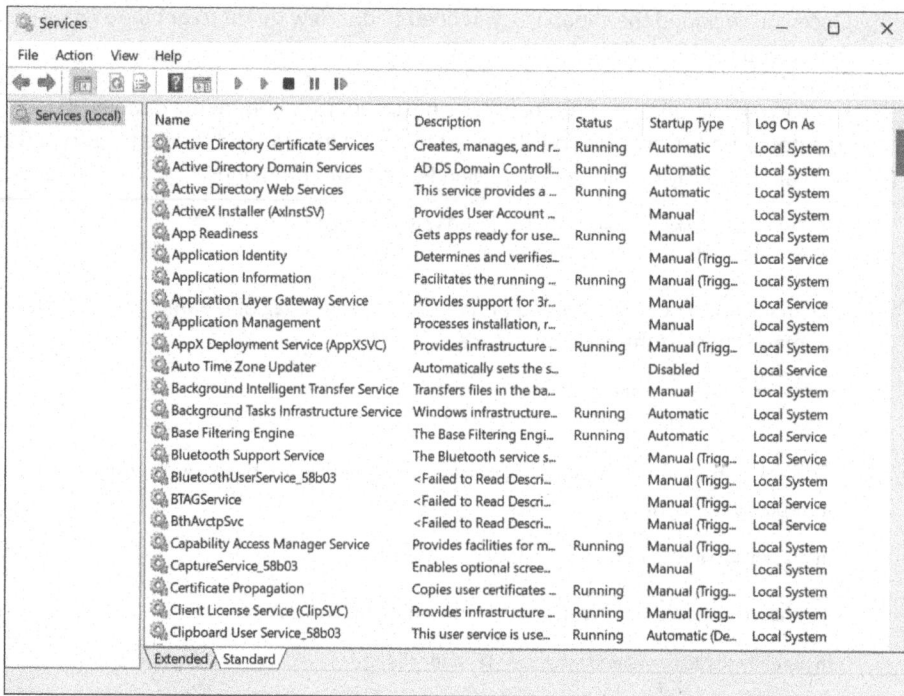

Figure 1-13   Services console

By editing the properties of a service, you can configure the following settings:

- On the General tab, you can configure the service startup type (automatic, automatic (delayed start), manual, disabled). You can also Start, Stop, Pause, and Resume the service.

- On the Log On tab, you can configure whether the service uses the Local System account or specify an account to be used by the service.

- On the Recovery tab, shown in Figure 1-14, you can configure what actions to take when the service fails. This can include performing no action, restarting the service, running a program, or even forcing a reboot.

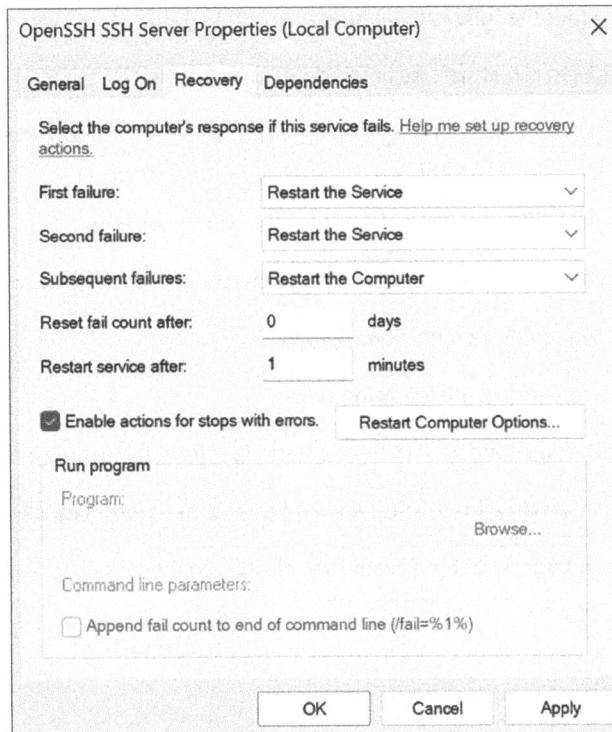

Figure 1-14   Services properties

Task Scheduler

Task Scheduler allows you to automatically run programs, scripts, or commands at predetermined times or when specific system events occur. A large number of existing tasks are already configured to run in Task Scheduler, as shown in Figure 1-15.

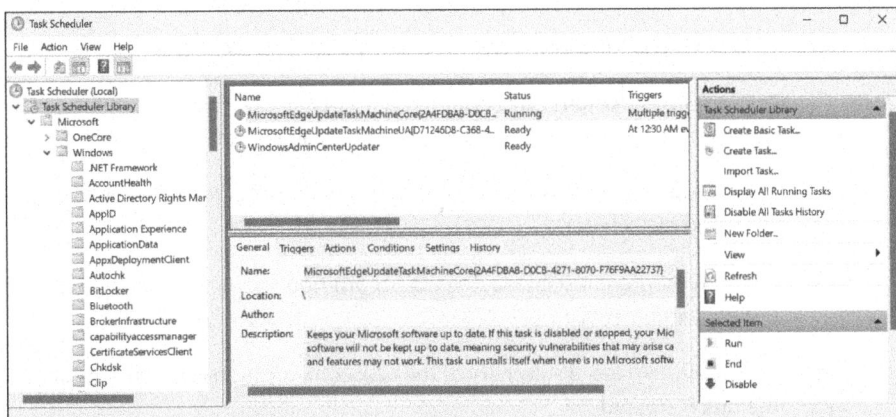

Figure 1-15   Task Scheduler

CHAPTER 1

Task Scheduler includes the following features:

- Schedule tasks to run at specific times, dates, or intervals

- Configure tasks to be triggered by events, including startup, logon, idle time, system event, and custom event triggers

- Run tasks under different user accounts with varying privileges.

- Set conditions on task execution, including network availability or power state

- Chain tasks together for complex workflows

To create a basic task, perform the following steps:

1. Open Task Scheduler and select Create a Basic Task from the actions pane.

2. Provide a unique name for the task and an optional description for clarity.

3. On the Trigger page, select the event that will initiate the task. You can choose from

   - Daily

   - Weekly

   - Monthly

   - One time

   - When the computer starts

   - When I log on

   - When a specific event is logged (a more advanced option within the basic wizard)

4. On the Action page, specify what the task will do. The primary options are

   - **Start A Program** Execute of an application, batch file, or script.

   - **Send An Email** This option is present in older interfaces but is generally considered deprecated due to security and reliability concerns.

   - **Display A Message** This action shows a message box to the currently logged-on interactive user.

5. If Start A Program is selected, the wizard prompts for the program/script path and any optional arguments.

6. On the Finish page, a summary of the task configuration is presented for review before the task is created.

If you choose to use Create Task, you get a multitabbed dialog interface, as shown in Figure 1-16. You can configure the following settings, as shown in Table 1-5.

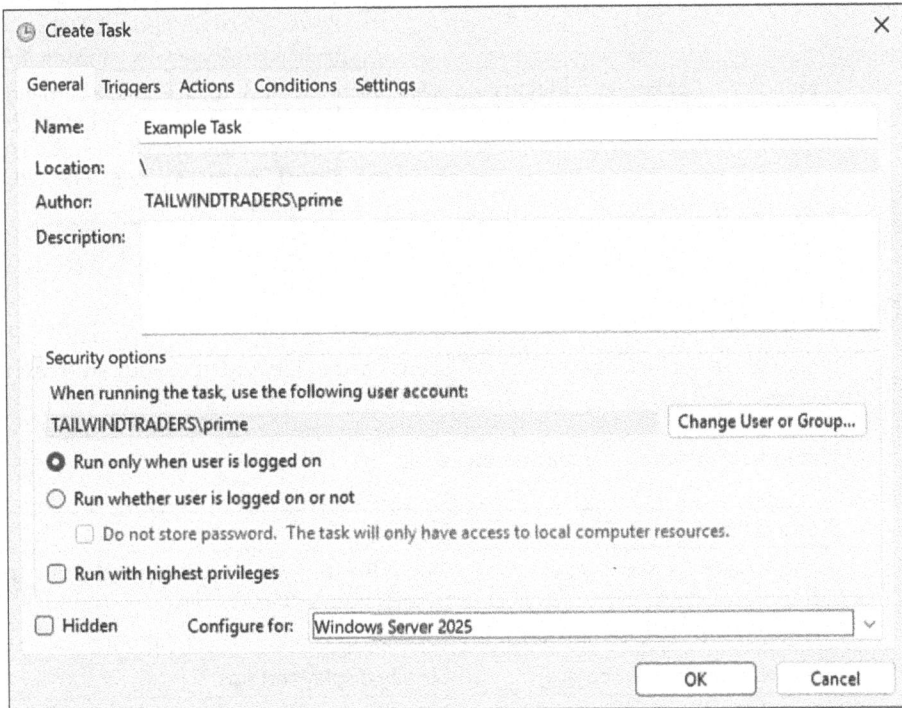

Figure 1-16   Create Task

Table 1-5   Create Task dialog settings

Tab	Purpose	Options
General	Defines basic task information and security context.	Name, Description, User Account To Run Task, Run Only When User Is Logged On / Run Whether User Is Logged On Or Not, Run With Highest Privileges, Hidden, Configure For (OS compatibility).
Triggers	Specifies the events or schedules that will initiate the task.	New/Edit/Delete Triggers (On A Schedule, At Startup, At Log On, On An Event, and so on), Advanced Settings (Delay, Repeat, Expire, Enabled).
Actions	Defines the operations the task will perform when triggered.	New/Edit/Delete Actions (Start a program, Send an email (deprecated)), Display A Message (deprecated), Program/Script Path, Arguments, Start In Directory.

Tab	Purpose	Options
Conditions	Sets criteria based on the computer's state that must be met to run.	Idle Settings (Start Only If Idle, Wait For Idle, Stop If Ceases To Be Idle), Power Settings (Ac Power, Wake Computer), Network Settings (Start Only If Specific Network Is Available).
Settings	Configures additional rules for task behavior and error handling.	Allow Task To Be Run On Demand; Run Task As Soon As Possible After Missed Schedule; Restart If Fails; Stop If Runs Too Long; Force Stop If Requested; Rule For Multiple Running Instances.

Control Panel tools

Windows Server includes the Control Panels listed in Table 1-6 that you can access directly from the command line.

Table 1-6   Windows Server Control Panels

Control Panel	Functionality
Control Panel (`control.exe`)	Opens the traditional control panel rather than the newer Settings dialog
Programs and Features (`appwiz.cpl`)	Uninstall or change installed programs
System Display (`desk.cpl`)	Modify display settings
Firewall (`firewall.cpl`)	Basic Firewall settings (rather than Advanced Firewall)
Device Manager (`Hdwwiz.cpl`)	Manage devices connected to the computer
Region settings (`intl.cpl`)	Configure region and language settings
Mouse settings (`main.cpl`)	Configure mouse settings
Network Connections (`ncpa.cpl`)	Network connections and adapters
System Properties (`sysdm.cpl`)	System Properties, including the ability to configure the server name and domain membership
Time and Date (`timedate.cpl`)	Configure time and date settings

This table only includes control panels that are directly available from the command line and does not include those available indirectly, either through the traditional Control Panel itself or the newer Settings dialogs.

Command-line tools

Windows Server includes a large number of command-line tools. While PowerShell is usually the first thing younger IT pros think of when someone suggests doing work at the Windows

Server command prompt, some of the older tools that are still included with the operating system can be useful when diagnosing and resolving problems. These commands can be a bit idiosyncratic, each having its own way of functioning; however, they often allow you to accomplish something with a single command that might take a short script in PowerShell.

Rather than provide a list of each command (which you can find on the *learn.microsoft.com* website), here are a few select commands that you're likely to find useful when troubleshooting. Once you find one that sounds like it might be useful, you can dig in and see how it works by running it from the command prompt or checking the online reference.

- `Arp.exe`   Manage the address resolution protocol cache.

- `At.exe`   Used to schedule tasks. Can also use schtasks for this purpose.

- `Attrib.exe`   Used to manage attributes assigned to files or directories.

- `Auditpol.exe`   Use this command to view information related to audit policies.

- `Bcdboot.exe`   Repair and manage the boot environment on the system partition.

- `Bcdedit.exe`   Manage the boot configuration data (BCD) stores.

- `Certreq.exe`   Manage certificate requests and interact with a certification authority.

- `Certutil.exe`   Can be used to configure, back up, and restore a certificate authority. Can also be used to manage local certificates.

- `Chkdsk.exe`   Troubleshoot the file system for logical and physical errors.

- `Chkntfs.exe`   Manage automatic disk checking when the system starts.

- `Cipher.exe`   Manage encryption of files and directories on NTFS volumes.

- `Clip.exe`   Redirects command-line output to the Windows clipboard.

- `Comp.exe`   Compare two files.

- `Compact.exe`   Manage the compression of files and directories on NTFS volumes.

- `Cscript.exe`   Starts a script that executes in the command-line environment.

- `Date.exe`   Sets the system date.

- `Dcgpofix.exe`   Regenerates the default group policy objects for a domain.

- `Dfsrmig.exe`   Migrates SYSVOL replication from file replication services to distributed file system replication (DFSR).

- `Diskshadow.exe`   Manage volume shadow copy services.

- `Dnscmd.exe`   Manage DNS servers.

- `Driverquery.exe`   Lists all device drivers installed on the computer.

- `Eventcreate.exe`   Create custom events in event logs.

- `Find.exe`   Search text files or text output for a specific string.

- `Findstr.exe`   Search text files and text output using regular expressions.

- `Format.exe`   Format a volume.

- `Fsutil.exe`   Manage volumes and file systems. `Fsutil.exe` with the "file" parameter allows you to find files by properties, such as locating all files owned by a specific user. `Fsutil.exe` with the "repair" parameter allows you to manage NTFS self-healing operations without having to run `chkdsk.exe`. `Fsutil.exe` with the "tiering" parameter allows you to manage storage tier functionality.

- `Getmac.exe`   Returns the MAC address and protocols associated with specific network adapters.

- `Gpfixup.exe`   Repair domain name dependencies in group policy objects and group policy links after a domain has been renamed.

- `Gpresult.exe`   Display cumulative group policy information for a specific user or computer.

- `Gpupdate.exe`   Refreshes group policy settings.

- `Hostname.exe`   View the computer's name.

- `Icacls.exe`   Manage discretionary access control lists on files.

- `Ipconfig.exe`   View TCP/IP configuration settings. Can also be used to refresh DHCP settings.

- `Klist.exe`   View a list of cached Kerberos tickets.

- `Ksetup.exe`   Manage the Kerberos protocol and key distribution center for Kerberos realms.

- `Ktmutil.exe`   Kernel transaction manager utility.

- `Ktpass.exe`   Configure the Service Principal Name for a host or service in Active Directory.

- `Lodctr.exe`   Configure performance counter registry settings.

- `Logman.exe`   Manage Event Trace Sessions and Performance logs.

- `Logoff.exe`   Kick a user off a Remote Desktop Session Host session and terminate their session.

- `Manage-bde.exe`   Manage BitLocker.

- `Mklink.exe`   Manage symbolic links.

- `Mountvol.exe`   Manage volume mount points.

- `Msiexec.exe`   Perform operations on Windows Installer files.

- `Nbtstat.exe`   Displays protocol information about NetBIOS over TCP/IP.

- `Netcfg.exe`   Manage the Windows Preinstallation Environment (WinPE).

- `Netsh.exe`   A command-line environment for managing network configuration.

- `Netstat.exe`   View information about TCP connections, networking statistics, and IP routing information.

- `Net print`   Manage print jobs and queues.

- `Nlbmgr.exe`   Manage network load balancing clusters.

- `Nslookup.exe`   View DNS information.

- `Openfiles.exe`   Display a list of open files and directories. Also can be used to disconnect a user from a remotely open file.

- `Pathping.exe`   Functions similarly to a combination of `traceroute.exe` and `ping.exe`.

- `Ping.exe`   Network diagnostic utility that uses ICMP to verify connectivity to another host.

- `Pnpunattend.exe`   Manage drivers installed on the system.

- `Pnputil.exe`   Manage the system's driver store.

- `Prndrvr.exe`   Manage printer drivers.

- `Prnjobs.exe`   Manage print jobs.

- `Prnmngr.exe`   Manage printers.

- `Prnqctl.exe`   Manage printer queues.

- `Pubprn.exe`   Manage the publication of printers to Active Directory.

- `Recover.exe`   Recover readable information from a defective volume.

- `Reg.exe`   Manage registry entries.

- `Regsvr32.exe`   Register dll files with the registry.

- `Repair-bde.exe`   Recover data from a damage BitLocker-encrypted volume.

- `Schtasks.exe` Manage scheduled tasks.

- `Secedit.exe` Analyze security configuration against a security template.

- `Servermanagercmd.exe` Menu-driven command-line utility for server configuration.

- `Sfc.exe` Verify the integrity of protected system files. Will replace problematic versions with updated versions.

- `Showmount.exe` View mounted directories.

- `Subst.exe` Allows you to associate a path with a volume letter.

- `Systeminfo.exe` View system information at the command line.

- `Takeown.exe` Recover access to a file by making an administrative account the owner of the file.

- `Taskkill.exe` Terminate a specific process from the command line.

- `Tasklist.exe` View a list of running processes.

- `Time.exe` Manage system time.

- `Tracerpt.exe` Manage Event Trace Logs as well as log files created by Performance Monitor.

- `Tracert.exe` Determine the path between the host and a remote system.

- `Tree.exe` View a graphical representation within the command-line environment of the directory structure.

- `Tzutil.exe` Manage the time zone settings.

- `Verifier.exe` Manage driver verification.

- `Wbadmin.exe` Manage backup.

- `Wdsutil.exe` Manage Windows Deployment Services.

- `Wecutil.exe` Manage event subscriptions.

- `Wevutil.exe` Manage information about event logs and publishers.

- `Where.exe` Locate files based on search keywords.

- `Whoami.exe` Provides information about the currently signed-on user identity.

- `Winrs.exe` Can be used to remotely manage and execute programs

- `Wmic` Manage WMI information from the command prompt.

- `Wscript.exe` Windows Script Host is an environment through which scripts can be run.

> ## More Info
>
> **Command-line tools**
>
> **You can learn more about the Windows Server command line tools as a whole at *https://learn.microsoft.com/windows-server/administration/windows-commands/ windows-commands.***

Sysinternals tools

The Sysinternals tools are a collection of utilities that you can use to diagnose and troubleshoot Windows Server and client operating systems. The tools are hosted on Microsoft's website and can be used to interact not only with the GUI version of Windows Server, but many of the tools can also be used with the Server Core version, either directly or remotely. In the following pages, you'll learn about several of the Sysinternals tools that you might find useful in troubleshooting and diagnosing your Windows Server deployment.

> ## More Info
>
> **Sysinternals tools**
>
> **You can learn more about the Sysinternals tools as a whole at *https://learn.microsoft. com/sysinternals/.***

Process Explorer

Process Explorer, shown in Figure 1-17, allows you to view real-time information about how processes are interacting with resources on a particular computer. Process Explorer can be thought of as a highly advanced version of the built-in Task Manager tool. You can use Process Explorer to determine which processes have a specific file open. Process Explorer also allows you to determine which handles a specific process has open, as well as allowing you to see which DLLs and memory-mapped files have been loaded by a specific process.

You can install Process Explorer using WinGet with the command

```
WinGet Install Microsoft.Sysinternals.ProcessExplorer
```

CHAPTER 1

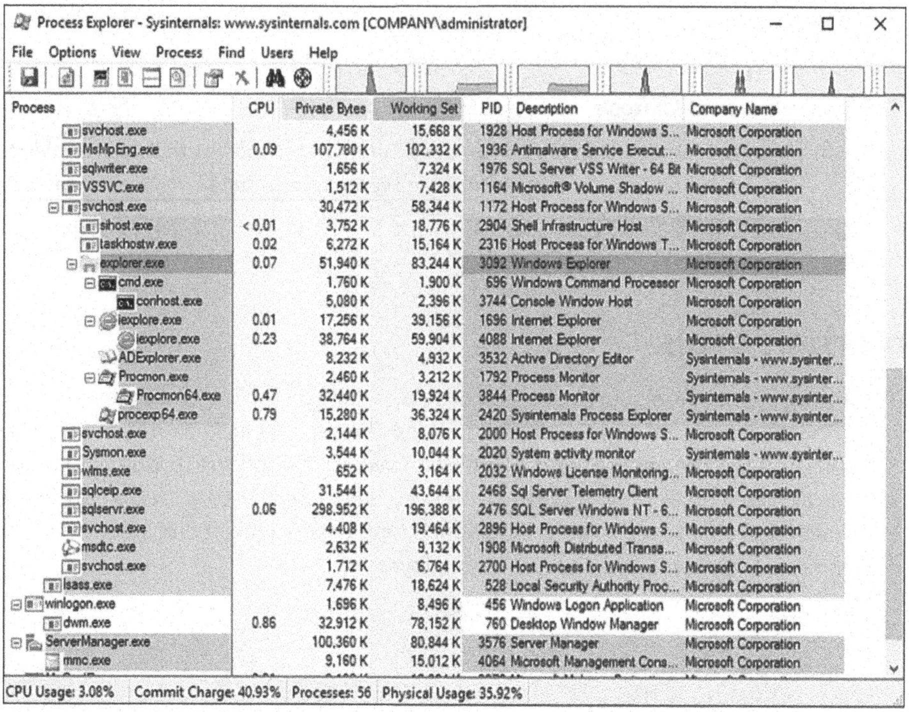

Figure 1-17   Process Explorer

Process Explorer includes the following functionality:

- **Tree view**   This allows you to see the parent/child relationships between processes.

- **Color coding**   Allows you to visually determine the process type and state, with services, .NET processes, suspended processes, and processes running using the same credentials as the user running Process Explorer each being assigned a separate color code.

- **Fractional CPU reporting**   Shows where processes are consuming minimal amounts of CPU resources, rather than being rounded down to zero, which might imply that the processes were completely inactive.

- **Suspicious process identification**   Process Explorer will highlight processes that are flagged as suspicious by *VirusTotal.com*, an antimalware service.

- **DLL and mapped file identification**   Identification of all DLLs and mapped files loaded by a process.

- **Kernel object handle identification**   Identification of all handles to kernel objects opened by a process.

- **Identifying open handles**   Ability to determine which processes have open handles to kernel objects, including files and folders.

- **Identifying processes loading specific DLLs**   Ability to determine which processes have loaded a specific DLL.

- **Viewing process threads**   View process threads, including start addresses and stacks.

- **Managing processes**   Modify a process's priority, suspend the process, and terminate a process or a process tree.

- **Process dumps**   Create a process dump.

> ## More Info
> ### Process Explorer
> You can learn more about Process Explorer at *https://learn.microsoft.com/sysinternals/downloads/process-explorer.*

Process Monitor

Process Monitor is a real-time monitoring tool that you can use to view file system, registry, and process/thread activity. You can configure Process Monitor to log data to a file for later analysis, and Process Monitor logging supports scaling to tens of millions of captured events and gigabytes of log data. Process Monitor also includes the ability to capture thread stacks for specific operations, allowing you to determine the root cause of an operation. You can also capture the details of processes, including image path, command line, related user or service account, and session ID. Process Monitor is shown in Figure 1-18.

You can install Process Monitor using WinGet with this command:

```
WinGet Install Microsoft.Sysinternals.ProcessMonitor
```

> ## More Info
> ### Process Monitor
> You can learn more about Process Monitor at *https://learn.microsoft.com/sysinternals/downloads/procmon.*

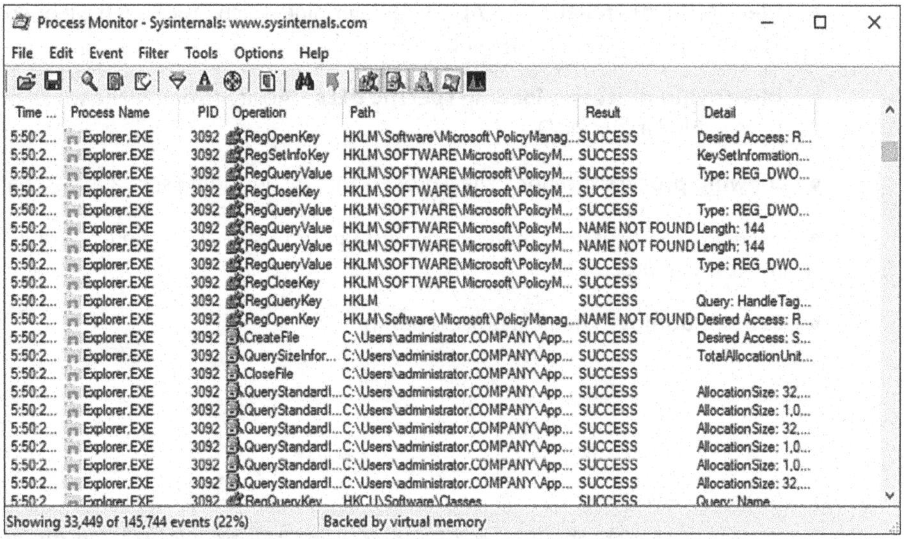

Figure 1-18   Process Monitor

ProcDump

ProcDump is a command-line utility that you can use to monitor a specific application for CPU utilization spikes. You can then generate diagnostic dumps during the spike that allow a developer to determine what causes the spike. ProcDump includes hung-window monitoring and unhandled exception monitoring, and it can be configured to trigger diagnostic dumps based on the values of specific system performance counters.

More Info

ProcDump

You can learn more about ProcDump at *https://learn.microsoft.com/sysinternals/downloads/procdump*.

PsTools

The PS Tools Suite is a collection of tools named after the UNIX operating system's PS utility rather than Microsoft's more recent PowerShell administrative scripting language. You can download the PS Tools Suite in its entirety from Microsoft's website or download individual tools as you need them. Some tools that are in the PS Tools Suite have functionality that is mirrored by Windows Server command-line utilities or PowerShell cmdlets. The PS Tools Suite has been around since the Sysinternals Tools were first released in the 1990s. The command-line utilities and PowerShell cmdlets only became available more recently. Tools included in the PS Tools Suite are as follows:

- **PsExec** Enact processes remotely.

- **PsFile** View files that have been opened remotely.

- **PsGetSid** View the SID of a user or computer.

- **PsInfo** View system information.

- **PsPing** Covered in detail later in this chapter; allows you to measure network performance.

- **PsKill** Terminate processes on the basis of name or process ID.

- **PsList** Determine detailed information about active processes on a system.

- **PsLoggedOn** Determine which accounts are signed on locally and through resource sharing.

- **PsLogList** Extract event log records.

- **PsPasswd** Change account passwords.

- **PsService** View and manage services.

- **PsShutdown** Shut down or reboot a computer.

- **PsSuspend** Suspends a running process.

Note that some antimalware tools will flag utilities in the PS Tools Suite as malware. This is because some malware toolchains include and leverage utilities in the PS Tools Suite. If you're concerned that one of the utilities in the PS Tools Suite is malware, use the SigCheck utility, covered later in this chapter, to verify the integrity of the tool in question.

More Info

PsTools

You can learn more about the PsTools collection at *https://learn.microsoft.com/sysinternals/downloads/pstools*.

CHAPTER 1

VMMap

VMMap allows you to analyze physical and virtual memory utilization. You can use VMMap to view a specific process's committed virtual memory types and the amount of physical memory (working set) that the operating system has allocated to the process. VMMap is useful when you need to troubleshoot application memory utilization. Figure 1-19 shows VMMap used to analyze the application ADExplorer.exe.

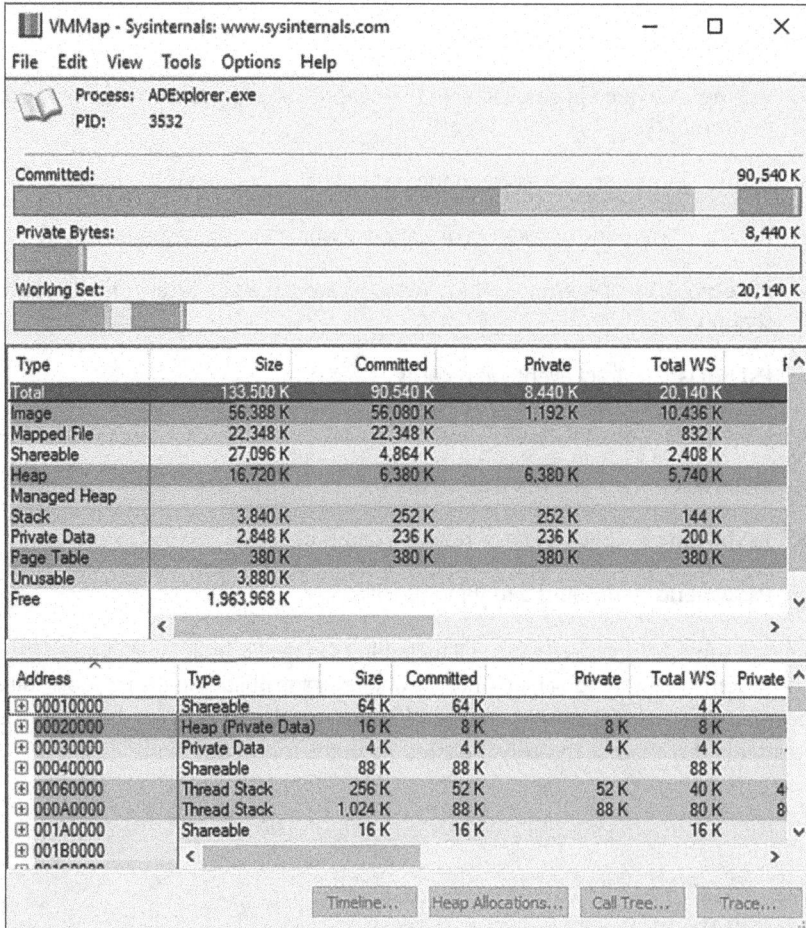

Figure 1-19   VMMap

More Info

VMMap

You can learn more about VMMap at *https://learn.microsoft.com/sysinternals/downloads/vmmap*.

SigCheck

Sigcheck is a command-line utility that allows you to view the following information:

- File version number

- Time stamp

- Digital signature details, including certificate chains

Sigcheck also allows you to check a file's status in VirusTotal, a database that scans against 40 separate antivirus engines. You can also use SigCheck to upload the file to be scanned by VirusTotal. Use SigCheck when you suspect a file may have been tampered with or may, for some other reason, not be legitimate.

You can install Sigcheck using WinGet with the following command:

```
WinGet install Microsoft.Sysinternals.Sigcheck
```

> **More Info**
>
> *SigCheck*
>
> **You can learn more about SigCheck at *https://learn.microsoft.com/sysinternals/downloads/sigcheck*.**

AccessChk

AccessChk is a command-line utility that allows you to determine what access user, service, or group accounts have to specific files, folders, registry keys, or Windows services. Using the `Accesschk -?` command provides a list of all options that can be used.

> **More Info**
>
> *AccessChk*
>
> **You can learn more about AccessChk at *https://learn.microsoft.com/sysinternals/downloads/accesschk*.**

Sysmon

System Monitor (Sysmon) is a service and device driver that you can install on Windows Server that monitors and logs system activity to the event logs. Sysmon will remain installed and running across reboots. Sysmon allows you to identify anomalous or malicious activity. Security experts use it to determine how malware and malicious actors operate when compromising a computer. It's important to understand that while Sysmon monitors and logs potentially hostile activity, it provides no method for you to analyze that activity. A competent attacker will be able to determine that Sysmon is present on a computer and will take appropriate countermeasures.

Sysmon includes the following functionality:

- **Logs the creation of processes**   This includes information about the command line for the currently created process as well as any parent process.

- **Creates a hash of the process image file**   The default is SHA1, but you can configure sysmon to use MD5, SHA256, or IMPHASH. You can have multiple hashes created for the same process image file.

- **Logs the loading of drivers and DLLS**   Records driver signatures and DLL hashes.

- **Includes a GUID for each process**   This allows you to track activity when Windows Server reuses process IDs for different processes over time.

- **Includes a GUID related to each session**   This allows you to correlate events to specific logon sessions.

- **Log raw disk access**   Logs open when raw read access to disks and volumes occurs.

- **Log network connections**   Data written to the log includes connection source processes, IP addresses, port numbers, hostnames used, and port names.

- **Detects modifications made to file creation time**   Malware and intruders often modify file creation timestamps when cleaning up evidence of a breach.

- **Reloads configuration**   Reloads configuration if the configuration is modified in the registry.

- **Supports rule filtering**   This allows you to include or exclude specific events from being monitored and logged.

- **Allows you to generate events during the system startup process**   This allows you to capture activity caused by kernel-mode malware.

Sysmon events are stored in the
`Applications and Services Logs\Microsoft\Windows\Sysmon\Operational` log folder.

Table 1-7 lists important event IDs generated by Sysmon.

Table 1-7   Important Sysmon event IDs

Event ID	Description
1: Process creation	Includes detailed information about newly created processes. Includes the ProcessGUID field that uniquely identifies the process. Hash generated is a full hash of the associated file using the configured hashing algorithms.
2: A process changed the file creation time	An event is generated when the file creation time is modified by a process. You can even use this to track the accurate creation time of a file. Intruders often alter file creation times in an attempt to mask malware to make it look as though it was part of the original operating system installation. It's important to note that many standard processes alter file creation times, and it will be necessary to investigate further to determine if the change was part of standard operating system behavior or malicious activity.
3: Network connection	Logs TCP and UDP connections to the server. This option is disabled by default when you install Sysmon. When enabled, each connection is associated with a `ProcessID` and `ProcessGUID`. The event will record source, destination host names, IP addresses, and port numbers.
4: Sysmon service state changed	Records when the Sysmon service starts or stops.
5: Process terminated	Records when a process terminates.
6: Driver loaded	Records when a driver has loaded. Provides hash and signature information for the driver. Signatures will be created asynchronously to minimize performance impact.
7: Image loaded	Records when a process loads a specific module. It's disabled by default when Sysmon is installed and must be manually enabled. It generates hash and signature information asynchronously to minimize performance impact. Only enable with appropriate filtering because enabling this process will cause a large number of events to be written to the monitoring log.
8: CreateRemoteThread	Records when one process creates a thread in another process. This is one strategy used by malware when it injects code to hide itself in the execution of another process. Event records both the source and target processes. Provides information on the code that runs in the new thread, including `StartAddress`, `StartModule`, and `StartFunction`.
9: RawAccessRead	Records when a process performs read operations from storage using the `\\.\` denotation. This technique is tracked because it is often used by malware when exfiltrating files locked for reading. It also avoids most file access auditing technologies. The event records the source process and target device.

CHAPTER 1

Event ID	Description
10: ProcessAccess	Records when one process opens another process, which may involve queries reading or writing data in the address space of the target process. This event ID often records hacking tools that copy the contents of memory used by processes such as the Local Security Authority (`Lsass.exe`) as part of a Pass-the-Hash attack. Enabling this type of auditing will generate a substantial number of events if diagnostic utilities that query the state of processes are being used on the server. In that case, create filters to remove this expected access.
11: FileCreate	Records when a file is created or overwritten. This is useful when investigating the status of autostart locations, as well as temporary and download locations. These locations are often used by attackers when storing malware during initial server compromise events.
12: RegistryEvent (Object create and delete)	Registry modification events, where keys and values are created or deleted, are mapped to this event. Use this event to determine if malware has made modifications to the registry.
13: RegistryEvent (Value Set)	Registry modification events, where values are changed. The changes are written as event data.
14: RegistryEvent (Key and Value rename)	Registry modification events, where keys and values are renamed. Name changes are written as event data.
15: FileCreateStreamHash	Records when a named file stream is created. Creates a hash of the contents of the file. Useful to track malware variants that use browser downloads to drop executables or configuration settings. This problem is less likely to occur if you deploy Server Core, as the web browser is not available.
255: Error	Generated when Sysmon experiences an error. May occur if Sysmon is under extreme load.

More Info

Sysmon

You can learn more about Sysmon at *https://learn.microsoft.com/sysinternals/downloads/sysmon.*

AccessEnum

AccessEnum allows you to determine where a file, directory, or registry key has separate permissions from its parent object. This allows you to view where permissions have been configured at the object level rather than where the object has inherited the permission from the parent level.

This sort of configuration is almost always done manually, though it won't be obvious unless surfaced by a tool such as AccessEnum. Figure 1-20 shows where one executable in a directory has different permissions applied to those of the parent directory.

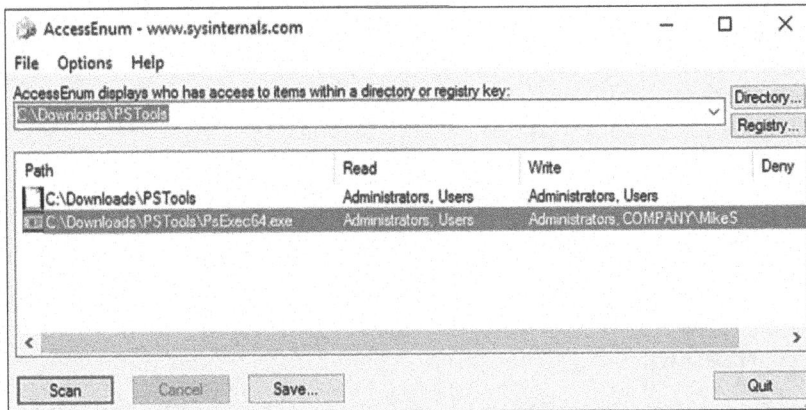

Figure 1-20   AccessEnum

CHAPTER 1

More Info

AccessEnum

You can learn more about AccessEnum at *https://learn.microsoft.com/sysinternals/ downloads/accessenum.*

ShellRunAs

ShellRunas provides you with the ability to quickly launch applications, including cmd.exe and PowerShell sessions, using the credentials of other users by right-clicking and selecting Run As Different User from the context menu. You must run shellrunas /reg from an elevated command prompt to register ShellRunas with the computer. Figure 1-21 shows ADExplorer.exe being configured to run with alternate credentials.

More Info

ShellRunAs

You can learn more about ShellRunAs at *https://learn.microsoft.com/sysinternals/ downloads/shellrunas.*

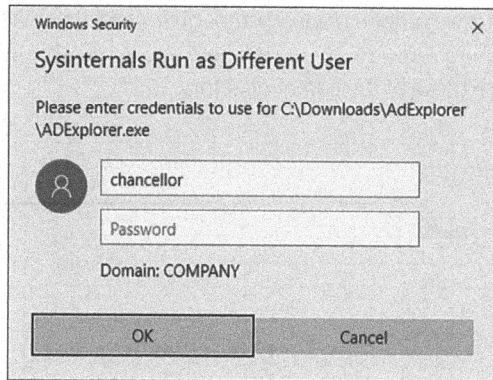

Figure 1-21   ShellRunAs

LogonSessions

LogonSessions is a command-line utility that allows you to view the activity of all active sessions on a Windows Server system. When used with the -p option, you're also able to see which processes are running in each session. This tool can also be used when connected to a remote PowerShell session to determine which active sessions are present on a server.

> ## More Info
> *LogonSessions*
>
> **You can learn more about LogonSessions at** *https://docs.microsoft.com/en-us/ sysinternals/downloads/logonsessions.*

Active Directory Explorer

Active Directory Explorer (AD Explorer) provides you with a detailed view of and the ability to edit Active Directory objects. It's in some ways a more advanced and substantially more user-friendly version of the ADSIEdit utility that's built into Windows Server. You can use AD Explorer to view Active Directory object properties and attributes as shown in Figure 1-22.

You can also use AD Explorer to save snapshots of the AD database for offline viewing. You can also use the tool to directly compare separate snapshots of the AD database, which can be very useful in recovery scenarios where you have several copies of the AD database and are unsure which version to restore to your production environment.

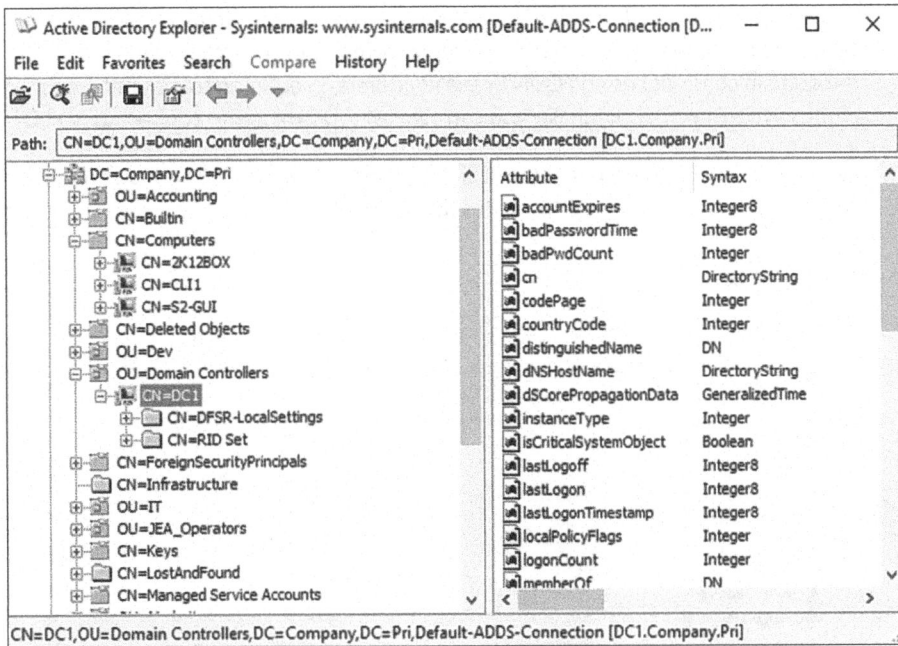

Figure 1-22   Active Directory Explorer

When connecting to a live AD instance, specify the domain name, user name, and password, as shown in Figure 1-23. You can also save connection properties, allowing you to reconnect to different domains as necessary.

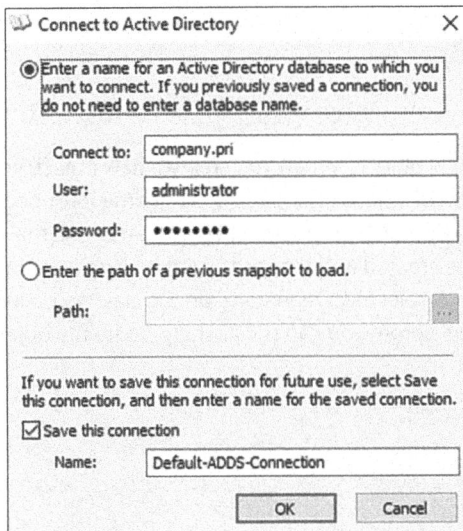

Figure 1-23   Connect to AD Database

When you specify the domain name, AD Explorer will connect to a domain controller in the same site. If you want to connect to a specific domain controller, you can specify the address of the domain controller using FQDN or the IP address. In addition to mounting existing snapshots of the Active Directory database, you can also use AD Explorer to connect to AD LDS instances.

You can use AD Explorer to rename or delete objects. You can also view and modify individual attributes of an object on the Attributes tab of the object's properties, as shown in Figure 1-24.

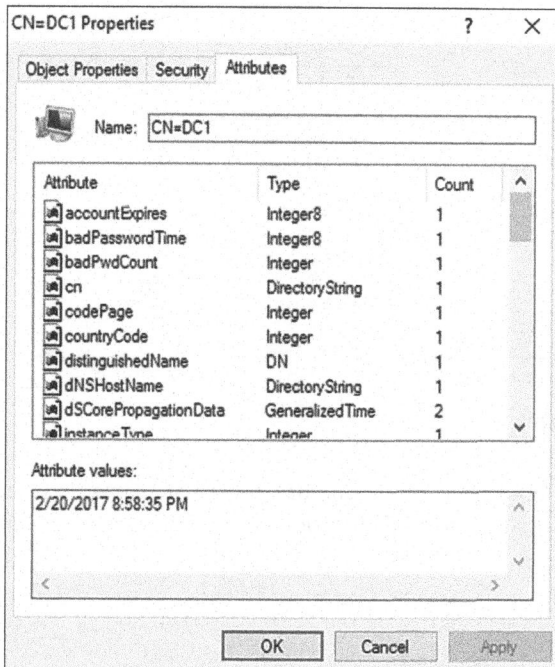

Figure 1-24   Object properties

You can also use AD Explorer to create new objects. When you create a new object, you must specify which class it belongs to, as shown in Figure 1-25. The object's name must begin with the designator CN= and must be unique within the container in which you create the object. The object's attribute list will automatically be created and set based on the attributes that are mandatory for the class of object that you have selected. Depending on the class you select, you'll need to configure several of these objects before you can successfully create the object.

More Info

Active Directory Explorer

You can learn more about ADExplorer at *https://learn.microsoft.com/sysinternals/downloads/adexplorer*.

Figure 1-25 Create object

Insight for Active Directory

ADInsight (Insight for Active Directory) allows you to monitor LDAP traffic. You can use ADInsight to resolve problems with Windows authentication, DNS, and other applications and services that interact with Active Directory.

ADInsight allows you to troubleshoot LDAP traffic by intercepting calls that applications make to the wldap32.dll library. This library is the foundation used for Active Directory APIs, including ADSI and LDAP. ADInsight differs from traditional network monitoring tools in that it will intercept and interpret all Active Directory–related client-side APIs. This includes those Active Directory–related client-side APIs that do not directly transmit data to a domain controller. When used with administrator privileges, ADInsight allows you to monitor Windows services and other system processes.

> ## More Info
> ### Insight for Active Directory
> **You can learn more about Insight for Active Directory at** *https://learn.microsoft.com/ sysinternals/downloads/adinsight.*

PsPing

You can use PsPing as an advanced network diagnostic utility that has a superset of the ping.exe utility's functionality. PsPing allows you to measure TCP ping, network latency, and network bandwidth. PsPing can report information to within 0.01 milliseconds, which is 100 times more accurate than the standard Ping utility. Use the following commands to determine information about each mode:

- **Psping -? i**   Provides information on ICMP ping functionality

- **Psping -? t**   Provides information on TCP ping functionality

- **Psping -? l**   Provides information on TCP/UDP latency tests

- **Psping -? b**   Provides information on TCP/UDP bandwidth tests

More Info

PsPing

You can learn more about PsPing at *https://learn.microsoft.com/sysinternals/downloads/psping*.

RAMMap

RAMMap provides advanced information about how physical memory is used on computers running Windows operating systems. You can install RAMMap using the following WinGet command:

```
WinGet install Microsoft.Sysinternals.RAMMap
```

The separate tabs of RAMMap provide the following information:

- **Use Counts**   Shown in Figure 1-26, this tab provides summary information by type. Categories include Process Private, Mapped File, Shareable, Page Table, Paged Pool, Nonpaged Pool, System PTE, Session Private, Metafile, Address Windowing Extension (AWE), Driver Locked, Kernel Stack, Large Page, and Unused.

- **Processes**   Provides information about the size of process working sets. Includes information about PID, Private memory, Standby, Modified, Page Table, and Total physical memory utilization.

- **Priority Summary**   Shows the size of prioritized standby lists. If items with priority 5 and higher show high repurpose counts, it's likely that the server is under memory pressure and would likely benefit from the addition of more physical memory.

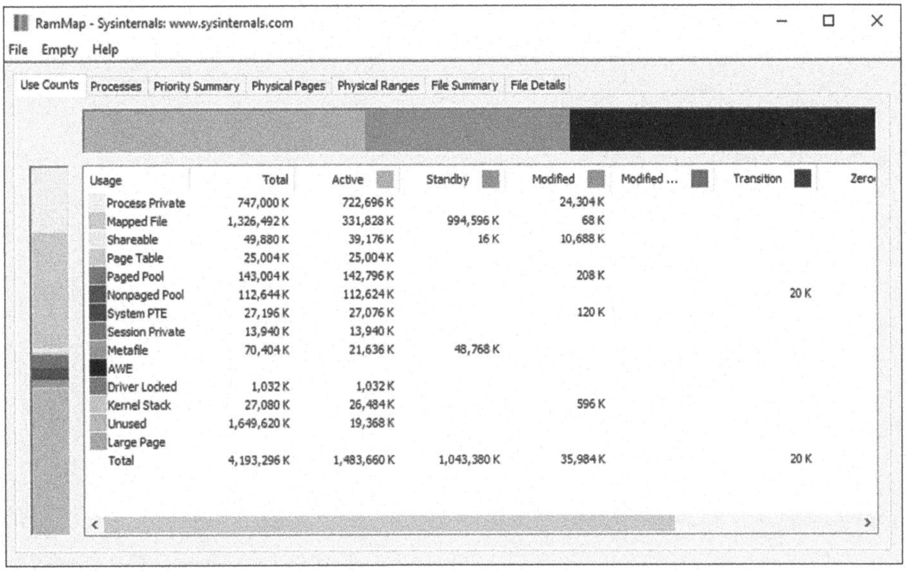

Figure 1-26   RAMMap

- **Physical Pages**   Shows per-page information about all physical memory in the computer. Provides physical page information including physical address, list membership, allocation type, priority, whether the page stores part of an image, offset within a page table, file name of mapped file, originating process, virtual address, and any paged and nonpaged memory pool tag.

- **Physical Ranges**   Lists the physical ranges used in terms of start address, end address, and overall size.

- **File Summary**   Provides details of files that are stored in physical memory.

- **File Details**   Displays memory pages in physical RAM on a per file basis.

You use RAMMap when you need to understand how Windows Server manages memory. For example, you can use it to determine how physical memory is allocated to a specific process or file. You can search memory for a specific file or process by using Ctrl+F. You can also use RAMMap to take snapshots of how physical memory is being allocated at a specific point in time for later analysis. You can also use RAMMap to purge portions of RAM when testing memory management scenarios.

More Info

RAMMap

You can learn more about RAMMap at *https://learn.microsoft.com/sysinternals/downloads/rammap*.

CHAPTER 1

CHAPTER 2

Installation options

Before you install Windows Server, you need to make a number of decisions about which edition you want to install, which version you want to install, and how you want to license the product. The choices that you make will be determined by the role that you want the server to play in hosting your organization's workloads. In this chapter, you'll learn about the different editions, channels, and versions of Windows Server. Chapter 3, "Deployment and configuration," covers the deployment process itself.

Windows Server editions

There are several editions of Windows Server. The primary editions are

- **Standard edition**   The standard edition of Windows Server is suitable for environments where most servers are deployed physically rather than as virtual machines. The Standard edition is licensed on a per-processor core basis and requires Windows Server CALs. Alternatively, it can be licensed using the Pay As You Go option through an associated Azure subscription.

- **Datacenter edition**   This edition is suitable for datacenters that include a high degree of virtualization. Licensed on a per-processor core basis and requires Windows Server CALs. Alternatively, it can be licensed using the Pay As You Go option through an associated Azure subscription. The primary benefit of the Datacenter edition is that it supports Automatic Virtual Machine Activation and licenses you to run an unlimited number of Windows Server virtual machines, with the only limit being the hardware capacity. Datacenter edition also includes the Network Controller, Hyper-V Host Guardian, Azure Extended Networking, and full Storage Spaces Direct feature support.

- **Azure edition**   Recent versions of Windows Server include a Datacenter edition that is specially configured to run in Azure or Azure Stack HCI and includes some features not present in the standard or datacenter editions. You generally have to install this edition from the Azure or Azure Stack HCI portal, and this edition is not supported outside the

Azure or Azure Stack environments. The Azure edition is licensed on a Pay As You Go basis through your Azure subscription. If you're running Windows Server in Azure, this is the edition you would choose to run. It can be configured for nested virtualization.

Windows Server 2025 has the following hardware limitations:

- **Maximum number of users**   Depends on the number of Client Access Licenses

- **Maximum SMB connections**   16,777,216

- **Maximum Remote Desktop Services connections**   65,535

- **Maximum number of 64-bit sockets**   64

- **Maximum number of cores**   Unlimited (Azure edition 2048 logical processors)

- **Maximum RAM**   4 Petabytes for hosts that support 5-level paging, 256 TB for hosts that support 4-level paging (Azure edition 240 TB for Gen 2 VM)

- **Windows Server Containers**   Unlimited

- **Hyper-V isolated containers**   Standard (2), Datacenter, and Azure edition unlimited

- **Storage replica**   Standard (1 partnership with 1 2 TB volume), Datacenter and Azure edition unlimited

Inside OUT

Additional editions

Windows Server 2019 also included an Essentials edition and a stripped-down Hyper-V server edition. These editions of Windows Server are not currently available for the more recent versions of Windows Server, such as Windows Server 2022 and Windows Server 2025.

Windows Server Licensing Options

Windows Server 2025 offers a Pay As You Go license option. Rather than pay for a standard or datacenter edition perpetual license, you instead associate the Windows Server instance with an Azure subscription through Azure Arc. You're billed through your Azure subscription on a monthly basis. This option is most appropriate for organizations that only infrequently require a Windows Server instance without wanting to pay for a perpetual license.

Windows Server servicing branches

Windows Server supports two separate servicing branches: the Long Term Servicing Channel (LTSC) and the Annual Channel (SAC).

Long Term Servicing Channel

LTSC versions are the versions of Windows Server that people usually think of as the main versions of Windows Server. Windows Server 2019 and Windows Server 2025 are LTSC versions. LTSC versions of Windows Server can be installed either as a Server with Desktop Experience or in the Server Core configuration.

LTSC provides five years of mainstream support with five years of extended support. This is similar to the support options provided for previous versions of Windows Server, such as Windows Server 2012 R2. Most organizations are likely to deploy this servicing branch. Microsoft also offers Extended Security Updates for Windows Server. Extended security updates allow support updates to be provided beyond the traditional 10-year support cycle.

Extended Security Updates are available for security bulletins rated Critical and Important. These updates are available for no additional fee for Windows Server instances deployed in Azure or in an Azure Stack HCI environment and are available for purchase if your servers are hosted elsewhere.

Annual Channel

The Annual Channel option is a version of Windows Server that's deployed as a container. These Windows Server container image versions are supported for 24 months instead of the LTSC version's 10 years. Annual Channel container images are activated through Windows Server Datacenter's activation keys.

> ## More Info
> ### Servicing Channels
> You can learn more about Windows Server servicing channels at *https://learn.microsoft. com/windows-server/get-started/servicing-channels-comparison*.

Insider Preview Builds

Windows Server Insider Preview builds are prerelease versions of the software that are similar to the old Release Candidate or Beta versions. Insider Preview Builds are for testing purposes only and should not be used in production environments. You get access to Windows Server Insider

Preview builds by joining the Windows Insider Program. New features appear in Insider Preview Builds before appearing in the SAC releases.

Inside OUT

At your own risk

Insider Preview Builds are very much a "run this at your own risk" proposition. Some builds will work perfectly well, and some will be less reliable than a teenager's promises to do the dishes.

More Info

Insider Previews

You can learn more about Windows Server Insider Preview Builds and sign up for the Insider program at *https://www.microsoft.com/en-us/software-download/ windowsinsiderpreviewserver*.

Server Core

Server Core is the default installation option for Windows Server. Because Server Core has fewer components, it doesn't need to have software updates applied as often as the Server With GUI installation option does. Because components such as the built-in web browser have been removed, Server Core is less vulnerable to malware than the Server with Desktop Experience installation option. Additionally, because it doesn't require all the components of the version that includes the GUI, it has a lower resource footprint.

The nature of Server Core is not explicitly called out by the Windows Server installation wizard shown in Figure 2-1. The version listed as Desktop Experience is the Server with Desktop Experience option. The Standard version is Server Core. Unless you are paying attention during a manual deployment, you might accidentally deploy Server Core rather than Server with Desktop Experience. I've done that more times than I can count, so you've been warned. These different versions cost the same to license, with the licensing cost difference being whether you choose the Standard or Datacenter edition.

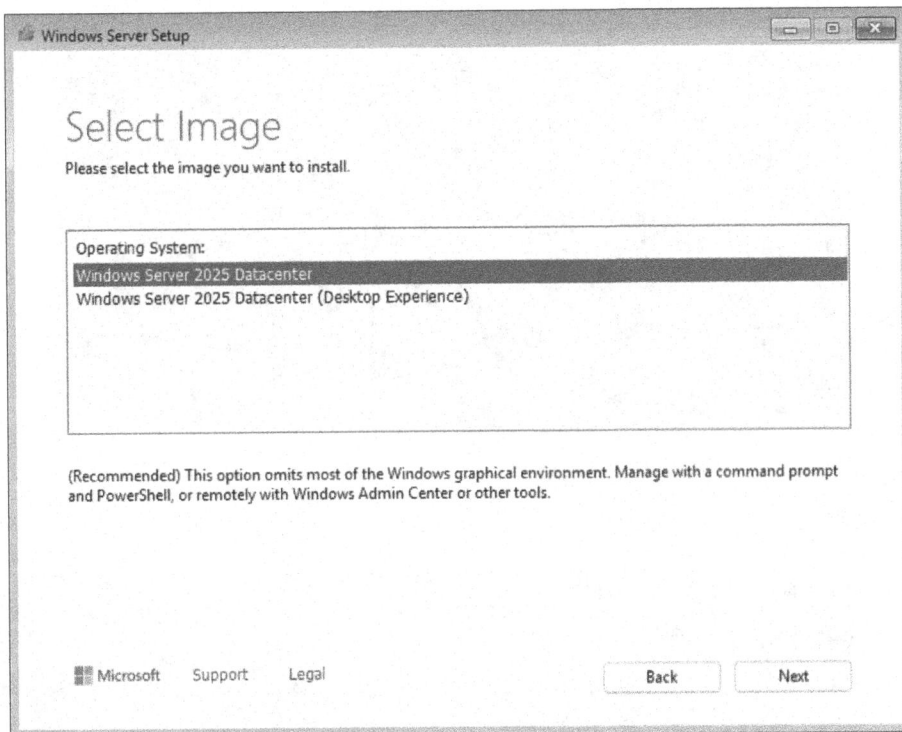

Figure 2-1   Windows Server 2025 installation options when a Datacenter edition key is provided

Server Core interface

The Server Core interface is a command prompt. As Figure 2-2 shows, to interact with the command prompt, you must press Ctrl+Alt+Delete to unlock. You can then sign in with a domain-based or local administrator account.

Once you sign on to Server Core with Windows Server 2022 and later, you are presented with the Sconfig interface. If you are using an earlier version, you can start Sconfig from the command line by typing **sconfig**. Sconfig is a menu-based administration tool that allows you to perform common tasks without having to remember PowerShell commands. This interface is shown in Figure 2-3.

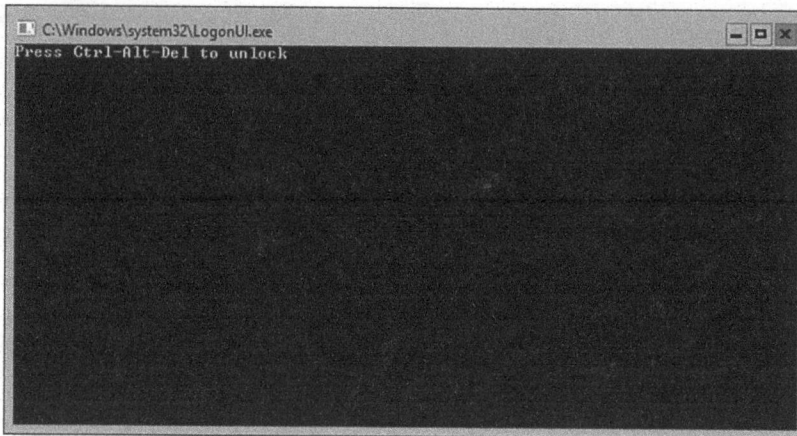

Figure 2-2   Server Core Desktop

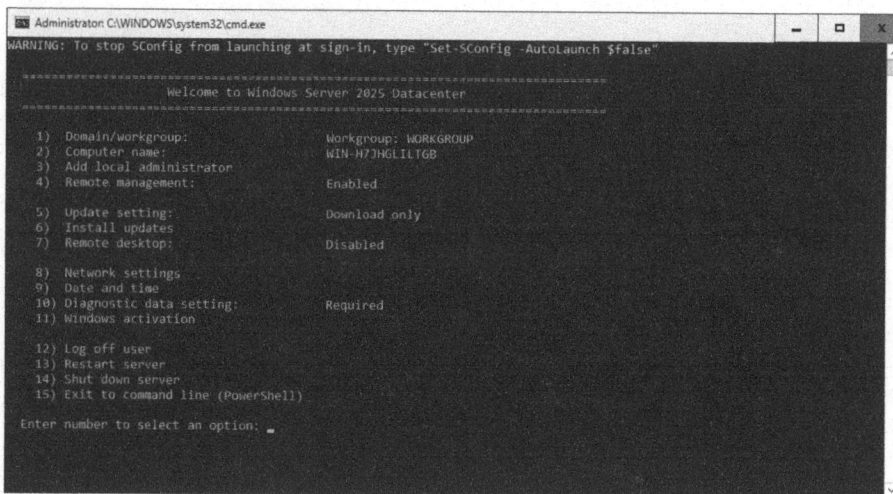

Figure 2-3   Sconfig menu

Sconfig allows you to perform the following tasks:

- Join an Active Directory Domain or switch back to a Workgroup

- Change the computer's name

- Add a local Administrator account

- Enable or disable remote management through PowerShell and Windows Admin Center

- Configure automatic Windows Update settings

- Install software updates

- Enable or disable access through Remote Desktop

- Configure network settings, including IP address and DNS server address information

- Configure data and time settings

- Configure diagnostic data reporting to Microsoft settings

- Configure Windows Activation

- Log off user

- Restart Server

- Shut down server

- Exit to PowerShell

Windows Server 2022 and Windows Server 2025 default to PowerShell in the Server Core environment when you drop to the command prompt. Windows Server 2019 and Windows Server 2016 default to cmd.exe as the command-line environment.

Updating PowerShell on Server Core

Windows Server 2025 defaults to PowerShell version 5.1 in the Server Core environment. If you want to update to the most recent version, download the version available on GitHub at *https://github.com/PowerShell/*. For example, to install PowerShell 7.4.4, perform the following steps:

1. Download the current version of PowerShell using `Invoke-WebRequest`, substituting the version number listed here for the current version:

   ```
   Invoke-WebRequest -Uri "https://github.com/PowerShell/PowerShell/releases/
   download/v7.4.4/PowerShell-7.4.4-win-x64.msi" -OutFile "C:\PowerShell-7.4.4-
   win-x64.msi"
   ```

2. Install PowerShell using the following command:

   ```
   Start-Process msiexec.exe -ArgumentList '/package C:\PowerShell-7.4.4-win-x64.msi
   /quiet' -Wait
   ```

3. By default, the package is installed to the `$env:ProgramFiles\PowerShell\<version>` folder. You can then add the new version of PowerShell to PATH using the following:

   ```
   $env:Path += ";C:\Program Files\PowerShell\7\"
   ```

You will then be able to launch the updated version of PowerShell from the version that ships with Windows Server by running the pwsh command and using the exit command to return

CHAPTER 2

to the default PowerShell environment. You can enter the cmd.exe environment by running the cmd.exe command and return to the default PowerShell environment by using the exit command.

Another way of achieving the same goal involves using Chocolatey and then installing the PowerShell-Core package using this tool. Chocolatey is covered more in Chapter 3.

Server Core graphical tools

While Server Core is primarily a command-line environment, there are some graphical tools that can be launched from the command prompt or Task Manager, including the following:

- **Task Manager**   Task Manager functions in the same way as Task Manager on Server with Desktop Experience or Windows 11, and it can use Task Manager to run tasks by selecting the Run New Task item from the File menu. To start Task Manager, run taskmgr.exe from the PowerShell prompt.

- **Notepad**   You can launch Notepad.exe to edit and view the contents of text files.

- **MSInfo32.exe**   This allows you to view information about the installation.

- **Regedit.exe and Regedt32.exe**   These allow you to edit the registry on a Server Core computer.

- **TimeDate.cpl**   This opens the Time And Date control panel.

- **Intl.cpl**   This opens the Regional Settings control panel.

- **Iscsicpl.exe**   This opens the iSCSI Initiator Properties control panel and allows you to connect to shared storage over iSCSI.

Installing Server Core App Compatibility Features on Demand, which you will learn more about later in this chapter, allows you to access even more GUI tools when signed on directly to the Server Core desktop.

Server Core roles

Server Core supports the following roles, which you can install using the Add-WindowsFeature PowerShell cmdlet, by using the Add Roles And Features Wizard, available in the Server Manager console, or by using Windows Admin Center from a remote computer. You can add the following features using Windows Admin Center:

- Active Directory Certificate Services

- Active Directory Domain Services

- Active Directory Federation Services

- Active Directory Lightweight Directory Services (AD LDS)

- Active Directory Rights Management Services

- Device Health Attestation

- DHCP Server

- DNS Server

- File and Storage Services

- Host Guardian Service

- Hyper-V

- Network Controller

- Print and Document Services

- Remote Access

- Remote Desktop Services

- Volume Activation Services

- Web Server (IIS)

- Windows Deployment Services

- Windows Server Update Services

Server Core also supports the following features:

- .NET Framework 3.5 Features

- .NET Framework 4.7 Features

- Background Intelligent Transfer Service (BITS)

- BitLocker Drive Encryption

- BranchCache

- Client for NFS

- Containers
- Data Center Bridging
- Enhanced Storage
- Failover Clustering
- Group Policy Management
- Host Guardian Hyper-V Support
- I/O Quality of Service
- IIS Hostable Web Core
- IP Address Management (IPAM) Server
- iSNS Server service
- Management OData IIS Extension
- Media Foundation
- Message Queuing
- Multipath I/O
- Network Load Balancing
- Network Virtualization
- Peer Name Resolution Protocol
- Quality Windows Audio Video Experience
- Remote Differential Compression
- RPC over HTTP Proxy
- Setup and Boot Event Collection
- Simple TCP/IP Services
- SMB 1.0/CIFS File Sharing Support
- SMB Bandwidth Limit

- SNMP Service

- Software Load Balancer

- Storage Replica

- Telnet Client

- VM Shielding Tools for Fabric Management

- Windows Defender Antivirus

- Windows Internal Database

- Windows PowerShell

- Windows Process Activation Service

- Windows Server Backup

- Windows Server Migration Tools

- Windows Standards-Based Storage Management

- Windows subsystem for Linux

- WinRM IIS Extension

- WINS Server

- WoW64 Support

While it is possible to install and manage these roles using PowerShell, either directly or through a remote PowerShell session, most administrators are likely to deploy and manage these roles and features remotely using Windows Admin Center or the appropriate Microsoft Management consoles.

As you learned in Chapter 1, Microsoft encourages organizations to manage all servers remotely. It doesn't really matter that Server Core doesn't have a GUI because if you follow best practice guidance, you'll almost never be logging on directly; instead, you will be connecting using remote administration tools.

CHAPTER 2

Inside OUT

Locked in

Older versions of Windows Server, including Windows Server 2012 and Windows Server 2012 R2 allowed you to switch between the Server Core and Server with Desktop Experience installation options. This gave administrators the ability to deploy the Server with Desktop Experience and then pare it back to Server Core if they found that they didn't need all the extra components included with Server with Desktop Experience. This gave server administrators who deployed the Server Core option an escape hatch. If they found that they couldn't run a specific application on Server Core, they could always bump it up to Server with Desktop Experience. Newer versions of Windows Server don't give you that option. The option you choose at deployment is the one you'll be stuck with. This makes sense in terms of Microsoft's philosophy around deployment, which is that if you want to make a substantive change, you should redeploy from scratch rather than reengineer the existing deployment. However, it probably means that fewer administrators will deploy Server Core because they know that applications will always work on a Server with Desktop Experience, but they can't be sure that they will work with Server Core.

Server Core App Compatibility Features on Demand

One of the big challenges many organizations had with deploying Server Core is that many applications that seemingly didn't require GUI components ended up having some form of dependency on the GUI. This meant that many people who wanted to deploy Server Core were unable to do so because of a dependency that either blocked installation or rendered the application non-functional.

App Compatibility Features on Demand (FOD) increases the compatibility of the Server Core installation option for a large number of applications. It also provides additional diagnostic tools for troubleshooting and debugging operations, including:

- Microsoft Management Console (mmc.exe)

- Event Viewer (Eventvwr.msc)

- Performance Monitor (PerfMon.exe)

- Resource Monitor (Resmon.exe)

- Device Manager (Devmgmt.msc)

- File Explorer (Explorer.exe)

- PowerShell Integrated Scripting Environment (PowerShell_ISE.exe)

- Disk Management (diskmgmt.msc)

- Failover Cluster Manager (CluAdmin.msc)

- Microsoft Edge browser (Chromium version)

If the computer has connectivity to Windows Update, you can perform an online installation of the Server Core App Compatibility FOD by running the following command from an elevated PowerShell session and then restarting the computer:

```
Add-WindowsCapability -Online -Name ServerCore.AppCompatibility~~~~0.0.1.0
```

If the Server Core instance doesn't have access to Windows Update, you can download the Feature On Demand ISO from Microsoft's website and deploy these features by running the following commands: the first mounts the ISO, and the second installs FOD.

```
Mount-DiskImage -ImagePath X:\ISO_Folder\ISO_filename.iso
Add-WindowsCapability -Online -Name ServerCore.AppCompatibility~~~~0.0.1.0 -Source
<Mounted_Server_FOD_Drive>
-LimitAccess
```

More Info

Server Core Features on Demand

You can learn more about Server Core Features on Demand and where to download the ISO file for offline installation at *https://learn.microsoft.com/en-us/windows-server/ get-started/server-core-app-compatibility-feature-on-demand*.

When to deploy Server Core

The key to deploying Server Core in your organization is determining whether it is suitable for a specific workload. Server Core is perfect for infrastructure-type roles such as Domain Controller, DNS server, DHCP server, and file server. Where Server Core may be less suitable is in hosting applications that have complex dependencies.

If you are thinking about deploying Server Core, you should perform tests to verify that each workload you intend to host on Server Core functions as expected. Even though Server Core is Microsoft's current preferred deployment option, third-party server-hosted applications often have dependencies that require them to be installed on the server with the GUI installation option.

CHAPTER 2

Inside OUT

Wget

Server Administrators often need to download files from a network or Internet location to a server computer to perform a task. This can get especially complicated if the server is on the perimeter network, meaning that you likely can't directly copy the file or files that you need from a network share. Server Core doesn't have a browser, which means that you can't use Internet Explorer to retrieve those files. What you can do is use the PowerShell wget command (which is just an alias to the *Invoke-WebRequest* cmdlet) with the *UseBasicParsing* parameter to download a file directly from a location on the Internet to the computer file system on which you are running the command. For example, to download the file at *https://www.contoso.com/folder/file.zip*, use the `wget -UseBasicParsing https://www.contoso.com/folder/file.zip file.zip` command.

Server Core can be installed from the Windows Server installation media, or it can be deployed using a variety of methods from the `install.wim` file that is located on the installation media. You'll learn more about deployment and configuration in Chapter 3, "Deployment and configuration."

Inside OUT

What happened to Nano?

Windows Server 2016 shipped with another installation option known as Nano Server. Nano Server was a very small version of the server operating system that only supported remote management and a limited number of roles. For a variety of reasons that Jeffrey Snover may (or may not) tell you about if you buy him some cake, Microsoft decided to discontinue Nano Server as an installation option you could deploy on physical hardware or as a virtual machine. Like the infamous parrot in a Monty Python sketch, Nano Server isn't dead, but it lives on as a container image option for Windows Server containers.

Server with Desktop Experience

Server with Desktop Experience, officially known as Server with Desktop Experience, is the version of Windows Server that IT pros who have been using and managing the product since the 1990s and 2000s are likely most familiar with. Server with Desktop Experience comes with a full desktop environment, including a web browser. You can also install software on a Server with

Desktop Experience that you would normally install on a computer running the Windows client operating system. In some cases, you can deploy Windows Server 2025 on computers that don't support Windows 11 because of the TPM requirements.

Microsoft recommends that you deploy Windows Server with the Desktop Experience only in situations where it is impractical to deploy Server Core. While many administrators who have worked with Windows Server for many years will choose the Server with Desktop Experience installation option out of habit, deploying this version of Windows Server should be the exception rather than the rule.

Roles and features

If you're new to Windows Server, you're likely to use the Add Roles And Features Wizard, shown in Figure 2-4, to add and remove roles and features from a computer running the Server with the Desktop Experience option. While you can use this feature of the Server Manager console locally or remotely, you can only use it to manage roles and features on one server at a time. Windows Admin Center has a similar one-server-at-a-time limitation.

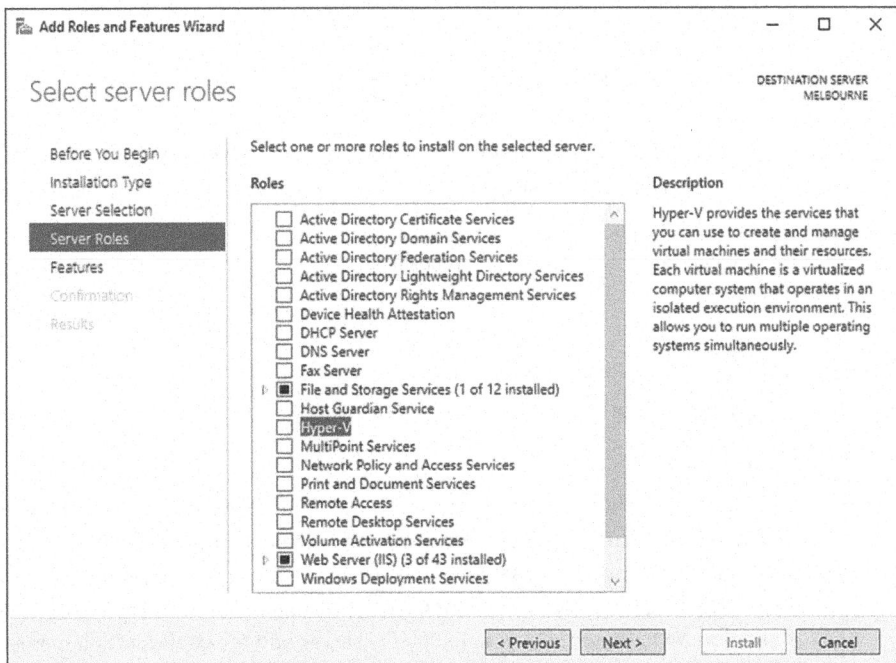

Figure 2-4   Add Roles And Features Wizard

PowerShell provides a better set of tools for adding, removing, and querying the status of features with the `Add-WindowsFeature`, `Get-WindowsFeature`, and `Remove WindowsFeature` cmdlets. For example, Figure 2-5 shows a list of all possible features on a computer, with several features, such as Active Directory Certificate Services, Active Directory Domain Services, DHCP Server, DNS Server, and File and Storage Services installed.

```
Administrator: Windows PowerShell                                          –   □   ×

[MEL-DC]: PS C:\> get-WindowsFeature | Out-Host -paging

Display Name                                      Name                   Install State
------------                                      ----                   -------------
[ ] Active Directory Certificate Services         AD-Certificate         Available
    [ ] Certification Authority                   ADCS-Cert-Authority    Available
    [ ] Certificate Enrollment Policy Web Service ADCS-Enroll-Web-Pol    Available
    [ ] Certificate Enrollment Web Service        ADCS-Enroll-Web-Svc    Available
    [ ] Certification Authority Web Enrollment    ADCS-Web-Enrollment    Available
    [ ] Network Device Enrollment Service         ADCS-Device-Enrollment Available
    [ ] Online Responder                          ADCS-Online-Cert       Available
[X] Active Directory Domain Services              AD-Domain-Services     Installed
[ ] Active Directory Federation Services          ADFS-Federation        Available
[ ] Active Directory Lightweight Directory Services ADLDS                Available
[ ] Active Directory Rights Management Services   ADRMS                  Available
    [ ] Active Directory Rights Management Server ADRMS-Server           Available
    [ ] Identity Federation Support               ADRMS-Identity         Available
[ ] Device Health Attestation                     DeviceHealthAttestat...Available
[X] DHCP Server                                   DHCP                   Installed
[X] DNS Server                                    DNS                    Installed
[ ] Fax Server                                    Fax                    Available
[X] File and Storage Services                     FileAndStorage-Services Installed
    [X] File and iSCSI Services                   File-Services          Installed
        [X] File Server                           FS-FileServer          Installed
        [ ] BranchCache for Network Files         FS-BranchCache         Available
        [ ] Data Deduplication                    FS-Data-Deduplication  Available
        [ ] DFS Namespaces                        FS-DFS-Namespace       Available
        [ ] DFS Replication                       FS-DFS-Replication     Available
        [ ] File Server Resource Manager          FS-Resource-Manager    Available
```

Figure 2-5 View installed features with PowerShell

For example, the following commands install the Hyper-V role on all computers listed in the virt-servers.txt text file and then restart those servers once the role installation is complete:

```
$Computers = Get-Content c:\virt-servers.txt
$Invoke-Command -ScriptBlock { Add-WindowsFeature Hyper-V -Restart } -Computername
$Computers
```

Inside OUT

Desired State

Adding and removing roles and features using Windows Admin Center, Server Manager, or PowerShell is a reasonable way to approach a small number of server modifications. If you need to deploy many servers that have a consistent configuration of roles and features, you're better off using configuration management tools like Desired State Configuration. With these tools, you deploy the server, and the configuration management system configures it with roles, features, and settings according to your specifications. You'll learn about using Desired State Configuration in Chapter 3, "Deployment and configuration."

Deployment and configuration

Depending on the size of your organization, you might deploy a couple of servers and then leave them in production for years. Other organizations deploy servers on a more frequent basis. Some even use a process where rather than applying software updates to a production server and incurring downtime as the update is applied and the server rebooted, they find it faster to deploy a newly patched computer, migrate the existing workload to the new host, and then decommission the original server.

This type of iterative deployment is possible because the tools used to manage the configuration of servers have evolved. Today, deploying and configuring a new server is no more bothersome than deploying an application would have been 20 years ago. In this chapter, you'll learn about how you can use Windows Server images, package management utilities, Desired State Configuration (DSC), Windows Deployment Services (WDS), and Virtual Machine Manager to deploy and manage the configuration of computers and virtual machines running the Windows Server operating system.

Bare-metal versus virtualized

Today, almost all new workloads are virtualized. For most organizations, virtualization hosts are the primary remaining physically deployed servers, with almost all other workloads running as virtual machines. Unless you have specific reasons not to virtualize a workload or are using it at the virtualization host operating system itself, you should run Windows Server as a VM rather than as a physically deployed server.

The security available with shielded VMs addresses one of the final objections that many organizations have had around deploying servers virtually rather than physically. With shielded VMs and VM encryption using virtual TPMs, you can provide the same level of security to a workload that you can to a physically deployed server sitting in a locked cage in a datacenter.

At present, your best bet with deploying virtualization hosts is to choose the Server Core instal-lation option because this has a smaller installation footprint and a reduced attack surface compared to the Server With Desktop Experience option. When you deploy a Server Core vir-tualization host, you manage Hyper-V remotely from a privileged access workstation or a tool such as Windows Admin Center or Virtual Machine Manager.

Windows images

With Windows *images*, the entire operating system, as well as associated drivers, updates, and applications, is stored within a single file known as an image file. During installation, this image is applied to the target volume. Windows images use the Windows Imaging (WIM) file format, which has the following benefits:

- **Multiple deployment methods** You can use a variety of ways to deploy Windows images. While unusual these days, you can deploy .wim files using a bootable USB drive, a traditional DVD-ROM, from a network share, or through specialized deployment tech-nologies such as Windows Deployment Services (WDS) or System Center Virtual Machine Manager. While it is possible to use Microsoft Configuration Manager to deploy Windows Server, Configuration Manager is primarily used with client operating systems rather than server operating systems.

- **Editable** You can mount an image and edit it, enabling, disabling, or removing operat-ing system roles and features as necessary.

- **Updatable** You can update an image without having to perform an operating system image capture.

The Windows Server installation media contains two .wim files in the Sources folder: Boot.wim and Install.wim. The installation media uses Boot.wim to load the preinstallation environ-ment that you use to deploy Windows Server. Install.wim stores one or more operating system images. Depending on the specifics of the hardware that you are attempting to install Windows Server on, you may need to add extra drivers to the boot.wim file. For example, you will need to do this if the Windows Server installation routine isn't able to access the storage device you want to install Windows Server on because that device's driver is included in the default boot image.

Modifying Windows images

The Deployment Image Servicing and Management (DISM) tool is a command-line tool that you can use to manage images in an offline state. You can use Dism.exe to perform the follow-ing tasks:

- Enable or disable roles and features

- List roles and features

- Add, remove, and list software updates

- Add, remove, and list software drivers

- Add, remove, and list software packages in `.appx` format to a Windows image

For example, you can take the `Install.wim` file from the Windows Server installation media and use `Dism.exe` to mount that image, add new drivers and recent software updates to that image, and save those changes to an image—all without having to perform an actual deployment. The advantage is that when you do use this updated image for deployment, the drivers and updates that you added are already applied to the image, and you won't have to install them as part of your post-installation configuration routine.

You can use the Microsoft Update Catalog (*https://catalog.update.microsoft.com*) to search for drivers for images that you use with physically deployed servers. This site stores all the certified hardware drivers, software updates, and hotfixes published by Microsoft. Once you download drivers and software updates, you can add them to your existing installation images by using `Dism.exe` or the appropriate PowerShell cmdlets in the `DISM` PowerShell module.

Servicing Windows images

As an IT professional responsible for deploying Windows Server, you need to ensure that your deployment images are kept up to date. The latest software updates should be applied to the image, and any new device drivers for commonly used server hardware should be included.

The main goals of an image servicing strategy are the following:

- Ensure that the latest software updates and hotfixes are applied to the image before the image is deployed to new servers.

- Ensure that the latest drivers are applied to the image before the image is deployed to new servers.

If you don't take these steps, you'll have to wait until after you've deployed the operating system before you can apply updates and drivers. While Windows Server updates are cumulative now, and you won't need to spend hours updating an image from RTM, it's quicker to have the most recent update already applied to the image than it is to wait for the server to deploy, retrieve the latest update, and then wait for it to download and install. Having updates apply after deployment has occurred consumes a significant amount of time and also substantively increases network traffic. If you aim to minimize the time between choosing to deploy and having the server available, ensure your deployment images are up to date.

You can use the DISM (Deployment Image Servicing and Management) utility or the associated PowerShell cmdlets in the `DISM` PowerShell module to service the current operating system in an online state or perform offline servicing of a Windows image.

Servicing images involves performing the following general steps:

1. Mount the image so that it can be modified.

2. Service the image.

3. Commit or discard the changes made to the image.

Mounting images

By mounting an image, you can make changes to that image. When you mount an image, you link it to a folder. You can use File Explorer, PowerShell, or Cmd.exe to navigate the structure of this folder and interact with it as you would any other folder located on the file system. Once the image is mounted, you can also use Dism.exe or PowerShell to perform servicing tasks, such as adding and removing drivers and updates.

A single WIM file can contain multiple operating system images. Each operating system image is assigned an index number, which you need to know before you can mount the image. You can determine the index number using Dism.exe with the /Get-wiminfo switch. For example, if you have an image named Install.wim located in the C:\Images folder, you can use the following command to get a list of the operating system images it contains:

```
Dism.exe /get-wiminfo /wimfile:c:\images\install.wim
```

You can accomplish the same task using the Get-WindowsImage PowerShell cmdlet. For example, to view the contents of the Install.wim image in the C:\Images folder, run the following command:

```
Get-WindowsImage -ImagePath c:\images\install.wim
```

Once you have determined which operating system image you want to service, you can use the /Mount-image switch with the Dism.exe command to mount that image. For example, to mount the Standard Edition of Windows Server 2025 from the Install.wim file that is available with the Evaluation Edition in the C:\Mount folder, issue this command:

```
Dism.exe /mount-image /imagefile:c:\images\install.wim /index:2 /mountdir:c:\mount
```

Alternatively, you can accomplish the same goal using the following Mount-WindowsImage command:

```
Mount-WindowsImage -ImagePath c:\images\install.wim -index 2 -path c:\mount
```

Adding drivers and updates to images

Once you have mounted an image, you can start to service that image. When servicing images used to deploy Windows Server, the most common tasks are adding device drivers and software updates to the image. You can use the /Add-Driver switch with the Dism.exe command to add a driver to a mounted image. When using the switch by itself, you need to specify the location of the driver's .inf file. Rather than adding a driver at a time, you can use the /Recurse option to have all drivers located in a folder and its subfolders added to an image. For example, to add all of the drivers located in and under the C:\Drivers folder to the image mounted in the C:\Mount folder, use the following command:

```
Dism.exe /image:c:\mount /Add-Driver /driver:c:\drivers\ /recurse
```

Similarly, you could use the Add-WindowsDriver cmdlet to accomplish the same objective by issuing this command:

```
Add-WindowsDriver -Path c:\mount -Driver c:\drivers -Recurse
```

You can use the /Get-Driver option to list all drivers that have been added to the image and the /Remove-Driver option to remove a driver from an image. In PowerShell, you use the Get-WindowsDriver cmdlet and the Remove-WindowsDriver cmdlets. You can remove only the drivers that you or someone else has added to an image. You can't remove any of the drivers that were present in the image when Microsoft published it. You might choose to remove an existing driver if the driver you added in the past has since been updated.

You can use Dism.exe with the /Add-Package switch to add packages that contain updates or packages in .cab or .msu format. Software updates are available from the Microsoft Update Catalog website in .msu format. For example, if you can download an update from the Microsoft Update Catalog website named 2025-05 Cumulative Update for Microsoft server operating system, version 22H2 for x64-based Systems (KB5058385) to the C:\ Updates folder on a computer.

If you mounted a WIM image of the Windows Server 2025 operating system in the C:\Mount folder, you could apply the update to the image by using this command:

```
Dism.exe /image:c:\mount /Add-Package /PackagePath:"c:\updates\windows10.0-kb5058385-x64
_344c2309880ca34fd35090fc7e09da335cb006cb.msu "
```

You can accomplish the same thing with the following Add-WindowsPackage command:

```
Add-WindowsPackage -path c:\mount -packagepath "c:\updates\windows10.0-kb5058385-x64_344
c2309880ca34fd35090fc7e09da335cb006cb.msu"
```

Adding roles and features

You can determine which features are available in a mounted operating system image by using the /Get-Features switch:

```
Dism.exe /image:c:\mount /Get-Features
```

You can enable or disable a specific feature using the /Enable-Feature switch. For example, to enable the NetFx3ServerFeatures feature, which enables the .NET Framework 3.5 server features in an image, use this command:

```
Dism.exe /image:c:\mount /Enable-Feature /all /FeatureName:NetFx3ServerFeatures
```

CHAPTER 3

Some features in the Windows Server image are in a state in which they're listed as having their payload removed, which means that the installation files for that feature are not included in the image. If you install a feature that had its payload removed when the operating system was deployed, the operating system can download the files from the Microsoft update servers on the Internet. You can also specify the location of the installation files. The installation files for the features that have had their payload removed in Windows Server are located in the \Sources\ sxs folder of the volume in which the installation media is located.

You can add these payload-removed features to an image by using Dism.exe and specifying the source directory. For example, to modify an image mounted in the C:\Mount folder so that the Microsoft .NET Framework 3.5 features are installed and available, issue this command when the installation media is located on volume D:

```
Dism.exe /image:c:\mount /Enable-Feature /all /FeatureName:NetFx3 /Source:d:\sources\sxs
```

Inside OUT

.NET Framework 3.5

While features like WINS remain available within Windows Server 2025, .NET Framework 3.5 is not only not installed by default but has been quarantined off into its own separate installation folder. One might suspect that Microsoft wants it to be difficult to install. The problem is that such a huge variety of software still depends on .NET Framework 3.5, which makes installing it more of a hassle than it needs to be.

Committing an image

When you finish servicing an image, you can save your changes using the /Unmount-Wim switch with the /Commit option. You can discard changes using the /Discard option. For example, to make changes and then commit the image mounted in the C:\Mount folder, use this command:

```
Dism.exe /Unmount-Wim /MountDir:c:\mount /commit
```

You can use the Save-WindowsImage PowerShell cmdlet to save changes to an image without dismounting the image. You use the Dismount-WimImage cmdlet with the Save parameter to save the modifications that you've made to an image and then dismount it. For example, to dismount and save the image mounted in the C:\Mount folder, run this command:

```
Dismount-WimImage -Path c:\mount -Save
```

Once you have committed the changes, the .wim file that you originally mounted is updated with these modifications. You can then import this .wim file into WDS, use it to build a virtual hard disk, use it with bootable USB installation media to deploy Windows Server, or use it with these updates and modifications already applied.

Build-and-capture

When you perform a build-and-capture, you deploy an operating system; provision that operating system with updates, applications, and drivers; and then capture that operating system for deployment. Build-and-capture is used less often with server operating systems because they rarely require the same sort of application deployment that is required for client operating systems. If you can just pull a container with an updated application down onto an operating system after deployment, there is little reason to include it in the image. Additionally, with tools such as Desired State Configuration, many post-installation and configuration tasks can be completely automated, reducing the hassle of post-installation configuration.

If your deployment strategy does involve the deployment and capture of Windows Server, you need to remember that you'll need to generalize the image prior to capture, removing any configuration information that is specific to the installation. You can perform this task using the Sysprep.exe utility. Sysprep.exe is included with Windows Server and is located in the `C:\Windows\System32\Sysprep` folder. When you use Sysprep.exe to prepare the image, you can configure the image to return to the System Out-of-Box Experience (OOBE), as shown in Figure 3-1. This is the same experience you get when Windows Server boots for the first time, though in this case, all the updates, applications, and drivers included in the captured image are included in the newly deployed image.

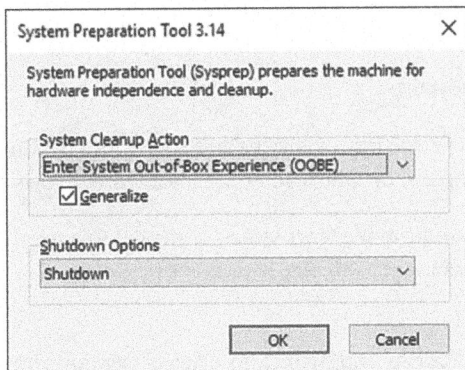

Figure 3-1   Sysprep

You can use `Dism.exe` with the `/Capture-Image` switch or the `New-WindowsImage` PowerShell cmdlet to capture an image.

Answer files

Answer files present a traditional method of performing operating system deployment and configuration. While not as comprehensive as newer technologies (such as Desired State Configuration that assists with deployment and ongoing configuration), answer files allow you to automate the process of deploying Windows Server.

CHAPTER 3

Instead of having to manually select specific installation options and perform post–installation configuration actions, such as joining a newly deployed server to an Active Directory Domain Services (AD DS) domain, you can automate the process with answer files. During setup, the Windows Server looks for a file on local and attached media named Autounattend.xml. If this file is present, Windows Server automatically uses the settings contained in the file to configure the new server deployment.

As its name suggests, Autounattend.xml uses the XML file format. Although it's certainly possible for you to manually edit this XML file using a text editor such as Notepad, this process is complicated, and you're likely to make errors that cause the file not to work. The Windows System Image Manager (known as Windows SIM) is a GUI-based tool that you can use to create an answer file. When using the tool, you must specify the image for which you want to create an answer file. Windows SIM then creates a catalog file for all the options that you can configure. After you configure all the settings that you want automated during installation and post-installation configuration, you can have the tool output an answer file using the correct XML syntax. Windows SIM is included with the Windows Assessment and Deployment Kit (Windows ADK), which you can download from the Microsoft website.

To create an answer file using Windows SIM, perform the following steps:

1. Download and install Windows ADK from the Microsoft website using the installation defaults. You can do this with WinGet, covered later in this chapter, by running the following command:

   ```
   winget install Microsoft.WindowsADK
   ```

2. Copy the \Sources\install.wim file from the Windows Server installation media to a temporary directory on the computer on which you have installed Windows ADK.

3. Open Windows SIM (imgmgr.exe) from the Start screen or the C:\Program Files (x86)\Windows Kits\10\Assessment and Deployment Kit\Deployment Tools\ WSIM\amd64 folder.

4. In the Windows SIM interface, click File, and then choose Select Windows Image. Open the Install.wim file.

5. Select an operating system image in the install image for which you want to create an answer file. For example, Figure 3-2 shows the selection of the Server Core version of Windows Server 2025 Standard edition.

6. When prompted to create a catalog file, click Yes.

7. Click File > New Answer File.

8. Use Windows SIM to select each component that you want to configure. Figure 3-3 shows how you can configure installation to join the *contoso.com* domain.

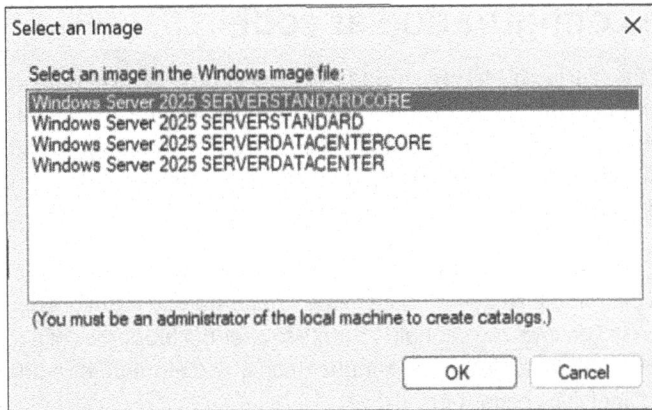

Figure 3-2   Select an image

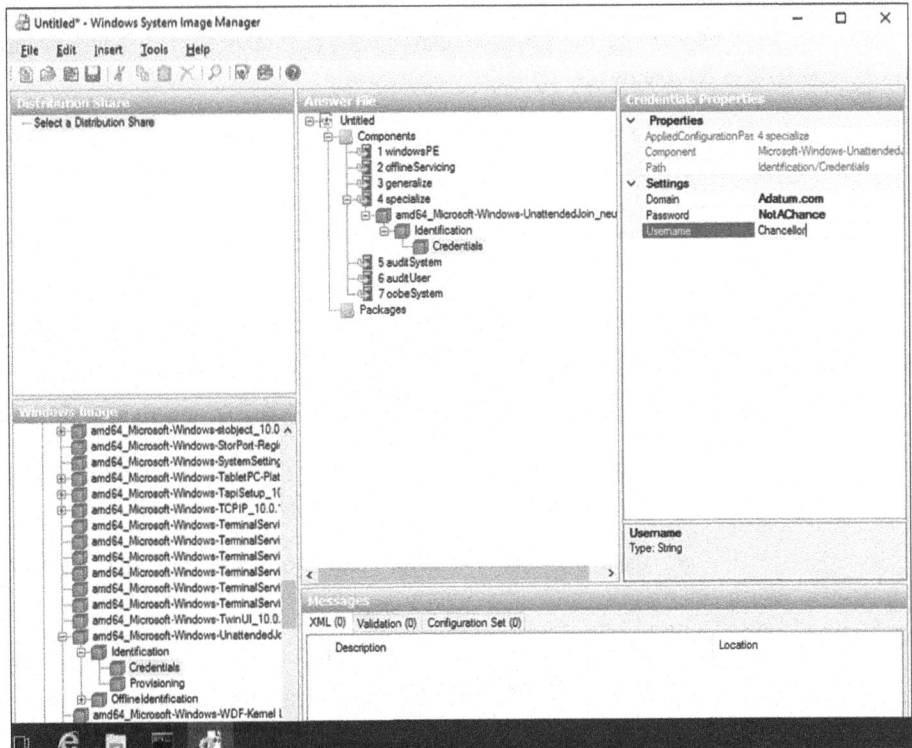

Figure 3-3   Windows System Image Manager

CHAPTER 3

Infrastructure configuration as code

As infrastructure (including servers, storage, and networks) has increasingly become virtualized, the configuration of that infrastructure has increasingly become defined by code. This means that rather than having to build out a template image, it's increasingly possible to define the properties of a server and the workload it hosts through a template written in a format such as JavaScript Object Notation (JSON), Ruby, or XML.

For example, with Azure, it's possible to load a JSON template that defines the properties of a virtual machine workload as well as the network and storage settings associated with that workload. It also becomes increasingly possible to alter the properties of a running workload by modifying and reapplying the template rather than going through the workload's management interface and applying changes manually.

Here are some other advantages of infrastructure configuration as code:

- You can version that code so that you can roll back changes by simply applying an earlier version of a set of templates in the event that a set of changes causes unforeseen problems.

- You can test the infrastructure code in a development environment before deploying it in a production environment. For example, you can ensure the infrastructure code to build your production VM workloads functions as expected on a test Hyper-V server before deploying the same code to your production Hyper-V failover cluster.

The MSLab project, hosted on GitHub at *https://github.com/microsoft/MSLab*, provides a set of PowerShell scripts that allow for the automatic creation of entire Hyper-V-based virtual machine testing labs. Running scripts allows you to do the following:

- Create updated base operating system virtual machine hard disk images by

  - Automatically downloading required operating system evaluation software from the Internet

  - Using the WIM images stored on those evaluation versions of Windows operating systems, create sysprepped, virtual machine parent disks

  - Applying the most recent software updates to ensure that the base operating system virtual machine hard disks are up to date

- Create Hyper-V internal and external networks

- Create fully functional virtual machines, including

  - Creating new virtual machines from the base operating system virtual hard disks

  - Connecting these newly created virtual machines to appropriate Hyper-V internal and external networks

- Injecting Desired State Configuration resources into the VMs from the host machine

- Injecting `Unattend.xml` files into the newly created VMs

- Using DSC to trigger the application of the DSC resources and configuration

Tools such as MSLab demonstrate that it's possible to deploy entire environments quickly from scratch just with scripts, tools such as DSC, and the base operating system's installation media.

Package-management utilities

Rather than the traditional process of downloading the current version of software from a vendor's website, vendors are increasingly publishing their software in centralized repositories that you can access through package-management utilities. The benefit of package-management utilities is that they provide a central location for obtaining software, updating, and removing software applications.

If you've used a Debian-derived flavor of Linux, you'll be familiar with the `Apt-get` utility. `Apt-get` allows you to install any package prepared for Debian. It also allows you to update packages and the operating system. You can even use `Apt-get` to perform an entire operating system upgrade.

Windows Server both directly and indirectly supports package management, either directly through WinGet, cmdlets in the `PackageManagement` Windows PowerShell module, or indirectly through package providers such as Chocolatey.

Winget

WinGet is included with the versions of Window Server 2025 that include the Desktop Experience. If you're using an older version of Windows Server or a Server Core version, you can instead use the third-party Chocolatey tool to perform many of the same tasks you can perform with WinGet. Chocolatey is covered later in this chapter.

The first time you perform a WinGet search or package install on Windows Server 2025, you may be asked to assent to the source agreement terms. Once you've done this, WinGet will run as normal.

Finding WinGet packages

To locate a page, use the `WinGet search` command. For example, to locate all Microsoft packages, use the following command:

```
WinGet search Microsoft
```

Sometimes, you'll want to be more specific; for example, to find the `PowerShell` WinGet package, use this command:

```
WinGet search PowerShell
```

Installing WinGet packages

You use the `WinGet install [package.name]` command to install WinGet packages (where `[package.name]` is replaced with the name of the package you want to install). WinGet is user account control aware, so it isn't necessary to run WinGet from an elevated PowerShell prompt to perform an installation.

For example, to install the most recent version of PowerShell, run this command:

```
WinGet install Microsoft.PowerShell
```

You can remove a package you installed using WinGet using the `WinGet Uninstall` command. For example, to remove the most recent version of PowerShell, run this command:

```
WinGet uninstall Microsoft.PowerShell
```

Winget upgrade

You can use the `WinGet upgrade -all` command to upgrade all WinGet packages on a Windows Server computer. You can use `WinGet upgrade Package.Name` to upgrade a specific package. For example, to upgrade the WinGet installed version of PowerShell to the latest version, run this command:

```
WinGet upgrade Microsoft.PowerShell
```

WinGet export

The `WinGet export` command allows you to export a list of all packages that you've currently installed using WinGet. The `WinGet configure export` command allows you to export the configuration settings used by WinGet into a file. You can then use this file to replicate the same environment or user settings on another computer or as a backup of your current configuration.

While `WinGet export` exports a list of installed applications to a JSON file, focusing on the packages themselves for migration or backup, `WinGet configure export` allows you to export user settings, the configuration, and potentially the entire environment setup, not just the list of apps that you've installed using WinGet.

You can also use `WinGet configure export` to export Desired State Configuration resources. For example, the following command would export a server's current configuration to a DSC YAML file, which can be used on another server:

```
winget configure export --output exported.configuration.dsc.yaml
```

PowerShell packages

Windows Server includes native support for the installation of a variety of different package-management providers through PowerShell. Some providers make PowerShell resources available, and others make prepackaged software available that you would otherwise download from the Internet and manually install. You can view which package providers are accessible by default to a Windows Server installation by using the `Find-PackageProvider` cmdlet.

PowerShell Gallery

PowerShell Gallery is a provider that functions as a clearinghouse for PowerShell-related tools and content. The PowerShell team publishes content to the gallery, as do other PowerShell enthusiasts and MVPs. This means that it's fairly likely that if there is a script, cmdlet, or module that does something you think quite a few people would need to do, someone has probably already created it and published it to the PowerShell gallery. You can interact with PowerShell Gallery with the `PowerShellGet` module. You can use this module to access cmdlets that do the following:

- Use `Find-Module` and `Find-Script` to find items in the gallery.

- Use `Save-Module` and `Save-Script` to save items from the gallery.

- Use `Install-Module` and `Install-Script` to install items from the gallery.

- Use `Publish-Module` and `Publish-Script` to publish items to the gallery.

- Add a custom repository to the gallery using `Register-PSRepository`.

More Info
PowerShell Gallery
You can learn more about PowerShell Gallery at *https://www.powershellgallery.com/*.

Chocolatey

Chocolatey is a third-party package provider available for Windows operating systems that works on Server Core and versions of Windows Server prior to Windows Server 2025.

To install Chocolatey, you'll need to set the PowerShell execution policy to `unrestricted` using the following command:

```
Set-ExecutionPolicy Unrestricted
```

Then, you'll need to run the following PowerShell command to install Chocolatey and all of its dependencies on the local computer:

```
iwr https://chocolatey.org/install.ps1 -UseBasicParsing | iex
```

Inside OUT

Package at your own risk

In a secure environment, you wouldn't set your execution policy to unrestricted, and you certainly wouldn't download and install packages from a public repository, no matter how reputable it may seem. In the long run, you don't know anything about the people building the packages, and while they're most likely simply helpful people trying to make your life easier by packaging software, they could also be a part of the great galactic space lizard malware conspiracy and simply finding a new vector to get malware deployed on your server. Before using a package in production, make sure you test it. When it comes to building secure servers, you'll need to validate the integrity of all software that you deploy, which means that the shortcuts provided by package providers are probably not an option.

You can update all Chocolatey packages on a system using the command:

```
Chocolatey update all
```

Chocolatey has the following disadvantages:

- Usually requires that the computer you are deploying software on be connected to the Internet. You can configure internal repositories, but you'll have to manage and maintain them yourself, including validating the quality of the software found in those repositories.

- Packages are usually installed in default locations with default settings. You don't get the installation customization options that you get when you install software manually.

- The provenance of the software isn't clear. While it's reasonable to assume that the software is safe, even large vendor app stores have apps that are infected with malware.

Using a simple script, you can install Chocolatey and then use it to download and install a common set of packages. You can also set up your own Chocolatey repository of packages that host only packages that you trust. You can then point a local Chocolatey instance at that repository and use it to quickly install software on newly deployed computers running a Windows operating system.

> ## More Info
>
> *Chocolatey*
>
> You can learn more about Chocolatey at *https://chocolatey.org/*. You can learn more about integrating Chocolatey with Puppet, Chef, and DSC at *https://chocolatey.org/docs/features-infrastructure-automation.*

Desired State Configuration

Microsoft Desired State Configuration v3 has some substantive changes compared to previous versions of the technology. Unlike PowerShell Desired State Configuration (PSDSC) v1.1 and v2, DSC v3 operates as a standalone command rather than a service, eliminating the need for a local configuration manager. This architectural change makes DSC v3 easier to use and scale, allowing any tool that can execute commands on Windows Server, such as Scheduled Tasks, to apply DSC configurations.

DSC v3 requires PowerShell 7.2 or later. You can install the most current version of PowerShell using the following WinGet command:

```
winget install microsoft.powershell
```

Once you've installed the latest version of PowerShell, you can open a new PowerShell session and install DSC using the following WinGet command:

```
Winget install Microsoft.DSC
```

Once DSC v3 is installed, restart the PowerShell session to begin using DSC commands. To view all available commands in DSC v3, run this command:

```
dsc --help
```

The output will display available commands, including

- `completer` Generate a shell completion script

- `config` Apply a configuration document

- `resource` Invoke a specific DSC resource

- `schema` Get the JSON schema for a DSC type

- `help` Display help information for commands

CHAPTER 3

View resources

Using the `dsc resource list` command allows you to determine what the local resources are that you can manage with Desired State Configuration. The output will provide information on the resource type, kind, version, capabilities, required adapter, and a brief description of the resource.

If you want to filter by resource name, you can use wildcards. For example, the following command will list all resources under the Microsoft.DSC namespace:

```
dsc resource list Microsoft.DSC/*
```

DSC v3 configurations

DSC v3 configurations can be written in YAML format. Previous versions of DSC used the MOF format. A DSC v3 configuration document must include

- A reference to the DSC resource schema

- At least one resource definition with properties

The following is a basic configuration that installs Internet Information Services when called by the `dsc.exe` command:

```
$schema: https://raw.githubusercontent.com/PowerShell/DSC/main/
schemas/2024/04/config/document.json
metadata:
 name: IIS-Configuration
resources:
 - name: Use Windows PowerShell resources
   type: Microsoft.Windows/WindowsPowerShell
   properties:
     resources:
       - name: Web server install
         type: PSDesiredStateConfiguration/WindowsFeature
         properties:
           Name: Web-Server
           Ensure: Present
```

To test a configuration to see what changes would be made, run the following command:

```
dsc config get -f .\iis-config.yaml
```

To apply a configuration, run a version of the command (with your YAML file specified):

```
dsc config set -f .\iis-config.yaml
```

Exporting DSC configuration

To export the current server's configuration, use the `dsc config export` command. This command generates a configuration document that captures every instance of a set of resources as currently configured on your server. When you do this, you need to specify a configuration document that lists the resource types you want to export.

For example, the following configuration document would allow you to export operating system information:

```
$schema: https://aka.ms/dsc/schemas/v3/bundled/config/document.json
resources:
 - name: Operating system information
   type: Microsoft/OSInfo
   properties: {}
```

If you named this file `exemplar.config.yaml`, you could create an exported configuration file using this command:

```
dsc config export --file ./exemplar.config.yaml > exported.config.yaml
```

You can determine which DSC resources can be exported by running the `dsc resource list` command and looking for the "e" output under the Capabilities column.

DSC shell completion scripts

The `dsc.exe` completer command is used to generate shell completion scripts that provide tab completion and command suggestions when using DSC with command-line shells, including PowerShell, Bash, and Zsh. On Windows Server, you would only use it for PowerShell. The functionality for other shells is a reminder that DSCv3 is cross-platform, and you can use the technology with Linux, including Windows Subsystem for Linux.

To use it with PowerShell on Windows Server, use the command

```
dsc completer powershell | Out-File dsc_completion.ps1
```

Then run the `dsc_completion.ps1` command. You'll now have tab completion for the `dsc` command.

CHAPTER 3

More Info

DSC

You can learn more about DSCv3 at *https://learn.microsoft.com/en-us/powershell/dsc/overview*.

Windows Deployment Services

Windows Deployment Services (WDS) is a server role that you can deploy on computers running Windows Server. WDS enables you to deploy operating systems to computers over the
network. WDS can send these operating systems across the network using multicast transmissions, which means that multiple computers receive the same operating system image while
minimizing the use of network bandwidth. When you use multicast transmissions, the same
amount of traffic crosses the network independently of whether you're deploying an operating
system to 1 or 50 computers. WDS can also use unicast transmissions. WDS is deprecated but
still available in Windows Server 2025.

Deploying Windows Server through WDS involves performing the following steps:

1. An operating system deployment transmission is prepared on the WDS server.

2. The media access control (MAC) addresses of Pre-boot Execution Environment (PXE)–
    compliant network adapters are made available to the WDS server.

3. The computers that are targets of the transmission boot using their PXE-compliant
    network adapters.

4. These computers locate the WDS server and begin the operating system setup process.
    If the WDS server has been provisioned with an answer file, the setup completes
    automatically. If the WDS server has not been provisioned with an answer file, an
    administrator must enter setup configuration information.

Each WDS server can have only one unattended installation file for each processor architecture.
Because unattended installation files differ between server and client, you either need to swap
unattended files when you're switching between client and server or have multiple WDS servers. WDS can be used in conjunction with other technologies, such as Desired State Configuration, where an answer file only performs basic configuration tasks, with the substantial tasks
completed by an advanced configuration technology.

WDS requirements

WDS clients need a PXE-compliant network adapter, which is rarely a problem because almost
all modern network adapters are PXE-compliant. You can also use WDS to deploy Windows
Server 2012 and later to virtual machines running under Hyper-V. The trick to doing this is to use
a legacy rather than a synthetic network adapter when creating the virtual machine as a Generation 1 virtual machine. This isn't necessary when using Generation 2 virtual machines because
the Generation 2 virtual machine network adapters support PXE booting.

If you have a computer that does not have a PXE-compliant network adapter, you can configure
a special type of boot image known as a discover image. A discover image boots an environment, loading special drivers to enable the network adapter to interact with the WDS server.

You create the boot image by adding the appropriate network adapter drivers associated with the computer that can't PXE boot to the Boot.wim file from the Windows Server installation media.

WDS has the following requirements:

- A Windows Server DNS server must be present on the local area network (LAN).

- You can host WDS and Dynamic Host Configuration Protocol (DHCP) on the same computer as long as you configure the options shown in Figure 3-4.

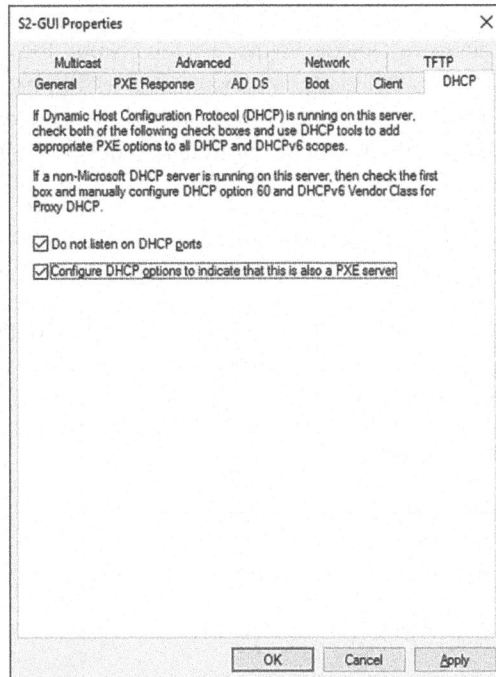

Figure 3-4   WDS DHCP settings

If you install WDS from the Add Roles And Features Wizard, you can configure these settings automatically. Although the WDS server does not require a static IP address, it's good practice to ensure that infrastructure roles such as WDS always use a consistent network address. You can install WDS on computers running the Server Core version of Windows Server.

When installing WDS on Server Core, you have to specify the location of the source files or ensure that the server has a connection to the Internet, which enables them to be downloaded automatically. Although it's possible to manage WDS from Windows PowerShell, most administrators use the graphical WDS Remote Server Administration Tools (RSAT) from a computer running Windows client or a version of Windows Server with desktop experience.

Managing images

Images contain either entire operating systems or a version of a special stripped-down operating system known as Windows PE. Windows PE functions as a type of boot disk, enabling a basic environment to be loaded from which more complex maintenance and installation tasks can be performed. WDS uses four image types: boot image, install image, discover image, and capture image:

- **Boot image**   A special image that enables the computer to boot and begin installing the operating system using the install image. A default boot image, named Boot.wim, is located in the sources folder of the Windows Server installation media.

- **Install image**   The main type of image discussed in this chapter. It contains the operating system as well as any other included components, such as software updates and additional applications. A default install image, named Install.wim, is present in the sources folder of the Windows Server installation media. Install images can be in .vhd or .vhdx format.

- **Discover image**   This special image is for computers that cannot PXE boot to load appropriate network drivers to begin a session with a WDS server.

- **Capture image**   A special image type that enables a prepared computer to be booted so that its operating system state can be captured as an install image. You add capture images as boot images in WDS.

To import an image into WDS, perform the following steps:

1. Open the Windows Deployment Services console.

2. Click Install Images. From the Action menu, click Add Install Image.

3. Choose whether to create a new image group or to use an existing image group.

4. Specify the location of the image file.

5. In the Available Images page of the Add Image Wizard, select the operating system images that you want to add. When the image or images are added, click Next, Finish.

Configuring WDS

The installation defaults for WDS are suitable when you deploy the role in small environments. If you are deploying WDS in larger environments and do not choose to implement System Center Virtual Machine Manager for server operating system deployments, you might want to configure the options discussed in the following sections, which are available by editing the properties of the WDS server in the Windows Deployment Services console.

PXE response settings

With PXE response settings, you can configure how the WDS server responds to computers. As Figure 3-5 shows, you can configure WDS not to respond to any client computers (this effectively disables WDS), to respond to known client computers, or to respond to all computers but require an administrator to manually approve an unknown computer. Known computers have prestaged accounts in Active Directory. You can prestage computers if you know the MAC address of the network interface card (NIC) that the computer uses. Vendors often supply a list of MAC addresses associated with computers when you purchase those computers, and you can use this list to prestage computer accounts.

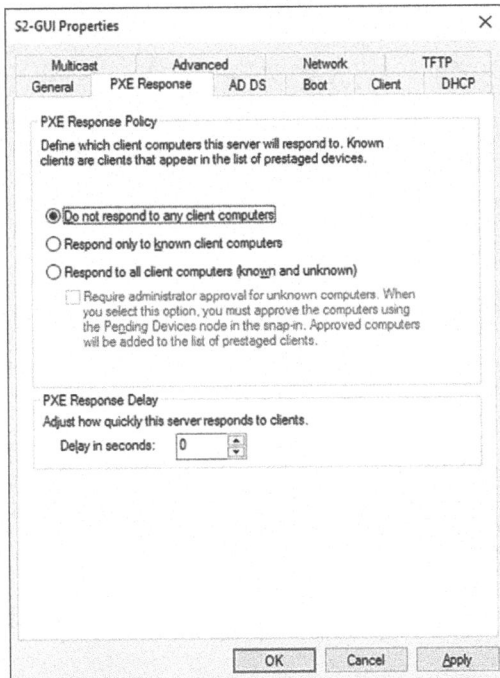

Figure 3-5   PXE Response settings

You use the PXE Response Delay setting when you have more than one WDS server in an environment. You can use this setting to ensure that clients receive transmissions from one WDS server over another, with the server configured with the lowest PXE response delay having priority over other WDS servers with higher delay settings.

Client Naming Policy

The Client Naming Policy enables you to configure how computers installed from WDS are named if you aren't using deployment options that perform the action. You can also use the settings on this tab, shown in Figure 3-6, to configure domain membership and organizational unit (OU) options for the computer account.

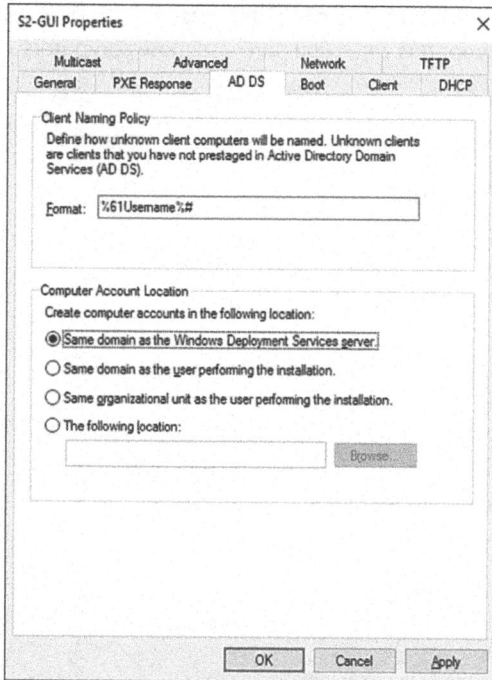

Figure 3-6   Client Naming Policy

WDS boot options

In the Boot Options tab of the WDS server's Properties dialog, shown in Figure 3-7, you can configure how clients that PXE boot interact with the WDS server. You can also configure a default boot image for each architecture supported by WDS. By default, once a client has connected to a WDS server, someone must press the F12 key to continue deploying the operating system. In environments in which you're performing a large number of simultaneous deployments, requiring this level of manual intervention might substantially delay the deployment.

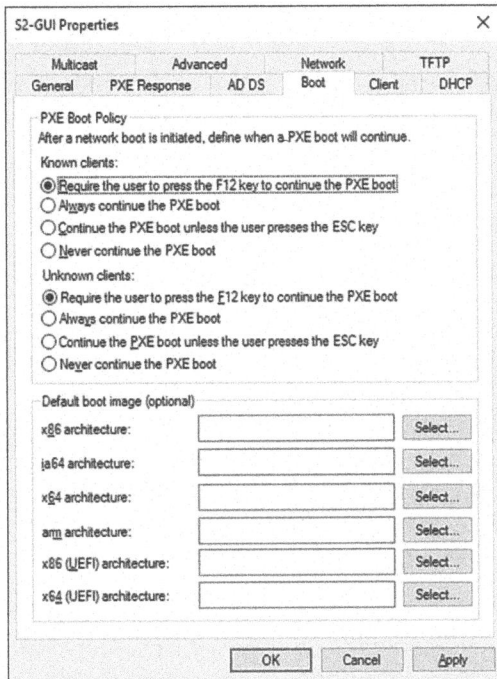

Figure 3-7   Boot options

Multicast options

The default settings of WDS have all computers that join the multicast transmission receiving the installation image at the same speed. If you frequently deploy operating systems, you're aware that sometimes transmission is slowed by the network adapters on a computer or two; transmissions that should take only 15 minutes take half a day. You can configure the transfer settings on the Multicast tab, shown in Figure 3-8, so that clients are partitioned into separate sessions, depending on how fast they can consume the multicast transmission. Those slow computers will still take a long time to receive the image, but the other computers connected to the transmission can complete the deployment quicker.

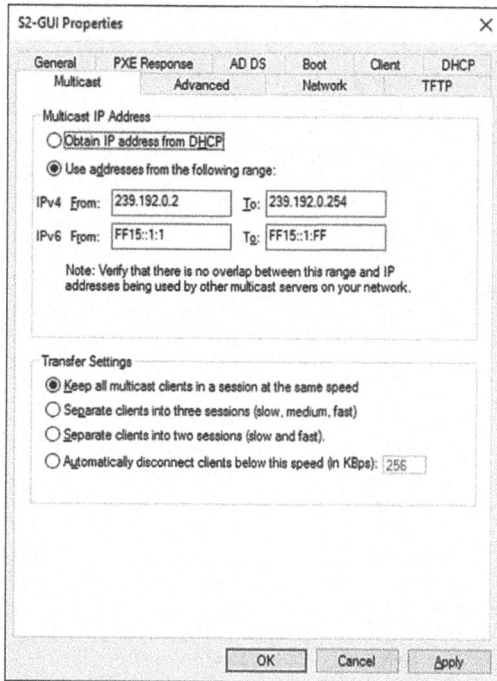

Figure 3-8   WDS Multicast tab

Other options

Although you are less likely to need them, you can configure other options on the following tabs:

- **Advanced tab**   You can configure WDS to use a specific domain controller and global catalog (GC) server. You can also configure whether WDS is authorized in DHCP. DHCP authorization occurs automatically when you install the WDS role.

- **Network tab**   You can specify a User Datagram Protocol (UDP) port policy to limit when UDP ports are used with transmissions. You can also configure a network profile to specify the speed of the network, minimizing the chance that WDS transmissions slow the network down.

- **TFTP tab**   You can specify the maximum block size and Trivial File Transfer Protocol (TFTP) window size.

Configuring transmissions

You use WDS transmissions to set WDS to transfer the operating system image to PXE clients. When configuring a WDS transmission, you need to decide what type of multicast transmission you're going to perform in the Multicast Type page of the Create Multicast Transmission Wizard, as shown in Figure 3-9.

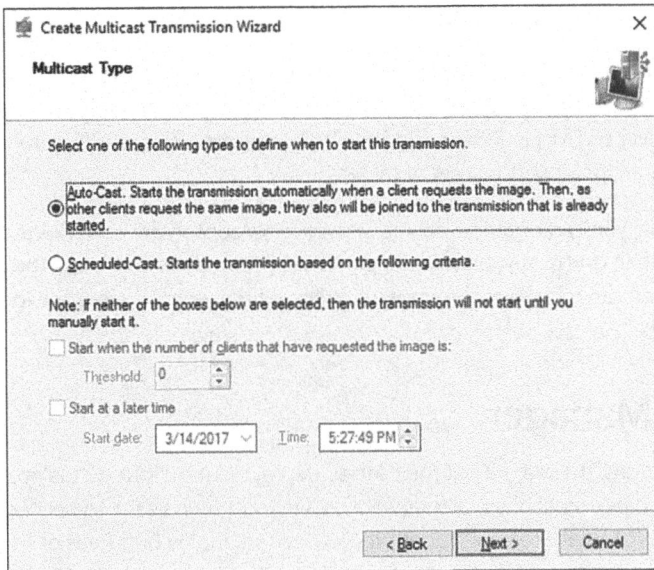

Figure 3-9   Multicast type

The difference between these options is as follows:

- **Auto-Cast**   A transmission starts when a client requests the image. If another client requests the same image, the client joins the existing transmission, caching data from the current transfer and then retrieving data that was transmitted before the client joined the transmission. This is the best option to use when you are performing one-off deployments.

- **Scheduled-Cast**   You choose either to start the transmission when a specified number of clients have joined, or you start the transmission at a particular date and time. Scheduled cast is the best option to use when you're deploying the same operating system image to a large number of computers.

To configure a WDS transmission, perform the following steps:

1. Open the Windows Deployment Services console, expand the WDS server from which you want to perform the deployment, and click Multicast Transmissions. In the Action menu, click Create Multicast Transmission.

2. Provide a name for the multicast transmission.

3. In the Image Selection page, specify which operating system image you want to deploy using the transmission.

4. In the Multicast Type page, specify whether you use Auto-Cast or Scheduled-Cast. If you choose Scheduled-Cast, select the number of clients or the transmission start time.

CHAPTER 3

Driver groups and packages

You can stage device drivers on a WDS server by importing the device driver as a package. A driver package contains the extracted driver files. You can import the driver package into WDS by locating the driver's .inf file. When using the WDS console, you can either import individual driver packages or all the drivers in a set of folders.

In the WDS console, you can organize drivers into driver groups. A driver package can be a member of more than one group, and deleting a driver group does not delete the associated driver packages. You can use driver groups with filters to limit which driver packages are available to WDS clients.

Virtual Machine Manager

For most organizations, the majority of their server deployments involve virtual machines rather than deploying to bare-metal physical hardware. While tools such as the Hyper-V console and WDS are adequate for smaller environments, if you need to deploy hundreds or thousands of virtual machines each year, you need a more comprehensive set of tools than those that are included with the Windows Server operating system.

System Center Virtual Machine Manager (VMM) is one tool that you can use to manage your organization's entire virtualization infrastructure, from virtualization hosts, clusters, and VMs to managing the entire networking and storage stack. In this section, you'll learn about VMM templates, storage, networking, and host groups.

Virtual machine templates

A Virtual Machine Manager VM template allows you to rapidly deploy virtual machines with a consistent set of settings. A VMM VM template is an XML object that's stored with a VMM library, and it includes one or more of the following components:

- **Guest operating system profile**   A guest operating system profile that includes operating system settings.

- **Hardware profile**   A hardware profile that includes VM hardware settings.

- **Virtual hard disk**   This can be a blank hard disk or a virtual hard disk that hosts a specially prepared, sysprepped disk, in the case of Windows-based operating systems version of an operating system.

You can create VM templates based on existing virtual machines deployed on a virtualization host managed by VMM, based on virtual hard disks stored in a VMM library, or by using an existing VM template.

VM templates have the following limitations:

- A VM template allows you to customize IP address settings, but you can only configure a static IP address for a specific VM from a pool when deploying that VM from the template.

- Application and SQL Server deployment are only used when you deploy a VM as part of a service.

- When creating a template from an existing VM, ensure that the VM is a member of a workgroup and is not joined to a domain.

- You should create a separate local administrator account on a VM before using it as the basis of a template. Using the built-in administrator account causes the Sysprep operation to fail.

More Info

Virtual machine templates

You can learn more about virtual machine templates at *https://learn.microsoft.com/en-us/system-center/vmm/vm-template?view=sc-vmm-2025*.

VMM storage

VMM can use local and remote storage, with local storage being storage devices that are directly attached to the server and remote storage being storage available through a storage area network. VMM can use

- **File storage**   VMM can use file shares that support the SMB 3.0 protocol. This protocol is supported by file shares on computers running Windows Server 2012 and later. SMB 3.0 is also supported by third-party vendors of network-attached storage (NAS) devices.

- **Block storage**   VMM can use block-level storage devices that host LUNs (Logical Unit Numbers) for storage using either the iSCSI, Serial Attached SCSI (SAS), or Fibre Channel protocols.

VMM supports automatically discovering local and remote storage, including the automatic discovery of the following:

- Storage arrays

- Storage pools

CHAPTER 3

- Storage volumes

- LUNs

- Disks

- Virtual disks

Using VMM, you can create new storage from the storage capacity discovered by VMM and assign that storage to a Hyper-V virtualization host or host cluster. You can use VMM to provision storage to Hyper-V virtualization hosts or host clusters using the following methods:

- **From available capacity**   Allows you to create storage volumes or LUNs from an existing storage pool.

- **From a writable snapshot of a virtual disk**   VMM supports creating storage from writable snapshots of existing virtual disks.

- **From a clone of a virtual disk**   You can provision storage by creating a copy of a virtual disk. This uses storage space less efficiently than creating storage from snapshots.

- **From SMB 3.0 file shares**   You can provision storage from SMB 3.0 file shares.

VMM supports the creation of a thin provisioned logical unit on a storage pool. This allows you to allocate a greater amount of capacity than is currently available in the pool, and it's only possible when

- The storage array supports thin provisioning

- The storage administrator has enabled thin provisioning for the storage pool

VMM supports the balancing of virtual disks across cluster-shared volumes to ensure that no single cluster-shared volume is overcommitted.

More Info

Storage in VMM

You can learn more about storage in VMM at *https://learn.microsoft.com/en-us/ system-center/vmm/manage-storage?view=sc-vmm-2025.*

Inside OUT

Storage classifications

Storage classifications allow you to assign a metadata label to a type of storage. For example, you might name a classification used with a storage pool that consists of high-speed solid-state disks as "Alpha," a classification used with Fibre Channel RAID 5 SAS storage as "Beta," and iSCSI SATA RAID 5 as "Gamma." The labels that you use should be appropriate to your environment.

VMM networking

A VMM logical network is a collection of network sites, VLAN (virtual local area network) information, and IP subnet information. A VMM deployment needs to have at least one logical network before you can use it to deploy VMs or services. When you add a Hyper-V-based virtualization host to VMM, one of the following happens:

- If the physical adapter is associated with an existing logical network, it remains associated with that network once added to VMM.

- If the physical adapter is not already associated with a logical network, VMM creates a new logical network, associating it with the physical adapter's DNS suffix.

You can create logical networks with the following properties:

- **One connected network**   Choose this option when network sites that comprise this network can route traffic to each other, and you can use this logical network as a single connected network. You have the additional option of allowing VM networks created on this logical network to use network virtualization.

- **VLAN-based independent networks**   The sites in this logical network are independent networks. The network sites that comprise this network can route traffic to each other, though this is not required.

- **Private VLAN (PVLAN) networks**   Choose this option when you want network sites within the logical network to be isolated independent networks.

You create network sites after you have created a VMM logical network. You use network sites to associate IP subnets, VLANs, and PVLANs with a VMM logical network.

CHAPTER 3

More Info

VMM logical network

You can learn more about VMM logical networks at *https://learn.microsoft.com/en-us/system-center/vmm/plan-network?view=sc-vmm-2025.*

Logical switches

VMM logical switches store network adapter configuration settings for use with VMM-managed virtualization hosts. You configure the properties of one or more virtualization host's network adapters by applying the logical switch configuration information.

You should perform the following tasks before creating a logical switch:

- Create logical networks and define network sites.

- Install the providers for any Hyper-V extensible virtual switch extensions.

- Create any required native port profiles for virtual adapters that you use to define port settings for the native Hyper-V virtual switch.

When you configure a VMM logical switch, you configure the following:

- Extensions

- Uplinks

- Virtual ports

Extensions

You use logical switch extensions to configure how the logical switch interacts with network traffic. VMM includes the following switch extensions:

- **Monitoring**   Allows the logical switch to monitor but not modify network traffic

- **Capturing**   Allows the logical switch to inspect but not modify network traffic

- **Filtering**   Allows the logical switch to modify, defragment, or block packets

- **Forwarding**   Allows the logical switch to alter the destination of network traffic based on the properties of that traffic

Uplink port profiles

Uplink port profiles specify which set of logical networks should be associated with physical network adapters. In the event that there are multiple network adapters on a virtualization host, an uplink port profile specifies whether and how those adapters should participate in teaming. Teaming allows network adapters to aggregate bandwidth and provide redundancy for network connections.

Virtual port profiles

You use port classifications to apply configurations based on functionality. The following port profiles are available:

- **SR-IOV**   Allows a virtual network adapter to use SR-IOV (Single Root Input Output Virtualization)

- **Host management**   For network adapters used to manage the virtualization host using RDP, PowerShell, or another management technology

- **Network load balancing**   To be used with network adapters that participate in Microsoft Network Load Balancing

- **Guest dynamic IP**   Used with network adapters that require guest dynamic IP addresses, such as those provided by DHCP

- **Live migration workload**   Used with network adapters that support VM live migration workloads between virtualization hosts

- **Medium bandwidth**   Assign to network adapters that need to support medium-bandwidth workloads

- **Host cluster workload**   Assign to network adapters that are used to support host clusters

- **Low bandwidth**   Assign to network adapters that need to support low-bandwidth workloads

- **High bandwidth**   Assign to network adapters that are used to support high-bandwidth workloads

- **iSCSI workload**   Assign to network adapters that are used to connect to SAN resources using the iSCSI protocol

More Info

Port profiles and logical switches

You can learn more about port profiles at *https://learn.microsoft.com/en-us/ system-center/vmm/network-port-profile?view=sc-vmm-2025.*

CHAPTER 3

Virtual machine networks

In VMM, virtual machines connect to a VMM logical network through a VMM virtual machine network. You connect a virtual machine's network adapter to the virtual machine network rather than the logical network. You can have VMM automatically create an associated virtual machine network when you create a logical network. If you have configured a logical network to support network virtualization, you can connect multiple VM networks to the logical network, and they will be isolated from each other. You can also configure virtual networks to support encryption.

You can use network virtualization to configure logical networks in such a manner that different VM tenants can utilize the same IP address space on the same virtualization host without collisions occurring. For example, tenant Alpha and tenant Beta use the 172.16.10.x address space when their workloads are hosted on the same virtualization host cluster. Even though tenant Alpha and tenant Beta have virtual machines that use the same IPv4 address, network virtualization ensures that conflicts do not occur.

When you configure network virtualization, each network adapter is assigned two IP addresses:

- **Customer IP address**   This IP address is the one used by the customer. The customer IP address is the address visible within the VM when you run a command such as `ipconfig` or `Get-NetIPConfiguration`.

- **Provider IP address**   This IP address is used by and is visible to VMM. It isn't visible within the VM operating system.

MAC address pools

A MAC address pool gives you a pool of MAC addresses that can be assigned to virtual machine network adapters across a group of virtualization hosts. Without MAC address pools, virtual machines are assigned MAC addresses on a per-virtualization host basis. While unlikely, the same MAC address may be assigned by separate virtualization hosts in environments with a very large number of virtualization hosts. Using a central MAC address pool ensures that doesn't happen. When creating a MAC address pool, you specify a starting and an ending MAC address range.

More Info

MAC address pools

You can learn more about MAC address pools at *https://learn.microsoft.com/en-us/system-center/vmm/network-mac?view=sc-vmm-2025*.

Static IP address pools

An IP address pool is a collection of IP addresses that, through an IP subnet, is associated with a network site. VMM can assign IP addresses from the static IP address pool to virtual machines running Windows operating systems if those virtual machines use the logical network associated with the pool. Static IP address pools can contain default gateway, DNS server, and WINS server information. Static IP address pools aren't necessary because VMs can be assigned IP address information from DHCP servers running on the network.

> ## More Info
> ### *IP address pools*
> **You can learn more about IP address pools at *https://learn.microsoft.com/en-us/ system-center/vmm/network-pool?view=sc-vmm-2025*.**

Private VLANS

VLANs segment network traffic by adding tags to packets. A VLAN ID is a 12-bit number, allowing you to configure VLAN IDS between the numbers 1 and 4095. While this is more than adequate for the majority of on-premises deployments, large hosting providers often have more than 5,000 clients, so they must use an alternate method to segment network traffic. A PVLAN is an extension to VLANs that uses a secondary VLAN ID with the original VLAN ID to segment a VLAN into isolated subnetworks.

You can implement VLANs and PVLANs in VMM by creating a Private VLAN logical network. Private VLAN logical networks allow you to specify the VLAN and/or PVLAN ID, as well as the IPv4 or IPv6 network.

Adding a WDS to VMM

In a scalable environment, you'll need to add additional Hyper-V host servers on a frequent basis as either a standalone server or as part of a failover cluster to increase your capacity. While it's possible to use another technology to deploy new Hyper-V host servers to bare-metal, the advantage of integrating virtualization host deployment with VMM is that you can fully automate the process. The process works in the following general manner:

1. Discovery of the chassis occurs. This may be through providing the chassis network adapter's MAC address to VMM.

2. The chassis performs a PXE boot and locates the Windows Deployment Services (WDS) server that you have integrated with VMM as a managed server role. When you integrate WDS with VMM, the WDS server hosts a VMM provider that handles PXE traffic from the bare-metal chassis started using the VMM provisioning tool.

3.   The VMM provider on the WDS server queries the VMM server to verify that the bare-metal chassis is an authorized target for managed virtualization host deployment. In the event that the bare-metal chassis isn't authorized, WDS attempts to deploy another operating system to the chassis. If that isn't possible, PXE deployment fails.

4.   If the bare-metal chassis is authorized, a special Windows PE (Preinstallation Environment) image is transmitted to the bare-metal chassis. This special Windows PE image includes a VMM agent that manages the operating system deployment.

5.   Depending on how you configure it, the VMM agent in the Windows PE image can run scripts to update firmware on the bare-metal chassis, configure RAID volumes, and prepare local storage.

6.   A specially prepared virtual hard disk (in either .vhdx or .vhd format) containing the virtualization host operating system is copied to the bare-metal chassis from a VMM library server.

7.   The VMM agent in the Windows PE image configures the bare-metal chassis to boot from the newly placed virtual hard disk.

8.   The bare-metal chassis boots into the virtual hard disk. If necessary, the newly deployed operating system can obtain additional drivers not included in the virtual hard disk from a VMM library server.

9.   Post-deployment customization of the newly deployed operating system occurs. This includes setting a name for the new host and joining an Active Directory Domain Services domain.

10.   The Hyper-V server role is deployed, and the newly deployed virtualization host is connected to VMM and placed in a host group.

The PXE server needs to provide the PXE service through Windows Deployment Services. When you add the VMM agent to an existing Windows Deployment Services server, VMM only manages the deployment process if the computer making the request is designated as a new virtualization host by VMM.

To integrate the WDS server with VMM to function as the VMM PXE server, you need to use an account on the VMM server that's a member of the local Administrators group on the WDS server. PXE servers need to be on the same subnet as the bare-metal chassis to which they deploy the virtualization host operating system.

VMM host groups

Host groups allow you to simplify the management of virtualization hosts by allowing you to apply the same settings across multiple hosts. VMM includes the All Hosts group by default. You can create additional host groups as required in a hierarchical structure. Child host groups inherit settings from the parent host group. However, if you move a child host group to a new host group, the child host group retains its original settings with the exception of any PRO configuration. When you configure changes to a parent host group, VMM provides a dialog asking if you would like to apply the changed settings to child host groups.

You can assign network and storage to host groups. Host group networks are the networks that are assigned to the host group. These resources include IP address pools, load balances, logical networks, and MAC address pools. Host group storage allows you to allocate logical units or storage pools that are accessible to the VMM server for a specific host group.

> # More Info
> *VMM host groups*
> You can learn more about VMM host groups at *https://learn.microsoft.com/en-us/ system-center/vmm/host-groups?view=sc-vmm-2025*.

VMM virtualization host requirements

To be able to configure a bare-metal hardware chassis so that it can function as a VMM-managed Hyper-V virtualization host, the hardware chassis needs to meet the following requirements:

- **X64 processor**   This needs to support hardware-assisted virtualization and hardware-enforced Data Execution Prevention (DEP). In some cases, it may be necessary to enable this support in BIOS.

- **PXE boot support**   The hardware chassis must be able to PXE boot from a PXE-enabled network adapter. The PXE-enabled network adapter needs to be configured as a boot device.

- **Out-of-band (OOB) management support**   System Center VMM can discover and manage the power states of the hardware chassis that supports BMC (Baseboard Management Controller). VMM supports the following protocols:

  - SMASH (Systems Management Architecture for Server Hardware) version 1 over WS-Management

  - DCMI (Datacenter Management Interface) version 1.0

  - IPMI (Microsoft Intelligent Platform Management Interface) version 1.5 or version 2.0

Placement rules

Placement rules allow you to configure how VMM identifies a suitable host for a VM deployment. Usually, this is based on the available resources on the virtualization host or the host cluster. By configuring host group placement rules, you can create rules that dictate the conditions under which a new VM can be placed on a virtualization host in the host group.

To add a placement rule, edit the properties of the host group, and on the placement tab, click Add. You then specify a custom property and one of the following requirements:

- Virtual Machine Must Match Host

- Virtual Machine Should Match Host

- Virtual Machine Must Not Match Host

- Virtual Machine Should Not Match Host

Host reserves

Host reserves allow you to configure the resources that VMM should set aside for the host operating system. When VMM is going to place a new VM on a host, that host must be able to meet the VM's resource requirements without exceeding the configured host reserves. You can configure host reserves for the following:

- CPU

- Memory

- Disk I/O

- Disk space

- Network I/O

Dynamic optimization

Dynamic optimization allows the virtualization of host clusters to balance workloads by transferring VMs between nodes according to the settings configured at the host group level. Whether the transfer occurs depends on whether the hardware resources on a node in the virtualization host cluster fall below the configured settings. Dynamic optimization only applies to clustered virtualization hosts and does not apply to hosts that are not members of a cluster.

More Info

Virtual Machine Manager

You can learn more about Virtual Machine Manager at *https://learn.microsoft.com/ en-us/system-center/vmm/overview?view=sc-vmm-2025.*

Active Directory

Active Directory, the identity glue that binds on-premises Microsoft networks, is at the center of almost all on-premises networks. Although each computer can have its own unique individual user and service accounts, Active Directory provides a central user, computer, and service account store.

But Active Directory is more than an identity store; it can also be used to store data for Active Directory–aware applications. One example of this is Microsoft Exchange Server, which stores server configuration information in Active Directory. Other applications, such as Microsoft Configuration Manager (formerly System Center Configuration Manager), are also highly dependent on Active Directory.

In this chapter, we look at managing Active Directory. We also cover deploying domain controllers, forests, domains, sites, Group Policy, user, computer, and service accounts, and a host of other Active Directory administrative tasks.

Managing Active Directory

Domain controllers are one of, if not the, highest value target for attackers on your network. An attacker who is able to take control of a domain controller has control over every domain-joined computer in the organization. Having control of a domain controller, which is also known as "domain dominance," means having control of all the authentication and authorization processes in the domain.

While we will discuss server hardening in more detail in Chapter 12 and Active Directory hardening in Chapter 13, one strategy for increasing server security is to reduce the attack surface. Where possible, you should deploy roles on computers installed in the Server Core configuration because this configuration has a smaller attack surface than a server that includes desktop components. Server Core is a great option for domain controller deployment because it provides a reduced attack surface, which strengthens the security of the installation.

Remote rather than local administration

You should perform Active Directory management tasks remotely using Windows Admin Center, management consoles, or PowerShell rather than signing on to the domain controller directly using RDP. If you're doing all your administrative tasks remotely, it won't make any difference to you that you've deployed the domain controller in the Server Core configuration. Using remote consoles also reduces the chance of malware being introduced to the domain controller. There are countless stories of organizations having their security compromised because an administrator signed in to a server using Remote Desktop, went to download a utility from the Internet using the built-in web browser, and ended up with more than they bargained for in terms of malware because they weren't careful about their browsing destinations.

There are a number of consoles that you can use to perform Active Directory administrative tasks. These include the following:

- Active Directory Administrative Center

- Active Directory Users And Computers

- Active Directory Sites And Services

- Active Directory Domains And Trusts

- Group Policy Management Console

Windows Admin Center provides some Active Directory administrative functionality, but not nearly enough that AD administrators could use it as their primary tool for managing Active Directory.

Active Directory Administrative Center

Active Directory Administrative Center was introduced with Windows Server 2008 R2, but it never really caught on as the primary method of managing Active Directory for most administrators. Active Directory Administrative Center (ADAC) allows you to manage users, computers, and service accounts to perform tasks with the Active Directory, such as the Recycle Bin, and to manage functionality, such as Dynamic Access Control.

Active Directory Administrative Center has better search functionality than the other consoles listed in this chapter, which haven't substantively changed since the release of Windows 2000.

You can use Active Directory Administrative Center to manage the following:

- User, computer, and service accounts

- Domain and forest functional level

- Fine-grained password policies

- Active Directory Recycle Bin GUI

- Authentication policies

- Dynamic Access Control

ADAC is built on PowerShell, meaning that it provides a graphical interface to build and enact PowerShell cmdlets. You can use the PowerShell History Viewer, shown in Figure 4-1, to see which cmdlets were used to carry out a task that you configured in the GUI. This simplifies the process of automating tasks because you can copy code straight out of the PowerShell history and then paste it into tools such as PowerShell ISE or Visual Studio Code.

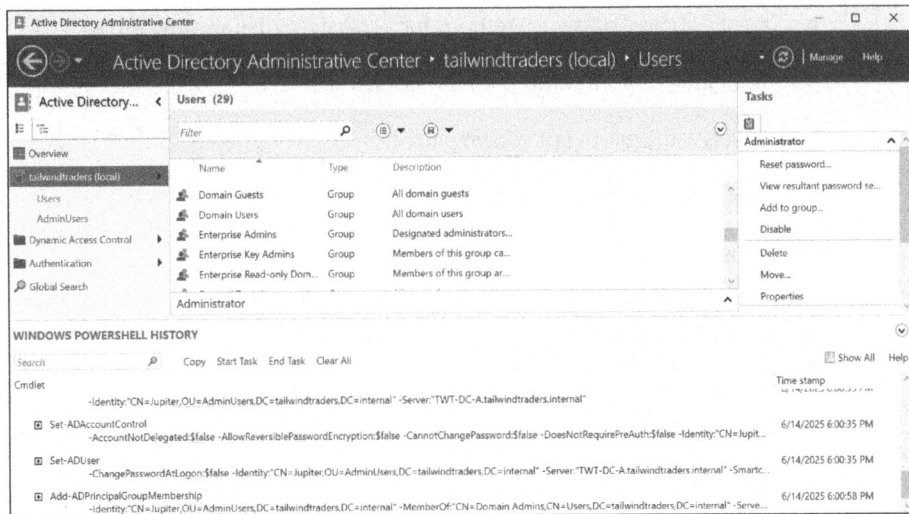

Figure 4-1   Active Directory Administrative Center

One of the most useful elements of Active Directory Administrative Center is the search functionality. You can use this functionality to locate accounts that might require further attention, such as users who haven't signed in for a certain period of time, users configured with passwords that never expire, or users with locked accounts. Using the Add Criteria option in the Global Search node of the Active Directory Administrative Center, you can search based on the following criteria:

- Users with disabled/enabled accounts

- Users with expired passwords

- Users whose passwords have an expiration date or no expiration date

- Users with enabled but locked accounts

- Users with enabled accounts who have not signed in for more than a given number of days

- Users with a password expiring in a given number of days

- Computers running as a given domain controller type

- Last modified between given dates

- Object type is user/inetOrgPerson/computer/group/organizational unit

- Directly applied password settings for a specific user

- Directly applied password settings for a specific global security group

- Resultant password settings for a specific user

- Objects with a given last known parent

- Resource property lists containing a given resource property

- Name

- Description

- City

- Department

- Employee ID

- First name

- Job title

- Last name

- SamAccountName

- State/province

- Telephone number

- UPN

- Zip/postal code

- Phonetic company name

- Phonetic department

- Phonetic display name

- Phonetic first name

- Phonetic last name

There are several tasks that you can't do with Active Directory Administrative Center or with PowerShell, such as running the Delegation Of Control Wizard.

Active Directory Users and Computers console

The Active Directory Users and Computers console is the one that many system administrators use to perform basic AD-related tasks. They use this console primarily out of habit because almost all functionality present in this console is also present in the Active Directory Administrative Center. Active Directory Users and Computers has been around since the days of Windows 2000 Server.

Active Directory Users and Computers allows you to perform tasks, including

- Running the Delegation Of Control Wizard

- Administering different domains within the forest

- Selecting which domain controller or LDAP port the tool connects to

- Finding objects within the domain

- Raising the domain functional level

- Managing the RID Master, PDC Emulator, and Infrastructure Master FSMO role locations

- Creating and editing the properties of

    - Computer accounts

    - User accounts

    - Contacts

    - Groups

    - InetOrgPerson

    - msDS-ShadowPrincipalContainers

- - `msDS-DelegatedManagedServiceAccount`

  - `msImaging-PSPs`

  - MSMQ Queue Alias

  - Organizational unit

  - Printers

  - Shared Folder

- Resultant Set of Policy planning

The View Advanced Features function allows you to see more details of the Active Directory environment. You enable this from the View menu of Active Directory Users And Computers. Enabling this view allows you to see containers that aren't visible in the standard view. If you've ever read a set of instructions that tell you to locate a specific object using Active Directory Users And Computers, and you haven't been able to find that object, chances are that you haven't enabled the View Advanced Features option as shown in Figure 4-2.

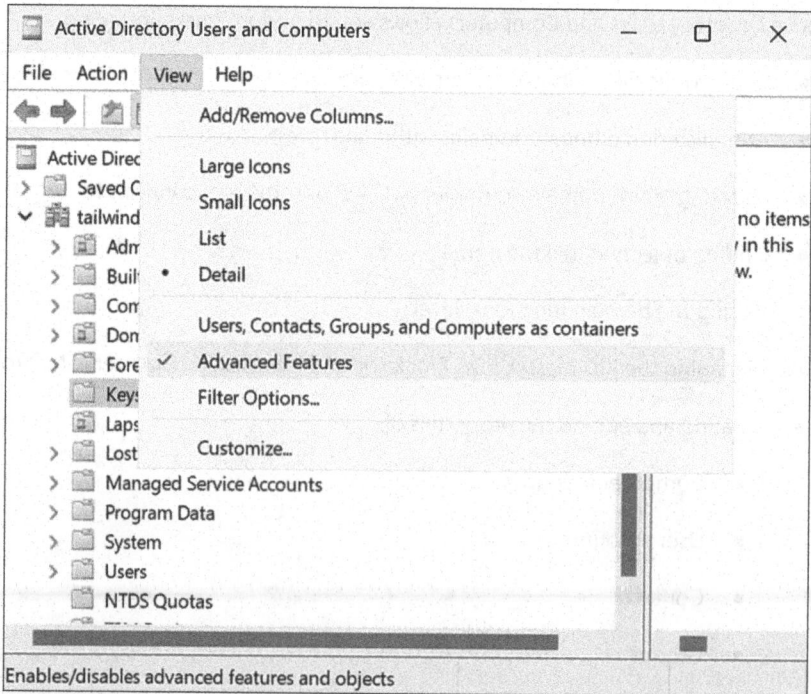

Figure 4-2   Active Directory Users and Computers Advanced Features

The Delegation Of Control Wizard is only available in Active Directory Users And Computers. This wizard allows you to delegate control over the domain and organizational units (OU). For example, you use this wizard to delegate the ability for a specific group to reset user passwords in an OU. This wizard is useful when you want to delegate some privileges to a group of IT ops staff, but you don't want to grant them all the privileges that they'd inherit if you made them a member of the Domain Admins group. You'll learn more about delegating permissions in Chapter 13, "Hardening Active Directory."

Active Directory Sites And Services console

You use the Active Directory Sites And Services console to manage Active Directory sites, which indirectly allows you to control a number of things, including replication traffic and which server a client connects to when using products such as Exchange Server. Sites are configured for the forest, with each domain in the forest sharing the same set of sites.

An Active Directory site is a collection of TCP/IP subnets. Sites allow you to define geographic locations for Active Directory on the basis of TCP/IP subnets. You can have multiple TCP/IP subnets in a site. You should put subnets together in a site where the hosts in that site have a high-bandwidth connection to each other. Usually, this means being in the same building, but it could also be multiple buildings with very-low-latency gigabit links between them.

You'll learn more about Active Directory sites and replication later in this chapter.

Active Directory Domains and Trusts console

You use the Active Directory Domains And Trusts console to configure and manage trust relationships. By default, all domains in a forest trust each other. Your primary use of this console is to create trust relationships between

- Domains in separate forests

- Separate forests

- Kerberos V5 realms

When creating a trust, you can choose between the following types:

- **One-Way: Incoming**   In this trust relationship, your local domain or forest is trusted by a remote domain or forest.

- **One-Way: Outgoing**   In this trust relationship, your local domain or forest trusts a remote domain or forest.

- **Two-way**   In this trust relationship, your local domain or forest trusts (and is trusted by) a remote domain or forest.

You'll learn about trust relationships later in this chapter.

CHAPTER 4

Group Policy Management console

The Group Policy Management console, shown in Figure 4-3, is the primary method by which Group Policy is managed in a standard Windows Server environment. This tool allows you to view Group Policy items from the forest level down. It provides information on which GPOs are linked at the domain, site, and OU levels. You can see a list of all GPOs in a domain under the Group Policy Objects node. There is also a WMI Filters node that contains all WMI filters configured for the domain, a Starter GPOs node that contains all starter GPOs, a Group Policy Modeling node, and a Group Policy Results node. By right-clicking a GPO and selecting Edit, you can edit a GPO in the Group Policy Management Editor. You can output information about a GPO, including which settings are configured and where the GPO is linked, to a file in HTML format using the Get-GPOReport cmdlet. You'll learn more about managing Group Policy later in this chapter.

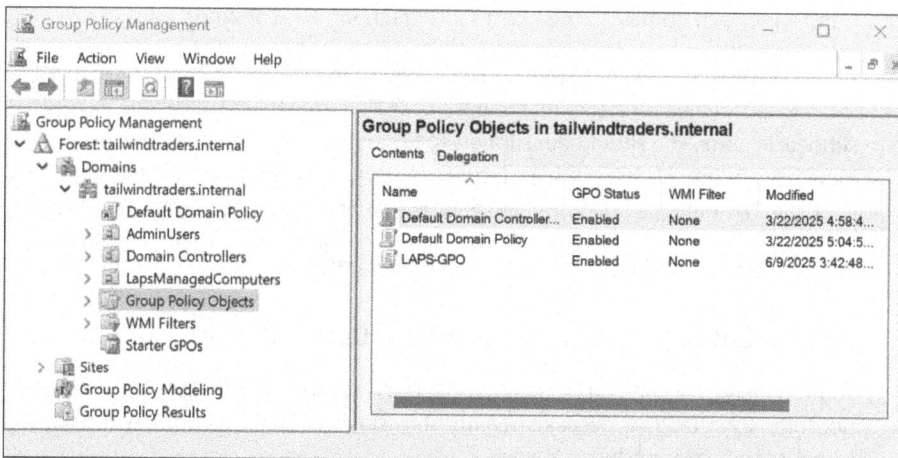

Figure 4-3   Group Policy Management Console

Domain controllers

Domain controllers (DCs) are the heart of Active Directory. Their primary role is to host the Active Directory database, stored in the ntds.dit file. Given their importance, you should limit who can sign on locally to a domain controller.

Inside OUT

Make sure you double-up!

Ensure that you have at least two domain controllers in each domain, and make sure you make regular backups and keep some of them offline. In the event that one domain controller fails, the other one is still there to perform all necessary functionality. Imagine you only have one domain controller and you don't have a backup. If that DC fails, you're going to need to rebuild your domain from scratch.

Deployment

Although the wizard for deploying a domain controller has been updated from what it looked like back in Windows Server 2008 R2, the process is still functionally the same. You choose whether you want to

- Add a domain controller to an existing domain

- Add a new domain to an existing forest

- Add a new forest

To deploy a domain controller, perform the following steps:

1. Using Add Roles and Features in Server Manager, add the Active Directory Domain services role. You need to add this role, shown in Figure 4-4, before you can promote a server to function as a domain controller.

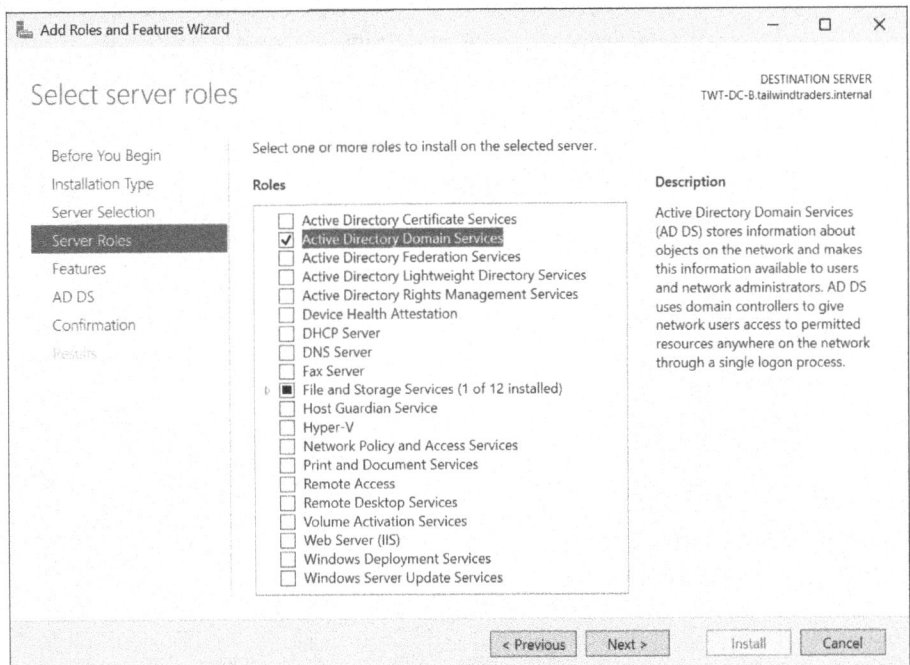

Figure 4-4   Add the Active Directory Domain Services role

2. Once the role files are installed, you'll be able to promote the server to function as a domain controller. You can do this from the Server Manager console by selecting the notification icon and then clicking Promote this server to a domain controller, as shown in Figure 4-5.

CHAPTER 4

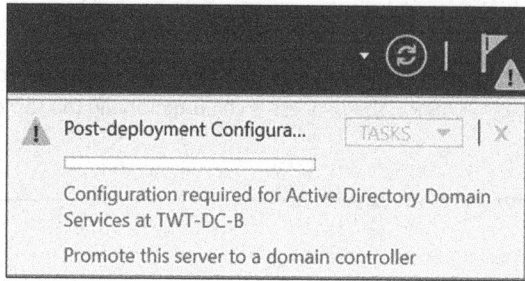

Figure 4-5   Promote this server to a domain controller in Server Manager

3. On the Deployment Configuration page of the Active Directory Domain Services Configuration Wizard, you'll be asked whether you want to add a domain controller to an existing domain, add a new domain to an existing forest, or add a new forest. To add a domain controller to an existing domain, you'll need to have the credentials of a member of the Domain Admins group. To add a new domain to an existing forest, you'll need an account that is a member of the Enterprise Admins group. You can specify this account on the Deployment Configuration page, as shown in Figure 4-6.

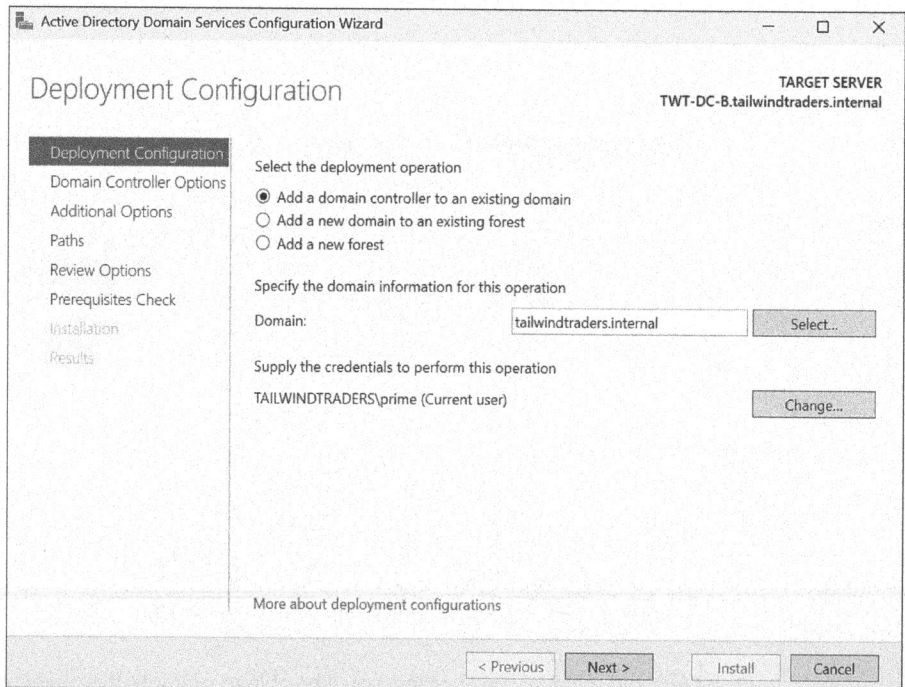

Figure 4-6   Deployment Configuration

If you're adding a domain controller to an existing domain, have the computer domain joined before promoting it. When you add a new domain to an existing forest, choose between adding a child domain or a tree domain. When you add a tree domain, you create a new namespace within an existing forest. For example, you can create the *Adatum.com* domain in the existing *contoso.com* forest. *Contoso.com* remains the root domain of the forest.

Microsoft's recommendation is that you use a registered root domain name, such as *Contoso.com* for the domain name, rather than a nonexternally resolvable domain name like *contoso.internal*. Having a registered externally resolvable domain name simplifies the process when configuring synchronization with Azure AD Connect.

Windows Server supports split DNS, which means that you can configure zones so that a subset of records is resolvable for clients on external networks. Many organizations still use non-resolvable domain names, and you should only take the Microsoft advice into account if you're deploying a new forest or reconfiguring a domain in preparation for synchronizing with Entra in Azure.

When you add a new child domain to an existing forest, you specify the parent domain. For example, you could add the *australia.contoso.com* child domain to the *contoso.com* domain. After you've done that, you can add the *victoria.australia.contoso.com* child domain to the *australia.contoso.com* parent domain. Adding a child domain requires Enterprise Administrator credentials in the forest.

Domain controllers can also host the DNS service and function as global catalog servers. In Windows Server environments, DNS is almost always hosted on domain controllers. You'll learn more about DNS configuration and options in Chapter 5, "DNS, DHCP, and IPAM." Global Catalog servers are covered later in this chapter.

When deploying a domain controller in an environment with multiple sites configured, you can select which site you want the domain controller to belong to. You can change this after deployment using the Active Directory Sites And Services console.

Generally, the default paths for the Database folder, log files folder, and SYSVOL folder are appropriate. The primary reasons to alter this location are for performance reasons or if you have concerns about the amount of storage available on the volume that hosts the Windows Server operating system.

Directory Services Restore Mode passwords

Directory Services Restore Mode (DSRM) allows you to perform an authoritative restore of deleted objects from the Active Directory database. You must perform an authoritative restore of deleted items because if you don't, the restored item is deleted the next time the AD database synchronizes with other domain controllers, where the item is marked as deleted. Authoritative restores are covered later in this chapter. You configure the Directory Services Restore Mode password on the Domain Controller Options page of the Active Directory Domain

Services Configuration Wizard, as shown in Figure 4-7. You can use Windows LAPs, covered in Chapter 12, "Hardening Windows Server," to centrally manage Directory Services Restore Mode Passwords and ensure they're unique for each domain controller.

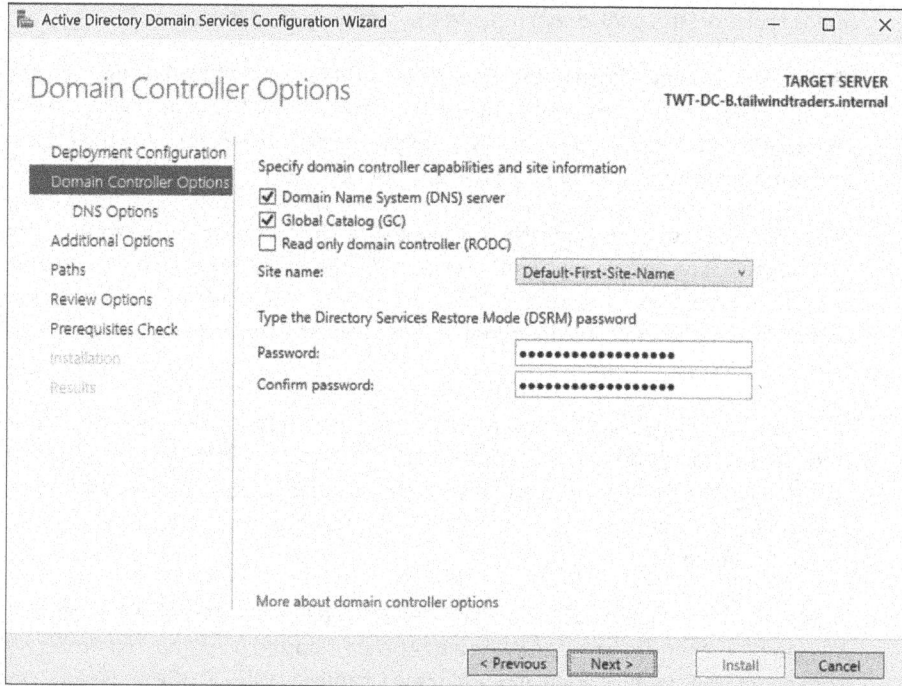

Figure 4-7   Configuring Domain Controller Options

In the event that you forget the DSRM password and you are not using Windows LAPs to manage them, you can reset it by running `ntdsutil.exe` from an elevated command prompt and entering the following command at the `ntdsutil.exe` prompt, at which point you are prompted to enter a new DSRM password:

```
Reset password on server null
```

Advanced installation options

One of the advanced installation options for domain controllers is to install from media. Installing from media gives you the option of prepopulating the AD DS database for a new DC from a backup of an existing DC's AD DS database, rather than having that database populated through synchronization from other domain controllers in your organization. This is very useful when you need to deploy a DC at a remote location that has limited WAN connectivity and you don't want to flood the WAN link with AD DS database synchronization traffic during domain controller deployment. Instead, you ship a backup of the AD DS database to the remote site, and that backup is used to perform the initial AD DS database population. After the newly installed DC connects to other domain controllers, it performs a synchronization, bringing the database up to date with a much smaller synchronization than what would be required when synchronizing from scratch.

Server Core

As the reduced attack surface area of Server Core deployments makes it more secure, domain controllers—which don't have a GUI dependency—are one of several perfect workloads for Server Core deployments. Microsoft recommends deploying domain controllers using the Server Core deployment option and managing those servers remotely.

To configure a computer running Server Core as a domain controller, you can

1. Remotely connect to the server using the Server Manager console.

2. Run the Add Roles And Features Wizard to remotely install the Active Directory binaries on the server.

3. Run the Active Directory Domain Services Configuration Wizard to promote the computer to a domain controller.

You can also use Windows Admin Center to deploy the AD DS feature, but at the time this book was written, you couldn't configure the feature once it was deployed. As an alternative to using the wizard or console, you can run the following PowerShell commands, either locally or remotely, to install the AD DS binaries and promote the server to a domain controller:

```
Install-WindowsFeature AD-Domain-Services -IncludeManagementTools
Install-ADDSDomainController -DomainName contoso.internal -InstallDNS:$True
-credential (Get-Credential)
```

In addition to running this set of commands, you also need to specify a Directory Service Restore Mode password before the computer running Server Core completes the domain controller promotion process. You'll need to use the `Install-ADDSForest` cmdlet if you're installing the first domain in a new forest, as shown here:

```
Install-ADDSForest -DomainName contoso.internal -InstallDNS
```

Virtualized domain controllers

Domain controllers can be run on supported virtualization platforms, including the latest version of VMware and Hyper-V. With the Production Checkpoints feature available in Windows Server 2019 and later Hyper-V, domain controllers can be restored from a checkpoint without causing problems. Microsoft recommends that you run virtualized domain controllers as shielded VMs on a guarded virtualization fabric because this will minimize the chance that a nefarious or compromised virtualization administrator account could be used to access the contents of the DC VM. You can learn more about production checkpoints, shielded VMs, and guarded fabrics in Chapter 6, "Hyper-V."

CHAPTER 4

Global catalog servers

Global catalog servers host a full copy of all objects stored in their host directory and a partial, read-only copy of all other objects in other domains in the same forest. They're used when it's necessary to perform a check of other objects in the forest, such as when a check is performed of a universal group's membership, which could contain members from other domains in the forest.

You can use the Active Directory Sites And Services console to configure a server to function as a global catalog server by right-clicking the NTDS settings of the server. Alternatively, you can run the Set-ADObject cmdlet. For example, to configure the DC MEL-DC1 in the Melbourne-Site site as a global catalog server, run the following command:

```
Set-ADObject "CN=NTDS Settings,CN=MEL-DC1,CN=Servers,CN=Melbourne-Site,CN=Sites,CN=Confi
guration,DC=Contoso,DC=Internal" -Replace @{options='1'}
```

Decommissioning a domain controller

In some circumstances, you want to remove an existing domain controller from your domain. When you do this, you want to ensure that all traces of the domain controller are removed from Active Directory and DNS. To demote a domain controller when the domain controller is accessible and online, perform the following steps:

1. Ensure that the server you want to demote hosts no FSMO roles. You'll learn how to locate and transfer these roles later in the chapter.

2. In Server Manager, go to Manage and then select Remove Roles and Features.

3. Select the server you want to demote and click Next.

4. On the Remove Server Roles screen, uncheck Active Directory Domain Services (AD DS) and choose Remove Features.

5. The wizard will prompt you to demote the domain controller. Click on Demote This Domain Controller as shown in Figure 4-8.

6. On the credentials page, provide the credentials. You don't need to use the Force The Removal Of This Domain Controller option unless the server is unable to contact the domain or this is the last domain controller in the domain or forest.

7. You'll be promoted on the Warnings page with a checkbox to proceed with removal, and you can't choose Next until you select this option.

8. On the Password page, you'll be asked to provide a password for the default local Administrator account. Unless the domain controller was the last in the domain or forest, the computer will still be domain-joined after the operation.

9. On the Review Options page, you'll be able to click Demote. The server will be restarted automatically upon completion. You can then remove the Active Directory Domain Services role files.

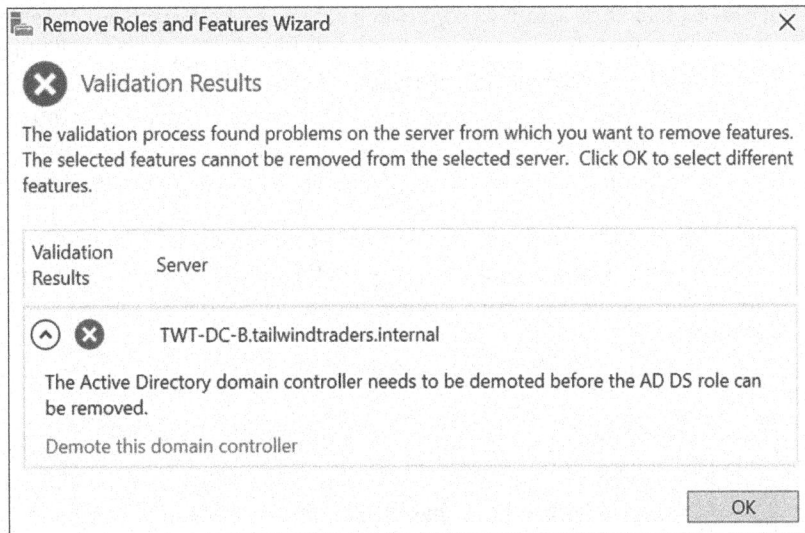

Figure 4-8   Configuring Domain Controller options

If you can't gracefully remove a domain controller because it's offline, forcibly seize any FSMO roles and then delete the domain controller's computer account using Active Directory users and computers. Deleting the account will remove the domain controller's metadata from Active Directory and DNS.

To remove server metadata using ntdsutil, issue the following command, where <ServerName> is the distinguished name of the domain controller whose metadata you want to remove from Active Directory:

```
Ntdsutil "metadata cleanup" "remove selected server <ServerName>"
```

Read Only Domain Controllers

Read Only Domain Controllers (RODC) are a special type of domain controller. They host a read-only copy of the AD DS database. Rather than storing the passwords for all users in the domain, RODCs only store the passwords of a specific set of accounts that you configure. The first domain controller in a new domain or forest cannot be an RODC.

The justification for RODCs is that DCs sometimes need to be located in places where servers have poor physical security and might be stolen. For example, many organizations had branch offices where servers were located under someone's desk. A good rule of thumb is that you should consider a location insecure if it is accessible to anyone other than IT. If a janitor can pull out a computer's power cord to power a vacuum cleaner, the computer isn't in a secure location.

If a server that hosts a domain controller is stolen, the best practice is to reset the account passwords that might have been compromised because it's possible, with the correct tools, to extract passwords from the AD DS database if you have direct access to it. If an ordinary DC is stolen, you would, in theory, need to reset the passwords of every account in the domain because you could never be sure that someone hadn't gained access to the Active Directory database and found a way to extract the passwords of people in your organization.

With shielded VMs and shielded fabrics, it's possible to run a DC in a manner where the VM itself is protected by encryption. In the event that the host server is stolen, the AD DS database cannot be recovered because the contents of the virtualization server's storage are encrypted using BitLocker.

Inside OUT

RODC and Writeable DC Deployment

Concerns about the physical security of a DC are the primary reason to deploy an RODC, so it's extremely unlikely that you would have both an RODC and a writable DC at the same site. RODCs are for sites where the domain controller was once placed in a location that wasn't secure. Though if you do have concerns about the security of a location, it's probably not a great idea to deploy a domain controller at that location!

Passwords on RODCs

One of the most important steps in configuring an RODC is limiting which passwords can be replicated down to the server from a writable domain controller. The default configuration of an RODC has it store almost everything from Active Directory except for user and computer account passwords. In the event that a user or computer account needs to be authenticated against Active Directory, the RODC acts as a proxy for a writable Windows Server DC. The authentication occurs, but it depends on the WAN link to be functional because if you could host a writable DC locally, you wouldn't need the RODC.

Although you can configure an RODC to not cache any passwords locally, you can configure an RODC to cache the passwords of select staff working at a branch office to speed their login. Caching passwords also allows branch office users to log in if the WAN link fails. If the WAN link fails and the user's credentials are not cached, the user is simply unable to log in to the domain.

You configure which accounts can authenticate using the RODC by using the Password Replication Policy, as shown in Figure 4-9. By default, only members of the Allowed RODC Password Replication group can use the RODC to authenticate. This is only the case if the user account is not a member of the Account Operators, Administrators, Backup Operators, Server Operators, or Denied RODC Password Replication Group groups.

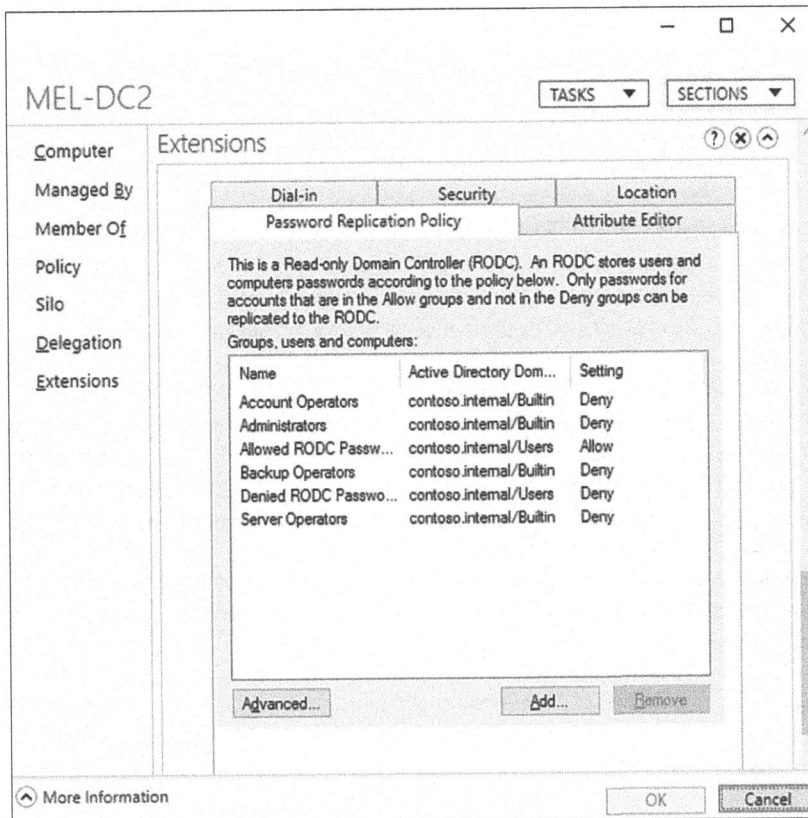

Figure 4-9   Password Replication Policy

RODC partial attribute set

You can configure Active Directory so that only specific attributes on AD DS objects are replicated to an RODC. You would do this because some applications are configured to store sensitive data, such as passwords or encryption keys, as attributes for an object. If you add these sensitive attributes to the filtered attributes set, you can ensure that this information will not be replicated and stored on an RODC.

It's not possible to add system-critical attributes to the RODC filtered attribute set. Attributes that cannot be added to the filtered attribute set are those required for AD DS, the Local Security Authority (LSA), Security Accounts Manager (SAM), and Microsoft-specific security services providers to be able to function correctly. You mark an attribute as confidential by removing the Read permission for that attribute for the Authenticated Users group.

RODC local administrators

Because you deploy RODCs as a security measure, they are almost always placed at branch office sites. Because resources at branch office sites are often sparse, it's also likely that you'll co-locate other services on the server hosting the RODC role. For example, a server that functions as an RODC can also function as a file server, DNS server, DHCP server, and local intranet server.

You can allow a user without Domain Admin privileges to deploy an RODC if you have pre-created an RODC account and added it to the appropriate Active Directory Domain Services site, and the user is a member of the local Administrators group on the computer. You can perform this task in PowerShell or the Active Directory Administrative Center.

If the computer hosting the RODC role also needs to host other roles, you might need to grant administrator access to a user who works at the branch office (but who is not a member of your organization's usual IT staff) in case your normal remote administration techniques don't work. RODCs differ from normal domain controllers in that you can grant local administrator access without having to make the user a member of the Domain Admins group.

To configure a user to function as a local administrator on the computer that hosts the RODC role, edit the properties of the RODC's computer account and configure a security group for the Managed By setting.

In Chapter 12, you learn about Just Enough Administration, a technology that you could use to allow a user to perform remote administrative tasks on an RODC without being made an RODC local administrator.

Decommissioning an RODC

If you suspect that an RODC has been compromised, you can delete the RODC's account from the Domain Controllers container in Active Directory Users And Computers. When you do this, you get the option of resetting all passwords for user and computer accounts that were cached on the RODC, as well as the option of exporting a list of all potentially compromised accounts.

Virtual domain controller cloning

Windows Server supports virtual domain controller cloning. Rather than redeploying domain controllers from scratch each time you need one, domain controller cloning allows you to take an existing virtual machine, make a copy of it, and deploy that copy.

Virtual domain controller cloning has the following prerequisites:

- Hypervisor must support VM-Generation ID. The version of Hyper-V included with all supported versions of Windows supports this technology, as do the most recent versions of VMware.

- The source domain controller needs to be running Windows Server 2012 or later.

- The domain controller that hosts the PDC Emulator role must be online and contactable by the cloned DC. The computer that hosts the PDC Emulator role must also be running Windows Server 2012 or later.

- The source DC must be a member of the Cloneable Domain Controllers group.

You also need to create the DCCloneConfig.xml file. You can do this by using the New-ADDC-CloneConfig cmdlet in PowerShell. When running this cmdlet, you need to specify the cloned DC's IPv4 address information and the site the cloned DC is deployed to. For example, to create the clone configuration file for a clone DC that has the IP address 10.10.10.42 with the subnet mask 255.255.255.0, default gateway of 10.10.10.1, DNS server address of 10.10.10.10, and site name MEL-SITE, issue this command:

```
New-ADDCCloneConfigFile -IPv4Address 10.10.10.42 -IPv4DefaultGateway 10.10.10.1
-IPv4SubnetMask 255.255.255.0 -IPv4DNSResolver 10.10.10.10 -Static -SiteName MEL-SITE
```

After the clone configuration file is created, you import the VM using this file and specify a copy of the source DC's exported virtual hard disk.

AD DS structure

Active Directory is made up of forests and domains. A forest is a collection of Active Directory domains that share a schema and some security principals. The majority of organizations in the world have a single forest domain. Larger, geographically dispersed organizations generally use multiple domain forests.

Domains

For the majority of organizations in the world, a single domain would be sufficient. There are two general reasons for having multiple domains in a forest. The first is that your organization is geographically dispersed, and there are issues around domain replication traffic. The second is that your organization is very large. A single domain can hold a staggering number of objects. Unless your organization has tens of thousands of users, a single domain is usually more than enough.

A domain tree is a collection of domains that share a namespace in a parent-child relationship. For example, the domains *australia.contoso.com* and *tonga.contoso.com* would be child domains of the *contoso.com* domain.

You should always deploy at least two domain controllers per domain for redundancy purposes. Make sure that if you have a multidomain forest, you are making regular backups of the domain controllers in the root domain. There has been more than one organization with a multidomain forest that has had the root domain controllers fail irreparably, making it necessary to redeploy the entire forest from scratch.

CHAPTER 4

Multidomain Active Directory environments

The majority of current AD DS deployments in small and medium-sized enterprises have a single domain. This hasn't always been the case because earlier versions of the Windows Server operating system, such as Windows NT 4, supported far fewer accounts. Supporting a smaller number of accounts often necessitated the use of multiple domains, and it wasn't unusual to see medium-sized organizations that used complicated domain structures.

Each Windows Server domain controller can create approximately 2.15 billion objects during its lifetime, and each domain supports the creation of up to approximately 2.15 billion relative identifiers (RIDs). Given this, however, few administrators implement multiple-domain forests because they need to support a large number of users.

There are many reasons why organizations implement multidomain forests. These can include (but are not limited to) the following:

- **Historical domain structure**   Even though newer versions of the Windows Server operating system handle large numbers of objects more efficiently, some organizations have retained the forest structure that was established when the organization first adopted AD DS.

- **Organizational or political reasons**   Some organizations are conglomerates, and they might be composed of separate companies that share a common administrative and management core. An example of this is a university faculty in Europe or Australia, such as a Faculty of Science, that consists of different departments or schools, such as the School of Physics and the Department of Botany. For political or organizational reasons, it might have been decided that each department or school should have its own domain that is a part of the overall faculty forest. AD DS gives organizations the ability to create domain namespaces that meet their needs, even if those needs might not directly map to the most efficient way of accomplishing a goal from a strict technical perspective.

- **Security reasons**   Domains enable you to create authentication and authorization boundaries. You can also use domains to partition administrative privileges so that you can have one set of administrators who are able to manage computers and users in their own domain, but who are not able to manage computers and users in a separate domain. Although it's possible to accomplish a similar goal by delegating privileges, many organizations prefer to use separate domains to accomplish this goal.

Domain trees

A *domain tree* is a set of names that share a common root domain name. For example, *contoso.com* can have *pacific.contoso.com* and *atlantic.contoso.com* as child domains, and these domains can have child domains themselves. A forest can have multiple domain trees. When you create a new tree in a forest, the root of the new tree is a child domain of the original root domain. In Figure 4-10, *adatum.com* is the root of the new domain tree in the *contoso.com* forest.

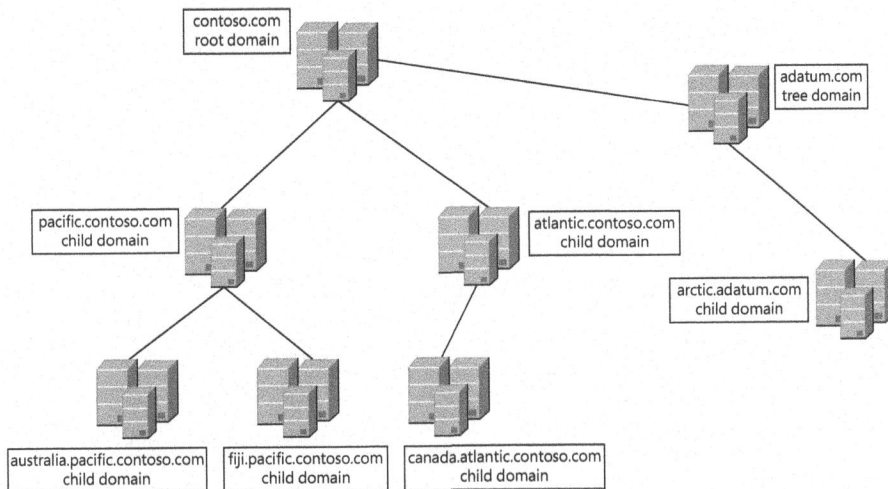

Figure 4-10 *Contoso.com* as the root domain in a two-tree forest

The depth of a domain tree is limited by a domain having a maximum fully qualified domain name (FQDN) length for a host of 64 characters.

Intra-forest authentication

All domains within the same forest automatically trust one another. This means that in the environment shown earlier in Figure 4-10, you can assign a user in the *Australia.pacific.contoso. com* permissions to a resource in the *arctic.adatum.com* domain without performing any extra configuration.

Because of the built-in automatic trust relationships, a single forest implementation is not appropriate for separate organizations, even when they're in partnership with one another. A single forest makes it possible for one or more users to have administrative control. Most organizations aren't comfortable even with trusted partners having administrative control over their IT environments. When you do need to allow users from partner organizations to have access to resources, you can configure trust relationships or federation.

Domain functional levels

The domain functional level determines which Active Directory features are available and which operating systems can participate as domain controllers within the domain. The domain functional level determines the minimum domain controller operating system. For example, if the domain functional level is set to Windows Server 2016, domain controllers must run Windows Server 2016 or later. This rule does not apply to member servers. You can have a domain running at the Windows Server 2016 functional level that still has servers running the Windows Server 2012 R2 operating system. Table 4-1 lists the maximum domain functional level given the minimum domain controller operating system. Assuming you are running supported versions of Windows Server and later, which means you are running domain controllers where the oldest operating system is Windows Server 2016, you can either have the domain functional level set to Windows Server 2016 or, if all your domain controllers are running Windows Server 2025, have the domain functional level set to Windows Server 2025.

Table 4-1   Maximum domain functional level

Minimum domain controller operating system	Maximum domain functional level
Windows Server 2016	Windows Server 2016
Windows Server 2019	Windows Server 2016
Windows Server 2022	Windows Server 2016
Windows Server 2025	Windows Server 2025

Inside OUT

Run DC at the highest OS level

Because domain controllers are so important to your network, Microsoft recommends that, from a security perspective, you always run domain controllers with the most recent operating system. Microsoft argues that the most recent operating system is the most secure and that you should pay special attention to the security of your organization's domain controllers.

You can introduce a DC running Windows Server 2025 to a domain at the Windows Server 2016 functional level as long as all the appropriate updates are installed. You can also perform an in-place upgrade of a Windows Server 2012 R2 domain controller to Windows Server 2025. You can raise the functional level after you've retired existing domain controllers running older versions of the Windows Server operating system. If all your domain controllers are running Windows Server 2025, you should update your domain functional level to the Windows Server 2025 functional level.

Inside OUT

Check your functional level

Even when older Windows Server DCs have long been removed, it's not unusual for people to have forgotten to elevate the functional level. Because you get greater functionality by raising functional levels, and there is no downside to doing so beyond not being able to introduce a domain controller running an operating system below that of the functional level, you should raise functional levels as high as possible.

Forests

A forest is a collection of domains that share a schema. There are automatic trust relationships between all domains in a forest. Accounts in one domain in a forest can be granted rights to resources in other domains. As mentioned earlier in this chapter, forests don't need to have a contiguous namespace. For example, a forest can contain both the *contoso.com* and *Adatum.com* domains.

There are several reasons why an organization might have multiple forests with trust relationships configured between those forests. The most common is that one organization has acquired another, and multiple forests exist until such a time that the users and resources hosted in the forest of the acquired organization are moved to the forest of the acquiring organization. A less common one is that an organization is splitting off a part of itself, and users need to be migrated out of the existing forest and into a new forest prior to the split occurring.

Forest functional levels are determined by the minimum domain functional level in the forest. After you've raised the domain functional levels in the forest, you can raise the forest functional level. Unlike in previous versions of Active Directory, it's possible to lower both the forest and domain functional levels after they have been raised. An important caveat with this is that the forest functional level must be lowered so that it's never higher than the lowest intended domain functional level.

Account and resource forests

Organizations are increasingly deploying what are known as Enhanced Security Administrative Environment (ESAE) forests. In an ESAE forest design, all of the accounts used for administrative tasks in the production forest are hosted in a second forest known as the ESAE, bastion, or administrative forest. The ESAE forest is configured with one-way trust relationships with the production forest.

In their native administrative forest, the accounts used for administrative tasks in the production forest are traditional unprivileged user accounts. These accounts and the groups that they are members of in the administrative forest are delegated privileges in the production forest.

The advantage of this approach is that, should one of these accounts become compromised, it can't be used to alter any permissions or settings in the administrative forest because the account only has privileges in the production forest.

Organizational units

The benefit of a comprehensive OU structure is that it simplifies the delegation of permissions over objects and allows you to apply GPOs closer to the accounts that they influence. While it's possible to filter GPOs based on security groups or WMI queries, it's important to remember that each GPO within a computer and user account's scope must be checked to see if it applies.

If you have all of your GPOs applied at the domain level and filtered on the basis of security group or WMI query, your Group Policy processing time at startup and sign-on is going to be substantially longer than if you apply GPOs as close to the accounts they influence as possible.

Better privilege delegation targeting is also a great reason to have a good OU structure. When delegating privileges, you want to ensure that you only delegate privileges over an appropriate set of objects. For example, imagine that you want to allow each department's administrative assistant to have the ability to reset passwords for users within their respective department. If all the user accounts for your organization are located in one OU, you won't be able to do this because, at best, you'll provide each administrative assistant with the ability to reset every user's password in the organization. If user accounts are located in department-specific OUs, you can then delegate the ability to reset passwords on a per-OU basis. This way, the administrative assistant for the Marketing department can be granted the ability to change passwords for user accounts located in the Marketing OU without granting them the ability to change passwords for user accounts located in the Accounting OU.

Inside OUT

OU structures don't always relate to organizational structure

Many organizations have had an AD deployment for more than a decade and a half. A big problem for many is that while the company goes through regular reorganizations, the OU structure doesn't go through a similar reorganization. This might mean that the OU structures don't in any way represent the organizational structure. You should peri-odically review your organization's OU structure to ensure that it maps sensibly to the organizational structure. While you might not implement GPOs at the OU level or del-egate privileges, it doesn't mean that you won't do so at some point in the future.

When you create OUs in Windows Server 2019 and later, the OUs are automatically configured so that accidental deletion protection is enabled.

Flexible Single Master Operations roles

The Flexible Single Master Operations (FSMO) roles are five special roles present on domain controllers. Two of these roles, the schema master and the domain naming master, are unique within each forest. The other three roles, PDC Emulator, infrastructure master, and RID master, must be present within each domain in the forest. For example, in a three-domain forest, there is only one schema master and domain naming master, but each domain in the forest has its own PDC emulator, infrastructure master, and RID master.

By default, FSMO roles are allocated to the first domain controller in a domain. After you have more than one domain controller in each domain, you should manually start to move the FSMO roles to other domain controllers. This protects you from a situation where the first domain controller deployed in each domain goes offline and all FSMO roles become unavailable. When you do need to take a domain controller offline for an extended period of time, ensure that you transition any FSMO roles that it hosts to another domain controller in the same domain.

Schema master

The schema master is the single server in the forest that is able to process updates to the Active Directory schema. The Active Directory schema defines the functionality of Active Directory. For example, by modifying the schema, you can increase the available attributes for existing objects as well as enable Active Directory to store new objects. Products, including Exchange Server and Configuration Manager, require that the default Active Directory schema be extended prior to product installation so that each product can store important data in Active Directory.

The domain controllers that host the schema master role should be located in the root domain of the forest. If you need to extend the schema prior to installing products such as Exchange Server, do so either on the computer that hosts the schema master role or on a computer in the same site. The account used to extend the schema needs to be a member of the Schema Admins security group.

You can determine which computer hosts the schema master role by running the following PowerShell command:

```
Get-ADForest contoso.internal | FT SchemaMaster
```

Domain naming master

The domain naming master is a forest-level role that is responsible for managing the addition and removal of domains from the forest. The domain naming master also manages references to domains in trusted forests. In a multidomain environment, the domain controller that hosts this forest-level role should be deployed in the root forest.

The domain naming master is also contacted when new instances of AD DS application directory partitions are added, such as when you configure a limited directory partition replication scope for an AD DS-integrated DNS zone. If you can't add new domains or partitions, the computer hosting this FSMO role may not be available.

You can determine which server hosts the domain naming master role by running the following PowerShell command:

```
Get-ADForest contoso.internal | FT DomainNamingMaster
```

PDC emulator

The PDC emulator role is a domain-level FSMO role that is responsible for handling both changes to account passwords as well as domain time synchronization. PDC emulators in child domains synchronize time against the PDC emulator in the forest root domain. You should ensure that the PDC emulator in the forest root domain synchronizes against a reliable external time source. If users are unable to change passwords or accounts can't be unlocked, the PDC emulator may have failed.

To determine which domain controller in a specific domain hosts the PDC emulator role, run the following PowerShell command:

```
Get-ADDomain contoso.internal | FT PDCEmulator
```

Infrastructure master

The computer that hosts the infrastructure master role keeps track of changes that occur in other domains in the forest as they apply to objects in the local domain. The infrastructure master FSMO role holder updates an object's SID (Security Identifier) and distinguished name in a cross-domain object reference. If group names or memberships for groups hosted in other domains don't appear current in the local domain, it may be that the infrastructure master has failed.

You should avoid having the infrastructure master role co-located with a domain controller that hosts the global catalog server role unless all domain controllers in the domain are configured as global catalog servers. You can determine which computer in a domain hosts the infrastructure master role by running the following PowerShell command:

```
Get-ADDomain contoso.internal | FT InfrastructureMaster
```

RID master

The RID master processes relative ID requests from domain controllers in a specific domain. Relative IDs and domain Security IDs are combined to create a unique Security ID (SID) for the object. There is an RID master in each domain in the forest. When a new security principal object, like a group or user account, is created, a unique SID is attached to that object. SIDs consist of

- The domain SID that will be the same for all SIDs created in the host domain

- An RID that is unique to each security principal SID created in a domain

Each AD DS DC has a pool of RIDs that it can allocate to security principals it creates. When this pool becomes exhausted, the DC will query the RID master for additional RIDs to add to this pool. If the RID master is not available, the pool cannot be replenished, and new accounts cannot be created.

You can use the following PowerShell command to determine which computer hosts the RID Master role:

```
Get-ADDomain contoso.internal | FT RidMaster
```

Seizing FSMO roles

In some cases, a domain controller hosting an FSMO role fails, and you need to seize the FSMO role to move it to another domain controller. For example, to move the RID Master, Infrastructure Master, and Domain Naming Master roles to a domain controller named MEL-DC2, run the following command:

```
Move-ADDirectoryServerOperationMasterRole -Identity MEL-DC2 -OperationMasterRole RIDMast
er,InfrastructureMaster,DomainNamingMaster -Force
```

Trust relationships

Trust relationships allow security principals in one Active Directory environment to access resources in another Active Directory environment. Trusts make it possible for users in one domain to be authenticated by domain controllers in a separate domain. For example, if there is a bidirectional trust relationship between the domains *contoso.local* and *adatum.remote*, users with accounts in the *contoso.local* domain are able to authenticate in the *adatum.remote* domain. By configuring a trust relationship, it's possible to allow users in one domain to access resources in another, such as being able to use shared folders and printers or being able to sign on locally to machines that are members of a different domain than the one that holds the user's account.

Some trusts are created automatically. For example, domains in the same forest automatically trust each other. Other trusts, such as external trusts, realm trusts, shortcut trusts, and forest trusts, must be created manually. Trusts use the Kerberos V5 authentication protocol by default, and they revert to NTLM if Kerberos V5 is not supported. You configure and manage trusts using the Active Directory Domains and Trusts console or the `netdom.exe` command-line utility with the `/trust` switch.

Although trusts themselves are relatively easy to come to terms with, the terminology around trusts tends to confuse many people. It's important that you understand the difference between a trusting and a trusted domain and how trust direction, incoming or outgoing, relates to which security principals are able to authenticate.

To understand trusts, you have to understand the difference between a trusting domain or forest and a trusted domain or forest. The trusting domain or forest contains the resources to which you want to grant security principals from the trusted domain or forest access. The trusted domain or forest hosts the security principals that you want to allow to access resources in the trusting forest. For example, if you want to grant users in the *adatum.remote* domain access to resources in the *contoso.local* domain, the *adatum.remote* domain is the trusted domain and the *contoso.local* domain is the trusting domain. In bidirectional trust relationships, a domain or forest is both trusting and trusted.

CHAPTER 4

Trust transitivity

A transitive trust extends beyond the original trusting domains. For example, if you have a trust between two domain forests and that trust is transitive, all of the domains in each of the forests trust each other. Forest trusts are transitive by default. External trusts are not transitive by default. When you create a trust, keep in mind that there may be domains beyond the one you're establishing the relationship with that may be included. You might trust the administrator of *adatum.remote* not to allow access by nefarious users, but do you trust the administrator of *subdomain.adatum.remote*?

Trust direction

When you create a new trust, you specify a trust direction. You can choose a two-way (or bidirectional) trust or a unidirectional trust, which is either one-way incoming or one-way outgoing.

When you configure a one-way incoming trust, users in the local domain are authenticated by their local domain and authorized for access to resources in the remote domain, realm, or forest. Remember that if you're configuring a one-way incoming trust between the single domain forests *contoso.local* and *adatum.remote*, users with accounts in *contoso.local* can access resources in *adatum.remote*. Similarly, if you're configuring a one-way outgoing trust between the single-domain forests *contoso.local* and *adatum.remote*, users with accounts in *adatum. remote* can access resources hosted in *contoso.local*.

The terminology around trusts can be a little confusing. The key thing to remember is that the direction of trust is the opposite of the direction of access, as shown in Figure 4-11. An outgoing trust allows incoming access, and an incoming trust allows outgoing access.

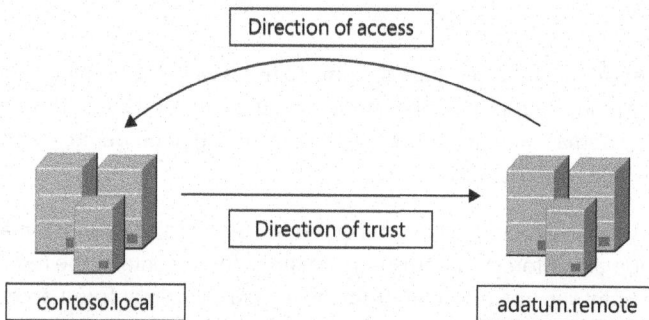

Figure 4-11   The direction of trust and direction of access

Forest trusts

When you configure a forest trust, one AD DS forest trusts the other one. Forest trusts are transitive. When you configure a forest trust, you can allow any domain in the trusting forest to be accessible to any security principal in the trusted forest. Forest trusts can be bidirectional or unidirectional. You are most likely to configure forest trusts if your organization has two or more AD DS forests. You can configure a trust between a forest hosted in Azure and one hosted on-premises.

You can configure one of two authentication scopes when you configure a forest trust. The type of authentication scope that you configure depends on your security requirements. The options are

- **Forest-wide authentication**   When you choose forest-wide authentication, users from the trusted forest are automatically authenticated for all resources in the local forest. You should use this option when both the trusted and trusting forests are part of the same organization.

- **Selective authentication**   When you configure this option, Windows does not auto-matically authenticate users from the trusted forest. You can then configure specific serv-ers and domains within the forest to allow users from the trusted forest to authenticate. Use this option when the two forests are from different organizations, or you have more stringent security requirements.

Configuring selective authentication

Configuring selective authentication means granting specific security principals in the trusted forest the Allowed To Authenticate (Allow) permission on the computer that hosts the resource to which you want to grant access. For example, assume you had configured a forest trust with selective authentication. You want to grant users in the Research universal group from the trusted forest access to a Remote Desktop Services (RDS) server in the trusting forest. To accomplish this goal, you can configure the properties of the RDS server's computer account in Active Directory Users And Computers and grant the Allowed To Authenticate permission to the Research universal group from the trusted forest. Doing this only allows users from this group to authenticate; you still have to grant them access to RDS by adding them to the appropriate local group on the RDS server.

External trusts

External trusts enable you to configure one domain in one forest to trust a domain in another forest without enabling a transitive trust. For example, you configure an external trust if you want to allow the *auckland.fabrikam.com* domain to have a trust relationship with the *welling-ton.adatum.com* domain without allowing any other domains in the *fabrikam.com* or *adatum.com* forests to have a security relationship with each other.

Shortcut trusts

Shortcut trusts enable you to speed up authentication between domains in a forest that might be in separate branches or even separate trees. For example, in the hypothetical forest shown in Figure 4-12, if a user in the *canada.atlantic.contoso.com* domain wants to access a resource in the *arctic.adatum.com* domain, authentication needs to travel up through the *atlantic.contoso.com* and *contoso.com* domains before passing across to the *adatum.com* domain and finally back to the *arctic.adatum.com*. If you implement a shortcut trust between the *canada.atlantic.contoso.com* and *arctic.adatum.com* domains, authentication traffic instead travels directly between these two domains without having to traverse the two domain trees in the forest.

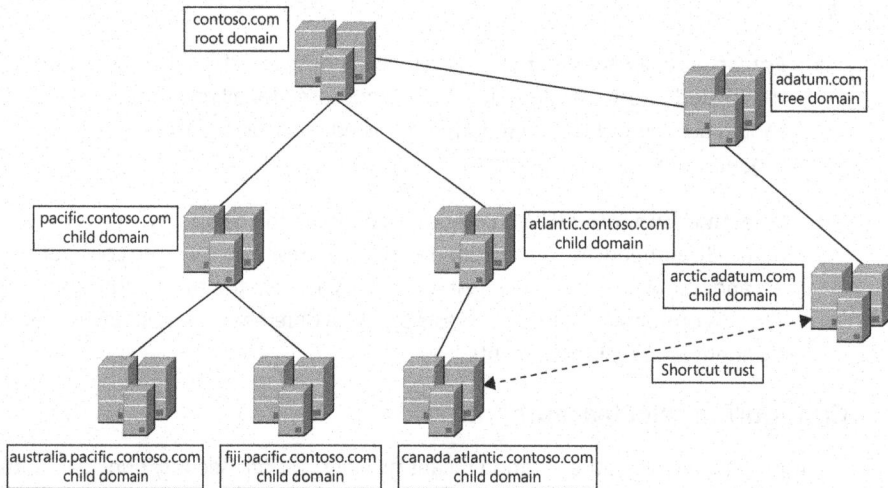

Figure 4-12 Shortcut trust

You configure a shortcut trust using the Active Directory Domains And Trusts console by editing the properties of one domain and triggering the New Trust Wizard on the Trusts tab. Shortcut trusts can be unidirectional or bidirectional. As is the case with the creation of other trusts, ensure that you have name resolution working properly between the trusting and the trusted domains, either by having the DNS zones propagate through the forest, by configuring conditional forwarders, or by configuring stub zones.

Realm trusts

You use a realm trust to create a relationship between an Active Directory Domain Services domain and a Kerberos V5 realm that uses a third-party directory service. Realm trusts can be transitive or nontransitive. They can also be unidirectional or bidirectional. You're most likely to configure a realm trust when you need to allow users who use a UNIX directory service to access resources in an AD DS domain or users in an AD DS domain to access resources in a UNIX Kerberos V5 realm.

You can configure a realm trust from the Active Directory Domains And Trust console. You do this by selecting the Realm Trust option, as shown in Figure 4-13. When configuring a realm trust, you specify a realm trust password that you use when configuring the other side of the trust in the Kerberos V5 realm.

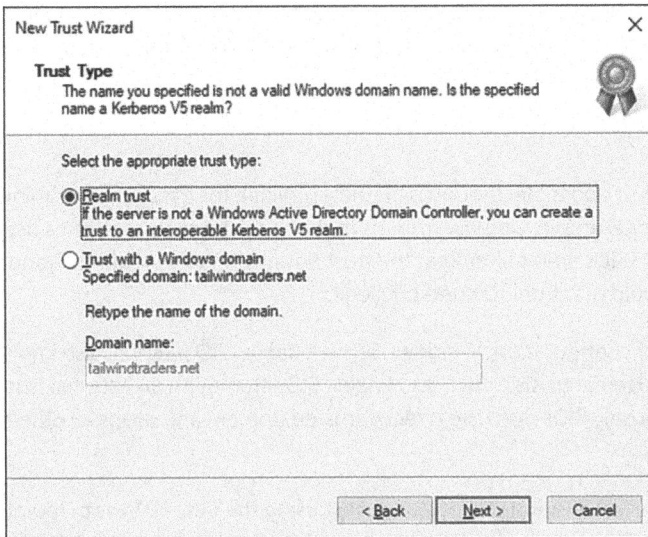

Figure 4-13   Configure the realm trust

Netdom.exe

You use netdom.exe with the trust switch to create and manage forest, shortcut, and realm trusts from the command line. When using netdom.exe, you specify the trusting domain name and the trusted domain name.

The syntax of netdom.exe with the /trust switch is shown in Figure 4-14.

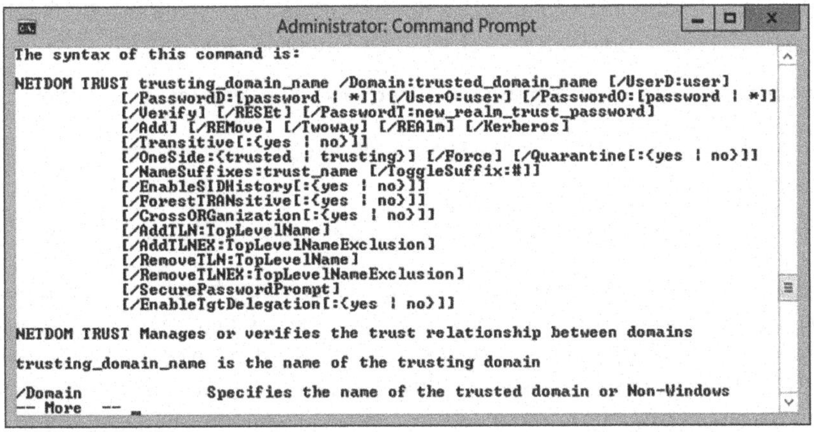

Figure 4-14   The command syntax for netdom.exe

CHAPTER 4

PowerShell doesn't include much in the way of cmdlets for creating and managing trust relationships beyond the `Get-ADTrust` cmdlet, which allows you to view the properties of an existing trust.

SID filtering

In a trusted domain, it's possible, though extremely difficult, for a malicious administrator to add foreign SIDs (for example, Domain Admins from the resource forest) into a user's sIDHistory. If those foreign SIDs aren't filtered at the trust boundary, they would be honored in the user's token and could grant unintended privileges.

To block this type of configuration, Windows Server enables *SID filtering*, also known as *domain quarantine*, on all external trusts. When you enable SID filtering on an external trust, the trusting domain accepts only SIDs from the directly trusted domain and drops all others (including foreign sIDHistory).

It's possible to verify SID filtering settings on a trust using the `Get-ADTrust` cmdlet in a PowerShell session run by a user with administrative privileges. For example, to verify that SID filtering is enabled on the trust with the *tailwindtraders.com* forest, issue the following command:

```
Get-ADTrust -identity tailwindtraders.com -properties SIDFilteringForestAware | fl *SID*
```

To disable SID filtering for the trusting forest, use the netdom trust command with the following option:

```
/enablesidhistory:Yes
```

Enabling SID history allows you to use SIDs that don't have the domain SID of the trusting domain. You enable or disable SID filtering on the trusting side of the trust. For example, if you are an administrator in the *contoso.com* domain and you want to disable SID filtering, you can issue the following command from an elevated command prompt:

```
Netdom trust contoso.com /domain:tailwindtraders.com /enablesidhistory:Yes
```

In the same scenario, if you want to reenable SID filtering, you can issue the following command:

```
Netdom trust contoso.com /domain:tailwindtraders.com /enablesidhistory:Yes
```

The default configuration, where SID filtering is enforced by default on trusts, is something that you should probably leave as it is. In the past, it was necessary to allow SID history when trusts were created with forests running Windows 2000 Server domain controllers. Since Windows 2000 is no longer supported by Microsoft, and SID history is not necessary for trust relationships with Windows Server 2003 or later domain controllers, you probably won't need to disable it.

Name suffix routing

Name suffix routing enables you to configure how authentication requests are routed when you configure a forest trust between two AD DS forests. When you create a forest trust, all unique name suffixes are routed. Name suffix routing assists when users sign on with a UPN, such as *rick_claus@contoso.com*. Depending on the UPNs that are configured, you might want to allow or disallow the use of specific UPN suffixes. You do this by configuring name suffix routing on the Name Suffix Routing tab of the trust's properties.

Managing sites

AD DS sites enable you to configure AD DS so that it understands which network locations have a fast local network connection. Generally, this means the computers are in the same building, although if your organization has a group of buildings in the same area that are connected by a high-speed network, you use a single AD DS site configuration.

An Active Directory site is a collection of TCP/IP subnets. Sites allow you to define geographic locations for Active Directory on the basis of TCP/IP subnets. You can have multiple TCP/IP subnets in a site. You should put subnets together in a site where the hosts in that site have a high-bandwidth connection to each other. Usually, this means being in the same building, but it could also mean multiple buildings with very-low-latency gigabit links between them.

For example, imagine that your organization has its head office in Melbourne and a branch office in Sydney. You can set up two sites: one site for Melbourne and the other for Sydney. This ensures that computers in the Melbourne location interact as much as possible with resources located in Melbourne, and computers in the Sydney location interact as much as possible with resources located in Sydney.

You associate the TCP/IP subnets in the head office with the Melbourne site and the TCP/IP subnets in the branch office with the Sydney site. After you do this, functionality such as replication topology is automatically configured.

You configure sites by associating them with IP address ranges. For example, you might associate the subnet 192.168.10.0 /24 with the AD DS Site BNE-Site. Any computers that have an IP address in this range would be located in that site. You can configure network addresses using IPv4 or IPv6 networks. When you install AD DS for the first time, a default site, named Default-First-Site-Name, is created. You configure sites using the Active Directory Sites And Services console, shown in Figure 4-15.

CHAPTER 4

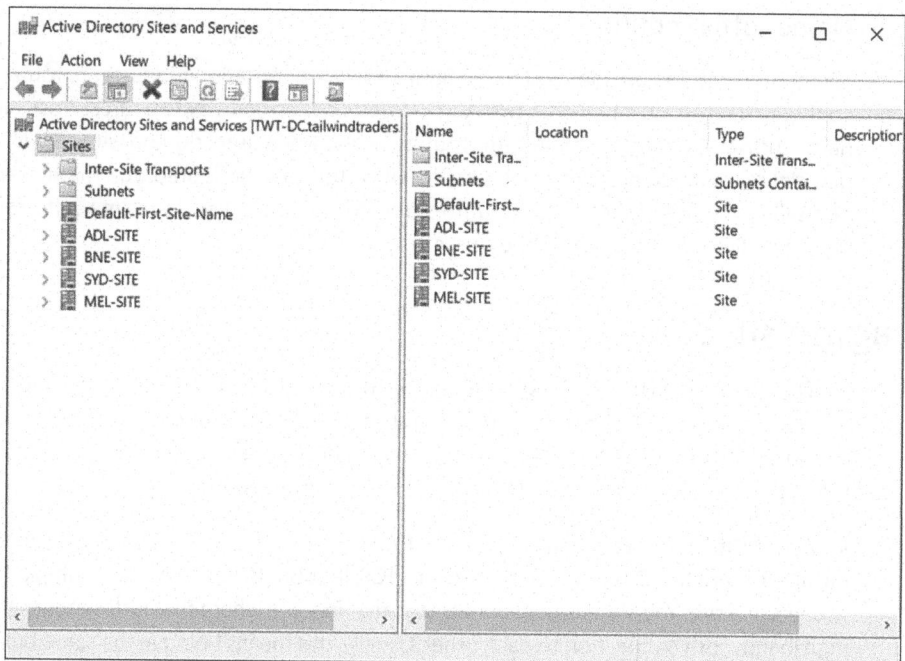

Figure 4-15   The Active Directory Sites And Services console

It's important that you add sites for each separate location in your organization. If you don't, AD DS assumes that all computers are located on the same fast network, and this might cause problems with other products as well as with AD DS. Microsoft products such as Exchange Server use AD DS site information when generating network topologies.

Sites enable you to do the following:

- **Separate different locations that are connected by a slow WAN or expensive WAN link**   For example, if your organization has a branch office in Sydney and another branch office in Melbourne, and these branch offices are connected by a WAN link that is rated at 512 kilobits per second (Kbps), you configure the Sydney and Melbourne branch offices as separate sites.

- **Control which domain controllers are used for authentication**   When users log on to the network, they perform authentication against an available domain controller located in their AD DS site. Although users are still able to sign on and authenticate against a DC in another site if one isn't available in their local site, you should strongly consider placing a domain controller at any site with a sufficient number of users. What counts as "a sufficient number of users" varies depending on the speed and reliability of the site's connection to the rest of the organization's network. In some cases, you might deploy an RODC to aid authentication at some branch office sites.

- **Control service localization**   Many Microsoft products, such as Exchange Server, and technologies, such as BranchCache and DFS, use AD DS sites as a way of determining network topology. To ensure that these products and technologies work well, you should ensure that each AD DS site is configured properly.

- **Control AD DS replication**   You can use AD DS sites to manage domain controller replication. The default settings make it possible for replication to occur 24 hours a day, 7 days a week. Instead, you can use AD DS site configuration to configure the replication to occur according to a specific schedule.

Creating sites

To add a new Active Directory site, right-click the Sites node in the Active Directory Sites And Services console and select New Site. Specify the site name and select a site link object, and then select OK twice.

A site link object represents a connection between two sites. The default site link object is named DEFAULTIPSITELINK. You can change the site link object later. Figure 4-16 shows the creation of a site named *Sydney*.

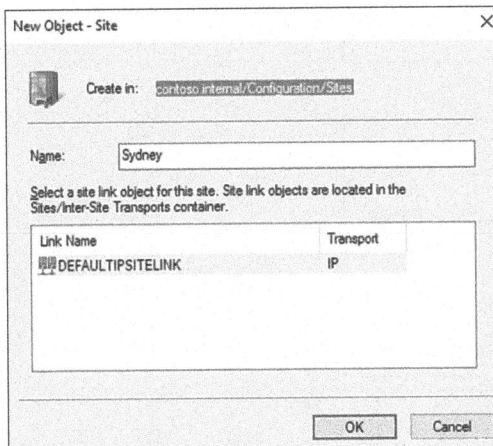

Figure 4-16   Creating a new site

You can use the New-ADReplicationSite PowerShell cmdlet to create a new site. For example, to create a new site named HBA-SITE that is associated with the default IP site link, issue this command:

```
New-ADReplicationSite HBA-SITE
```

After you've created a site, you need to associate it with IP address ranges. You can't do that until you've added IP address ranges as subnets. When you create a subnet, you specify an

IPv4 or IPv6 network prefix. For an IPv4 network, you specify the network address and the subnet in CIDR notation. For example, you specify network 192.168.15.0 with a subnet mask of 255.255.255.0 as 192.168.15.0 /24.

Creating subnets

To add a subnet, right-click the Subnets node in Active Directory Sites And Services and then select New Subnet. You can specify the new subnet in IPv4 or IPv6 format. After you've specified the subnet, you have to specify which site the subnet is associated with. Figure 4-17 shows the 10.10.10.0/24 subnet associated with the Melbourne site.

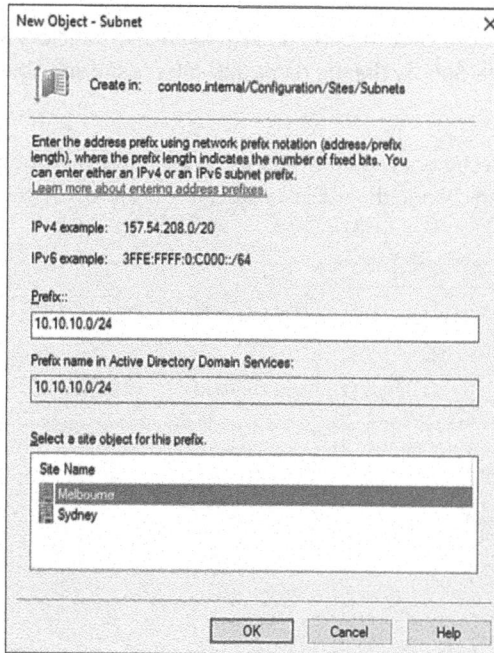

Figure 4-17   New subnet

You can create a new subnet from PowerShell with the New-ADReplicationSubnet cmdlet. For example, to create a new subnet that has the address 192.168.16.0/24 and associate it with the HBA-SITE site, issue the command:

```
New-ADReplicationSubnet -Name "192.168.16.0/24" -Site HBA-SITE
```

You can verify which subnets are associated with a particular AD DS site by viewing the properties of that site. You can't change which subnets are associated with a site by editing the site properties; you can only do so by editing the subnet properties. You can associate multiple subnets with an AD DS site, but you can't associate multiple AD DS sites with a specific subnet.

Creating site links

Site links enable you to specify how different AD DS sites are connected. When you add a site, you're asked to specify the site link, and the DEFAULTIPSITELINK site link is the default option even if another site link is available. Sites that are connected to the same site link are able to replicate with each other directly. For example, if all the sites in Figure 4-18 are associated with the DEFAULTIPSITELINK site link, each site assumes that it could replicate directly with the others. When troubleshooting replication, determine whether you want all sites connected to DEFAULTIPSITELINK or if you want them to use separate site links for alternative replication paths. For example, a domain controller in the Melbourne site attempts to replicate directly with a domain controller in the Canberra site. With this topology, you instead configure site links for Melbourne-Sydney, Adelaide-Sydney, and Canberra-Sydney. This way, domain controllers in Canberra, Melbourne, and Adelaide only replicate with the Sydney site rather than attempting to replicate with each other directly.

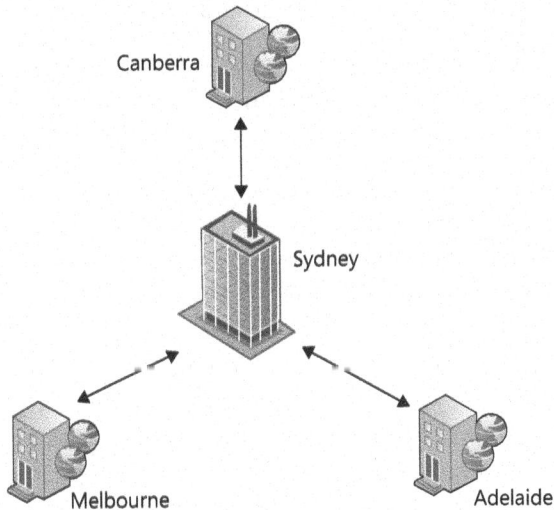

Figure 4-18   Configuring site links that mirror network topology

You can create a new IP site link using the Active Directory Sites And Services console. When you create a site link, you specify the sites that use the link. You can configure the cost and replication schedule of a site link after it's created by editing the Site Link properties. The default Cost is 100, and site links that have lower costs are preferred for replication over site links that have a higher cost. Replication occurs every 180 minutes by default, 24 hours a day. You can modify when replication occurs by configuring a replication schedule.

If you want replication to occur as quickly as possible, you can enable the Use Notify replication option by modifying a site link's options attribute. You can perform this task by using the Attribute Editor tab in the site link's properties.

You can create a site link using the `New-ADReplicationSiteLink` cmdlet. For example, to create a new site link named ADL-CBR that links the ADL-SITE and CBR-SITE sites, issue this command:

```
New-ADReplicationSiteLink "ADL-CBR" -SitesIncluded ADL-SITE, CBR-SITE
```

Members of the Enterprise Admins security group can create and modify site links. Members of the Domain Admins security group in the forest root domain can also perform site link management tasks. User accounts that are only members of the child domain but not the forest root domain's Domain Admins security group are unable to manage site links.

Creating site link bridges

Site link bridges create transitive links between site links. Each site link in a bridge must have a site in common with another site link in the bridge. It's only necessary to create a site link bridge with complex network topologies, as site link bridges are automatically created based on the topology created when you configure site links. You likely need to create a site link bridge if

- Your IP network is not fully routed. If you disable the Bridge All Site Links option, all site links will be treated as nontransitive. You can then use your own site link bridges to reflect the manner in which traffic is routed across your network.

- You need to control replication flow between sites. By disabling the Bridge All Site Links for the site link IP transport and creating a site link bridge, you can create a disjointed network. This ensures that site links within the bridge can route AD DS traffic transitively, but they will not route traffic outside of the site link bridge.

Moving domain controllers

When you deploy a new domain controller, the domain controller promotion process performs a lookup to determine which AD DS site the domain controller should be a member of based on its IP address. If you haven't created a subnet in the Active Directory Sites And Services console that maps to the IP address of the server that you are promoting to the domain controller, the domain controller is instead assigned to the first AD DS site, which is Default-First-Site-Name unless you have changed it.

The domain controller does not automatically reassign itself to a new site if you create the subnet and site objects in the Active Directory Sites And Services console, if it has already been added to the Default-First-Site-Name site. In this instance, you need to move the domain controller to the new site manually. You can move the domain controller using the Active Directory Sites And Services console by right-clicking the domain controller that you want to move, selecting Move, and selecting the destination site in the Move Server dialog.

You can also move a domain controller to a different site using the `Move-ADDirectoryServer` PowerShell cmdlet. For example, to move the server PERTH-DC to the Perth-Site AD DS site, execute the following command:

```
Move-ADDirectoryServer -Identity "PERTH-DC" -Site "Perth-Site"
```

Managing replication

Replication makes it possible for changes that are made on one AD DS domain controller to be replicated to other domain controllers in the domain and, in some cases, to other domain controllers in the forest. Rather than replicating the AD DS database in its entirety, the replication process is made more efficient by splitting the database into logical partitions. Replication occurs at the partition level, with some partitions only replicating to domain controllers within the local domain, some partitions replicating only to enrolled domain controllers, and some partitions replicating to all domain controllers in the forest. AD DS includes the following default partitions:

- **Configuration partition**   This partition stores forest-wide AD DS structure information, including domain, site, and domain controller location data. The configuration partition also holds information about DHCP server authorization and Active Directory Certificate Services certificate templates. The configuration partition replicates to all domain controllers in the forest.

- **Schema partition**   The schema partition stores definitions of all objects and attributes as well as the rules for creating and manipulating those objects. There is a default set of classes and attributes that cannot be changed, but it's possible to extend the schema and add new attributes and classes. Only the domain controller that holds the Schema Master FSMO role is able to extend the schema. The schema partition replicates to all domain controllers in the forest.

- **Domain partition**   The domain partition holds information about domain-specific objects such as organizational units, domain-related settings, user, group, and computer accounts. A new domain partition is created each time you add a new domain to the forest. The domain partition replicates to all domain controllers in a domain. All objects in every domain partition are stored in the Global Catalog, but these objects are stored only with some, not all, of their attribute values.

- **Application partition**   Application partitions store application-specific information for applications that store information in AD DS. There can be multiple application partitions, each of which is used by different applications. You can configure application partitions so that they replicate only to some domain controllers in a forest. For example, you can create specific application partitions to be used for DNS replication so that DNS zones replicate to some, but not all, domain controllers in the forest.

Active Directory supports attribute-level replication. Rather than replicate the entire object when a change is made to an attribute on that object, such as when group membership changes for a user account, only the attribute that changes is replicated to other domain controllers. Attribute-level replication substantially reduces the amount of data that needs to be transmitted when objects stored in AD DS are modified.

CHAPTER 4

Understanding multimaster replication

AD DS uses multimaster replication. This means that any writable domain controller is able to make modifications to the AD DS database and to have those modifications propagate to the other domain controllers in the domain. Domain controllers use *pull replication* to acquire changes from other domain controllers. A domain controller may pull changes after being notified by replication partners that changes are available. A domain controller notifies its first replication partner that a change has occurred within 15 seconds and additional replication partners every 3 seconds after the previous notification. Domain controllers also periodically poll replication partners to determine whether changes are available so that those changes can be pulled and applied to the local copy of the relevant partition. By default, polling occurs once every 60 minutes. You can alter this schedule by editing the properties of the connection object in the Active Directory Sites And Services console.

Knowledge Consistency Checker (KCC)

The Knowledge Consistency Checker (KCC) runs on each domain controller. The KCC is responsible for creating and optimizing the replication paths between domain controllers located at a specific site. In the event that a domain controller is added or removed from a site, the KCC automatically reconfigures the site's replication topology. The KCC topology organization process occurs every 15 minutes by default. Although you can change this value by editing the registry, you can also trigger an update using the repadmin command-line tool with the KCC switch.

Store and forward replication

AD DS supports store-and-forward replication. For example, the Canberra and Melbourne branch offices are enrolled in a custom application partition. These branch offices aren't connected, but they are connected to the Sydney head office. In this case, changes made to objects stored in the application partition at Canberra can be pulled by the domain controller in Sydney. The Melbourne domain controller can then pull those changes from the domain controller in Sydney, as shown in Figure 4-19.

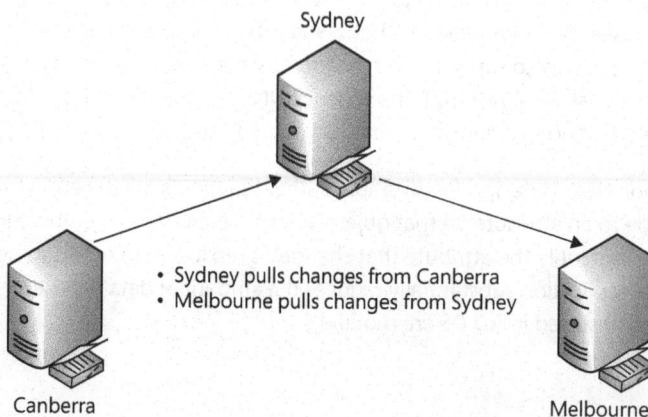

Sydney

- Sydney pulls changes from Canberra
- Melbourne pulls changes from Sydney

Canberra

Melbourne

Figure 4-19   An example of store-and-forward replication

Conflict resolution

In an environment that supports multimaster replication, updates may be made to the same object at the same time in two or more different places. Active Directory includes sophisticated technologies that minimize the chance that these conflicts will cause problems, even when conflicting updates occur in locations that are distant from each other.

Each domain controller tracks updates by using *update sequence numbers (USNs)*. Each time a domain controller updates, either by processing an update performed locally or by processing an update acquired through replication, it increments the USN and associates the new value with the update. USNs are unique to each domain controller, as each domain controller processes a different number of updates to every other domain controller.

When this happens, the domain controller that wrote the most recent change, known as the last writer, wins. Because each domain controller's clock might not be precisely synchronized with every other domain controller's clock, the last write isn't simply determined by a comparison of time stamps. Similarly, because USNs are unique to each domain controller, a direct comparison of USNs is not made. Instead, the conflict resolution algorithm looks at the attribute version number. This is a number that indicates how many times the attribute has changed and is calculated using USNs. When the same attribute has been changed on different domain controllers, the attribute with the higher attribute version number wins. If the attribute version number is the same, the attribute modification time stamps are compared, with the most recent change being deemed authoritative.

If you add or move an object to a container that was deleted on another domain controller at the same time, the object is moved to the LostAndFound container. You can view this container when you enable the Advanced Features option in the Active Directory Users and Computers console.

RODC replication

The key difference between an RODC and a writable domain controller is that RODCs aren't able to update the Active Directory database, and they only host password information for a subset of security principals. When a client in a site that only has RODCs needs to make a change to the Active Directory database, that change is forwarded to a writable domain controller in another site. When considering replication, remember that all RODC-related replication is incoming and that other domain controllers do not pull updates from the AD DS database hosted on an RODC.

RODCs use the usual replication schedule to pull updates from writable domain controllers, except in certain cases, RODCs perform inbound replication using a replicate-single-object (RSO) operation. These cases include

- The password of a user whose account password is stored on the RODC is changed.

- A DNS record update occurs where the DNS client performing the update attempts to use the RODC to process the update and is then redirected by the RODC to a writable DC that hosts the appropriate Active Directory Integrated DNS zone.

- Client attributes, including client name, DnsHostName, OsName, OsVersionInfo, supported encryption types, and LastLogonTimeStamp, are updated.

These updates occur outside the usual replication schedule because they involve objects and attributes that are important to security. An example is when a user at a site that uses RODCs calls the service desk to have their password reset. The service desk staff member, located in another site, resets the password using a writable domain controller. If a special RSO operation isn't performed, it's necessary to wait for the change to replicate to the site before the user is able to sign on with the newly reset password.

Monitor and manage replication

You can use the Active Directory Sites And Services console to trigger replication. You can trigger replication on a specific domain controller by right-clicking the connection object and selecting Replicate Now. When you do this, the domain controller replicates with all of its replication partners.

You can also monitor replication as it occurs using DirectoryServices performance counters in Performance Monitor. Through Performance Monitor, you can view inbound and outbound replication, including the number of inbound objects in the queue and pending synchronizations.

Repadmin

You can use the `repadmin` command-line tool to manage and monitor replication. This tool is especially useful at enabling you to diagnose where there are problems in a replication topology. For example, you can use `repadmin` with the following switches:

- `replsummary`   Generates information showing when replication between partners has failed. You can also use this switch to view information about the largest interval between replication events.

- `showrepl`   Views specific inbound replication traffic, including objects that were replicated and the date stamps associated with that traffic.

- `prp`   Determines which user account passwords are being stored on an RODC.

- `kcc`   Forces the KCC to recalculate a domain controller's inbound replication topology.

- `queue`   Enables you to display inbound replication requests that a domain controller must make to reach a state of convergence with source replication partners.

- `replicate`   Forces replication of a specific directory partition to a specific destination domain controller.

- `replsingleobj`   Use this switch when you need to replicate a single object between two domain controllers.

- `rodcpwdrepl`   Enables you to populate RODCs with the passwords of specific users.

- `showutdvec`   Displays the highest USN value recorded for committed replication operations on a specific DC.

Accounts

Accounts represent the identities of security principals in an Active Directory environment. The most common type of account is a user account, which represents a person as they interact with the Windows environment. IT Ops personnel also need to regularly deal with computer accounts, group accounts, and service accounts.

User accounts

User accounts almost always represent real people in an Active Directory environment, with the caveat that some user accounts are used for services rather than traditional users signing in to their desktop computers.

In many organizations, a user account is nothing more than a username, a password, and a collection of group memberships. User accounts can contain substantial additional information, including

- First name
- Last name
- Middle initial
- Full name
- Office information
- Email address
- Web page
- Job title
- Department
- Company
- Manager
- Phone numbers (main, home, mobile, fax, pager, IP phone)
- Address
- User profile location
- Log-on script
- Home folder

- Remote desktop service profile

- Dial-in permissions

- Published certificates

- Remote Desktop Sessions settings

- Remote Control settings

You should configure important accounts to be protected from deletion by enabling the Protect From Accidental Deletion option, as shown in Figure 4-20. Unless this option is removed, the account can't be deleted. This setting doesn't stop an account from being removed deliberately, but it does stop the account from being deleted accidentally.

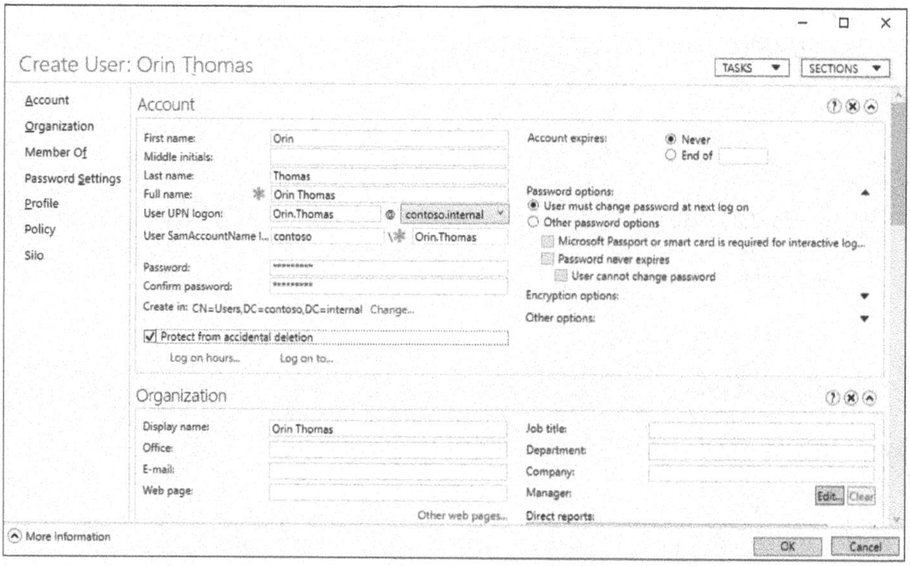

Figure 4-20   User account properties

Computer accounts

Computer accounts represent the computer within Active Directory. You often move computer accounts to specific OUs and then apply group policies to those OUs as a way of configuring the computer. When you join a computer to the domain, the computer account is automatically placed in the default Computers container.

If a computer account becomes desynchronized from the domain of which it is a member and loses its trust relationship, you can repair the relationship by signing in with the local Administrator account and running the following PowerShell command:

```
Test-ComputerSecureChannel -Credential Domain\<AdminAccount> -Repair
```

If you don't know the local Administrator account password but suspect that cached domain administrator credentials might be present, disconnect the computer from the network, either by physically removing the Ethernet connection or disconnecting the virtual network adapter, sign in using those credentials, and then run the PowerShell command previously mentioned. The Local Administrator Password Solution, which ensures that you don't forget the local Administrator account password, is covered in Chapter 12.

Group accounts

Active Directory supports three different types of group account scopes: domain local, global (the default), and universal. It also supports two group types: Security and Distribution. You use security groups to control access to resources, delegate permissions, and for email distribution. Distribution groups can only be used for email distribution. If your organization uses Exchange Server, you manage distribution groups through Exchange. Best practice is to place users within global groups, add those global groups to domain local groups, and assign permissions and rights directly to the domain local groups. By default, members of the Account Operators, Domain Admins, or Enterprise Admins groups can modify the membership of groups.

Universal

A universal group can hold accounts and groups from the same forest. Universal groups are stored in the global catalog. If you change the membership of a universal group, this change replicates to all global catalog servers in the forest. Universal groups are great in single forest environments where replication traffic isn't an issue or where there are few changes to universal group membership. Universal groups can be nested within other universal groups, or they can be added to domain local groups.

Global

Global groups can contain user accounts from their home domains. Global groups can also contain other global groups from its home domain. Global groups can be members of universal groups and domain local groups.

Domain local

Domain local groups can have universal groups, global groups, and domain local groups as members. Domain local groups can host accounts from any domain in the forest and accounts from domains in trusted forests. Domain local groups can only be added to domain local groups within their own domain. A domain local group can only be assigned rights and permissions within its own domain. Domain local groups cannot be added to global or universal groups.

Default groups

The groups listed in Table 4-2 are included in a Windows Server domain by default.

CHAPTER 4

Table 4-2   Important groups

Group	Function
Access Control Assistance Operators	Members can query authorization attributes and permissions for resources on the computer.
Account Operators	Members can manage domain user and group accounts.
Administrators	Built-in administrators group. On a DC, this provides unlimited access to the computer and domain.
Allowed RODC Password Replication Group	Members can have their passwords replicated to RODCs.
Backup Operators	Members can override security restrictions to back up or restore files.
Cert Publishers	Members can publish certificates to AD DS.
Certificate Services DCOM Access	Members can connect to Certification Authorities.
Cloneable Domain Controllers	Domain controllers that can be cloned.
Cryptographic Operators	Can perform cryptographic operations.
Denied RODC Password Replication Group	Members cannot have their passwords replicated to RODCs.
Distributed COM Users	Can launch, activate, and use Distributed COM objects.
DNSAdmins	DNS administrators group.
DNSUpdateProxy	Group for DNS clients who are able to perform dynamic updates on behalf of services, such as DHCP servers.
Domain Admins	Members can administer the domain. Automatically add members of the local Administrators group on every computer in the domain. The default owner of all objects created in Active Directory.
Domain Computers	All computers that are members of the domain.
Domain Controllers	All domain controllers in the domain.
Domain Guests	Hosts the built-in domain guest account.
Domain Users	Hosts all user accounts in the domain.
Enterprise Admins	Only present in the root domain of a forest. Can make forest-wide changes, such as raising the forest functional level or adding domains.
Enterprise Key Admins	Members can perform administrative tasks on key objects at the forest level.
Enterprise Read-only Domain Controllers	Group for enterprise read-only domain controllers.
Event Log Readers	Can view the contents of event logs on the computer.
Group Policy Creator Owners	Members can create and modify GPOs.
Hyper-V Administrators	Can manage Hyper-V on the local machine.

Group	Function
IIS_IUSRS	Internet Information Services built-in group.
Incoming Forest Trust Builders	Members can create incoming, one-way trusts to the forest.
Key Admins	Members can perform administrative tasks on key objects at the domain level.
Network Configuration Operators	Members can configure networking features.
Performance Log Users	Members can schedule logging of performance counters and collect event traces.
Performance Monitor Users	Members can access performance counter data locally and remotely.
Pre-Windows 2000 Compatible Access	A group that exists for backward compatibility.
Print Operators	Members can manage printers deployed on domain controllers.
Protected Users	Members of this group have stricter security controls applied to their accounts.
RAS and IAS Servers	Members in this group are able to access the remote access settings of user accounts.
RDS Endpoint Servers	Servers in this group host VMs used with RemoteApp programs and personal virtual desktops.
RDS Management Servers	Servers in this group can perform administrative actions on other servers running the Remote Desktop Services role.
RDS Remote Access Servers	Servers in this group enable users of RemoteApp programs and personal virtual desktops to access resources.
Read-only Domain Controllers	Read-only domain controllers in the domain.
Remote Desktop Users	Granted the right to sign on using Remote Desktop.
Remote Management Users	Members can access WMI resources over management protocols.
Replicator	Group supporting file replication at the domain level.
Schema Admins	Root domain group. Members are authorized to make changes to the Active Directory Schema.
Server Operators	Members can administer domain member servers.
Storage Replica Administrators	Members can manage storage replicas.
Terminal Server License Servers	Members can update Active Directory information about terminal services licensing.
Users	Built-in Users group.
Windows Authorization Access Group	Have access to the computed `tokenGroupGlobalAndUniversal` attribute on User objects.

CHAPTER 4

Service accounts

Service accounts are functionally user accounts used by services to interact with the operating system and resources on the network. By assigning rights to the service account, you can limit what the service can or cannot do.

One of the key things to remember about a service account is that it should not have the right to log on locally to a computer but should have the log on as a service right. This is important because administrators in many organizations have bad habits where they grant service accounts unnecessary rights and even go as far as to give all service accounts the same non-expiring password. Sophisticated attackers know this and use this to compromise service accounts and use them as a way to gain privileged access.

Local System

The Local System (NT AUTHORITY\SYSTEM) account is a built-in account. It has privileges equivalent to a local administrator account on the local computer. It acts with the computer account's credentials when interacting on the network. This is the most powerful service account, and generally, you should be reluctant to assign this service account manually to a service given its extensive privileges.

Local Service

The Local Service (NT AUTHORITY\LocalService) account has the same level of privilege as user accounts that are members of the local Users group on a computer. This account has fewer local privileges than the Local System account. Any services assigned to this account access network resources as a null session without credentials. Use this account when the service doesn't require network access or can access network resources as an anonymous user and requires only minimal privileges on the computer it is being used on.

Network Service

The Network Service (NT AUTHORITY\NetworkService) account is similar to the Local Service account in that it has privileges on the local computer equivalent to those assigned to a member of the local Users group. The primary difference is that this account interacts with the computer account's credentials to access resources on the network.

GMSA

A group managed service account (GMSA) is a service account that is managed by the domain. This means that rather than having to update the service account's password manually, Active Directory updates the password in line with the domain password policy. Many organizations that use regular user accounts as service accounts tend to set a static password for these accounts, which is often simple rather than complex.

Group Managed Service Accounts require the forest functional level to be Windows Server 2012 or higher. Forests at the Windows Server 2008 level support a version of a GMSA called an MSA, but this is more limited than a GMSA, with each MSA only being able to be installed on a single machine.

Prior to using GMSAs, you'll need to create a Key Distribution Services (KDS) root key. You can do this with the following command:

```
Add-KdsRootKey -EffectiveTime ((get-date).addhours(-10))
```

You manage GMSAs using Windows PowerShell. To create a GMSA, specify the name of the account, a DNS hostname associated with the account, and the name of the security principals that are allowed to use the account. For example, to create a GMSA named MEL-SQL-GMSA for the contoso.internal domain that can be used by servers in the MEL-SQL-Servers security group, enact the following command:

```
New-ADServiceAccount MEL-SQL-GMSA -DNSHostname MEL-SQL-GMSA.contso.internal
-PrincipalsAllowedToRetrieveManagedPassword MEL-SQL-Servers
```

To install the account on a specific server so that you can use it, run the Install-ADService-Account cmdlet. For example, to install the MEL-SQL-GMSA account on a server so that you can assign the account to services, enact the command:

```
Install-ADServiceAccount MEL-SQL-GMSA
```

Prior to running this command, you may need to install the RSAT ADDS Tools on the local server. You can do this by running the command:

```
Install-WindowsFeature RSAT-ADDS-Tools
```

When assigning the account to a service, you should clear the Password and Confirm Password textbox. You'll need to append $ to the account name when configuring it as shown in Figure 4-21. Windows Server recognizes that the account is a GMSA and manages the password settings.

Figure 4-21   GMSA configuration

CHAPTER 4

dMSA

A Delegated Managed Service Account (dMSA) is a new type of service account introduced in Windows Server 2025. dMSAs are tied to specific machine identities in Active Directory, ensuring that only designated devices can authenticate using the account. This binding enhances security by preventing unauthorized use of service account credentials. dMSAs benefit from automatic password management, with secrets stored exclusively on domain controllers.

When used with Credential Guard, dMSAs leverage virtualization-based security to protect secrets, mitigating risks associated with credential theft techniques like Kerberoasting.

To install and configure a dMSA, ensure that the KDS root key exists using

```
Add-KdsRootKey -EffectiveTime ((get-date).addhours(-10))
```

Create the dMSA using the following PowerShell command:

```
$params = @{
  Name = "ServiceAccountName"
  DNSHostName = "DNSHostName"
  CreateDelegatedServiceAccount = $true
  KerberosEncryptionType = "AES256"
}
New-ADServiceAccount @params
```

Use the following command to allow a specific computer account to interact with the dMSA password, substituting `Machine$` with `ComputerName$`:

```
$params = @{
  Identity = "DMSA Name"
  PrincipalsAllowedToRetrieveManagedPassword = "Machine$"
}
Set-ADServiceAccount @params
```

Configure the appropriate delegation state using the following command:

```
$params = @{ Identity = "dMSAsnmp"; Properties = @{ "msDS-DelegatedMSAState" = 3 } }
Set-ADServiceAccount @params
```

Then, on the target computer, run the following command to install the dMSA:

```
Install-ADServiceAccount -Identity "ServiceAccountName"
```

You can then configure a service to use the dMSA by setting the service to log on as the dMSA account in the format `domain\dMSA$`.

Virtual account

A virtual account is the local equivalent of a group-managed service account. Virtual accounts are supported by products such as SQL Server as an alternative to the default built-in accounts.

You can create virtual service accounts by editing the properties of a service and setting the account name to NT Service\<ServiceName>.

Kerberos delegation

Kerberos constrained delegation restricts how and where application services can act on a user's behalf. You can configure accounts so that they can be used only for specific tasks. For example, Figure 4-22 shows configuring the delegation of the account for computer SYD-B, for delegation through Kerberos, for the time service on computer SYD-A. You can configure Kerberos delegation using the Set-ADComputer, Set-ADServiceAccount, and Set-ADUser cmdlets with the PrincipalsAllowedToDelegateAccount parameter.

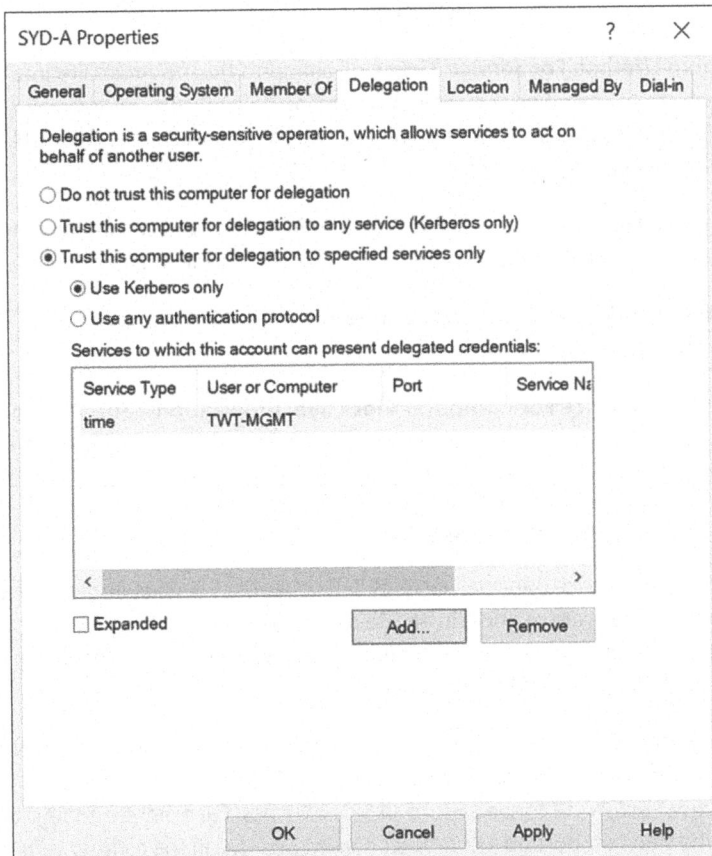

Figure 4-22   Kerberos delegation

CHAPTER 4

Kerberos policies

Kerberos policies determine how the service and user tickets are used in the Authentication function in an Active Directory domain. Like password and account lockout policy, Kerberos policy is applied at the domain level. Kerberos policies applied at the site and organizational level do not affect the resultant Kerberos policy. Kerberos policies are located in the `Computer Configuration\Policies\Windows Settings\Security Settings\Account Policies\Kerberos Policy` node.

You can configure the following Kerberos policies:

- **Enforce User Logon Restrictions**   Ensures that Kerberos checks every request for a session ticket, also known as a service ticket.

- **Maximum Lifetime For Service Ticket**   Configures the maximum lifetime of a service ticket, which is also known as a session ticket. The default value for this policy is 10 hours. The value of this policy must be less than or equal to the value specified in the Maximum Lifetime For User Ticket policy.

- **Maximum Lifetime For User Ticket**   Determines the maximum lifetime of a user ticket, also known as a ticket-granting ticket (TGT). The default value of this policy is 10 hours.

- **Maximum Lifetime For User Ticket Renewal**   Specifies the maximum TGT renewal period. The default is seven days.

- **Maximum Tolerance For Computer Clock Synchronization**   Specifies how much drift there can be in domain controller clocks before ticket errors occur. The default setting is five minutes.

Service principal name management

Kerberos clients use a service principal name (SPN) to identify a unique instance of a service on a given computer. If there are multiple instances of the same service hosted on computers in a domain or forest, each service requires a unique SPN. Service instances can be configured with multiple SPNs, as long as those SPNs are unique.

You can use the SetSPN command-line utility to configure SPNs for computers running Windows Server. SetSPN uses this syntax: `setspn serviceclass/host:portnumber servicename`. You can use `SetSPN /?` to see a list of all SPN switches. For example, to register the HTTP service using the standard port on a computer named MEL-DC in the *contoso.com* domain using a GMSA named SYD-SRVC, issue this command:

```
setpspn -s http/MEL-DC.contoso.com CONTOSO\SYD-SRVC
```

Group Policy

Group Policy provides a central way of managing user and computer configuration. You can use Group Policy to configure everything from password and auditing policies to software deployment, desktop background settings, and mappings between file extensions and default applications.

> ## Inside OUT
> ### Not the only configuration management option
> It's fair to say that Group Policy is really starting to show its age. On the server side, Microsoft is pushing Desired State Configuration as the primary method of managing server configuration. On the client side, you often get a better result using tools such as Configuration Manager for on-premises deployments and Intune for clients that aren't domain joined.

GPO management

After you get beyond editing GPOs to configure settings, you need to start thinking about issues such as GPO maintenance. For example, if an important document is lost, you need to know how to recover it from backup. Do you know what to do if someone accidentally deletes a GPO that has hundreds of settings configured over a long period of time?

The main tool you'll use for managing GPOs is the Group Policy Management Console (GPMC), shown in Figure 4-23. You can use this console to back up, restore, import, copy, and migrate. You can also use this console to delegate GPO management tasks.

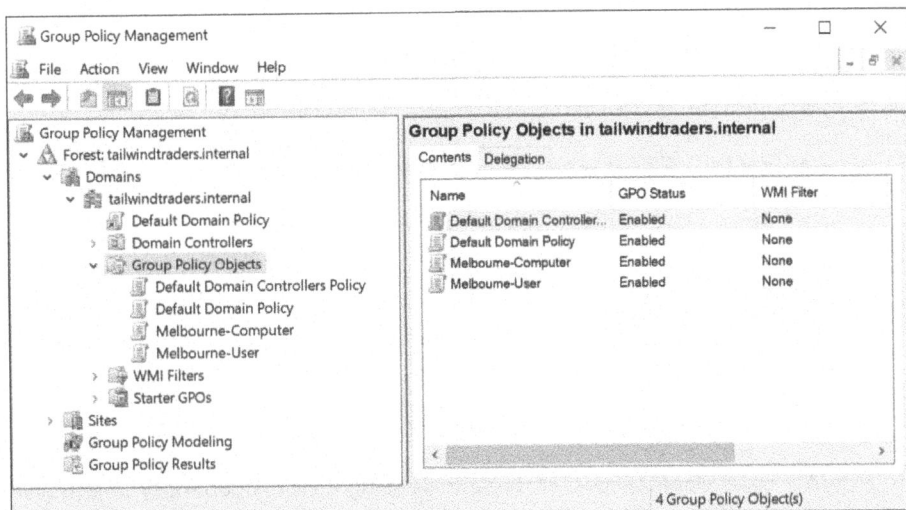

Figure 4-23   Group Policy Management Console

In larger environments, there is more than one person in the IT department. In very large organizations, one person's entire job responsibility might be creating and editing GPOs. Delegation enables you to grant permission to perform specific tasks to a specific user or group of users. You can delegate some or all of the following Group Policy management tasks:

- GPO creation

- GPO modification

- GPO linking to specific sites, organizational units (OUs), or domains

- Permission to perform Group Policy Modeling analysis at the OU or domain level

- Permission to view Group Policy Results information at the OU or domain level

- Windows Management Instrumentation (WMI) filter creation

Users in the Domain Admins and Enterprise Admins groups can perform all Group Policy management tasks. Users who are members of the Group Policy Creator Owners domain group can create GPOs. They also have the right to edit and delete any GPOs that they've created. You can delegate permissions to GPOs directly using the GPMC.

There are also a substantial number of cmdlets available in the PowerShell Group Policy module, including the following:

- `Get-GPO`   Enables you to view GPOs

- `Backup-GPO`   Enables you to back up GPOs

- `Import-GPO`   Enables you to import a backed-up GPO into a specified GPO

- `New-GPO`   Enables you to create a new GPO

- `Copy-GPO`   Enables you to copy a GPO

- `Rename-GPO`   Enables you to change a GPO's name

- `Restore-GPO`   Enables you to restore a backed-up GPO to its original location

- `Remove-GPO`   Enables you to remove a GPO

Creating GPOs

Creating a GPO is simply creating a new Group Policy Object. Newly created GPOs have no settings applied. Follow these steps to create a new GPO:

1. Open the Group Policy Management Console.

2. Under `Forest\Domains\Domain Name`, right-click Group Policy Objects and select New.

3. Provide a name for the new GPO and select OK.

If you want to delegate the ability for users to create GPOs, you can add them to the Group Policy Creator Owners group. You can also explicitly permit them to create GPOs using the GPMC. To do this, perform the following steps:

1. Open the GPMC from the Tools menu of Server Manager.

2. Expand the domain in which you want to delegate the ability to create GPOs, select Group Policy Objects, and select the Delegation tab.

3. Select Add and select the group or user that you want to give the ability to create GPOs in that domain.

Editing GPOs

To edit a GPO, users must be either a member of the Domain Admins or Enterprise Admins group. Users can edit a GPO if they

-   Created it

-   Have been given Read/Write permissions on the GPO through the GPMC

To grant a user permission to edit a GPO, perform the following steps:

1. Select the GPO in the GPMC.

2. Select the Delegation tab.

3. Select Add, specify the user or group that should have permission to edit the GPO, and then specify the permissions that you want to give this user or group. You can choose from one of the following permissions:

    -   Read

    -   Edit Settings

    -   Edit Settings, Delete, Modify Security

Linking GPOs

Linking a GPO to an object such as a domain or OU involves navigating to the location in the Group Policy Management Console, right-clicking on that location, and selecting Link Existing GPO. You then select which of the existing GPOs you want to link to the domain or OU. You can also create and link a GPO using this method.

To enable a user to link a GPO to a specific object, you need to edit the permission on that object. You can perform this task in the GPMC. For example, to grant a user or group permission to link a GPO to an OU, select the OU in the GPMC, select the Delegation tab, select Add, and then select the user or group to which you want to grant this permission.

CHAPTER 4

Backup GPOs

Backing up a GPO enables you to create a copy of a GPO as it exists at a specific point in time. A user must have read permission on a GPO to back it up. When you back up a GPO, the backup version of the GPO is incremented. It's good practice to back up GPOs prior to editing them so that if something goes wrong, you can revert to the unmodified GPO.

You should back up GPOs before you or other people modify them. If a problem occurs, it's quicker to restore a backup than it is to reconfigure the modified GPO with the existing settings.

To back up a GPO, perform the following steps:

1.   Open the GPMC.

2.   Right-click the GPO that you want to back up and select Back Up. In the Back Up Group Policy Object dialog, enter the location of the backup and a description for the backup, and then select Back Up.

You can restore a GPO using the `Restore-GPO` cmdlet. Restoring a GPO overwrites the current version of the GPO if one exists or re-creates the GPO if the GPO has been deleted. To restore a GPO, follow these steps:

1.   Right-click the Group Policy Objects node in the GPMC and select Manage Backups.

2.   In the Manage Backups dialog, select the GPO you want to restore and select Restore.

3.   If multiple backups of the same GPO exist, you can select which version of a GPO to restore.

Import and copy GPOs

Importing a GPO enables you to take the settings in a backed-up GPO and import them into an existing GPO. To import a GPO, perform the following steps:

1.   Right-click an existing GPO in the GPMC and select Import Settings.

2.   In the Import Settings Wizard, you are given the option of backing up the destination GPO's settings. This enables you to roll back the import.

3.   Specify the folder that hosts the backed-up GPO.

4.   On the Source GPO page of the Import Settings Wizard, select the source GPO. You can view the settings that have been configured in the source GPO prior to importing it. Complete the wizard to finish importing the settings.

Remember that when you import settings from a backed-up GPO, the settings in the backed-up GPO overwrite the settings in the destination GPO.

Copying a GPO creates a new GPO and copies all configuration settings from the original to the new. You can copy GPOs from one domain to another. You can also use a migration table when copying a GPO to map security principals referenced in the source domain to security principals referenced in the destination domain.

To copy a GPO, perform the following steps:

1. Right-click the GPO that you want to copy and select Copy.

2. Right-click the location that you want to copy the GPO to and select Paste.

3. In the Copy GPO dialog, choose between using the default permissions and preserving the existing permissions assigned to the GPO.

Fixing GPO Problems

Windows Server includes command-line utilities that allow you to repair a GPO after you perform a domain rename or re-create default GPOs. If you need to re-create the default GPOs for a domain, use the DCGPOFix command. If you perform a domain rename, you can use the GPFixup command to repair name dependencies in GPOs and Group Policy links.

Migrate Group Policy Objects

When moving GPOs between domains or forests, you need to ensure that any domain-specific information is accounted for, so locations and security principals in the source domain aren't used in the destination domain. You can account for these locations and security principals using migration tables. You use *migration tables* when copying or importing GPOs.

Migration tables enable you to alter references when moving a GPO from one domain to another, or from one forest to another. An example is when you are using GPOs for software deployment and need to replace the address of a shared folder that hosts a software installation file so that it's relevant to the target domain. You can open the Migration Table Editor (MTE) by right-clicking Domains in the GPMC and selecting Open Migration Table Editor.

When you use the MTE, you can choose to populate from a GPO that's in the current domain or to populate the MTE from a backed-up GPO. When you perform this action, the MTE will be populated with settings that reference local objects. If there are no results, then no local locations are referenced in the GPO that you're going to migrate.

Inside OUT

Restoring GPO doesn't restore links

Note that restoring a GPO does not restore the GPO's links, such as links to specific OUs. You can, however, determine where the GPO was linked prior to restoring the GPO by viewing information about the backed-up GPO.

Policy processing

Group policy is processed in the following order, with subsequent policies overriding previously applied policies where conflicts exist:

- **Local**   Settings configured at the local level apply first. If multiple local policies apply, settings in machine policies apply first, settings in admin and nonadmin local policies override them, and settings in per-user policies override any configured at the machine and admin/nonadmin levels.

- **Site**   Policies based on location apply next. Any settings configured at the site level override settings configured at the local level. You can link multiple GPOs at the site level. When you do this, policies with a lower numerical link order override policies with a higher numerical link order.

- **Domain**   Settings applied at the domain level override settings applied at the site and local levels. You can link multiple GPOs at the domain level. The Default Domain Policy is linked at this level.

- **Organizational unit (OU)**   Settings applied at the organizational unit level override settings applied at the domain, site, and local levels. When an account is a member of a child OU, policies applied at the child OU level override policies applied at the parent OU level. You can apply multiple GPOs at the OU level. Policies with a lower numerical link order override policies with a higher numerical link order.

For example, if one policy configures a setting at the AD site level and another policy configures the same setting at the OU level, the policy that configures the setting at the OU level is applied.

The exception to this is when you configure one of the following settings:

- **Block Inheritance**   The Block Inheritance option allows you to block upstream policies from applying. You can configure this option at the Domain or OU level. It blocks all upstream settings except those configured through a policy that has the No Override setting.

- **No Override**   You use the No Override setting to stop the Block setting. Use this on policies that you need to have enforced.

Every setting that is configured in a Group Policy item will be examined during the Group Policy processing. Configuring settings you don't need increases Group Policy processing times, which can increase startup and logon times.

Resultant Set of Policy tool

The Resultant Set of Policy tool allows you to generate a model of Group Policy application, allowing you to figure out which policies apply to particular objects within the domain. Resultant Set of Policy allows you to figure out why the Group Policy application isn't behaving in the way that you expect and allows you to resolve Group Policy conflicts.

There are two ways you can calculate the Resultant Set of Policy. The first is to use Group Policy Modeling. The second is to use Group Policy Results. The difference between these is as follows:

- **Group Policy Modeling**   Allows you to view the impact of altering site membership, security group membership, filtering, slow links, loopback processing, and the movement of accounts to new OUs on the application of policy.

- **Group Policy Results**   Allows you to troubleshoot the application of policy by telling you which settings apply to a specific user or computer account.

By default, members of the Domain Admins and Enterprise Admins groups can generate Group Policy Modeling or Group Policy Results information. You can delegate permissions so users can perform these tasks at the OU or domain level.

> ## Inside OUT
> ### Policy in multidomain forests
> Policies linked at the site level in multidomain forests are stored in the root domain. This can cause challenges with Group Policy application in scenarios in which a site-linked policy applies but where no DC with a root domain membership is present in the local site.

Filtering

GPO filtering allows you to determine whether a linked GPO applies based on group membership or the results of a WMI query. By default, a linked GPO will have the security filter set so it applies to Authenticated Users and no WMI filter set, as shown in Figure 4-24. If a GPO is only supposed to apply to a specific group of users or computers in the domain, site, or OU, specify the security group and remove the Authenticated Users group.

CHAPTER 4

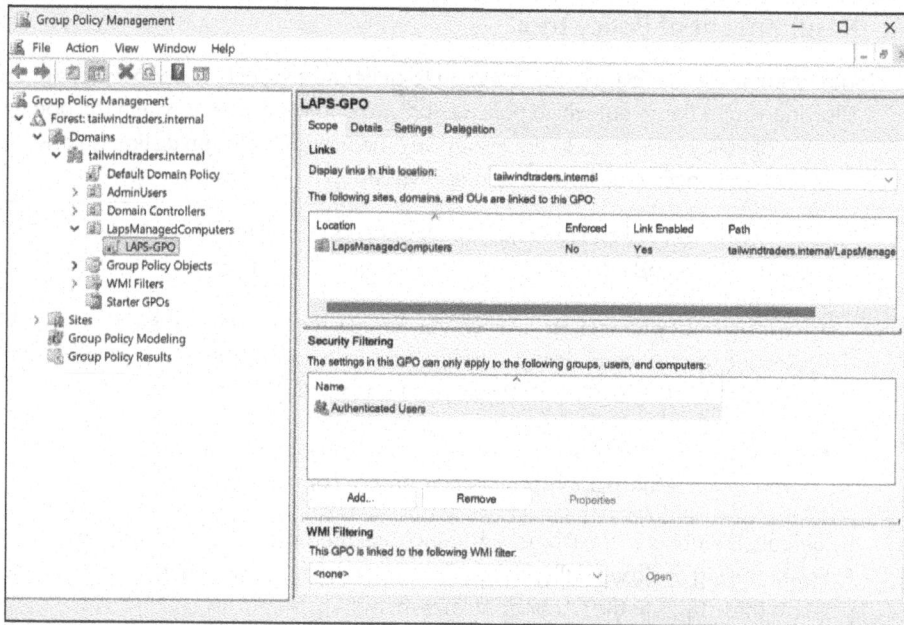

Figure 4-24   GPO filtering

For example, you could write a WMI query that performs a check so that a GPO only applies if the computer has more than 4 GB of RAM. If the computer has more than 4 GB of RAM, the policy applies normally. If the computer has less than 4 GB of RAM, the GPO does not apply. WMI filters must be assessed, which can slow down Group Policy processing. Many of the scenarios in which WMI filtering might have been appropriate 20 years ago can be better accomplished using PowerShell scripts.

Inside OUT

Site-linked GPOs

If Group Policy processing takes too long because of site-linked GPOs, the simplest solution is not to link polices at the site level; instead, you apply the links at the domain level and use Group Policy filtering through a WMI query to ensure location-specific GPOs are applied. An alternative is to place domain controllers that have root domain membership at each site, although this is likely to be more expensive than the policy filtering option.

Loopback processing

Each GPO has two distinct sections: Computer Configuration and User Configuration. The resultant policies for a user are based on the cumulative user configuration settings in GPOs that apply to the user's accounts at the site, domain, and OU settings. The resultant computer policies are applied based on the cumulative computer configuration settings in GPOs that apply to the computer's account at the site, domain, and OU level.

In some situations, you'll want only the GPOs that apply to the computer account to apply. You might want to do this with conference room computers, for which you want people to be able to sign on with domain accounts but to have a very controlled configuration. When you enable loopback processing, user settings are determined based on the settings in the User Configuration settings area of GPOs that apply to the computer account.

There are two types of loopback processing that you can configure by setting the Group Policy loopback processing mode policy. This policy is located under the `Computer Configuration\ Administrative Templates\System\Group Policy` node and can be configured with the following settings:

- **Replace**   When you configure Replace, only the GPOs that apply to the computer account will apply. Settings in the User Configuration area of the GPOs that apply to the computer account will apply.

- **Merge**   The settings in the User Configuration area of GPOs that apply to the user account will still apply but will be overridden by settings in the User Configuration area of GPOs that apply to the computer account.

Slow-link processing enables you to configure Group Policy application to be performed differently, depending on the speed of the connection from the client to the domain controller. It enables you to block activities such as software deployment when the connection between Active Directory and the client is detected as falling below a particular threshold. You configure slow-link detection by configuring the Group Policy slow-link detection policy located under `Computer Configuration\Administrative Templates\System\Group Policy`. When a slow link is detected, Registry settings from administrative templates, security policies, EFS recovery policy, and firewall policies are applied. Policies related to application deployment, scripts, folder redirection, and disk quotas will not be applied.

Group Policy caching

Group Policy caching reduces the amount of time taken to process Group Policy during computer startup and user sign-on. Rather than retrieve the Group Policies that apply to the computer from a domain controller when a computer starts up or a user signs on, the client will use a cached copy of the last Group Policies downloaded from the domain controller. After this initial application of the cached policies during startup and user sign-on, policies will be retrieved and applied normally from a domain controller. You enable Group Policy caching by configuring the Configure Group Policy Caching policy. This policy is located under `Computer Configura- tion\Policies\Administrative Templates\System\Group Policy`.

CHAPTER 4

Force Remote Group Policy update

Remote Group Policy update allows you to force a remote computer to perform a Group Policy update without having to sign on to the computer and run the `GPUpdate` command or the `Invoke-GPUpdate` PowerShell cmdlet. Remote Group Policy requires that the following firewall rules be enabled on clients:

- Remote Scheduled Tasks Management (RPC)

- Remote Scheduled Tasks Management (RPC-EPMAP)

- Windows Management Instrumentation (WMI-In)

You can run a remote Group Policy update from the Group Policy Management Console by right-clicking on a container or OU. An update will run on all computers within the container or OU, as well as on any computer accounts stored within child OUs. You can also use the `Invoke-GPUpdate` PowerShell cmdlet to trigger a remote Group Policy update. The advantage of the PowerShell cmdlet is that you can target a specific computer rather than all computer accounts in an OU.

Group Policy preferences

Group Policy preferences work around the idea of eliminating (or at least substantially reducing) the need for traditional start-up and log-in scripts. Log-in scripts have a way of becoming convoluted over time. Group Policy preferences allow simplification of common log-in and start-up script tasks, such as drive mappings and setting environment variables.

By reducing or eliminating some of the complexity of log-in scripts, you can use Group Policy preferences to reduce configuration errors. You can use Group Policy preferences to configure the following settings:

- Applications

- Drive mappings

- Environment variables

- File updates

- Folders

- Ini files

- Registry settings

- Shortcuts

- Data sources

- Devices

- Folder options

- Internet settings

- Local users and groups

- Network options

- Network shares

- Power options

- Printer settings

- Regional options

- Scheduled tasks

- Start Menu settings

Some of these items can also be configured using a traditional Group Policy. In the event that an item is configured in the same GPO using both policy and preferences, the traditional setting takes precedence. The difference between a Group Policy preference and a normal Group Policy setting is that users can change a Group Policy preference if they have the appropriate permissions. For example, users can unmap a mapped network drive. The drive would remain unmapped until the user logged in again, at which point it would be remapped. Generally, if you want to enforce a setting, use a standard Group Policy. If you want to apply the setting and allow users to change it, use a Group Policy preference. The closest you can come to enforcing a Group Policy preference is to disable the Apply Once And Do Not Reapply setting in the policy item's configuration. This way, the preference is applied each time Group Policy refreshes.

You can target Group Policy preferences so that different preferences can apply to the same item types within a single GPO. You can use the following items to restrict how a Group Policy preference applies:

- The computer has a battery.

- The computer has a specific name.

- The computer has a specific CPU speed.

- Apply by or after a specific date.

- The computer has a certain amount of disk space.

CHAPTER 4

- The computer is a member of a domain.

- The computer has a particular environment variable set.

- A certain file is present on the computer.

- The computer is within a particular IP address range.

- The computer uses specific language settings.

- The computer meets the requirements of an LDAP query.

- The computer has a MAC address within a specific range.

- The computer meets the requirements of a WMI query.

- The computer uses a specific type of network connection.

- The computer is running a specific operating system.

- The computer is a member of a specific OU.

- The computer has PCMCIA.

- The computer is portable.

- The computer uses a specific processing mode.

- The computer has a certain amount of RAM.

- The computer has a certain registry entry.

- User or computer is a member of a specific security group.

- The computer is in a specific Active Directory site.

- The computer has a Remote Desktop Setting.

- That a specific time range is present.

- The user has a specific name.

Administrative templates

Group Policy Administrative Templates allow you to extend Group Policy beyond the settings available in GPOs. Common software packages, such as Microsoft Office, often include Administrative Templates that you can import to manage software-specific settings. In early versions of Windows Server, Administrative Templates were available as files in ADM format. Since the release of Windows Server 2008, Administrative Templates are available in a standards-based XML file format called ADMX.

To be able to use an Administrative Template, you can import it directly into a GPO using the Add/Remove Templates option when you right-click the Administrative Templates node. A second option is to copy the Administrative Template files to the Central Store, located in the `c:\Windows\Sysvol\sysvol\<domainname>\Policies\PolicyDefinitions` folder on any domain controller. You might need to create this folder if it does not already exist. After the folder is present, the template is then replicated to all domain controllers, and you can access the newly imported Administrative Templates through the Administrative Templates node of a GPO.

Reverting settings configured by Group Policy

Removing or unlinking a GPO does not always revert the affected settings on client machines. The outcome depends on the type of policy, how it was applied, and the nature of the setting. Consider the following when trying to revert settings applied using Group Policy:

- Group Policy Preferences write their values directly into the standard registry or system configuration areas, not the special policy areas. This process is sometimes termed "tattooing." When the GPO or preference is removed, the setting remains at its last-applied value and is not reverted or reset to the previous or default state. The original value is overwritten and lost, so the system retains the "tattooed" configuration until it's changed by another means.

- Some policy settings do not revert to their previous or default state when the GPO is set to "Not Configured" or removed. Instead, the system keeps the last value set by the policy. This is especially common with certain registry-based settings.

- Changes to service startup types, file/folder permissions, or other system configurations that are not managed exclusively through policy areas may persist after a GPO is removed.

CHAPTER 4

Inside OUT
Like that before I got here

In scenarios where group policies have been used with systems that have been in production for some time, settings might have been configured long ago by policies that have since been removed. You might need to use Desired State Configuration or manual tools to change settings back to defaults that were altered by a no longer applied Group Policy Object.

Active Directory database optimization

There are several steps you can take to optimize your Active Directory database, including defragmenting the database, performing a file integrity check, and performing a semantic integrity check.

When you defragment the Active Directory database, a new copy of the database file, Ntds.dit, is created. You can defragment the Active Directory database or perform other operations only if the database is offline. You can take the Active Directory database offline by stopping the AD DS service, which you can do from the Update Services console or by issuing the following command from an elevated PowerShell prompt:

```
Stop-Service NTDS -force
```

You use the ntdsutil.exe utility to perform the defragmentation using the following command:

```
ntdsutil.exe "activate instance ntds" files "compact to c:\\" quit quit
```

After the defragmentation has completed, copy the defragmented database over the original located in C:\windows\NTDS\ntds.dit and delete all log files in the C:\windows\NTDS folder.

You can check the integrity of the file that stores the database using the ntdsutil.exe by issuing the following command from an elevated prompt when the AD DS service is stopped:

```
ntdsutil.exe "activate instance ntds" files integrity quit quit
```

To verify that the AD DS database is internally consistent, you can run a semantic consistency check. The semantic check can also repair the database if problems are detected. You can perform a semantic check using ntdsutil.exe by issuing the following command:

```
ntdsutil.exe "activate instance ntds" "semantic database analysis" "verbose on" "go fixup" quit quit
```

Active Directory snapshots

You can use ntdsutil.exe to create snapshots of the Active Directory database. A *snapshot* is a point-in-time copy of the database. You can use tools to examine the contents of the database as it existed at that point in time. It's also possible to transfer objects from the snapshot of the Active Directory database back into the version currently used with your domain's domain controllers. The AD DS service must be running to create a snapshot.

To create a snapshot, execute the following command:

```
Ntdsutil snapshot "Activate Instance NTDS" create quit quit
```

A GUID identifies each snapshot. You can create a scheduled task to create snapshots on a regular basis. You can view a list of all current snapshots on a domain controller by running the following command:

```
Ntdsutil snapshot "list all" quit quit
```

To mount a snapshot, make a note of the GUID of the snapshot that you want to mount and then issue the following command:

```
Ntdsutil "activate instance ntds" snapshot "mount {GUID}" quit quit
```

When mounting snapshots, you must use the {} braces with the GUID. You can also use the snapshot number associated with the GUID when mounting the snapshot with the ntdsutil.exe command. This number is always odd.

When the snapshot mounts, take a note of the path associated with the snapshot. You use this path when mounting the snapshot with dsamain. For example, to use dsamain with the snapshot mounted as c:\$SNAP_201212291630_VOLUMEc$\, issue this command:

```
Dsamain /dbpath 'c:\$SNAP_201212291630_VOLUMEC$\Windows\NTDS\ntds.dit' /ldapport 50000
```

You can choose to mount the snapshot using any available TCP port number; 50000 is just easy to remember. Leave the PowerShell windows open when performing this action. After the snapshot is mounted, you can access it using Active Directory Users And Computers. To do this, perform the following steps:

1. Open Active Directory Users And Computers.

2. Right-click the root node and select Change Domain Controller.

3. In the Change Directory Server dialog, enter the name of the domain controller and the port, and select OK. You can then view the contents of the snapshot using Active Directory Users And Computers in the same way that you would the contents of the current directory.

You can dismount the snapshot by using Ctrl+C to close dsamain, and then executing the following command to dismount the snapshot:

```
Ntdsutil.exe "activate instance ntds" snapshot "unmount {GUID}" quit quit
```

Active Directory backup

AD DS is backed up when you perform a backup of the server's system state. This occurs when you back up all critical volumes on a domain controller. The primary tool you use for backing up this data is Windows Server Backup, which is not installed by default on computers running Windows Server. You can install Windows Server Backup using the following PowerShell command:

```
Install-WindowsFeature -IncludeAllSubFeature -IncludeManagementTools
Windows-Server-Backup
```

The majority of restore operations occur because Active Directory objects were accidentally (rather than deliberately) deleted. You can configure objects to be protected from accidental deletion by editing the object properties. When you attempt to delete an object that is protected from accidental deletion, a dialog will inform you that the object can't be deleted because it's protected from accidental deletion. This protection option must be removed before you or anyone else can delete the object.

Restoring deleted items

Sometimes, an Active Directory account, such as a user account or even an entire OU, is accidentally—or on occasion, maliciously—deleted. Rather than re-create the deleted item or items, you can restore the items. Deleted items are retained within the AD DS database for a period of time specified as the *tombstone lifetime*. You can recover a deleted item without having to restore the item from a backup of Active Directory as long as the item was deleted within the Tombstone Lifetime window.

The default tombstone lifetime for an Active Directory environment at the Windows Server 2008 forest functional level or higher is 180 days. You can check the value of the tombstone lifetime by issuing the following command from an elevated command prompt (substituting dc=Contoso,dc=Internal for the suffix of your organization's forest root domain):

```
Dsquery * "cn=Directory Service,cn=Windows NT,cn=Services,cn=Configuration,dc=Contoso,dc
=Internal" -scope base -attr tombstonelifetime
```

For most organizations, the 180-day default is fine, but some administrators might want to increase or decrease this value to give them a greater or lesser window for easily restoring deleted items. You can change the default tombstone lifetime by performing the following steps:

1. From an elevated command prompt or PowerShell session, type **ADSIEdit.msc**.

2. From the Action menu, click Connect To. In the Connection Settings dialog, click Configuration, as shown in Figure 4-25, and then click OK.

3. Right-click the CN=Services, CN=Windows NT, CN=Directory Service node and click Properties.

4. In the list of attributes, select tombstoneLifetime, as shown in Figure 4-26, and click Edit.

5. On the Integer Attribute Editor dialog, enter the new value for the tombstone lifetime and click OK twice.

6. Close the ADSI Edit console.

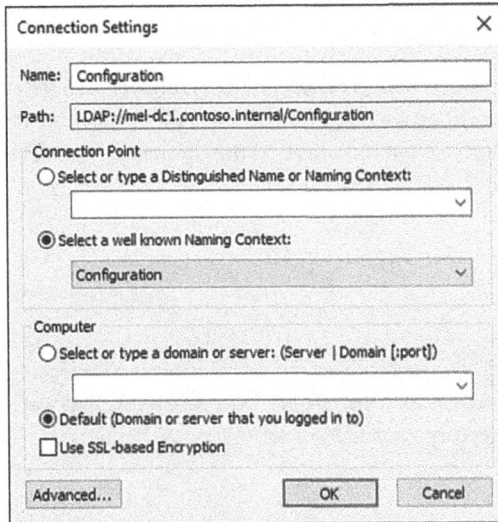

Figure 4-25   Connection settings

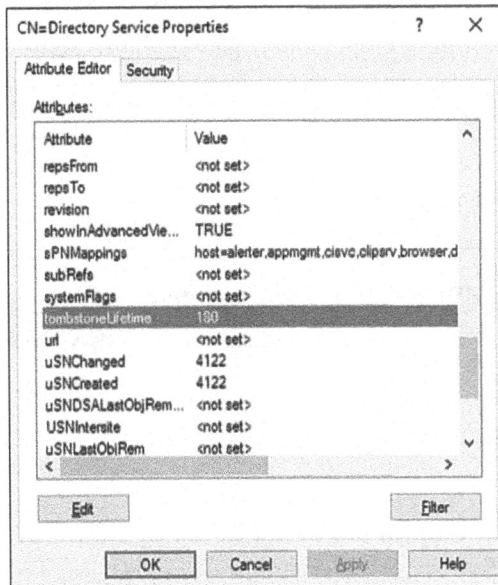

Figure 4-26   Tombstone lifetime

Active Directory Recycle Bin

Active Directory Recycle Bin allows you to restore items that have been deleted from Active Directory but are still present within the database because the tombstone lifetime has not been exceeded. Active Directory Recycle Bin requires that the domain functional level be set to Windows Server 2008 R2 or higher.

Inside OUT

Enable AD Recycle Bin first

You can't use the Active Directory Recycle Bin to restore items that were deleted before you enabled Active Directory Recycle Bin.

Once activated, you can't deactivate the Active Directory Recycle Bin. There isn't any great reason to want to deactivate AD Recycle Bin once it's activated. You don't have to use it to restore deleted items if you still prefer to go through the authoritative restore process.

To activate the Active Directory Recycle Bin, perform the following steps:

1. Open the Active Directory Administrative Center and select the domain that you want to enable.

2. In the Tasks pane, click Enable Recycle Bin, as shown in Figure 4-27.

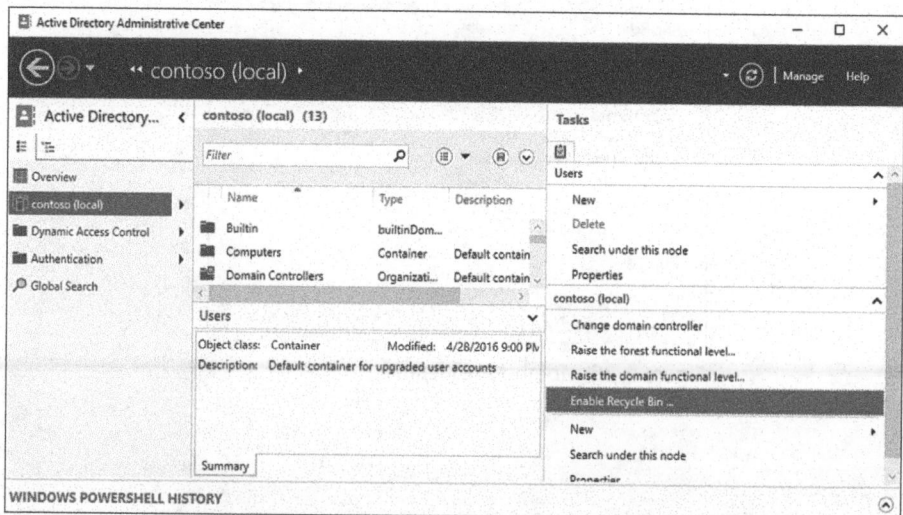

Figure 4-27   Enable Recycle Bin

CHAPTER 4

After you've enabled the AD Recycle Bin, you can restore an object from the newly available Deleted Objects container. This is, of course, assuming that the object was deleted after the Recycle Bin was enabled and assuming that the tombstone lifetime value has not been exceeded. To recover the object, select the object in the Deleted Items container and then click Restore or Restore To. Figure 4-28 shows a deleted item being selected, which can then be restored to its original location. The Restore To option allows you to restore the object to another available location, such as another OU.

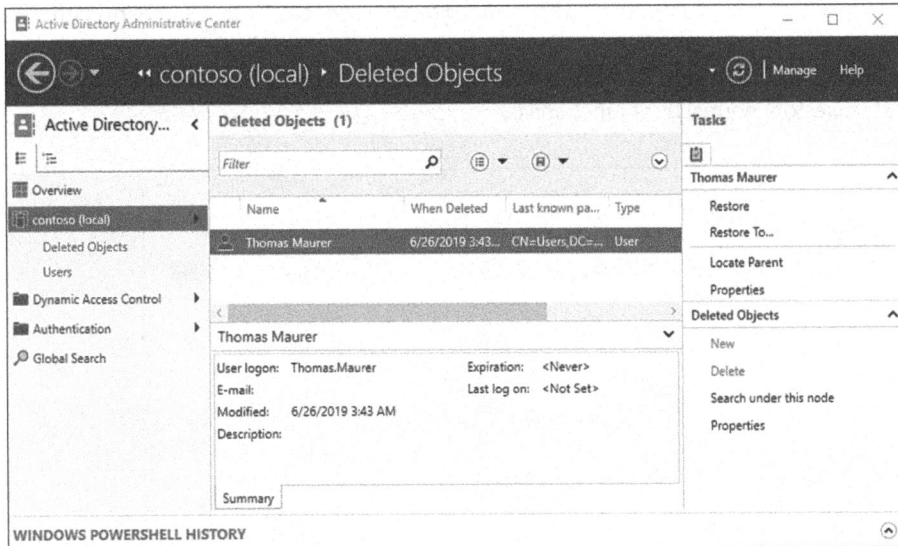

Figure 4-28   Deleted Objects container

Authoritative restore

An authoritative restore is performed when you want the items you are recovering to overwrite items that are in the current Active Directory database. If you don't perform an authoritative restore, Active Directory assumes that the restored data is simply out of date and overwrites it when it's synchronized from another domain controller. If you perform a normal Restore on an item that was backed up last Tuesday, when it was deleted the following Thursday, the item is deleted the next time the Active Directory database is synchronized. You do not need to perform an authoritative restore if you only have one domain controller in your organization because there is no other domain controller that can overwrite the changes.

An authoritative restore is useful in the following scenarios:

- You haven't enabled Active Directory Recycle Bin.

- You have enabled Active Directory Recycle Bin, but the object you want to restore was deleted before you enabled Active Directory Recycle Bin.

- You need to restore items that are older than the tombstone lifetime of the AD DS database.

To perform an authoritative restore, you need to reboot a DC into Directory Services Restore Mode. If you want to restore an item that's older than the tombstone lifetime of the AD DS database, you also need to restore the AD DS database. You can do this by restoring the system state data on the server. You'll likely need to take the DC temporarily off the network to perform this operation, because if you restore a computer with old system state data and the DC synchronizes, all the data that you want to recover will be deleted when the domain controller synchronizes.

You can configure a server to boot into Directory Services Restore Mode from the System Configuration utility. To do this, select the Active Directory Repair option on the Boot tab as shown in Figure 4-29. After you've finished with Directory Services Restore Mode, use this same utility to restore normal boot functionality.

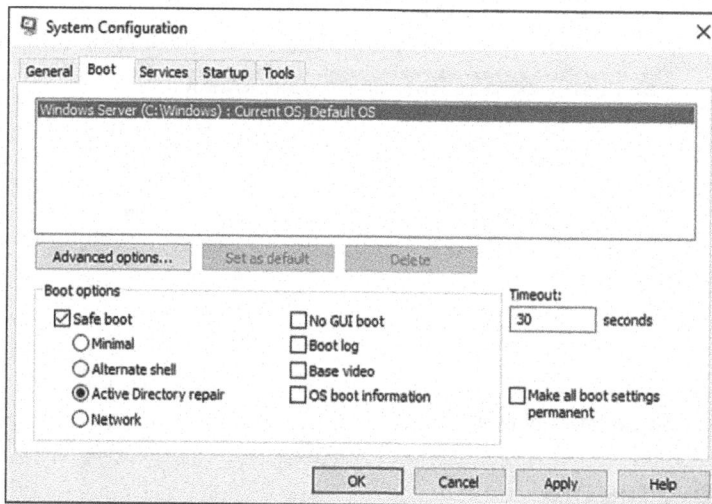

Figure 4-29   System Configuration

To enter Directory Services Restore Mode, you need to enter the Directory Services Restore Mode password.

To perform an authoritative restore, perform the following general steps:

1.   Choose a computer that functions as a global catalog server. This DC functions as your restore server.

2.   Locate the most recent system state backup that contains the objects that you want to restore.

3.   Restart the restore server in DSRM mode. Enter the DSRM password.

4. Restore the system state data.

5. Use the following command to restore items (where Mercury is the object name, Planets is the OU that it is contained in, and *contoso.com* is the host domain):

    ```
    Ntdsutil "authoritative restore" "restore object
    cn=Mercury,ou=Planets,dc=contoso,dc=com" q q
    ```

6. If an entire OU is deleted, you can use the Restore Subtree option. For example, if you deleted the Planets OU and all the accounts that it held in the *contoso.com* domain, you could use the following command to restore it and all the items it contained:

    ```
    Ntdsutil "authoritative restore" "restore subtree OU=Planets,DC=contoso,DC=com" q
    q
    ```

Active Directory snapshots

You can use the Active Directory database mounting tool, dsamain.exe, to mount the contents of the AD DS database as it exists in snapshots or in backups so that you can interact with it using the Active Directory Users and Computers console. This provides you with a quick way of checking the state of a snapshot or backup without actually having to restore it to a production or development environment. For example, you might do this if you want to check what the AD DS database looked like at a specific point in time to determine the state of particular accounts or organizational units.

If you restored the AD DS database file, ntds.dit, to the location c:\restore, you could mount this file using the dsamain.exe utility on port 51389 by entering the following command:

```
Dsamain.exe /dbpath C:\restore\ntds.dit /ldapport 51389
```

You can then use Active Directory Users And Computers to connect to the specified port, in this case, port 51389, to view the mounted version of the AD DS database.

You can also create snapshots of the AD DS database that you can interact with without having to make a backup. A snapshot is a copy of the AD DS database as it exists at a specific point in time. You create a snapshot of the AD DS database by running the following command from an elevated command prompt on a domain controller:

```
Ntdsutil "Activate Instance NTDS" snapshot create quit quit
```

You can list all current snapshots of the AD DS database on a domain controller by running the following command:

```
Ntdsutil snapshot "list all" quit quit
```

Each snapshot has an odd number associated with it next to the date the snapshot was taken. To select and mount a snapshot, use the command:

```
Ntdsutil snapshot "list all" "mount 1" quit quit
```

This mounts snapshot 1. Make a note of the path on which the snapshot is mounted. You can then use the dsadmin.exe command to mount the snapshot so that it is accessible as an LDAP server. For example, to make the snapshot at path C:\$SNAP_201606100306_VOLUMEC$\ accessible on port 51389, use the command

```
Dsamain.exe /dbpath C:\$SNAP_201606100306_VOLUMEC$\WINDOWS\NTDS\ntds.dit /ldapport 51389
```

You can then use Active Directory Users And Computers to connect to the specified port to view the mounted snapshot. Only members of the Domain Admins and Enterprise Admins groups can view snapshots. While you can't directly copy objects from a snapshot to the production version of the AD DS database, you can use utilities such as CSVDE and LDIFDE to export information from a snapshot and then later import it into the production AD DS database.

Managing AD DS with PowerShell

Many Active Directory administrative tasks are repetitive. If you're likely to perform a task more than once, it's better to script it in PowerShell than work your way through the appropriate wizard multiple times.

There are three PowerShell modules related to Active Directory. The Active Directory PowerShell module (Table 4-3) is the one you're likely to use on a regular basis when managing Active Directory. The GroupPolicy module (Table 4-4) allows you to manage Group Policy from PowerShell.

Active Directory module

As already mentioned, the Active Directory PowerShell module (see Table 4-3) is the one you're likely to use regularly when managing Active Directory.

Table 4-3   Active Directory module cmdlets

Noun	Verbs	Function
ADAccount	Unlock, Search, Enable, Disable	Allows you to find, unlock, enable, or disable a user, computer, or service account.
ADAccountAuthentication-PolicySilo	Set	Allows you to configure the authentication policy or authentication policy silo of an account.
ADAccountAuthorizationGroup	Get	Gets the security groups for a specified user, computer, or service account based on its token. Uses the global catalog to determine this information.

Noun	Verbs	Function
`ADAccountControl`	`Set`	Modifies the user account control values of an Active Directory user or computer account.
`ADAccountExpiration`	`Set, Clear`	Configure account expiration.
`ADAccountPassword`	`Set`	Configure the password of a user, computer, or service account.
`ADAccountResultant-` `PasswordReplicationPolicy`	`Get`	Gets the password replication policy for a user, computer, or service account on a specific RODC.
`ADAuthenticationPolicy`	`Set, Remove,` `New, Get`	Manipulate the properties of the AD DS authentication policy.
`ADAuthenticationPolicy-` `Expression`	`Show`	Displays Edit Access Control Conditions, Windows Update, or SSDL security descriptors.
`ADAuthenticationPolicySilo`	`New, Remove,` `Get, Set`	Manipulate Active Directory Domain Services authentication policy silos.
`ADAuthenticationPolicy-` `SiloAccess`	`Revoke, Grant`	Manage membership of authentication policy silos.
`ADCentralAccessPolicy`	`Remove, Get,` `Set, New`	Manage central access rules and policies.
`ADCentralAccessPolicyMember`	`Remove, Add`	Add and remove rules from a central access policy.
`ADCentralAccessRule`	`New, Set,` `Remove, Get`	Manage central access rules.
`ADClaimTransformLink`	`Set, Clear,` `Remove`	Manage claims transforms from being applied to one or more cross-forest trust relationships.
`ADClaimTransformPolicy`	`New, Set, Get`	Manage claim transformation policy objects from Active Directory.
`ADClaimType`	`New, Get,` `Remove, Set`	Manage Active Directory claim types.
`ADComputer`	`Remove, New,` `Set, Get`	Manage Active Directory computer accounts.
`ADComputerServiceAccount`	`Remove, Add,` `Get`	Add service accounts from Active Directory to a local computer.
`ADDCCloneConfigFile`	`New`	Generates a clone configuration file for a domain controller.
`ADDCCloningExcluded-` `ApplicationList`	`Get`	Manage which Active Directory applications are excluded when cloning the configuration of a domain controller.

CHAPTER 4

Noun	Verbs	Function
ADDefaultDomainPassword-Policy	Set, Get	Manage the default password policy for a domain.
ADDirectoryServer	Move	Use this cmdlet to move a DC to another AD site.
ADDirectoryServerOperation-MasterRole	Move	Move an operations master role to another computer.
ADDomain	Set, Get	View and manage the properties of a domain.
ADDomainController	Get	View the properties of a domain controller.
ADDomainController-PasswordReplicationPolicy	Remove, Get, Add	Manage which accounts can be replicated to an RODC.
ADDomainMode	Set	Set the domain functional level.
ADFineGrainedPasswordPolicy	Remove, Get, Set, New	Manage AD fine-grained password policy.
ADFineGrainedPassword-PolicySubject	Get, Remove, Add	Manage the application of fine-grained password policies.
ADForest	Set, Get	Manage forest properties.
ADForestMode	Set	Configure the forest functional level.
ADGroup	Get, Set, Remove, New	Manage AD groups.
ADGroupMember	Get, Remove, Add	Manage AD group membership.
ADObject	Get, Restore, Rename, Set, Move, Remove, Sync, New	Manage AD objects.
ADOptionalFeature	Disable, Get, Enable	Configure AD optional features.
ADOrganizationalUnit	Set, Get, New, Remove	Manage AD OUs.
ADPrincipalGroupMembership	Remove, Add, Get	Manage group membership on the basis of the user account.
ADReplicationAttribute-Metadata	Get	View replication metadata for AD object attributes.
ADReplicationConnection	Get, Set	Manage the properties of an AD replication connection.
ADReplicationFailure	Get	View information about AD replication failure.

Noun	Verbs	Function
ADReplicationPartnerMetadata	Get	View information about AD replication partners.
ADReplicationQueueOperation	Get	View all operations in the AD replication queue.
ADReplicationSite	Set, Get, Remove, New	Manage AD replication sites.
ADReplicationSiteLink	Set, New, Get, Remove	Manage AD replication site links.
ADReplicationSiteLinkBridge	Get, Remove, New, Set	Manage AD replication site link bridges.
ADReplicationSubnet	New, Get, Set, Remove	Manage AD replication subnets.
ADReplicationUpToDateness-VectorTable	Get	Displays Update Sequence Numbers (USNs) for domain controllers.
ADResourceProperty	Set, New, Remove, Get	Manage Active Directory resource properties.
ADResourcePropertyList	Remove, Set, New, Get	Manage Active Directory resource property list.
ADResourcePropertyListMember	Remove, Add	Add and remove resource properties from an Active Directory resource property list.
ADResourcePropertyValueType	Get	View a resource property value type.
ADRootDSE	Get	View the root of a Directory Server information tree.
ADServiceAccount	Get, Test, Set, Install, New, Remove, Uninstall	Manage the AD Managed Service Account.
ADServiceAccountPassword	Reset	Reset the AD Managed Service Account password.
ADTrust	Get	View the properties of an AD Trust.
ADUser	New, Set, Get, Remove	Manage an Active Directory user.
ADUserResultantPassword-Policy	Get	Use this cmdlet to determine the resultant password policy for an account that has multiple fine-grained password policies applied to it.

CHAPTER 4

Group Policy module

As mentioned earlier, the GroupPolicy module (see Table 4-4) allows you to manage Group Policy from PowerShell.

Table 4-4   Group Policy module cmdlets

Noun	Verbs	Function
GPInheritance	Get, Set	View and manage which GPOs are applied and whether inheritance is blocked.
GPLink	Remove, New, Set	Manage whether a GPO is linked.
GPO	Restore, Import, New, Remove, Rename, Backup, Get, Copy	Manage GPOs, including backup restore and copy.
GPOReport	Get	Generate a report on a GPO.
GPPermission	Set, Get	Manage permissions on policies.
GPPrefRegistryValue	Remove, Set, Get,	Manage registry-based policy preference settings. Microsoft maintains spreadsheets that map Group Policy settings to registry settings. To use this cmdlet to set registry settings, you need to consult the spreadsheet.
GPRegistryValue	Remove, Get, Set,	Manage registry-based policy settings.
GPResultantSetOf-Policy	Get	View the resultant set of policy information.
GPStarterGPO	New, Get	Manage the starter GPO.
GPUpdate	Invoke	Triggers a Group Policy update.

ADDSDeployment module

As previously mentioned, you use the ADDSDeployment (see Table 4-4) module when performing deployment tasks.

Table 4-4   Active Directory module cmdlets

Noun	Verbs	Function
ADDSDomain	Install	Installs a new Active Directory Domain Services domain.
ADDSDomainController	Install, Uninstall	Use to add or remove a domain controller.
ADDSDomainControllerInstallation	Test	Runs a prerequisite check prior to installing a domain controller.
ADDSDomainControllerUninstallation	Test	Runs a prerequisite check prior to removing a domain controller.

Noun	Verbs	Function
`ADDSDomainInstallation`	`Test`	Checks the prerequisites for a new Active Directory Domain Services domain.
`ADDSForest`	`Install`	Allows you to install a new Active Directory Forest configuration.
`ADDSForestInstallation`	`Test`	Allows you to perform a prerequisite check prior to performing an Active Directory forest installation.
`ADDSReadOnlyDomainController-Account`	`Add`	Use this cmdlet to create an RODC account in the AD DS database.
`ADDSReadOnlyDomainController-AccountCreation`	`Test`	Allows you to check that the necessary prerequisites are in place before you create an RODC account.

DNS, DHCP, and IPAM

DNS and DHCP servers are a part of all networks' core infrastructure. It doesn't matter if your organization has hosts running on Windows, Linux, Mac OS, or Internet of Things (IoT) devices because DHCP and DNS are likely managing the name and address information for those hosts. While you can get a network device to provide DNS and DHCP services to your network, Windows Server's implementation offers seamless integration with Active Directory, enabling centralized management and enhanced security through features like dynamic DNS updates and secure DHCP. Administration through common Windows Server administrative tools, including management consoles and PowerShell, simplifies administration for IT staff already versed in Microsoft technologies.

DNS

At the most basic level, DNS servers translate host names to IP addresses and translate IP addresses to host names. By querying special records on DNS servers, it's possible to locate mail servers and name servers, verify domain ownership, and locate servers such as domain controllers. While DNS servers are usually deployed on a domain controller on a Windows Server network, it's also possible to deploy them on member servers or standalone computers.

DNS zone types

Zones store DNS resource record information. The DNS Server service in Windows Server supports several zone types, each of which is appropriate for a different set of circumstances. These zone types include primary, secondary, stub, and GlobalNames zones. You can integrate zones into Active Directory, or you can use the traditional primary or secondary architecture.

Active Directory–integrated zones

Active Directory–integrated zones can be replicated to all domain controllers in a domain, all domain controllers in a forest, or all domain controllers enrolled in a specific Active Directory partition. You can create an Active Directory–integrated zone only on a writable domain controller, but you can also configure primary and stub zones as Active Directory–integrated zones.

Domain controllers with DNS servers that host Active Directory–integrated zones can process updates to those zones.

When you choose to make a zone Active Directory–integrated, you have the option to configure a replication scope. You can configure the zone to be replicated so that it's present on all domain controllers in the domain, in the forest, or within the scope of a custom Active Directory partition. When determining the appropriate replication scope, consider which clients need regular, direct access to the zone and which clients require only occasional, indirect access.

You can use custom directory partitions to replicate a zone to some, but not all, domain controllers. You can only select this option if there is an existing custom DNS application directory partition. You can use the Add-DNSServerDirectoryPartition cmdlet to create a directory partition. For example, to create a DNS Server directory partition called Tasmania on a subset of your organization's domain controllers, execute this command:

```
Add-DNSServerDirectoryPartition -Name Tasmania
```

The most common choice for Active Directory–integrated zones is to configure DNS replication to all domain controllers in a forest, enabling clients to access DNS information seamlessly without the need for additional forwarding configuration.

Active Directory–integrated zones use multimaster replication, meaning any domain controller that hosts the DNS zone can process updates to the zone. When creating a DNS zone, you must specify whether the zone supports dynamic updates, which allow clients to update DNS records. This is useful in environments in which clients change IP addresses on a regular basis. When a client gets a new IP address, it can update the record associated with its host name in the appropriate DNS zone. There are three dynamic update configuration options:

- **Allow Only Secure Dynamic Updates**   You can use this option only with Active Directory–integrated zones. Only authenticated clients can update DNS records.

- **Allow Both Non-Secure And Secure Dynamic Updates**   With this option, any client can update a record. Although this option is convenient, it's also insecure because any client can update the DNS zone, which could potentially redirect clients that trust the quality of the information stored on the DNS server.

- **Do Not Allow Dynamic Updates**   When you choose this option, all DNS updates must be performed manually. This option is very secure, but it's also labor-intensive.

An Active Directory–integrated zone can replicate to a read-only domain controller (RODC). With this configuration, the RODC-hosted zone is read-only, and the RODC cannot process updates to the zone. RODCs are also unable to perform DNS scavenging for these zones. When you replicate an Active Directory–integrated zone to an RODC, the RODC forwards any client that wants to update the zone to a writable domain controller.

You can create an Active Directory–integrated primary zone by using the `Add-DnsServerPri-maryZone` cmdlet with the `ReplicationScope` parameter. For example, to create the Active Directory–integrated zone *tailwindtraders.com* so that it replicates to all domain controllers in the forest, issue this command:

```
Add-DnsServerPrimaryZone -Name tailwindtraders.com -ReplicationScope Forest
```

You can configure an Active Directory–integrated primary zone by using the `Set-Dns-ServerPrimaryZone` cmdlet. For example, to configure the Active Directory–integrated zone `tailwindtraders.com` so that it only allows secure dynamic updates, use the following command:

```
Set-DnsServerPrimaryZone -Name "tailwindtraders.com" -DynamicUpdate "Secure"
```

When you first install Active Directory, the installation process ensures that the DNS zone associated with the root domain is automatically configured as an Active Directory–integrated zone. This root domain zone is automatically replicated to all domain controllers in the forest.

You can use the `Get-DnsServerZone` cmdlet to view the replication scope. For example, to check the replication scope and dynamic update settings of the `tailwindtraders.com` zone hosted running on an AD DS DC named DC1, which hosts the zone, use the following PowerShell command:

```
Get-DnsServerZone -Name "tailwindtraders.com" -ComputerName "DC1" | Select-Object
-Property ZoneName, ReplicationScope,DynamicUpdate
```

Primary and secondary zones

Windows Server supports two types of primary zones: Active Directory–integrated zones and standard primary zones. As mentioned earlier, Active Directory–integrated zones can only be hosted on computers that also function as domain controllers.

In traditional DNS implementations, a single server hosts a primary zone, which processes all zone updates, and a collection of secondary servers replicates zone data from the primary zone. One drawback to this model is that if the primary server fails, no zone updates can occur until the primary zone is restored.

Computers running Windows Server that are configured as standalone computers or domain member servers can host standard primary zones.

Inside OUT

All zone types on a domain controller

The DNS server service on a domain controller supports all zone types. This means that you can choose to deploy a standard or Active Directory–integrated primary zone, a stub zone, a reverse lookup zone, or a secondary zone on a domain controller.

A secondary zone is a read-only copy of a primary zone. Secondary zones cannot process updates and can only retrieve updates from a primary zone. Also, secondary zones cannot be Active Directory–integrated zones, but you can configure a secondary zone for an Active Directory–integrated primary zone. Secondary zones provide you with a more secure way of providing DNS resolution to clients on untrusted networks. Through secondary zones, you can make any primary zone available on a Windows Server standalone server. In the event that the DNS server hosting a secondary zone is compromised, updates to the DNS zone can't be pushed to the primary zone.

Prior to configuring a secondary zone, you need to configure the primary zone from which you want it to replicate to enable transfers to that zone. You can do this on the Zone Transfers tab of the Zone Properties dialog. Secondary zones work best when the primary zone that they replicate from does not update frequently. If the primary zone updates frequently, be aware that the secondary zone might have out-of-date records. To allow a primary zone to be replicated to a specific server, use the `Set-DnsServerPrimaryZone` cmdlet. For example, to allow transfers from `tailwindtraders.com` to the server at `10.10.10.100`, use this command:

```
Set-DnsServerPrimaryZone -Name "tailwindtraders.com" -SecureSecondaries
TransferToSecureServers -SecondaryServers 10.10.10.100
```

Use the `Add-DNSServerSecondaryZone` cmdlet to create a secondary zone. For example, to create a secondary zone for the `australia.contoso.com` zone, where a DNS server hosting the primary zone is located at `192.168.15.100`, issue the following command:

```
Add-DnsServerSecondaryZone -Name "australia.contoso.com" -ZoneFile "australia.contoso.
com.dns" -MasterServers 192.168.15.100
```

Reverse lookup zones

Reverse lookup zones translate IP addresses into FQDNs. You can create IPv4 or IPv6 reverse lookup zones, and you can also configure reverse lookup zones as Active Directory–integrated zones, standard primary zones, secondary zones, or stub zones. The domain controller promotion process automatically creates a reverse lookup zone based on the IP address of the first domain controller promoted in the organization.

Reverse lookup zones are dependent on the network ID of the IP address range that they represent. IPv4 reverse lookup zones can only represent /8, /16, or /24 networks, which are the old Class A, Class B, and Class C networks. You can't create a single reverse lookup zone for IP subnets that don't fit into one of these categories, and the smallest reverse lookup zone you can create is for subnet mask /24, or `255.255.255.0`.

Use the `Add-DNSPrimaryZone` cmdlet and the `NetworkID` parameter to create a reverse lookup zone. For example, to create an Active Directory–integrated reverse lookup zone for the `192.168.15.0/24` subnet, issue the following command:

```
Add-DnsServerPrimaryZone -NetworkID "192.168.15.0/24" -ReplicationScope "Forest"
```

Inside OUT

Reverse lookup zones

Few applications actually require that you configure reverse lookup zones. In most organizations, the only reverse lookup zone is the one that is automatically created when Active Directory is installed. One of the few times when reverse lookup zones seem necessary is when you configure Simple Mail Transfer Protocol (SMTP) gateways. This is because some anti-SPAM checks perform a reverse IP address lookup to verify the identity of the SMTP gateway. Often, the SMTP gateway's IP address, being a public address, belongs to the ISP, which means creating the reverse lookup zone entry is beyond your direct control as a systems administrator.

Zone delegation

Zone delegations function as pointers to the next subordinate DNS layer in the DNS hierarchy. For example, if your organization uses the contoso.com DNS zone and you want to create a separate australia.contoso.com DNS zone, you can perform a zone delegation so that the DNS servers for the contoso.com DNS zone point to the DNS servers for the australia.contoso.com DNS zone. When you create a new child domain in an Active Directory forest, zone delegation occurs automatically. When you are performing a manual delegation, create the delegated zone on the target DNS server prior to performing the delegation from the parent zone.

Although you can delegate several levels, remember that the maximum length of an FQDN is 255 bytes, and the maximum length of an FQDN for an Active Directory Domain Services domain controller is 155 bytes.

Use the Add-DnsServerZoneDelegation cmdlet to add a delegation. For example, to add a delegation for the australia.contoso.com zone to the contoso.com zone pointing at the name server ausdns.australia.contoso.com, which has the IP address 192.168.15.100, use the following command:

```
Add-DnsServerZoneDelegation -Name "contoso.com" -ChildZoneName "australia" -NameServer
"ausdns.australia.contoso.com" -IPAddress 192.168.15.100 -PassThru
-Verbose
```

Forwarders and conditional forwarders

Forwarders and conditional forwarders enable your DNS server to forward traffic to specific DNS servers when a lookup request cannot be handled locally. For example, you might configure a conditional forwarder to forward all traffic for resource records in the tailspintoys.com zone to a DNS server at a specific IP address. If you don't configure a forwarder or if a configured forwarder can't be contacted, the DNS Server service forwards the request to a DNS root server, and the request is resolved normally.

Forwarders

When you want to have a specific DNS server on the Internet handle your organization's DNS resolution traffic, you are likely to use a DNS forwarder rather than have your DNS server use the root server. Most organizations configure their ISPs' DNS servers as forwarders. When you do this, the ISP's DNS server performs all the query work, returning the result to your organization's DNS server. Your organization's DNS server then returns the result of the query back to the original requesting client.

You configure forwarders on a per-DNS server level. You can configure a forwarder using the DNS Manager. You can do this by editing the properties of the DNS server and then configuring the list of forwarders on the Forwarders tab.

You can create a DNS forwarder by using the `Add-DnsServerForwarder` cmdlet. For example, to create a DNS forwarder for a DNS server with `10.10.10.111` as the IP address, issue this command:

```
Add-DnsServerForwarder 10.10.10.111
```

You can't create a forwarder on one DNS server and then have it replicate to all other DNS servers in the forest or the domain; however, this is possible with conditional forwarders and stub zones.

Conditional forwarders

Conditional forwarders only forward address requests from specific domains rather than forwarding all requests that the DNS server can't resolve. When configured, a conditional forwarder takes precedence over a forwarder. Conditional forwarders are useful when your organization has a trust relationship or partnership with another organization. You can configure a conditional forwarder that directs all traffic to host names within that organization instead of having to resolve those host names through the standard DNS resolution process.

You can create conditional forwarders using the `Add-DnsServerConditionalForwarderZone` PowerShell cmdlet. For example, to create a conditional forwarder for the DNS domain `tailspintoys.com` that forwards DNS queries to the server at IP address `10.10.10.102` and also replicates that conditional forwarder to all DNS servers within the Active Directory forest, issue this command:

```
Add-DnsServerConditionalForwarderZone -MasterServers 10.10.10.102 -Name tailspintoys.com
-ReplicationScope Forest
```

Stub zones

A stub zone is a special zone that stores authoritative name server records for a target zone. Stub zones have an advantage over forwarders when the address of a target zone's authoritative DNS server changes on a regular basis. Stub zones are often used to host the records for authoritative DNS servers in delegated zones. Using stub zones in this way ensures that delegated zone information is up to date. If you create the stub zone on a writable domain controller, it can be stored with Active Directory and replicated to other domain controllers in the domain or forest.

You can add a stub zone using the Add-DnsServerStubZone cmdlet. For example, to add a DNS stub zone for the fabrikam.com zone using the DNS server at 10.10.10.222 and to also replicate that stub zone to all DNS servers in the forest, execute this command:

```
Add-DnsServerStubZone -MasterServers 10.10.10.222 -Name fabrikam.com -ReplicationScope
Forest -LoadExisting
```

GlobalNames zones

GlobalNames zones are a single-label, name-resolution replacement for WINS that can utilize existing DNS infrastructure. Deploying GlobalNames zones enables organizations to retire their existing WINS servers. You can use GlobalNames zones as long as your organization's DNS servers are running Windows Server 2008 or later.

Your organization should consider deploying GlobalNames zones instead of WINS in the following situations:

- Your organization is transitioning to IPv6. WINS does not support IPv6, and you need to support single-label name resolution.

- Single-label name resolution is limited to a small number of hosts that rarely change. GlobalNames zones must be updated manually.

- You have a large number of suffix search lists because of a complex naming strategy or disjoined namespace.

Entries in the GlobalNames zones must be populated manually. GlobalNames zone entries are alias (CNAME) records to existing DNS A or AAAA records. The existing DNS A and AAAA records can be dynamically updated, with these updates flowing on to records in the GlobalNames zone.

To deploy a GlobalNames zone in a forest, perform the following steps:

1. On a domain controller that's configured as a DNS server, create a new Active Directory–integrated forward lookup zone and configure it to replicate to every domain controller in the forest using the New Zone Wizard.

CHAPTER 5

2. On the Zone Name page, enter **GlobalNames** as the zone name. You can also accomplish the same task by running the following Windows PowerShell command:

```
Add-DnsServerPrimaryZone -Name GlobalNames -ReplicationScope Fores
```

3. Next, activate the `GlobalNames` zone on each authoritative DNS server hosted on a domain controller in the forest. To do this, execute the following Windows PowerShell command (where `DNSServerName` is the name of the domain controller hosting DNS):

```
Set-DnsServerGlobalNameZone -ComputerName DNSServerName -Enable $True
```

4. To populate the `GlobalNames` zone, create alias (CNAME) records in the `GlobalNames` zone that point to A or AAAA records in existing zones.

Resource records

DNS supports a large number of resource records. The most basic resource record maps an FQDN to an IP address. More complex resource records provide information about the location of services, such as SMTP servers and domain controllers.

Host records

Host records are the most common form of record and can be used to map FQDNs to IP addresses. There are two types of host records:

*   The A record, which is used to map FQDNs to IPv4 addresses

*   AAAA records, which are used to map FQDNs to IPv6 addresses

You can add a new host record to a zone by right-clicking the zone in DNS Manager and then clicking New Host (A or AAAA). You also have the option of creating a pointer (PTR) record in the appropriate reverse lookup zone—if one exists. You can add host records with the Add-DnsServerResourceRecordA cmdlet and AAAA records with the Add-DnsServerResourceRecordAAAA cmdlet.

Alias (CNAME)

An alias—or CNAME—record enables you to provide an alternate name when there is an existing host record. You can create as many aliases for a particular record as you need. To create a new alias in a zone, right-click the zone in DNS Manager and then click New Alias (CNAME). When you create an alias, you must point the alias to an existing host record. You can use the Browse button to navigate to the target host record or enter it manually. You can also add an alias record to a zone from Windows PowerShell by using the Add-DnsServerResourceRecordCName cmdlet.

Mail exchanger

Mail exchanger (MX) records are used to locate mail gateways. For example, when a remote mail gateway wants to forward an email message to an email address associated with your organization's DNS zone, it performs an MX lookup to determine the location of the mail gateway. After that determination has been made, the remote mail gateway contacts the local gateway and transmits the message. MX records must map to existing host records. To create an MX record, right-click the zone in DNS Manager, click New Mail Exchanger (MX), and enter information in the New Resource Record dialog. The Mail Server Priority field is available to allow for the existence of more than one MX record in a zone and is often used when organizations have multiple mail gateways. This is done so that if an organization's primary mail gateway fails, remote mail servers can forward message traffic to other mail gateways. You can add MX records using the Add-DnsServerResourceRecordMX PowerShell cmdlet.

Pointer record

Pointer (PTR) records enable you to connect IP addresses to FQDNs and are hosted in reverse lookup zones. When you create a host record, a PTR record is automatically created by default if an appropriate reverse lookup zone exists. To create a PTR record, right-click the reverse lookup zone in DNS Manager, click New Pointer (PTR), and enter the PTR record information in the New Resource Record dialog. You can create a PTR record from Windows PowerShell by using the Add-DnsServerResourceRecordPtr cmdlet.

Inside OUT
Unknown Records

Windows Server DNS supports "unknown records," which are resource records whose RDATA format is unknown to the DNS server. "Unknown records" are defined in RFC 3597 and can be added to Windows Server DNS zones when they're hosted on computers running the Windows Server operating system.

Zone aging and scavenging

Aging and scavenging provide a technique to reduce the incidence of stale resource records in a primary DNS zone. Stale records are records that are out of date or no longer relevant. If your organization has zones that relate to users with portable computers, such as laptops and tablets, those zones might end up accumulating stale resource records. This can lead to the following problems:

- DNS queries return stale rather than relevant results.

- Large zones can cause DNS server performance problems.

- Stale records might prevent DNS names from being reassigned to different devices.

To resolve these problems, you can configure the DNS Server service to do the following:

- Timestamp resource records that are dynamically added to primary zones. This occurs when you enable aging and scavenging.

- Age resource records based on a refresh period.

- Scavenge resource records that are still present beyond the refresh period.

After you configure the DNS Server service, aging and scavenging occur automatically. It's also possible to trigger scavenging by right-clicking the DNS server in DNS Manager and then clicking Scavenge Stale Resource Records. You can also configure aging and scavenging using the `Set-DnsServerScavenging` cmdlet. For example, to enable stale resource record scavenging on all zones of a DNS server and to set the `ScavengingInterval` and `RefreshInterval` to 10 days, issue this command:

```
Set-DnsServerScavenging -ApplyOnAllZones -RefreshInterval 10.0:0:0 -ScavengingInterval
10.0:0:0 -ScavengingState $True
```

DNSSEC

Domain Name System Security Extensions (DNSSEC) add security to DNS by enabling DNS servers to validate the responses given by other DNS servers. DNSSEC enables digital signatures to be used with DNS zones. When the DNS resolver issues a query for a record in a signed zone, the authoritative DNS server provides both the record and a digital signature, enabling validation of that record.

To configure DNSSEC, perform the following steps:

1. Right-click the zone in DNS manager, click DNSSEC, and then click Sign The Zone.

2. On the Signing Options page, select Use Default Settings To Sign The Zone.

3. When you configure DNSSEC, three new resource records are available with the following properties:

   - **Resource Record Signature (RRSIG) record**   This record is stored within the zone, and each is associated with a different zone record. When the DNS server is queried for a zone record, it returns the record and the associated RRSIG record.

   - **DNSKEY**   This is a public key resource record that enables the validation of RRSIG records.

   - **Next Secure (NSEC/NSEC3) record**   This record is used as proof that a record does not exist. For example, the *contoso.com* zone is configured with DNSSEC. A client issues a query for the `tasmania.contoso.command` host record if there is no record for `tasmania.contoso.com`. The NSEC record returns, informing the host making the query that no such record exists.

4. In addition to the special resource records, a DNSSEC implementation has the following components:

    ■ **Trust anchor**   This is a special public key associated with a zone. Trust anchors enable a DNS server to validate DNSKEY resource records. If you deploy DNSSEC on a DNS server hosted on a domain controller, the trust anchors can be stored in the Active Directory forest directory partition. This replicates the trust anchor to all DNS servers hosted on domain controllers in the forest.

    ■ **DNSSEC Key Master**   This is a special DNS server that you use to generate and manage signing keys for a DNSSEC-protected zone. Any computer running Windows Server 2012 or later that hosts a primary zone, whether standard or integrated, can function as a DNSSEC Key Master. A single computer can function as a DNSSEC Key Master for multiple zones. The DNSSEC Key Master role can also be transferred to another DNS server that hosts the primary zone.

    ■ **Key Signing Key (KSK)**   You use the KSK to sign all DNSKEY records at the zone root. You create the KSK by using the DNSSEC Key Master.

    ■ **Zone Signing Key (ZSK)**   You use the ZSK to sign zone data, such as individual records hosted in the zone. You create the ZSK by using the DNSSEC Key Master.

You can configure Group Policy to ensure that clients only accept records from a DNS server for a specific zone if those records have been signed using DNSSEC. You do this by configuring the Name Resolution Policy Table, which is located in the `Computer Configuration\Policies\ Windows Settings\Name Resolution Policy` node of a GPO. You create entries in the table, for example, requiring that all queries against a specific zone require DNSSEC validation. You can configure the NRPT by using Group Policy or through Windows PowerShell.

DNSSEC is appropriate for high-security environments, such as those where IPSec and authenticating switches are in use. DNSSEC protects against attacks where clients are fed false DNS information. In many small- to medium-sized environments, the likelihood of such an attack is minimal; however, in high-security environments, enabling DNSSEC is a prudent precaution.

DNS event logs

The DNS server log is located in the Applications And Services Logs folder in Event Viewer. Depending on how you configure event logging on the Event Logging tab of the DNS server's properties, this event log can record information, including

● Changes to the DNS service, such as when the DNS server service is stopped or started

● Zone-loading and signing events

● Modifications to the DNS server configuration

● DNS warning and error events

CHAPTER 5

CHAPTER 5

By default, the DNS server records all these events. It's also possible to configure the DNS server to log only errors, or you can have it log errors and warning events. The key with any type of logging is that you should only enable logging for information that you might need to review at some point in time. Many administrators log everything "just in case," even though they are only ever interested in a specific type of event.

In the event that you need to debug how a DNS server performs, you can enable Debug Logging on the Debug Logging tab of the DNS server's Properties dialog. Debug logging is resource-intensive, and you should only use it when you have a specific problem related to the functionality of the DNS server. You can configure debug logging to use a filter so that only traffic from specific hosts is recorded instead of recording traffic from all hosts that interact with the DNS server. You can view DNS analytic logs in the Event Viewer under `Applications and Services Logs\Microsoft\Windows\DNS-Server\Analytical`.

For real-time monitoring, you can use the PowerShell `Get-Content` cmdlet with the `-Wait` parameter:

```
Get-Content -Path "C:\Windows\System32\DNS\dns.log" -Wait
```

If you have `LogParser.exe` installed, covered in Chapter 23, "Monitoring and Maintenance," you can use the following query against the log:

```
LogParser.exe "SELECT * FROM dns.log WHERE Text LIKE '%example.com%'"
```

DNS options

In high-security environments, there are a number of steps that you can take to make a DNS server more secure from attackers who attempt to spoof it. Spoofing can cause the server to provide records that redirect clients to malicious sites. While DNSSEC provides security for zones hosted on the server, most DNS server traffic involves retrieving information from remote DNS servers and passing that information on to clients. In this section, you learn about settings that you can configure to ensure that the information relayed to clients retains its integrity in the event that a nefarious third party attempts to spoof your organization's DNS servers.

DNS socket pool

DNS socket pool is a technology that makes cache-tampering and spoofing attacks more difficult by using source port randomization when issuing DNS queries to remote DNS servers. To spoof the DNS server with an incorrect record, the attacker needs to guess which randomized port was used as well as the randomized transaction ID that was issued with the query. By default, one DNS server running on Windows Server uses a socket pool size of 2,500. You can use the dnscmd command-line tool to change the socket pool size to a value between 0 and 10,000. For example, to set the socket pool size to 4,000, issue the following command:

```
Dnscmd /config /socketpoolsize 4000
```

You must restart the DNS service before you can use the reconfigured socket pool size.

DNS cache locking

DNS cache locking provides you with control over when information stored in the DNS server's cache can be overwritten. For example, when a recursive DNS server responds to a query for a record that's hosted on another DNS server, it caches the results of that query so that it doesn't have to contact the remote DNS server if the same record is queried again within the Time to Live (TTL) value of the resource record. DNS cache locking prevents record data in a DNS server's cache from being overwritten until a configured percentage of the TTL value has expired. By default, the cache-locking value is set to 100 percent, but you can reset it by using the Set-DNS-ServerCache cmdlet with the LockingPercent option. For example, to set the cache-locking value to 80 percent, issue the following command and then restart the DNS server service:

```
Set-DNSServerCache -LockingPercent 80
```

DNS recursion

By default, Windows Server DNS servers perform recursive queries on behalf of clients. This means that when the client asks the DNS server to find a record that isn't stored in a zone hosted by the DNS server, the DNS server then goes out and finds the result of that query and passes it back to the client. It's possible, however, for nefarious third parties to use recursion as a denial-of-service attack vector, which could slow a DNS server to the point where it becomes unresponsive. You can disable recursion on the Advanced Tab of the DNS server's properties, or you can configure it by using the Set-DNSServerRecursion cmdlet. For example, to configure the recursion retry interval to 3 seconds, use the following command:

```
Set-DNSServerRecursion -RetryInterval 3 -PassThru
```

Netmask ordering

Netmask ordering ensures that the DNS server returns the host record on the requesting client's subnet if such a record exists. For example, imagine that the following host records exist on a network that uses 24-bit subnet masks:

```
10.10.10.105  wsus.contoso.com
10.10.20.105  wsus.contoso.com
10.10.30.105  wsus.contoso.com
```

If netmask ordering is enabled and a client with the IP address 10.10.20.50 performs a lookup of *wsus.contoso.com*, the lookup always returns the record 10.10.20.105 because this record is on the same subnet as the client. If netmask ordering isn't enabled, the DNS server returns records in a round-robin fashion. If the requesting client is not on the same network as any of the host records, the DNS server also returns records in a round-robin fashion. Netmask ordering is useful for services, such as WSUS, that you might have at each branch office. When you use netmask ordering, the DNS server redirects the client in the branch office to a resource on the local subnet when one exists.

Netmask ordering is enabled by default on Windows Server DNS servers. You can verify that netmask ordering is enabled by viewing the Advanced Properties of the DNS server.

Response rate limiting

Distributed denial-of-service attacks against DNS servers are becoming increasingly common. One method of ameliorating such attacks is by configuring response rate limiting. Response rate limiting determines how a DNS server responds to clients sending an unusually high number of DNS queries. You can configure the following response rate limiting settings:

- **Responses Per Second**   Determines the maximum number of times an identical response can be returned to a client per second.

- **Errors Per Second**   Determines the maximum number of error responses returned to a client per second.

- **Window**   The timeout period for any client that exceeds the maximum request threshold.

- **Leak Rate**   Determines how often the DNS server responds to queries if a client is in the suspension window. The leak rate is the number of queries it takes before a response is sent. A leak rate of 42 means that the DNS server only responds to one query out of every 42 when a client is in the suspension window period.

- **TC Rate**   Tells the client to try connecting with TCP when the client is in the suspension window. The TC rate should be below the leak rate to give the client the option of attempting a TCP connection before a leak response is sent.

- **Maximum Responses**   The maximum number of responses that a DNS server issues to a client during the timeout period.

- **White List Domains**   Domains that are excluded from response rate limiting settings.

- **White List Subnets**   Subnets that are excluded from response rate limiting settings.

- **White List Server Interfaces**   DNS server interfaces that are excluded from response rate limiting settings.

DANE

DNS-based Authentication of Named Entities (DANE) allows you to configure records that use Transport Layer Security Authentication (TLSA) to inform DNS clients of which certificate authorities (CA) they should accept certificates from for your organization's domain name DNS zone. DANE blocks attackers from using attacks where a certificate is issued from a rogue CA and is used to provide validation for a rogue website when a DNS server is compromised. When DANE is implemented, a client requesting a TLS connection to a website, such as www.tail-spintoys.com, knows that it should only accept a TLS certificate from a specific CA. If the TLS certificate for www.tailwindtraders.com is from a different CA, the client knows that the website that appears to be at www.tailwindtraders.com might have been compromised or that the client might have been redirected by an attacker corrupting a DNS cache.

DNS policies

You use DNS policies to control how DNS servers respond to queries based on the properties of that query. You can configure DNS policies to achieve the following:

- **Application load balancing**   Allows you to apply weight to which endpoint is returned when multiple endpoints exist for an address. For example, returning one IP address 75 percent of the time and another IP address 25 percent of the time. This differs from DNS round-robin, where multiple IP addresses associated with a specific address would be returned to clients on an equal basis (netmask ordering being the exception).

- **Traffic management**   The DNS server responds to the client, directing them to the datacenter closest to them. For example, clients making DNS requests from Australia are redirected to an application endpoint in Australia, and clients making DNS requests from Canada are redirected to an application endpoint in Canada.

- **Split Brain DNS**   DNS records can be segmented into zone scopes. Records can be placed in different scopes. This allows external clients to query the DNS zone and be able to access only a specific number of DNS records that are members of a scope designed for external clients. Internal clients have access to a more comprehensive internal scope.

- **Filtering**   Allows you to block DNS queries from specific IP addresses, IP address ranges, or FQDNs.

- **Forensics**   Redirects malicious clients to a sinkhole host rather than to the host they are trying to reach. For example, if clients appear to be attempting a denial-of-service attack, redirect them to a static page rather than the site they are attempting to attack.

- **Time of day–based redirection**   Allows you to configure a policy where clients are redirected to specific hosts based on the time of day when the query is received.

To accomplish most of these tasks, you create a zone scope, which is a collection of records within a zone. For example, in a split-brain scenario, you'd create a zone scope for the internal records. You'd then use the Add-DNSServerQueryResolutionPolicy cmdlet to create a policy that allowed all queries from the DNS server's internal network interface to have access to records in the internal zone scope; queries that came through any other interface on the DNS server would only have access to the Default scope, which would only be comprised of those records in the zone to which you wanted public clients to have access. Similarly, in the time of day–based redirection scenario, you'd create scopes for each period of time and then create policies that were triggered based on the time of day that would direct clients to records within the particular scope associated with that period of time.

CHAPTER 5

Delegated administration

In some larger environments, you might want to separate administrative privileges so that the people responsible for managing your organization's DNS servers don't have other permissions, such as the ability to create user accounts or reset passwords. By default, members of the Domain Admins group can perform all DNS administration tasks on DNS servers within a domain. Members of the Enterprise Admins group can perform all DNS administration tasks on any DNS server in the forest.

You can use the DNSAdmins domain local group to grant users the ability to view and modify DNS data, as well as view and modify server configurations of DNS servers within a domain. Add users to this group when you want to allow them to perform DNS administration tasks without giving them additional permissions. You can assign permissions that allow users or security groups to manage a specific DNS server on the Security tab of the server's Properties dialog.

You can also configure permissions at the zone level. To do this, assign security principal permissions on the Security tab of the zone's Properties dialog. You might do this when you want to allow a specific person to manage host records without assigning them any other permissions. Today, most organizations allow DNS records to be updated dynamically. This means that the only zones where you might need to configure special permissions to allow manual management are ones where security is especially important, such as those that are accessible to clients on the Internet.

Managing DNS with PowerShell

You can manage almost all aspects of DNS server operations using the DnsServer module of Windows PowerShell. Table 5-1 lists the DNS server PowerShell cmdlets.

Table 5-1   DNS PowerShell cmdlets

Noun	Verbs	Function
DnsServer	Set, Get, Test	View and manage DNS server configuration
DnsServerCache	Get, Set, Show, Clear	Manage DHS server cache configuration
DnsServerClientSubnet	Set, Get, Add, Remove	Manage DHS server client subnets for use in DNS policies
DnsServerConditional-ForwarderZone	Set, Add	Manage conditional forwarders
DnsServerDiagnostics	Set, Get	View DNS event log information
DnsServerDirectoryPartition	Unregister, Remove, Get, Register, Add	Manage DNS server directory partitions

Noun	Verbs	Function
DnsServerDnsSecPublicKey	Export	Export the DS and DNSKEY data for a DNSSEC-signed zone
DnsServerDnsSecZoneSetting	Get, Set, Test	Configure DNSSEC settings for a zone
DnsServerDsSetting	Set, Get	Configure Active Directory server settings
DnsServerEDns	Get, Set	Manage CacheTimeout, EnableProbes, and EnableReception settings
DnsServerForwarder	Add, Set, Get, Remove	Manage DNS server forwarders
DnsServerGlobalNameZone	Set, Get	Manage the global names zone
DnsServerGlobalQueryBlockList	Get, Set	Manage the global query block list
DnsServerKeyStorageProvider	Show	View key storage provider information
DnsServerPolicy	Disable, Enable	Enable or disable DNS server policies
DnsServerPrimaryZone	Restore, Set, Add, ConvertTo	Manage DNS server primary zones
DnsServerQueryResolution-Policy	Add, Get, Remove, Set	Configure DNS server query resolution policy
DnsServerRecursion	Set, Get	Manage DNS server recursion settings
DnsServerRecursionScope	Remove, Set, Get, Add	Configure DNS server recursion scopes
DnsServerResourceRecord	Add, Set, Remove, Get	Manage DNS server resource records
DnsServerResourceRecordA	Add	Add an IPv4 host record
DnsServerResourceRecordAAAA	Add	Add an IPv6 host record
DnsServerResourceRecordAging	Set	Configure resource record aging
DnsServerResourceRecordCName	Add	Add a CNAME record
DnsServerResourceRecordDnsKey	Add	Add a DNSKey resource record
DnsServerResourceRecordDS	Import, Add	Manage delegation signer (DS) resource records
DnsServerResourceRecordMX	Add	Add a mail exchanger (MX) resource record
DnsServerResourceRecordPtr	Add	Add a pointer (PTR) resource record
DnsServerResponseRateLimiting	Get, Set	Configure response rate limiting

CHAPTER 5

CHAPTER 5

Noun	Verbs	Function
DnsServerResponseRate-LimitingExceptionlist	Add, Remove, Get, Set	Configure response rate limit exceptions
DnsServerRootHint	Remove, Get, Add, Set, Import	Manage DNS server root hints
DnsServerScavenging	Start, Set, Get	Manage DNS server scavenging setting
DnsServerSecondaryZone	Add, Restore, ConvertTo, Set	Manage DNS server secondary zones
DnsServerSetting	Get, Set	Configure DNS server settings
DnsServerSigningKey	Get, Add, Set, Remove	Manage DNS Server signing keys
DnsServerSigningKeyRollover	Invoke, Enable, Step, Disable	Configure signing key rollover
DnsServerStatistics	Clear, Get	Manage DNS server statistics
DnsServerStubZone	Set, Add	Configure stub zones
DnsServerTrustAnchor	Get, Import, Remove, Add	Configure DNSSEC trust anchor
DnsServerTrustPoint	Get, Update	Configure DNSSET trust point
DnsServerVirtualization-Instance	Remove, Get, Set, Add	Manage virtualization instances
DnsServerZone	Get, Export, Sync, Suspend, Remove, Resume	Manage zones, including export and import
DnsServerZoneAging	Set, Get	Configure zone record aging
DnsServerZoneDelegation	Remove, Add, Get, Set	Configure zone delegation
DnsServerZoneKeyMasterRole	Reset	Transfers the key master role for a DNS zone
DnsServerZoneScope	Remove, Get, Add	Manage zone scopes
DnsServerZoneSign	Invoke	Sign a DNS zone (DNSSEC)
DnsServerZoneTransfer	Start	Manage zone transfers
DnsServerZoneTransferPolicy	Add, Get, Set, Remove	Configure zone transfer policies
DnsServerZoneUnsign	Invoke	Unsign a DNS zone (DNSSEC)

DHCP

DHCP is a network service that most administrators barely pay attention to after they've configured it. Many organizations use a basic DHCP service on a hardware device to lease addresses and pay the service no more attention unless a problem arises. DHCP is a service that you can deploy on Windows Server that allows you to extend the humble DHCP server beyond what is available on a basic network device. DHCP in Windows Server can be seamlessly integrated with the Active Directory identity platform and with the DNS Server service. This allows you to integrate address leases with the computer name and user logon information, which you can then make highly available through DHCP failover.

Scopes

A DHCP scope is a collection of IP address settings that a client uses to determine its IP address configuration. You configure a DHCP scope for every separate IPv4 subnet to which you want the DHCP servers to provide IP address configuration information. When configuring an IPv4 scope, specify the following information:

- **Scope Name**   The name of the scope. The name should be descriptive enough that you recognize which hosts the scope applies to. For example, Level 2, Old Arts Building.

- **IP Address Range**   This is the range of IP addresses encompassed by the scope, and it should be a logical subnet.

- **IP Address Exclusions**   This includes which IP addresses within the IP address range you do not want the DHCP server to lease. For example, you could configure exclusions for several computers that have statically assigned IP addresses.

- **Delay**   This setting determines how long the DHCP server waits before offering an address. This provides you with a method of DHCP server redundancy, with one DHCP server offering addresses immediately and another only offering addresses after a certain period of time has elapsed.

- **Lease Duration**   The lease duration determines how long a client has an IP address before the address returns to the lease pool.

- **DHCP Options**   There are 61 standard options that you can configure. These include settings, such as DNS server address and default gateway address, that apply to leases in the scope.

You can add a DHCP server scope using the Add-DHCPServer4Scope or Add-DHCPServer-6Scope PowerShell cmdlets. For example, to create a new scope for the 192.168.10.0/24 network named MelbourneNet, enact the following PowerShell command:

```
Add-DHCPServerv4Scope -Name "MelbourneNet" -StartRange 192.168.10.1 -Endrange
192.168.10.254 -SubnetMask 255.255.255.0
```

CHAPTER 5

Inside OUT

IPv6 DHCP

Most organizations are still using IPv4 with their DHCP server. For the sake of brevity, all PowerShell examples are for IPv4, with the cmdlets for managing IPv6 DHCP scopes listed later in the chapter.

Server and scope options

DHCP options include additional configuration settings, such as the address of a network's default gateway or the addresses of DNS servers. You can configure DHCP options at two levels: the scope level and the server level. Options configured at the scope level override options configured at the server level.

Common scope options include

- **003 Router**   The address of the default gateway for the subnet.

- **006 DNS Servers**   The address of DNS servers that the client should use for name resolution.

- **015 DNS Domain Name**   This is the DNS suffix assigned to the client.

- **058 Renewal time**   This determines how long after the lease is initially acquired that the client waits before it attempts to renew the lease.

You can configure IPv4 scope options using the `Set-DHCPServer4OptionValue` cmdlet. For example, to configure the scope with ID `192.168.10.0` on DHCP server `dhcp.contoso.com` with the value for the DNS server set to `192.168.0.100`, issue the following command:

```
Set-DHcpServerv4OptionValue -Computername dhcp.contoso.com -ScopeID 192.168.10.0
-DNSServer 192.168.0.100
```

Reservations

Reservations allow you to ensure that a particular computer always receives a specific IP address. You can use reservations to allow servers to always have the same address, even when they're configured to retrieve that address through DHCP. If you don't configure a reservation for a computer, it can be assigned any available address from the pool. Although you can configure DHCP to update DNS to ensure that other hosts can connect using the client's hostname, it's generally a good idea to ensure that a server retains the same IP address.

There are two ways to configure a DHCP reservation:

- The simplest way is to locate an existing IP address lease in the DHCP console, right-click it, and then select Add To Reservation. This ties that specific network adapter address to that IP address. The only drawback of this method is that the reservation is for the assigned IP address, and you cannot customize it.

- If you know the network adapter address of the computer for which you want to configure a reservation, you can right-click the Reservations node under the scope that you want to configure the reservation, and then click New Reservation. In the New Reservation dialog, enter the Reservation Name, IP Address, and Network Adapter Address, and then click Add to create the reservation. You can also configure a reservation using the `Add-DhcpServerv4Reservation` cmdlet. For example, to configure a reservation, issue the following command:

```
Add-DhcpServerv4Reservation -ScopeId 192.168.10.0 -IPAddress 192.168.10.8
-ClientId A0-FE-C1-7A-00-E5 -Description "A4 Printer"
```

DHCP filtering

You can configure DHCP filtering on the Filters tab of the IPv4 Properties dialog in the DHCP console. DHCP filtering is used in high-security environments to restrict the network adapter addresses that can utilize DHCP. For example, you can have a list of all network adapter addresses in your organization and use the Enable Allow List option to lease only IP addresses to this list of authorized adapters. This method of security is not entirely effective because unauthorized people can fake an authorized adapter address to gain network access. You can add a specific network adapter to the allowed list of MAC addresses using the `Add-DHCPServerv-4Filter` cmdlet. For example, to allow a laptop with the MAC address `D1-F2-7C-00-5E-F0` to the authorized list of adapters, issue the following command:

```
Add-DhcpServerv4Filter -List Allow -MacAddress D1-F2-7C-00-5E-F0 Description "Rooslan's
Laptop"
```

Superscopes

A superscope is a collection of individual DHCP scopes. You might create a superscope when you want to bind existing scopes for administrative reasons. For example, imagine that you have a subnet in a building that's close to fully allocated. You can add a second subnet to the building and then bind them into a superscope. The process of binding several separate logical subnets on the same physical network is known as multinetting.

There needs to be at least one existing scope present on the DHCP server before you can create a superscope. After you have created a superscope, you can add new subnets or remove subnets from that scope. It's also possible to deactivate some subnets within a scope while keeping others active. You might use this technique when migrating clients from one IP address range to another. For example, you could have both the source and destination scopes as part of the same superscope, activate the new scope, and deactivate the original scope as necessary when performing the migration. You can create superscopes using the `Add-DHCPServerv4Super-scope` cmdlet. For example, to add the scopes with ID `192.168.10.0` and `192.168.11.0` to a superscope named `MelbourneCBD`, run the following command:

```
Add-DhcpServerv4Superscope -SuperscopeName "MelbourneCBD" -ScopeId 192.168.10.0,
192.168.11.0
```

Multicast scopes

A multicast address is an address that allows one-to-many communications on a network. When you use multicast, multiple network hosts listen for traffic on a single multicast IP address. Multicast addresses are in the IPv4 range of 224.0.0.0 through 239.255.255.255. Multicast scopes are collections of multicast addresses. You can configure a Windows Server DHCP server to host multicast scopes. Multicast scopes are also known as Multicast Address Dynamic Client Allocation Protocol (MADCAP) scopes because applications that require access to multicast addresses support the MADCAP API.

The most common use for multicast addresses using the default Windows Server roles is for Windows Deployment Services. You can, however, configure the WDS server with its own set of multicast addresses, and you don't need to configure a special multicast scope in DHCP to support this role.

Split scopes

A split scope is one method of providing fault tolerance for a DHCP scope. The idea behind a split scope is that you host one part of the scope on one DHCP server and a second, smaller part of the scope on a second DHCP server. Usually, this split has 80 percent of the addresses on the first DHCP server and 20 percent of the addresses on the second server. In this scenario, the DHCP server that hosts the 20 percent portion of the address space is usually located on a remote subnet. In the split-scope scenario, you also use a DHCP relay agent configured with a delay so that most addresses are leased from the DHCP server that hosts 80 percent of the address space. Split scopes are more likely in older deployments that haven't transitioned to using DHCP failover.

Name protection

DHCP name protection is a feature that allows you to ensure that the hostnames a DHCP server registers with a DNS server are not overwritten in the event that a non-Windows operating system has the same name. DHCP name protection also protects names from being overwritten by hosts that use static addresses that conflict with DHCP-assigned addresses.

For example, imagine that in the `tailwindtraders.com` domain, there is a computer running the Windows 11 operating system that has the name `Auckland` and receives its IP address information from a Windows Server DHCP server. The DHCP server registers this name in DNS and creates a record in the `contoso.com` DNS zone that associates the name `Auckland.tailwindtraders.com` with the IP address assigned to the computer running Windows 11. A newly installed computer running a distribution of Linux is also assigned the name `Auckland`. Because name protection has been enabled, this new computer is unable to overwrite the existing record with a new record that associates the name `Auckland.tailwindtraders.com` with the Linux computer's IP address. If name protection had not been enabled, it's possible that the record would have been overwritten.

You can enable name protection on a scope by clicking Configure on the DNS tab of the IPv4 or IPv6 Properties dialog. You can also do this by using the `Set-DhcpServerv4DnsSetting` or the `Set-DhcpServerv6DnsSetting` cmdlet. For example, to configure the DHCP server on computer MEL-DC so that name protection is enabled on all IPv4 scopes, issue the following command:

```
Set-DhcpServerv4DnsSetting –Computer MEL-DC –NameProtection $true
```

DHCP failover

DHCP failover allows you to configure DHCP to be highly available without using split scopes. You have two options when configuring DHCP failover:

- **Hot Standby mode**   This relationship is a traditional failover relationship. When you configure this relationship, the primary server handles all DHCP traffic unless it becomes unavailable. You can configure DHCP servers to be in multiple separate relationships, so it's possible that a DHCP server can be the primary server in one relationship and a hot standby server in another relationship. When configuring this relationship, you specify a percentage of the address ranges to be reserved on the standby server. The default value is 5 percent. These 5 percent of addresses are instantly available after the primary server becomes unavailable. The hot standby server takes control of the entire address range when the figure specified by the state switchover interval is reached. The default value for this interval is 60 minutes.

- **Load Sharing mode**   This is the default mode when you create a DHCP failover relationship. In this mode, both servers provide IP addresses to clients according to the ratio defined by the load balance percentage figure. The default is for each server to share 50 percent of the load. The maximum client lead time figure enables one of the partners to take control of the entire scope in the event that the other partner is not available for the specified time.

Prior to configuring DHCP failover, you need to remove any split scopes between the potential partners. You can also choose a shared secret to authenticate replication traffic, but you don't have to enter this secret on the partner DHCP server.

To configure two servers that already have the DHCP server role installed for DHCP failover, perform the following steps:

1. Configure DHCP scopes and options for the scopes you want to configure failover for on the primary server.

2. On the primary server, open the DHCP console and right-click IPv4, then select "Configure Failover."

CHAPTER 5

3. In the Configure Failover wizard, do the following:

    1. Select the scopes you want to configure for failover.

    2. Specify the partner (secondary) server.

    3. Choose a name for the failover relationship.

    4. Select either Load Balance or Hot Standby mode.

    5. Configure settings like shared secret, load balance percentage, and so on.

4. Complete the wizard to establish the failover relationship between the two servers.

5. The scopes and settings will be automatically replicated to the secondary server.

DHCP server authorization

DHCP servers need to be authorized in Active Directory before they start leasing addresses. DHCP servers on Microsoft operating systems must always be authorized before they start working, simply because this reduces the chance that a rogue DHCP server might start leasing IP addresses. Only the following can authorize DHCP servers:

- Members of the Enterprise Admins group

- Members of the Domain Admins group in the forest root domain

- Accounts delegated the ability to add, modify, or delete new objects of the DHCP class type on the NetServices folder in Active Directory

To authorize a DHCP server, ensure that you're signed on with an account that's a member of one of these groups and run the following PowerShell command from an elevated PowerShell prompt, substituting the DHCP server's FQDN and IP address:

```
Add-DhcpServerInDC -DnsName "dhcp_server_name.domain.com" -IPAddress
"dhcp_server_ip_address"
```

When you deploy the DHCP server role, the following local groups are created. You can use membership in these groups to delegate DHCP server management permissions to users or groups:

- **DHCP Administrators**   Members of this group can view or modify any DHCP server settings, including configuring DHCP options, failover, and scopes.

- **DHCP Users**   Members of this group have only read-only access to the DHCP server. They can view, but not modify, DHCP server settings, including scope information and data.

DHCP relay agent

A DHCP relay agent forwards DHCP requests from a subnet that doesn't have a DHCP server to a DHCP server on another subnet that has a scope that's appropriate for that subnet. DHCP relay agents are only necessary on networks that don't have routers that forward DHCP request traffic. To install the DHCP relay agent on Windows Server, you need to deploy the Remote Access server role. To deploy and configure a DHCP relay agent on a Windows Server computer on a remote subnet, perform the following steps:

1. In the Server Manager console, select Add Roles And Features.

2. On the Roles page, expand the Remote Access role by selecting the accompanying checkbox or arrow.

3. In Role Services, select Routing, and then choose Add Features when prompted.

4. Complete the Add Roles And Features Wizard, selecting Install to perform the installation.

5. After the installation completes, select Open The Getting Started Wizard.

6. In the Routing And Remote Access Microsoft Management Console (MMC), right-click the server and then select Configure And Enable Routing And Remote Access to open the Routing And Remote Access Server Setup Wizard.

7. In the Welcome To The Routing And Remote Access Server Setup Wizard, select Next.

8. In Configuration, select LAN routing, and then choose Next.

9. In Custom Configuration, select VPN Access, and then select Next.

10. Select Finish to close the wizard, and then choose Start Service when prompted.

11. In the left pane, expand the server name, right-click General under IPv4 or IPv6, and then select New Routing Protocol.

12. In the left pane, right-click DHCP Relay Agent under IPv4 or IPv6, and then select New Interface.

13. Select the network interface you want to use for the DHCP relay agent. Select OK.

14. In the left pane, right-click DHCP Relay Agent under IPv4 or IPv6, and then select Properties.

15. Enter the IP address of the DHCP server you want to relay DHCP requests to, and then select Add.

16. Select OK to save your settings.

CHAPTER 5

17. The computer will now forward requests from its local subnet to the DHCP server on the remote subnet.

Managing DHCP with PowerShell

You can manage the DHCP role by using the PowerShell cmdlets listed in Table 5-2.

Table 5-2   DHCP PowerShell cmdlets

Noun	Verbs	Function
DhcpServer	Restore, Export, Backup, Import	Backup, recover, export, and import DHCP server configuration
DhcpServerAuditLog	Get, Set	Manage the DHCP server audit log
DhcpServerDatabase	Get, Set	Manage the DHCP server database
DhcpServerDnsCredential	Get, Remove, Set	Configure the account that the DHCP server uses to manage DHS server records
DhcpServerInDC	Add, Get, Remove	Manage DHCP server authorization in Active Directory
DhcpServerSecurityGroup	Add	Add security groups to a DHCP server
DhcpServerSetting	Set, Get	Manage the DHCP server database configuration parameters
DhcpServerv4Binding	Get, Set	Manage the network interfaces to which the DHCP server services are bound
DhcpServerv4Class	Add, Remove, Get, Set	Manage IPv4 vendor or user classes for the DHCP server service
DhcpServerv4DnsSetting	Set, Get	Configure DNS settings at the scope, reservation, or server level
DhcpServerv4ExclusionRange	Add, Get, Remove	Manage IPv4 exclusion ranges
DhcpServerv4Failover	Set, Add, Remove, Get	Configure IPv4 failover relationships
DhcpServerv4FailoverReplication	Invoke	Replicate scope configuration between failover partners
DhcpServerv4FailoverScope	Add, Remove	Configure DHCP IPv4 failover scopes
DhcpServerv4Filter	Remove, Add, Get	Manage DHCP IPv4 MAC address filters

Noun	Verbs	Function
`DhcpServerv4FilterList`	Set, Get	Manage the filter list status
`DhcpServerv4FreeIPAddress`	Get	Find free IP addresses in a scope
`DhcpServerv4IPRecord`	Repair	Reconcile inconsistent records in the DHCP database.
`DhcpServerv4Lease`	Add, Remove, Get	Manage IPv4 DHCP leases
`DhcpServerv4MulticastExclusion-Range`	Get, Remove, Add	Manage multicast exclusions
`DhcpServerv4MulticastLease`	Get, Remove	Manage IPv4 multicast lease
`DhcpServerv4MulticastScope`	Remove, Get, Add, Set	Manage IPv4 multicast scopes
`DhcpServerv4MulticastScope-Statistics`	Get	View IPv4 multicast scope statistics
`DhcpServerv4OptionDefinition`	Add, Set, Remove, Get	Manage IPv4 option definitions
`DhcpServerv4OptionValue`	Get, Remove, Set	Configure IPv4 option values
`DhcpServerv4Policy`	Add, Remove, Get, Set	Manage IPv4 policies
`DhcpServerv4PolicyIPRange`	Get, Add, Remove	Manage bindings between IP ranges and policies
`DhcpServerv4Reservation`	Add, Set, Get, Remove	Configure IPv4 reservations
`DhcpServerv4Scope`	Get, Remove, Set, Add	Manage IPv4 DHCP scopes
`DhcpServerv4ScopeStatistics`	Get	View IPv4 DHCP scope statistics
`DhcpServerv4Statistics`	Get	View IPv4 DHCP statistics
`DhcpServerv4Superscope`	Remove, Rename, Get, Add	Manage IPv4 DHCP superscopes
`DhcpServerv4Superscope-Statistics`	Get	View IPv4 DHCP superscope statistics
`DhcpServerv6Binding`	Set, Get	Manage the binding of the DHCP server to IPv6 interfaces
`DhcpServerv6Class`	Remove, Set, Get, Add	Manage IPv6 vendor or user classes
`DhcpServerv6DnsSetting`	Get, Set	Configure IPv6 DNS settings at the scope, reservation, or server
`DhcpServerv6ExclusionRange`	Get, Add, Remove	Manage IPv6 exclusions
`DhcpServerv6FreeIPAddress`	Get	Locate free IPv6 addresses
`DhcpServerv6Lease`	Add, Remove, Get	Manage IPv6 leases

CHAPTER 5

Noun	Verbs	Function
DhcpServerv6OptionDefinition	Add, Remove, Get, Set	Manage IPv6 option definitions
DhcpServerv6OptionValue	Set, Remove, Get	Manage IPv6 option values
DhcpServerv6Reservation	Remove, Add, Get, Set	Manage IPv6 DHCP reservations
DhcpServerv6Scope	Remove, Add, Get, Set	Manage IPv6 scope
DhcpServerv6ScopeStatistics	Get	View IPv6 scope statistics
DhcpServerv6StatelessStatistics	Get	View IPv6 stateless statistics
DhcpServerv6StatelessStore	Set, Get	Manage the properties of the stateless store
DhcpServerv6Statistics	Get	View IPv6 server statistics
DhcpServerVersion	Get	View DHCP server version information

IPAM

IPAM allows you to centralize the management of DHCP and DNS servers. Rather than manage each server separately, you can use IPAM to manage them from a single console. You can use a single IPAM server to manage up to 150 separate DHCP servers and up to 500 individual DNS servers. Also, it can manage 6,000 separate DHCP scopes and 150 separate DNS zones. You can perform tasks such as creating address scopes, configuring address reservations, and managing DHCP and DNS options globally instead of having to perform these tasks on a server-by-server basis. IPAM supports both Active Directory and file-based DNS zones. IPAM can also be integrated into System Center Virtual Machine Manager (VMM) and can keep track of VMM IP address pools.

Deploy IPAM

You can only install the IPAM feature on a computer that is a member of an Active Directory domain. You can have multiple IPAM servers within a single Active Directory forest. You are likely to do this if your organization is geographically dispersed. It's important to note that IPAM cannot manage a DHCP or DNS server if the role is installed on the same computer that hosts IPAM. For this reason, you should install the IPAM feature on a server that doesn't host the DNS or DHCP roles. IPAM is also not supported on computers that host the Domain Controller server role. Additionally, if you want to use the IPAM server to manage IPv6 address ranges, you need to ensure that IPv6 is enabled on the computer hosting the IPAM server.

Configure server discovery

Server discovery is the process where the IPAM server checks with Active Directory to locate Domain Controllers, DNS servers, and DHCP servers. You select which domains to discover on the Configure Server Discovery dialog. After you've completed server discovery, you need to run a special PowerShell cmdlet that creates and provisions Group Policy objects that allow these servers to be managed by the IPAM server. When you set up the IPAM server, you choose a GPO name prefix. Use this prefix when executing the `Invoke-IpamGpoProvisioning` Windows PowerShell cmdlet that creates the appropriate GPOs.

If you use the GPO prefix IPAM, the three GPOs are named:

- IPAM_DC_NPS
- IPAM_DHCP
- IPAM_DNS

Until these GPOs apply to the discovered servers, these servers are listed as having an IPAM Access status of blocked. After the GPOs are applied to the discovered servers, the IPAM Access status is set to Unblocked. After the discovered service has an IPAM Access Status set to Unblocked, you can edit the properties of the server and set it to Managed. After you do this, you can use IPAM to manage the selected services on the server.

IPAM supports managing DNS and DHCP servers in forests where a two-way trust relationship has been configured. You perform DHCP and DNS server discovery in a trusted forest on a per-domain basis.

IPAM administration

You can delegate administrative permissions by adding user accounts to one of five local security groups on the IPAM server. By default, members of the Domain Admins and Enterprise Admins groups are able to perform all tasks on the IPAM server. The following local security groups are present on the IPAM server after you deploy the role, and they allow you to delegate the following permissions:

- **DNS Record Administrator** Members of this role can manage DNS resource records.
- **IP Address Record Administrator** Members of this role can manage IP addresses but not address spaces, ranges, subnets, or blocks.
- **IPAM Administrators** Members of this role can perform all tasks on the IPAM server, including viewing IP Address tracking information.
- **IPAM ASM Administrators** ASM stands for Address Space Administrator. Users added to this group can perform all tasks that members of the IPAM Users group can perform,

but they're also able to manage the IP address space. They cannot perform monitoring tasks and are unable to perform IP address tracking tasks.

- **IPAM DHCP Administrator**   Members of this role can manage DHCP servers using IPAM.

- **IPAM DHCP Reservations Administrator**   Members of this role can manage DHCP reservations using IPAM.

- **IPAM DHCP Scope Administrator**   Members of this role can manage DHCP scopes.

- **IPAM MSM Administrators**   MSM stands for Multi-Server-Management. Members of this role can manage all DNS and DHCP servers managed by IPAM.

- **IPAM DNS Administrator**   Members of this role can manage DHCP servers using IPAM.

Managing the IP address space

The benefit of IPAM is that it allows you to manage all the IP addresses in your organization. IPAM supports the management of IPv4 public and private addresses, whether they're statically or dynamically assigned. IPAM allows you to

- Detect whether there are overlapping IP address ranges defined in DHCP scopes on different servers

- Determine IP address utilization and whether there are free IP addresses in a specific range

- Create DHCP reservations centrally without having to configure them on individual DHCP servers

- Create DNS records based on IP address lease information

IPAM separates the IP address space into blocks, ranges, and individual addresses. An IP address block is a large collection of IP addresses that you use to organize the address space that your organization uses at the highest level. An organization might only have one or two address blocks: one for its entire internal network and another smaller block that represents the public IP address space used by the organization. An IP address range is part of an IP address block. An IP address range cannot map to multiple IP address blocks. Generally, an IP address range corresponds to a DHCP scope. An individual IP address maps to a single IP address range. IPAM stores the following information with an IP address:

- Any associated MAC addresses

- How the address is assigned (static/DHCP)

- Assignment date

- Assignment expiration

- Which service manages the IP address

- DNS records associated with the IP address

IP address tracking

One of the most important features of IPAM is its ability to track IP addresses by correlating DHCP leases with user and computer authentication events on managed domain controllers and NPS servers. IP address tracking allows you to figure out which user was associated with a specific IP address at a particular point in time, which can be important when trying to determine the cause of unauthorized activity on the organizational network.

You can search for IP address records using one of the following four parameters:

- **Track by IP address** You can track by IPv4 address, but IPAM doesn't support tracking by IPv6 address.

- **Track by client ID** You can track by client ID in IPAM, which allows you to track IP address activity by MAC address.

- **Track by host name** You can track by the computer's name as registered in DNS.

- **Track by username** You can track a username, but to do this, you must also provide a host name.

Naturally, you can only track data that has been recorded since IPAM has been deployed. So, while it is possible to store several years of data in the Windows Internal Database that IPAM uses, you are limited to only being able to retrieve events recorded after IPAM was configured.

Microsoft estimates that the Windows Internal Database IPAM can store 3 years of IP address utilization data for an organization that has 100,000 users before data must be purged.

You can use IPAM to locate free subnets and IP address ranges in your existing IP address scheme. For example, if you need 50 consecutive free IP addresses for a project, you can use the Find-IpamFreeRange PowerShell cmdlet to determine whether such a range is present in your current environment.

Managing IPAM with PowerShell

You can manage IPAM with Windows PowerShell cmdlets that are contained in the IPAMServer module. Table 5-3 outlines the functionality of these cmdlets.

Table 5-3   IPAM PowerShell cmdlets

Noun	Verbs	Function
IpamAccessScope	Set	Configure an IPAM access scope
IpamAddress	Export, Remove, Get, Import, Add, Set	Use this set of cmdlets to manage IPAM addresses
IpamAddressSpace	Set, Remove, Get, Add	Use this set of cmdlets to manage an IPAM address space
IpamAddressUtilization-Threshold	Set, Get	Configure the IPAM address utilization thresholds
IpamBlock	Remove, Get, Add, Set	Manage IPAM address blocks
IpamCapability	Disable, Get, Enable	Manage optional IPAM capabilities
IpamConfiguration	Set, Get	Manage the configuration of the IPAM server
IpamConfigurationEvent	Get, Remove	View IPAM configuration events stored in the IPAM database
IpamCustomField	Rename, Add, Remove, Get	Manage IPAM custom fields
IpamCustomFieldAssociation	Remove, Add, Set, Get	Configure the association between custom field values
IpamCustomValue	Remove, Add, Rename	Manage values assigned to custom fields in IPAM
IpamDatabase	Move, Get, Set	Manage the IPAM database
IpamDhcpConfigurationEvent	Remove, Get	Manage DHCP configuration events stored in the IPAM database
IpamDhcpScope	Get	View IPAM DHCP scope information
IpamDhcpServer	Get	View IPAM DHCP server information
IpamDhcpSuperscope	Get	View IPAM DHCP superscope information
IpamDiscoveryDomain	Set, Remove, Add, Get	Configure IPAM discovery domains
IpamDnsConditionalForwarder	Get	View information about IPAM DNS conditional forwarders
IpamDnsResourceRecord	Get	View information about IPAM DNS resource records
IpamDnsServer	Get	View information about IPAM DNS servers
IpamDnsZone	Get	View information about IPAM DNS zones

Noun	Verbs	Function
IpamFreeAddress	Find	Locate available IP addresses from the IPAM database
IpamFreeRange	Find	Locate ranges of free IP addresses from the IPAM database
IpamFreeSubnet	Find	Locate free subnets in the IPAM database
IpamGpoProvisioning	Invoke	Configures GPOs necessary to prepare DNS and DHCP servers managed by the IPAM server
IpamIpAddressAuditEvent	Remove, Get	Manage IPAM audit events in the IPAM database
IpamRange	Export, Import, Add, Get, Remove, Set	Manage IPAM IP address ranges
IpamServer	Update	Updates an IPAM server after you update the host server's operating system
IpamServerInventory	Remove, Add, Get, Set	Manage the properties of an infrastructure server stored in the IPAM server inventory
IpamServerProvisioning	Invoke	Use this cmdlet to automate the provisioning of an IPAM server
IpamSubnet	Add, Get, Set, Import, Export, Remove	Manage an IP subnet stored in the IPAM server database
IpamUtilizationData	Remove	Remove existing IPAM IP address utilization information

CHAPTER 5

Hyper-V

Hyper-V is a virtualization platform that is built into Windows Server. Not only can you use Hyper-V to host virtual machines and a special type of containers, but Hyper-V is also integrated into the very fabric of Microsoft's Azure cloud. Hyper-V is also available on the Pro, Enterprise, and Education editions of Windows 11. This means that it's possible to transfer a virtual machine from Windows 11 to Windows Server to Azure and back without needing to alter the virtual machine's format.

In this chapter, we look at many topics, including memory configuration, Generation 2 VMs, nested virtualization, virtual hard disks, replicas and failovers, live migration, storage migration, guarded virtualization fabrics, and shielded virtual machines.

Dynamic memory

You have two options when assigning memory to VMs. You can assign a static amount of memory, or you can configure dynamic memory. When you assign a static amount of memory, the amount of memory assigned to the VM remains the same, whether the VM is starting up, it is currently running, or it is in the process of shutting down.

When you configure dynamic memory, you can configure the following values in Windows Admin Center (WAC):

- **Startup Memory**   This is the amount of memory allocated to the VM during startup. This can be the same as the minimum amount of memory, or it can be as large as the maximum amount of allocated memory. Once the VM has started, it will instead use the amount of memory configured as the Minimum Memory.

- **Minimum Memory**   This is the minimum amount of memory that the VM will be assigned by the virtualization host when dynamic memory is enabled. When multiple VMs are demanding memory, Hyper-V may reallocate memory away from the VM until the Minimum Memory value is met. You can reduce the Minimum Memory setting while the VM is running, but you cannot increase it while the VM is running.

- **Maximum Memory**   This is the maximum amount of memory that the VM will be allocated by the virtualization host when dynamic memory is enabled. You can increase the Maximum Memory setting while the VM is running, but you cannot decrease it while the VM is running.

- **Memory Buffer**   This is the percentage of memory that Hyper-V should allocate to the VM as a buffer.

- **Memory Weight**   This setting allows you to configure how memory should be allocated to this particular VM as compared to other VMs running on the same virtualization host.

Generally, when you configure dynamic memory, the amount of memory used by a VM will fluctuate between the Minimum Memory and Maximum Memory values. You should monitor VM memory utilization and tune these values so that they accurately represent the VM's actual requirements. If you allocate a Minimum Memory value below what the VM would actually need to run, this shortage might cause the virtualization host to reduce the amount of memory allocated to this Minimum Memory value, which will cause the VM to stop running.

Hot Add Memory allows you to alter the memory allocation of a running VM that is not configured to use Dynamic Memory. Hot-add of memory in HyperV requires the host to be Windows Server 2016 or later, and where the VM's configuration version is at version 8.0 or later. You can modify the memory of Generation 1 or Generation 2 VMs. vNUMA is supported with runtime memory resize. You can hot-add memory by performing the following steps:

1. Open the VM settings in Hyper-V Manager while the VM is running. In the Settings dialog, select the Memory section. You will see the VM's current Assigned Memory and the configuration for Startup RAM.

2. Increase the memory value to the desired amount. For example, if the VM is currently assigned 4 GB and you want to add 2 GB more, change the value to 6,144 MB. Click Apply. HyperV will immediately allocate the additional RAM to the VM.

3. Verify inside the guest OS that the memory was added.

To hot-remove memory, follow a similar process:

- The guest OS will relinquish the specified memory down to a minimum of 1 GB.

- Always ensure the guest actually can give up that memory.

- If the RAM is heavily in use or the OS doesn't support removal, the operation will fail.

Smart paging

Smart paging is a special technology in Hyper-V that functions under certain conditions when a VM is restarting. Smart paging uses a file on the disk to simulate memory to meet Startup Memory requirements when the Startup Memory setting exceeds the Minimum Memory setting. Startup Memory is the amount of memory allocated to the VM when it starts, but not when it's running. For example, you could set Startup Memory to 2,048 MB and the Minimum Memory to 512 MB for a specific virtual machine. In a scenario where 1,024 MB of free memory was available on the virtualization host, smart paging would allow the VM to access the required 2,048 MB of memory.

Because it uses storage to simulate memory, smart paging is only active if the following three conditions occur at the same time:

- The VM is being restarted.

- There is not enough memory on the virtualization host to meet the Startup Memory setting.

- Memory cannot be reclaimed from other VMs running on the same host.

Smart paging doesn't allow a VM to perform a "cold start" if the required amount of Startup Memory is not available, but the Minimum Memory amount is available. Smart paging is only used when a VM that was already running restarts and the preceding three conditions have been met.

CHAPTER 6

You can configure the location of the smart paging file on a per-VM basis. By default, smart paging files are written to the `C:\ProgramData\Microsoft\Windows\Hyper-V` folder. The smart paging file is created only when needed and is deleted within 10 minutes of the VM restarting.

Resource metering

Resource metering allows you to track the consumption of processor, disk, memory, and network resources by individual VMs. To enable resource metering, use the `Enable-VMResource-Metering` Windows PowerShell cmdlet. You can view metering data using the `Measure-VM` Windows PowerShell cmdlet. Resource metering allows you to record the following information:

- Average CPU use

- Average memory use

- Minimum memory use

- Maximum memory use

- Maximum disk allocation

- Incoming network traffic

- Outgoing network traffic

Average CPU use is measured in megahertz (MHz). All other metrics are measured in megabytes. Although you can extract data using the `Measure-VM` cmdlet, you need to use another solution to output this data into a visual form, such as a graph.

Guest integration services

Integration services allow the virtualization host to extract information and perform operations on a hosted VM. By default, Windows Server and the Pro, Enterprise, and Education editions of Windows Client include Hyper-V integration services. If you're running a Linux guest VM on your Hyper-V Server, you can download the Linux Integration Services for Hyper-V and Azure from Microsoft's website. Integration services installation files are available for all operating systems that are supported on Hyper-V. You can enable the following integration services:

- **Operating System Shutdown**   This integration service allows you to shut down the VM from the virtualization host, rather than from within the VM's OS.

- **Time Synchronization**   Synchronizes the virtualization host's clock with the VM's clock. Ensures that the VM clock doesn't drift when the VM is started, stopped, or reverted to a checkpoint.

- **Data Exchange**   Allows the virtualization host to read and modify specific VM registry values.

- **Heartbeat**   Allows the virtualization host to verify that the VM OS is still functioning and responding to requests.

- **Backup (Volume Checkpoint)**   For VMs that support Volume Shadow Copy, this service synchronizes with the virtualization host, allowing backups of the VM while the VM is in operation.

- **Guest Services**   Guest services allow you to copy files from the virtualization host to the VM using the Copy-VMFile Windows PowerShell cmdlet.

Generation 2 VMs

Generation 2 VMs are a special type of VM that differs in configuration from the VMs that are now termed "Generation 1 VMs," which could be created on Hyper-V virtualization hosts running the Windows Server 2008, Windows Server 2008 R2, and Windows Server 2012 operating systems. Generation 2 VMs are supported on Windows Server 2012 R2 and later operating systems. Generation 2 VMs are also now supported in Azure.

Generation 2 VMs provide the following functionality:

- Can boot from a SCSI virtual hard disk

- Can boot from a SCSI virtual DVD

- Supports UEFI firmware on the VM

- Supports VM Secure Boot

- Support virtual TPM (vTPM)

- PXE boot using a standard network adapter

There are no legacy network adapters with Generation 2 VMs, and the majority of legacy devices, such as COM ports and the diskette drive, are no longer present. Generation 2 VMs are "virtual first" and are not designed to simulate hardware for computers that have undergone physical-to-virtual (P2V) conversion. If you need to deploy a VM that requires an emulated component such as a COM port, you'll need to deploy a Generation 1 VM.

You configure the generation of a VM during the VM creation. Once a VM is created, Hyper-V doesn't allow you to modify the VM's generation. Windows Server 2016 and later support both Generation 1 and Generation 2 VMs.

CHAPTER 6

Generation 2 VMs boot more quickly and allow the installation of operating systems more quickly than Generation 1 VMs. Generation 2 VMs have the following limitations:

- You can only use Generation 2 VMs if the guest operating system is running an x64 version of Windows 10 or later client operating systems and Windows Server 2012 R2 or later operating systems.

- Generation 2 VMs only support virtual hard disks in VHDX format.

Enhanced Session Mode

Enhanced Session Mode allows you to perform actions, including cutting and pasting, audio redirection, and volume and device mapping when using Virtual Machine Connection windows. You can also sign in to a VM with a smart card through Enhanced Session Mode. You enable Enhanced Session Mode on the Hyper-V server by selecting Allow Enhanced Session Mode in the Enhanced Session Mode Policy section of the Hyper-V server's Properties dialog.

You can only use Enhanced Session Mode with Windows Server 2012 R2 and later guest VMs and Windows 10 and later guest VMs. To utilize Enhanced Session Mode, you must have permission to connect to the VM using Remote Desktop through the account you use to sign in to the guest VM. You can grant permission to the VM by adding the user to the Remote Desktop Users group. A user who is a member of the local Administrators group also has this permission. The Remote Desktop Services service must be running on the guest VM.

Discrete Device Assignment

Discrete Device Assignment (DDA) is available in Windows Server 2016 and later and allows you to directly assign a physical GPU or an NVMe storage device to a specific virtual machine. Each physical GPU or NVMe storage device can only be associated with one VM. DDA involves installing the device's native driver in the VM associated with that GPU. This process works for both Windows and Linux VMs as long as the drivers are available for the VM's operating system. DDA is supported for Generation 1 or 2 VMs running Windows Server 2012 R2 or later, Windows 10, and some Linux guest operating systems.

Before assigning the physical GPU or storage device to a specific VM, you need to dismount the device from the Hyper-V host. Some device vendors provide partitioning drivers for the Hyper-V host. Partitioning drivers are different from the standard device drivers and improve the security of the DDA configuration. If a partitioning driver is available, you should install this driver prior to dismounting the device from the Hyper-V host. If no driver is available, you'll have to use the -Force option with the Dismount-VMHostAssignableDevice cmdlet.

Once you've dismounted the physical device from the Hyper-V host, you can assign it to a specific guest VM using the Add-VMAssignableDevice cmdlet.

Enabling DDA requires that you disable the VM's automatic stop action. You can do this using the following command:

```
Set-VM -Name VMName -AutomaticStopAction TurnOff
```

In addition to disabling the automatic stop action, the following functionality is also not available to VMs configured with DDA:

- VM Save and Restore
- VM live migration
- Use of dynamic memory
- Deployment of a VM to a high-availability cluster

CHAPTER 6

More Info

Direct Device Assignment

You can learn more about Direct Device Assignment at *https://learn.microsoft.com/windows-server/virtualization/hyper-v/plan/plan-for-deploying-devices-using-discrete-device-assignment*.

Inside OUT

RemoteFX

RemoteFX is a technology available in Windows Server 2016 that performs a similar function to Discrete Device Assignment. RemoteFX provides a 3D virtual adapter and USB redirection support for VMs. You can only use RemoteFX if the virtualization host has a compatible GPU. RemoteFX allows one or more compatible graphics adapters to perform graphics processing tasks for multiple VMs. Like Discrete Device Assignment, you can use RemoteFX to provide support for graphically intensive applications, such as CAD, in VDI scenarios. RemoteFX is not available in Windows Server 2019 and later versions, in favor of DDA.

GPU partitioning

GPU Partitioning (GPU-P) is a feature in Windows Server 2025 Hyper-V that allows multiple virtual machines to share a single physical GPU by dividing it into isolated fractions. Each VM can be allocated a dedicated fraction of the GPU's resources instead of being allocated the entire GPU. When you use GPU-P, each VM is only able to access its allocated GPU partition.

When you configure Discrete Device Assignment (DDA), you allocate an entire physical GPU exclusively to one VM. GPU-P allows higher utilization and VM density for graphics or compute workloads compared to DDA, which provides maximum performance for a single VM.

GPU-P supports live VM migration and failover clustering. VMs configured with DDA VMs are unable to live-migrate and must be shut down when moved to another host. GPU Partitioning in Windows Server 2025 is only supported on select GPU hardware. These GPUs are specialized, and you are unable to use a retail gaming GPU with GPU-P.

GPU-P requires the following:

- **CPU with IOMMU**   The host processors must support Intel VT-d or AMD-Vi with DMA remapping (IOMMU). This is crucial for mapping device memory securely between the host and VMs.

- **BIOS Settings**   Ensure that in each host's UEFI/BIOS, Intel VT-d/AMD-Vi, and SR-IOV are enabled.

- **Host GPU Drivers**   Use vendor-provided drivers that support GPU virtualization. Microsoft advises following the GPU vendor's documentation for installation.

- **Guest VM Drivers**   The guest VMs also need appropriate GPU drivers installed (within the VM's OS) to make use of the virtual GPU.

After hardware setup and driver installation, it's important to verify that the host recognizes the GPU as "partitionable." You can check this with PowerShell with the following command:

```
Get-VMHostPartitionableGpu | FL Name, ValidPartitionCounts, PartitionCount
```

This will list each GPU device's identifier and what partition counts it supports. The `ValidPartitionCounts` values are the only partition sizes you can choose from. For example, a result might show a device with {16, 8, 4, 2}— meaning the GPU can be split into 2, 4, 8, or 16 virtual GPUs.

If no GPUs are listed, or the list is empty, the GPU is not recognized as partitionable. If the GPU is listed but ValidPartitionCounts is blank or shows only "1," then it might not support SR-IOV and can only be used via DDA.

When using GPU-P with a VM, each physical GPU must be configured with a partition count. You can allocate all partitions to a VM, though you could just use DDA in that scenario. To partition a GPU-P-capable GPU before assigning those GPU partitions to individual VMs:

1. Run the `Set-VMHostPartitionableGpu` cmdlet. Provide the GPU's device ID (from the Name field of the earlier `Get-VMHostPartitionableGpu` output) and the desired `-PartitionCount`:

```
Set-VMHostPartitionableGpu -Name "<GPU-device-ID>" -PartitionCount 4
```

2. Verify the setting by running `Get-VMHostPartitionableGpu | FL Name,PartitionCount` again. It should now show the PartitionCount set to your chosen value (for example, PartitionCount : 4 for each listed GPU).

You can also configure the partition count via the WAC GUI. In WAC's GPU partitions tool, select the GPU and choose Configure Partition Count. WAC will present a dropdown of valid partition counts. Selecting a number will show a tooltip showing how much VRAM each partition would have. WAC helps ensure that you apply the change to all similar GPUs in the cluster. After applying the changes, it will update the partition count on each host automatically.

With the GPU partitioned at the host level, the next step is to attach a GPU partition to a VM. This is analogous to plugging a virtual GPU device into the VM. Each VM can have at most one GPU partition device attached. To add the GPU Partition to the VM, use the `Add-VMGpuPartitionAdapter` cmdlet to attach a partitioned GPU to the VM:

```
Add-VMGpuPartitionAdapter -VMName "<VMName>"
```

This will allocate one of the available GPU partitions on the host to the specified VM. There is no parameter to specify which partition or GPU. Hyper-V will auto-select an available partition from a compatible GPU. If no partition is free or the host GPUs aren't partitioned, this cmdlet will return an error.

You can check that the VM has a GPU partition attached by running:

```
Get-VMGpuPartitionAdapter -VMName "<VMName>" | FL InstancePath,PartitionId
```

This will show details like the GPU device instance path and a PartitionId for the VM's GPU device. Once the GPU partition is attached, you can start the VM, and the VM's OS will detect a new display adapter. You can then install and configure the appropriate GPU driver inside the VM.

VM resource groups

Instead of instituting resource constraints on a per-virtual machine basis, virtual machine resource controls allow you to create groups of virtual machines where each group is allocated a different proportion of the Hyper-V host's total CPU resources. For example, you can have a group of six virtual machines used by a specific department that are limited to a specific pro-portion of the Hyper-V host's CPU capacity that they cannot exceed. VM resource groups also allow you to limit what resources the Hyper-V host can use; for example, you can configure that the Hyper-V host has a limit on processor and memory use that can't be exceeded, which would limit the processor and memory available to VMs.

VM CPU groups

VM CPU groups allow you to isolate VM groups to specific host processors; for example, on a multiprocessor Hyper-V host, you might choose to allow a group of VMs exclusive access to specific processor cores. This can be useful in scenarios where you must ensure that different VMs are partitioned from one another, with Hyper-V network virtualization providing com-pletely separate tenant networks and VM CPU groups, ensuring that separate VM groups never share the same physical CPUs.

CPU groups are managed through the Hyper-V Host Compute Service (HCS). You cannot directly manage CPU groups through PowerShell or the Hyper-V console and instead need to download the cpugroups.exe command-line utility from the Microsoft Download Center.

> ## More Info
>
> *Hyper-V CPU groups*
>
> **You can learn more about Hyper-V CPU groups at *https://learn.microsoft.com/windows-server/virtualization/hyper-v/manage/manage-hyper-v-cpugroups*.**

Hypervisor scheduling types

Hyper-V supports a "classic" scheduler and a newer Hypervisor core scheduler. The differences between them are as follows:

- **Classic scheduler**   Uses a fair-share round-robin method of scheduling processor tasks across the Hyper-V host, including processors used by the host and those used by guest VMs. The classic scheduler is the default type used on all versions of Hyper-V until Win-dows Server 2019. When used on a host with Symmetric Multi-Threading (SMT) enabled, the classic scheduler will schedule guest virtual processors from any VM running on the host so that one VM runs on an SMT processor core thread while another VM runs on another SMT thread of the same processor core.

- **Core scheduler**   The core scheduler uses SMT to ensure isolation of guest workloads. This means that a CPU core is never shared between VMs, which is not the case if SMT is enabled and the classic scheduler is used. The core scheduler ensures a strong security boundary for guest workload isolation. It also allows the use of SMT within guest VMs, allowing programming interfaces to control and distribute tasks across SMT threads. By default, Windows Server 2019 and later versions of Hyper-V use the core scheduler. New virtual machines created using VM version 9.0 or later will inherit the SMT properties of the physical host. VMs that may have been migrated to Windows Server 2019 or later and have been updated to VM version 9.0 or later will need to have SMT enabled in their settings using the `Set-VMProcessor` cmdlet with the `HWThreadCountPerCore` parameter.

More Info

Hyper-V scheduling types

You can learn more about Hyper-V scheduling types at *https://learn. microsoft.com/windows-server/virtualization/hyper-v/manage/ about-hyper-v-scheduler-type-selection*.

Nested virtualization

Hyper-V on Windows Server 2016 and later supports nested virtualization, which allows you to enable Hyper-V and host virtual machines within a virtual machine running under Hyper-V as long as that VM is running Windows Server 2016 or later.

Nested virtualization is generally enabled when you install the Hyper-V role, but some advanced features require you to run the following command on the Hyper-V host before enabling nested virtualization on its guest VMs.

```
bcdedit /set Hypervisorlaunchtype auto
```

Nested virtualization can be enabled on a per-VM basis by running the following PowerShell command:

```
Set-VMProcessor -VMName NameOfVM -ExposeVirtualiationExtensions $true
```

Nested virtualization dynamic memory

Once you've run this command, you'll be able to enable Hyper-V on the VM. You won't be able to adjust the memory of a virtual machine that is enabled for nested virtualization while that virtual machine is running. While it is possible to enable dynamic memory, the amount of memory allocated to a virtual machine configured for nested virtualization will not fluctuate while the VM is running.

Nested virtualization networking

To route network packets through the multiple virtual switches required during nested virtualization, you can either enable MAC address spoofing or configure network address translation (NAT). To enable MAC address spoofing on the virtual machine that you have configured for nested virtualization, run the following PowerShell command:

```
Get-VMNetworkAdapter -VMName NameOfVM | Set-VMNEtworkAdapter -MacAddressSpoofing On
```

To enable NAT, create a virtual NAT switch in the VM that has been enabled for nested virtualization using the following PowerShell commands:

```
New-VMSwitch -name VMNAT -SwitchTypeInternal
New-NetNAT -Name LocalNAT -InternalIPInterfaceAddressPrefix "192.168.15.0/24"
Get-NetAdapter "vEthernet (VmNat)" | New-NetIPAddress -IPAddress 192.168.15.1
-AddressFamily IPv4 -PrefixLength 24
```

Once you've done this, you'll need to manually assign IP addresses to VMs running under the VM enabled for nested virtualization, using the default gateway of 192.168.15.1. You can use a separate internal addressing scheme other than 192.168.15.0/24 by altering the appropriate PowerShell commands in the preceding example.

> ## More Info
>
> *Nested Virtualization*
>
> **You can learn more about Hyper-V nested virtualization at *https://learn.microsoft.com/ virtualization/hyper-v-on-windows/user-guide/nested-virtualization*.**

PowerShell Direct

PowerShell Direct allows you to create a remote PowerShell session directly from a Hyper-V host to a virtual machine hosted on that Hyper-V host without requiring the virtual machine to be configured with a network connection. PowerShell Direct requires that both the Hyper-V host and the VM be running Windows Server 2016 or later or Windows 10 or later.

To use PowerShell Direct, you must be signed in locally to the Hyper-V host with Hyper-V Administrator privileges. You also must have access to valid credentials for the virtual machine. If you do not have credentials for the virtual machine, you will not be able to establish a Power-Shell Direct connection.

To establish a PowerShell Direct connection, use this command:

```
Enter-PSSession -vmname NameOfVM
```

You exit the PowerShell Direct session by using the Exit-PSSession cmdlet.

> ## More Info
> ### PowerShell Direct
> You can learn more about PowerShell Direct at *https://learn.microsoft.com/en-us/virtualization/hyper-v-on-windows/user-guide/powershell-direct*.

HVC for Linux

HVC.exe, which is included with Windows Server 2019 and later, allows you to make a remote SSH connection from a Hyper-V host to a Linux virtual machine guest without requiring the Linux VM to have a functioning network connection. It provides similar functionality to PowerShell Direct. For HVC.exe to work, you'll need to ensure that the Linux virtual machine has an updated kernel and that the Linux integration services are installed. You'll also need the SSH server on the Linux VM to be installed and configured before you'll be able to use HVC.exe to initiate an SSH connection.

Virtual hard disks

Hyper-V supports two separate virtual hard disk formats. Virtual hard disk files in .vhd format are limited to 2,040 GB. Virtual hard disks in this format can be used on all supported versions of Hyper-V. Other than the size limitation, the important thing to remember is that you cannot use virtual hard disk files in .vhd format with Generation 2 VMs. Windows Server 2025 allows you to attach up to 256 disks per VM across 4 SCSI controllers.

Virtual hard disk files in .vhdx format are an improvement over virtual hard disks in .vhd format. The main limitation of virtual hard disks in .vhdx format is that they cannot be used with Hyper-V on Windows Server 2008 or Windows Server 2008 R2, which shouldn't be as much of a problem now as these operating systems no longer have mainstream support. Virtual hard disks in .vhdx format have the following benefits:

- Can be up to 64 TB in size

- Has a larger block size for dynamic and differential disks

- Provides 4 KB logical sector virtual disks

- Has an internal log that reduces the chance of corruption

- Supports trim to reclaim unused space

CHAPTER 6

You can convert hard disks between .vhd and .vhdx format. You can create virtual hard disks at the time you create the VM by using the New Virtual Hard Disk Wizard or the New-VHD Windows PowerShell cmdlet.

Fixed-size disks

Virtual hard disks can be dynamic, differencing, or fixed. When you create a fixed-size disk, all space used by the disk is allocated on the hosting volume at the time of creation. Fixed disks increase performance if the physical storage medium does not support Windows Offloaded Data Transfer. Improvements in Windows Server reduce the performance benefit of fixed-size disks when the storage medium supports Windows Offloaded Data Transfer. The space to be allocated to the disk must be present on the host volume when you create the disk. For example, you can't create a 3 TB fixed disk on a volume that only has 2 TB of space.

Dynamically expanding disks

Dynamically expanding disks use an initial small file and then grow as the VM allocates data to the virtual hard disk. This means you can create a 3 TB dynamic virtual hard disk on a 2 TB volume because the entire 3 TB will not be allocated at disk creation. However, in this scenario, you would need to ensure that you extend the size of the 2 TB volume before the dynamic virtual disk outgrows the available storage space.

Differencing disks

Differencing disks are a special type of virtual hard disk that have a child relationship with a parent hard disk. Parent disks can be fixed-size or dynamic virtual hard disks, but the differencing disk must be the same type as the parent disk. For example, you *can* create a differencing disk in .vhdx format for a parent disk that uses .vhdx format, but you *cannot* create a differencing disk in .vhd format for a parent disk in .vhdx format.

Differencing disks record the changes that would otherwise be made to the parent hard disk by the VM. For example, differencing disks are used to record Hyper-V VM checkpoints. One parent virtual hard disk can have multiple differencing disks associated with it.

For example, you can create a specially prepared parent virtual hard disk by installing Windows Server on a VM by running the sysprep utility within the VM and then shutting the VM down. You can use the virtual hard disk created by this process as a parent virtual hard disk. In this scenario, when you create new Windows Server VMs, you would configure the VMs to use a new differencing disk that uses the sysprepped virtual hard disk as a parent. When you run the new VM, it will write any changes that it would normally make to the full virtual hard disk to the differencing disk. In this scenario, deploying new Windows Server VMs becomes a simple matter of creating new VMs that use a differencing disk that uses the sysprepped Windows Server virtual hard disk as a parent.

You can create differencing hard disks using the New Virtual Hard Disk Wizard or the New-VHD Windows PowerShell cmdlet. You need to specify the parent disk during the creation process.

The key to using differencing disks is to ensure that you don't make changes to the parent disk; doing so will invalidate the relationship with any child disks. Generally, differencing disks can provide storage efficiencies because the only changes are recorded on child disks. For example, rather than storing 10 different instances of Windows Server 2019 in its entirety, you could create one parent disk and have 10 much smaller differencing disks to accomplish the same objective. If you store VM virtual hard disks on a volume that has been deduplicated, these efficiencies are reduced.

Hot-add virtual hard disks

Any virtual disk on a SCSI controller can be added or removed while the VM is running. This applies to both Generation 1 and Generation 2 VMs, because both support SCSI controllers for data drives. The key requirement is that the VM has an available SCSI controller. Hyper-V VMs can have up to four SCSI controllers, each supporting up to 64 devices and an available slot on one. To hot-add a disk, use the following steps:

1. In Hyper V Manager, open Settings for the running VM. Under one of the SCSI Controller entries in the hardware list, click Hard Drive and then click Add.

2. In the Hard Drive settings, choose an existing Virtual Hard Disk or create a New one. Click Apply/OK to attach the disk to the VM. The new virtual disk will be connected to the VM's SCSI controller on the next available location.

3. Inside the VM's guest OS, bring the new disk online. On Windows, you can do this in Disk Management. In Linux, use commands like `fdisk -l` or `lsblk` to see the new drive, and then create a file system and mount it as needed.

To remove a virtual disk on the fly, in the VM's Settings, select the hard disk in question, and click Remove. Make sure you prepare for safe removal at the OS level if applicable. Linux typically requires unmounting volumes before removal.

Modifying virtual hard disks

You can perform the following tasks to modify existing virtual hard disks:

- Convert a virtual hard disk from `.vhd` to `.vhdx` format

- Convert a virtual hard disk from `.vhdx` to `.vhd` format

- Change the disk from fixed size to dynamically expanding or from dynamically expanding to fixed size

- Shrink or enlarge the virtual hard disk

CHAPTER 6

You convert virtual hard disk type (.vhd to .vhdx, .vhdx to .vhd, dynamic to fixed, or fixed to dynamic) either using the Edit Virtual Hard Disk Wizard or the Convert-VHD Windows Power-Shell cmdlet. When converting from .vhdx to .vhd, remember that virtual hard disks in .vhd format cannot exceed 2,040 GB in size. So, while it is possible to convert virtual hard disks in .vhdx format that are smaller than 2,040 GB to .vhd format, you will not be able to convert virtual hard disks that are larger than 2,040 GB.

You can only perform conversions from one format to another and from one type to another while the VM is powered off. You must shrink the virtual hard disk using the disk manager in the VM operating system prior to shrinking the virtual hard disk using the Edit Virtual Hard Disk Wizard or the Resize-VHD cmdlet. You can resize a virtual hard disk while the VM is running under the following conditions:

- The virtual hard disk is in .vhdx format.
- The virtual hard disk is attached to a virtual SCSI controller.
- The virtual hard disk must have been shrunk. Prior to shrinking the virtual hard disk, you must shrink the virtual hard disk using the disk manager in the host operating system using the Edit Virtual Hard Disk Wizard or the Resize-VHD cmdlet.

Pass-through disks

Pass-through disks, also known as directly attached disks, allow a VM to directly access the underlying storage rather than accessing a virtual hard disk that resides on that storage. For example, with Hyper-V, you normally connect a VM to a virtual hard disk file hosted on a volume formatted with NTFS or ReFS. With pass-through disks, the VM instead accesses the disk directly, and there is no virtual hard disk file.

Pass-through disks allow VMs to access larger volumes than are possible when using virtual hard disks in .vhd format. In earlier versions of Hyper-V—such as the version available with Windows Server 2008—pass-through disks provide performance advantages over virtual hard disks. The need for pass-through disks has diminished with the availability of virtual hard disks in .vhdx format because .vhdx format allows you to create much larger volumes.

Pass-through disks can be directly attached to the virtualization host, or they can be attached to Fibre Channel or iSCSI disks. When adding a pass-through disk, you will need to ensure that the disk is offline. You can use the Disk Management console or the diskpart.exe utility on the virtualization host to set a disk to be offline.

To add a pass-through disk using Windows PowerShell, use the Get-Disk cmdlet to get the properties of the disk that you want to add as a pass-through disk. Next, pipe the result to the Add-VMHardDiskDrive cmdlet. For example, to add physical disk 3 to the VM named Alpha-Test, execute the following command:

```
Get-Disk 3 | Add-VMHardDiskDrive -VMName Alpha-Test
```

A VM that uses pass-through disks will not support VM checkpoints. Pass-through disks also cannot be backed up with backup programs that use the Hyper-V VSS writer.

Managing checkpoints

Checkpoints represent the state of a VM at a particular point in time. You can create checkpoints when the VM is running or when the VM is shut down. When you create a checkpoint of a running VM, the running VM's memory state is also stored in the checkpoint. Restoring a checkpoint taken of a running VM returns the running VM to a restored state. Creating a checkpoint creates either an .avhd or .avhdx file (depending on whether the VM is using virtual hard disks in the VHD or VHDx format).

Windows Server 2016 and later support two types of checkpoints:

- **Standard checkpoints**   These function just as checkpoints have functioned in previous versions of Hyper-V. These checkpoints capture the state, date, and hardware configuration of a virtual machine. They're designed for development and test scenarios.

- **Production checkpoints**   Available only in Windows Server 2016 and later, production checkpoints use backup technology inside the guest as opposed to the saved-state technology used in standard checkpoints. Production checkpoints are fully supported by Microsoft and can be used with production workloads, which is something that was not supported with the standard version of checkpoints available in previous versions of Hyper-V.

You can switch between standard and production checkpoints on a per-virtual machine basis by editing the Properties of the virtual machine; in the Management section of the Properties dialog, choose between Production and Standard checkpoints.

You can create checkpoints from Windows PowerShell with the Checkpoint-VM cmdlet. The other checkpoint-related Windows PowerShell cmdlets in Windows Server actually use the VMSnapshot noun, though on Windows 10, they confusingly have aliases for the VMCheckPoint noun.

The Windows Server checkpoint-related cmdlets are as follows:

- Restore-VMSnapshot   Restores an existing VM checkpoint.

- Export-VMSnapshot   Allows you to export the state of a VM as it exists when a particular checkpoint was taken. For example, if you took checkpoints at 2 PM and 3 PM, you could choose to export the checkpoint taken at 2 PM and then import the VM in the state that it was in at 2 PM on another Hyper-V host.

- Get-VMSnapshot   Lists the current checkpoints.

- `Rename-VMSnapshot`   Allows you to rename an existing VM checkpoint.

- `Remove-VMSnapshot`   Deletes a VM checkpoint. If the VM checkpoint is part of the chain but not the final link, changes are merged with the successive checkpoint, so that the checkpoint remains a representation of the VM at the point in time when the snapshot was taken. For example, if checkpoints were taken at 1 PM, 2 PM, and 3 PM, and you delete the 2 PM checkpoint, the `.avhd` and `.avhdx` files associated with the 2 PM snapshot would be merged with the `.avhd` and `.avhdx` files associated with the 3 PM snapshot, so that the 3 PM snapshot retains its integrity.

Checkpoints do not replace backups. Checkpoints are almost always stored on the same volume as the original VM hard disks, so a failure of that volume will result in all VM storage files being lost—including both original disks and checkpoint disks. If a disk in a checkpoint chain becomes corrupted, then that checkpoint and all subsequent checkpoints will be lost. Disks earlier in the checkpoint chain will remain unaffected. Hyper-V supports a maximum of 50 checkpoints per VM.

Virtual Fibre Channel adapters

Virtual Fibre Channel allows you to make direct connections from VMs running on Hyper-V to Fibre Channel storage. Virtual Fibre Channel has the following requirements:

- The computer functioning as the Hyper-V virtualization host must have a Fibre Channel host bus adapter (HBA) that has a driver that supports virtual Fibre Channel.

- SAN must be NPIV (N_Port ID) enabled.

- The VM must be running a supported version of the guest operating system.

- Virtual Fibre Channel LUNs cannot be used to boot Hyper-V VMs

VMs running on Hyper-V support up to four virtual Fibre Channel adapters, each of which can be associated with a separate Storage Area Network (SAN).

Before you can use a virtual Fibre Channel adapter, you will need to create at least one virtual SAN on the Hyper-V virtualization host. A virtual SAN is a group of physical Fibre Channel ports that connect to the same SAN.

VM live migration and VM failover clusters are supported; however, virtual Fibre Channel does not support VM checkpoints, host-based backup, or live migration of SAN data.

Storage QoS

Storage Quality of Service (QoS) allows you to limit the maximum number of IOPS (input/output operations per second) for virtual hard disks. IOPS are measured in 8 KB increments. If you specify a maximum IOPS value, the virtual hard disk will be unable to exceed this value. You use Storage QoS to ensure that no single workload on a Hyper-V virtualization host consumes a disproportionate amount of storage resources.

It's also possible to specify a minimum IOPS value for each virtual hard disk. You would do this if you wanted to be notified that a specific virtual hard disk's IOPS has fallen below a threshold value. When the number of IOPS falls below the specified minimum, an event is written to the event log. You configure Storage QoS on a per-virtual hard disk basis.

Hyper-V storage optimization

Several technologies built into Windows Server allow you to optimize the performance and data storage requirements for files associated with VMs.

Deduplication

In Windows Server 2019 and later, both ReFS and NTFS volumes support deduplication (on Windows Server 2016, only NTFS supports deduplication). Deduplication is a process by which duplicate instances of data are removed from a volume and replaced with pointers to the original instance. Deduplication is especially effective when used with volumes that host virtual hard disk files because many of these files contain duplicate copies of data, such as the VM's operating system and program files.

Once installed, you can enable deduplication through the Volumes node of the File And Storage Services section of the Server Manager Console. When enabling deduplication, you specify whether you want to use a general file server data deduplication scheme or a virtual desktop infrastructure scheme. For volumes that host VM files, the VDI scheme is appropriate. You can't enable deduplication on the operating system volume; deduplication may only be enabled on data volumes. For this reason, remember to store VM configuration files and hard disks on a volume that is separate from the operating system volume.

Storage tiering

Storage tiering is a technology that allows you to mix fast storage, such as solid-state disk (SSD), with traditional spinning magnetic disks to optimize both storage performance and capacity. Storage tiering works on the premise that a minority of the data stored on a volume is responsible for the majority of read and write operations. Storage tiering can be enabled through the storage spaces functionality, and rather than creating a large volume that consists entirely of SSDs, you create a volume comprised of both solid-state and spinning magnetic disks. In this configuration, frequently accessed data is moved to the parts of the volume hosted on the SSDs, and less frequently accessed data is moved to the parts of the volume hosted on the slower spinning magnetic disks. This configuration allows many of the performance benefits of an SSD-only volume to be realized without the cost of using SSD-only storage.

When used in conjunction with deduplication, frequently accessed deduplicated data is moved to the faster storage, providing reduced storage requirements while improving performance over what would be possible if the volume hosting VM files were solely comprised of spinning magnetic disks. You also have the option of pinning specific files to the faster storage, which overrides the algorithms that move data according to accumulated utilization statistics. You configure storage tiering using Windows PowerShell.

Hyper-V virtual switches

Hyper-V virtual switches, called Hyper-V virtual networks in previous versions of Hyper-V, represent network connections to which the Hyper-V virtual network adapters can connect. You can configure three types of Hyper-V virtual switches: external switches, internal switches, and private switches. Windows Server 2025 supports individual VMs with up to 68 virtual NICs.

External switches

An external switch connects to a physical or wireless network adapter. Only one virtual switch can be mapped to a specific physical or wireless network adapter or NIC team. For example, if a virtualization host had four physical network adapters configured as two separate NIC teams, you could configure two external virtual switches. If a virtualization host had three physical network adapters that did not participate in any NIC teams, you could configure three external virtual switches. VMs connected to the same external switch can communicate with each other as well as external hosts connected to the network to which the network adapter mapped to the external switch is connected. For example, if an external switch is connected to a network adapter that is connected to a network that can route traffic to the Internet, a VM connected to that external virtual switch will also be able to connect to hosts on the Internet. When you create an external switch, a virtual network adapter that maps to this switch is created on the virtualization host unless you clear the option that allows the management operating system to share the network adapter. If you clear this option, the virtualization host will not be able to communicate through the network adapter associated with the external switch.

Internal switches

An internal switch allows communication between the VM and the virtualization host. All VMs connected to the same internal switch can communicate with each other and the virtualization host. For example, you could successfully initiate an RDP connection from the virtualization host to an appropriately configured VM or use the `Test-NetConnection` Windows PowerShell cmdlet from a Windows PowerShell prompt on the virtualization host to get a response from a VM connected to an internal network connection. VMs connected to an internal switch are unable to use that virtual switch to communicate with hosts on a separate virtualization host that is connected to an internal switch with the same name.

Private switches

VMs connected to the same private switch on a VM host can communicate with one another, but they cannot communicate directly with the virtualization host. Private switches only allow communication between VMs on the same virtualization host. For example, VMs alpha and beta are connected to private switch p_switch_a on virtualization host h_v_one. VM gamma is connected to private switch p_switch_a on virtualization host h_v_ two. VMs alpha and beta will be able to communicate with each other, but they won't be able to communicate with h_v_one or VM gamma.

Virtual machine network adapters

Generation 1 VMs support two types of network adapters—synthetic network adapters and legacy network adapters. A synthetic network adapter uses drivers that are provided when you install integration services in the VM operating system. If a VM operating system doesn't have these drivers or if integration services are not available for this operating system, then the network adapter will not function. Synthetic network adapters are unavailable until a VM operating system that supports them is running. This means that you can't perform a PXE boot from a synthetic network adapter if you have configured a Generation 1 VM.

Legacy network adapters emulate a physical network adapter, similar to a multiport DEC/Intel 21140 10/100TX 100 MB card. Many operating systems support this network adapter, including those that do not support virtual machine integration services. This means that if you want to run an operating system in a VM that doesn't have virtual machine integration services support—such as a version of Linux or BSD that isn't officially supported for Hyper-V—you'll need to use a legacy network adapter because it's likely to be recognized by the guest VM operating system.

Legacy network adapters on Generation 1 VMs also function before the VM guest operating system is loaded. This means that if you want to PXE boot a Generation 1 VM—for example, if you wanted to use WDS to deploy an operating system to the VM—you'd need to configure the VM with a legacy network adapter.

Generation 2 VMs don't separate synthetic and legacy network adapters and only have a single network adapter type. Generation 2 VMs support PXE booting from this single network adapter type. Generation 2 VMs also support "hot-add" network adapters, allowing you to add or remove network adapters to or from a virtual machine while it's running. It's important to remember that only recent Windows client and server operating systems and only certain Linux operating systems are supported as Generation 2 VMs.

Optimizing network performance

You can optimize network performance for VMs hosted on Hyper-V in a number of ways. For example, you can configure the virtualization host with separate network adapters connected to separate subnets. You do this to separate network traffic related to the management of the Hyper-V virtualization host from network traffic associated with hosted VMs. You can also use NIC teaming on the Hyper-V virtualization host to provide increased and fault-tolerant network connectivity. You'll learn more about NIC teaming later in this chapter.

Bandwidth management

An additional method of optimizing network performance is to configure bandwidth management at the virtual network adapter level. Bandwidth management allows you to specify a minimum and maximum traffic throughput for a virtual network adapter. The minimum bandwidth allocation is an amount that Hyper-V will reserve for the network adapter. For example, if you set the minimum bandwidth allocation to 10 Mbps for each VM, Hyper-V would ensure that when other VMs needed more, they would be able to increase their bandwidth utilization until they reached a limit defined by the combined minimum bandwidth allocation of all VMs hosted on the server. Maximum bandwidth allocations specify an upper limit for bandwidth utilization. By default, no minimum or maximum limits are set on virtual network adapters.

You configure bandwidth management by selecting the Enable Bandwidth Management option on a virtual network adapter and specifying a minimum and maximum bandwidth allocation in megabits per second (Mbps).

SR-IOV

SR-IOV (Single Root I/O Virtualization) increases network throughput by bypassing a virtual switch and sending network traffic straight to the VM. When you configure SR-IOV, the physical network adapter is mapped directly to the VM. As such, SR-IOV requires that the VM's operating system include a driver for the physical network adapter. You can only use SR-IOV if the physical network adapter and the network adapter drivers used with the virtualization host support the functionality. You can only configure SR-IOV for a virtual switch during switch creation. Once you have an SR-IOV-enabled virtual switch, you can then enable SR-IOV on the virtual network adapter that connects to that switch.

Dynamic virtual machine queue

Dynamic virtual machine queue is an additional technology that you can use to optimize network performance. When a VM is connected through a virtual switch to a network adapter that supports virtual machine queue, and virtual machine queue is enabled on the virtual network adapter's properties, the physical network adapter can use Direct Memory Access (DMA) to forward traffic directly to the VM. With a virtual machine queue, network traffic is processed by the CPU assigned to the VM rather than by the physical network adapter used by the Hyper-V virtualization host. The dynamic virtual machine queue automatically adjusts the number of CPU cores used to process network traffic. The dynamic virtual machine queue is automatically enabled on a virtual switch when you enable virtual machine queue on the virtual network adapter.

Virtual machine NIC teaming

NIC teaming allows you to aggregate bandwidth across multiple network adapters while also providing a redundant network connection in the event that one of the adapters in the team fails. NIC teaming allows you to consolidate up to 32 network adapters and to use them as a single network interface. You can configure NIC teams using adapters that are from different manufacturers and that run at different speeds (though it's generally a good idea to use the same adapter make and model in production environments).

You can configure NIC teaming at the virtualization host level if the virtualization host has multiple network adapters. The drawback is that you can't configure NIC teaming at the host level if the network adapters are configured to use SR-IOV. If you want to use SR-IOV and NIC teaming, create the NIC team instead in the VM. You can configure NIC teaming within VMs by adding adapters to a new team using the Server Manager console or the New-NetLbfoTeam Power-Shell cmdlet.

When configuring NIC teaming in a VM, ensure that each virtual network adapter that will participate in the team has MAC address spoofing enabled.

Virtual machine MAC addresses

By default, VMs running on Hyper-V hosts use dynamic MAC addresses. Each time a VM is powered on, it will be assigned a MAC address from a MAC address pool. You can configure the properties of the MAC address pool through the MAC Address Range settings available through Virtual Switch Manager.

When you deploy operating systems on physical hardware, you can use two methods to ensure that the computer is always assigned the same IP address configuration. The first method is to assign a static IP address from within the virtualized operating system. The second is to configure a DHCP reservation that always assigns the same IP address configuration to the MAC address associated with the physical computer's network adapter.

This won't work with Hyper-V VMs in their default configuration because the MAC address may change if you power the VM off and then on. Rather than configure a static IP address using the VM's operating system, you can instead configure a static MAC address on a per-virtual network adapter basis. This will ensure that a VM's virtual network adapter retains the same MAC address whether the VM is restarted or even if the VM is migrated to another virtualization host.

To configure a static MAC address on a per-network adapter basis, edit the network adapter's advanced features. When entering a static MAC address, you will need to select a MAC address manually. You shouldn't use one from the existing MAC address pool because there is no way for the current virtualization hosts or other virtualization hosts on the same subnet to check whether a MAC address that is to be assigned dynamically has already been assigned statically.

Network isolation

Hyper-V supports VLAN (Virtual Local Area Network) tagging at both the network adapter and virtual switch levels. VLAN tags allow the isolation of traffic for hosts connected to the same network by creating separate broadcast domains. Enterprise hardware switches also support VLANs as a way of partitioning network traffic. To use VLANs with Hyper-V, the virtualization hosts' network adapter must support VLANs. A VLAN ID has 12 bits, which means you can configure 4,095 VLAN IDs.

You configure VLAN tags at the virtual network adapter level by selecting Enable Virtual LAN Identification in the Virtual Network Adapter Properties dialog. VLAN tags applied at the virtual switch level override VLAN tags applied at the virtual network adapter level. To configure VLAN tags at the virtual switch level, select the Enable Virtual LAN Identification For Management Operating System option and specify the VLAN identifier.

Hyper-V replica

Hyper-V replica provides a replica of a VM running on one Hyper-V host that can be stored and updated on another Hyper-V host. For example, you could configure a VM hosted on a Hyper-V failover cluster in Melbourne to be replicated through Hyper-V replica to a Hyper-V failover cluster in Sydney. Hyper-V replication allows for replication across site boundaries and does not require access to shared storage in the way that failover clustering does.

Hyper-V replication is asynchronous. While the replica copy is consistent, it's a lagged copy with changes sent only as frequently as once every 30 seconds. Hyper-V replication supports multiple recovery points, with a recovery snapshot taken every hour. (This incurs a resource penalty, so it's off by default.) This means that when activating the replica, you can choose to activate the most up-to-date copy or a lagged copy. You would choose to activate a lagged copy in the event that some form of corruption or change made the up-to-date copy problematic.

When you perform a planned failover from the primary host to the replica, you need to switch off the primary host. This ensures that the replica is in an up-to-date and consistent state. This is a drawback compared to failover or live migration, where the VM will remain available during the process. A series of checks is completed before performing a planned failover to ensure that the VM is off, that reverse replication is allowed back to the original primary Hyper-V host, and that the state of the VM on the current replica is consistent with the state of the VM on the current primary. Performing a planned failover will start the replicated VM on the original replica, which will now become the new primary server.

Hyper-V replica also supports unplanned failover. You perform an unplanned failover in the event that the original Hyper-V host has failed or the site that hosts the primary replica has become unavailable. When performing unplanned failover, you can either choose the most recent recovery point or a previous recovery point. Performing an unplanned failover will start the VM on the original replica, which will now become the new primary server.

Hyper-V extended replication allows you to create a second replica of the existing replica server. For example, you could configure Hyper-V replication between a Hyper-V virtualization host in Melbourne and Sydney, with Sydney hosting the replica. You could then configure an extended replica in Brisbane using the Sydney replica.

Configuring Hyper-V replica servers

To configure Hyper-V replication, you need to configure the Replication Configuration settings. The first step is to select Enable This Computer As A Replica Server. Next, select the authentication method you're going to use. If the computers are part of the same Active Directory environment, you can use Kerberos. When you use Kerberos, Hyper-V replication data isn't encrypted when transmitted across the network. If you're concerned about encrypting network data, you could configure IPsec. If you are concerned about encrypting replication traffic, another option is to use certificate-based authentication. This is useful if you're transmitting data across the public Internet without using an encrypted VPN tunnel. When using certificate-based authentication, you'll need to import and select a public certificate issued to the partner server.

The final step when configuring a Hyper-V replica is to select the servers from which the Hyper-V virtualization host will accept incoming replicated VM data. One option is to have the Hyper-V virtualization host accept replicated VMs from any authenticated Hyper-V virtualization host, using a single default location to store replica data. The other option is to configure VM replica storage on a per-server basis. For example, if you want to store VM replicas from one server on one volume and VM replicas from another server on a different volume, you'd configure VM replica storage on a per-server basis.

Once replication is configured on the source and destination servers, you'll also need to enable the predefined firewall rules to allow the incoming replication traffic. There are two rules: one for replication using Kerberos (HTTP) on port 80 and the other for using certificate-based authentication on port 443.

Configuring VM replicas

Once you've configured the source and destination replica servers, you need to configure replication on a per-VM basis. You do this by running the Enable Replication Wizard, which you can trigger by clicking Enable Replication when the VM is selected in Hyper-V Manager. To configure VM replicas, you must perform the following steps:

- **Select Replica Server**   Select the replica server name. If you are replicating to a Hyper-V failover cluster, you'll need to specify the name of the Hyper-V replica broker. You'll learn more about Hyper-V replica broker later in this chapter.

CHAPTER 6

- **Choose Connection Parameters**   Specify the connection parameters. The options will depend on the configuration of the replica servers. On this page, depending on the existing configuration, you can choose the authentication type and whether replication data will be compressed when transmitted over the network.

- **Select Replication VHDs**   When configuring replication, you have the option of not replicating some of a VM's virtual hard disks. In most scenarios, you should replicate all of a VM's hard disk drives. One reason not to replicate a VM's virtual hard disk would be if the virtual hard disk only stores frequently changing temporary data that wouldn't be required when recovering the VM.

- **Replication Frequency**   Use this to specify the frequency with which changes are sent to the replica server. You can choose between intervals of 30 seconds, 5 minutes, and 15 minutes.

- **Additional Recovery Points**   You can choose to create additional hourly recovery points. Doing this gives you the option of starting the replica from a previous point in time rather than the most recent. The advantage is that this allows you to roll back to a previous version of the VM in the event that data corruption occurs and has replicated to the most recent recovery point. The replica server can store a maximum of 24 recovery points.

- **Initial Replication**   The last step in configuring Hyper-V replica is choosing how to seed the initial replica. Replication works by sending changed blocks of data, so the initial replica, which sends the entire VM, will be the largest transfer. You can perform an offline transfer with external media, use an existing VM on the replica server as the initial copy (the VM for which you're configuring a replica must have been exported and then imported on the replica server), or transfer all VM data across the network. You can perform replication immediately or at a specific time in the future, such as 2 AM when network utilization is likely to be lower.

Replica failover

You perform a planned replica failover when you want to run the VM on the replica server rather than on the primary host. Planned failover involves shutting down the VM, which ensures that the replica will be up to date. Contrast this with Hyper-V live migration, which you perform while the VM is running. When performing a planned failover, you can configure the VM on the replica server to automatically start once the process completes; you can also configure reverse replication, so that the current replica server becomes the new primary server, and the current primary becomes the new replica server.

In the event that the primary server becomes unavailable, you can trigger an unplanned failover. You would then perform the unplanned failover on the replica server (as the primary is not available). When performing an unplanned failover, you can select any of the up to 24 previously stored recovery points.

Hyper-V replica broker

You need to configure and deploy a Hyper-V replica broker if your Hyper-V replica configuration includes a Hyper-V failover cluster as a source or destination. You don't need to configure and deploy a Hyper-V replica broker if both the source and destination servers are not participating in a Hyper-V failover cluster. You install the Hyper-V Replica Broker role using Failover Cluster Manager after you've enabled the Hyper-V role on cluster nodes.

Hyper-V failover clusters

One of the most common uses for failover clustering is to host a Hyper-V virtual machine. The Hyper-V and failover clustering roles are even supported in Nano Server, which allows organizations to deploy failover clustering–capable virtualization hosts that have a minimal operating system footprint.

Hyper-V host cluster storage

When deployed on Hyper-V host clusters, the configuration and virtual hard disk files for highly available VMs are hosted on shared storage. This shared storage can be one of the following:

- **Serial Attached SCSI (SAS)**   Suitable for two-node failover clusters where the cluster nodes are in close proximity to each other.

- **iSCSI storage**   Suitable for failover clusters with two or more nodes. Windows Server includes iSCSI Target Software, allowing it to host iSCSI targets that can be used as shared storage by Windows failover clusters.

- **Fibre Channel**   Fibre Channel/Fibre Channel over Ethernet storage requires special network hardware. While generally providing better performance than iSCSI, Fibre Channel components tend to be more expensive.

- **SMB 3.0 file shares configured as continuously available storage**   This special type of file share is highly available, with multiple cluster nodes able to maintain access to the file share. This configuration requires multiple clusters. One cluster hosts the highly available storage used by the VMs, and the other cluster hosts the highly available VMs.

- **Cluster Shared Volumes (CSVs)**   CSVs can also be used for VM storage in Hyper-V failover clusters. As with continuously available file shares, multiple nodes in the cluster have access to the files stored on CSVs, ensuring that failover occurs with minimal disruption. As with SMB 3.0 file shares, multiple clusters are required, with one cluster hosting the CSVs and the other cluster hosting the VMs.

When considering storage for a Hyper-V failover cluster, remember the following:

- Ensure volumes used for disk witnesses are formatted as either NTFS or ReFS.

- Avoid allowing nodes from separate failover clusters to access the same shared storage by using LUN masking or zoning.

- Where possible, use storage spaces to host volumes presented as shared storage.

Cluster quorum

Hyper-V failover clusters remain functional until they do not have enough active votes to retain a quorum. Votes can consist of nodes that participate in the cluster as well as disk or file share witnesses. The calculation on whether the cluster maintains a quorum is dependent on the cluster quorum mode. When you deploy a Windows Server failover cluster, one of the following modes will automatically be selected, depending on the current cluster configuration:

- Node Majority

- Node and Disk Majority

- Node and File Share Majority

- No Majority: Disk Only

You can change the cluster mode manually. With Dynamic Quorum in Windows Server 2019 and later, the cluster mode will change automatically when you add or remove nodes, a witness disk, or a witness share.

Node Majority

The Node Majority cluster quorum mode is chosen automatically during setup if a cluster has an odd number of nodes. When this cluster quorum mode is used, a file share or disk witness is not used. A failover cluster will retain quorum as long as the number of available nodes is more than the number of failed nodes that retain cluster membership. For example, if you deploy a nine-node failover cluster, the cluster will retain a quorum as long as five cluster nodes are able to communicate with each other.

Node and Disk Majority

The Node and Disk Majority model is chosen automatically during setup if the cluster has an even number of nodes and shared storage is available to function as a disk witness. In this configuration, cluster nodes and the disk witness each have a vote when calculating a quorum. As with the Node Majority model, the cluster will retain a quorum as long as the number of votes that remain in communication exceeds the number of votes that cannot be contacted. For example, if you deployed a six-node cluster and a witness disk, there would be a total of seven votes. As long as four of those votes remained in communication with each other, the failover cluster would retain a quorum.

Node and File Share Majority

The Node and File Share Majority model is used when a file share is configured as a witness. Each node and the file share have a vote when it comes to determining if a quorum is retained. As with other models, a majority of the votes must be present for the cluster to retain a quorum. Node and File Share Majority is suitable for organizations that are deploying multisite clusters, such as placing half the cluster nodes in one site, half the cluster nodes in another site, and the file share witness in a third site. If one site fails, the other site is able to retain communication with the site that hosts the file share witness, in which case, a quorum is retained.

No Majority: Disk Only

The No Majority: Disk Only model must be configured manually and must only be used in testing environments because the only vote that counts toward a quorum is that of the disk witness on shared storage. The cluster will retain the quorum as long as the witness is available, even if every node but one fails. Similarly, the cluster will be in a failed state if all the nodes are available, but the shared storage hosting the disk witness goes offline.

Cluster node weight

Rather than every node in the cluster having an equal vote when determining quorum, you can configure which cluster nodes can vote to determine a quorum by running the Configure Cluster Quorum Wizard. Configuring node weight is useful if you are deploying a multisite cluster and you want to control which site retains a quorum in the event that communication between the sites is lost. You can determine which nodes in a cluster are currently assigned votes by selecting Nodes in the Failover Cluster Manager.

Dynamic quorum

Dynamic quorum allows the cluster quorum to be recalculated automatically each time a node is removed from or added to a cluster. By default, dynamic quorum is enabled on Windows Server clusters. Dynamic quorum works in the following manner:

- The vote of the witness is automatically adjusted based on the number of voting nodes in the cluster. If the cluster has an even number of nodes, the witness has a vote. If a cluster has an even number of nodes and a node is added or removed, the witness loses its vote.

- In the event of a 50 percent node split, the dynamic quorum can adjust a node's vote. This is useful in avoiding "split-brain" syndrome during site splits with multisite failover clusters.

An advantage of a dynamic quorum is that as long as nodes are evicted gracefully, the cluster will reconfigure a quorum appropriately. This means that you could change a nine-node cluster so that it was a five-node cluster by evicting nodes, and the new quorum model would automatically be recalculated, assuming that the cluster only had five nodes. With a dynamic quorum, it's a good idea to specify a witness even if the initial cluster configuration has an odd number of nodes; doing so means a witness vote will automatically be included in the event that an administrator adds or removes a node from the cluster.

Cluster networking

In lab and development environments, it's reasonable to have failover cluster nodes that are configured with a single network adapter. In production environments with mission-critical workloads, you should configure cluster nodes with multiple network adapters, institute adapter teaming, and leverage separate networks. Separate networks should include

- A network dedicated to connecting cluster nodes to shared storage

- A network dedicated to internal cluster communication

- The network that clients use to access services deployed on the cluster

When configuring IPv4 or IPv6 addressing for failover cluster nodes, ensure that addresses are assigned either statically or dynamically to cluster node network adapters. Avoid using a mixture of statically and dynamically assigned addresses because this will cause an error with the Cluster Validation Wizard. Also, ensure that cluster network adapters are configured with a default gateway. While the Cluster Validation Wizard will not provide an error if a default gateway is not present for the network adapters of each potential cluster node, you will be unable to create a failover cluster unless a default gateway is present.

Force Quorum Resiliency

Imagine you have a five-node, multisite cluster in Melbourne and Sydney, with three nodes in Sydney. Also, imagine that Internet connectivity to the Sydney site is lost. Within the Sydney site itself, the cluster will remain running because with three nodes, it has retained quorum. But if external connectivity to the Sydney site is not available, you may instead need to forcibly start the cluster in the Melbourne site (which will be in a failed state because only two nodes are present) using the /fq (forced quorum) switch to provide services to clients.

In the past, when connectivity was restored, this would have led to a "split-brain" or partitioned cluster because both sides of the cluster would be configured to be authoritative. To resolve this with failover clusters running Windows Server 2012 or earlier, you would need to manually restart the nodes that were not part of the forced quorum set using the /pq (prevent quorum) switch. Windows Server provides a feature known as Force Quorum Resiliency that automatically restarts the nodes that were not part of the forced quorum set, so that the cluster does not remain partitioned.

Cluster Shared Volumes

Cluster Shared Volumes (CSVs) are a high-availability storage technology that allows multiple cluster nodes in a failover cluster to have read-write access to the same LUN. This has the following advantages for Hyper-V failover clusters:

- VMs stored on the same LUN can be run on different cluster nodes. This reduces the number of LUNs required to host VMs because the VMs stored on a CSV aren't tied to one specific Hyper-V failover cluster node; instead, the VMs can be spread across multiple Hyper-V failover cluster nodes.

- Switch-over between nodes is almost instantaneous in the event of failover because the new host node doesn't have to go through the process of seizing the LUN from the failed node.

CSVs are hosted from servers running the Windows Server 2012 or later operating system and allow multiple nodes in a cluster to access the same NTFS- or ReFS-formatted file system. CSVs support BitLocker, with each node performing decryption of encrypted content using a cluster computer account. CSVs also integrate with SMB (Server Message Block) Multichannel and SMB Direct, allowing traffic to be sent through multiple networks and to leverage network cards that include Remote Direct Memory Access (RDMA) technology. CSVs can also automatically scan and repair volumes without requiring storage to be taken offline. You can convert cluster storage to a CSV using the Disks node of the Failover Cluster Manager.

Preferred owner and failover settings

Cluster role preferences settings allow you to configure a preferred owner for a cluster role. When you do this, the role will be hosted on the node listed as the preferred owner. You can specify multiple preferred owners and configure the order in which a role will attempt to return to a specific cluster node.

Failover settings allow you to configure how many times a service will attempt to restart or failover in a specific period. By default, a cluster service can failover twice in a six-hour period before the failover cluster will leave the cluster role in a failed state. The failback setting allows you to configure the amount of time a clustered role that has failed over to a node that is not its preferred owner will wait before falling back to the preferred owner.

Hyper-V guest clusters

A guest cluster is a failover cluster that consists of two or more VMs as cluster nodes. You can run a guest cluster on a Hyper-V failover cluster, or you can run guest clusters with nodes on separate Hyper-V failover clusters. While deploying a guest cluster on Hyper-V failover clusters may seem as though it's taking redundancy to an extreme, there are good reasons to deploy guest clusters and Hyper-V failover clusters together, including the following:

- **Failover clusters monitor the health of clustered roles to ensure that they are functioning.** This means that a guest failover cluster can detect when the failure of a clustered role occurs and can take steps to recover the role. For example, you deploy a SQL Server failover cluster as a guest cluster on a Hyper-V failover cluster. One of the SQL Server instances that participates in the guest cluster suffers a failure. In this scenario, failover occurs within the guest cluster, and another instance of SQL Server hosted on the other guest cluster node continues to service client requests.

- **Deploying guest and Hyper-V failover clusters together allows you to move applications to other guest cluster nodes while you're performing servicing tasks.** For example, you may need to apply software updates that require a restart of the operating system that hosts a SQL Server instance. If this SQL Server instance is participating in a Hyper-V guest cluster, you could move the clustered role to another node, apply software updates to the original node, perform the restart, and then move the clustered SQL Server role back to the original node.

- **Deploying guest and Hyper-V failover clusters together allows you to live migrate guest cluster VMs from one host cluster to another host cluster while ensuring clients retain connectivity to clustered applications.** For example, a two-node guest cluster hosting SQL Server is hosted on one Hyper-V failover cluster in your organization's datacenter. You want to move the guest cluster from its current host Hyper-V failover cluster to a new Hyper-V failover cluster. By migrating one guest cluster node at a time from the original Hyper-V failover cluster to the new Hyper-V failover cluster, you'll be able to continue to service client requests without interruption, failing over SQL Server to the guest node on the new Hyper-V failover cluster after the first node completes its migration and before migrating the second node across.

Using GPU-P with clusters

GPU-P can be used with live migration and failover clustering. To accomplish this, all hosts in the cluster should have identical GPU hardware and partitioning setups. You can't use a mix of GPU models or partition sizes when using GPU-P for failover clustering or live migration.

If a host crashes or goes down, a clustered VM with a GPU partition will be automatically restarted on another node, much like any highly available VM. A key difference is that a GPU-P configured VM cannot save its state, so the VM will be subject to a cold start on the new node, attaching to a new GPU partition there, and the VM's active state on the original failed node will be lost.

In this scenario, when the VM comes up on the new node, it will request a GPU partition. Hyper-V will allocate one if available. If the second node has no free partition, the VM may start but not be allocated a GPU.

Hyper-V guest cluster storage

Just as you can configure a Hyper-V failover cluster where multiple Hyper-V hosts function as failover cluster nodes, you can configure failover clusters within VMs, where each failover cluster node is a VM. Even though failover cluster nodes must be members of the same Active Directory domain, there is no requirement that they be hosted on the same cluster. For example, you could configure a multisite failover cluster where the cluster nodes are hosted as highly available VMs, each hosted on its own Hyper-V failover cluster in each site.

When considering how to deploy a VM guest cluster, you will need to choose how you will provision the shared storage that is accessible to each cluster node. The options for configuring shared storage for VM guest clusters include

- iSCSI

- Virtual Fibre Channel

- Cluster Shared Volumes

- Continuously Available File Shares

- Shared virtual hard disks

The conditions for using iSCSI, Virtual Fibre Channel, Cluster Shared Volumes, and Continuously Available File Shares with VM guest clusters are essentially the same for VMs as they are when configuring traditional, physically hosted failover cluster nodes.

Shared virtual hard disk

Shared virtual hard disks are a special type of shared storage only available to VM guest clusters. With shared virtual hard disks, each guest cluster node can be configured to access the same shared virtual hard disk. Each VM cluster node's operating system will recognize the shared virtual hard disk as shared storage when building the VM guest failover cluster.

Shared virtual hard disks have the following requirements:

- Can be used with Generation 1 and Generation 2 VMs.

- Can only be used with guest operating systems running Windows Server 2012 or later. If the guest operating systems are running Windows Server 2012, they must be updated to use the Windows Server 2012 R2 integration services components.

- Can only be used if virtualization hosts are running the Windows Server 2012 R2 or later version of Hyper-V.

- Must be configured to use the .vhdx virtual hard disk format.

- Must be connected to a virtual SCSI controller.

- When deployed on a failover cluster, the shared virtual hard disk itself should be located on shared storage, such as a Continuously Available File Share or Cluster Shared Volume. This is not necessary when configuring a guest failover cluster on a single Hyper-V server that isn't part of a Hyper-V failover cluster.

- VMs can only use shared virtual hard disks to store data. You can't boot a VM from a shared virtual hard disk.

The configuration of shared virtual hard disks differs from the traditional configuration of VM guest failover clusters because you configure the connection to shared storage by editing the VM properties rather than connecting to the shared storage from within the VM. Windows Server supports shared virtual hard disks being resized and used with Hyper-V replica.

Hyper-V VHD Sets

VHD Sets are a newer version of shared virtual hard disks. Hyper-V VHD Sets use a new virtual hard disk format that uses the .vhds extension. VHD Sets support online resizing of shared virtual disks and Hyper-V Replica and also support application-consistent Hyper-V checkpoints.

You can create a VHD Set file from Hyper-V Manager or by using the New-VHD cmdlet with the file type set to .vhds when specifying the virtual hard disk name. You can use the Convert-VHD SharedVirtualHardDiskName to convert an existing shared virtual hard disk file to a VHD Set file as long as you've taken the VMs that use the shared virtual hard disk file offline and removed the shared virtual hard disk from the VM using the Remove-VHHardDiskDrive cmdlet.

> ## More Info
>
> **Hyper-V VHD Sets**
>
> **You can learn more about Hyper-V VHD Sets at *https://learn.microsoft.com/en-us/windows-server/virtualization/hyper-v/manage/create-vhdset-file.***

Live migration

Live migration is the process of moving an operational VM from one physical virtualization host to another with no interruption to VM clients or users. Live migration is supported between cluster nodes that share storage between separate Hyper-V virtualization hosts that are not participating in a failover cluster using an SMB 3.0 file share as storage; live migrations are even supported between separate Hyper-V hosts that are not participating in a failover cluster using a process called "shared nothing live migration."

Live migration has the following prerequisites:

- There must be two or more servers running Hyper-V that use processors from the same manufacturer (for example, all Hyper-V virtualization hosts configured with Intel processors or all Hyper-V virtualization hosts configured with AMD processors).

- Hyper-V virtualization hosts need to be members of the same domain, or they must be members of domains that have a trust relationship with each other.

- VMs must be configured to use virtual hard disks or virtual Fibre Channel disks; pass-through disks are not allowed.

It is possible to perform live migration with VMs configured with pass-through disks under the following conditions:

- VMs are hosted on a Windows Server Hyper-V failover cluster.

- Live migration will be within nodes that participate in the same Hyper-V failover cluster.

- VM configuration files are stored on a Cluster Shared Volume.

- The physical disk that is used as a pass-through disk is configured as a storage disk resource that is controlled by the failover cluster. This disk must be configured as a dependent resource for the highly available VM.

If performing a live migration using shared storage, the following conditions must be met:

- The SMB 3.0 share needs to be configured so that the source and the destination virtualization host's computer accounts have read and write permissions.

- All VM files (virtual hard disks, configuration files, and snapshot files) must be located on the SMB 3.0 share. You can use storage migration to move VM files to an SMB 3.0 share while the VM is running, prior to performing a live migration using this method.

You must configure the source and destination Hyper-V virtualization hosts to support live migrations by enabling live migrations in the Hyper-V settings. When you do this, you specify the maximum number of simultaneous live migrations and the networks that you will use for live migration. Microsoft recommends using an isolated network for live migration traffic, though this is not a requirement.

The next step in configuring live migration is choosing which authentication protocol and live migration performance options to use. You select these in the Advanced Features area of the Live Migrations settings. The default authentication protocol is CredSSP (Credential Security Support Provider). CredSSP requires local sign-in to both the source and destination Hyper-V virtualization host to perform live migration. Kerberos allows you to trigger live migration remotely. To use Kerberos, you must configure the computer accounts for each Hyper-V virtualization host with constrained delegation for the CIFS and Microsoft Virtual System Migration Service services, granting permissions to the virtualization hosts that will participate in the live migration partnership. The performance options allow you to speed up live migration. Compression increases processor utilization. SMB will use SMB Direct if both the network adapters used for the live migration process support Remote Direct Memory Access (RDMA) and RDMA capabilities are enabled.

Storage migration

With storage migration, you can move a VM's virtual hard disk files, checkpoint files, smart paging files, and configuration files from one location to another. You can perform storage migration while the VM is running or while the VM is powered off. You can move data to any location that is accessible to the Hyper-V host. This allows you to move data from one volume to another, from one folder to another, or even to an SMB 3.0 file share on another computer. When performing storage migration, choose the Move The VM's Storage option.

For example, you could use storage migration to move VM files from one Cluster Share Volume to another on a Hyper-V failover cluster without interrupting the VM's operation. You have the option of moving all data to a single location, moving VM data to separate locations, or moving only the VM's virtual hard disk. To move the VM's data to different locations, select the items you want to move and the destination locations.

Exporting, importing, and copying VMs

A VM export creates a duplicate of a VM that you can import on the same or a different Hyper-V virtualization host. When performing an export, you can choose to export the VM, which includes all its VM checkpoints, or you can choose to export just a single VM checkpoint. Windows Server supports exporting a running VM.

Exporting a VM with all of its checkpoints will create multiple differencing disks. When you import a VM that was exported with checkpoints, these checkpoints will also be imported. If you import a VM that was running at the time of export, the VM is placed in a saved state. You can resume from this saved state, rather than having to restart the VM.

When importing a VM, you can choose from the following options:

- **Register The Virtual Machine In Place (Use The Existing ID)**   Use this option when you want to import the VM while keeping the VM files in their current locations. Because this method uses the existing VM ID, you can only use it if the original VM on which the export was created is not present on the host to which you want to import the VM.

- **Restore The Virtual Machine (Use The Existing Unique ID)**   Use this option when you want to import the VM while moving the files to a new location; for example, you would choose this option if you're importing a VM that was exported to a network share. Because this method also uses the existing VM ID, you can only use it if the original VM on which the export was created is not present on the host to which you want to import the VM.

- **Copy The Virtual Machine (Create A New Unique ID)**   Use this method if you want to create a separate clone of the exported VM. The exported files will be copied to a new location, leaving the original exported files unaltered. A new VM ID is created, meaning that the cloned VM can run concurrently on the same virtualization host as the original progenitor VM. When importing a cloned VM onto the same virtualization host as the original progenitor VM, ensure that you rename the newly imported VM; otherwise, you may confuse the VMs.

Exporting and migrating VMs with virtual TPMs

A challenge with performing a migration, failover, or import and export of a VM that has a virtual TPM (vTPM) is that you can only have the VM run on a host that has the appropriate certificates. These certificates are created on the Hyper-V host in which the VM with the vTPM is first created, but they have to be manually imported on any other host where you want to run the VM.

When you added a vTPM to a VM, Hyper-V automatically created a pair of certificates, one for encryption and one for signing, in the host's Local Machine certificate store under Shielded VM Local Certificates. These certificates (with their private keys) protect the VM's TPM data and must be present on any host that runs the VM. If the vTPM certificates aren't present, the VM won't start. Even when you add additional VMs with vTPMs to the same Hyper-V host, the same certificates are used.

To export these certificates so that you can use the VMs with vTPMs on other hosts, perform the following steps:

1. Run `mmc.exe` and add the Certificates snap-in for the Local Computer account on the Hyper-V host that has the VM with the vTPM you want to export.

2. In the certificates snap-in, navigate to Certificates (Local Computer)\Shielded VM Local Certificates\Certificates.

3. You will see two certificates listed here. These represent the Encryption Certificate and Signing Certificate used by the vTPM (often created under a default guardian name like "UntrustedGuardian").

4. Export each certificate with its private key by right-clicking each certificate, choosing All Tasks, and choosing Export. In the Certificate Export Wizard, ensure that

- You choose Yes, Export The Private Key.

- If prompted for the export format, choose PFX (Personal Information Exchange) and include all certificates in the path, if that option appears.

- Assign a strong password to protect the PFX file and save each exported certificate with a meaningful name.

- Do not select Delete The Private Key If Export Is Successful" unless you're permanently moving and want to remove this key from the current host.

5. To do this using PowerShell, run the command:

```
Get-ChildItem -Path Cert:\LocalMachine\Shielded VM Local Certificates | Export-
PfxCertificate -FilePath C:\Temp\HostCerts.pfx -Password (ConvertTo-SecureString
"YourPassword" -AsPlainText -Force) -CryptoAlgorithmOption AES256_SHA256
```

6. The next step is to bring the exported certificate files to the destination Hyper-V host. If the destination Hyper-V host has never hosted a VM with a vTPM, you'll need to run the command:

```
New-Item -Path 'Cert:\LocalMachine\Shielded VM Local Certificates'
```

7. Once this location exists, you can import the necessary certificates using the following PowerShell command:

```
Import-PfxCertificate -FilePath C:\Temp\HostCerts.pfx -CertStoreLocation Cert:\
LocalMachine\Shielded VM Local Certificates -Password (ConvertTo-SecureString
"YourPassword" -AsPlainText -Force) -Exportable
```

8. Alternatively, you can use mmc.exe on the destination computer and add the Certificates snap-in for the Local Computer account, and then perform an import of the certificate files. Importing will create the Shielded VM Local Certificates store. You should also mark the imported key as exportable, which will allow you to export it in the future if required.

Once the certificates are imported on the destination host, you'll be able to import the exported VM with a vTPM. As the certificates support all vTPM-enabled VMs from the original host, you might use this technique to populate all Hyper-V servers in your organization with a common set of certificates. This way, you'll be able to move VMs as necessary without being concerned about certificate management.

VM Network Health Detection

VM Network Health Detection is a feature for VMs that are deployed on Hyper-V host clusters. With VM Network Health Detection, you configure a VM's network adapter settings and mark certain networks as being protected. You do this in the Advanced Features section of the Network Adapter properties dialog.

In the event that a VM is running on a cluster node where the network marked as protected becomes unavailable, the cluster will automatically live migrate the VM to a node where the protected network is available. For example, you have a four-node Hyper-V failover cluster. Each node has multiple network adapters and a virtual switch named Alpha maps as an external virtual switch to a physical network adapter on each node. A VM, configured as highly available and hosted on the first cluster node, is connected to virtual switch Alpha. The network adapter on this VM is configured with the protected network option. After the VM has been switched on and has been running for some time, a fault occurs, causing the physical network adapter mapped to virtual switch Alpha on the first cluster node to fail. When this happens, the VM will automatically be live migrated to another cluster node where virtual switch Alpha is working.

VM drain on shutdown

VM drain on shutdown is a feature that will automatically live migrate all running VMs off a node if you shut down that node without putting it into maintenance mode. If you're following best practice, you'll be putting nodes into maintenance mode and live migrating running workloads away from nodes that you will restart or intend to shut down anyway. The main benefit of VM drain on shutdown is that, in the event that you're having a bad day and forget to put a cluster node into maintenance mode before shutting it down or restarting it, any running VMs will be live migrated without requiring your direct intervention.

Domain controller cloning

Windows Server supports creating copies of domain controllers that are running as VMs as long as certain conditions are met. Cloned domain controllers have the following prerequisites:

- The virtualization host supports VM-GenerationID, a 128-bit random integer that identifies each VM checkpoint. VM-GenerationID is supported by the version of Hyper-V available with Windows Server 2012 and later, as well as some third-party hypervisors.

- The server that hosts the PDC emulator Flexible Single Master Operations Role (FSMO) must be contactable.

- The computer account of the domain controller that will serve as the template for cloning must be added to the Cloneable Domain Controllers security group.

Once you have met these conditions, you'll need to create an XML configuration file named DCCloneConfig.xml using the New-ADDCCloneConfigFile Windows PowerShell cmdlet. Once created, you'll need to edit this file and specify settings such as computer name, network settings, and Active Directory site information. You should also check the template DC using the

Get-ADDCCloningExcludedApplicationsList cmdlet to determine whether any services that will cause problems with the cloning are present on the template DC, such as the DHCP server service.

Dynamic Processor Compatibility Mode

Dynamic Processor Compatibility Mode is a Windows Server 2025 Hyper-V feature that improves the existing processor compatibility functionality for virtual machines. In earlier versions of Hyper-V, enabling "processor compatibility mode" on a VM would hide most advanced CPU features, forcing the VM to run on a minimal, static baseline CPU feature set for maximum compatibility. This old approach ensured a live-migrated VM could run on older processors, but at the cost of significant performance loss, since many CPU optimizations were disabled.

With Dynamic Processor Compatibility mode, Hyper-V dynamically calculates the common denominator of CPU features across all hosts in a cluster and exposes the maximum set of features that all those processors support to each VM. This improves VM performance compared to the old static compatibility mode, since fewer CPU capabilities are masked out.

Dynamic compatibility determination happens automatically at the cluster level. Hyper-V continuously determines the supported processor features of each node and derives a common feature set that is replicated across the cluster. Whenever you enable processor compatibility on a VM in a Windows Server 2025 Hyper-V cluster, the VM will use this dynamically calculated cluster-wide feature set, and no setting needs to be configured at the cluster level.

When a live migration is initiated, Hyper-V will compare the source and target hosts' CPU feature sets. As long as the VM's presented feature set is a subset of what the target host supports, the migration can proceed without issue. If a VM is running with dynamic compatibility, it should already be constrained to instructions present on all cluster nodes, so any intracluster migration will succeed by design.

All hosts must use the same processor vendor for compatibility mode to work, and you cannot live migrate between Intel and AMD CPUs using this feature. The CPU architectures must be the same; if you need to move a VM between different CPU manufacturers, you still have to power it off first. Within a vendor line, dynamic compatibility can span different generations/families (such as Intel Haswell to Intel Ice Lake, or AMD Zen2 to Zen4), as long as those CPUs share some common instruction baseline.

Dynamic Processor Compatibility Mode is configured per virtual machine, but a VM must be shut down before changing the processor compatibility settings.

You can enable Dynamic Processor Compatibility Mode using Windows Admin Center or Hyper-V Manager. You can also use the following PowerShell:

```
Get-VM -Name "<VMName>" | Set-VMProcessor -CompatibilityForMigrationEnabled $true
-CompatibilityForMigrationMode CommonClusterFeatureSet
```

To use Dynamic Processor Compatibility mode,

- Hyper-V hosts must be running Windows Server 2025 or later.

- VM must use configuration version 10.0 or later.

Shielded virtual machines

Shielded virtual machines are a special type of virtual machine that has a virtual Trusted Platform Module (TPM) chip that is encrypted using BitLocker and can only run on specific approved hosts that support what is known as a guarded fabric. Shielded VMs allow sensitive data and workloads to be run on virtualization hosts without the concern that an attacker or the administrator of the virtualization host might export the virtual machine to gain access to the sensitive data stored there. Only certain operating systems can be used for shielded guest virtual machines.

Managing Hyper-V using PowerShell

The Hyper-V PowerShell module contains a large number of cmdlets that you can use to manage all aspects of Hyper-V and virtual machines on Windows Server. These cmdlets are described in Table 6-1.

Table 6-1   Remote Access PowerShell cmdlets

Noun	Verbs	Function
VFD	New	Create a new virtual floppy disk.
VHD	Convert, Merge, Resize, Optimize, Dismount, New, Mount, Set, Get, Test	Manage virtual hard disks.
VHDSet	Optimize, Get	Manage virtual hard disk set files. These are an update to the VHDX files from previous versions of Hyper-V.
VHDSnapshot	Get, Remove	Used to manage snapshots with VHDSets.
VM	Wait, Move, Get, Export, Debug, Measure, Import, Save, Resume, Restart, Set, Suspend, Stop, Start, Repair, Checkpoint, Remove, New, Compare, Rename	Use to manage virtual machines.
VMAssignableDevice	Add, Get, Remove	Manage VM assignable devices.

CHAPTER 6

CHAPTER 6

Noun	Verbs	Function
VMBios	Set, Get	Manage VM BIOS settings.
VMComPort	Set, Get	Manage VM COM Port settings.
VMConnectAccess	Grant, Revoke, Get	Manage which users can connect to specific VMs.
VMConsoleSupport	Enable, Disable	Manage HID device support for virtual machines.
VMDvdDrive	Add, Set, Get, Remove	Manage VM DVD drive settings.
VMEventing	Disable, Enable	Enable or disable VM eventing.
VMFailover	Complete, Stop, Start	Manage VM failover.
VMFibreChannelHba	Set, Get, Remove, Add	Manage VM fibre channel HBA settings.
VMFile	Copy	Copy a file from the virtualization host to a location within the virtual machine.
VMFirmware	Set, Get	Manage VM virtual firmware settings.
VMGpuPartitionAdapter	Set, Add, Remove, Get	Manage VM GPU settings.
VMGroup	New, Get, Remove, Rename	Allows you to manage VM Groups, which you use to manage groups of machines that might make up a multitier application.
VMGroupMember	Remove, Add	Add and remove VMs from a specific group.
VMHardDiskDrive	Set, Add, Remove, Get	Manage VM hard disk drive settings.
VMHost	Set, Get	Configure VM host settings.
VMHostAssignableDevice	Add, Mount, Get, Remove, Dismount	Manage VM host assignable devices.
VMHostCluster	Get, Set	Configure VM host cluster settings.
VMHostNumaNode	Get	View VM host numa node information.
VMHostNumaNodeStatus	Get	View VM host Numa node status.
VMHostSupportedVersion	Get	View VM host supported information data.
VMIdeController	Get	Manage VM IDE controller settings.

Noun	Verbs	Function
VMInitialReplication	Import, Start, Stop	Configure initial VM replication settings.
VMIntegrationService	Enable, Disable, Get	Manage VM integration services.
VMKeyProtector	Get, Set	Manage VM key protector settings.
VMKeyStorageDrive	Set, Remove, Get, Add	Manage VM key storage drive settings.
VMMemory	Set, Get	Manage VM memory.
VMMigration	Enable, Disable	Manage VM Migration.
VMMigrationNetwork	Add, Remove, Get, Set	Configure VM migration network settings.
VMNetworkAdapter	Disconnect, Connect, Remove, Test, Add, Set, Rename, Get	Configure VM network adapters.
VMNetworkAdapterAcl	Remove, Add, Get	Manage VM network adapter ACLs.
VMNetworkAdapterExtendedAcl	Remove, Add, Get	Manage VM Network adapter extended ACL settings.
VMNetworkAdapterFailover-Configuration	Get, Set	Manage VM network adapter failover settings.
VMNetworkAdapterIsolation	Set, Get	Manage VM network adapter isolation settings.
VMNetworkAdapterRdma	Set, Get	Manage virtual network adapter RDMA settings.
VMNetworkAdapterRouting-DomainMapping	Set, Get, Remove, Add	Configure virtual network adapter routing domains.
VMNetworkAdapterTeamMapping	Remove, Get, Set	Configure virtual network adapter team mapping.
VMNetworkAdapterVlan	Get, Set	Manage VM network adapter VLAN settings.
VMPartitionableGpu	Get, Set	Manage VM GPU settings.
VMProcessor	Get, Set	Configure VM Processor settings.
VMRemoteFx3dVideoAdapter	Remove, Set, Get, Add	Manage RemoteFX3d video adapters.
VMRemoteFXPhysicalVideo-Adapter	Disable, Get, Enable	Manage RemoteFX physical adapters.

CHAPTER 6

Noun	Verbs	Function
VMReplication	Get, Stop, Suspend, Remove, Measure, Enable, Resume, Set	Manage VM replication.
VMReplicationAuthorizationEntry	Set, Remove, New, Get	Manage VM replication authorization entries.
VMReplicationConnection	Test	Check VM replication.
VMReplicationServer	Get, Set	Configure VM replication server settings.
VMReplicationStatistics	Reset	Reset VM replication statistics.
VMResourceMetering	Reset, Disable, Enable	Configure VM resource metering.
VMResourcePool	Set, Rename, Get, Measure, New, Remove	Manage VM resource pool settings.
VMSan	Remove, Disconnect, Connect, New, Set, Rename, Get	Manage VM SAN settings.
VMSavedState	Remove	Remove saved state data.
VMScsiController	Remove, Add, Get	Manage the VM's SCSI controller.
VMSecurity	Get, Set	Manage VM security information.
VMSecurityPolicy	Set	Configure VM security policies.
VMSnapshot	Rename, Restore, Export, Get, Remove	Manage VM checkpoints.
VMStorage	Move	Move VM storage.
VMStoragePath	Get, Remove, Add	Configure VM storage path.
VMSwitch	Set, Get, Rename, Remove, Add, New	Manage virtual switches.
VMSwitchExtension	Enable, Disable, Get	Manage extensions on a virtual switch.
VMSwitchExtensionPortData	Get	View port extensions on a virtual switch.
VMSwitchExtensionPortFeature	Set, Add, Remove, Get	Manage switch port features.
VMSwitchExtensionSwitchData	Get	View switch port data.
VMSwitchExtensionSwitchFeature	Add, Get, Set, Remove	Manage switch features.
VMSwitchTeam	Set, Get	Manage switch teams.

CHAPTER 6

Noun	Verbs	Function
VMSwitchTeamMember	Add, Remove	Manage switch team membership.
VMSystemSwitchExtension	Get	View switch extensions installed on the VM host.
VMSystemSwitchExtension-PortFeature	Get	View port-level features supported by switch extensions on the VM host.
VMSystemSwitchExtension-SwitchFeature	Get	View switch-level features supported by virtual switch extensions on the VM host.
VMTPM	Disable, Enable	Manage virtual TPM settings.
VMTrace	Stop, Start	Manage trace settings for VM debugging.
VMVersion	Update	Update the version of the VM.
VMVideo	Get, Set	Configure video settings for virtual machines.

CHAPTER 6

Windows Server provides a number of software-defined storage solutions that allow you to have complex storage configurations managed by the Windows Server operating system rather than having to manage storage solutions using storage hardware–specific vendor management tools. Many of the storage service solutions available in Windows Server are used by Microsoft in its Azure datacenters, where storage provisioning, performance, resiliency, and redundancy are all managed through software rather than through specific hardware devices.

Storage spaces and storage pools

A *storage pool* is a collection of storage devices that you can use to aggregate storage. You expand the capacity of a storage pool by adding storage devices to the pool. A storage space is a virtual disk that you create from the free space that's available in a storage pool. Depending on how you configure it, a storage space can be resilient to failure and have improved performance through storage tiering.

You manage storage spaces and storage pools through Windows Admin Center, PowerShell, the RSAT Tools, or Server Manager.

Inside OUT

Persistent memory support

Windows Server 2019 and later support persistent memory, also termed storage-class memory. Examples include Intel Optane DC PM and NVDIMM-N modules.

Storage pools

A storage pool is a collection of storage devices, usually disks, but can also include items such as virtual hard disks from which you can create one or more storage spaces. A storage space is a special type of virtual disk that has the following features:

- **Resilient storage**   Configure to use disk mirroring or parity in the structure of the underlying storage (if available). Resilience is discussed later in this chapter.

- **Tiering**   Configure to leverage a combination of SSD and HDD disks to achieve maximum performance. Tiering is discussed later in this chapter.

- **Continuous availability**   Storage spaces integrate with failover clustering, and you can cluster pools across separate nodes within a single failover cluster.

- **Write-back cache**   If a storage space includes SSDs, a write-back cache can be configured in the pool to buffer small random writes. These random writes are then later offloaded to SSDs or HDDs that make up the virtual disk in the pool.

- **Multitenancy**   You can configure Access Control Lists on each storage pool. This allows you to configure isolation in multitenant scenarios.

To add storage to a storage pool, perform the following general steps:

1. In Server Manager, navigate to the Storage Pools node under the Volumes node of the File And Storage Services workspace. In this workspace, you will see available storage that hasn't been allocated in the Primordial pool, as shown in Figure 7-1. The Primordial pool is the collection of disks that have not been provisioned.

2. On the Tasks menu, click New Storage Pool. You can also use the Tasks menu to rescan storage. You might need to use that option if you can't see the storage in the Primordial pool that you want to add to a potential storage pool.

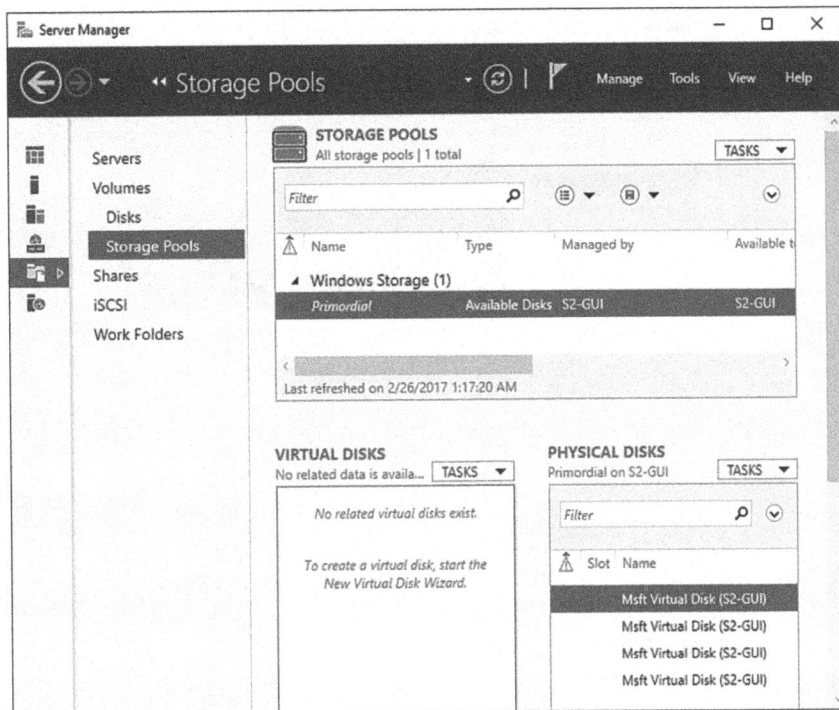

Figure 7-1   Primordial storage

3. On the Storage Pool Name page of the New Storage Pool Wizard, specify a name for the storage pool and select which group of available disks you want to allocate to the storage pool. By default, the disks in the Primordial pool will be selected.

4. On the Physical Disks page, specify which available disks you want to add to the new pool. Figure 7-2 shows three disks being allocated using the Automatic allocation type and one disk being allocated as a Hot Spare type. Hot Spares will be swapped in if the existing disk in the storage pool fails.

5. On the confirmation page, review your settings and click Create. When the pool is created, click Close.

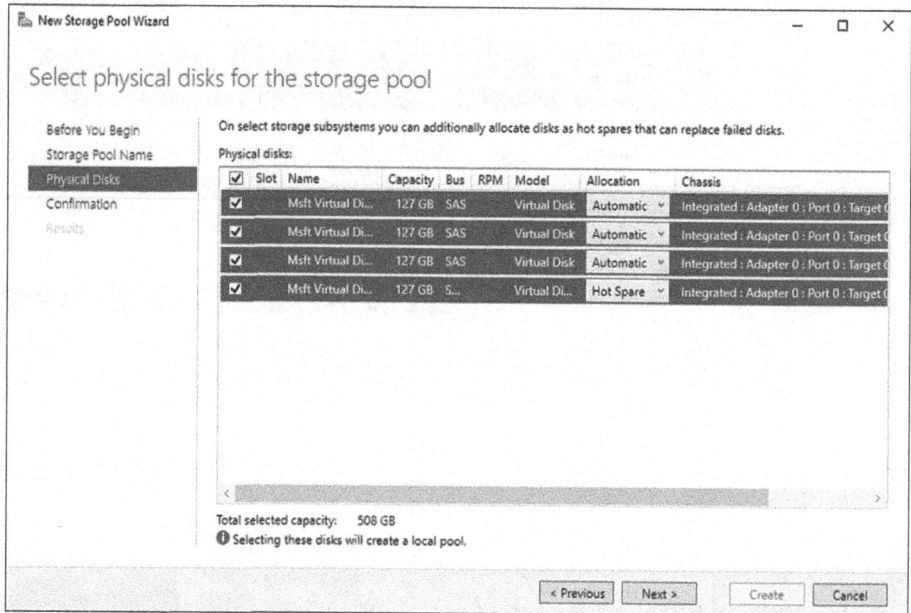

Figure 7-2   Adding disks

You can add and remove disks from an existing storage pool. To add disks to an existing storage pool, perform the following steps:

1. In the Storage Pools node, verify that the disks that you want to add to the pool are available in the Primordial pool.

2. Right-click the storage pool where you want to add the additional disks and click Add Physical Disk.

3. In the Add Physical Disk dialog, select the disks from the Primordial pool that you want to add to the existing storage pool and specify which Allocation type they will use. You can choose between Automatic, Hot Spare, and Manual. Figure 7-3 shows two disks being added using the Automatic allocation type.

To remove a disk from an existing storage pool, perform the following steps:

1. In the Storage Pools node, select the storage pool from which you want to remove the disk.

2. In the list of physical disks, select the disk that you want to remove. You can right-click the disk within the pool and select the Toggle Drive Light option, shown in Figure 7-4, to ensure that you are removing the correct disk.

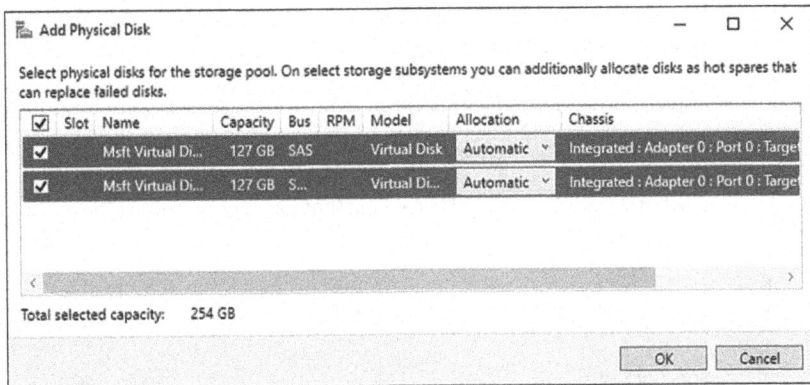

Figure 7-3 Adding disks to the existing pool

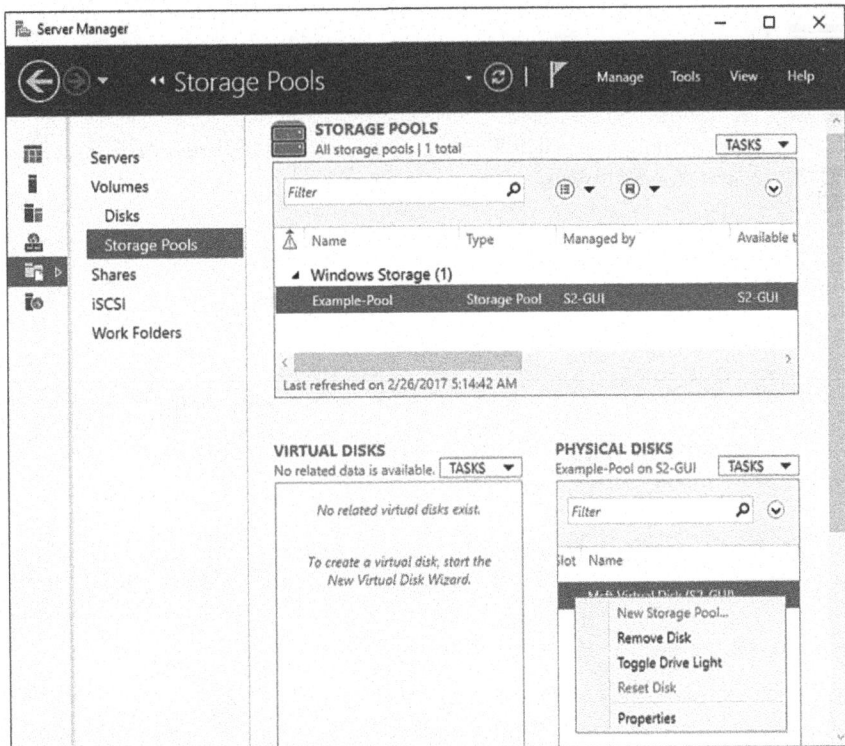

Figure 7-4 Toggle Drive Light

3. Once you are ready to remove the appropriate disk from the pool, right-click the disk and select the Remove Disk option.

4. You will be presented with a warning message informing you that the operating system will attempt to rebuild virtual disks that store data on the disk that you're removing from the pool. This can only happen if enough disks remain in the pool to store the data that is currently stored on the physical disk that has been removed from the pool.

More Info

Storage spaces

To learn more about storage spaces, consult the following link: *https://learn.microsoft.com/windows-server/storage/storage-spaces/overview*.

Storage space resiliency

When creating a virtual disk on a storage pool that has enough disks, you can choose between several Storage Layouts, as shown in Figure 7-5.

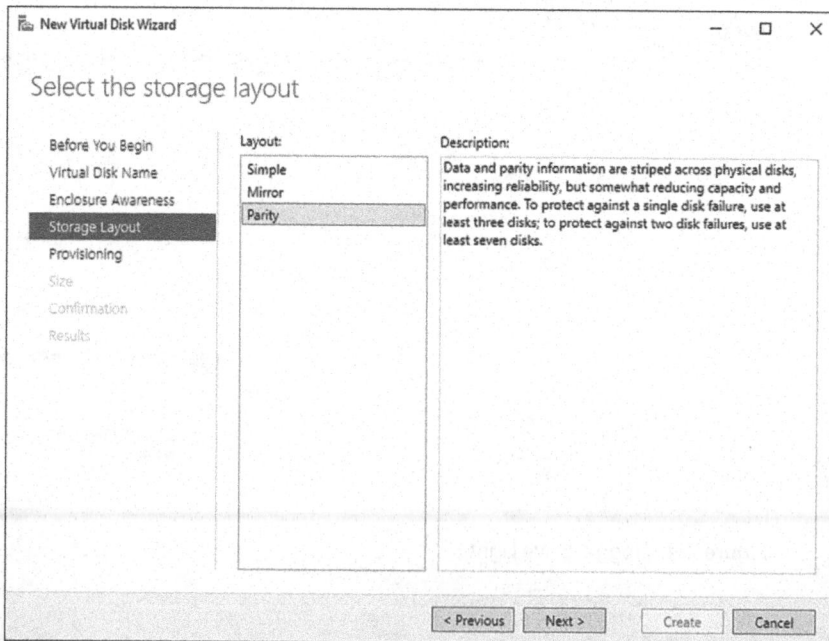

Figure 7-5   Choosing the Storage Layout

These options provide the following benefits:

- **Mirror**   Multiple copies of data are written across separate disks in the pool. This protects the virtual disk from failure of the physical disks that constitute the storage pool. Mirroring can be used with storage tiering. Depending on the number of disks in the pool, Storage Spaces on Windows Server 2019 and later provide two-way or three-way mirroring. Two-way mirroring writes two copies of data, and three-way mirroring writes three copies of data. Three-way mirroring provides better redundancy, but it also consumes more disk space.

- **Parity**   Similar to RAID 5, parity data is stored on disks in the array that are separate from where data is stored. Parity provides greater capacity than using the Mirror option, but it has the drawback of slower write performance. Windows Server provides two types of parity: Single Parity and Dual Parity. Single Parity protects against one failure at a time. Dual Parity protects against two failures at a time. You need to have a minimum of three disks for Single Parity and a minimum of seven disks for Dual Parity. You get the option to select between Single Parity and Dual Parity when configuring storage layout when there are more than seven disks.

- **Simple**   This option provides no resiliency for the storage, which means that if one of the disks in the storage pool fails, the data on any virtual hard disks built from that pool will also be lost.

If you configure disks in the storage pool that use the Hot Spare option, storage spaces will be able to automatically repair virtual disks that use the Mirror or Parity resiliency options. It's also possible for automatic repairs to occur if spare unallocated capacity exists within the pool.

Storage space tiering

Storage space tiering allows you to create a special type of virtual disk from a pool of storage that is a combination of SSD and traditional HDD disks. Storage tiering provides the virtual disk with performance similar to that of an array built out of SSD disks but without the cost of building a large capacity array comprised of SSD disks. It accomplishes this by moving frequently accessed files to faster physical disks within the pool, thus moving less-frequently accessed files to slower storage media.

You can only configure storage tiers when creating a virtual disk if there is a mixture of physical disks with the HDD and the SSD disk type in the pool upon which you want to create the disk. Once the disk is created, you cannot undo storage tiering from a virtual disk. You configure storage tiering for a virtual disk by selecting the Create Storage Tiers On This Virtual Disk option during virtual disk creation, as shown in Figure 7-6.

One challenge when configuring storage tiering is ensuring that you have media marked as SSD and HDD in the pool. While media will usually be recognized correctly, in some cases, you must specify that a disk is of the SSD type, which allows storage tiering to be configured.

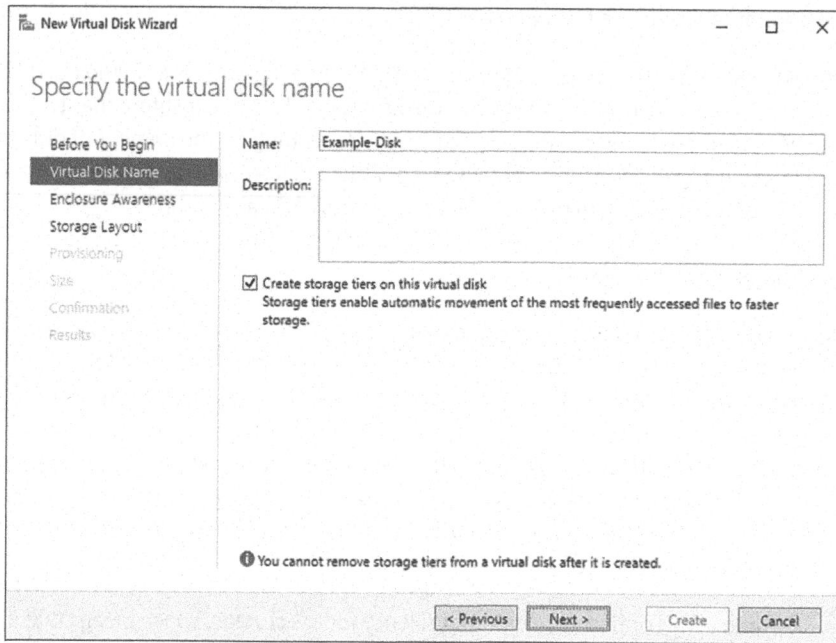

Figure 7-6 Enable storage tiering

You can specify the disk media type using the following PowerShell procedure:

1. First, determine the storage using the `Get-StoragePool` cmdlet.

2. To view whether physical disks are configured as SSD or HDD, use the `Get-StoragePool` cmdlet and then pipe that cmdlet to the `Get-PhysicalDisk` cmdlet, as shown in Figure 7-7.

Figure 7-7 View disk media types

3.   For example, to view the identity and media type of physical disks in the storage pool
     named `Example-Pool`, issue this command:

```
Get-StoragePool -FriendlyName ExamplePool | Get-PhysicalDisk | Select UniqueID,
MediaType, Usage
```

4.   Once you have determined the UniqueIDs of the disks that you want to configure as the
     SSD type, you can configure a disk to have the SSD type by using the `Set-PhysicalDisk`
     cmdlet with the `UniqueID` parameter and the `MediaType` parameter set to SSD. Similarly,
     you can change the type back to HDD by setting the `MediaType` parameter to HDD.

Thin provisioning and trim

Thin provisioning allows you to create virtual disks where you specify a total size for the disk,
but only the space that is actually used will be allocated. For example, with thin provisioning,
you might create a virtual hard disk that can grow to 500 GB in size but is currently only 10 GB in
size because only 10 GB of data is currently stored on the volumes hosted on the disk. Figure 7-8
shows where you select the Provisioning Type in the New Virtual Disk Wizard.

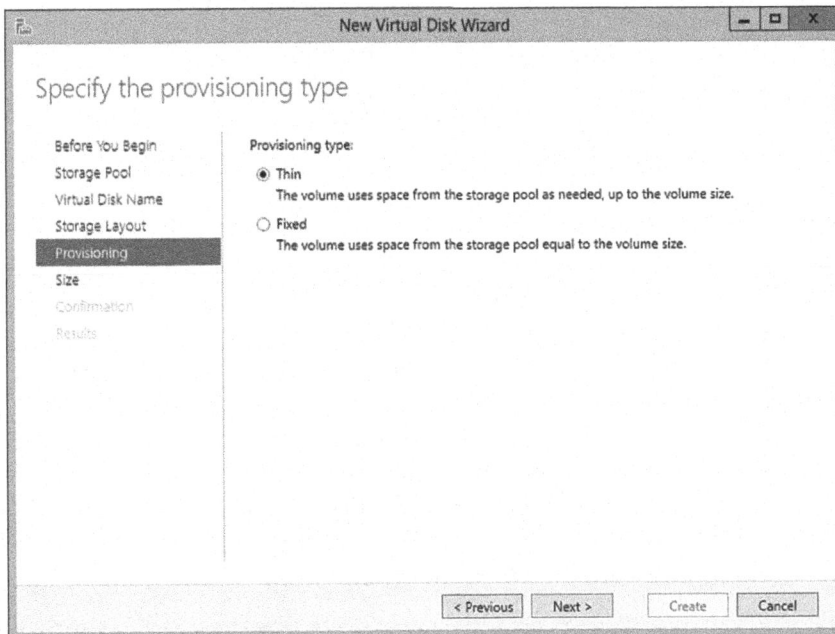

Figure 7-8   Thin provisioning

You can view the amount of space that has been allocated to a thin-provisioned virtual disk,
and you can see the total capacity in the Virtual Disks area when the Storage Pools node is
selected in the Server Manager console, as shown in Figure 7-9. When you create a virtual disk,

the maximum disk size available is determined by the amount of free space on the physical disks that make up the storage pool, rather than the maximum capacity of the existing thin-provisioned disks. For example, if you have a storage pool with two 10 TB physical disks, you can create more than two thin-provisioned disks that have a maximum size of 10 TB. You can create thin-provisioned disks 10 TB in size as long as the actual allocated space on the storage pool doesn't exceed 10 out of the 20 available. It's possible to create thin-provisioned disks in such a way that the total thin-provisioned disk capacity exceeds the storage capacity of the underlying storage pool. If you do overallocate space, you'll need to monitor how much of the underlying storage pool capacity is consumed and add disks to the storage pool because that capacity is exhausted.

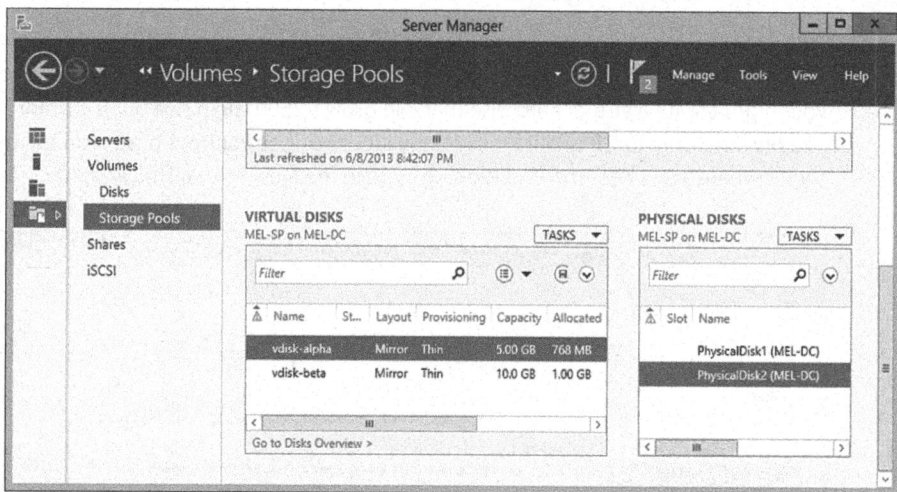

Figure 7-9 Capacity and allocation

Trim is an automatic process that reclaims space when data is deleted from thin-provisioned disks. For example, if you have a 10 TB thin-provisioned virtual disk that stores 8 TB of data, 8 TB will be allocated from the storage pool that hosts that virtual disk. If you delete 2 TB of data from that thin-provisioned virtual disk, Trim ensures that the storage pool that hosts that virtual disk will be able to reclaim that unused space. The 10 TB thin-provisioned virtual disk will appear to be 10 TB in size, but after the trim process is complete, it will only consume 6 TB of space on the underlying storage pool. Trim is enabled by default.

More Info

Thin provisioning and Trim storage

To learn more about thin provisioning, consult the following link: *https://learn.microsoft. com/windows-hardware/drivers/storage/thin-provisioning.*

Creating virtual disks

A storage space virtual disk comprises the capacity available in the storage pool. As long as there's available capacity, you can create multiple virtual disks from a single storage pool. To create a new virtual disk using an existing storage pool, perform the following steps:

1. In Server Manager, navigate to the Storage Pools node under the Volumes node of the File And Storage Services workspace. In the Tasks menu of the Virtual Disks area, select New Virtual Disk.

2. On the list of available storage pools, shown in Figure 7-10, select an available storage pool upon which to create a new virtual disk and click OK.

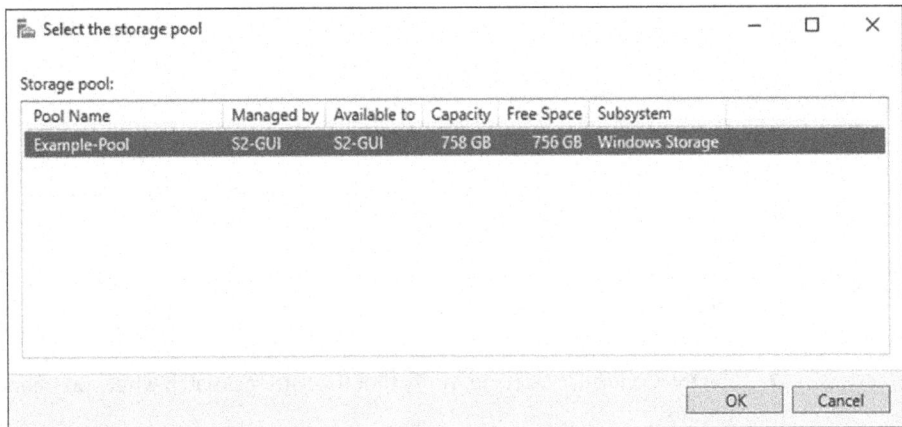

Figure 7-10   Select a storage pool

3. On the Enclosure Awareness page, select whether you want to enable Enclosure Awareness. Doing so will mean that copies of data are stored across separate storage enclosures. For enclosure awareness to work, you'll need multiple enclosures to host the disks that make up the storage pool.

4. On the Storage Layout page, you will be presented with the available layout options. Depending on the type and number of disks, you can choose between Simple, Mirror, and Parity.

5. On the Provisioning Type page, you can choose between thin and fixed provisioning.

6. On the Size page, shown in Figure 7-11, you can choose a size for the disk. If you choose the thin provisioning option, which you saw back in Figure 7-8, the maximum amount of space in the storage pool is not listed. If you choose the fixed option, the total amount of storage currently available in the pool is listed.

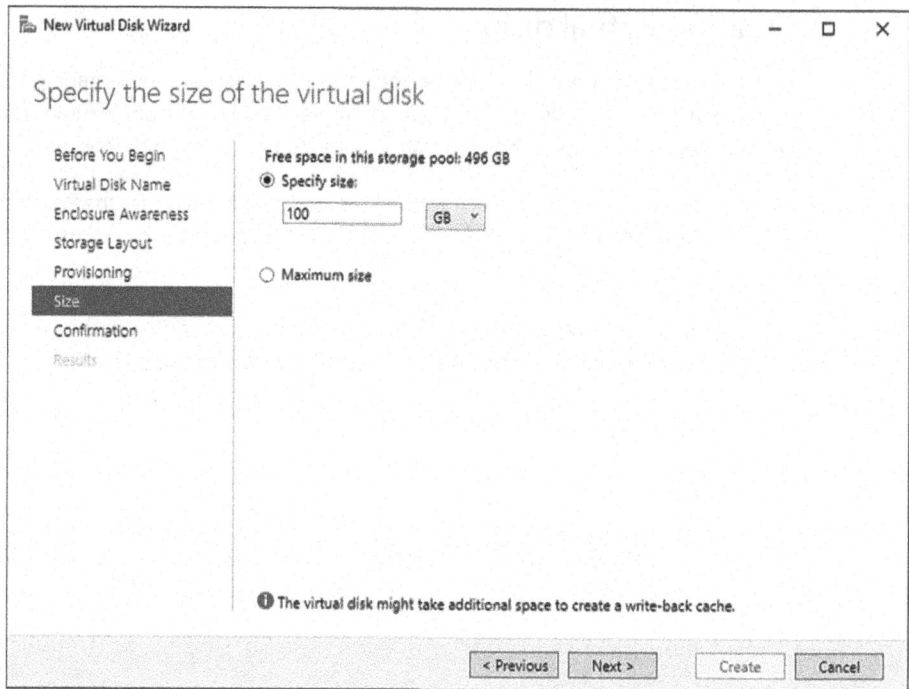

Figure 7-11   Specify the virtual disk size

7. On the Confirmation page, verify that the settings match what you intend and click
    Create.

Storage Spaces Direct

Storage Spaces Direct allows you to use Windows Server with locally attached storage to create
highly available software-defined storage. Storage Spaces Direct (which uses the acronym S2D
because the SSD abbreviation is already used for solid-state disks) provides a form of distributed, software-defined, shared-nothing storage that has similar characteristics to RAID in terms
of performance and redundancy. S2D allows you to create volumes from a storage pool of
physical drives that are attached to multiple nodes that participate in a Windows Server failover
cluster. Storage Spaces Direct functions as a replacement for expensive, large-scale hardware
storage arrays. S2D is only available with the Datacenter edition of Windows Server.

Inside OUT

Supported hardware

Although you can probably figure out a way to get an S2D cluster up and running on hardware that isn't officially supported, it's a terrible idea if you're intending to handle production workloads and data. Check with your vendor to determine whether its hardware includes support for S2D.

Storage Spaces Direct has the following properties:

- You can scale out by adding additional nodes to the cluster.

- When you add a node to a cluster configured for Storage Spaces Direct, all eligible drives on the cluster node will be added to the Storage Spaces Direct pool.

- You can have between 2 and 16 nodes in a Storage Spaces Direct failover cluster.

- It requires each node to have at least two solid-state drives and at least four additional drives.

- A cluster can have more than 400 drives and can support more than 4 petabytes of storage.

- Storage Spaces Direct works with locally attached SATA, SAS, persistent memory, or NVMe drives.

- Cache is automatically built from SSD media. All writes up to 256KB and all reads up to 64KB will be cached. Writes are then de-staged to HDD storage in optimal order.

- Storage Spaces Direct volumes can be part mirror and part parity. To have a three-way mirror with dual parity, it is necessary to have four nodes in the Windows Server failover cluster that hosts Storage Spaces Direct.

- If a disk fails, the plug-and-play replacement will automatically be added to the storage space pool when connected to the original cluster node.

- A Storage Spaces Direct cluster can be configured with rack and chassis awareness as a way of further ensuring fault tolerance.

- Storage Spaces Direct clusters are not supported where nodes span multiple sites.

- While NTFS is supported for use with S2D clusters, Resilient File System (ReFS) is recommended.

CHAPTER 7

S2D supports two deployment options:

- **Hyper-Converged**   With the Hyper-Converged deployment option, both storage and compute resources are deployed on the same cluster. This has the benefit of not requiring you to configure file server access and permissions, and is most commonly used in small to medium-sized Hyper-V deployments.

- **Converged**   With the converged (also known as *disaggregated*) deployment option, storage and compute resources are deployed in separate clusters. Often used with Hyper-V Infrastructure as a Service (IaaS) deployments, a scale-out file server is deployed on S2D to provide network-attached storage over SMB3 file shares. The compute resources for the IaaS virtual machines are located on a separate cluster from the S2D cluster.

Storage Spaces Direct in Windows Server 2019 and later supports nested resiliency. Nested resiliency is a capability designed for two-server S2D clusters that allows storage to remain available in the event of multiple hardware failures. When nested resiliency is configured, volumes can remain online and accessible even if one server goes offline and a drive fails. Nested resiliency only works when a cluster has two nodes. Nested resiliency requires a minimum of four capacity drives per server node and two cache drives per server node.

More Info

Storage Spaces Direct

To learn more about Storage Spaces Direct, consult the following link: *https://learn. microsoft.com/windows-server/storage/storage-spaces/storage-spaces-direct-overview*.

S2D resiliency types

S2D resiliency options are dependent on how many fault domains are present, the failure tolerance required, and the storage efficiency that can be achieved. A fault domain is a collection of hardware, such as a rack of servers, where a single failure can affect every component in that collection.

Table 7-1 lists the different resiliency types, failure tolerances, storage efficiencies, and minimum fault domains.

Table 7-1 S2D resiliency

Resiliency	Failure tolerance	Storage efficiency	Minimum fault domains
Two-way mirror	1	50.0%	2
Three-way mirror	2	33.3%	3
Dual parity	2	50.0%–80.0%	4
Mixed	2	33.3%–80.0%	4

More Info

S2D Resiliency

To learn more about S2D resiliency, consult the following link: *https://learn.microsoft.com/windows-server/storage/storage-spaces/fault-tolerance*.

Deploying S2D clusters

Deploying an S2D cluster is essentially the same as deploying a normal Windows Server failover cluster, with the extra step of enabling S2D once the cluster has been created. To deploy an S2D cluster, perform the following general steps:

1. Ensure that the drives that you will use for S2D are empty and contain no existing partitions or data.

2. Install the Failover Clustering, Hyper-V, File Server, Data Center Bridging, and roles and features; also, you install the Hyper-V and clustering PowerShell cmdlets on each cluster node by using the following command:

   ```
   Install-WindowsFeature -Name "Failover-Clustering", "Hyper-V", "Data-Center-Bridging", "RSAT-Clustering-PowerShell", "Hyper-V-PowerShell", "FS-FileServer"
   ```

3. Use the `Test-Cluster` cmdlet with the `-Include Storage Spaces Direct`, `Inventory`, `Network`, and `System Configuration` parameters to verify that the cluster configuration is valid.

4. Use the `New-Cluster` cmdlet with the `-NoStorage` parameter to create the cluster. For example, run this command to create a new cluster named `TestS2DCluster` with machines S2DN1 and S2DN2:

   ```
   New-Cluster -Name TestS2DCluster -Node S2DN1,S2DN2 -NoStorage
   ```

CHAPTER 7

5. Configure a cluster witness—cloud witness, file share witness, or disk witness.

6. Enable Storage Spaces Direct using the `Enable-ClusterStorageSpacesDirect` cmdlet. For example, to enable S2D on a cluster named `TestS2DCluster`, run the following command:

```
Enable-ClusterStorageSpacesDirect -CimSession TestS2DCluster
```

7. The next step is to create volumes and optionally enable the CSV cache.

> ## More Info
> ### S2D deployment
> To learn more about S2D deployment, consult the following link: *https://learn.microsoft.com/windows-server/storage/storage-spaces/deploy-storage-spaces-direct*.

Managing S2D volumes

You can use Windows Admin Center to manage S2D cluster volumes. To add a volume to an S2D cluster, perform the following steps:

1. Use Windows Admin Center to connect to the S2D cluster by name.

2. Select Volumes in the Tools pane.

3. On the Volume page, click Inventory, as shown in Figure 7-12, and then click Create Volume.

4. On the Create Volume page, shown in Figure 7-13, provide a Name for the volume, and then configure the volume Resiliency, volume size (Size On HDD), and whether options such as Deduplication will be enabled.

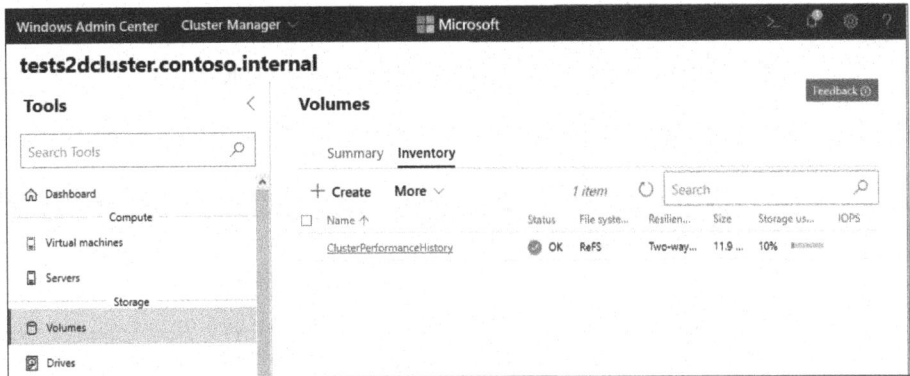

Figure 7-12   S2D cluster volume inventory

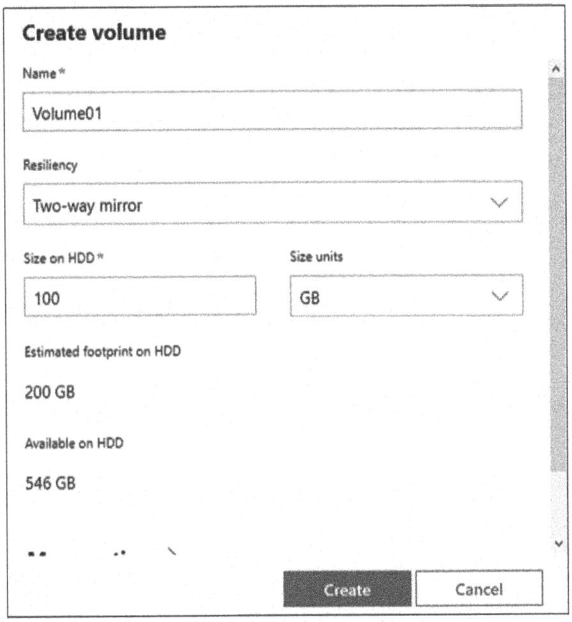

Figure 7-13   New S2D volume

You might want to make an S2D volume larger. You can do this by expanding the volume. To expand an S2D volume, perform the following steps:

1. Use Windows Admin Center to connect to the S2D cluster by name.

2. Select Volumes in the Tools pane and click the Volume.

3. On the Volume Properties page, shown in Figure 7-14, click Expand.

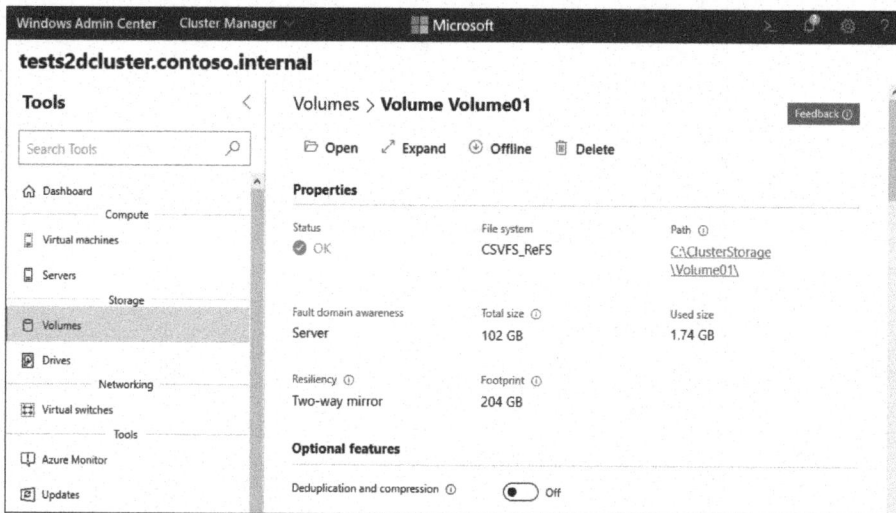

Figure 7-14   S2D volume properties

4. On the Expand page, shown in Figure 7-15, specify the size you want to expand the volume to (up to the Available limit) and click Expand.

You can also use the Volume Properties page to take a volume offline or delete the volume.

More Info

Add S2D volumes

To learn more about adding S2D volumes, consult the following link: *https://learn.microsoft.com/windows-server/storage/storage-spaces/create-volumes.*

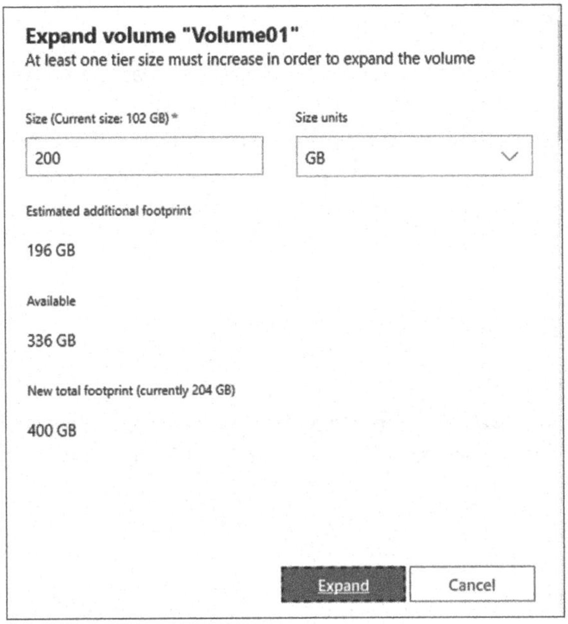

Figure 7-15   Expand the S2D volume

Adding S2D cluster nodes

Before adding a server to an existing S2D cluster, run the `test-cluster` cluster validation cmdlet while including current and existing nodes. For example, run this command to test the configuration of cluster node S2DN3 with a cluster that includes nodes S2DN1 and S2DN2:

```
Test-Cluster -Name TestS2DCluster -node S2DN1,S2DN2,S2DN3 -Include "Storage Spaces
Direct", "Inventory", "Network", "System Configuration"
```

Once the validation has completed, run the `Add-Clusternode` cmdlet on one of the existing cluster nodes and specify the new cluster node name.

More Info

Adding nodes to S2D clusters

To learn more about adding nodes to S2D clusters, consult the following link: *https://learn.microsoft.com/windows-server/storage/storage-spaces/add-nodes.*

CHAPTER 7

S2D cluster node maintenance

Prior to performing maintenance on a cluster node, you should pause and drain the node. You can do this with the `Suspend-ClusterNode` cmdlet with the `-Drain` parameter. Once the node is drained, which will also put it in a paused state, you can either shut the node down or perform other maintenance operations, such as restarting the node. When you have completed maintenance on the node, you can return it to operation by using the `Resume-Clusternode` cmdlet.

> ## More Info
>
> ### S2D cluster node maintenance
>
> To learn more about S2D cluster node maintenance, consult the following link: *https://learn.microsoft.com/azure/azure-local/manage/maintain-servers.*

Storage Replica

Storage Replica allows you to replicate volumes between servers, including clusters, for the purposes of disaster recovery. You can also use Storage Replica to configure asynchronous replication to provision failover clusters that span two geographically disparate sites, while all nodes remain synchronized.

You can configure Storage Replica to support the following types of replication:

- **Synchronous Replication**   Use this when you want to mirror data and you have very low latency between the source and the destination. This allows you to create crash-consistent volumes. Synchronous replication ensures zero data loss at the file system level should a failure occur.

- **Asynchronous Replication**   Asynchronous Storage Replica is suitable when you want to replicate storage across sites where you are experiencing higher latencies.

Storage Replica is available for single volumes under 2 TB in the standard edition of Windows Server 2019 and later. Volume limits do not apply to the datacenter edition of the operating system. Participant servers must be members of the same Active Directory Domain Services Forest.

Storage Replica operates at the partition layer. This means that it replicates all VSS snapshots created by the Windows Server operating system or by backup software that leverages VSS snapshot functionality.

Storage replica has the following features:

- **Zero data loss, block-level replication**   When used with synchronous replication, there is no data loss. By leveraging block-level replication, even files that are locked will be replicated at the block level.

- **Guest and host**   Storage Replica works when Windows Server is a virtualized guest or when it functions as a host operating system. It's possible to replicate from third-party virtualization solutions to IaaS virtual machines hosted in the public cloud as long as Windows Server functions as the source and target operating system.

- **Supports manual failover with zero data loss**   You can perform manual failover when both the source and destination are online, or you can have failover occur automatically if the source storage fails.

- **Leverage SMB3**   This allows Storage Replica to use multichannel, SMB direct support on RoCE, iWARP, and InfiniBand RDMA network cards.

- **Encryption and authentication support**   Storage Replica supports packet signing, AES-128-GCM full data encryption, support for Intel AES-NI encryption acceleration, and Kerberos AES 256 authentication.

- **Initial seeding**   You can perform initial seeding by transferring data using a method other than Storage Replica between the source and destination. This is especially useful when transferring large amounts of data between disparate sites, where it may make more sense to use a courier to transport a high-capacity hard disk drive than it does to transmit data across a WAN link. The initial replication will then only copy blocks that have been changed since the replica data was exported from the source to the destination.

- **Consistency groups**   Consistency groups implement write ordering guarantees. This ensures that applications such as Microsoft SQL Server, which may write data to multiple replicated volumes, will have that data replicated such that it remains replicated sequentially and consistently.

Supported configurations

Storage replica is supported in the following configurations:

- **Server-to-server**   In this configuration, Storage Replica supports both synchronous and asynchronous replication between two standalone services. Local drives, storage spaces with shared SAS (Serial Attached SCSI) storage, SAN (Subject Alternative Name), and iSCSI-attached LUNs (Logical Unit Numbers) can be replicated. You can manage this configuration either using Server Manager or PowerShell. Failover can only be performed manually.

- **Cluster-to-cluster**   In this configuration, replication occurs between two separate clusters. The first cluster might use Storage Spaces Direct, Storage Spaces with shared SAS storage, SAN, and iSCSI-attached LUNs. You manage this configuration using PowerShell and Azure Site Recovery. Failover must be performed manually.

- **Stretch cluster**   A single cluster where nodes are located in geographically disparate sites. Some nodes share one set of asymmetric storage, and other nodes share another set of asymmetric storage. Storage is replicated either synchronously or asynchronously, depending on bandwidth considerations. This scenario supports Storage Spaces with shared SAS storage, SAN, and iSCSI-attached LUNs. You manage this configuration using PowerShell and the Failover Cluster Manager GUI tool. This scenario allows for automated failover.

The following configurations are not supported on Windows Server, though they may be supported at some point in the future:

- Storage Replica only supports one-to-one replication in Windows Server. You cannot configure Storage Replica to support one-to-many replication or transitive replication. Transitive replication is where there is a replica of the replica server.

- Storage Replica on Windows Server does not support bringing a replicated volume online for read-only access in Windows Server 2016. In Windows Server 2019 and later, you can perform a test failover and temporarily mount a snapshot of the replicated storage on an unused NTFS or ReFS-formatted volume.

- Deploying Scale-out File Servers on stretch clusters participating in Storage Replica is not a supported configuration.

- Deploying Storage Spaces Direct in a stretch cluster with Storage Replica is not supported.

Configuring replication

To configure replication between two servers that are members of the same domain, perform the following steps:

1. Ensure that each server meets the following requirements:

    - It must have two volumes—one volume hosts the data that you want to replicate, and another that hosts the replication logs.

    - Ensure that both log and data disks are formatted as GPT and not MBR.

    - Data volume on the source and destination servers must be the same size and use the same sector sizes.

    - Log volume on the source and destination volumes should be the same size and use the same sector sizes. The log volume should be a minimum of 9 GB in size.

    - Ensure that the data volume does not contain the system volume, page file, or dump files.

    - Install the File Server role service and Storage Replica feature on each server as shown in Figure 7-16. Installing these features requires that you restart the computer.

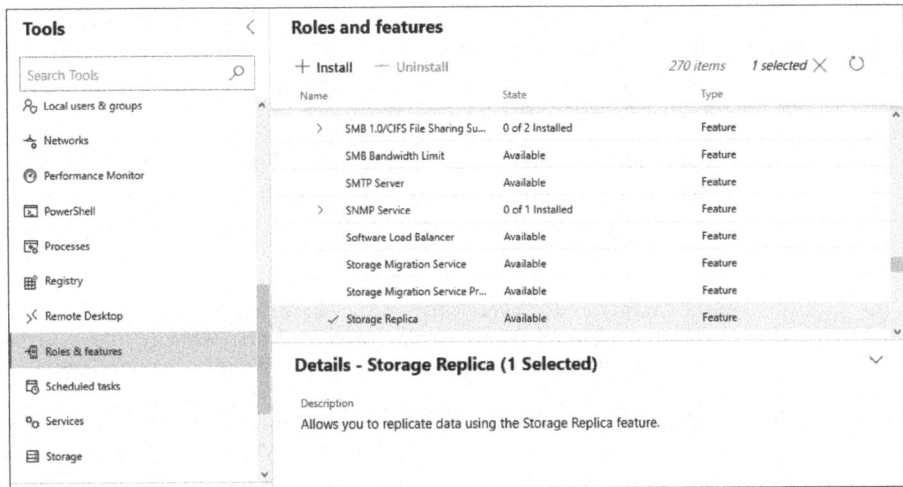

Figure 7-16   Install Storage Replica feature

2. Use the `Test-SRTopology` cmdlet to verify that all Storage Replica requirements have been met. To do this, perform the following steps:

    1. Create a temp directory on the source server that will store the Storage Replica Topology Report.

    2. Make a note of the drive letters of the source storage, the log volumes, and the destination storage and log volumes.

3. The following command will test Storage Topology for a source computer with the following details:

    ■ It is named S3-DCenter.

    ■ The source volume is E:, and the log volume is F:.

    ■ The destination computer is named S4-DCenter.

    ■ The volume is E:, and the destination log volume is F:.

    ■ The duration is 15 minutes.

    ■ The results are written to the c:\temp folder.

```
Test-SRTopology -SourceComputerName  S3-DCenter -SourceVolumeName e:
-SourceLogVolumeName f: -DestinationComputerName S4-DCenter -DestinationVolumeName
e: -DestinationLogVolumeName f: -DurationInMinutes 15 -ResultPath c:\temp
```

4. When the test completes, view the `TestSrTopologyReport.html` file to verify that your configuration meets Storage Replica requirements. Once you have verified that the configuration meets requirements, you can use the `New-SRPartnerShip` cmdlet to create a Storage Replica partnership.

    For example, the following command will configure a Storage Replica group named SR71 for a source computer named S3-DCenter with the source volume of E: and the log volume of F: to a destination computer named S4-DCenter with the destination volume of E: and the destination log volume of F:

    ```
    New-SRPartnerShip -SourceRGName SR71 -DestinationRGName SR72 -SourceComputerName
    S3-DCenter -SourceVolumeName e: -SourceLogVolumeName f: -DestinationComputerName
    S4-DCenter -DestinationVolumeName e: -DestinationLogVolumeName f:
    ```

5. You can check the status of Storage Replica replication by running the `Get-SRGroup`, `Get-SRPartnership` and `(Get-SRGroup).replicas` cmdlets. Once Storage Replica is active, you won't be able to access the replica storage device on the destination computer unless you reverse replication or remove replication.

6. To switch direction, use the `Set-SRPartnerShip` cmdlet. For example, to reverse the replication direction of the Storage Replica partnership configured in step 5, use the following command:

    ```
    Set-SRPartnerShip -NewSourceComputerName S4-DCenter -SourceRGName SR72
    -DestinationComputerName S3-DCenter -DestinationRGName SR71
    ```

    When you run this command, you will receive a warning that data loss may occur, and you will be asked whether you want to complete the operation.

7. To remove replication, run the following commands on the source node:

    ```
    Get-SRPartnership | Remove-SRPartnership
    Get-SRGroup | Remove-SRGroup
    ```

    Then, run the following command on the destination node:

    ```
    Get-SRGroup | Remove-SRGroup
    ```

8. By default, all replication when Storage Replica is configured is synchronous. You can switch between synchronous and asynchronous replication using the `Set-SRPartnership` cmdlet with the `ReplicationMode` parameter.

    Storage Replica uses the following ports:

    - **445** Used for SMB, which is the replication transport protocol

    - **5985** Used for WSManHTTP, which is the management protocol for WMI/CIM/PowerShell

    - **5445** Used for SMB with iWARP. This port is only required if using iWARP RDMA networking

> ## More Info
> ***Storage Replica***
>
> To learn more about Storage Replica, consult the following link: *https://learn.microsoft.com/windows-server/storage/storage-replica/storage-replica-overview*.

Configuring SMB

The most recent version of SMB is 3.1.1, which has been available since Windows Server 2016. SMB 3.1.1 contains substantial security and performance improvements over previous versions of the SMB protocol. You can determine which version of SMB a server is using by running the `Get-SmbConnection` cmdlet, as shown in Figure 7-17.

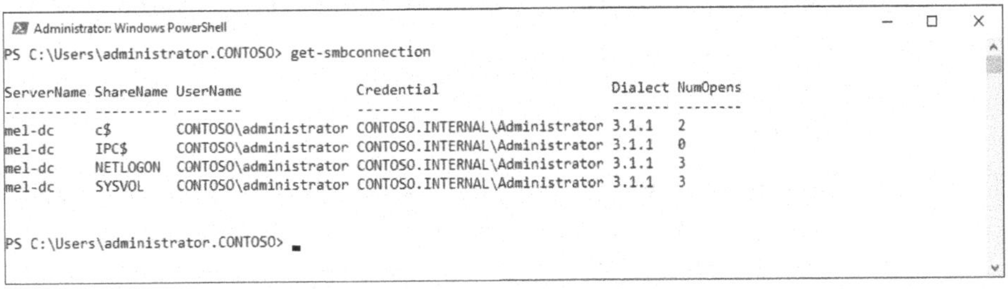

```
Administrator: Windows PowerShell
PS C:\Users\administrator.CONTOSO> get-smbconnection

ServerName ShareName UserName               Credential                          Dialect NumOpens
---------- --------- --------               ----------                          ------- --------
mel-dc     c$        CONTOSO\administrator CONTOSO.INTERNAL\Administrator 3.1.1   2
mel-dc     IPC$      CONTOSO\administrator CONTOSO.INTERNAL\Administrator 3.1.1   0
mel-dc     NETLOGON  CONTOSO\administrator CONTOSO.INTERNAL\Administrator 3.1.1   3
mel-dc     SYSVOL    CONTOSO\administrator CONTOSO.INTERNAL\Administrator 3.1.1   3


PS C:\Users\administrator.CONTOSO>
```

Figure 7-17 Check SMB version

The version of SMB that is used depends on the operating system of the client. Because newer versions of SMB perform much better and are much more secure than older versions, updating clients and server operating systems to the most recent version ensures that you are running the fastest version of SMB. Table 7-2 lists which version of SMB is used when clients or servers communicate with one another.

Table 7-2 Protocol negotiation

OS	Win 10+ / WS 2016+	Win 8.1 / WS 2012 R2	Win 8 / WS 2012	Win 7 / WS 2008 R2	Win Vista / WS 2008	Older versions
Win 10+ / WS 2016+	SMB 3.1.1	SMB 3.0.2	SMB 3.0	SMB 2.1	SMB 2.0.2	SMB 1.x
Win 8.1 / WS 2012 R2	SMB 3.0.2	SMB 3.0.2	SMB 3.0	SMB 2.1	SMB 2.0.2	SMB 1.x
Win 8 / WS 2012	SMB 3.0	SMB 3.0	SMB 3.0	SMB 2.1	SMB 2.0.2	SMB 1.x
Win 7 / WS 2008 R2	SMB 2.1	SMB 2.1	SMB 2.1	SMB 2.1	SMB 2.0.2	SMB 1.x
Win Vista / WS 2008	SMB 2.0.2	SMB 2.0.2	SMB 2.0.2	SMB 2.0.2	SMB 2.0.2	SMB 1.x
Older versions	SMB 1.x	SMB 1.x	SMB 1.x	SMB 1.x	SMB 1.x	SMB 1.x

SMB 1 is an old protocol that doesn't include key protections available in later versions of SMB, including preauthentication integrity, secure dialect negotiation, encryption, insecure guest authentication blocking, and improved message signing. SMB 1 is less efficient than version SMB 3 or later, with SMB 3 supporting larger read and writes, peer caching of folder and file properties, durable handles, the client oplock leasing model, SMB direct, and directory leasing. SMB 1 is only necessary if your organization is running older versions of Windows that are no longer in mainstream support.

By default, SMB 1 is disabled on Windows Server 2019 and later. If your organization has servers running Windows Server 2016 or earlier, you'll need to configure the operating system so that SMB 1 is not present. If you are worried that you have applications on the network that use SMB 1, you can audit SMB 1 utilization by running the following command on any file server that has SMB 1 enabled, and check the SMBServer\Audit event log:

```
Set-SmbServerConfiguration -AuditSmb1Access $true
```

Run the following command to remove SMB 1 from a computer running Windows Server:

```
Remove-WindowsFeature -Name FS-SMB1
```

SMB compression

SMB compression allows for files to be compressed as they are transferred across the network. The drawback of SMB compression is that there is increased CPU utilization during the transfer. You should use SMB compression on low-bandwidth networks, as there will be less benefit on file transfer speeds on uncongested networks that exceed 100 Gbps.

SMB compression requires Windows Server 2022 or later and clients running Windows 11 or later. To configure SMB compression, perform the following steps:

1. Use Windows Admin Center to connect to the file server.

2. On the Files And File Sharing menu, select File Shares.

3. Select the share on which you want to enable SMB compression and select Edit Share.

4. On the Share Permissions page, select the Compress Data checkbox and choose Edit to apply the changes.

To enable SMB compression using PowerShell, use the Set-SmbShare cmdlet with the CompressData parameter. For example, to enable compression on the Engineering share, run the following command:

```
Set-SmbShare -Name "Engineering" -CompressData $true
```

To configure SMB compression at the file server level using Windows Admin Center, navigate to Files And File Sharing, select the File Shares tab, and then choose File Server Settings. On the File Server Settings page, select the Request SMB Compression checkbox.

> ## More Info
>
> *SMB compression*
>
> To learn more about SMB compression, consult the following link: *https://learn.micro-soft.com/windows-server/storage/file-server/smb-compression*.

SMB encryption

The SMB clients for Windows Server 2025 and Windows 11 support requiring encryption for all outbound SMB connections. SMB Encryption supplies SMB data end-to-end protection from interception attacks and snooping. When you enable this option, SMB clients will not connect to an SMB server that doesn't support SMB encryption.

You can require SMB encryption for outbound connections by editing the Require encryption policy located in a GPO under the `Computer Configuration\Administrative Templates\ Network\Lanman Workstation` node. You can configure the SMB client to require encryption using the `Set-SmbClientConfiguration` PowerShell cmdlet with the `RequireEncryption` parameter. For example, to require SMB encryption on Windows 11 or Windows Server 2025, run the following command:

```
Set-SmbClientConfiguration -RequireEncryption $true
```

When you enable SMB Encryption for a file share or server, only SMB 3.0, 3.02, and 3.1.1 and later clients are allowed to access that file share. To enable SMB encryption on a file share using Windows Admin Center, perform the following steps:

1. Use Windows Admin Center to connect to the file server.

2. On the Files And File Sharing menu, select File Shares.

3. Select the share on which you want to enable SMB compression and select Edit Share.

4. On the Share Permissions page, select the Enable SMB Encryption checkbox and choose Edit to apply the changes.

To enable SMB Encryption with PowerShell, use the `Set-SmbShare` cmdlet with the `Encrypt-Data` parameter. For example, to enable SMB encryption on the Engineering share, run the following command:

```
Set-SmbShare -Name "Engineering" -EncryptData $true
```

CHAPTER 7

To configure SMB encryption at the file server level using Windows Admin Center, navigate to Files And File Sharing, select the File Shares tab, and then choose File Server Settings. On the File Server Settings page, set SMB 3 Encryption to either Required From Clients That Support It or Required From All Clients.

More Info

SMB encryption

To learn more about SMB encryption, consult the following link: *https://learn.microsoft. com/windows-server/storage/file-server/smb-security*.

SMB signing

SMB signing is a security feature that uses a session key and cipher suite to add a signature to a transmission across the network. This signature contains a cryptographic hash of the entire message in the SMB header. This means that if someone tampers with the transmission, the hash calculated at the other end will not match the hash in the signature. The hash also includes the identities of the original sender and intended recipient. Windows 11 Enterprise, Pro, and Education require outbound and inbound SMB signing. Windows Server 2025 requires outbound SMB signing only.

You configure SMB signing in Group Policy by configuring the `Microsoft network client: Digitally Sign Communications (Always)` policy located under `Computer Configuration\Windows Settings\Security Settings\Local Policies\Security Options`.

To configure SMB signing on a file server using Windows Admin Center, navigate to Files And File Sharing, select the File Shares tab, and then choose File Server Settings. On the File Server Settings page, set SMB Signing to Required.

More Info

SMB signing

To learn more about SMB signing, consult the following link: *https://learn.microsoft. com/windows-server/storage/file-server/smb-signing*.

SMB NTLM blocking

SMB NTLM blocking allows you to block NTLM authentication for remote outbound connections. SMB NTLM blocking requires clients running Windows 11 or Windows Server 2025 or later. Also, the destination SMB server must support Kerberos authentication. NTLM blocking is configurable at the client level, though you can disable NTLM for all authentication on a server as well. You can configure SMB blocking by editing the Block NTLM (LM, NTLM, NTLMv2) policy located in the `Computer Configuration\Administrative Templates\Network\ Lanman Workstation` node of a GPO or by running the following PowerShell command:

```
Set-SMbClientConfiguration -BlockNTLM $true
```

> **More Info**
>
> **SMB NTLM blocking**
>
> To learn more about SMB signing, consult the following link: *https://learn.microsoft.com/windows-server/storage/file-server/smb-ntlm-blocking*.

SMB over QUIC

SMB over QUIC provides secure connectivity to edge file servers over the internet. QUIC is an industry standard protocol, and SMB over QUIC functions similar to an SMB VPN without requiring an explicit VPN client connection from the host to the destination server. When SMB over QUIC is implemented, the server certificate on the file server is used to create a TLS 1.3 encrypted tunnel over UDP port 443. SMB traffic passes through this tunnel between the client and the server. Windows SMB client only attempts SMB over QUIC if they are unable to establish a TCP connection or if a connection is made using the New-SmbMapping cmdlet with the TransportType parameter set to QUIC.

SMB over QUIC was only supported in the Azure edition of Windows Server 2022, but is supported by all editions of Windows Server 2025. SMB over QUIC also requires that a domain-joined Windows 11 client or that the client has a local user account on the remote file server. Microsoft recommends using SMB over QUIC in Active Directory domain-joined scenarios, as workgroup scenarios use NTLM for authentication.

The file server that functions as the SMB over QUIC endpoint needs to be accessible to clients on UDP port 443 inbound. The FQDN (fully qualified domain name) of the file server needs to be able to be resolved by the SMB over the QUIC client.

The file server that functions as the SMB over QUIC endpoint also needs to have a certificate from a trusted third-party certificate authority or Active Directory Certificate Services. A certificate issued by Active Directory Certificate Services needs to have the following properties:

- **Key usage** Digital signature.

- **Purpose** Server authentication (EKU 1.3.6.1.5.5.7.3.1).

- **Signature algorithm** SHA256RSA (or greater).

- **Signature hash** SHA256 (or greater).

- **Public key algorithm** ECDSA_P256 (or greater). Can also use RSA with at least a 2,048 key length.

- **Subject Alternative Name (SAN)** A DNS name entry is required for each fully qualified DNS name used to reach the SMB server.

- **Subject** (CN= anything name; cannot be left blank).

- **Private key included** Yes.

You should not use an IP address for SMB over QUIC server SANs when configuring the certificate. SMB over QUIC does not support the use of an IP address for the server name when traversing network address translation (NAT). IP address names will also default to NTLM rather than Kerberos if NAT is not present between the client and server.

1. To configure SMB over QUIC, ensure that these requirements are met:

    - Name resolution is configured for clients when they are on untrusted networks, so that they are able to resolve the file server address.

    - Firewalls are configured as appropriate to allow inbound connections on UDP port 443.

    - A certificate with the appropriate configuration is installed on the file server.

2. Then, perform the following steps on the file server:

    1. Store the details of the installed certificate in a PowerShell variable using the following command:

        ```
        $serverCert = Get-ChildItem -Path Cert:\LocalMachine\My | Where-Object {$_.
        Subject -Match "<subject name>"}
        ```

    2. Run the following command using the FQDN of the server that clients on untrusted networks will use to connect:

        ```
        New-SmbServerCertificateMapping -Name <server FQDN> -ThumbPrint $serverCert.
        Thumbprint -Storename My
        ```

> ## More Info
> ### SMB over QUIC
>
> To learn more about SMB over QUIC, consult the following link: *https://learn.microsoft. com/windows-server/storage/file-server/smb-over-quic.*

SMB Direct

SMB Direct allows you to leverage the capabilities of network adapters that have Remote Direct Memory Access (RDMA) capability. The benefit of SMB Direct is that it reduces the CPU utilization required to process large amounts of file server traffic on the network adapter, rather than requiring as many CPU cycles. SMB Direct has been enabled by default on all versions of Windows Server since Windows Server 2012. You can disable SMB Direct by running the following PowerShell command:

```
Disable-WindowsOptionalFeature -Online -FeatureName SMBDirect
```

> ## More Info
> ### SMB Direct
>
> To learn more about SMB Direct, consult the following link: *https://learn.microsoft. com/windows-server/storage/file-server/smb-direct.*

iSCSI

iSCSI allows access to storage devices across a TCP/IP network. The iSCSI initiator is a special software component that allows connections to iSCSI targets, which are storage devices to which an iSCSI initiator connects over the network. When you install the iSCSI Target Server role service on a computer running the Windows Server operating system, you can configure virtual hard disks as iSCSI targets. When an iSCSI initiator connects to this virtual hard disk, it appears on the client as a local disk. While you can use iSCSI targets as local storage, you can also use an iSCSI-connected disk as shared storage in failover clusters.

By default, the iSCSI Initiator component is installed on all computers running supported versions of Windows Server. When you select the iSCSI Initiator for the first time in the Tools menu of the Server Manager console, it will prompt you to start the service and to configure it to start automatically in the future. Once the service is started, you can configure the iSCSI initiator on the iSCSI Initiator Properties dialog, which is available when you select the iSCSI Initiator in the Tools menu of the Server Manager console. In most cases, the configuration involves entering the FQDN of the server that hosts the iSCSI target in the Target text box and clicking Quick Connect. The iSCSI Initiator Properties dialog is shown in Figure 7-18.

Figure 7-18   iSCSI Initiator Properties

You can only connect to an iSCSI target that has been configured to accept connections from the iSCSI initiator to which you are attempting to connect. When creating an iSCSI target, you specify which iSCSI initiators can access the target, as shown in Figure 7-19. You can specify initiators on the basis of IQN, DNS name, IP address, or MAC address.

If the initiator is running on a domain-joined computer running a Windows 8 client operating system (or later) or a Windows Server 2012 server operating system (or later), you can query Active Directory to determine the initiator ID, as shown in Figure 7-20. When configuring an initiator ID for a client running a Microsoft operating system, the format is iqn.1991-05.com.microsoft:FQDN. For example, if you are specifying the initiator ID of cbr.contoso.internal, you would type **iqn.199-05.com.microsoft:cbr.contoso.internal**.

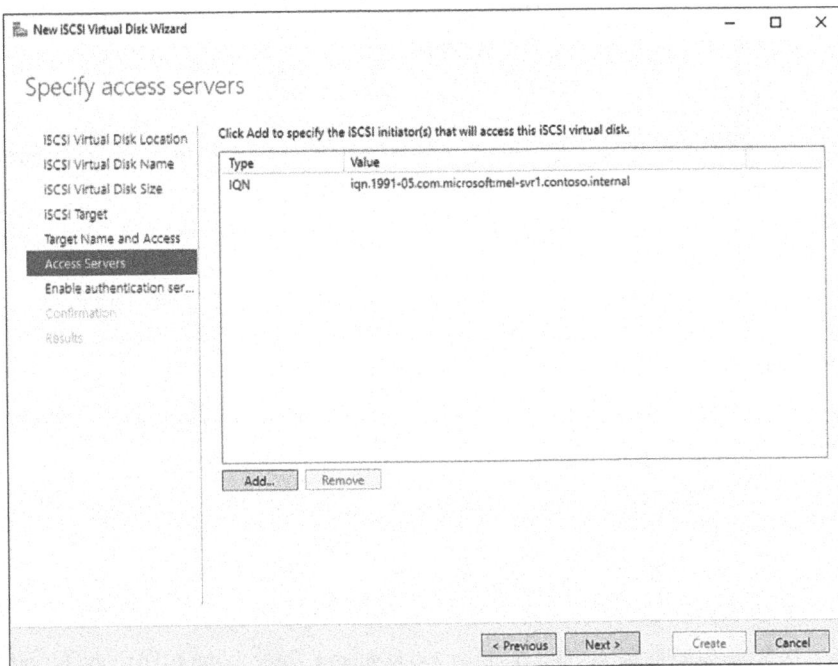

Figure 7-19   Configuring access servers

You can create a new iSCSI virtual disk using the New-IscsiVirtualDisk cmdlet. For example, to create a new 10GB iSCSI virtual disk that has the path E:\Disks\Disk1.vhd, you can use this command:

```
New-IscsiVirtualDisk -Path "e:\disks\disk1.vhd" -Size 10GB
```

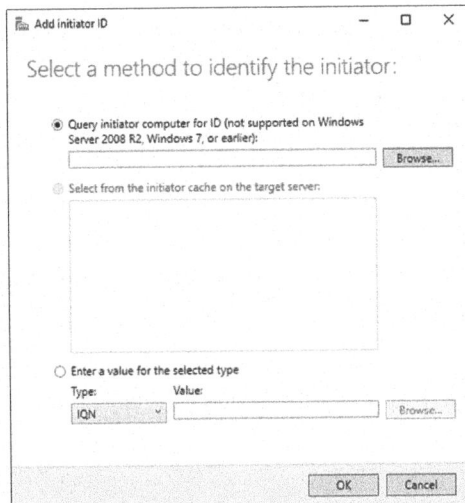

Figure 7-20   Identify the initiator

More Info

iSCSI Target

To learn more about iSCSI Target, consult the following link: *https://learn.microsoft.com/windows-server/storage/iscsi/iscsi-target-server.*

You can use the `New-IscsiServerTarget` cmdlet to create an iSCSI server target. For example, to configure an iSCSI target that allows computers `syd-a.contoso.com` and `syd-b.contoso.com` to access an iSCSI virtual disk, you can use this command:

```
New-IscsiServerTarget -Targetname "Syd-A-Syd-B-Target" -InitiatorIDs DNSName:Syd-a.
contoso.com,DNSName:syd-b.contoso.com
```

More Info

Scale-Out File Servers

A Scale-Out File Server (SoFS) allows you to share a single folder from multiple nodes of the same cluster. You can use SoFS to deploy file shares that are continuously available for file-based server application storage. This storage is suitable for hosting Hyper-V virtual machine files or Microsoft SQL Server databases with a level of reliability, availability, manageability, and performance that equates to what is possible with a storage area network.

The benefits of an SoFS deployment include

- **Active-Active file share topology**   SoFS allows the same folder to be accessed from multiple nodes of the same cluster. An SoFS file share remains online should one or more cluster nodes fail or be taken down for planned maintenance.

- **Scalable bandwidth**   You can respond to a requirement for increased bandwidth by adding nodes.

- **Automatic rebalancing of clients**   SMB client connects are tracked on a per-per-file-share basis, with clients being redirected to the cluster node that has the best access to the storage device used by the file share.

- **CHKDSK with zero downtime**   The Cluster Shared Volume File System, used with SoFS, allows CHKDSK operations to occur without affecting applications that have open handles on the file system.

You should consider SoFS file shares for the following scenarios:

- Store the Hyper-V configuration and live virtual disks

- Store live SQL Server database files

- Store shared IIS configuration data

SoFS has the following requirements:

- The storage configuration must be explicitly supported by failover clustering. This means that you must be able to successfully run the Cluster Validation Wizard prior to adding an SoFS.

- SoFS requires Cluster Shared Volumes.

Windows Server 2019 introduced a new SoFS role called the Infrastructure File Server. An infrastructure SoFS uses a single namespace share for the Cluster Shared Volume drive. The benefit of the Infrastructure File Server role is that it allows the Hyper-V host to communicate using guaranteed continuous availability to the Infrastructure SoFS SMB server. A failover cluster can only support a single Infrastructure SoFS instance. To create an Infrastructure SoFS, run the following PowerShell command:

```
Add-ClusterScaleOutFileServerRole -Cluster ClusterName -Infrastructure -Name
InfrastructureSoFSName
```

> ## More Info
>
> **SoFS**
>
> **To learn more about SoFS, consult the following link: *https://learn.microsoft.com/windows-server/failover-clustering/sofs-overview*.**

Server for NFS

Server for NFS allows clients that use the Network File System (NFS) protocol to access data stored on computers running Windows Server. NFS is primarily used by UNIX and Linux clients, but some third-party hypervisors also use it. You can configure Server for NFS to leverage Windows-to-UNIX user mappings from Active Directory Domain Services, User Name Mapping, or both. Identity Management for UNIX can also be deployed to update the Active Directory schema to support UNIX user account data.

CHAPTER 7

Server for NFS supports continuous availability when deployed on a Windows Server failover cluster. Once installed, you configure Server for NFS by editing the properties of the Server For NFS node of the Services For Network File System tool, which is available from the Tools menu of the Server Manager console (see Figure 7-21) when Server for NFS is installed.

You can use this dialog to configure the following:

- Support for NFS version 3

- Transport protocol (TCP/UPD, TCP, or UDP)

- Authentication cache renewal

- Filename translation for file characters supported by NFS. (NTFS does not support file-name translation.

- File locking wait period

- Activity logging

- Netgroups for managing access to NFS shares

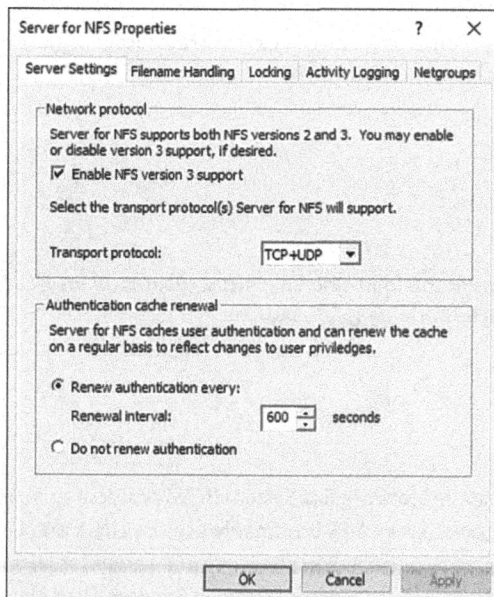

Figure 7-21   Server For NFS Properties

Even though the Server For NFS dialog mentions NSF versions 2 and 3, Server for NFS in Windows Server 2016 and later also includes support for NFS version 4.1. There is also support in the NFS server implementation of Windows Server for the Pseudo file system, sessions, session trunking, and compound RPCs.

> ## More Info
>
> *Server for NFS*
>
> To learn more about Server for NFS, consult the following link: *https://learn.microsoft.com/windows-server/storage/nfs/nfs-overview*.

Deduplication

Deduplication works by analyzing files, locating the unique chunks of data that make up those files, and only storing one copy of each unique data chunk on the volume. (A chunk is a collection of storage blocks.) Deduplication can reduce the amount of storage consumed on the volume because, when analyzed, it turns out that a substantial number of data chunks stored on a volume are identical. Rather than store multiple copies of the same identical chunk, deduplication ensures that one copy of the chunk is stored with placeholders in other locations pointing at the single copy of the chunk, rather than storing the chunk itself. Windows Server supports deduplication on both NTFS- and ReFS-formatted volumes.

Before you can enable deduplication, you need to install the Data Deduplication role service, as shown in Figure 7-22.

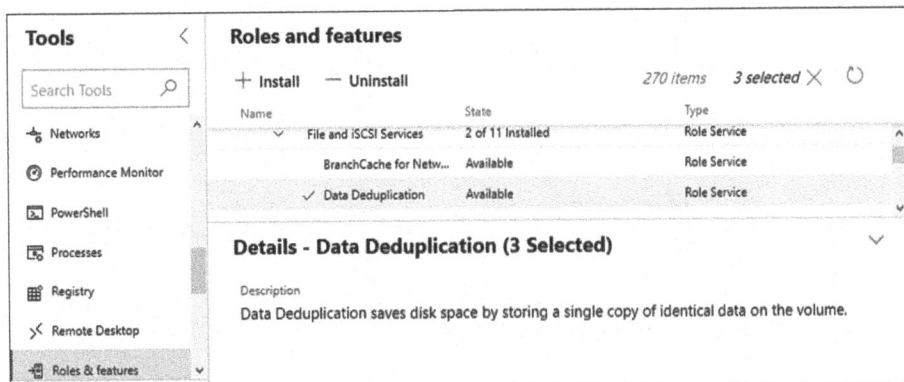

Figure 7-22   Enable deduplication

CHAPTER 7

When you configure deduplication, you choose from one of the following usage types, as shown in Figure 7-23:

- **General Purpose File Server**   Appropriate for general-purpose file servers, optimization is performed in the background on any file that is older than three days. Files that are in use and partial files are not optimized.

- **Virtual Desktop Infrastructure (VDI) server**   Appropriate for VDI servers, optimization is performed in the background on any file that is older than three days, but files that are in use and partial files will also be optimized.

- **Virtualized Backup Server**   This usage type is suitable for backup applications such as System Center Data Protection Manager or an Azure Backup Server. Performs priority optimization on files of any age. It will optimize in-use files, but it will not optimize partial files.

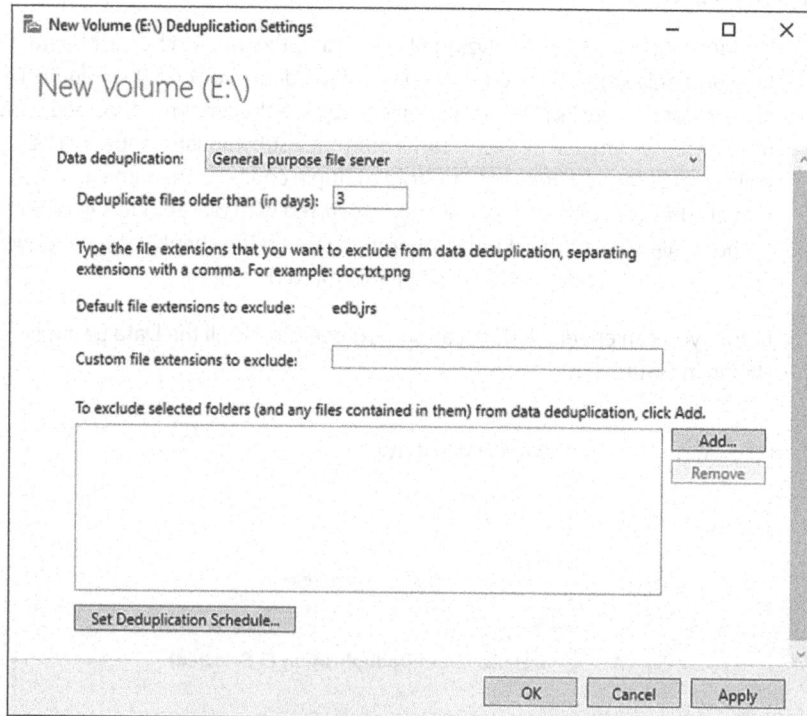

Figure 7-23   Deduplication Settings

When configuring deduplication settings, you can configure files to be excluded on the basis of file extension, or you can exclude entire folders from data deduplication. Deduplication involves running a series of jobs outlined in Table 7-3.

Table 7-3   Deduplication jobs

Name	Description	Schedule
Optimization	Deduplicates and optimizes the volume.	Once per hour
Garbage collection	Reclaims disk space by removing unnecessary chunks. You may want to run this job manually after deleting a substantial amount of data in an attempt to reclaim space by using the `Start-DedupeJob` cmdlet with the `Type` parameter set to `GarbageCollection`.	Every Saturday at 2:35 AM
Integrity scrubbing	Identifies corruption in the chunk store and uses volume features where possible to repair and reconstruct corrupted data.	Every Saturday at 3.35 AM
Unoptimization	A special job that you run manually when you want to disable deduplication for a volume.	Run manually

More Info

Deduplication

To learn more about deduplication, consult the following link: *https://learn.microsoft.com/windows-server/storage/data-deduplication/overview.*

Storage Quality of Service

Storage Quality of Service (QoS) allows you to centrally manage and monitor the performance of storage used for virtual machines that leverage the Scale-Out File Server and Hyper-V roles. The Storage QoS feature will automatically ensure that access to storage resources is distributed equitably between virtual machines that use the same file server cluster. It allows you to configure minimum and maximum performance settings as policies in units of IOPS (input/output operations per second).

Storage QoS allows you to accomplish the following goals:

- **Reduce the impact of noisy neighbor VMs**   A noisy neighbor VM is a virtual machine that is consuming a disproportionate amount of storage resources. Storage QoS allows you to limit the extent to which such a VM can consume storage bandwidth.

- **Monitor storage performance**   When you deploy a virtual machine to a Scale-Out File Server, you can review storage performance from a central location.

CHAPTER 7

- **Allocate the minimum and maximum available resources**   Through Storage QoS policies, you can specify the minimum and maximum resources available. This allows you to ensure that each VM has the minimum storage performance it requires to run reserved for it.

There are two types of Storage QoS policy:

- **Aggregated**   An aggregated policy applies maximum and minimum values for a combined set of virtual hard disk files and virtual machines. For example, by creating an aggregated policy with a minimum of 150 IOPS and a maximum of 250 IOPS and applying it to three virtual hard disk files, you can ensure that the three virtual hard disk files will have a minimum of 150 IOPS between them when the system is under load and will consume a maximum of 250 IOPs when the virtual machines associated with those hard disks are heavily using storage.

- **Dedicated**   A dedicated policy applies a minimum and maximum value to each virtual hard disk. For example, if you apply a dedicated policy to each of three virtual hard disks that specify a minimum of 150 IOPS and a maximum of 250 IOPS, each virtual hard disk will individually be able to use up to 250 IOPS, while having a minimum of 150 IOPS reserved for use if the system is under pressure.

You create policies with the `New-StorageQosPolicy` cmdlet, which is specified by using the `PolicyType` parameter if the policy is Dedicated or Aggregated; also, you must specify the minimum and maximum IOPS. For example, run this command to create a new policy called `Alpha` of the Dedicated type that has a minimum of 150 IOPS and a maximum of 250 IOPS:

```
New-StorageQosPolicy -Name Alpha -PolicyType Dedicated -MinimumIops 150 -MaximumIops 250
```

Once you've created a policy, you can apply it to a virtual hard disk using the `Set-VMHardDiskDrive` cmdlet.

More Info

Storage Quality of Service

To learn more about Storage QoS, consult the following link: *https://learn.microsoft.com/windows-server/storage/storage-qos/storage-qos-overview*.

ReFS

ReFS (Resilient File System) is a file system that is appropriate for very large workloads where you need to maximize data availability and integrity and ensure that the file system is resilient to corruption. ReFS in Windows Server 2019 and later supports deduplication.

The ReFS file system is suitable for hosting specific types of workloads, such as virtual machines and SQL Server data, because it includes the following features that improve upon NTFS:

- **Integrity** ReFS uses checksums for both metadata and file data, meaning can detect data corruption.

- **Storage spaces integration** When integrated with storage spaces that are configured with Mirror or Parity options, ReFS can automatically detect and repair corruption using a secondary or tertiary copy of data stored by Storage Spaces. The repair occurs without downtime.

- **Proactive error correction** ReFS includes a data integrity scanner that scans the volume to identify latent corruption and proactively repairs corrupt data.

- **Scalability** ReFS is specifically designed to support data sets in the petabyte range.

- **Advanced VM operations** ReFS includes functionality specifically to support virtual machine operations. Block cloning accelerates copy operations, which accelerate VM checkpoint merges. Sparse VDL allows ReFS to substantially reduce the amount of time required to create very large fixed-size virtual hard disks.

It's important to note that ReFS is suitable only for hosting specific types of workloads. It isn't suitable for many workloads used in small and medium enterprises that aren't hosting large VMs or huge SQL Server databases. You won't choose to deploy ReFS for a file server because it doesn't support functionality such as File Server Resource Manager, file compression, file encryption, extended attributes, and quotas.

When used with Storage Spaces Direct and Windows Server 2019 and later, ReFS allows mirror-accelerated parity. Mirror-accelerated parity provides fault tolerance without impacting performance. To create a mirror-accelerated parity volume for use with Storage Spaces Direct, use the following PowerShell command:

```
New-Volume -FriendlyName "ExampleVolume" -filesystem CSVFS_ReFS -StoragePoolFriendlyName
"ExamplePool" -StorageTierFriendlyNames Performance, Capacity -StorateTierSizes 200GB,
800GB
```

More Info
Resilient File System

To learn more about ReFS, consult the following link: *https://learn.microsoft.com/windows-server/storage/refs/refs-overview.*

Storage-related PowerShell cmdlets

There are a number of different modules that contain cmdlets that are relevant to storage services. These are listed in the coming pages.

Deduplication

Table 7-4 lists the PowerShell cmdlets in the deduplication module.

Table 7-4   Deduplication module cmdlets

Noun	Verbs	Function
Dedupfile	Expand	Expand a deduplicated file or directory
DedupFileMetadata	Measure	View the file deduplication information
DedupJob	Stop, Get, Start	Manage deduplication jobs
DedupMetadata	Get	View deduplication metadata
DedupSchedule	New, Remove, Get, Set	Configure the deduplication schedule
DedupStatus	Update, Get	View deduplication status
DedupVolume	Disable, Enable, Get, Set	Configure deduplication for a volume

iSCSI

Table 7-5 lists the PowerShell cmdlets in the iSCSI module.

Table 7-5   iSCSI module cmdlets

Noun	Verbs	Function
iSCSIChapSecret	Set	Configure the iSCSI secret
iSCSIConnection	Get	View the iSCSI connection
iSCSISession	Unregister, Register, Get	Configure an iSCSI session
iSCSITarget	Connect, Update, Disconnect, Get	Manage iSCSI Target
iSCSITargetPortal	Update, Get, New, Remove	Configure iSCSI Target Portal

iSCSITarget

Table 7-6 lists the PowerShell cmdlets in the iSCSI Target module.

Table 7-6 iSCSI Target module cmdlets

Noun	Verbs	Function
iSCSIServerTarget	Get, Remove, New, Set	Manage the iSCSI Server Target
iSCSITargetServer-Configuration	Import, Export	Backup and recover the iSCSI target server configuration
iSCSITargetServerSetting	Set, Get	View and manage iSCSI target server settings
iSCSIVirtualDisk	Import, New, Remove, Restore, Convert, Checkpoint, Set, Get, Resize	Manage iSCSI virtual disks
iSCSIVirtualDiskOperation	Stop	Stop the iSCSI virtual disk operation
iSCSIVirtualDiskSnapshot	Set, Export, Dismount, Mount, Get, Remove	Configure iSCSI virtual disk snapshots
iSCSIVirtualDiskTarget-Mapping	Add, Remove, Expand	Manage the iSCSI virtual disk target mapping

NFS

Table 7-7 lists the PowerShell cmdlets in the NFS module.

Table 7-7 NFS module cmdlets

Noun	Verbs	Function
NFSClientConfiguration	Get, Set	View and configure NFS client settings
NFSClientGroup	Remove, Rename, Set, Get, New	Manage NFS client groups
NFSClientLock	Get, Remove	Manage NFS client locks
NFSMappedIdentity	Set, Test, Remove, New, Get, Resolve	Configure NFS mapped identities
NfsMappingStore	Revoke, Get	Configure the NFS mapping store
NfsMountedClient	Get, Revoke	Manage clients connected to the NFS server.
NfsNetgroup	Remove, Get, Set, New	Configure the NFS net groups

CHAPTER 7

Noun	Verbs	Function
NfsNetgroupStore	Set, Get	Configure the NFS net group store
NfsOpenFile	Revoke, Get	Manage NDF open files
NfsServerConfiguration	Get, Set	Manage the NFS server configuration
NfsSession	Get, Disconnect	Manage NFS sessions
NfsShare	Remove, Get, Set, New	Configure NFS shares
NfsSharePermission	Get, Revoke, Grant	Manage NFS share permissions
NfsStatistics	ReSet, Get	View and reset NFS statistics

Storage

Table 7-8 lists the PowerShell cmdlets in the X module.

Table 7-8   Storage module cmdlets

Noun	Verbs	Function
DedupProperties	Get	View deduplication properties
Disk	Clear, Initialize, Get, Set, Update	Configure disk
DiskImage	Mount, Get, Dismount	Mount, dismount, and view the disk image
DiskStorageNodeView	Get	View the disk storage node view
FileIntegrity	Set, Repair, Get	Manage file integrity
FileShare	Get, Remove, Debug, Set, New	Manage file shares
FileShareAccess	Revoke, Grant, Block, Unblock	Manage file share access
FileShareAccessControlEntry	Get	View file share access control entries
FileStorageTier	Clear, Set, Get	Configure and view file storage tiers
HostStorageCache	Update	Update the host storage cache
InitiatorID	Remove, Get	View and remove the initiator ID
InitiatorIdFromMaskingSet	Remove	Remove the initiator ID from the masking set

Noun	Verbs	Function
InitiatorIDToMaskingSet	Add	Add the initiator ID to the masking set
InitiatorPort	Set, Get	View and configure the initiator port
MaskingSet	Get, Remove, New, Rename	Manage the masking set
OffloadDataTransferSetting	Get	View offload data transfer settings
Partition	Resize, New, Get, Remove, Set	Manage partitions
PartitionAccessPath	Remove, Add	Manage partition access paths
PartitionSupportSize	Get	View the partition support size
PhysicalDisk	Add, Set, Remove, Reset, Get	Manage physical disks
PhysicalDiskIdentification	Enable, Disable	Enable or disable physical disk identification
PhysicalDiskStorageNodeView	Get	View the physical disk storage node view data
PhysicalExtent	Get	View the physical extent information
PhysicalExtentAssociation	Get	View the physical extent association
ResiliencySetting	Get, Set	View and configure the resiliency setting
StorageAdvancedProperty	Get	View the storage advanced properties
StorageDiagnosticInfo	Clear, Get	View and reset the storage diagnostic information
StorageDiagnosticLog	Start, Stop	Start and stop diagnostic logs
StorageEnclosure	Get	View the storage enclosure information
StorageEnclosureIdentification	Disable, Enable	Enable or disable the storage enclosure identification
StorageEnclosureStorage-NodeView	Get	View the storage enclosure storage node view information
StorageEnclosureVendorData	Get	View the storage enclosure vendor data
StorageFaultDomain	Get	View the storage fault domain information

CHAPTER 7

Noun	Verbs	Function
StorageFileServer	Remove, Get, New, Set	Configure the storage file server
StorageFirmware	Update	Update the storage firmware
StorageFirmwareInformation	Get	View the storage firmware information
StorageHealthAction	Get	View the storage health action
StorageHealthReport	Get	View the storage health report
StorageHealthSetting	Get, Set, Remove	Configure and manage the storage health settings
StorageHighAvailability	Disable, Enable	Enable or disable storage high availability
StorageJob	Stop, Get	Stop or view the storage job
StorageMaintenanceMode	Enable, Disable	Enable or disable the storage maintenance mode
StoargeNode	Get	View the storage node information
StoragePool	Optimize, Set, Update, Remove, New, Get	Manage the storage pool
StorageProvider	Set, Get	View and configure the storage provider
StorageProviderCache	Update	Update the storage provider cache
StorageReliabilityCounter	Get, Reset	Manage the storage reliability counter
StorageSetting	Set, Get	View and configure the storage settings
StorageSubSystem	Get, Unregister, Set, Register, Debug	Manage the storage subsystem
StorageSubsystemVirtualDisk	New	Manage the new storage subsystem virtual disk
StorageTier	Get, Remove, New, Resize, Set	Manage the storage tiers
StorageTierSupportedSize	Get	View the storage tier supported size
SupportedClusterSizes	Get	View the supported cluster sizes
SupportedFileSystems	Get	View the supported file system information
TargetPort	Get	View the target port information

CHAPTER 7

Noun	Verbs	Function
TargetPortal	Get	View the target portal information
TargetPortFromMaskingSet	Remove	Remove the target port from a masking set
VirtualDisk	Show, New, Get, Hide, Resize, Remove, Repair, Set, Disconnect, Connect	Manage the virtual disk
VirtualDiskClone	New	Create a new virtual disk clone
VirtualDiskFromMaskingSet	Remove	Remove a virtual disk from a masking set
VirtualDiskSnapshot	New	Create a virtual disk snapshot
VirtualDiskSupportedSize	Get	View the virtual disk supported size
VirtualDiskToMaskingSet	Add	Add the virtual disk to the masking set
Volume	Optimize, Set, Repair, Format, Get, Debug, New	Manage volumes
VolumeCache	Write	Flush the volume cache to storage
VolumeCorruptionCount	Get	View the volume corruption data
VolumeScrubPolicy	Get, Set	View and configure the volume scrub policy

Storage Replica

Table 7-9 lists the PowerShell cmdlets in the Storage Replica module.

Table 7-9   Storage Replica module cmdlets

Noun	Verbs	Function
SRAccess	Get, Grant, Revoke	Manage Storage Replica access
SRConfiguration	Export	Back up the existing Storage Replica configuration
SRDelegation	Grant, Revoke, Get	Configure Storage Replica delegation
SRGroup	Suspend, Sync, Remove, Set, Get, New	Manage Storage Replica groups
SRMetadata	Clear	Clear the Storage Replica metadata

Noun	Verbs	Function
SRNetworkConstraint	Get, Set, Remove	Manage the Storage Replica network constraints
SRPartnership	Set, Get, New, Remove	Configure Storage Replica partnerships
SRTopology	Test	Verify the Storage Replica topology

File servers

Traditionally, the most common use for Windows servers has been as a file server. No matter how advanced technology gets, people who work in an organization need a way to share files that's less chaotic than emailing them or handing them over on USB drives. Even with cloud storage options such as SharePoint Online and OneDrive, many organizations still make use of the humble file server as a way of storing and sharing documents. Shared folders also provide a central location that can be backed up on a regular basis, something that gives them utility beyond just being a central location to store documents.

In this chapter, you'll learn about how you can get more out of your Windows Server 2025 file server by taking advantage of the functionality of File Server Resource Manager, Distributed File System, and BranchCache. Azure File Sync, which allows you to take advantage of the cloud to assist with file tiering and replication, is covered in Chapter 17, "Azure Arc and hybrid services."

Inside OUT

Enable deduplication

We talked about deduplication in detail in Chapter 7, "Storage." As mentioned there, deduplication is a really useful technology to use with file servers. This is because a surprising number of files stored on file servers are duplicates of one another. Some organizations that have implemented deduplication on file servers found that they reduced storage utilization by up to 80 percent. Remember, to enable deduplication, you need to have all the file shares on a volume that is separate from the OS volume. Both NTFS and ReFS support deduplication in Windows Server 2025.

Shared folder permissions

The basic idea with shared folders is that you create a folder and assign permissions to a group, such as a department within your organization, and the people in that group use that space on the file server to store files to be shared with the group.

For example, you create a shared folder named Managers on a file server named FS1. Next, you set share permissions on the shared folder and file system permissions on the files and folders within the shared folder. Permissions allow you to control who can access the shared folder and what users can do with that access. For example, permissions determine whether they are limited to just read-only access or whether they can create and edit new and existing files.

When you set share permissions and file system permissions for a shared folder, the most restrictive permissions apply. For example, if you configure the Share permission so that the Everyone group has Full Control and then configure the file permission so that the Domain Users group has Read Access, a user who is a member of the Domain Users group accessing the file over the network has Read Access.

Things get a little more complicated when a user is a member of multiple groups; in this case, the most cumulative permission applies. For example, in a file where the Domain Users group has Read Access, but the Managers group has Full Control, a user who is a member of both the Domain Users and Managers groups who accesses the file over the network has the Full Control permission. This is great for a certification exam question, but it can be needlessly complex when you're trying to untangle permissions to resolve a service desk ticket.

Inside OUT

We need to talk about permissions

If you've ever studied for a Microsoft certification and come across file servers, you'll have learned about the difference between shared folders and file system permissions. The general problem with these permissions is that they tend to confuse people, which is why permissions are often incorrectly applied manually and why service desks are inundated with calls about the wrong people having access to a file while the right people can't open it. There are several solutions to the permissions problem. The first is to have permissions set automatically using Dynamic Access Control, where access is determined by rules around the nature of the file and the user trying to access the file. You'll learn about Dynamic Access Control and how you can use it to solve the permissions problem in Chapter 20, "Active Directory Rights Management Services." The next permissions-related technology is AD RMS, covered in Chapter 20, which ensures that permissions stay with the file even when the file is moved away from the file share. More useful in today's "Cloud First" world is Microsoft Purview Information Protection, which you'll learn about in Chapter 9, "Azure Arc and hybrid services."

Using File Explorer

You can create shared folders in a variety of ways. The way that many administrators do it, often out of habit, is by using the built-in functionality of File Explorer. If you're using File Explorer to share folders, you have two general options when it comes to permissions:

- **Simple Share Permissions**   When you use the Simple Share Permissions option, you specify whether a user or group account has Read or Read/Write permissions to a shared folder. Figure 8-1 shows this for the Managers group. When you use Simple Share Permissions, both the share permissions and the file and folder level permissions are set at the same time. It's important to note that any files and folders in the shared folder path have their permissions reset to match those configured through the File Sharing dialog. This, however, doesn't happen with other forms of share permission configurations.

- **Advanced Share Permissions**   Advanced Share Permissions are what administrators who have been managing Windows file servers since the days of Windows NT 4 are likely to be more familiar with. With Advanced Permissions, you configure share permissions separately from file system permissions. You configure Advanced Share Permissions through the Advanced Sharing button on the Sharing tab of a folder's Properties dialog. Figure 8-2 shows how you configure Advanced Sharing Permissions. When you configure Advanced Sharing Permissions, permissions are only set on the share and are not reset on the files and folders within the share. If you're using Advanced Sharing Permissions, you set the file system permissions separately.

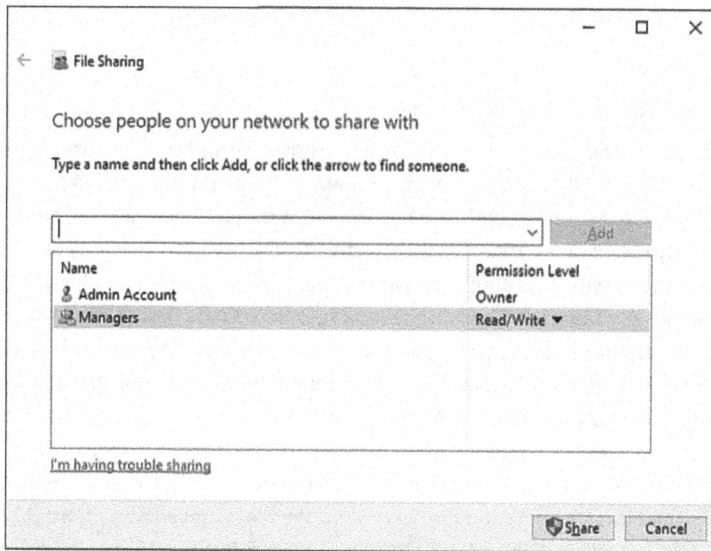

Figure 8-1   Simple share permissions

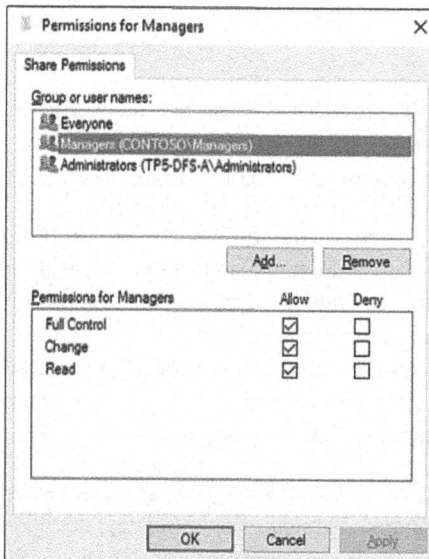

Figure 8-2   Share Permissions dialog

Windows Admin Center

Windows Admin Center (WAC) also provides basic file share–configuration functionality, though this is not currently as sophisticated as what can be accomplished through Server Manager or

File Explorer. As WAC evolves, more file-sharing functionality will likely be added to the tool. At the moment, file sharing is accessible through the Files node of WAC. To access the permissions of a share, you must select the host folder in the WAC interface and then use the More dropdown to view share permissions. Share Permissions for a folder named Shared-WAC are displayed in Figure 8-3.

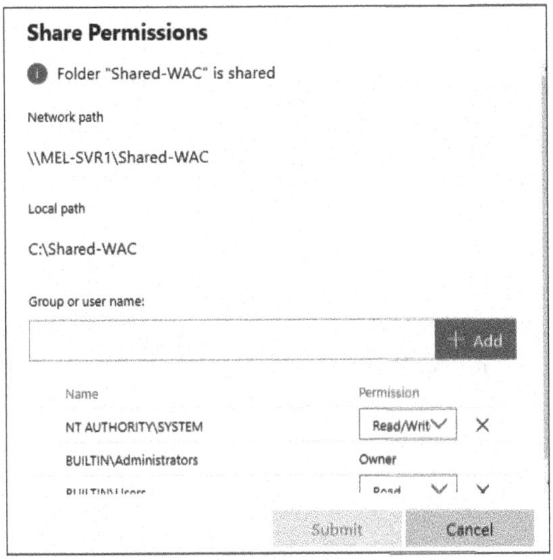

Figure 8-3   Windows Admin Center Share Permissions dialog

Server Manager

You can manage shares centrally through the Shares area of the Server Manager console, as shown in Figure 8-4. The advantage of the Server Manager console is that you can use it to connect to and manage shares on remote servers, including servers running the Server Core installation option.

When you edit the properties of a share through Server Manager, you can also edit the permissions, as shown in Figure 8-5. This functions in the same way as editing Advanced Share Permissions through File Explorer in that it won't reset the permissions on the file system itself; permissions are only reset on the share.

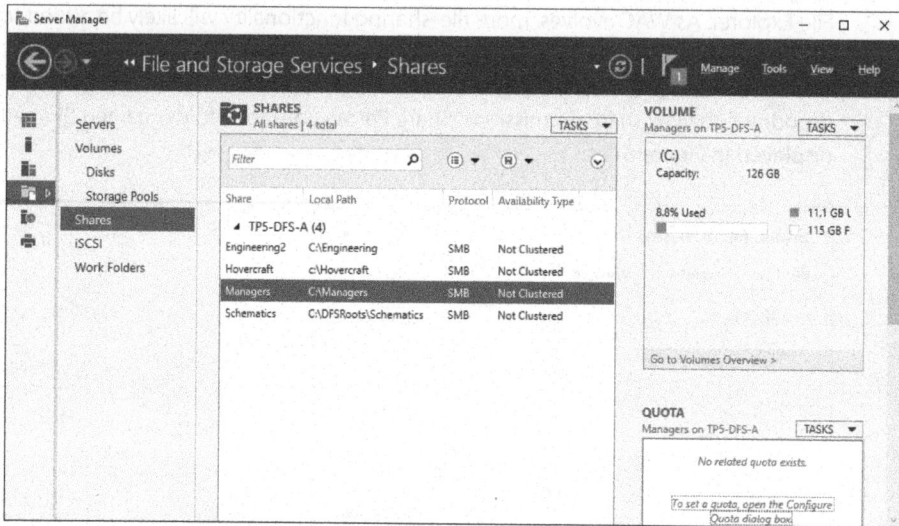

Figure 8-4   Server Manager for share management

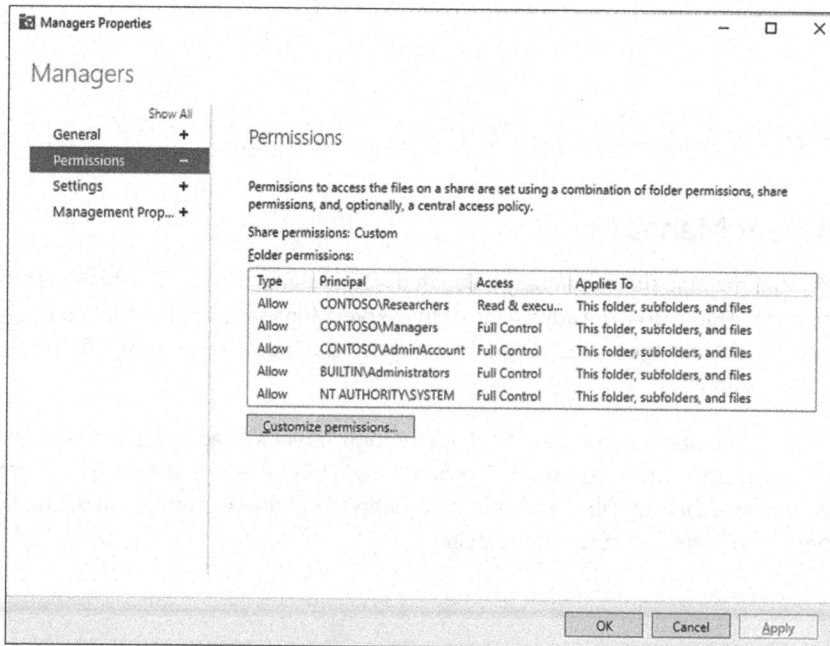

Figure 8-5   Server Manager Permissions management

CHAPTER 8

You can also use the Server Manager's share properties interface when File Server Resource Manager is installed to edit the following settings:

- **Enable Access-Based Enumeration**   Enabled by default, this setting ensures that users can only see files and folders to which they have access. This is shown as enabled in Figure 8-6.

- **Allow Caching Of Share**   Allows files to be used offline. An additional setting, Enable BranchCache On The File Share, allows the use of BranchCache if the appropriate group policies are applied. You'll learn more about BranchCache later in this chapter. You can configure this option when the Settings tab is selected.

- **Encrypt Data Access**   When you enable this option, traffic to and from the shared folder is encrypted if the client supports SMB 3.0 (Windows 8 and later). You can configure this option when the Settings tab is selected.

- **Specify Folder Owner Email Address**   Setting the folder owner's email address can be useful when resolving access-denied assistance requests. You can configure this when the Permission tab is selected.

- **Configure Folder Usage Properties**   Folder-usage properties allow you to apply metadata to the folder that specifies the nature of the files stored there. You can choose between User Files, Group Files, Application Files, and Backup and Archival files. You can use folder usage properties with data classification rules.

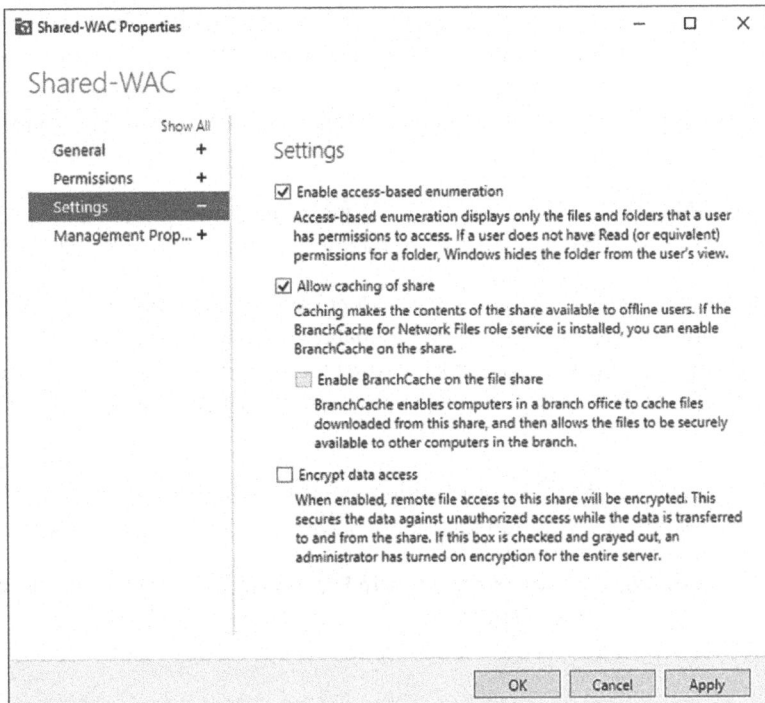

Figure 8-6   Server Manager share settings management

File Server Resource Manager

File Server Resource Manager (FSRM) is a tool that allows you to perform advanced file server management. You can use FSRM to configure the following:

- Quotas at the volume and folder level
- File screens
- Storage reports
- File classification
- File management tasks
- Access denied assistance

Folder-level quotas

Quotas are important. If you don't use them, file shares tend to end up consuming all available storage. Some users dump as much as possible onto a file share unless quotas are in place and unless you are monitoring storage; the first you'll hear about it is when the service desk gets calls about people being unable to add new files to the file share.

NTFS has had rudimentary quota functionality since the Windows NT days. The reason that most Windows server administrators don't bother with it is that it can't be applied only to individual user accounts, and it applies at the volume level. Needless to say, if you have 500 users for whom you want to configure quotas, you don't want to have to configure a quota for each one individually. Even with command-line utilities, you still need to create an entry for each user.

Luckily, FSRM provides far more substantial quota functionality that makes quotas more practical to implement as a way of managing storage utilization on Windows file servers.

Quotas in FSRM can be applied on a per-folder basis and are not cumulative across a volume. You can also configure quotas in FSRM so that users are sent warning emails should they exceed a specific quota threshold, but before they're blocked from writing files to the file server. You manage quotas using FSRM by creating a quota template and then applying that quota template to a path.

Creating a quota template involves setting a limit, specifying a quota type, and then configuring notification thresholds. You can choose between the following quota types:

- **Hard Quota. Do Not Allow Users To Exceed Limit**   A hard quota blocks users from writing data to the file share after the quota value is exceeded.

- **Soft Quota. Allow Users To Exceed Limit (Use For Monitoring)**   A soft quota allows you to monitor when users exceed a specific storage utilization value, but it doesn't block users from writing data to the file share after the quota value is exceeded.

Notification thresholds allow you to configure actions to be taken after a certain percentage of the assigned quotas is reached. As shown in Figure 8-7, you can configure notifications via email, get an item written to an event log, run a command, or have a report generated.

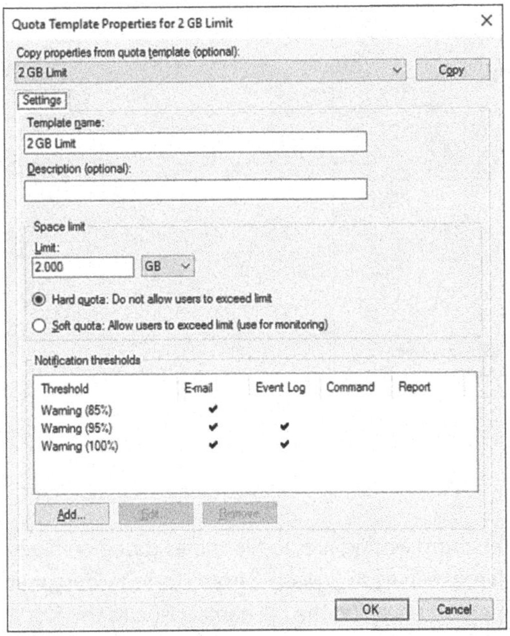

Figure 8-7   Quota template

After you have the quota template created, you apply it to a folder. To do this, select the Quotas node under Quota Management, and from the Action menu, click Create Quota. In the Create Quota dialog, shown in Figure 8-8, select the path to which the quota applies and the quota template to apply. You then choose between applying the quota to the whole path or setting up an auto-apply template. Auto-apply templates allow separate quotas to be applied to any new and existing quota path subfolders. For example, if you applied a quota to the C:\Example path using the 2 GB template, the quota would apply cumulatively for all folders in that path. If you choose an auto-apply template, a separate 2 GB quota would be configured for each new and existing folder under C:\Example.

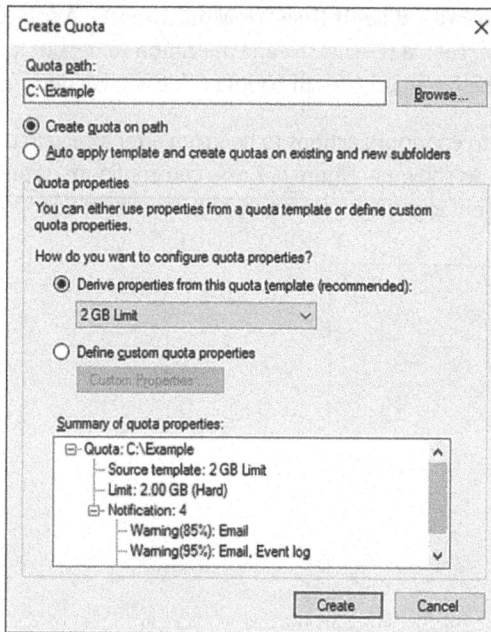

Figure 8-8   Create Quota dialog

File screens

File screens allow you to block users from writing files to file shares based on file name extension. For example, you can use a file screen to stop people from storing video or audio files on
file shares. File screens are implemented based on the file name. Usually, this just means file
screens are implemented by file extension, but you can configure file screens based on a pattern
match of any part of a file name. You implement file screens using file groups and file screen
templates.

Inside OUT

Doesn't block what is already there

A file screen doesn't block files that are already there; file screens just stop new files from
being written to the share. File screens also only work based on the file name. If you
have especially cunning users, they might figure out that it's possible to get around a file
screen by renaming files so they don't get blocked by the screen.

CHAPTER 8

File groups

A file group is a preconfigured collection of file extensions related to a specific type of file. For example, the Image Files file group includes file name extensions related to image files, such as `.jpg`, `.png`, and `.gif`. While file groups are usually fairly comprehensive in their coverage, they aren't always complete. Should you need to, you can modify the list to add new file extensions.

The file groups included with FSRM are shown in Figure 8-9 and include the following:

- **Audio And Video Files**   Blocks file extensions related to audio and video files, such as `.avi` and `.mp3`

- **Backup Files**   Blocks file extensions related to backups, including `.bak` and `.old` files

- **Compressed Files**   Blocks file extensions related to compressed files, such as `.zip` and `.cab`

- **Email Files**   Blocks file extensions related to email storage, including `.pst` and `.mbx` files

- **Executable Files**   Blocks file extensions related to executable files and scripts, such as `.exe` or `.ps1` extensions

- **Image Files**   Blocks file extensions related to images, such as `.jpg` or `.png` extensions

- **Office Files**   Blocks file extensions related to Microsoft Office files, such as `.docx` and `.pptx` files

- **System Files**   Blocks file extensions related to system files, including `.dll` and `.sys` files

- **Temporary Files**   Blocks file extensions related to temporary files, such as `.tmp`. Also blocks files starting with the ~ character

- **Text Files**   Blocks file extensions related to text files, including `.txt` and `.asc` files

- **Web Page Files**   Blocks file extensions related to web page files, including `.html` and `.htm` files

To edit the list of files in a file group, right-click the file group and click Edit File Group Properties. Using the dialog shown in Figure 8-10, you can modify the list of files to include and exclude files based on the file name pattern. For example, you can do a simple exclusion or inclusion based on the file name suffix, such as `*.bak`. You also have the option of creating a more complex exclusion or inclusion based on the file name, such as `backup *.*`, which would exclude all files with the word backup at the start of any extension.

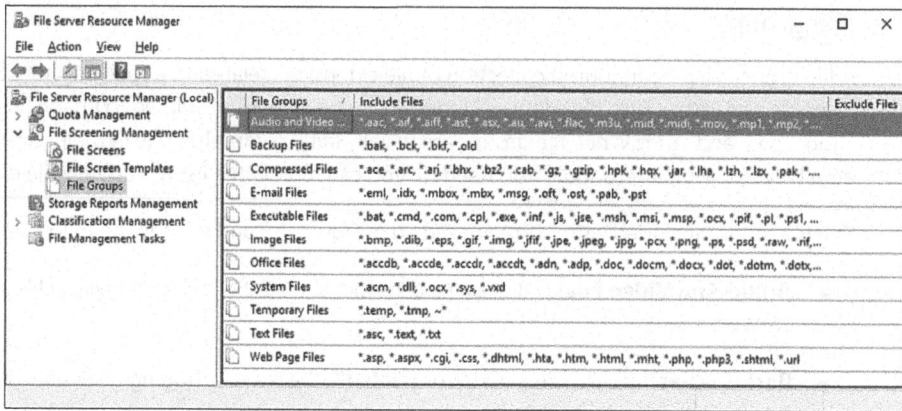

Figure 8-9   File groups

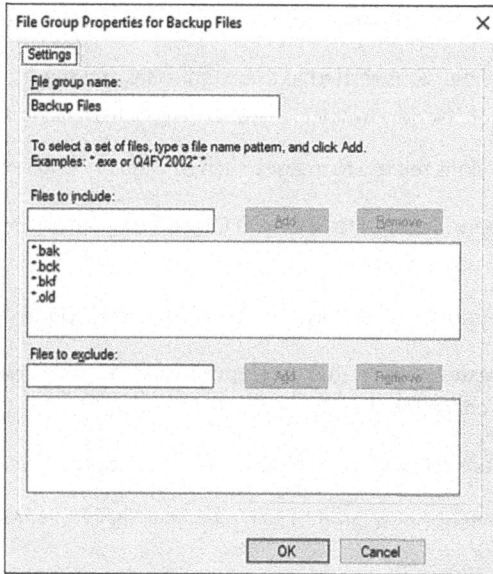

Figure 8-10   File group properties

Exclusions allow you to add exceptions to an existing block rule. For example, you could configure a file screen to block all files that have the extension .vhdx. You might then create an exception for the name server2019.vhdx. When implemented, all files with the .vhdx extension would be blocked from being written to the share, except for files with the name server2019.vhdx.

While the NTFS and ReFS file systems are case-sensitive, file screens are not.

To create a new file group, right-click the File Groups node in the File Server Resource Manager console and click Create File Group. Provide the following information:

- **File Group Name**   The name of the file group.

- **Files To Include**   Provide patterns that match the names of files you want to block from being written to the file server.

- **Files To Exclude**   Provide patterns that match the names of files you want to exclude from the block.

File screen templates

File screen templates are made up of a screening type, a collection of file groups, and a set of actions to perform when a match is found. File screen templates support the following screening types:

- **Active Screening**   An active screen blocks users from writing files to the file share that have names that match those patterns listed in the file group.

- **Passive Screening**   A passive screen doesn't block users from writing files to the file share that have names that match patterns listed in the file group. Instead, you use a passive screen to monitor such activity.

The actions you can configure include sending an email, writing a message to the event log, running a command, or generating a report. Figure 8-11 shows the Create File Screen Template dialog.

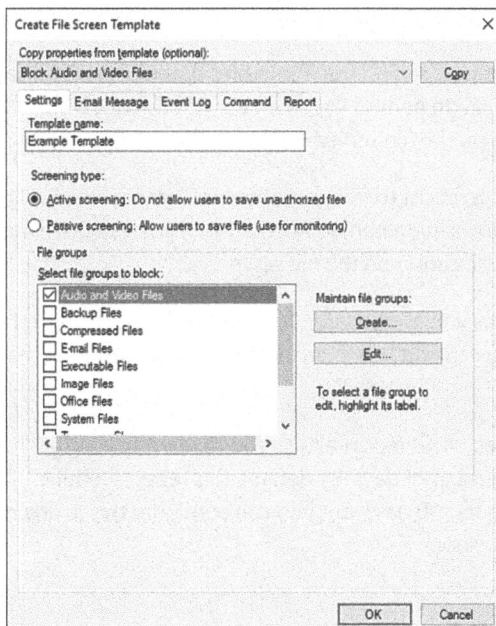

Figure 8-11   Creating a template

After you have configured the appropriate file screen template, create the file screen by applying the template to a specific path. You can also create file screen exceptions, which exempt specific folders from an existing file screen. For example, you might apply a file screen at the root of a shared folder that blocks audio and video files from being written to the share. If you want to allow users to write audio and video files to one folder in the share, you could configure a file screen exception and apply it to that folder.

Storage reports

The Storage Reports functionality of FSRM allows you to generate information about the files that are being stored on a particular file server. You can use FSRM to create the following storage reports:

- **Duplicate Files**   This report locates multiple copies of the same file. If you've enabled deduplication on the volume hosting these files, these additional copies do not consume additional disk space as they are deduplicated.

- **File Screening Audit**   This report allows you to view which users or applications are triggering file screens (for example, users who have tried to save music or video files to a shared folder).

- **Files By File Group**   This report allows you to view files sorted by file group. You can view files by all file groups, or you can search for specific files (such as a report on .zip files stored in a shared folder).

- **Files By Owner**   This report allows you to view files by owner. You can search for files by all owners or run a report that provides information on files by one or more specific users.

- **Files By Property**   Use this report to find out about files based on a classification. For example, if you have a classification named Top_Secret, you can generate a report about all files with that classification on the file server.

- **Folders By Property**   Use this report to find out about folders based on a classification. For example, if you have a classification named Accounting, you can generate a report about all folders with that classification on the file server.

- **Large Files**   This report allows you to find large files on the file server. By default, it finds files larger than 5 MB, but you can edit this to locate all files that are larger than a certain size.

- **Least Recently Accessed Files**   This report allows you to identify files that have not been accessed for a certain number of days. By default, this report identifies files that have not been accessed in the last 90 days, but you can configure this to any number that is appropriate for your organization.

- **Most Recently Accessed Files**   Use this report to determine which files have been accessed most recently. The default version of this report finds files that have been accessed in the last seven days.

- **Quota Usage**   Use this report to view how a user's storage usage compares against the assigned quota. For example, you could run a report to determine which users have exceeded 90 percent of their quota.

You can configure storage reports to run and be stored locally on file servers. You also have the option of configuring storage reports to be emailed to one or more email addresses. You can generate storage reports in DHTML, HTML, XML, CSV, and text formats.

To run a storage report, perform the following steps:

1. In the File Server Resource Manager console, select the Storage Reports Management node, and then on the Action menu, click Generate Reports Now.

2. On the Settings page of the Storage Reports Task Properties dialog shown in Figure 8-12, select the reports you want to run. You can click Edit Parameters to modify the properties of the report.

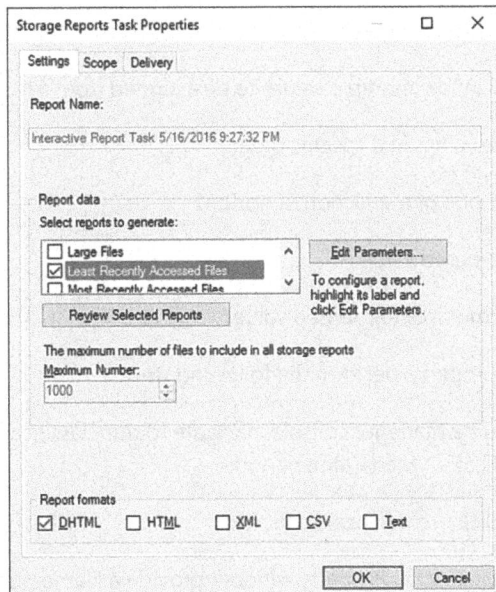

Figure 8-12   Storage reports

3. On the Scope tab of the Storage Reports Tasks Properties dialog, you can configure which folders the report runs on.

4. On the Delivery tab of the Storage Reports Task Properties dialog, you can configure the location where reports are saved and the email addresses to which the reports are sent.

File classification

File classification allows you to apply metadata to files based on file properties. For example, you can apply the tag Top_Secret to a file that has specific properties, such as who authored it or whether a particular string of characters appeared in the file.

The first step to take when configuring file classification is to configure classification properties. After you've done this, you can create a classification rule to assign the classification property to a file. You can also allow users to manually assign classification properties to a file. By specifying the values allowed, you limit which classification properties the user can assign.

Classification properties

You can configure the following file classification property types:

- **Yes/No**   Provide a Boolean value

- **Date-Time**   Provide a date and time

- **Number**   Provide an integer value

- **Multiple Choice List**   Allow multiple values to be assigned from a list

- **Ordered List**   Provide values in a specific order

- **Single Choice**   Select one of a selection of options

- **String**   Provide a text-based value

- **Multi-string**   Assign multiple text-based values

To configure a classification property, perform the following steps:

1. In the File Server Resource Manager console, navigate to the Classification Properties node under the Classification Management node.

2. On the Action menu, click Create Local Property.

3. In the Create Local Classification Property window, provide a Name, select a Property Type, and configure properties. Figure 8-13 shows a classification property named Sensitivity that gives a Single Choice property type and has the available values Top_Secret and Not_Sensitive. Click OK to save the new classification.

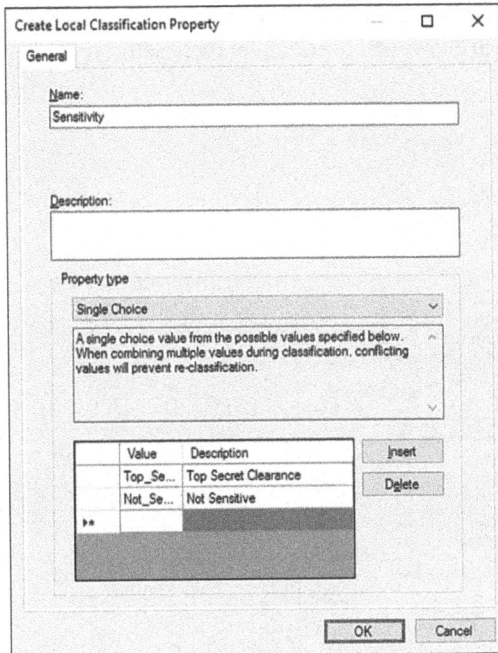

Figure 8-13   Create classification property

Classification rules

Classification rules allow you to assign classifications to files based on the properties of a file. You can configure three separate methods to classify a file:

- **Content Classifier**   When you choose this method of classification, you configure a regular expression to scan the contents of a file for a specific string or text pattern. For example, you could use the content classifier to automatically assign the Top_Secret classification to any file that contains the text Project_X.

- **Folder Classifier**   When you choose this method of classification, all files in a particular path are assigned the designated classification.

- **Windows PowerShell Classifier**   When you choose this method of classification, a PowerShell script is run to determine whether a file is assigned a particular classification.

You can configure classification rules to run against specific folders. When configuring a classification rule, you can also choose to recheck files each time the rule is run. This allows you to change a file's classification in the event that the properties that triggered the initial classification change. When configuring reevaluation, you can also choose to remove user-assigned classifications in case there is a conflict. Figure 8-14 shows the Evaluation Type tab of the Create Classification Rule dialog, which allows you to configure these settings.

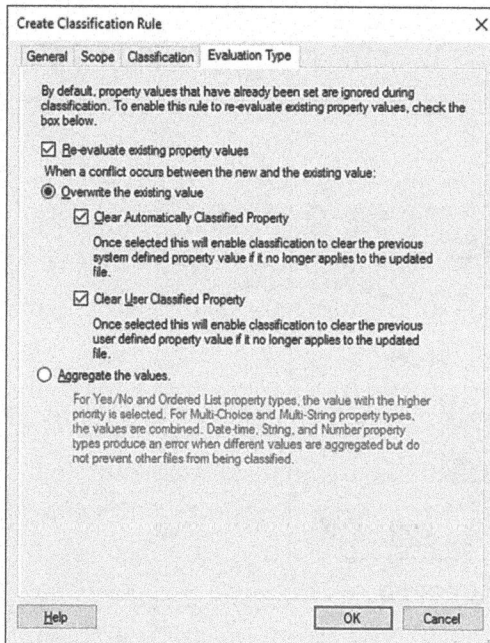

Figure 8-14   Evaluation type

File management tasks

File management tasks are automated tasks that FSRM performs on files according to a schedule. FSRM supports three types of file management tasks. These are

- **File Expiration**   This moves all files that match the conditions to a specific directory. The most common usage of a file expiration task is to move files that haven't been accessed by anyone for a specific period (such as 365 days) to a specific directory.

- **Custom**   Allows you to run a specific executable against a file. You can specify which executable is to be run, any special arguments to be used when running the executable, and the service account permissions, which can be Local Service, Network Service, or Local System.

- **RMS Encryption**   Allows you to apply an RMS template or a set of file permissions to a file based on conditions. For example, you might want to automatically apply a specific set of file permissions to a file that has the Top_Secret classification or apply a specific RMS template to a file that has the Ultra_Secret classification.

When configuring a file management task, you also need to provide the following information:

- **Scope**   The path where the task is run.

- **Notification**   Any notification settings that you want to configure, such as sending an email, running a command, or writing an event to an event log. With file expiration, you can configure an email to be sent to each user who has files that are subject to the expiration task.

- **Report**   Generating a report each time the task is run. A notification is sent to the user who owns the file; reports are sent to administrators.

- **Schedule**   When you want the file management task to be run.

- **Condition**   The condition that triggers the management task. For example, Figure 8-15 shows a task that's triggered when the Sensitivity classification property is set to `Top_Secret`.

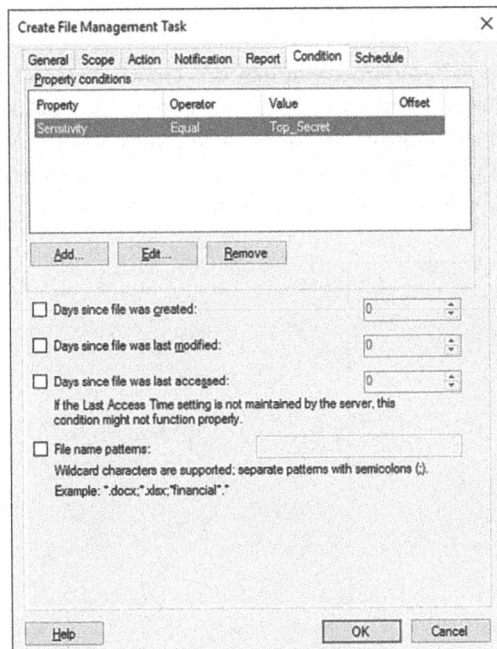

Figure 8-15   Create file management task

Inside OUT

Cleaning up file servers

Most files become stale after a few months. If a file hasn't been accessed for a year, there's a very good chance that it might never be accessed again. If you're responsible for managing file servers, you should come up with a way of identifying and removing these files on a periodic basis. Storage reports can help you identify them, and FSRM file management tasks allow you to move them off the file server in an automated way. Just remember that you might need to keep some files around for a certain amount of time to meet your organization's compliance obligations. Another option is to adopt Azure File Sync, a solution that can automatically tier derelict files to the cloud, where they can be synced back if required, but otherwise aren't actually present on the file server. You'll learn about Azure File Sync in Chapter 9.

Access-denied assistance

Access-denied assistance allows users to be informed why they don't have access to a specific file. Access denied assistance gives you the option of allowing the user to send an email message to the file owner so that they can, if appropriate, grant access to the file. You can configure Access-Denied Assistance using FSRM, as shown in Figure 8-16, or by configuring group policy. You configure Access-Denied Assistance for a single server in FSRM by editing the FSRM options.

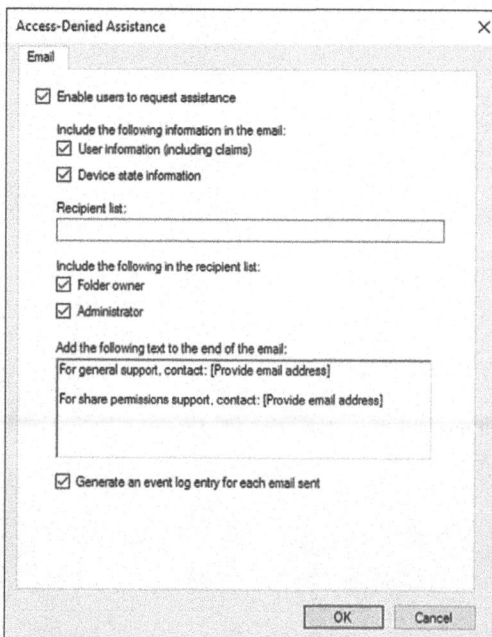

Figure 8-16   Access-Denied Assistance

If you want to use Access-Denied Assistance across all file servers in your organization, you can choose to use Group Policy. To configure Access-Denied Assistance using Group Policy, edit the policies located in the `Computer Configuration\Policies\Administrative Templates\ System\Access-Denied Assistance` mode. This node contains the following policies:

- **Customize Message For Access Denied Errors**   Use this policy to specify the message users see when they're blocked from accessing a file.

- **Enable Access-Denied Assistance On Client For All File Types**   When enabled, Access-Denied Assistance functions for all file types where the user is blocked from accessing the file.

Distributed File System

Distributed File System (DFS) has two advantages over a traditional file share. The first is that DFS automatically replicates to create copies of the file share and its content on one or more other servers. The second is that clients connect to a single UNC address, with the client directed to the closest server and redirected to the next closest server in the event that a server hosting a DFS replica fails. Azure File Sync provides most of the first functionality, but does not provide the second functionality. You'll learn more about Azure File Sync in Chapter 9.

Using DFS, you can push a single shared folder structure out across an organization that has multiple branch offices. Changes made to files on one file share replica propagate across to the other file share replicas, with a robust and built-in conflict-management system present to ensure that problems do not occur when users are editing the same file at the same time.

DFS namespace

A DFS namespace is a collection of DFS shared folders. It uses the same UNC pathname structure, except instead of `\\ServerName\FileShareName` with DFS, it is `\\domainname` with all DFS shared folders located under this DFS root. For example, instead of

```
\\FS-1\Engineering
\\FS-2\Accounting
\\FS-3\Documents
```

You could have

```
\\Contoso.com\Engineering
\\Contoso.com\Accounting
\\Contoso.com\Documents
```

CHAPTER 8

In this scenario, the `Engineering`, `Accounting`, and `Documents` folders could all be hosted on separate file servers, and you could use a single namespace to locate those shared folders instead of needing to know the identity of the file server that hosts them.

As shown in Figure 8-17, DFS supports the following types of namespaces:

- **Domain-Based Namespace**   Domain-based namespaces store configuration data in Active Directory. You deploy a domain-based namespace when you want to ensure that the namespace remains available even if one or more of the servers hosting the namespace go offline.

- **Stand-Alone Namespace**   Stand-alone namespaces have namespace data stored in the registry of a single server and not in Active Directory, as is the case with domain-based namespaces. You can only have a single namespace server with a standalone namespace. Should the server that hosts the namespace fail, the entire namespace is unavailable even if servers that host individual folder targets remain online.

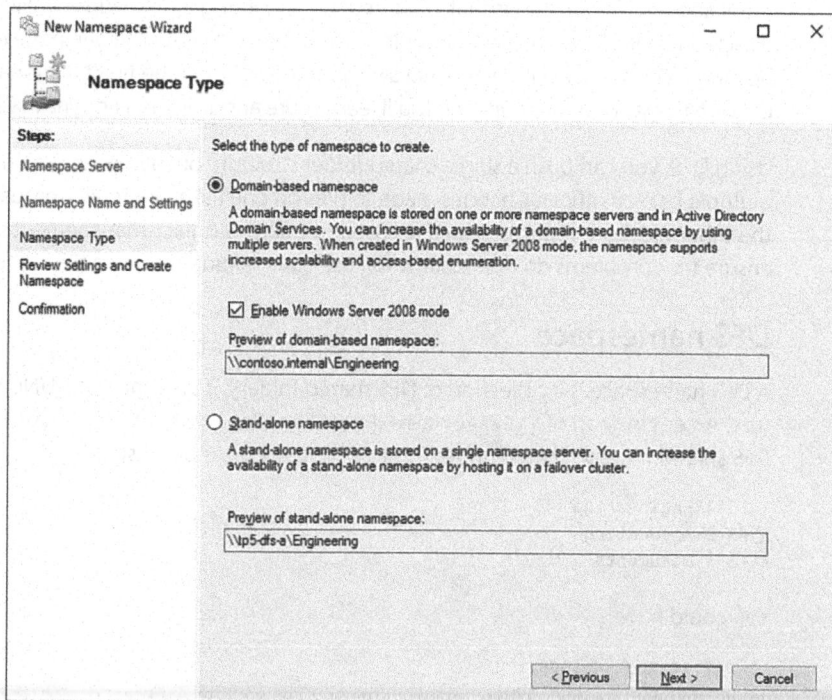

Figure 8-17   Namespace Type

Inside OUT

Windows Server 2008 mode

From the perspective of deploying modern versions of Windows Server, Windows Server 2008 mode might sound like an option that you'd use for backward compatibility. It's actually the opposite, because if you don't select Windows Server 2008 mode, DFS uses Windows 2000 mode. Windows Server 2008 mode supports 50,000 folder targets and access-based enumeration, which means users can only see files and folders that they have access to. The requirement for Windows Server 2008 mode is that you have a domain functional level of Windows Server 2008 or higher and a forest functional level of Windows Server 2003 or higher. As you should be running at the most recent domain and forest functional levels, this shouldn't be a problem.

To create a DFS namespace, perform the following steps:

1. In the DFS console, click the Namespaces node. In the Action menu, click New Namespace.

2. On the Namespace Server page, select a server that has the DFS Namespaces feature installed. You can install this feature with the following PowerShell cmdlet:

```
Install-WindowsFeature FS-DFS-Namespace
```

3. On the Namespace Name And Settings page, provide a meaningful name for the namespace. This is located under the Domain name. For example, if you added the name Schematics and you were installing DFS in the contoso.internal domain, the namespace would end up as \\contoso.internal\Schematics. By default, a shared folder is created on the namespace server, although you can edit settings on this page of the wizard and specify a separate location for the shared folder that hosts the content you want to replicate.

4. On the Namespace Type page, you should generally select a domain-based namespace because this gives you the greatest flexibility and allows you to add namespace servers later on for redundancy.

To add a namespace server to an existing namespace, ensure that the DFS Namespace role feature is installed on the server you want to add and then perform the following steps:

1. In the DFS Console, select the namespace to which you want to add the additional namespace server; on the Action menu, click Add Namespace Server.

2. On the Add Namespace Server page, specify the name of the namespace server or browse and query Active Directory to verify that the name is correct; then click OK. This creates a shared folder on the new namespace server with the name of the namespace.

DFS replication

A replica is a copy of a DFS folder. Replication is the process that ensures each replica is kept up to date. DFS uses block-level replication, which means that only blocks in a file that have changed are transmitted to other replicas during the replication process.

You install the DFS replication feature by running the following PowerShell command:

```
Install-WindowsFeature FS-DFS-Replication
```

If different users on different replicas are editing the same file, DFS uses a "last writer wins" conflict-resolution model. In the unlikely event that two separate users create files with the same name in the same location on different replicas at approximately the same time, conflict resolution uses "earliest creator wins." When conflicts occur, files and folders that "lose" the conflict are moved to the Conflict And Deleted folder, located under the local path of the replicated folder in the DfsrPrivate\ConflictandDeleted directory.

Replicated folders and targets

One of the big advantages of DFS is that you can create copies of folders across multiple servers that are automatically updated. Each copy of that replica is called a folder target. Only computers that have the DFS replication role feature installed can host folder targets. A replicated folder can have multiple folder targets. For example, you might have a replicated folder named \\contoso.com\Engineering that you have configured targets for in

- Sydney on \\SYD-FS1\Engineering

- Melbourne on \\MEL-FS1\Engineering

- Auckland on \\AKL-FS1\Engineering

To create a new folder to replicate, perform the following steps:

1. In the DFS console, select the namespace to which you want to add the folder.

2. On the Action menu, click New Folder. In the New Folder dialog, provide a folder name and click Add.

3. If you've already created a shared folder to host the target, enter that address in the Add Folder Target dialog. Otherwise, click Browse, select the server you want to host the folder, and click New Shared Folder.

4. On the Create Share dialog, shown in Figure 8-18, provide a share name, a local path, and the permissions that you want to apply. The advantage of using the DFS console to create the share is that it ensures all the appropriate folders are created, and permissions are applied. You need an account that has local Administrator access on the server that hosts the share to perform these actions. To create the new folder, click OK until all dialogs are dismissed.

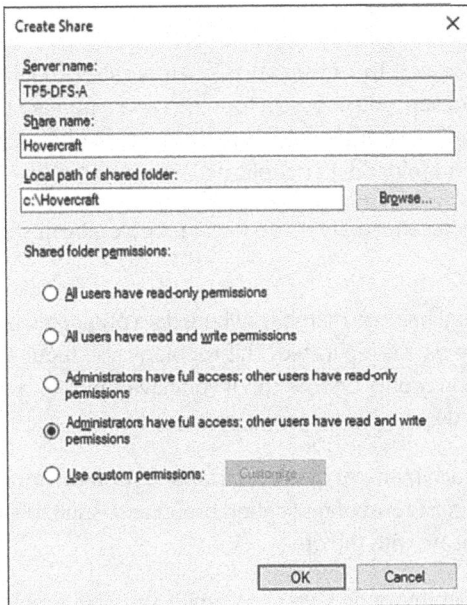

Figure 8-18   Create Share dialog

To add a folder target to an existing folder, perform the following steps:

1.   In the DFS console, select the folder under the namespace to which you want to add a folder target.

2.   On the Action menu, click Add Folder Target.

3.   If you've already created the share, enter the address of the shared folder. Otherwise, click Browse.

4.   On the Browse For Shared Folders dialog, click Browse again and use Active Directory to query for the address of the server that you want to host the folder target. Remember, this server must have the DFS Replication role service installed on it.

5.   Click New Shared Folder. In the Create Share dialog, provide a share name, a local path, and the permissions that you want to apply. These should be the same as the permissions you've chosen for other replicas.

6.   You need an account that has local Administrator access on the server that hosts the share to perform these actions. To create the new folder target, click OK until all dialogs are dismissed.

If this is the first additional target that you've created, you need to configure a replication topology and a replication group.

Replication topology

A replication group is a collection of servers that host copies of a replicated folder. When configuring replication for a replication group, you choose a topology and a primary member. The topology dictates how data replicates between the folders that each server hosts. The primary member is the seed from which file and folder data is replicated.

When creating a replication group, you can specify the following topologies, as shown in Figure 8-19:

- **Hub And Spoke**   This topology has hub members where data originates, and spoke members to the location where data is replicated. This topology also requires at least three members of the replication group. Choose this if you have a hub-and-spoke topology for your organizational WAN.

- **Full Mesh**   In this topology, each member of the replication group can replicate with other members. This is the simplest form of replication group and is suitable when each member can directly communicate with the other.

- **No Topology**   When you select this option, you can create a custom topology where you specify how each member replicates with others.

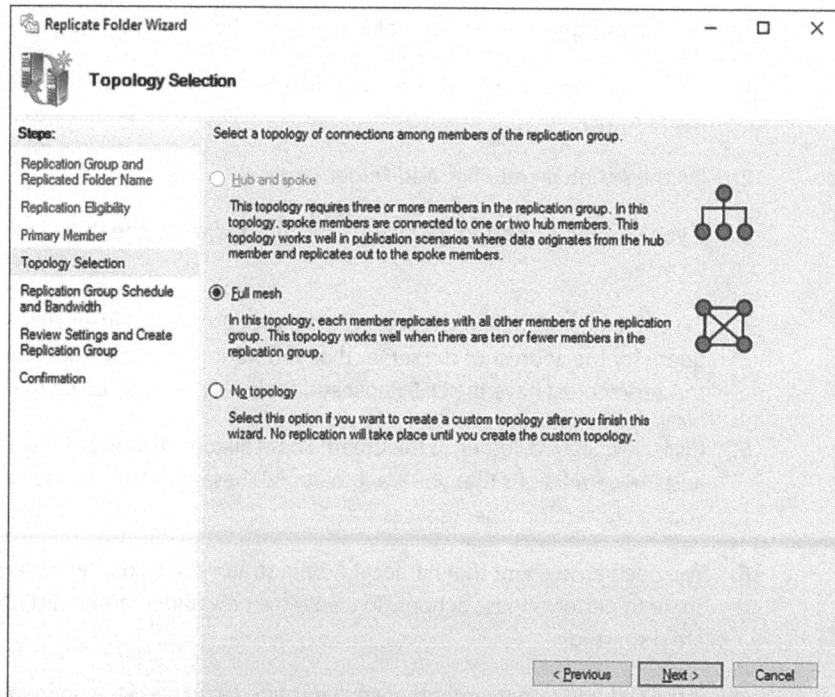

Figure 8-19   Replication topology

Replication schedules

You use replication schedules to determine how replication partners communicate with each other. You use a replication schedule to specify when replication partners communicate and whether replication traffic is throttled so that it doesn't flood the network.

You can configure replication to occur continuously and specify bandwidth utilization, with a minimum value of 16 Kbps and an upper value of 256 Mbps and the option of setting it to Unlimited. If necessary, you can also set different bandwidth limitations for different periods of the day. Figure 8-20 shows that the cap is set to 512 Kbps during work hours and to 64 Mbps after hours.

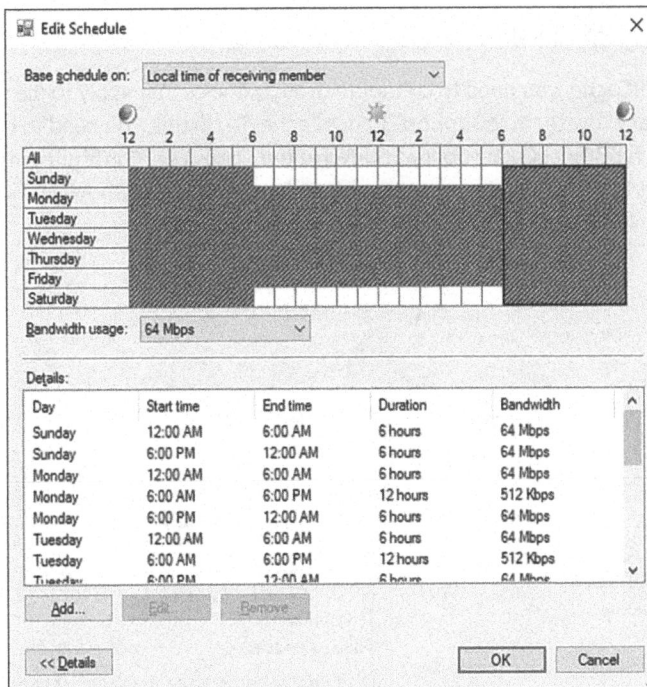

Figure 8-20   Edit Schedule dialog

BranchCache

BranchCache speeds up access to files stored on shared folders that are accessed across medium- to high-latency WAN links. For example, several users in a company's Auckland, New Zealand, branch office need regular access to several files stored on a file server in the Sydney, Australia, head office. The connection between the Auckland and Sydney offices is low band-width and high latency. The files are also fairly large and need to be stored on the Sydney file server. Additionally, the Auckland branch office is too small for a DFS replica to make sense. In a scenario such as this, you would implement BranchCache.

BranchCache creates a locally cached copy of files from remote file servers that can be accessed by other computers on the local network, assuming the file hasn't been updated at the source. In the example scenario, after one person in the Auckland office accesses the file, the next person to access the same file in the Auckland office accesses a copy that is cached locally rather than retrieving it from the Sydney file server. The BranchCache process performs a check to verify that the cached version is up to date. If it isn't, the updated file is retrieved and stored in the Auckland network's BranchCache.

You add BranchCache to a file server by using the following PowerShell command:

```
Install-WindowsFeature FS-BranchCache
```

After installing BranchCache, you need to configure group policies that apply to file servers in your organization that allow them to support BranchCache. To do this, you need to configure the Hash Publication for BranchCache policy, located in the `Computer Configuration\Policies\Administrative Templates\Network\Lanman Server` node, as shown in Figure 8-21.

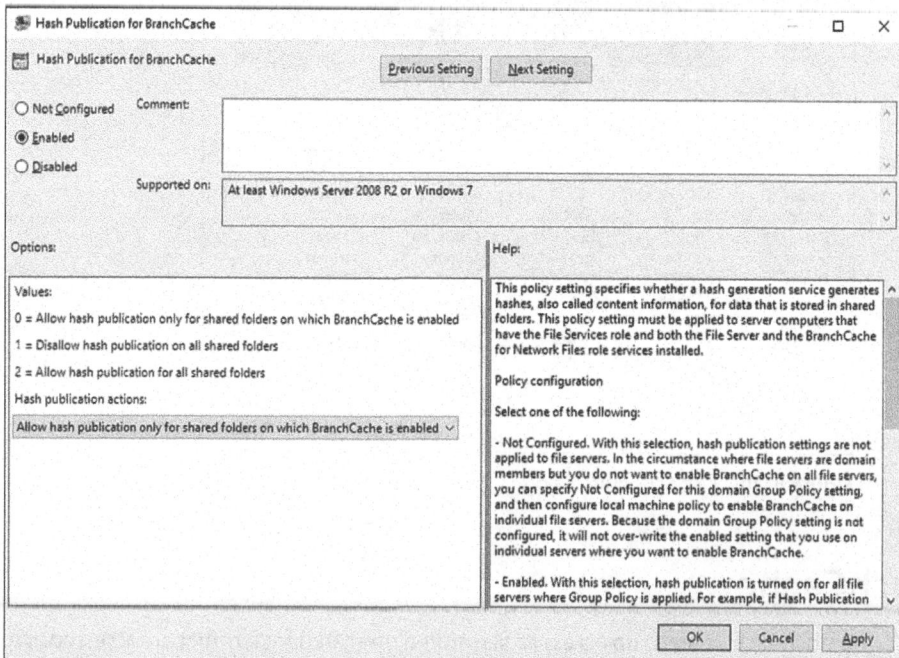

Figure 8-21   Hash Publication For BranchCache

You have three options when configuring this policy:

- **Allow Hash Publication Only For Shared Folders On Which BranchCache Is Enabled**   This option allows you to selectively enable BranchCache.

- **Disallow Hash Publication On All Shared Folders**   Use this option when you want to disable BranchCache.

- **Allow Hash Publication For All Shared Folders**   Use this option if you want to enable BranchCache on all shared folders.

Generally, there's rarely a great reason not to enable BranchCache on all shared folders, but should you want to be selective, you do have that option. Should you choose to be selective and only enable BranchCache on some shares, you need to edit the properties of the share and enable BranchCache. You do this by clicking Caching on the Advanced Sharing page and then using the Offline Settings dialog, which is shown in Figure 8-22.

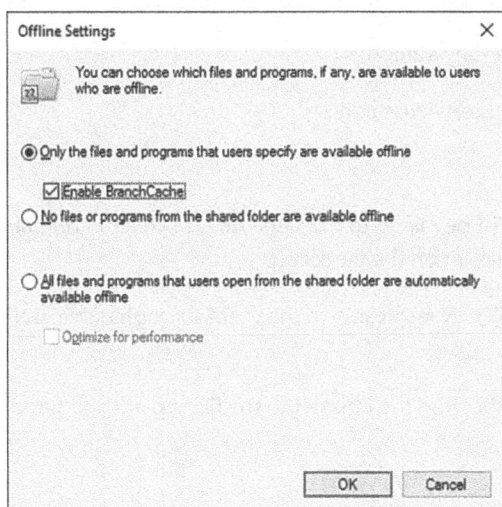

Figure 8-22   Offline Settings dialog

After you've configured your file server to support BranchCache, you need to configure client computers to support branch cache. You do this by configuring group policy in the `Computer Configuration\Policies\Administrative Templates\Network\BranchCache` node of a GPO. Which policies you configure depends on how you want BranchCache to work at each branch office. You can choose between the following options:

- **Distributed Cache Mode**   When client computers are configured for Distributed Cache mode, each Windows 7 or later computer hosts part of the cache.

- **Hosted Cache Mode**   When you configure Hosted Cache mode, a server at the branch office hosts the cache in its entirety. Any server running Windows Server 2008 R2 or later can function as a hosted cache mode server.

To configure a branch office server to function as a hosted cache mode server, run the following PowerShell commands:

```
Install-WindowsFeature BranchCache
Start-Service BranchCache
Enable-BCHostedServer
```

SMB over QUIC

SMB over QUIC allows you to make file shares securely accessible over the internet without requiring a VPN connection. Windows Server 2025 allows SMB over QUIC servers to be published from hosts on a perimeter network over UDP port 443. SMB over QUIC has the following requirements:

- Windows Server 2025 or later (any edition).

- Windows Server 2022 Datacenter: Azure edition.

- Windows 11 Client.

- Both the server and client must be joined to the same Active Directory domain, or the client must have a local user account on the file server.

- The file server must have an FQDN resolvable to the client through public DNS, private DNS, or the hosts file.

- UDP port 443 must allow traffic from the internet to the file server configured for SMB over QUIC.

Certificate requirements

SMB over QUIC requires a server certificate trusted by both the file server and the client computer with the following properties:

- **Key usage**   Digital signature.

- **Purpose**   Server authentication (EKU 1.3.6.1.5.5.7.3.1).

- **Signature algorithm**   SHA256RSA (or greater).

- **Signature hash**   SHA256 (or greater).

- **Public key algorithm** ECDSA_P256 (or greater). Can also use RSA with at least a key length of 2,048).

- **Subject Alternative Name (SAN)** A DNS name entry for each fully qualified DNS name used to reach the SMB server.

- **Subject** CN = anything, but one must be present.

- **Private key included** Yes.

A trusted third-party certificate authority can issue this certificate. You can also configure an Active Directory Certificate Services server configured as an enterprise root or subordinate CA to issue certificates that support SMB over QUIC by configuring a certificate template in the following manner by duplicating the Computer template as a starting point and then configuring the following properties:

- **Compatibility** Set to the latest version for best security.

- **General tab** Set a clear display name and template name.

- **Request Handling tab** Set the Purpose to Signature.

- **Subject Name tab** Allow information to be supplied in the request.

- **Extensions tab** Ensure Server Authentication (EKU 1.3.6.1.5.5.7.3.1) is included.

- **Security tab** Grant the necessary permissions for enrollment.

- **Key usage** Digital signature.

- **Signature algorithm** SHA256RSA or greater.

- **Signature hash** SHA256 or greater.

- **Public key algorithm** ECDSA_P256 or greater. (An RSA with at least 2048-bit length is also acceptable.)

- **Subject Alternative Name (SAN)** Include all fully qualified DNS names used to reach the SMB server.

- **Subject** Must exist, but can be anything.

- **Private key included** Yes.

Configuring the file server for SMB over QUIC

To configure the file server for SMB over QUIC, install the certificate on the file server and then perform the following steps in PowerShell:

```
# Retrieve the installed certificate thumbprint
$cert = Get-ChildItem Cert:\LocalMachine\My | Where-Object {$_.Subject -like "*CN=SMB over QUIC*"}
$thumbprint = $cert.Thumbprint
# Map the certificate to the SMB server
New-SmbServerCertificateMapping -Name "your-server-fqdn" -Thumbprint $thumbprint -Store My
# Enable SMB over QUIC on the file server
Set-SmbServerConfiguration -EnableSMBQUIC $true
# Verify SMB over QUIC is enabled
netstat -a | Select-String 443
```

Configure SMB-over-QUIC client access control

You can use the SMB over QUIC client access control feature to restrict which clients can access an SMB-over-QUIC-enabled file server. Access restrictions occur based on the client certificate. You use the following PowerShell cmdlets to manage client access to SMB over QUIC-enabled file servers:

- `Grant-SmbClientAccessToServer`   Provides access by creating an allow access control list entry for a client

- `Revoke-SmbClientAccessToServer`   Removes a client's allow access control list entry

- `Block-SmbClientAccessToServer`   Add a deny access control list entry for a client

- `Unblock-SmbClientAccessToServer`   Remove a deny access control list entry for a client

- `Get-SmbClientAccessToServer`   View the access control list entries

You can audit which clients have accessed an SMB over a QUIC-enabled file server by running the following PowerShell command:

```
Set-SmbServerConfiguration -AuditClientCertificateAccess $true
```

Once you have enabled auditing, client access-related events are stored in the following event logs:

- `Applications and Services Logs\Microsoft\Windows\SMBServer\Audit` (event IDs 3007, 3008, 3009)

- `Applications and Services Logs\Microsoft\Windows\SMBClient\Connectivity` (event ID 30831)

> ## More Info
>
> *SMB over QUIC*
>
> You can learn more about SMB over QUIC at *https://learn.microsoft.com/en-us/ windows-server/storage/file-server/smb-over-quic.*

PowerShell commands

While you can remotely manage file servers using the Remote Server Administration Tools, if you need to manage a large number of servers, it's more efficient to use PowerShell. In the next few pages, you'll learn which PowerShell cmdlets are available for managing Windows Server file servers.

Shared folder cmdlets

Shared folder cmdlets are in the `SmbShare` PowerShell module. This is because traditional file shares use the SMB protocol. Sometimes, the documentation refers to SMB servers, which is another way of saying "file servers." Table 8-1 lists the shared folder-related cmdlets available in Windows Server.

Table 8-1   Shared folder cmdlets

Noun	Verbs	Functionality
`SMBBandwidthLimit`	`Get, Remove, Set`	Manage shared folder bandwidth caps
`SMBClientConfiguration`	`Get, Set`	View client SMB configuration
`SMBClientNetworkInterface`	`Get`	View the network interfaces used by the client
`SMBConnection`	`Get`	View connections from the client to shared folders
`SMBDelegation`	`Disable, Enable, Get`	Manage constrained delegation authorization for SMB clients
`SMBMapping`	`Get, New, Remove`	Manage SMB mappings
`SMBMultiChannelConnection`	`Get, Update`	Manage multichannel connections to SMB shares
`SMBMultichannelConstraint`	`Get, New, Remove`	Manages SMB multichannel constraints on shared folders
`SMBOpenFile`	`Get, Close`	Manage files that are open from shared folders
`SMBPathAcl`	`Set`	Configure the ACL for the file system folder to match the ACL of the shared folder

Noun	Verbs	Functionality
SMBServerConfiguration	Get, Set	Manage SMB server configuration
SMBServerNetworkInterface	Get	View network interfaces used by the SMB server
SMBSession	Get, Close	View and terminate SMB sessions
SMBShare	Get, New, Remove, Set	Manage shared folders
SMBShareAccess	Block, Get, Grant, Revoke, Unblock	Manage permissions on shared folders

File Server Resource Manager cmdlets

One of the challenges with FSRM is that you need to configure it on a per-server basis. When you have complex FSRM configurations, this can make it challenging to deploy the same configuration across multiple servers. One way of simplifying the process of deploying FSRM across multiple file servers is to use PowerShell. By creating and running a PowerShell script or by using DSC, you can apply the same FSRM settings across multiple file servers.

Table 8-2 lists the FSRM-related cmdlets on the basis of PowerShell noun, available verbs, and functionality.

Table 8-2   FSRM cmdlets

Noun	Verbs	Functionality
FSRMAction	New	Create a new action, such as sending an email, creating an event log entry, running a command, or generating a report.
FsrmAdrSetting	Get, Set	Manage access denied remediation settings, which display information for users when they're denied access to a file.
FSRMAutoQuota	Get, New, Remove, Set, Update	Manage auto apply quotas. Auto apply quotas are quota templates that you can apply at the volume or folder level.
FSRMClassification	Get, Set, Start, Stop, Wait	Manage classification processes, such as starting and stopping them.
FSRMClassification-PropertyDefinition	Get, New, Remove, Set, Update	Manage classification property definitions.
FSRMClassification-PropertyValue	New	Manage classification property values.
FSRMClassificationRule	Get, New, Remove, Set	Manage classification property rules.

Noun	Verbs	Functionality
FSRMEffectiveNamespace	Get,	Provides a list of paths that match FSRM namespaces.
FSRMFileGroup	Get, New, Remove, Set	Manage FSRM file groups for file screens.
FSRMFileManagementJob	Get, New, Remove, Set, Start, Stop, Wait	Manage FSRM file management jobs.
FSRMFileScreen	Get, New, Remove, Reset, Set	Manage FSRM file screens.
FSRMFileScreenException	Get, New, Remove, Set	Manage FSRM file screen exceptions.
FSRMFileScreenTemplate	Get, New, Remove, Set	Manage FSRM file screen templates.
FSRMFmjAction	New	Create file management job actions.
FSRMFmjCondition	New	Create file management job conditions.
FSRMFmjNotification	New	Create file management job notifications.
FSRMFmjNotificationAction	New	Create file management notification actions.
FSRMMacro	Get,	Lists FSRM macros.
FSRMMgmtProperty	Get, Remove, Set	Manage FSRM management properties.
FSRMQuota	Get, New, Remove, Reset, Set, Update	Manage FSRM quotas.
FSRMQuotaTemplate	Get, New, Remove, Set	Manage FSRM quota templates.
FSRMQuotaThreshold	New	Manage FSRM quota thresholds.
FSRMRmsTemplate	Get,	View available RMS templates that you can apply using FSRM.
FSRMScheduledTask	New	Create an FSRM Scheduled Task.
FSRMSetting	Get, Set	Manage FSRM settings.
FSRMStorageReport	Get, Remove, New, Set, Start, Stop, Wait	Manage FSRM storage reports.
FSRMTestEmail	Send	Send a test alert email using FSRM settings.

BranchCache cmdlets

You can use the BranchCache cmdlets, available when you install the BranchCache feature, to configure and manage BranchCache on both file servers and clients. These cmdlets are listed in Table 8-3.

Table 8-3   BranchCache cmdlets

Noun	Verbs	Function
BC	Disable, Reset	Disable or reset BranchCache
BCAuthentication	Set	Configure BranchCache Computer Authentication mode
BCCache	Clear, Set	Manage cache files
BCCachePackage	Export, Import	Export and import cache packages
BCClientConfiguration	Get	View client computer settings
BCContentServerConfiguration	Get	View the content server configuration
BCDataCache	Get	Get information about the data cache
BCDataCacheEntryMaxAge	Set	Manage the amount of time data can be stored in the cache
BCDataCacheExtension	Add, Get	Manage cache storage space
BCDistributed	Enable	Configure a computer to operate in distributed cache mode
BCDowngrading	Enable, Disable	Manage whether computers can use Windows 7 BranchCache mode
BCFileContent	Publish	Creates hashes for files on the file server that have BranchCache enabled
BCHashCache	Get	View the BranchCache hash cache
BCHostedCacheServer-Configuration	Get	View hosted cache server settings
BCHostedClient	Enable	Configure BranchCache to function in hosted cache client mode
BCHostedServer	Enable	Configure BranchCache to function in hosted cache server mode
BCLocal	Enable	Enable the BranchCache service to function in local caching mode
BCMinSMBLatency	Set	Configure the minimum latency requirement for activation of Branch-Cache functionality
BCNetworkConfiguration	Get	View BranchCache network settings
BCSecretKey	Export, Import, Set	Manage the cryptographic key used for the generation of BranchCache segment secrets
BCServeOnBattery	Disable, Enable	Configure whether content discovery requests are responded to depending on whether a computer is running on battery power
BCStatus	Get	View BranchCache status and configuration information
BCWebContent	Publish	Creates hashes for web content

DFS cmdlets

DFS cmdlets are available across two separate PowerShell modules. You use the first set of cmdlets, listed in Table 8-4, to manage DFS namespaces and namespace servers. You use the second set of cmdlets, listed in Table 8-5 to manage DFS replication and folder targets.

Table 8-4   DFS namespace cmdlets

Noun	Verbs	Function
DfsnAccess	Get, Grant, Remove, Revoke	Manage permissions for DFS namespace folders
DfsnFolder	Get, Move, New, Remove, Set	Manage DFS namespace folder settings
DfsnFolderTarget	Get, New, Remove, Set	Manage the DFS namespace folder target settings
DfsnRoot	Get, New, Remove, Set	Manage settings for DFS roots
DfsnRootTarget	Get, New, Remove, Set	Manage settings for DFS root targets
DfsnServer-Configuration	Get, Set	Manage DFS namespace settings for the DFSN root server

Table 8-5   DFS Replication cmdlets

Noun	Verbs	Function
DfsrBacklog	Get	Provides a list of pending file updates between replication partners.
DfsrClone	Export, Get, Import, Reset	Manage a cloned DFS replication database.
DfsrConfiguration-FromAD	Update	Updates the DFS Replication service by checking the Active Directory database.
DfsrConnection	Add, Get, Remove, Set	Manage connections between members of a replication group.
DfsrConnectionSchedule	Get, Set	Manage the connection schedule between members of a replication group.
DfsrDelegation	Get, Grant, Revoke	Manage replication group permissions.
DfsReplicatedFolder	Get, New, Remove, Set	Manage replicated folders in a replication group.
DfsReplicationGroup	Get, New, Remove, Set, Suspend, Sync	Manage replication groups.
DfsrFileHash	Get	View a file hash.
DfsrGroupSchedule	Get, Set	Manage replication group schedules.
DfsrGuid	ConvertFrom	Translates GUIDs to friendly names for a specific replication group.

CHAPTER 8

Noun	Verbs	Function
DfsrHealthReport	Write	Generates a replication health report that you can use for diagnostic purposes.
DfsrIdRecord	Get	View ID records for replicated files or folders from the DFS replication database.
DfsrMember	Add, Get, Set	Manage the computer members of the DFS replication group.
DfsrMembership	Get, Set	View and configure replication group membership settings.
DfsrPreservedFiles	Get, Restore	Manage preserved files and folders. Preserved files are ones where there has been a conflict or where files have been deleted.
DfsrPropagationReport	Write	Create reports based on the propagation of test files.
DfsrPropagationTest	Remove, Start	Manage propagation test files.
DfsrService-Configuration	Get, Set	Manage DFS Replication service settings.
DfsrState	Get	View the DFS Replication state for a member.

Dynamic Access Control cmdlets

You can use the cmdlets listed in Table 8-6 to manage Dynamic Access Control.

Table 8-6   Dynamic Access Control cmdlets

Noun	Verbs	Function
ADCentralAccessPolicy	Get, New, Remove, Set	Manage central access policies
ADCentralAccessPolicyMember	Add. Remove	Add and remove central access rules to a central access policy in AD DS
ADCentralAccessRule	Get, New, Remove, Set	Manages central access rules
ADClaimType	Get, New, Remove, Set	Manage claim types
ADResourceProperty	Get, New, Remove, Set	Manage resource properties
ADResourcePropertyList	Get, New, Remove, Set	Manage resource property lists
ADResourcePropertyList-Member	Add, Remove	Manage resource properties in a resource property list
ADResourcePropertyValueType	Get	View resource property value type

Azure Arc and hybrid services

Windows Server is designed to integrate with Microsoft's Azure and Microsoft 365 clouds. In this chapter, you'll learn about this integration from the hybrid perspective, with coverage of hybrid identity and hybrid management services that can be connected under the umbrella of Azure Arc.

Microsoft Entra ID

Microsoft Entra ID is Microsoft's identity and access management service hosted in Azure. It's mostly used as the identity service for products such as Office 365, but you can also integrate it with Azure services such as Microsoft Entra Domain Services, which allows you to domain join IaaS VMs and replicate some of the functionality of on-premises Active Directory instance. You will learn more about Microsoft Entra Domain Services in Chapter 10, "Windows Server in Azure."

You can also configure synchronization between an on-premises Active Directory instance and an Entra ID instance, which allows the same username and password to be used on-premises and in Azure. You can also configure self-service password reset, which allows your on-premises users to navigate to a web page hosted in Azure to reset their on-premises passwords.

Microsoft Entra Connect

Microsoft Entra Connect is designed to streamline configuring connections between the on-premises deployment and a Microsoft Entra ID instance. The Microsoft Entra Connect tool is designed to make configuring synchronization between an on-premises Active Directory deployment and Microsoft Entra ID as frictionless as possible.

Microsoft Entra Connect can automatically configure and install simple password synchronization or Federation/single sign-on, depending on your organizational needs. When you choose the Federation with AD FS option, Active Directory Federation Services is installed and configured along with a web application proxy server to facilitate communication between the on-premises AD FS deployment and Microsoft Entra ID.

The Microsoft Entra Connect tool supports the following optional features:

- **Exchange Hybrid Deployment** This option is suitable for organizations with an Office 365 deployment in which mailboxes are hosted on-premises and in the cloud.

- **Exchange Mail Public Folders** This feature allows organizations to synchronize mail-enabled public folder objects from an on-premises Active Directory environment to Microsoft 365.

- **Entra ID App And Attribute Filtering** Selecting this option allows you to be more selective about which attributes are synchronized between the on-premises environment and Entra ID.

- **Password Synchronization** This synchronizes the user's on-premises password hash with Entra ID. When the user authenticates to Entra ID, the submitted password is hashed using the same process, and if the hashes match, the user is authenticated. Each time the user updates their password on-premises, the updated password hash synchronizes to Entra ID.

- **Password Writeback** Password writeback allows users to change their passwords in the cloud and have the changed password written back to the on-premises Active Directory instance.

- **Device Writeback** Here, information about devices the user registers in Entra ID is written back to the on-premises AD instance.

- **Directory Extension Attribute Sync** This option allows you to extend the Entra ID schema based on extensions made to your organization's on-premises Active Directory instance.

More Info

Microsoft Entra Connect

You can learn more about Microsoft Entra Connect at *https://learn.microsoft.com/entra/identity/hybrid/connect/whatis-azure-ad-connect*.

Microsoft Entra Connect supports a variety of user sign-in options related to the method you use to synchronize directory information from Active Directory Domain Services to Entra ID. You configure which sign-in option to use when setting up Microsoft Entra Connect. The default method—password sync—is appropriate for most organizations that will use Microsoft Entra Connect to synchronize identities to the cloud.

Password synchronization

Hashes of on-premises Active Directory user passwords synchronize to Microsoft Entra ID, and changed passwords immediately synchronize to Microsoft Entra ID. Actual passwords are never sent to Microsoft Entra ID and are not stored in Microsoft Entra ID. This allows for single sign-on for users of computers that are joined to an Active Directory domain that synchronizes to Microsoft Entra ID. Password synchronization also enables password writeback for self-service password reset functionality through Microsoft Entra ID.

Pass-through authentication

The user's password is validated against an on-premises Active Directory domain controller when authenticating to Microsoft Entra ID. Passwords and password hashes are not present in Microsoft Entra ID. Pass-through authentication allows for on-premises password policies to apply. Pass-through authentication requires Microsoft Entra Connect to have an agent on a computer joined to the domain that hosts the Active Directory instance containing the relevant user accounts. Pass-through authentication also allows single sign-on for users of domain-joined machines.

Pass-through authentication validates the user's password against the on-premises Active Directory controller. The password doesn't need to be present in Microsoft Entra ID in any form. This allows for on-premises policies, such as sign-in hour restrictions, to be evaluated during authentication to cloud services.

Pass-through authentication uses a simple agent on a Windows Server domain-joined machine in the on-premises environment. This agent listens for password-validation requests. It doesn't require any inbound ports to be open to the Internet.

You can also enable single sign-on for users on domain-joined machines that are on the corporate network. With single sign-on, enabled users only need to enter a username to help them securely access cloud resources.

Active Directory Federation

Active Directory Federation allows users to authenticate to Microsoft Entra ID resources using on-premises credentials. It also requires the deployment of an Active Directory Federation Services infrastructure. This is the most complicated identity synchronization configuration for Entra ID and is only likely to be implemented in environments with complicated identity configurations.

> ## More Info
> ### Microsoft Entra Connect sign-in options
> To learn more about sign-in options, consult the following article: *https://learn.micro-soft.com/entra/identity/hybrid/connect/plan-connect-user-signin*.

CHAPTER 9

CHAPTER 9

Microsoft Entra Connect prerequisites

To configure Microsoft Entra Connect synchronization, install the Microsoft Entra Connect software and then run the Microsoft Entra Connect Installation Wizard. Installing Microsoft Entra Connect is simply a matter of installing the appropriate MSI file on a Windows Server computer in an environment that meets the necessary prerequisites. After installing the software, you use the Microsoft Entra Connect Setup Wizard to perform the initial configuration. Run the Setup Wizard again if you want to change any Microsoft Entra Connect synchronization settings. You can also use PowerShell or the Synchronization Service Manager to configure synchronization settings, which you'll learn about later in this section.

Before installing Microsoft Entra Connect, you should ensure that your environment, Microsoft Entra Connect computer, and account used to configure Microsoft Entra Connect meet the software, hardware, and privilege requirements. So, you need to ensure that your Active Directory environment is configured at the appropriate level, that the computer on which you will run Microsoft Entra Connect has the appropriate software and hardware configuration, and that the account used to install Microsoft Entra Connect has been added to the appropriate security groups.

> ## More Info
>
> ### Microsoft Entra Connect prerequisites
>
> You can learn more about Microsoft Entra Connect prerequisites at *https://learn.microsoft.com/entra/identity/hybrid/connect/how-to-connect-install-prerequisites*.

Before installing and configuring Microsoft Entra Connect, you must ensure that you have configured an additional DNS domain for Entra. By default, a Microsoft Entra ID tenant will allow 50,000 objects; however, when you add and verify an additional domain, this limit increases to 300,000. You can open a support ticket with Microsoft if you require more than 300,000 objects in your Microsoft Entra ID instance. If you require more than 500,000 objects in your Microsoft Entra ID instance, you must acquire a Microsoft Entra P1 or P2 license or Enterprise Mobility and Security license. Having the DNS domain configured before you set up identity synchronization will allow you to ensure that user UPNs aren't using the default onmicrosoft.com DNS domain.

Microsoft Entra Connect Server requirements

Microsoft Entra Connect is software installed on a computer that manages synchronizing objects between the on-premises Active Directory and the Microsoft Entra ID instance. You can install Microsoft Entra Connect on computers running all supported versions of the Windows Server operating system.

Microsoft Entra Connect has the following requirements:

- It must be installed on a Windows Server instance with the GUI version of the operating system. You cannot install Microsoft Entra Connect on a Server Core operating system computer.

- You can deploy Microsoft Entra Connect on a computer that is a domain controller, a member server, or a standalone server if you use the custom options. Because it's best practice not to allow AD DS domain controllers to be able to contact hosts on the Internet directly and to have AD DS domain controllers run the Server Core version of the Windows Server operating system, you should generally avoid domain controller deployment.

- The server hosting Microsoft Entra Connect requires .NET Framework 4.6.2 or later.

- Microsoft Entra Connect's server hosting must not have PowerShell Transcription enabled through Group Policy.

- If you're deploying Microsoft Entra Connect with Active Directory Federation Services, you must use Windows Server 2012 R2 or later for the web application proxy, and Windows remote management must be enabled on the servers that will host AD FS roles.

- If Global Administrators enable multifactor authentication (MFA), then the *https://secure.aadcdn.microsoftonline-p.com* URL must be configured as a trusted site.

- The computer with Microsoft Entra Connect installed must be a member of a domain in the forest that you want to synchronize, and it must have connectivity to a writable domain controller in each domain of the forest you want to synchronize on the following ports:

  - **DNS**   TCP/UDP port 53

  - **Kerberos**   TCP/UDP port 88

  - **RPC**   TCP port 135

  - **LDAP**   TCP/UDP port 389

  - **SSL**   TCP port 443

  - **SMB**   TCP port 445

The computer with Microsoft Entra Connect installed must be able to establish communication with the Microsoft Azure servers on the Internet over TCP port 443. This computer can be located on an internal network if it can initiate communication on TCP port 443. It doesn't need a publicly routable IP address. The computer hosting Microsoft Entra Connect always initiates synchronization communication to Microsoft Azure. Microsoft Entra ID doesn't initiate synchronization communication to the computer hosting Microsoft Entra Connect on the on-premises network.

Although you can install Microsoft Entra Connect on a domain controller, Microsoft recommends deploying Microsoft Entra Connect on a computer that doesn't have the domain controller role. If you will be replicating more than 50,000 objects, Microsoft recommends deploying SQL Server on a computer that's separate from the one that will host Microsoft Entra Connect. If you plan to host the SQL Server instance on a separate computer, ensure that communication is possible between the computer hosting Microsoft Entra Connect and the computer hosting the SQL instance on TCP port 1433.

If you will use a separate SQL Server instance, ensure that the account used to install and configure Microsoft Entra Connect has systems administrator rights on the SQL instance and that the service account used for Microsoft Entra Connect has public permissions on the Microsoft Entra Connect database.

SQL Server requirements

When you deploy Microsoft Entra Connect, you can have Microsoft Entra Connect install an SQL Server Express instance, or you can choose to have Microsoft Entra Connect leverage a full instance of SQL Server. SQL Server Express is limited to a maximum database size of 10 GB. In terms of Microsoft Entra Connect, this means that Microsoft Entra Connect can only manage 100,000 objects. This is likely to be adequate for all but the largest environments.

For environments that require Microsoft Entra Connect to manage more than 100,000 objects, you'll need to have Microsoft Entra Connect leverage a full instance of SQL Server. Microsoft Entra Connect can use all supported versions of Microsoft SQL Server. If deploying a full instance of SQL Server to support Microsoft Entra Connect, ensure that the following prerequisites are met:

- **Use a case-insensitive SQL collation.** Case-insensitive collations have the _CI_ identifier in their name. Case-sensitive collations (those that use the _CS_ designation) are not supported for use with Microsoft Entra Connect.

- **You can only use one sync engine per SQL instance.** If you have an additional Microsoft Entra Connect sync engine, or if you are using Microsoft Identity Manager in your environment, each sync engine requires its own separate SQL instance.

Installation account requirements

The accounts that you use to install and configure Microsoft Entra Connect have the following requirements:

- The account configuring Microsoft Entra Connect must have the Global Administrator permission in the Entra ID tenant. If you create a service account in Microsoft 365 to use in place of the account with tenant administrator permissions, be sure to configure the account with a password that does not expire.

- If you use express installation settings, the account used to install and configure Microsoft Entra Connect must have enterprise administrator permissions within the on-premises Active Directory forest. This account is required only during installation and configuration. Once Microsoft Entra Connect is installed and configured, this account no longer needs enterprise administrator permissions. Best practices are creating a separate account for Microsoft Entra Connect installation and configuration and temporarily adding this account to the enterprise administrators group during the installation and configuration process. After installing and configuring Microsoft Entra Connect, this account can be removed from the enterprise administrators group. You shouldn't attempt to change the account used after Microsoft Entra Connect is set up and configured because Microsoft Entra Connect always attempts to run using the original account.

- The account used to install and configure Microsoft Entra Connect must be a member of the Local Administrators group on the computer on which Microsoft Entra Connect is installed.

- Microsoft Entra Connect installation can create a new account specifically for synchronization. To do this, you will have to provide Enterprise Administrator credentials.

Installing Microsoft Entra Connect

Installing Microsoft Entra Connect with express settings is appropriate if your organization has a single Active Directory forest and you want to use password sync for authentication. The Microsoft Entra Connect express settings are appropriate for most organizations.

To install Microsoft Entra Connect with Express settings, perform the following steps:

1. Double-click the installation file downloaded from the Microsoft Download Center or the Microsoft Entra portal to the computer hosting the synchronization service. You will be presented with a security warning and then installation will complete, prompting you to perform configuration. You'll be asked to agree to the license terms and privacy notice before performing configuration.

2. You must use custom settings if your organization has an internal nonroutable domain. To use custom settings, select Customize.

3. On the Install Required Components page, choose from the following options:

   - **Specify A Custom Installation Location**   Choose this option to install Microsoft Entra Connect in a separate location, such as on another volume.

   - **Specify An Existing SQL Server**   Choose this option to specify an alternative SQL server instance. By default, Microsoft Entra Connect will install an SQL Server Express instance.

CHAPTER 9

- **Use An Existing Service Account**   You can configure Microsoft Entra Connect to use an existing service account. By default, Microsoft Entra Connect will create a service account. If you install Microsoft Entra Connect on a computer running Windows Server 2012 or later, you can configure Microsoft Entra Connect to use a group-managed service account. You'll need to use an existing service account if you're using Microsoft Entra Connect with a remote SQL Server instance or if communication with Azure will occur through a proxy server that requires authentication.

- **Specify Custom Sync Groups**   When you deploy Microsoft Entra Connect, it creates four local groups on the server that hosts the Microsoft Entra Connect instance: the Administrators group, operators group, password reset group, and browse groups. If you want to use your own set of groups, you can specify them here. These groups must be local to the host server and not a member of the domain.

4. You don't have to select any custom options, but if you have a nonroutable domain on-premises, you must perform a custom installation; select Install.

5. On the User Sign-In page, specify what type of sign-in you want to allow. You can choose between the following options, the details of which were covered earlier in this chapter (except for PingFederate, which is a third-party tool and not addressed by the MS-102 exam). Most organizations choose Password Synchronization because it's the most straightforward.

    - Password Synchronization
    - Pass-Through Authentication
    - Federation With AD FS
    - Federation With PingFederate
    - Do Not Configure
    - Enable Single Sign-On

6. On the Connect To Microsoft Entra ID page, provide the credentials of a Global Administrator account. Microsoft recommends using an account in the default onmicrosoft.com domain associated with the Microsoft Entra ID instance you'll be connecting to. If you choose the Federation With AD FS option, ensure you don't sign in using an account in a domain you'll enable for Federation.

7. After Microsoft Entra Connect has connected to Microsoft Entra ID, you can specify the directory to synchronize as well as the forest. Select Add Directory to add a specific forest. When you add a forest by selecting Add Directory, you must specify the credentials of

an account that will perform periodic synchronization. Unless you're certain that you've applied the minimum necessary privileges to an account, you should provide enterprise administrator credentials and allow Microsoft Entra Connect to create the account (choose Create New AD Account). Doing so will ensure that the account is assigned only the privileges necessary to perform synchronization tasks.

8. After verifying the credentials, select Next and review the UPN suffix on the Microsoft Entra ID Sign-In Configuration page. Inspect the on-premises attribute to use as the Microsoft Entra ID username. When doing this, you must ensure that accounts use a routable Microsoft Entra ID username.

9. On the Domain And OU Filtering page, select whether you want to sync all objects (Sync All Domains And OUs) or just objects in specific domains and OUs (Sync Selected Domains and OUs).

10. On the Uniquely Identifying Your Users page, specify how users will be identified. By default, users should have only one representation across all directories (Users Are Represented Only Once Across All Directories). If users exist in multiple directories, you can have matches identified by a specific Active Directory attribute (User Identities Exist Across Multiple Directories. Match Using), with the default being the Mail Attribute.

11. On the Filter Users And Devices page, specify whether you want to synchronize all users and devices or only members of a specific group.

12. On the Optional Features page, select any optional features that you want to configure. These features include the following:

    - Exchange Hybrid Deployment

    - Exchange Mail Public Folders

    - Microsoft Entra ID App And Attribute Filtering

    - Password Hash Synchronization

    - Password Writeback

    - Group Writeback

    - Device Writeback

    - Directory Extension Attribute Sync

13. On the Ready To Configure page, you can choose to start synchronization (Start The Synchronization Process When Configuration Completes) or enable staging mode (Enable Staging Mode: When Selected, Synchronization Will Not Export Any Data to AD or Microsoft Entra ID), where synchronization will prepare to be run but won't synchronize any data with Microsoft Entra ID.

CHAPTER 9

> ## More Info
> ### Microsoft Entra Connect Custom Installation
> To install Microsoft Entra Connect with the custom settings, consult the article at *https://learn.microsoft.com/entra/identity/hybrid/connect/how-to-connect-install-custom*.

Microsoft Entra Connect Health

Microsoft Entra Connect Health is a tool available in the Microsoft Entra admin center that allows you to monitor the health of synchronization between your organization's on-premises directory and Microsoft Entra ID.

You can use Microsoft Entra Connect Health to view the following information:

- **Synchronization Errors**   These include duplicate attributes, data mismatches, data validation failure, large attributes, Federated domain change, and existing admin role conflicts.

- **Synchronization Services**   This handles information about which services synchronize with Microsoft Entra ID.

- **AD FS Services**   This is information about AD FS when Microsoft Entra Connect is configured for Federation, including information about errors and issues.

- **AD DS Services**   This is information about domains and forests connected to Microsoft Entra ID.

> ## More Info
> ### Microsoft Entra Connect Health
> You can learn more about Microsoft Entra Connect Health at *https://learn.microsoft.com/azure/active-directory/hybrid/whatis-azure-ad-connect*.

By default, synchronization occurs between the on-premises instance of Active Directory and Microsoft Entra ID every 30 minutes. However, in some cases, you'll change a user account or create a collection of user accounts and want to get those changes or new accounts into the Microsoft Entra ID instance that supports the Microsoft 365 tenancy as fast as possible. You can force synchronization by running the Microsoft Entra Connect Wizard again or using the Synchronization Service Manager.

To perform a full synchronization using the Synchronization Service Manager, follow these steps:

1. Open the Synchronization Service Manager by selecting Synchronization Service in the Start menu or running the `miisclient.exe` file in the `C:\Program Files\Microsoft Microsoft Entra ID Sync\UIShell` folder.

2. Select the Connectors tab.

3. On the Connectors tab, select the name of your Active Directory domain service.

4. In the Actions pane, select Run.

5. The Run Connector dialog contains a list of synchronization options:

   - **Full Synchronization**   Performs a full synchronization

   - **Delta Import**   Imports changed schema and objects

   - **Delta Synchronization**   Synchronizes only objects that have changed since the last sync

   - **Export**   Writes data from the Azure instance to the on-premises instance

   - **Full Import**   Suitable for initiating the first full synchronization or the first full synchronization after you have changed the filtering parameters

6. Select Full Synchronization and click OK.

You can also use the Synchronization Service Manager to configure extensive filtering options. However, for tasks such as configuring OU-based filtering, Microsoft recommends first attempting to configure filtering using the Microsoft Entra Connect Setup Wizard and relying on a tool such as the Synchronization Service Manager only if problems arise.

More Info

Synchronization Service Manager

You can learn more about the Synchronization Service Manager at *https:// learn.microsoft.com/en-us/azure/active-directory/hybrid/connect/ how-to-connect-sync-service-manager-ui.*

CHAPTER 9

Configure object filters

When you use Microsoft Entra Connect to synchronize on-premises Active Directory to a Microsoft Entra ID instance, the default setting is to have all user accounts, group accounts, and mail-enabled contact objects synchronized to the cloud. For some organizations, synchronizing everything is exactly what they want. Other organizations want to be more selective about which objects are synchronized from the on-premises Active Directory environment to the Microsoft Entra ID instance.

With Microsoft Entra Connect, you can choose to filter based on the following options:

- **Domain-based**   In a forest with multiple domains, you can configure filtering so that only objects from some domains, and not others, are filtered.

- **Organizational unit (OU) based**   With this filtering type, you choose which objects are filtered based on their location within specific organizational units.

You can also configure filtering based on group membership, as shown in the Filter Users And Devices dialog. Using Microsoft Entra Connect, you can configure separate group-based filters for each forest or domain that's synchronized.

> ## More Info
> *Configure filtering*
>
> **You can learn more about Microsoft Entra ID sync filtering at *https://learn.microsoft.com/azure/active-directory/hybrid/how-to-connect-sync-configure-filtering*.**

Although Microsoft Entra Connect will address most organizations' synchronization requirements, the Synchronization Rules Editor is the most comprehensive tool you can use to filter synchronization. You can use this tool to modify and create new synchronization rules. Rather than configuring synchronization on a per-domain or per-OU basis, you can tailor rules for individual objects and specific Active Directory attributes.

> ## More Info
> *Synchronization Rules Editor*
>
> **You can learn more about the Synchronization Rules Editor at *https://learn.microsoft.com/entra/identity/hybrid/connect/how-to-connect-sync-change-the-configuration*.**

Configure password synchronization

Password sync allows the synchronization of user account passwords from an on-premises Active Directory to the Microsoft Entra ID instance. The advantage of this is that users can sign in to access Microsoft 365 and Azure resources using the same password that they use to sign in to computers on the on-premises environment. Password sync does not provide single sign-on or Federation.

When you enable password sync, the on-premises password complexity policies override password complexity policies configured for the Microsoft Entra ID instance. This means that any password valid for an on-premises user will be valid within Entra ID, even if it normally wouldn't be.

Password expiration works as follows: The password of the account of the cloud user object is set to never expire. Each time the user account password is changed in the on-premises Active Directory instance, this change replicates to the Microsoft Entra ID instance that supports the Microsoft 365 tenancy. So, a user account's password can expire on the on-premises Active Directory instance, but that user can still use the same password to sign in to Microsoft 365. The next time they sign in to the on-premises environment, they are forced to change their password, and that change replicates to the Microsoft Entra ID instance that supports the Microsoft 365 tenancy.

If you disable a user's account in the on-premises Active Directory instance when password sync is enabled, the user's account in the Microsoft Entra ID instance that supports the Microsoft 365 tenancy is disabled within a few minutes. If password sync isn't enabled and you disable a user account in the on-premises Active Directory instance, the user's account in the Microsoft Entra ID instance that supports the Microsoft 365 tenancy isn't disabled until the next full synchronization.

More Info

Password sync

You can learn more about password sync at *https://learn.microsoft.com/azure/active-directory/hybrid/how-to-connect-password-hash-synchronization.*

Implement multiforest AD DS scenarios

The Microsoft Entra Connect tool supports synchronization from multiple on-premises Active Directory forests to a single Microsoft Entra ID instance. Multiforest synchronization to a single Microsoft Entra ID instance is supported only when a single Microsoft Entra Connect server is used. Microsoft doesn't support multiple Microsoft Entra Connect servers synchronizing with a single Microsoft Entra ID instance, whether one or multiple forests are being synchronized.

By default, Microsoft Entra Connect assumes that

- A user has a single enabled account. Also, the forest where this account is located must host the directory that is used to authenticate the user. This assumption is used in both password sync and Federation scenarios. Based on this assumption, the UserPrincipal-Name and sourceAnchor/immutableID attributes are drawn from this forest.

- Each user has a single mailbox, and the forest that hosts that mailbox is the best source of attributes visible in the Exchange global address list (GAL). If a user doesn't have an associated mailbox, any configured forest can function as the source for the attribute values.

If a user account has a linked mailbox, an account in an alternate forest will be used for the sign-in process.

The key to synchronizing user accounts from multiple forests is that only one user account from all synchronized forests should represent the user, meaning the synchronization engine should have a way to determine when accounts in separate forests represent the same user. You can configure how the Microsoft Entra Connect sync engine identifies users on the Uniquely Identifying Your Users page using one of the following options:

- Matching users using the Mail Attribute

- Matching users using ObjectSID and msExchangeMasterAccountSID/msRTCIP-Origina-torSID attributes

- Matching users using the SAMAccountName and MailNickName attributes

- Specifying a custom attribute on which to match names

More Info

Multiforest synchronization

You can learn more about multiforest synchronization and supported topologies for Microsoft Entra Connect at *https://learn.microsoft.com/entra/identity/hybrid/connect/plan-connect-topologies*.

Microsoft Entra Cloud Sync

Microsoft Entra Cloud Sync is a separate product from Microsoft Entra Connect. The product is still in development and far from feature parity with the more established Microsoft Entra Connect. Like Microsoft Entra Connect, Microsoft Entra Cloud Sync synchronizes users, groups, and contacts from an on-premises AD DS instance to Microsoft Entra ID. The primary architectural difference between the two products is that the synchronization engine is hosted on an on-premises server with Microsoft Entra Connect. With Microsoft Entra Cloud Sync, the synchronization engine runs in Azure. Microsoft Entra Cloud Sync can be deployed alongside Microsoft Entra Connect.

> ## More Info
> ### Microsoft Entra Cloud SYNC
> You can learn more about Microsoft Entra Cloud Sync at *https://learn.microsoft.com/azure/active-directory/cloud-sync/what-is-cloud-sync.*

Installing Microsoft Entra Cloud Sync

To install the Microsoft Entra Cloud Sync agent, perform the following steps:

1. In the Microsoft Entra admin center (entra.microsoft.com), select Microsoft Entra Connect > Manage Microsoft Entra Cloud Sync.

2. On the Microsoft Entra Cloud Sync page, click Download Agent > Accept Terms & Download. The installation file will be downloaded to your computer.

3. Open this file on the computer that you want to have as your Microsoft Entra Cloud Sync server. You can have multiple computers in this role. While you can install the Microsoft Entra Cloud Sync agent on a domain controller, the best practice is to avoid allowing AD DS domain controllers to communicate directly with any host on the Internet. It is also a best practice to have AD DS Domain Controllers run the Server Core version of Windows Server to minimize the operating system's attack surface.

4. On the Microsoft Entra Connect Provisioning Agent Package page, agree to the license terms and conditions and click Install. On the User Account Control dialog, click Yes.

5. On the Microsoft Microsoft Entra Connect Provisioning Agent Configuration page, click Next.

6. On the Select Extension page, select HR-Driven Provisioning (Workday And SuccessFactors) / Microsoft Entra Cloud Sync and click Next.

7. You'll then be prompted to sign in to your Microsoft 365 tenancy with an account with Global Administrator permissions. Authenticate with your Microsoft 365 or Microsoft Entra ID credentials.

8. On the Configure Service Account page, provide domain administrator credentials for the on-premises AD DS domain you want to synchronize with Microsoft Entra ID.

9. On the Connect Active Directory page, select the domain you want to synchronize and click Add Directory. Add each directory in the forest you want to synchronize and then click Next.

10. On the Confirm Page, review the configuration and then click Confirm.

You can verify that the agent is running by opening the Services console and verifying that the following services are present and running:

- Microsoft Microsoft Entra Connect Agent Updater

- Microsoft Microsoft Entra Connect Provisioning Agent

More Info

Install Microsoft Entra Cloud SYNC

You can learn more about installing Microsoft Entra Cloud Sync at *https://learn.micro-soft.com/entra/identity/hybrid/cloud-sync/how-to-install.*

Comparing Microsoft Entra Cloud Sync with Microsoft Entra Connect

The primary benefit of Microsoft Entra Cloud Sync is that it has a minimal on-premises footprint. The drawback is that it doesn't support all the same features as Microsoft Entra Connect. Most organizations that need the full feature set will continue to use Microsoft Entra Connect. For example, if you need support for Pass-Through Authentication, you'll need Microsoft Entra Connect. Organizations with new synchronization requirements or that are reducing their on-premises footprints and only needing Microsoft Entra Cloud Sync's features should deploy Microsoft Entra Cloud Sync.

Table 9-1 compares Microsoft Entra Connect and Microsoft Entra Cloud Sync features.

Table 9-1   Feature comparison between Microsoft Entra Connect and Microsoft Entra Cloud Sync

Feature	Microsoft Entra Connect	Microsoft Entra Cloud Sync
Connect to a single on-premises AD forest	Yes	Yes
Connect to multiple on-premises AD forests	Yes	Yes
Connect to multiple disconnected on-premises AD forests	No	Yes
Lightweight agent installation model	No	Yes
Multiple active agents for high availability	No	Yes

Feature	Microsoft Entra Connect	Microsoft Entra Cloud Sync
Connect to LDAP directories	Yes	No
Support for user objects	Yes	Yes
Support for group objects	Yes	Yes
Support for contact objects	Yes	Yes
Support for device objects	Yes	No
Allow basic customization for attribute flows	Yes	Yes
Synchronize Exchange online attributes	Yes	Yes
Synchronize extension attributes	Yes	Yes
Synchronize customer-defined AD attributes (directory extensions)	Yes	Yes
Support for Password Hash Sync	Yes	Yes
Support for Pass-Through Authentication	Yes	No
Support for federation	Yes	Yes
Seamless Single Sign-on	Yes	Yes
Supports installation on a Domain Controller	Yes	Yes
Filter on Domains/OUs/groups	Yes	Yes
Filter on objects' attribute values	Yes	No
Allow a minimal set of attributes to be synchronized (MinSync)	Yes	Yes
Allow removing attributes from flowing from AD to Microsoft Entra ID	Yes	Yes
Allow advanced customization for attribute flows	Yes	No
Support for password writeback	Yes	Yes
Support for device writeback	Yes	No
Support for group writeback	Yes	No
Support for merging user attributes from multiple domains	Yes	No
Microsoft Entra Domain Services support	Yes	No
Exchange hybrid writeback	Yes	No
Unlimited number of objects per AD domain	Yes	No
Support for up to 150,000 objects per AD domain	Yes	Yes
Groups with up to 50,000 members	Yes	Yes
Large groups with up to 250,000 members	Yes	No
Cross-domain references	Yes	Yes
On-demand provisioning	No	Yes

CHAPTER 9

Troubleshooting Microsoft Entra Cloud Sync

When troubleshooting the Microsoft Entra Cloud Sync, first verify that the agent is installed and running on the server on which you deployed it by checking the Microsoft Entra Connect Agent Updater and Microsoft Entra Connect Provisioning Agent services.

The next step is determining whether the agent is in the Microsoft Entra admin center. You can do this by opening the Microsoft Entra admin center (entra.microsoft.com), selecting Microsoft Entra Connect, and then clicking Manage Microsoft Entra Cloud Sync. Click Review All Agents to view deployed agents and their status.

The agent cannot communicate with Azure if it cannot open a TCP port 80 or 443 connection to Azure services on the Internet or resolve the DNS addresses of Azure services on the Internet.

The agent stores log files in the `C:\ProgramData\Microsoft\Microsoft Entra Connect Provisioning Agent\Trace` folder. You can use the `Export-AADCloudSyncToolsLogs` cmdlet to interrogate these logs. This cmdlet is located in the `AADCloudSyncTools` PowerShell module you learned about earlier in this chapter.

If you need to repair the cloud sync service account, use the `Repair-AADCloudsyncTools-Account` cmdlet. This cmdlet is also found in the `AADCloudSyncTools` PowerShell module.

The Provisioning Logs page, available from the Microsoft Entra Cloud Sync page of the Microsoft Entra ID portal, shows details of object synchronization between on-premises AD DS and Entra ID. If there are synchronization problems for specific objects, you can review these logs to determine more information.

More Info

Troubleshoot Entra Cloud SYNC

You can learn more about troubleshooting Microsoft Entra Cloud Sync at *https://learn.microsoft.com/entra/identity/hybrid/cloud-sync/how-to-troubleshoot*.

Self-Service Password Reset

Self-Service Password Reset (SSPR) allows users to safely reset or change their passwords using Azure while having the updated password sync back to on-premises Active Directory Domain Services (AD DS).

SSPR has the following requirements:

- Each account must have a Microsoft Entra ID Premium P1 or P2 or a Microsoft 365 Business Premium license. Ensure licenses are assigned before enabling SSPR.

- Identity synchronization is configured between on-premises AD and Entra ID.

- Password writeback must be enabled in this tool to allow cloud-initiated password changes to flow to AD DS).

- The AD DS account used by Entra ID Connect must have permissions in Active Directory to perform password resets. Verify that this account has the ability to reset passwords, change passwords, write to the lockoutTime and pwdLastSet attributes, and the "Unexpire Password" extended right on the domain object (applied to user objects).

- Ensure on-prem AD password policies don't block frequent resets by setting Minimum password age = 0 in Group Policy so that users can reset their password more than once in a day if needed.

To enable SSPR, in the Azure portal, access the Microsoft Entra admin center and configure the following:

1. Using an account with Global Administrator or Authentication Policy Administrator privileges, Navigate to Password reset in the Entra ID blade of the Azure portal; on the Properties page, choose which users will be enabled for SSPR.

2. Under Authentication methods, specify how many methods a user must verify to reset their password and which methods are allowed. For stronger security, requiring two methods is recommended.

3. Under Registration, you can enforce that users register their authentication info. Require users to register when signing in to Yes to prompt unregistered users to provide backup contact methods at their next sign-in. You can also set a periodic reconfirmation so users keep their info up to date.

4. On the On-premises integration tab. Check the Write Back Passwords To Your On-Premises Directory option. This allows Azure to write the new password back to AD DS through Entra ID Connect. If you're using Entra Connect Cloud Sync, also check Write Back Passwords with Microsoft Entra Connect Cloud Sync.

5. Additionally, set Allow Users To Unlock Accounts Without Resetting Their Password to Yes. This unlock option lets users clear an AD account lockout via SSPR without having to change their passwords.

To ensure that password resets in the cloud synchronize to your on-prem AD, you must enable the password writeback feature in Microsoft Entra ID Connect. To do this, run the Entra ID Connect Configuration Wizard, and on the Optional features page, select the check the box for Password Writeback and complete the wizard. Once Entra ID Connect is configured with writeback and the portal setting is enabled, any user-initiated password reset from Azure will trigger the sync service to immediately push the new password to the on-prem AD.

Microsoft Entra Password Protection

Microsoft Password Protection allows you to block commonly used passwords as well as your own custom password list from being used in your on-premises Active Directory environment. Deploying Entra Password Protection involves deploying the Entra Password Protection Proxy Service on computers in your environment that are located on your organization's perimeter network and the Entra Password Protection DC agent on each domain controller in your environment. The proxy service allows you to ensure that your domain controllers are not directly communicating with the Internet.

Microsoft recommends that you deploy Entra Password Protection in audit mode. This will allow you to determine how many users are currently using insecure passwords and will also allow you to notify users about when you'll be implementing the solution to block the use of commonly known passwords.

To deploy Entra Password Protection, you need the following:

- You need an account that has Windows Active Directory domain administrator privileges in the forest root domain of your Windows Active Directory environment. This will be used to register the forest with Entra ID.

- You need an account that has Global Administrator privileges for your organization's Azure tenant. This account will be used to register the Entra Password Protection Proxy service with Entra ID.

- You must enable the Key Distribution Service on all domain controllers.

- You must have network connectivity between at least one domain controller in each domain in the forest and a server that hosts the Entra Password Protection Proxy service.

- The computers that host the Entra Password Protection Proxy service must be able to access the following endpoints on the Internet:

    - *https://login.microsoftonline.com*

    - *https://enterpriseregistration.windows.net*

    - *https://autoupdate.msappproxy.net*

- Deploy the Entra Password Protection Proxy service prior to installing the agents on domain controllers. Register the proxy service against Entra ID using the *Register-Azure-ADPasswordProtectionProxy* cmdlet. Then register the on-premises Active Directory forest with the *Register-AzureADPasswordProtectionForest* PowerShell cmdlet.

- Deploy the Windows Server Active Directory Domain Controller agent on each domain controller in your organization. The agent must be deployed on each domain controller because you cannot predict which domain controller in your organization will be used to process a password change.

Once the agents are installed, you switch on-premises password protection on by performing the following steps:

1. In the Azure portal, open Entra ID; in the Manage section, click Security > Authentication Methods> Password Protection.

2. Select the Yes option under Enable Password Protection On Windows Server Active Directory. You'll be able to do this only after you've registered the proxy service with Entra ID.

3. You can then use this console to switch between Audit mode, which will report on problematic password, and Enforced mode, which will block users from setting a problematic password.

More Info

Entra Password Protection

You can learn more about Entra Password Protection at *https://learn.microsoft.com / entra/identity/authentication/howto-password-ban-bad-on-premises-deploy.*

Inside OUT

A lot more than identity synchronization

Entra ID does far more than what is mentioned here. It can function as the identity service for applications, supports conditional access to web applications, and can be easily integrated with third-party identity providers.

Understanding Entra identities

Microsoft Azure and Microsoft 365 use Microsoft Entra ID as their identity store. In hybrid environments, you'll manage identities primarily using on-premises management tools such as Active Directory Users and Computers. In environments where Microsoft Entra ID is the primary authority source, you can use the Microsoft Entra admin center to manage user identities. You can also use the Entra blade of the Azure portal to perform these tasks.

Manage Entra users

To create a new Microsoft Entra ID user, perform the following steps:

1. In the Entra blade of the Azure portal or Microsoft Entra admin center, select Users > All Users > New User.

2. On the New User blade, provide the following information:

    - **Display Name** The user's actual name.

    - **User Principal Name** The user's sign-in name in UPN format.

    - **Profile** The user's first name, last name, job title, and department.

    - **Properties** The user's source of authority. By default, if you're creating the user using the Entra blade of the Azure portal, Entra admin center or the Microsoft 365 admin center, this will be Entra ID.

    - **Groups** The groups the user should be a member of.

    - **Directory Role** Whether the account has User, Global Administrator, or a limited administrator role.

    - **Password** The automatically generated password. With the Show Password option, you can transmit the password to the user through a secure channel.

You can also use the Entra blade of the Azure portal to perform the following user administrator tasks:

- Update profile information

- Assign directory roles

- Manage group membership

- Manage licenses

- Manage devices

- Manage access to Azure resources

- Manage authentication methods

When you delete a user from Entra ID, the account remains in the Entra ID Recycle Bin for 30 days. The Entra ID Recycle Bin for users is present in the Users blade of the Entra section of the Azure portal. The Entra ID recycle bin allows you to recover deleted accounts should it be necessary to do so. If you delete a user from your on-premises Active Directory environment but have enabled the on-premises Active Directory Recycle Bin, recovering the user from the on-premises Active Directory Recycle Bin will recover the user account in Entra ID. If you don't have the Active Directory Recycle Bin enabled, you will need to create another account with a new GUID.

You can use the Audit Logs section of the Users blade to view activities related to user management, including user creation and updates. You can use the Sign-In Logs section of the Users blade to view user sign-in activity.

You configure default user role permissions in the User Settings section of the Users blade. Using these controls, you can configure whether users can perform the following actions:

- **Users Can Register Applications** Determines whether users can register applications with the Entra tenancy.

- **Restrict Non-Admin Users From Creating Tenants** Determines whether users without administrative privileges can create tenants.

- **Users Can Create Security Groups** Configure whether a user can create security groups and manage the membership of those groups.

Manage Entra groups

Groups enable you to collect users and assign them privileges and access to workloads or services. Rather than assign privileges and access to workloads or services directly to users, you can assign these rights to a group and then indirectly assign them to users by adding the user accounts to the appropriate group. Using groups in this way is a long-standing administrative practice because it allows you to determine a user's level of access and rights by looking at the user's group memberships rather than checking each workload and service to determine if the user account has been assigned rights to that service. You can use the Manage Groups section of the Microsoft Entra admin console or the All Groups section of the Entra blade of the Azure portal.

Entra supports two group types: security groups and Microsoft 365 groups. Microsoft 365 groups are used for collaboration between users where organizations use services such as Microsoft 365 or Office 365. Users in groups can be internal or external to the organization. Microsoft 365 group types can be configured as assigned or dynamic. When the dynamic option is selected, group membership is determined based on the results of a query against user or device attributes. For example, with Microsoft 365 groups, group membership can be determined by user attributes such as location or manager.

CHAPTER 9

More Info

Entra ID Groups

You can learn more about Entra ID Groups at *https://learn.microsoft.com/entra/fundamentals/groups-view-azure-portal*.

To create an Entra group, perform the following steps:

1. In the Azure portal, open the Entra menu blade.

2. Under Manage in the Entra menu blade, select Groups.

3. On the Groups page control bar, click New Group.

4. On the New Group page, provide the following information and select Create:

    - **Group Type**   Choose between Security and Microsoft 365.

    - **Group Name**   Provide a name for the group. It's often a good idea to come up with a system for naming groups rather than naming the group based on whatever comes to mind when filling out the form. Use this system for all groups in the subscription. One strategy is to name groups in a way that indicates how they collect accounts, such as Research Users for user accounts related to research. Group names need to be unique within an Azure Active Directory instance.

    - **Group Description**   Provide a meaningful description for the group. This description should be meaningful enough that if you won the lottery and retired to Tahiti, the person who replaced you could understand the group's purpose.

    - **Microsoft Entra Roles Can Be Assigned To The Group**   Allows you to specify if Entra roles can be assigned to the group.

    - **Membership Type**   If you choose a Security group, group members must be added manually. If you choose the Microsoft 365 group type, you'll have the following options:

        ▼ **Owners**   Users designated as group owners can modify the membership of the group.

        ▼ **Members**   Allows you to specify group membership, including users, groups, service principals, and managed identities.

More Info

Creating groups

You can learn more about creating groups at *https://learn.microsoft.com/entra/fundamentals/concept-learn-about-groups*.

Entra ID allows you to add a security group as a member of another security group known as a nested group. When you do this, the member group will inherit the attributes and properties of the parent group. Nesting groups allows you to further simplify the management of large amounts of users. For example, you might have groups for Melbourne, Sydney, and Adelaide managers. You could add these three groups to an Australian Managers group and then assign top-level group rights and permissions to Australian Managers rather than assigning those rights to each city-level Managers group. This also provides flexibility if you later add additional city-level managers groups, such as Brisbane and Perth, because you'd just add these groups to the Australian Managers group to assign the same permissions.

At the time this book was written, Entra ID does not support the following nesting scenarios:

- Adding an Entra ID group to a group synchronized from on-premises Active Directory
- Adding Entra ID security groups to Microsoft 365 groups
- Adding Microsoft 365 to groups other than other Microsoft 365 groups
- Assigning apps to nested groups
- Assigning licenses to nested groups
- Nesting distribution groups

To nest groups using the Azure portal, perform the following steps:

1. On the Groups | All Groups page of the Entra blade of the Azure portal, click the group you want to nest.
2. On the group's properties page, select Members > Add Members. Select the group you want to nest.
3. Click Select to nest the group. A group can be nested within multiple groups.

To remove a group from another group, open the parent group's group membership page and then remove the nested group by selecting that group and clicking Remove Memberships.

More Info

Nesting groups

You can learn more about nesting groups at *https://learn.microsoft.com/en-us/entra/fundamentals/how-to-manage-groups*.

Manage administrative units

Entra ID administrative units are containers for Entra users, groups, and devices that you can use to limit administrative permissions. For example, if you want to limit administrative rights to a specific set of users and groups, you could place those users and groups in an administrative unit and assign permissions using the administrative unit as the permission scope. All the user and group objects in that administrative unit will be subject to the permissions assigned at the administrative unit level.

The administrative unit structure will be dependent on the needs of each organization. Some organizations might create an administrative unit structure based on geographical boundaries; others might create an administrative unit structure based on their company divisions. Administrative units in Entra are analogous to Organizational Units in Active Directory Domain Services. Users with the Global Administrator or Privileged Role Administrators can do the following:

- Create administrative units

- Add users and groups to administrative units

- Delegate administrative roles to administrative units

To add an administrative unit through the Azure portal, perform the following steps:

1. In the Entra blade of the Azure portal, select Administrative Units under Manage.

2. In the Administrative Units blade, select Add. You will be asked to provide a name for the administrative unit in the Name box and have the option to provide a description for the administrative unit.

3. You can create the Administrative Unit by clicking Review + Create or choose Next: Assign Roles to assign roles to the administrative unit.

4. On the Assign Roles page, choose which roles to assign to the Administrative unit.

5. Click Add to complete the process of adding the administrative unit.

Once you have created the administrative unit, you can add users and groups and assign roles and administrators. To add a user using the Azure portal, open the Administrative Unit, select Users, and then click Add Member.

To add a group using the Azure portal, navigate to the administrative unit, select Groups, and click Add. You will need an Azure AD P1 or P2 license to add roles and administrators for the Administrative Unit. By default, the following administrative roles are assigned permissions to the Administrative Unit:

- Authentication Administrator

- Cloud Device Administrator

- Groups Administrator

- Helpdesk Administrator

- License Administrator

- Password Administrator

- Printer Administrator

- Privileged Authentication Administrator

- SharePoint Administrator

- Teams Administrator

- Teams Devices Administrator

- User Administrator

Perform the following steps to add a user or group to one of the existing roles scoped only with permissions to objects within the Administrative Unit:

1. Open the Administrative Unit in the Azure portal and select Roles And Administrators.

2. Select the role you want to assign over the objects within the administrative unit and then select Add Assignments.

3. On the Add Assignments pane, select the users or groups you want to assign to the role.

The best practice when using role-based access control technologies is to assign roles to specially created groups and then add users to that group. Removing a user's privileges is a matter of removing their account from specific groups. This process is simpler than removing privileges for a specific user on a resource-by-resource basis.

Restricted management administrative units allow you to limit the management of specific users, groups, and devices in your Entra tenancy to specific administrative users. For example, you may want to allow only some, and not all, of the users that have been assigned the Helpdesk Administrator role to be able to reset the password of your senior administrators' team or the CEO of the organization. To do this, you would add the senior administrators to a restricted management administrative unit and limit which security principals can reset their passwords.

More Info

Entra ID administrative units

You can learn more about Entra ID administrative units at *https://learn.microsoft.com/entra/identity/role-based-access-control/administrative-units*.

Azure Arc–enabled servers

Azure Arc–enabled servers extend Azure's management capabilities to hybrid Windows server instances. You can use Azure Arc to perform the following tasks:

- **Govern**   Assign Azure machine configurations to audit and enforce desired settings within the hybrid machines.

- **Protect**   Integration with Microsoft Defender for Cloud allows for threat detection, vulnerability management, and proactive security monitoring. Connecting Arc allows for utilizing Microsoft Sentinel to collect and correlate security-related events from diverse data sources. Microsoft Defender for Cloud will be covered in more detail in Chapter 14, "Security systems and services."

- **Configure**   Azure Automation can be used to perform frequent and time-consuming management tasks through PowerShell and Python runbooks. The Azure Monitor Agent facilitates the assessment of configuration changes for installed software, Microsoft services, Windows registry, and files. Post-deployment configuration and automation tasks are further enabled through supported Azure Arc–enabled servers VM extensions.

- **Update**   Operating system updates can be managed using Azure Update Manager. Applying software updates is covered in more detail by Chapter 23, "Monitoring and maintenance."

- **Monitor**   Operational performance of the operating system can be monitored, and application components can be discovered to visualize processes and dependencies with other resources using VM insights. The Azure Monitor Agent collects additional log data, such as performance metrics and events, from the operating system or workloads, storing this information in a designated Log Analytics workspace. Azure Monitor integration is covered in more detail by Chapter 23.

- **Inventory**   All Azure Arc resources, regardless of their native hosting environment, can be viewed and managed from a single, unified dashboard within the Azure portal or through programmatic interfaces such as Azure CLI, PowerShell, or the REST API.

For Windows Server 2025 and later versions, Azure Arc Setup is integrated as a Features On Demand component that you can install from Windows Server.

More Info

Azure Arc-enabled servers

You can learn more about Azure Arc for Servers at *https://learn.microsoft.com/azure/azure-arc/servers/overview.*

Onboarding

Prior to onboarding computers to Azure Arc, you'll need to ensure that connectivity between your Windows Server instances and Azure is possible. The Azure Connected Machine agent used by Azure Arc communicates outbound securely to Azure Arc over TCP port 443. The URLs that the agent needs to communicate with are

- *download.microsoft.com* for downloading the Windows installation package

- *login.microsoftonline.com*, **.login.microsoft.com*, and *pas.windows.net* for Microsoft Entra ID authentication

- *management.azure.com* for Azure Resource Manager operations, such as creating or deleting the Arc server resource

- **.his.arc.azure.com* for metadata and hybrid identity services

- **.guestconfiguration.azure.com* for extension management and guest configuration services

- *guestnotificationservice.azure.com* and *azgn*.servicebus.windows.net* for notification services related to extensions and connectivity

- **.blob.core.windows.net* as the download source for Azure Arc–enabled servers extensions

- **.<region>.arcdataservices.com* specifically for Azure Arc–enabled SQL Server, which exclusively supports TLS 1.2 or 1.3

- *www.microsoft.com/pkiops/certs* for intermediate certificate updates, particularly when using Extended Security Updates (ESUs)

- *dls.microsoft.com* for license validation when using features like Hotpatching or Windows Server Azure Benefits

The Azure Connected Machine agent can be configured to use a proxy server if required by the network environment.

Azure Arc Entra ID managed identity

Every Azure Arc–enabled server is automatically associated with a system-assigned Microsoft Entra ID managed identity. This identity is fundamental for the Azure Connected Machine agent to authenticate securely with Azure services. The system-assigned managed identity provides a mechanism for authentication to Azure services without the need for manual credential management on the hybrid server. This managed identity can also be leveraged by extensions or other authorized applications running on the hybrid server to access Azure resources that support OAuth tokens.

CHAPTER 9

The managed identity appears in the Microsoft Entra ID portal as an enterprise application, bearing the same name as the Azure Arc–enabled server resource. The agent fully manages the lifecycle of this identity, including automatic credential rotation, with the underlying certificate valid for 90 days and renewed when 45 or fewer days of validity remain. If the agent remains offline for an extended period and the certificate expires, a reonboarding process will be necessary.

The managed identity certificate is stored locally on the Windows Server instance in the `C:\ProgramData\AzureConnectedMachineAgent\Certs\` folder. The agent automatically applies an Access Control List (ACL) to this directory, restricting access to local administrators and the himds account.

Azure Role-Based Access Control (RBAC) is utilized to control which accounts can view and manage Azure Arc–enabled servers. Two built-in roles are specifically designed for this purpose:

- **Azure Connected Machine Onboarding**   This role is intended for accounts used to connect new machines to Azure Arc. It grants permissions to view and create new Arc servers but explicitly disallows extension management. This role is recommended for assignment to the Microsoft Entra service principal used for at-scale machine onboarding.

- **Azure Connected Machine Resource Administrator**   This role is for accounts that will manage servers once they're connected. It permits reading, creating, and deleting Arc servers, VM extensions, licenses, and private link scopes.

Generic Azure built-in roles such as Reader, Contributor, and Owner also apply to Azure Arc–enabled servers. Security principals assigned the Contributor role or an administrator role to a resource can make changes, including deploying or deleting extensions on the machine. Since extensions can execute arbitrary scripts in a privileged context, any Contributor on the Azure resource should be considered an indirect administrator of the server.

Connecting to Azure Arc

There are several methods that you can use to connect a Windows Server computer to Azure Arc. The following permissions are required:

- **Azure**   Azure Connected Machine Onboarding or Contributor role

- **Windows Server**   Local Administrator permissions

The following Azure resource providers must be registered in the subscription that the Arc-enabled servers connect to

- Microsoft.HybridCompute

- Microsoft.GuestConfiguration

- Microsoft.HybridConnectivity

- Microsoft.AzureArcData

Azure Arc–enabled SQL

When a Windows server with Microsoft SQL Server installed is connected to Azure Arc, the SQL Server instances will automatically be connected to Azure Arc as well. This automatic connection provides detailed inventory and additional management capabilities for SQL Server. Organizations that want to opt out of this automatic SQL Server connection can do so by adding a tag to the Windows server with the name ArcSQLServerExtensionDeployment and the value Disabled during the initial connection to Azure Arc.

If Azure Arc–enabled SQL Server instances are planned, the Microsoft.AzureArcData resource provider must be registered in the subscription that the Arc-enabled server connects to.

Onboarding from Windows Server

Windows Server 2022 and later include a built-in Azure Arc Setup wizard. This wizard simplifies the onboarding process by automating prerequisite checks, agent download, and installation. To use this wizard, perform the following steps:

1. The wizard can be launched from the system tray icon, which is enabled by default or from the Windows Server Start menu.

2. The wizard automatically performs prerequisite checks and installs the Azure Connected Machine agent. Once this process is complete, select Configure.

3. You're asked to sign in to Azure: Select the applicable Azure cloud and then click Sign In to Azure. Provide your Azure sign-in credentials.

4. Once you're signed in, the wizard determines which subscriptions you have access to. Enter the resource details, including selecting the Azure Subscription and Resource group that will host the server object.

5. Once the configuration is finished and the machine is onboarded to Azure Arc, click Finish.

You can confirm the machine's enrollment status by checking the Azure Arc Management field in Server Manager (under Local Server), which should display Enabled. You can also view the server in the Azure Arc blade of the Azure portal.

Onboarding Azure Arc using PowerShell

Rather than manually onboarding from Windows Server, you can create a PowerShell script from the Azure portal, which then automates the agent download, installation, and configuration on a target server in your environment. To do this, perform the following steps:

1. Sign in to the Azure portal and navigate to Azure Arc. In the Azure Arc blade, select Machines - Azure Arc. Then select Add/Create and choose Add A Machine from the dropdown.

2. On the Add Servers With Azure Arc page, locate the Add A Single Server tile and select Generate Script.

3. On the Basics page, specify the following:

    - **Project details**   Select the Azure Subscription and Resource group where the machine's metadata will be managed.

    - **Server details**   Choose the Azure Region to store the server's metadata and select Windows from the Operating System dropdown.

    - **Connectivity method**   Determine how the Azure Connected Machine agent will connect to the Internet. Options include Public Endpoint, Private Endpoint (requiring selection or creation of a private link scope), or Proxy Server (requiring the proxy server's IP address or name and port number in the format *http://<proxyURL>:<proxyport>*).

4. (Optional) Proceed to the Tags page to review suggested default physical location tags or specify custom tags.

5. Click Next to navigate to the Download And Run Script page. Review the summary information and then select Download to save the `OnboardingScript.ps1` file.

6. Once the script is downloaded, run the script on the target Windows Server using local administrator privileges.

7. After the agent installation and configuration are complete, verify the server's successful connection by navigating to Azure Arc > Servers in the Azure portal.

Service principal-based deployment

Service principal-based deployment allows you to automate the onboarding of multiple machines, leveraging an Azure service principal for authentication. To do this you must perform the following steps:

1. In the Azure Arc blade of the Azure portal, select Service Principals under the Management section. Select Add to create a new service principal. Provide a name and choose the scope of access (an entire subscription or a specific resource group). Make a note of the service principal ID (application ID) and the service principal secret (password) because you'll need these values for the script.

2. Grant the newly created service principal the Azure Connected Machine Onboarding role. Limit the scope of this role to a resource group or subscription if appropriate.

3. In the Machines section of the Azure Arc blade, select Add/Create and then Add A Machine.

4. On the Add Servers With Azure Arc page, select the Add Multiple Servers tile and then Generate Script.

5. Configure the project details, server details, and connectivity method as before. In the Authentication section, select the service principal created in the previous step for authentication.

6. Download the generated script and execute the script on target machines with local administrator privileges.

Virtual machine extensions

Virtual machine (VM) extensions are applications and services that allow you to perform post-deployment configuration and automation tasks on Azure Arc–enabled servers. They function in the same manner through Azure Arc as they do with native Azure VMs.

VM extensions can be deployed using various Azure management tools: the Azure portal, Azure PowerShell, Azure CLI, or Azure Resource Manager (ARM) templates. Some extensions, such as the Azure Key Vault VM extension, do not support deployment directly from the Azure portal, necessitating the use of PowerShell, Azure CLI, or ARM templates.

To deploy an extension, use the following general guidance:

1. Navigate to Machines - Azure Arc in the Azure portal and select the target machine.

2. Under the Settings blade, select Extensions.

3. Click + Add, choose the desired extension (for example, Azure Monitor Agent for Windows), and select Next.

4. Provide any required configuration information specific to the extension (for example, proxy settings for the Azure Monitor Agent).

5. Review the deployment summary and select Create.

To perform this step in Azure PowerShell, use the `New-AzConnectedMachineExtension` cmdlet. For example, to deploy the Azure Monitor extension to a computer named WinServ2025A in the resource group ArcMachines in the WestUS region, run this command:

```
New-AzConnectedMachineExtension -Name "AzureMonitorWindowsAgent" -ResourceGroupName
"ArcMachines" -MachineName "WinServ2025A" -Location "WestUS" -Publisher "Microsoft.
Azure.Monitor" -ExtensionType "AzureMonitorWindowsAgent" -EnableAutomaticUpgrade
```

You can accomplish the same task using Azure CLI by running the following command:

```
az connectedmachine extension create --name AzureMonitorWindowsAgent --publisher
Microsoft.Azure.Monitor --type AzureMonitorWindowsAgent --machine-name WinServ2025A
--resource-group ArcMachines --location WestUS --enable-auto-upgrade true
```

To view currently installed VM extensions on an Azure Arc–enabled server, navigate to Machines - Azure Arc, select the machine, and then go to Settings > Extensions. You can also do this with the `Get-AzConnectedMachine` extension cmdlet:

```
Get-AzConnectedMachineExtension -MachineName "WinServ2025A" -ResourceGroupName
"ArcMachines"
```

Many VM extensions can be configured for automatic upgrades. To enable automatic upgrades on VM extensions, on the Extensions tab of the Arc-enabled server, select the specific extension and then choose Enable Automatic Upgrade. You can do this with the `Update-AzConnected-MachineExtension` PowerShell cmdlet by including the `EnableAutomaticUpgrade` parameter when updating an extension. You can do this from Azure CLI by using the `--enable-auto-upgrade true` option when using `az connectedmachine` extension update.

Azure Policy

Machine Configuration is the component of Azure Policy that audits and enforces settings such as application presence, environment variables, and specific operating system configurations. This includes ensuring secure communication protocols are used, adherence to the Azure compute security baseline, or enabling Windows Defender Exploit Guard. Machine Configuration policies operate with elevated privileges (Local System on Windows). The Microsoft.GuestConfiguration resource provider must be registered in the Azure subscription where machines are onboarded; this often occurs automatically when a machine configuration policy is assigned or through Microsoft Defender for Cloud.

Azure Policy can be utilized to deploy the Azure Monitor Agent (AMA) VM extension at scale across an environment and to maintain its configuration compliance. This is particularly valuable because it can reinstall the extension if it's removed and automatically install it when a new Azure Arc–enabled server registers with Azure.

The policy named Configure *operating system* Arc-Enabled Machines To Run Azure Monitor Agent specifically installs the AMA extension and configures it to report to a designated Log Analytics workspace. This policy *does not* create Data Collection Rules (DCRs); DCRs must be created separately and associated with the agent to define what data is collected. There's more about DCRs in Chapter 23. The standard compliance evaluation cycle for Azure Policy is typically every 24 hours.

To assign an Azure Policy definition to Azure Arc–enabled servers, use the following steps:

1. In the Azure portal, search for Policy, and select the Policy service.

2. In the service menu, under Authoring, select Assignments.

3. Select Assign Policy from the top of the Assignments pane.

4. On the Assign Policy page, select the scope by choosing a management group, subscription, or resource group. This scope determines which resources the policy assignment will be enforced on. If you've put all your Azure Arc servers in a resource group, this should be your scope.

5. Select the Policy Definition ellipsis to open the list of available definitions. For example, search for and select the desired definition, such as Configure Windows Arc-Enabled Machines To Run Azure Monitor Agent.

6. The Assignment Name will be automatically populated. You need to enter the resource ID of the log analytics workspace to which Azure Monitor Agent will report.

7. On the Remediation tab, choose Create A Managed Identity and ensure the option Monitoring Metrics Publisher & Log Analytics Contributor on the workspace are configured.

8. Review the settings and create the assignment.

After a policy assignment, its compliance status can be monitored. In the Azure Policy service menu, select Compliance. Locate the policy assignment, and any existing resources that do not comply with the new assignment will be marked as Non-Compliant.

To remove a policy assignment, do the following:

1. In the Azure Policy service menu, select Compliance or Assignments under Authoring.

2. Locate the specific policy assignment.

3. Right-click the policy assignment and select Delete Assignment.

Azure Automation and Hybrid Runbook Workers

You can use Azure Automation with Hybrid Runbook Workers (HRWs) to extend Azure's orchestration capabilities to Azure Arc–enabled servers. Using this method, you can allow PowerShell and Python runbooks to execute locally on Arc-enabled hybrid computers. HRWs function as local agents that execute runbooks, providing direct access to resources on the host server.

The recommended and currently supported type of HRW is extension-based because agent-based HRWs were retired in August 2024. To deploy an extension-based HRW, perform the following steps:

1. In the Azure portal, navigate to your Automation account.

2. Obtain the AutomationHybridServiceURL from your Automation Account properties.

3. Under Process Automation, select Hybrid Worker Groups.

4. Select + Create Hybrid Worker Group and provide a name for the group.

5. Choose whether to use Default (local system account) or Custom (select a credential asset) for Hybrid Worker Credentials.

6. Select Add Machines and choose your Azure Arc–enabled server(s) from the list. The HRW extension will be installed on the selected machines as part of this process.

390 Chapter 9 Azure Arc and hybrid services

7. Confirm the successful installation of the HybridWorkerExtension by checking its status under the Extensions tab of your Azure Arc–enabled server in the Azure portal.

Azure Arc–enabled servers possess a built-in System Managed Identity. This identity can be granted permissions to access to resources in Azure by adding appropriate role assignments in the Access control (IAM) blade for the target resource. If the Automation Account itself has a Managed Identity enabled, only the Automation Account's System-Assigned Managed Identity can be used for Azure resource access from runbooks. The Arc-enabled server's managed identity will not be used by the runbook.

For Windows Hybrid Workers, a custom credential asset with local resource access can be defined. The Hybrid Worker Group can then be configured to use this custom credential. Specific folder permissions (`C:\ProgramData\AzureConnectedMachineAgent\Tokens` for Arc-enabled servers) must be set for the custom user account.

To initiate a runbook from the Azure portal, select the Run On: Hybrid Worker option and then choose the specific Hybrid Runbook Worker group from the dropdown.

Azure network adapter

Azure network adapter allows you to create a point-to-site VPN connection to an Azure virtual network directly from Windows Admin Center on a computer running Windows Server 2019 and later. Because it's a point-to-site VPN, the computer that you're configuring with Azure Network Adapter only needs a connection to the Internet; it doesn't need to have a public IP address.

While it's possible to create point-to-site VPN connections from the Azure console, as is the case with creating an Azure VM from Windows Admin Center, this allows you to perform all the necessary tasks from the primary tool that you use to manage Windows Server. Windows Admin Center will also assist in the creation of Azure VPN gateways if one isn't already present on the virtual network to which you're creating a connection.

Once you've configured Azure Network Adapter, you'll be able to connect to and manage IaaS VMs running Windows Server operating systems connected to the virtual network the adapter connects to. You can configure multiple Azure virtual network adapters, each of which connects to a different virtual network.

More Info

Azure Network Adapter

You can learn more about Azure Network Adapter at *https://learn.microsoft.com/azure/virtual-network/accelerated-networking-mana-overview.*

Azure File Sync

Azure File Sync is one of the most useful hybrid technologies available for Windows Server. Anyone who has managed a file server knows the challenges they pose: having to remove disused files on a regular basis to ensure that there is enough space for new files, ensuring that files are regularly backed up, and even being able to restore a file that you might have removed at some point to save space because someone actually needs it now. Azure File Sync helps you address all these problems, reducing the amount of time you need to spend maintaining file servers so you can get on with the million other things on your to-do list.

Create Azure File Sync Service

The backbone of Azure File Sync is the Storage Sync Service. The storage sync service is the service that runs in Azure that manages Azure. You should deploy as few storage sync services as necessary since a Windows Server file server can only be registered with one sync service and file servers that are connected to different storage sync services are unable to synchronize with each other.

You should plan to deploy the storage sync service and the Azure File Share endpoints used by each sync group in the same Azure region and resource group. To deploy a storage sync service, perform the following steps:

1. In the Azure portal select Create a resource and then search for Azure File Sync. In the list of results select Azure File Sync and then select Create.

2. On the Deploy Storage Sync page, provide the following:

    - **Name** A name for the storage sync service. This name only needs to be unique on a per-region basis, but it's a good idea to have it unique for your organization.

    - **Subscription** The name of the subscription that will host the storage sync service. This will be the subscription where costs accrue for the service.

    - **Resource Group** The resource group that will host the storage sync service. You should also plan to host the storage account used with the sync service in the same resource group.

    - **Location** The location where you will deploy Azure File Sync. This location should be geographically proximate to where your server endpoints are. Remember that clients will be accessing files through the file server endpoints close to them. Bandwidth and latency between the server endpoint and the file share is generally an issue only when there is a substantive delay between a file that is tiered being requested and it's synchronizing back to the endpoint.

Create sync groups

A sync group allows you to replicate a specific folder and file structure across server and Azure File Share endpoints. Each sync group has a single Azure file share endpoint but can have multiple server endpoints. An Azure file storage sync service can host multiple sync groups, and a Windows Server endpoint can participate in multiple sync groups as long as those sync groups belong to the same storage sync service. To create a sync group, you need to specify a sync group name, which is separate from the sync service name; the name of the storage account that will be used; and the name of the Azure File Share that will be used. You should create the storage account and Azure File Share before creating the sync group.

Create cloud endpoints

The back end of Azure File Sync is an *Azure File Share*, also termed a *cloud endpoint*. This is a cloud file share that will store any file that is written to an Azure File Sync endpoint. The back-end Azure File Share stores the entire contents of what appears to be on the file share that is the front end for Azure File Sync. Creating a file share involves creating a storage account and then creating the file share within the storage account.

To create an Azure File Share, consider the following:

- **Performance requirements**   In most cases, the only computers interacting with the file share in an Azure File Sync deployment are the server endpoints. This means that you're unlikely to require the higher I/O performance capabilities of a premium file share that's hosted on solid-state disk (SSD)-based hardware.

- **Redundancy requirements**   Standard file shares can use locally redundant, zone-redundant, or geo-redundant storage. Large file shares of the type you're likely to use with Azure File Sync are only available with locally redundant and zone-redundant storage.

- **File share size**   Local and zone redundant storage accounts allow for file shares that span up to 100 TiB. The file share size will need to be able to hold all the tiered data from your file share endpoints and should be substantially larger than the storage on any on-premises server. The amount of storage you allocate to a file share will depend on the amount of data you need to tier and how much storing that data costs. Storage and transfer costs are billed separately, and even if you create a file share that's larger than you need, your organization will only be billed by the storage capacity actually used.

You can configure Azure Backup to back up this file share endpoint. The advantage of this is that in the event of data corruption or deletion, you can just recover data to the Azure File Share in the cloud from the Azure console, and it will replicate down to all the Azure File Sync endpoints.

Register servers

The Azure File Sync agent allows you to register a server with a storage sync service. To register a server, download and install the Azure File Sync agent from the Microsoft Download Center. As part of the installation process, you can configure the agent to be automatically updated through Microsoft Update. When the installation completes, you perform registration with a storage sync service. To register a server, you need local Administrator privileges on the server you want to register, and you need an Azure account that is a member of the Owner or Contributor management role for the Storage Sync Service in Azure. You can delegate these roles to an Entra account under Access Control (IAM) on the Storage Sync Service properties page in the Azure console. During the registration process, you must specify the Azure subscription, resource group, and storage sync service that will be used with the server endpoint.

Registration will use Azure credentials to create a trust relationship between the storage sync service and the Windows Server computer. The Windows Server instance will then create an identity separate from the user account used to create the registration that will function as long as the server remains registered and the current share Access Signature token associated with the storage account remains valid.

Create server endpoints

An Azure File Sync endpoint consists of a server and a path that are enrolled in an Azure File Sync service. A Windows Server can host multiple endpoints, each of which has a different path as long as those endpoints are in different sync groups associated with the same sync service. An Azure File Sync endpoint functions as the folder structure that underlies a normal file share. Administrators create a traditional shared folder and point it at the path that the Azure File Sync endpoint replicates to. You can also point a Distributed File System (DFS) namespace at this path, replacing Distributed File System Replication (DFSR) with Azure File Sync replication while still keeping the navigational advantages of the DFS way of identifying shared folders.

Create a server endpoint by adding the server that you registered with the Storage Sync Service and specifying the local path to the files that you want to replicate using Azure File Sync. When creating the server endpoint, you also specify the cloud tiering settings in terms of how much free space should always be available on the local volume that hosts the files and how many days after a file was last accessed should pass before the file is tiered. After the endpoint is created, any files in the path specified will be replicated up to the Azure File Share that functions as the cloud endpoint. If you create an endpoint that points to the system volume of the registered server, you can't enable cloud tiering on that endpoint.

File shares that serve as front ends for Azure File Sync endpoints should have the same share permissions. If you're using Azure File Sync with a failover cluster, ensure that the agent is installed on each node in the cluster and that each node in the cluster is registered to the same storage sync service.

CHAPTER 9

> ## Need More Review?
> ### Deploy Azure File Sync
>
> You can learn more about deploying Azure File Sync at *https://learn.microsoft.com/en-us/azure/storage/file-sync/file-sync-deployment-guide*.

Configure cloud tiering

Azure File Sync uses a process called *cloud tiering* to ensure that there is capacity on the volume that hosts the share. Cloud tiering means that you don't need to worry about constantly freeing up space for new files. You can configure Azure File Sync on a per-file share basis to tier files based on when the file was last accessed, how much free space there is on the volume that hosts the share, or both. For example, you might configure Azure File Sync so that any file that hasn't been accessed in 14 days on a particular share is automatically tiered to Azure. You could also specify that the least recently accessed files be automatically tiered to Azure in the event that the volume has only 30 percent free space remaining. If you have both a policy to tier files that exceed a certain age and a requirement that a certain amount of space still be available on the volume, Azure File Sync will ensure that requirement for free space is met by tiering least recently accessed files until the free space requirement is met.

From the users' perspective, a tiered file still appears as though it's on the file server that they're accessing. If users try to open the file, it syncs down from the back-end Azure File Share to the Azure File Sync file share endpoint and then opens normally. Cloud tiering can be configured on a per-server endpoint basis in the Azure console.

Monitor File Sync

You can monitor Azure File Sync using Azure Monitor, the Storage Sync Service, and Windows Server. Azure Monitor provides the following data:

- Bytes synced
- Cloud tiering cache hit rate
- Cloud tiering recall size
- Cloud tiering recall size by application
- Cloud tiering recall success rate
- Cloud tiering recall throughput
- Files not syncing

- Files synced

- Server cache size

- Server online status

- Sync session results

The Storage Sync Service in the Azure portal provides you with the following data:

- Registered server health

- Server endpoint health

  - Files not syncing

  - Sync activity

  - Cloud tiering efficiency

  - Files not tiering

  - Recall errors

- Metrics

You can also view the Telemetry event log in Event Viewer on a server endpoint under Applications and Services\Microsoft\FileSync\Agent to view sync health information. Azure File Sync performance counters are available in Performance Monitor that allow you to view bandwidth utilization and performance of the Azure File Sync agent.

Need More Review?

Monitor Azure File Sync

You can learn more about monitoring Azure File Sync at *https://learn.microsoft.com/azure/storage/file-sync/file-sync-monitoring*.

Migrate DFS to Azure File Sync

When you migrate DFS to Azure File Sync, you replace the older DFS file replication technology with Azure File Sync. The technology that is relevant to Azure File Sync is the namespace technology.

CHAPTER 9

When you use DFS Namespaces, you can configure a single UNC path to map to multiple SMB shares. For example \\adatum\shares\hovercraft can map to \\Adelaide-fs01\ hovercraft as well as \\Melbourne-fs01\hovercraft. When a client attempts to access the DFS UNC path, they are directed by DFS to the closest SMB endpoint. When used with DFS replication, it means that a user attempting to access a share would be connected to the closest DFS endpoint. When you use DFS Namespaces with Azure File Sync, a client that navigates to the DFS address will be directed to the closest Azure File Sync endpoint.

To migrate from DFS replication to Azure File Sync Replication, perform the following steps:

1. Create a new sync group that will be used as the substitute for the DFS replication topology you are replacing.

2. Start on the server that has the full set of data in your DFS replication topology to migrate. Install Azure File Sync on that server.

3. Register that server and create a server endpoint for the first server to be migrated. Do not enable cloud tiering.

4. Let all the data on that server sync to your Azure File Share cloud endpoint.

5. Install and register the Azure File Sync agent on each of the remaining servers that host DFS replicas.

6. Disable DFS replication on each server.

7. Create an Azure File Sync server endpoint on each of the previous servers that participated in DFS replication. Do not enable cloud tiering.

8. Ensure that the sync process completes and test your topology.

9. Retire DFS-R.

10. Enable cloud tiering on any server endpoint as desired.

Need More Review?

Using DFS namespaces with Azure files

You can learn more about using DFS namespaces with Azure files at *https://docs.micro-soft.com/en-us/azure/storage/files/files-manage-namespaces*.

Windows Server in Azure

In this chapter, you'll learn about deploying and managing Azure Infrastructure as a Service (IaaS) VMs running Windows Server. You'll then learn about Entra Domain Services and how you can domain join Azure IaaS VMs running Windows Server to this cloud-based identity service.

Windows Server IaaS VMs

IaaS allows you to host your IT infrastructure in the cloud. Rather than deploy the virtual machine in an on-premises hypervisor, which you must pay for and maintain yourself, IaaS allows you to run your virtual machines in a cloud provider's infrastructure, which the cloud provider is responsible for maintaining.

There are several benefits to running Windows Server in an Azure virtual machine over running a Windows Server VM on-premises, including

- **Efficient costing** You will be charged on a per-minute and, in some cases, per-second basis for the hosted virtual machine. You aren't charged for deallocated virtual machines. In certain circumstances, it might be cheaper to run the virtual machine in the cloud than to pay for the infrastructure to host the virtual machine in your own datacenter.

- **Efficient use of licensing** When you deploy Windows Server on IaaS, the operating system license is included in your charges. If you have an existing software assurance license, you can use Bring Your Own License (BYOL) functionality.

- **Up-to-date deployment images** When deployed, the operating system will be fully patched with the latest software updates. This means that the operating system will be secure at deployment. When you maintain your own images, you need to either make sure that they are up to date or spend time after deployment ensuring that they are up to date. Gallery images also include the Azure virtual machine agent. The Azure virtual machine agent enables the VM extensions. The VM extensions enable post-VM deployment configuration and VM recovery features, and they can reset the default VM admin account password.

- **Azure features**   IaaS VMs running in Azure can use hotpatching, which reduces the number of times each year that you have to reboot to apply software updates, without the additional costs involved in using the technology through Azure Arc, where it is configured as an add-on. It is also simpler to configure integration with other Azure services. The Azure Edition of Windows Server is a special version of Datacenter Edition that includes features that aren't always available to Windows Server outside of an Azure or Azure Local deployment.

Creating Azure IaaS VMs

To create an Azure IaaS VM using the Azure portal, perform the following steps:

1. On the Azure portal home page, click Create A Resource, click Compute, and then click Create next to Virtual Machine.

2. On the Create A Virtual Machine page, configure the following:

   - **Subscription**   Specify which subscription the VM will belong to

   - **Resource Group**   Specify the resource group in which you want to place the VM. You can create a new resource group or use an existing resource group. Resource groups should host resources that share a common lifecycle, such as VMs that function as tiers of a multitier application.

   - **Virtual Machine Name**   This is a name that identifies the virtual machine.

   - **Region**   This is where you choose the Azure region that will host the virtual machine. Choose a region that is proximate to where you want the application to run.

   - **Availability Options**   This is where you choose whether you want to use replicated VMs in Availability Zones or Availability Sets. To get the strongest Azure SLA, you will need to choose an availability option. The cheapest option is to choose No Infrastructure Redundancy Required.

   - **Image**   This is where you choose the image you want to deploy. You have the option of choosing a version of the Azure Edition that includes Hotpatch functionality.

   - **Run With Azure Spot Discount**   Choose this option for a discounted rate, though your VM may be shut down if Azure needs to recall capacity for traditional pay-as-you-go workloads.

   - **Size**   This is where you specify the virtual CPU, memory, data disks, maximum IOPS, and whether the VM supports premium disks. The Size will give an estimate of the cost of running the VM. Some, but not all, VM SKUs support hibernation.

- **Administrator Account Username** Cannot be set to *Administrator*, *Admin*, or *Root*. Make this name something consistent that you will remember, such as *Prime* or *Chancellor*.

- **Password** Create a complex password that is a minimum of 12 and a maximum of 123 characters in length.

- **Public Inbound Ports** Choose whether you want to have the VM accessible on specific ports to hosts on the Internet. There is no need to open these ports unless the workload is serving content to hosts on the Internet, such as having it host a public web server. You can also configure which ports are open after deployment.

- **Specify Whether You Have A Windows Server License** If your organization has Software Assurance, you can reduce your licensing costs by specifying that you have an existing Windows Server license.

From this point, you can click Review And Create to create the VM, or you can keep navigating through the deployment wizard.

Inside OUT

Inbound port configuration

By default, when you enable public inbound ports at deployment, Azure will open the chosen ports to all hosts on the Internet. If you want to limit the port to a specific IP address range, you'll need to configure additional options such as a network security group or Azure Firewall. You can also configure Windows firewall within the VM after the VM has been deployed. Unless you have a pressing reason, it's usually best not to enable public ports at deployment, and to come back and configure them in a more granular way once the VM is operational.

If you choose to keep navigating through the deployment wizard, you'll be asked to configure the following:

- **Disks** Allows you to configure the properties of the operating system disk, the temp disks, and any data disks. You can also choose whether disk encryption will use a platform-managed key, or you provide your own key for disk encryption or a mix of both.

- **Networking** On the networking page, you can choose to connect the VM's network adapter to an existing virtual network or create a new one. You can also choose to configure a basic or advanced network security group for the network adapter and configure which public inbound ports are open. You can also choose whether to delete the assigned public IP and NIC when the VM is deleted and whether accelerated networking is enabled. The networking page also allows you to configure whether inbound traffic will use load balancing through the Azure load balancer or application gateway.

- **Management** On the management page of the Create A Virtual Machine Wizard, you can configure whether the VM will be connected to Microsoft Defender for Cloud. You can also enable a system-assigned managed identity, which functions in Entra in the same manner as a Computer account does in Active Directory. You can choose whether or not to allow Entra ID login, auto shutdown, backup, site recovery, guest OS updates, hotpatch, and patch orchestration. These options are discussed in more detail later in this chapter.

You should only allocate a VM a public IP address if the VM needs to serve content to hosts directly on the public Internet. Technologies such as Azure Bastion or VPNs, covered later in this chapter, allow you to make administrative connections to VMs that only have private IP addresses.

On the Management page, you can choose whether you want to have the VM monitored by Azure Security Center, whether you want to enable boot diagnostics, operating system guest diagnostics, and specify a storage account to store diagnostic data. Boot diagnostics allow you to make an EMS connection and view screenshots of the VM running on the Azure host. Guest OS diagnostics allow you to get up-to-date performance counter information from the VM displayed in the Azure portal.

You can also configure a system-assigned managed identity, which is similar to an Active Directory Computer account and allows the VM to access cloud resources without having to store credentials. You can configure whether you want to be able to sign in to the VM using Entra ID credentials and whether the VM automatically shuts down at a specific time each day if it has been left running. You can also enable a backup for the VM during creation. You'll learn about configuring Azure Backup for a VM later in the chapter.

On the Advanced page of the Create A Virtual Machine Deployment Wizard, you can specify whether you want to run the VM on a private Azure host, whether you want the VM to be in proximity with other resources deployed in the same region, and whether you want the VM to be a Generation 1 or a Generation 2 VM. The choice of generations provides similar benefits to choosing between Generation 1 or Generation 2 VMs when deploying in Hyper-V.

Run the following set of commands to deploy a Windows Server 2025 VM named WSIO-C using Cloud Shell to the resource group WSIO-RG, where the username is set to Prime and the administrator password is set to &&Tailwind&&Tailwind. Connect the VM to the subnet Alpha on virtual network VNet1:

```
adminPassword='&&Tailwind&&Tailwind'
az vm create --resource-group WSIO-RG --name WSIO-C --image 2025-datacenter-azure-
edition --vnet-name VNet1 --subnet Alpha --admin-username prime --admin-password
$adminPassword
```

Later in the chapter, you'll learn how to create an Azure IaaS VM running Windows Server using Windows Admin Center.

> ## More Info
>
> ### Windows VMs in Azure
>
> You can learn more about Windows VMs in Azure at *https://learn.microsoft.com/azure/virtual-machines/*.

Login with Entra ID

You can configure a Windows Server IaaS VM running in Azure to allow login with an Entra ID account. This account is separate from a local computer account and doesn't require that you domain join the Windows Server IaaS VM to Entra Domain Services. You'll learn about Entra Domain Services later in the chapter.

Users must be assigned either the Virtual Machine Administrator Login or Virtual Machine User Login Azure roles for the VM. If using Conditional Access with MFA, exclude the Azure Windows VM Sign-in application in Entra Conditional Access to avoid login blocks.

Follow these steps to enable Entra Login with Entra ID:

1. Navigate to the VM in the Azure portal.

2. Under Management, find and select the Login With Entra ID (Azure AD) option.

IaaS VM networking

IaaS VMs connect to virtual networks. An IaaS virtual network is a collection of subnets that share a common private IP address space in the RFC 1918 range. For example, you might create a virtual network that uses the 192.168.0.0/16 address space and create subnets, such as 192.168.10.0/24. Azure IaaS virtual machines connect to the subnets in an Azure virtual network.

IaaS virtual networks

Azure IaaS VMs can only use virtual networks that are in the same location as the IaaS virtual machine. For example, if you are deploying an IaaS VM to Australia South East, you'll only be able to connect the IaaS VM directly to a virtual network in Australia South East.

To create a new network, perform the following steps:

1. In the Azure console, click Create A Resource, and in the Search bar, type **Network**. In the results, click Virtual Network and then click Create.

2. On the Create Virtual Network blade, provide the following information:

    - **Name**   This is the name of the virtual network, and it needs to be unique to the subscription

    - **Address space**   This is the IPv4 address space that will be used by hosts on the virtual network. You have the option to add an IPv6 address space.

    - **Subscription**   Choose which Azure subscription the virtual network will be associated with.

    - **Resource Group**   Choose an existing resource group within the subscription or create a new resource group.

    - **Subnet Name**   This is the first subnet within the address space. Because you might want to add a gateway subnet for a VPN at some point in the future, it is a good idea to avoid creating a subnet that starts right at the beginning of the address space. For example, if your address space is 192.168.0.0/16, create the first subnet as 192.168.1.0/24 or 192.168.10.0/24 rather than 192.168.0.0/24. This ensures that you always have extra space for special subnet types, such as gateway subnets or Azure bastion subnets.

    - **Subnet Address Range**   This is the address range of the first subnet within the address space. This range can consume the entire address space.

    - **DDoS Protection**   Select between the basic Distributed Denial Of Service Protection or enable the Standard Distributed Denial Of Service Protection. The basic Distributed Denial Of Service Protection level incurs no extra fee, while the Standard Distributed Denial Of Service Protection level incurs extra fees.

    - **Service Endpoints**   This setting allows you to configure access to Azure IaaS service endpoints, such as Azure Key Vault, from the virtual network. You'll learn about using Azure Key Vault to enable BitLocker later in this chapter.

Once you have deployed the virtual network, you can configure the following properties for the virtual network using the Azure console:

- **Address Space**   This property allows you to add additional address spaces to the Azure virtual network. You partition these address spaces using subnets.

- **Connected Devices**   This property lists the current devices that are connected to the Azure virtual network. This property includes a list of VM network adapters and the internal IP address to which those adapters are assigned.

- **Subnets**   This property shows subnets that you create within the address space and allows you to put different Azure virtual machines on separate subnets within the same virtual network.

- **DNS Servers**   This property allows you to configure the IP address of the DNS servers assigned by the DHCP server used by the Azure virtual network. Use this to configure DNS settings when you deploy a domain controller on an Azure IaaS VM or when you deploy Azure AD DS for an Azure virtual network.

- **Properties**   This property allows you to change which subscription the Azure virtual network is associated with.

- **Locks**   This setting allows you to apply configuration locks, which block changes being made to the settings of the resource unless the lock is first removed.

- **Automation Script**   This setting allows you to access the JSON template file that you can use to reproduce and redeploy virtual networks with similar settings.

By default, hosts that are located on one subnet in a virtual network will automatically be able to communicate with other subnets on a virtual network. You can modify this behavior by configuring user-defined routes, network security groups, Azure Firewall, or Network Virtual Appliances, which allow you to configure the subnets within a virtual network in a similar manner to the way that you might segment traffic on an on-premises network.

CHAPTER 10

More Info

Azure Virtual Networks

You can learn more about Azure Virtual Networks at *https://learn.microsoft.com/en-us/azure/virtual-network/virtual-networks-overview.*

IP addressing

A virtual machine on an Azure network will have an internally assigned IP address in the range specified by the virtual network it is associated with. You can configure this assignment to be static or dynamic. It is important to remember that when you assign an IP address as dynamic or static on the network adapter object within Azure, you don't manage IP address configuration from within the IaaS virtual machine operating system.

Inside OUT

Setting Azure IaaS VM addresses

You never configure the IP address for an Azure IaaS VM through virtual network adapter settings inside the VM. Instead, you configure the IP address for the IaaS VM on the network adapter properties in either the Azure portal or other management tools, such as Cloud Shell. An IaaS VM should always be configured to use dynamic IP addressing. If you stuff this up and manually assign an IP address within the VM, you'll almost always (depending on what setting you configured) be unable to communicate with the VM. You can fix this by removing the existing virtual network adapter in Azure and replacing it with a new one. The new one will be configured for DHCP, and your networking problem will be fixed.

You may also assign a public IP address to the VM, but you should only do this in the event that the VM needs to be directly accessible to hosts on the Internet. A VM with an internally assigned IP address can perform outbound communication to hosts on the Internet without a public IP address, so a public address is only necessary if hosts on the Internet need to communicate directly with the IaaS VM.

Even VMs that do need to be accessible to hosts on the Internet can avoid having a public IP address if they're sitting behind a load balancer, web application, or network virtual appliance. A network virtual appliance (NVA) is similar to a traditional perimeter firewall or application gateway device and mediates traffic flow through to a web application or VM running in the cloud.

You can determine which IP addresses are assigned to an Azure virtual machine on the Network Interfaces blade of the VM's properties. You can also apply a region-specific DNS name to the network interface so that you can connect to the VM using a FQDN rather than an IP address. If you have a DNS server or you have configured an Azure DNS zone, you can then create a CNAME record that points to the region-specific DNS name for future connections. This saves you from always connecting to a *cloudapp.azure.com* address, and it will also remain pointing to the VM if the VM changes IP address.

More Info

IP addressing

You can learn more about IP addressing at Azure at *https://learn.microsoft.com/azure/virtual-network/ip-services/public-ip-addresses*.

Network Security Groups

A Network Security Group (NSG) is a packet filter for mediating traffic at the virtual network subnet level and also at the level of an IaaS VM's network adapter. When you create a virtual machine, an NSG is automatically applied to the VM's network adapter interface, and you can choose whether you want to allow traffic on management ports, such as TCP port 3389 and through to the VM.

An NSG rule has the following elements:

- **Priority** NSG rules are processed in order, with lower numbers processed before higher ones. The moment traffic meets the conditions of a rule, that rule is enforced, and no further rules are processed.

- **Source** Specifies the source address or subnet of traffic. Can also include a service tag, which allows you to specify a particular Azure service or an application security group (a way of identifying the network identity of a series of workloads that make up an application).

- **Destination** Specifies the destination address or subnet of traffic. Can also include a service tag, which allows you to specify a particular Azure service or an application security group (a way of identifying the network identity of a series of workloads that make up an application).

- **Protocol** Can be configured to TCP, UDP, ICMP, or Any.

- **Port Range** Allows you to specify either an individual port or a range of ports.

- **Direction** Specifies whether the rule applies to inbound or outbound traffic.

- **Action** Allows you to specify whether you want to allow or deny the traffic.

Network security groups are fairly basic in that they only work on the basis of IP address information and cannot be configured on the basis of a fully qualified domain name. Azure offers more advanced ways of mediating traffic flow, including Azure Firewall and Network Virtual Appliances, which can be used in conjunction with NSGs; however, these topics are beyond the scope of this book.

Inside OUT

Windows Firewall

You must also configure Windows Firewall to allow access to any application or service that you want to make available that is hosted on your Windows Server IaaS VM. Remember when trying to troubleshoot that there are multiple layers where a packet may be blocked between a host and the destination service running on an IaaS VM in Azure.

CHAPTER 10

> ## More Info
> ### NSGs
>
> You can learn more about NSGs at *https://learn.microsoft.com/azure/virtual-network/network-security-groups-overview*.

Default outbound access

In late 2025, Microsoft changed the configuration of new Azure VMs so that by default, they do not receive automatic Internet access via a default outbound IP. If your VM requires outbound Internet connectivity, you will need to explicitly configure one of these methods:

- Assigning a public IP address directly to the VM

- Configuring a subnet with a NAT Gateway

- Using an Azure Load Balancer with an outbound rule

- Using Network Virtual Appliances (NVAs) to control and manage egress

VPNs and IaaS virtual networks

You can configure IaaS virtual networks to support VPN connections by configuring a VPN gateway. IaaS virtual network VPN gateways support site-to-site connections. A site-to-site connection allows you to connect an IaaS virtual network to an existing network, just as you might connect a branch office network to a head office network in your on-premises environment. IaaS virtual network VPN gateways also support point-to-site VPN connections. This allows you to connect individual host computers to IaaS virtual networks. Windows Server 2019 and later even includes a simplified setup of a point-to-site VPN connection through the deployment of an Azure Network Adapter, which is covered later in this chapter.

> ## More Info
> ### Azure VPN gateways
>
> You can learn more about Azure VPN gateways at *https://learn.microsoft.com/en-us/azure/vpn-gateway/*.

IaaS VM administration

Once you've deployed an IaaS VM, there are a variety of tasks that you need to perform, from configuring how users will connect to the virtual machine to ensuring the VM is regularly backed up.

In your on-premises environment, you would not allow most users of a VM to have access to a VM in Hyper-V Manager and would only allow them to connect directly to the VM using RDP or PowerShell. You should do the same thing in Azure, as most people who use VMs in Azure don't need to interact with them in the Azure console.

Azure IaaS VMs are only visible to users in the Azure portal if they have a role that grants them that right. The default Azure IaaS VM Role-Based Access Control (RBAC) roles are

- **Virtual Machine Contributor**   Users who hold this role can manage virtual machines through the Azure console and perform operations such as restarting and deleting virtual machines. Membership in this role does not provide the user with access to the virtual machine itself. It also does not provide access to the virtual network or storage account to which the virtual machine is connected.

- **Virtual Machine Administrator Login**   If the VM is configured to allow login using Azure AD accounts, assigning this role grants the user local administrator privileges in the virtual machine. Users who hold this role can view the details of a virtual machine in the portal but not change the properties of the virtual machine.

- **Virtual Machine User Login**   Users who hold this role are able to view the details of a virtual machine in the Azure portal and can log in using their Azure AD account with user permissions. Users who hold this role cannot change the properties of the virtual machine.

Users who aren't members of the Virtual Machine Administrator Login or Virtual Machine User Login roles can still access virtual machines if they have a local account on the virtual machine. Put another way, just because you can't see it in the portal doesn't mean you can't RDP to it if you have the address and the correct ports are open.

Windows Admin Center

You can configure Windows Admin Center to be available as a blade from the Azure portal. This gives you Windows Admin Center access to the VM from the portal without having to establish a Remote Desktop session or install Windows Admin Center on your management system.

To use Windows Admin Center from the Azure portal, the target VM must run Windows Server 2016 or later, must have at least 3 GB of RAM, and be in a supported region. You need Owner or Contributor rights at the resource group or VM level to install the WAC extension, as well as

CHAPTER 10

Reader and Windows Admin Center Administrator Login roles at the VM level to connect using WAC to manage the VM. You should ensure that the following network settings are configured:

- Outbound Internet access is enabled, or an outbound port rule allowing HTTPS traffic to the WindowsAdminCenter and AzureActiveDirectory service tags has been set up.

- If you will be connecting to the portal using a public IP, an inbound port rule tightly scoped to port 6516 is required. Microsoft recommends using a private IP address within the VM's virtual network for enhanced security, which you can do via a bastion host or VPN.

To enable Windows Admin Center from the Azure portal, perform the following steps:

1. In the VM's settings in the Azure portal, scroll to the Settings group and select Windows Admin Center.

2. Click Set Up to begin the WAC extension installation.

3. Accept the required permissions for WAC to manage the VM. This includes allowing the extension to install components and configure the VM.

4. Choose whether to connect via Public IP (for testing) or Private IP (recommended).

5. If you are using a public IP, you can check Open This Port For Me to automatically open port 6516 (not recommended for production). As this doesn't always work, you should ensure the inbound port rule is manually configured as described earlier.

6. Click Install to deploy the WAC extension. The installation process takes a few minutes. Wait for the completion notification in the Azure portal.

7. After installation, return to the Windows Admin Center blade in the VM's settings in the Azure portal.

8. Select the IP address to connect (Public IP for testing or Private IP for production) and click Connect.

9. You'll be prompted to enter credentials. You can use a Microsoft Entra ID account with the Windows Admin Center Administrator Login role for single sign-on, or a local account configured on the VM that is a member of the Administrators local group if Entra ID sign-in is not configured.

10. Once authenticated, the WAC interface will load, and you'll be able to manage the Windows Server VM.

Remote PowerShell

You can initiate a remote PowerShell session from hosts on the Internet. Another option is to run a Cloud Shell session in a browser and perform PowerShell remote administration in this manner. Cloud Shell is a browser-based CLI and a lot simpler to use than adding the Azure CLI to your local computer. There is a Cloud Shell icon on the top panel of the Azure Console.

You can enable Remote PowerShell on an Azure IaaS Windows VM by performing the following steps from Cloud Shell:

1. Ensure that Cloud Shell has PowerShell enabled by running the pwsh command.

2. From the PowerShell prompt in Cloud Shell, type the following command to enter local Administrator credentials for the Azure IaaS Windows VM:

   ```
   $cred=get-credential
   ```

3. From the PowerShell prompt in Cloud Shell, type the following command to enable PowerShell remoting on the Azure IaaS Windows VM, where the VM name is WS-IO-A and the resource group that hosts the VM is WS-IO-RG:

   ```
   Enable-AzVMPSRemoting -Name WS-IO-A -ResourceGroupName WS-IO-RG -Protocol https
   ```

4. Once this command has completed executing, you can use the Enter-AzVM cmdlet to establish a remote PowerShell session. For example, run this command to connect to the VM named WS-IO-A in resource group WS-IO-RG:

   ```
   Enter-AzVM -name WS-IO-A -ResourceGroupName WS-IO-RG -Credential $cred
   ```

Azure Bastion

Azure Bastion allows you to establish an RDP session to a Windows Server IaaS VM through a standards-compliant browser such as Microsoft Edge, Mozilla Firefox, or Google Chrome rather than having to use a remote desktop client. You can think of Azure Bastion as "jumpbox as a service" because it allows access to IaaS VMs that do not have a public IP address. Prior to the release of Azure Bastion, the only way to gain access to an IaaS VM that didn't have a public IP address was either through a VPN to the virtual network that hosted the VM or by deploying a jump box VM with a public IP address from which you then created a secondary connection through to the target VM. If you have configured an SSH server on the IaaS VM, Bastion also supports creating SSH connections to Linux IaaS VMs or Windows Server.

Prior to deploying Azure Bastion, you need to create a special subnet named AzureBastion-Subnet on the virtual network that hosts your IaaS VMs. Once you deploy Azure Bastion, the service will manage the network security group configuration to allow you to successfully make connections.

> ## More Info
> ### Azure Bastion
> You can learn more about Azure Bastion at *https://learn.microsoft.com/azure/bastion/bastion-overview.*

Just In Time VM Access

Just-In-Time (JIT) VM Access in Microsoft Defender for Cloud allows temporary opening of management ports (for example, RDP on TCP 3389, SSH on 22) for Azure IaaS VMs, restricted to specific IP ranges and durations, reducing exposure to the Internet. JIT is ideal for VMs requiring public IP access; for private IPs or browser-based access, Azure Bastion is a better alternative because it avoids exposing management ports.

JIT requires Microsoft Defender for Servers, which incurs an additional cost. To configure JIT, follow these steps:

1. In Microsoft Defender for Cloud, go to Environment Settings, select your subscription/workspace, and click Just-in-Time VM Access under Cloud Security.

2. On the Recommended tab, select a VM, and then click Enable JIT On X VMs.

3. On the JIT Access Configuration page, choose a port (such as 3389) and configure source IPs. (Per Request uses the requesting device's IP; CIDR Block specifies a range.) Set a Max Request Time (1–24 hours) for new connections (existing sessions remain active).

To request JIT access once it is configured for a VM, do this:

1. In Microsoft Defender for Cloud, navigate to Just-in-Time VM Access. Navigate to the Configured tab, select the VM, and click Request Access.

2. Select the port, toggle it to On, choose My IP or IP Range, optionally add a log message, and click Open Ports.

3. The port will be opened, and you will be able to establish a connection.

> ## More Info
> ### Just in Time VM Access
> You can learn more about Just in Time VM access at *https://learn.microsoft.com/en-us/azure/defender-for-cloud/just-in-time-access-usage.*

IaaS VM operations

Azure includes many services that support virtual machines that you'd have to configure and manage manually if you were running those VMs in an on-premises private cloud. One of the substantial advantages to running a Windows Server VM in Azure is the supporting ecosystem of services, including monitoring, backup, security, and update management.

Azure Automanage

Azure Automanage is a service that simplifies and automates the management of Windows IaaS VMs. Azure Automanage automatically configures and applies Azure best practices for Windows Server VMs, including

- **Automated onboarding**   Integrates VMs with essential Azure services like Azure Monitor, Azure Backup, Microsoft Defender for Cloud, and Update Management.

- **Configuration management**   Enforces consistent configurations (for example, security baselines, patch management, and monitoring) based on Azure's recommended settings.

- **Drift detection and remediation**   Continuously monitors VMs for configuration drift and automatically corrects deviations to maintain compliance with best practices.

- **Simplified operations**   Reduces manual setup and maintenance tasks by automating routine management processes.

Automanage eliminates the need to manually configure and manage multiple Azure services. It allows you to automatically apply security configurations. Automanage allows you to configure VMs according to Azure's recommended practices. You can configure all of these services individually for your VM if you choose, but if you have to deploy large numbers of VMs on a regular basis, it can make more sense to allow Automanage to handle the configuration and enrollment.

> ## More Info
> ### *Azure Automanage*
> You can learn more about Azure Automanage at *https://learn.microsoft.com/ azure/ automanage/.*

Azure Monitor

Azure Monitor enables you to collect performance metrics, gather system and application logs, and set up proactive alerts. By using integrating Azure Monitor with Windows Server IaaS VMs, the following things are possible:

- All telemetry from VMs can be collected in a central Azure Monitor Log Analytics workspace for analysis.

- You can configure alerts on metrics, including high CPU usage or event log items.

- Azure Monitor can be integrated with Azure Dashboards for visualizing data and Power BI for advanced reporting. Azure Monitor can trigger actions through Action Groups, including emailing admins or running scripts when thresholds are breached.

Deploy Log Analytics Workspace

The first step in integrating Azure Monitor with Windows Server IaaS VMs is deploying a Log Analytics workspace. You can do this by performing the following steps:

1. In the Azure portal, search for Log Analytics workspaces. Click + Create to start a new workspace creation.

2. On the Basics Tab – Workspace Details, select the appropriate Subscription and Resource Group for the workspace. Enter a Name for the workspace and choose an Azure Region close to the IaaS VM deployment.

3. On the Pricing Tier page, select a pricing tier and configure data retention and caps settings.

4. Click Review + Create > Create to deploy the workspace.

Install Azure Monitor Agent

You connect Windows Server IaaS VMs to Log Analytics by installing the Azure Monitor Agent. You can do this by performing the following steps:

1. In the Azure portal, navigate to your Windows Server VM and under Monitoring, select Insights. Click Enable to open the Monitoring configuration pane.

2. In the enablement pane, choose Azure Monitor Agent. You will be asked to select a Data Collection Rule (DCR) and Log Analytics workspace.

3. You can use the Default option, which automatically creates a DCR and uses either an existing default workspace or lets you choose one. By default, the VM Insights DCR will collect basic guest OS performance metrics (CPU, memory, disk, network) but not detailed processes or event logs.

4. Click Create (this creates the DCR and associates the VM) and then Configure to start the onboarding. Azure will deploy the Azure Monitor Agent extension to the VM and apply the DCR for data collection.

5. Once enabled, the Insights view for the VM will show performance charts.

Configure data collection rules

You can customize data collection by creating or editing a DCR. To do this, perform the following steps:

1. In the Azure portal, navigate to Azure Monitor, choose Data Collection Rules, and click + Create. Provide a rule name, and select your Subscription, Resource Group, and Region. Set the Platform type as Windows.

2. Select Target Resources and specify the VMs to which the rule will apply.

3. Under Collect and deliver, click Add Data Source and choose Performance Counters as the Data Source Type. For Collection mode, you can start with Basic, which provides a preset selection of common counters (CPU, memory, disk, network, and so on). Select the performance counter categories or specific counters you want to collect. If you want to record a counter not listed in the Basic set, choose Custom and enter the performance counter's XPath (such as `\Process(<process_name>)\Thread Count`). Adjust the sample interval as needed.

4. Click the Destination tab for this data source, choose Azure Monitor Logs, and select your Log Analytics workspace. You can also enable Azure Monitor Metrics as a destination. This makes the data available in Metrics Explorer, and you can use it for metric alerts. Click Add Data Source to save the performance counter configuration.

5. To collect Windows Event Logs, in the DCR Collect and deliver step, add another data source for Windows events. Click Add Data Source and select Windows Event Logs. Choose the logs and event severity levels you want to collect. You can also add specific event logs or custom log channels by name.

6. On the Destination tab, select Azure Monitor Logs and your Log Analytics workspace. Click Add Data Source to save the event log configuration.

Create alert rules

Azure Monitor allows you to set up alert rules that trigger actions when certain conditions occur. For example, you want to be alerted when a specific event or error occurs on the VM (as recorded in the Windows Event Log). Once you've configured those logs to be collected in your Log Analytics workspace, you can create a log search alert on that data. To do this, perform the following steps:

1. Navigate to the VM's Logs (Log Analytics) page. In the VM menu, click Logs. This opens the Log Analytics query editor scoped to that VM.

2. Write a Kusto Query Language (KQL) query that captures the condition you care about. For example, to alert on any error in the System event log, use this:

```
Event
| where LogName == "System" and Level == "Error"
| where TimeGenerated >= ago(5m)
```

3. Above the query results, click New Alert Rule. (This button appears after running a query, allowing you to create an alert directly from that query.) The Alert Creation pane opens. The Scope will be set, and the Condition is prefilled with your log query.

4. Set the Evaluation Period and Frequency. Ensure that the Frequency is equal to or shorter than the time window in your query so each run catches new events.

5. Under Alert Logic, choose the Operator and Threshold. For log alerts, a common pattern is to trigger when the number of results is greater than 0 (meaning at least one event was found). By default, if your query does not include an aggregation (summarize), the alert will count the number of records. So you can simply set Greater Than 0 to fire an alert when any matching event is found.

6. Configure the Action Group, Severity, and Alert Name. For example, name the alert **System Error Event - VM01** and maybe use a higher severity (2 or 3) since this indicates an error event occurred. Ensure that an Action Group is selected to notify the right team.

7. Click Create Alert Rule to save it. Now, Azure Monitor will run the query every five minutes; if any error events appear in the System Log, an alert will be fired. You can adapt this approach for other event logs or specific Event IDs. (Just modify the KQL query accordingly.) For instance, you could alert on critical Application Log Events or security audit failures.

Resizing a VM

Azure allows you to resize an IaaS VM. Resizing a VM allows you to change the IaaS VM's processor and memory allocation. Resizing a VM might also alter the number of disks that can be associated with a VM; cheaper SKUs will be limited to less storage, and in some cases, they will be limited to standard rather than premium storage types. If the Azure IaaS VM is running, the only drawback is that the VM will need to restart for the resize to occur.

To resize an Azure IaaS VM, perform the following steps:

1. Open the VM's page in the Azure portal under Virtual Machines

2. In the left menu under Settings, click Size.

3. Select the new size that you want to apply to the virtual machine.

4. Click Resize.

The virtual machine will then restart, and the new size will be applied.

More Info

Resizing an Azure IaaS VM

You can learn more about resizing an Azure IaaS VM at *https://learn.microsoft.com/azure/virtual-machines/sizes/resize-vm*.

IaaS VM backup

An advantage to running an IaaS VM in Azure is that it is far simpler to set up a daily backup than it is when you have to manage all the backup and recovery infrastructure yourself. This is because Azure IaaS VM Backup is a feature of Azure. Essentially, all you need to do is turn Azure IaaS VM Backup on, and it looks after itself.

To enable backup and recovery of an Azure IaaS VM, perform the following steps:

1. In Cloud Shell, run the following command to create a recovery services vault to host the backup data:

    ```
    az backup vault create --resource-group VMResourceGroup --name
    IaaSVMRecoveryServicesVault --location southeasteasia
    ```

2. Run the following command to enable backup for an Azure VM:

    ```
    az backup protection enable-for-vm --resource-group VMResourceGroup --vault-name
    IaaSVMRecoveryServicesVault --vm $(az vm show --resource-group VMResourceGroup
    --name NameOfVM --query id -o tsv) --policy-name DefaultPolicy
    ```

3. Run the following command to trigger a manual backup for an Azure VM:

    ```
    az backup protection backup-now --resource-group VMResourceGroup --vault-name
    IaaSVMRecoveryServicesVault --container-name "iaasvmcontainerv2;vmresourcegroup;na
    meofvm" --item-name "vm;nameofvm" --retain-until 12-12-2027
    ```

More Info

Azure IaaS VM Backup

You can learn more about Azure IaaS VM Backup at *https://learn.microsoft.com/azure/backup/quick-backup-vm-cli*.

CHAPTER 10

IaaS VM encryption

To support IaaS VM disk encryption, the Windows Server IaaS VM must be able to do the following. (By default, IaaS VM can do this unless you remove the default network security group rules.)

- The server must be able to connect to the key vault endpoint so that the Windows Server IaaS VM can store and retrieve encryption keys.

- The server must be able to connect to an Entra ID endpoint at *login.microsoftonline.com* so that it can retrieve a token that allows it to connect to the key vault that holds the encryption keys.

- The server must be able to connect to an Azure storage endpoint that hosts the Azure extension repository and the Azure storage account that stores the VM's virtual hard disks.

- Enable Managed Identity on the VM.

- If the Windows Server IaaS VM is domain joined, do not configure BitLocker-related Group Policies, other than the Configure User Storage Of BitLocker Recovery Information: Allow 256-Bit Recovery Key policy. This policy is usually configured automatically during the encryption process, and Azure Disk Encryption will fail if a Group Policy conflict in any TPM or BitLocker-related policies exists.

Perform the following steps to encrypt the hard disk drives of a Windows Server IaaS VM:

1. Enable Managed Identity on the VM

    ```
    az vm identity assign --resource-group "VMResourceGroup" --name "VMName"
    ```

2. Create an Azure Key Vault to store the encryption key used to encrypt the hard disk of the VM. You can do this with the following code:

    ```
    az keyvault create --name "KeyVaultName" --resource-group "VMResourceGroup"
    --location AzureRegion --enabled-for-disk-encryption
    ```

3. Once the key vault is created, provide the VM's identity access to the Key Vault:

    ```
    object_id=$(az vm show --name "VMName" --resource-group "VMResourceGroup" --query
    identity.principalId -o tsv)
    az keyvault set-policy --name "KeyVaultName" --resource-group "VMResourceGroup"
    --object-id $object_id --key-permissions get unwrapKey wrapKey
    ```

4. Encrypt the VM:

    ```
    keyvault_url=$(az keyvault show --name "KeyVaultName" --query properties.vaultUri
    -o tsv)
    az vm encryption enable --resource-group "VMResourceGroup" --name "VMName" --disk-
    encryption-keyvault "KeyVaultName" --disk-encryption-keyvault-url "$keyvault_url"
    --volume-type "ALL"
    ```

More Info

Encrypt Azure IaaS VM disks

You can learn more about encrypting Azure IaaS VM disks at *https://learn.microsoft.com/en-us/azure/virtual-machines/disk-encryption-overview*.

Azure Site Recovery

Azure Site Recovery (ASR) allows you to replicate physical and virtual machines from one site to a secondary location. The primary and secondary locations can be on-premises, Azure, or a mixture of both. ASR is designed so that when an outage occurs at the primary location, you can initiate a failover to the secondary location. Once you restore service to the primary location, you can use the failback process to return the workloads to that site. Azure Site Recovery integrates with Azure Backup and uses Recovery Services vaults (RSVs).

ASR includes the following functionality:

- Set up and manage replication, failover, and failback from a primary site to a secondary site using a single location in the Azure portal.

- Manage disaster recovery for Azure IaaS VMs from a primary region to a secondary region.

- Site recovery provides continuous replication.

- Support for application-consistent snapshot replication so that data in memory and transactions in process shift to the alternate site.

- Support for running disaster recovery drills without impacting ongoing replication of virtual machine data and state.

- Planned failovers can be initiated with zero loss of data.

- Unplanned failovers can be triggered with minimal data loss depending on replication frequency.

- Customized recovery plans allow you to orchestrate the sequence of failover and recovery for multitier applications.

- Network integration to reserve IP addresses and configure load-balancers and utilization of Azure Traffic Manager for efficient network switchovers.

CHAPTER 10

Configure Site Recovery for Azure virtual machines

You can use ASR to manage the process of replicating and failing over Azure IaaS VMs from one Azure datacenter to another. Replication is continuous when replicating IaaS VMs to another Azure region.

To configure ASR for an Azure VM, perform the following steps:

1. Select the IaaS VM you want to replicate.

2. In the Operations section, select Disaster Recovery.

3. On the Basics tab, select the target region to which you want to replicate the VM.

4. Select Review + Start Replication. Replication will occur according to the default ASR IaaS VM replication policy.

ASR replication policies define the retention history of ASR recovery points. The default replication policy retains recovery points for one day, and application-consistent snapshots are disabled. You can configure an ASR recovery policy that has a longer ASR recovery point and that has application-consistent recovery points. Application-consistent recovery points can be created at a minimum frequency of once an hour. You can configure recovery points to be stored up to 15 days with managed disks and three days with unmanaged disks. Rather than specifying a longer ASR recovery point retention policy, it's generally simpler to use Azure Backup and cross-region restore functionality if you want to recover older versions of a replicated VM.

ASR for Azure IaaS virtual machines supports the following replication features:

- Replication of VMs to different subscriptions associated with the same Entra tenant.

- VMs that have Azure Disk Encryption (ADE) enabled. Replication will copy the required disk encryption keys and secrets from the source region to the target region using the user context. If the account configuring ASR doesn't have the appropriate security, it's also possible for a person with the required permissions to script the transfer of keys and secrets.

- Azure IaaS VM disks can be excluded from replication.

- Azure IaaS VM disks can be added to a VM replication configuration.

- ASR for IaaS VMs between regions does not support the VM retaining the same public IP address after failover. As public IP addresses are specific to each Azure region, a new one will be assigned after failover. IaaS VMs can retain their private IP address information.

Configure Azure Site Recovery networking

When configuring ASR replication between Azure sites, you should create a network service endpoint in the virtual network that hosts the VMs that you're protecting to ensure that replication traffic does not leave the Azure boundary. You should also configure IP addressing between the primary and target virtual networks prior to enabling replication.

To configure network mapping, perform the following steps:

1. In the Site Recovery Infrastructure section of the RSV, select Network Mapping.

2. Add a network mapping and then specify the source virtual network and the target virtual network.

If you don't create a network mapping prior to configuring disaster recovery for Azure IaaS VMs, you can specify a target network when you configure replication. When you do this, a mapping is automatically created, and a network in the target region that is identical to the source network is created. This target network will have the -asr suffix.

The subnet assigned within the virtual network for the target VM will be selected based on the name of the subnet for the source VM. If there is no subnet in the target network that has the same name as a subnet in the source network, then the first subnet in alphabetical order in the target network will be assigned to the VM. If the source and destination subnets are configured with the same address space, then the source and destination IaaS VMs will have the same IP addresses. If the source and destination subnets have different address spaces, the target VM will be assigned the next available IP address in the target subnet.

Entra Domain Services

A simple option for domain-joining an IaaS VM is to deploy an IaaS domain controller VM and then join other VMs to the domain in the same way that you would in an on-premises environment. The challenge with this is that it means that you have to deploy, maintain, and pay for an IaaS VM configured as a domain controller. Or you can deploy, maintain, and pay for two IaaS VMs if you're following the best practice of having at least two domain controllers for any single domain.

Entra Domain Services provides a managed domain service for IaaS VMs running in Azure. This service provides domain join, Group Policy, lightweight directory access protocol (LDAP), and Kerberos and NTLM authentication, and it is compatible with Windows Server Active Directory. Because Entra Domain Services is a managed service, Microsoft takes care of the management of the back-end domain controller infrastructure.

Entra Domain Services pulls identity data from Entra ID. This includes identities synchronized from an on-premises Windows Active Directory instance through Microsoft Entra Connect.

When you deploy Entra Domain Services, you select an Azure virtual network on which to make the service available. IaaS VMs placed on that virtual network can then domain join to Entra Domain Services in the same manner as a computer running on a traditional network with a domain controller would.

An Azure AD DS–managed domain can also be configured in a trust relationship with an on-premises AD DS domain. This allows you to deploy resources in an Azure AD DS–managed domain that functions as a resource forest that is accessible to on-premises accounts stored and managed in an on-premises trusted account forest. You'll learn more about this configuration later in the chapter.

More Info

Entra Domain Services

You can learn more about Entra Domain Services at *https://learn.microsoft.com/entra/identity/domain-services/*.

Deploying Entra Domain Services

Entra Domain Services can be enabled within a subscription and can leverage an Entra tenancy. Entra Domain Services has the following prerequisites:

- To enable Entra Domain Services, you'll need Global Administrator, or Application Administrator, Domain Service Contributor, and Groups Administrator privileges within the Entra tenancy.

- Creating resources in Entra Domain Services requires that you have contributor privileges in the Azure subscription.

- You must have a virtual network with DNS servers that can resolve Azure infrastructure resources, including storage. You can use Azure's DNS servers. If you use custom DNS servers that are unable to resolve Internet hosts, you may be unable to create an Entra Domain Services domain.

Before creating an Entra Domain Services domain, you should decide on the properties of the DNS name that you will assign. Take into account the following:

- The default option will be to use the built-in domain name of the Entra directory associated with the managed domain. (This will have an *.onmicrosoft.com* DNS suffix.) The challenge with this option is that if you want to enable secure LDAP, you won't be able to create a digital certificate that allows a connection to this default domain because Microsoft owns the domain name associated with the DNS suffix.

- Nonroutable domain names (such as *.local* and *.internal*) will cause problems with DNS resolution and should be avoided.

- A custom domain name that you have registered publicly is the best option. Microsoft recommends that you use a domain name separate from any existing Azure or on-premises DNS namespace. For example, use *addstailwindtraders.com* for the managed domain, whereas you use *tailwindtraders.com* for an on-premises domain as well as for some resources in Azure.

The following additional restrictions apply for domain names associated with Entra Domain Services managed domains:

- The domain prefix element of the domain name (*domainprefix.tailwindtraders.com*) cannot be longer than 15 characters. The domain suffix (*tailwindtraders.com*) is not counted toward this limit.

- The DNS domain name of the managed domain should not already exist in the virtual network. You cannot already have an AD DS domain with the same DNS domain name present, an Azure cloud service with that name, or a VPN connection to an on-premises network with that name.

Deploying an Azure AD Domain Services managed domain involves performing the following steps:

1. In the Azure portal, select Create A Resource and search for **Entra Domain Services**:

2. On the Entra Domain Services page, select Create.

3. Choose the Azure subscription and resource group that will host the managed domain.

4. Enter the selected DNS name for the Entra Domain Services domain.

5. Choose the location in which the domain should be created. If the region supports Azure Availability Zones, the Entra Domain Services resources will be distributed across zones for additional redundancy.

6. Choose a SKU (this determines the performance and backup frequency and can be altered after deployment). You can choose between Standard and Enterprise.

7. Select between a user forest and a resource forest:

   - User forests synchronize all objects from Entra, including any user account synchronized from an on-premises AD DS environment.

   - Resource forests only synchronize objects created in Entra and will not include any accounts synchronized from an on-premises AD DS environment. A resource forest can be configured in a one-way trust relationship with an on-premises Windows

CHAPTER 10

Server AD DS forest. This allows accounts that aren't synchronized to Azure to access resources hosted on Azure IaaS VMs that are domain-joined to an Entra Domain Services domain.

8. If you select Review and Create and have selected a User forest, the following occurs:

    ■   A new virtual network named aadds-vnet that uses the IP address range 10.0.0.0/24 is created.

    ■   A new subnet named aadds-subnet that uses the IP address range 10.0.0.0/24 is deployed within the newly created aadds-vnet.

    ■   A new network security group is created that contains rules that allow for service communication.

    ■   You can provide alternate options for virtual network and subnet and should extend the vNet's range at this point if you want to add a VPN gateway.

9. After deployment has completed, you will need to update the DNS server settings for the Azure Virtual Network associated with the Entra Domain Services domain so that the DNS server addresses match those associated with the Entra Domain Services domain. You can do this automatically by selecting Configure on the overview page of the Entra Domain Services domain.

Entra Domain Services domain join

You can only perform a domain join to an Entra Domain Services instance with an account that is part of the Entra tenant. You can't perform a domain join using an account that has been synchronized from an on-premises Windows AD DS instance to perform this task. As is the case when configuring Microsoft Entra Connect, you should consider creating a special account using the default tenancy *onmicrosoft.com* suffix for performing domain-join operations rather than any custom domain name that you have assigned to the tenancy.

You perform the domain-join operation from within the Windows Server VM, either directly by connecting through an RDP or Azure Bastion session or through a remote PowerShell session, either by changing the domain membership on the Computer Name tab of the System Properties dialog or by using the Add-Computer PowerShell cmdlet with the DomainName parameter.

Need More Review?

IaaS VM domain join

You can learn more about domain-joining a Windows Server IaaS VM at *https://learn.microsoft.com/entra/identity/domain-services/join-windows-vm*.

Integrate AD DS and Entra Domain Services

You can configure Entra Domain Services so that an account created on-premises synchronizes using Microsoft Entra Connect to Entra and is configured with the appropriate hash synchronization that this account can, in turn, be used to sign on to an Entra Domain Services joined VM.

By default, Entra does not automatically generate NTLM or Kerberos password hashes for users. For users to log on to computers that are members of an Entra Domain Services domain, they need to have passwords stored in a hash format that can be used by NTLM or Kerberos authentication.

You can configure accounts that are only hosted in Entra to support authentication on computers joined to an Entra Domain Services domain by changing the account's password once an Entra Domain Services instance associated with the Azure AD tenancy is created. Once this is done, generating a new password will create the appropriately stored password hash.

If you are synchronizing accounts and passwords to Azure using Microsoft Connect, you'll need to perform the following steps:

1. Open the Synchronization Service on the computer that hosts Microsoft Connect.

2. On the list of connectors, take note of the connector names.

3. Run the following script, adding the connector names to the location in the script that defines the $azureadConnector and $adConnector variables:

```
# Define the Entra Connect connector names
$entraConnector = "<CASE SENSITIVE ENTRA CONNECTOR NAME>"
$adConnector = "<CASE SENSITIVE AD DS CONNECTOR NAME>"

# Import the required PowerShell module
try {
    Import-Module "C:\Program Files\Microsoft Azure AD Sync\Bin\ADSync\ADSync.
psd1" -ErrorAction Stop
    Import-Module "C:\Program Files\Microsoft Azure AD Sync\Bin\AdSyncConfig\
AdSyncConfig.psm1" -ErrorAction Stop
}
catch {
    Write-Error "Failed to import required modules: $_"
    exit
}
# Create a new ForceFullPasswordSync configuration parameter object
try {
    $connector = Get-ADSyncConnector -Name $adConnector -ErrorAction Stop
    $param = New-Object Microsoft.IdentityManagement.PowerShell.ObjectModel.
ConfigurationParameter '
        "Microsoft.Synchronize.ForceFullPasswordSync", String, ConnectorGlobal,
$null, $null, $null
    $param.Value = 1
```

```
        # Update connector configuration
        $connector.GlobalParameters.Remove($param.Name)
        $connector.GlobalParameters.Add($param)
        $connector = Add-ADSyncConnector -Connector $connector -ErrorAction Stop
}
catch {
        Write-Error "Failed to update connector configuration: $_"
        exit
}

# Disable and re-enable password sync to force a full synchronization
try {
        Set-ADSyncAADPasswordSyncConfiguration -SourceConnector $adConnector '
            -TargetConnector $entraConnector -Enable $false -ErrorAction Stop
        Start-Sleep -Seconds 2
        Set-ADSyncAADPasswordSyncConfiguration -SourceConnector $adConnector '
            -TargetConnector $entraConnector -Enable $true -ErrorAction Stop

        Write-Output "Full password synchronization successfully triggered."
}
catch {
        Write-Error "Failed to trigger full password sync: $_"
        Exit
}
```

Need More Review?

Hybrid password synchronization for Entra Domain Services

You can learn more about domain-joining a Windows Server IaaS VM at *https://learn. microsoft.com/entra/identity/domain-services/tutorial-configure-password-hash-sync.*

Create a forest trust between on-premises AD DS and Entra Domain Services

You can create a forest trust between an on-premises AD DS domain and Entra Domain Services. The virtual network that hosts the Entra Domain Services forest needs a VPN or ExpressRoute connection to your on-premises Active Directory environment. Applications and services also need network connectivity to the virtual network hosting the Entra Domain Services forest. You'll also need to ensure there's continuous DNS name resolution between your Entra Domain Services forest name and your on-premises Active Directory forest name. You can configure resolution from the on-premises environment to Entra Domain Services by configuring a conditional forwarder from the on-premises DNS servers to the DNS servers used by your instance of Entra Domain Services.

To create the two-way forest trust, perform the following steps:

1. Open Active Directory Domains and Trusts on a computer connected to a domain controller for the on-premises AD DS instance.

2. Right-click the domain, such as *onprem.tailwindtraders.com*, and then select Properties.

3. Choose the Trusts tab, and then select New Trust.

4. Enter the Domain Services domain name, such as *entradstailwindtraders.com*, and then select Next.

5. Select the option to create a Forest Trust, then to create a Two-Way Trust.

6. Choose to create the trust for This Domain Only.

7. Choose to use forest-wide authentication, and then enter and confirm a trust password. Remember this password, as you'll need to enter it later in the Microsoft Entra admin center.

8. Step through the next few windows with the default options, and then choose No, Do Not Confirm The Outgoing Trust. Select Finish to end the wizard.

9. In the Microsoft Entra admin center, search for and select Microsoft Entra Domain Services, and then select your managed domain, such as *entradstailwindtraders.com.com*.

10. From the menu on the left side of the managed domain, select Trusts, and then click + Add A Trust.

11. Select Two-Way as the Trust Direction.

12. Enter a Display Name that identifies your trust, and then enter the On-Premises Trusted Forest DNS Name, such as *onprem.tailwindtraders.com*.

13. Provide the same trust password that was used to configure the inbound forest trust for the on-premises AD DS domain.

14. Provide at least two DNS servers for the on-premises AD DS domain, such as 10.1.1.4 and 10.1.1.5.

15. When ready, choose Save to save the outbound forest trust.

Managing the Entra Domain Services Active Directory Domain Services instance

The AAD DC Administrators group is a privileged security group automatically provisioned in Entra Domain Services that grants administrative permissions within the managed domain.

Members of this group can perform common Active Directory tasks such as creating and managing users and groups, resetting passwords, joining computers to the domain, and administering Group Policy Objects (GPOs) within custom organizational units (OUs). The AAD DC Administrators group does not grant full domain administrator privileges as in a traditional on-premises Active Directory. Its permissions are scoped to specific administrative tasks within the constraints of Entra DS's managed environment.

Users who are members of this group can also remotely access and manage domain-joined virtual machines. Members of this group cannot manage domain controllers, FSMO roles, or schema-level configurations because these are managed by Entra DS.

Membership in the AAD DC Administrators group is managed from the Entra portal and not from within Entra Domain Services. To add users to this group, an Entra ID administrator must assign them to the AAD DC Administrators security group, which is then synchronized into Entra Domain Services. Changes to group membership may take several minutes to propagate.

Managing Group Policy and Organizational Units in Entra Domain Services differs from traditional Active Directory due to the managed nature of the service. Administrators can create custom OUs and define Group Policy Objects (GPOs) within those OUs, enabling them to apply policies to users and computers in a controlled scope. However, the default OUs, AADDC Computers, and AADDC Users are read-only, and you cannot link or apply new GPOs to them or restructure their hierarchy. You cannot modify or delete the built-in GPOs that Microsoft manages, and you cannot affect domain-level policies or create site-linked GPOs.

Windows Subsystem for Linux

Windows Subsystem for Linux (WSL) allows you to run a variety of Linux distributions on Windows computers. Windows Subsystem for Linux is available for Windows client with a variety of distributions available from the Microsoft Store. Though you can't use the Microsoft Store with Windows Server, WSL is available and relatively easy to install from the command line. In this chapter, you'll learn how to set up Windows Subsystem for Linux on Windows Server and how to install, configure, and manage Linux distributions.

Linux on Windows Server

Linux has been available on Windows Server through a variety of methods over the years, including Windows Services for UNIX that were available with Windows NT and Windows 2000 and third-party products, such as Cygwin; also, you can run Linux or BSD virtual machine on Hyper-V.

WSL is more about providing access to Linux tools on Windows computers than it is about having Windows computers host Linux services on the network. For example, you may install tools like ffmpeg on Linux to convert multimedia files and call them using Windows Server command-line scripts. Although you can host Linux workloads such as nginx on WSL, in production environments, Linux virtual machines are far more robust solutions.

Installing WSL

The first step involved in installing WSL on Windows Server is to enable the Windows Subsystem for Linux optional feature. You can do this by running the following command and then restarting the server:

```
wsl --install
```

Unlike Windows 10, where you can install a WSL distribution directly from the store, WSL on Windows Server requires that you install prepared WSL distros using the command line. You can determine which WSL distros are available using the command

```
wsl --list --online
```

This command will list both the distribution name and the distribution's friendly name for use in operations such as installation. At the time of writing, the distributions available for Windows Server are

- AlmaLinux OS 8

- AlmaLinux OS 9

- AlmaLinux OS Kitten 10

- AlmaLinux OS 10

- Debian GNU/Linux

- Fedora Linux 42

- SUSE Linux Enterprise 15 SP6

- SUSE Linux Enterprise 15 SP7

- Ubuntu

- Ubuntu 24.04 LTS

- Arch Linux

- Kali Linux Rolling

- openSUSE Tumbleweed

- openSUSE Leap 15.6

- Ubuntu 18.04 LTS

- Ubuntu 20.04 LTS

- Ubuntu 22.04 LTS

- Oracle Linux 7.9

- Oracle Linux 8.10

- Oracle Linux 9.5

You can install a Linux distribution in WSL by determining its friendly name and using the command `wsl --install friendlyname`. For example, to install Ubuntu, run the command `wsl --install ubuntu`; to install Kali Linux, run the command `wsl --install kali-linux`.

You can install multiple Linux distributions and run those distros concurrently.

Inside OUT

Linux containers on Windows

Linux Containers on Windows was an early version of running Linux containers on Windows without using WSL or a Hyper-V virtual machine. Linux Containers on Windows was an experimental option on Windows Server prior to the introduction of WSL 2. Microsoft's focus for containers support on Windows Server is Windows Server containers. You can run Linux containers using WSL, but this architecture will only be useful in very specific use cases, such as having a workload run in a container where you don't want to go to the effort of deploying a separate Linux host or virtual machine.

When you run a WSL distribution, the Windows file system will be located in the `/mnt/<drive letter>` folder from the perspective of the Linux command line.

Once WSL is installed, you can run Linux utilities directly from the Windows Server command line by using the `wsl.exe <command>` syntax.

Inside OUT

Remember to update

WSL will not be automatically updated by running Windows Update, and you need to manually update the distribution using the appropriate distribution update tools, such as apt-get for Ubuntu or Debian. Once you've installed a WSL distribution, the first thing you should do is run a software update!

WSL 2.0

WSL 2.0 is the default version of Windows Subsystem for Linux. WSL 2.0 uses virtualization to enable WSL to interact with a Linux kernel, which leads to better performance. Unlike WSL 1, which uses a translation layer to allow Linux workloads to run on Windows, WSL 2 leverages virtualization to host a lightweight kernel to achieve this goal.

WSL 2 requires that the host supports virtualization. If you want to install WSL 2 on a Windows Server virtual machine, the virtual machine will need to be configured to support nested virtualization.

You can verify which Linux version your WSL distributions are configured for by using the following command.

```
Wsl --list --verbose
```

> ## More Info
> ### WSL 2
> You can find out more about WSL at *https://learn.microsoft.com/en-us/windows/wsl/compare-versions*.

WSL networking

By default, WSL2 uses a NAT networking architecture. The WSL instance is hidden behind the Windows host's network, where it runs in a lightweight VM with its own virtual Ethernet adapter and IP address. The WSL VM does not share the same IP as the Windows host and uses a unique private IP on a NAT network managed by the Windows Server operating system. By default, on the Windows Server itself, you can connect to a Linux service using the address localhost:port, but other devices on the LAN cannot directly reach that service without additional configuration.

You can determine the WSL IP address from Windows Server by running this command:

```
wsl hostname --all-ip-addresses
```

You can determine the IP address of the Windows Server computer from within WSL by running the command

```
ip route show | grep -i default | awk '{print $3}'
```

Configuring port forwarding for WSL

You can configure port forwarding to relay ports from the Windows Server network interface through to the server or application running in WSL. To do this, perform the following steps:

1. Ensure that the service is listening on all interfaces. For example, if you're running Nginx in WSL, set the listen address to 0.0.0.0 and ensure that the service is started.

2. In Windows, determine the WSL instance's IP using `wsl hostname --all-ip-addresses`.

3. Use the netsh interface `portproxy` command to forward a port on the Windows Server network interface to WSL. For example, to forward all incoming traffic on port 80 of the Windows Server host to port 80 in WSL, run the command (substituting WSL's address for WSL_IP):

```
netsh interface portproxys add v4tov4 listenport=80 listenaddress=0.0.0.0
connectport=80 connectaddress=WSL_IP
```

4. Ensure that Windows Firewall allows inbound traffic on the chosen port.

The WSL instance can have a different IP each time it starts, so if you want this port forwarding configuration to persist, you need to write a script that retrieves the WSL instance's IP address each time the system restarts.

Configure mirrored networking for WSL

An alternative to port forwarding is a networking mode termed *mirrored* or *bridge networking*. In mirrored mode, the network interface of the WSL VM is essentially bridged with the host's network interface, making the WSL instance appear as if it's on the same LAN as the Windows Server computer.

To use this mode, you create or edit a file named `.wslconfig` in your Windows user profile directory and add the following lines:

```
[wsl2]
networkingMode=mirrored
```

With this setting, WSL will start in mirrored networking mode. The WSL VM's network interface will now mirror the host's NIC.

In mirrored mode, the WSL instance shares the host's IP. For example, if your Windows Server has IP 192.168.1.50 and you run Nginx in WSL on port 80 with mirrored networking, another host can connect to 192.168.1.50:80, and WSL will respond. You'll need to enable Windows Firewall rules to allow access to the ports hosting the service you're publishing.

CHAPTER 11

CHAPTER 12

Hardening Windows Server

Windows Server 2025 is Microsoft's most secure version of the Windows Server operating system, but you can configure the operating system to be far more secure than it is in a default deployment.

Hardening is the process of configuring security controls to improve security. The drawback of hardening Windows Server is that it reduces compatibility. Applying security controls is always a matter of balancing security with the requirements of the environment.

Always perform hardening activities that are commensurate with your organization's risk profile. If you're managing Windows Server for a federal government department, you have a substantially different risk profile than if you're managing Windows Server for the local school district.

Inside OUT

Tighten and test slowly

Be sure to implement security controls incrementally. Most security controls aren't enabled by default because turning them on often breaks compatibility with something. If you turn on all possible security controls at once, it's likely that a raft of compatibility problems will arise, and you'll have a substantial amount of trouble figuring out which control caused them. If you implement one security control at a time and a compatibility problem arises, you'll easily be able to guess which control was responsible for the problem.

Hardening Windows Server

You should secure Windows Server hosts as tightly as possible without triggering compatibility issues. Beyond the advice offered in this chapter, multiple third-party guides exist that list recommended security configurations for Windows Server. These guides are extremely lengthy and provide an excellent way of understanding exactly which security controls are available to harden Windows Server. The two most important organizations providing guides are

- **Center for Internet Security** Benchmarks exist in Microsoft Exchange, Microsoft SQL Server, and Windows Server. You can find out more at *https://www.cisecurity.org/ cis-benchmarks*.

- **Defense Information Systems Agency (DISA)** DISA Security Technical Implementation Guide (STIG) is a respected security benchmark. You can access benchmarks for workloads including Active Directory, .NET Framework, Microsoft Exchange, Microsoft SharePoint, Microsoft SQL Server, and Windows Server. You can find out more at *https://public.cyber.mil/stigs/downloads/*.

User rights

Rather than adding a user or service account to the local Administrators group, you should use Group Policy to assign the specific rights that a user account needs to perform the tasks it needs to perform. Assign rights as close to the object as possible. For example, don't give a user account the ability to log in through Remote Desktop Services to all computers in an OU if the user account needs remote desktop access to only one or two computers. You can use Group Policy to configure the rights outlined in Table 12-1.

Table 12-1 User rights assignment policy

User rights assignment policy	Function
Access Credential Manager As A Trusted Caller	Used by Credential Manager during backup and restore. Do not assign this privilege to user accounts.
Access This Computer From The Network	Specifies which accounts and groups may connect to the computer from the network. Does not affect Remote Desktop Services.
Act As Part Of The Operating System	Allow a process to impersonate an account without requiring authentication. Processes that require this privilege are often assigned the Local System account.
Add Workstations To Domain	Grants the ability to join workstations to the domain.
Adjust Memory Quotas For A Process	Configures which security principals can adjust the maximum amount of memory assigned to a process.
Allow Log On Locally	Specify which accounts can sign in locally to a computer. Alter this policy on privileged access workstations to remove members of the Users group. This limits which accounts can sign in to a computer. By default, any authenticated user can sign in to any workstation or server except for a domain controller.
Allow Log On Through Remote Desktop Services	Determines which accounts and groups can sign in remotely to the computer using Remote Desktop. Configure this policy to allow users to access enhanced session mode for Hyper-V VMs.

User rights assignment policy	Function
Back Up Files And Directories	Grant permission to back up files, directories, registry, and other objects that the user account wouldn't normally have permission to. Assigning this right gives indirect access to all data on a computer. A person that holds the right can back up that data and then recover it in an environment over which they have complete control.
Bypass Traverse Checking	Gives users with this right the ability to traverse directories on which they don't have permission. Does not allow the user to list the contents of that directory.
Change The System Time	Accounts with this right can alter the system time. System time is separate from the computer's time zone.
Change The Time Zone	Accounts with this right can alter the time zone but not the system time.
Create A Pagefile	Allows the account assigned this right the ability to create and modify the page file.
Create A Token Object	Specifies which accounts can be used by processes to create tokens that allow accesses to local resources. You should not assign this right to any user who you do not want to give complete control of the system. This privilege can be used to elevate to local Administrator privileges.
Create Global Objects	Determines which accounts can create global objects that are available to all sessions. You should not assign this right to any user who you do not want to give complete control of the system. This privilege can be used to elevate to local Administrator privileges.
Create Permanent Shared Objects	Specify which accounts can create directory objects by using the object manager.
Create Symbolic Links	Specify which accounts can create symbolic links from the computer they are signed in to. Assign this right only to trusted users because symbolic links can expose security vulnerabilities in apps that aren't configured to support them.
Debug Programs	Specify which accounts can attach a debugger to processes within the operating system kernel. Only required by developers writing new system components. Rarely, if ever, necessary for developers writing applications. Removing the default Administrator from this account will substantially limit the likelihood that utilities, such as Mimikatz, can be used to scrape credentials.
Deny Access To This Computer From The Network	Blocks specified accounts and groups from accessing the computer from the network. This setting overrides the policy that allows access from the network.
Deny Log On As A Batch Job	Blocks specified accounts and groups from signing in as a batch job. Overrides the Log On As A Batch job policy.

CHAPTER 12

User rights assignment policy	Function
Deny Log On As A Service	When assigned, blocks service accounts from registering a process as a service. Overrides the Log On As A Service policy. Does not apply to Local System, Local Service, or Network Service accounts.
Deny Log On Locally	When assigned, blocks accounts from signing on locally. This policy overrides the allow Log On Locally policy.
Deny Log On Through Remote Desktop Services	When assigned, blocks accounts from signing in by using Remote Desktop Services. This policy overrides the allow sign in through Remote Desktop Services policy.
Enable Computer And User Accounts To Be Trusted For Delegation	Determines whether you can configure the Trusted For Delegation setting on a user or a computer object.
Force Shutdown From A Remote System	Accounts assigned this right are allowed to shut down computers from remote locations on the network.
Generate Security Audits	Determines which accounts can use processes to add items to the security log. Because this right allows interaction with the security log, it presents a security risk when you assign this to a user account.
Impersonate A Client After Authentication	Allows apps running on behalf of a user to impersonate a client. This right can be a security risk and you should assign it only to trusted users.
Increase A Process Working Set	Accounts assigned this right can increase or decrease the number of memory pages visible to the process in RAM.
Increase Scheduling Priority	Accounts assigned this right can change the scheduling priority of a process.
Load And Unload Device Drivers	Accounts assigned this right can dynamically load and unload device drivers into kernel mode. This right is separate from the right to load and unload Plug and Play drivers. Assigning this right is a security risk because it grants access to the kernel mode.
Lock Pages In Memory	Accounts assigned this right can use a process to keep data stored in physical memory, blocking that data from being paged to virtual memory.
Log On As A Batch Job	Accounts assigned this right can be signed in to the computer by means of a batch-queue facility. This right is only relevant to older versions of the Windows operating system, and you should not use it with current versions.
Log On As A Service	Allows a security principal to sign in as a service. You need to assign this right to any account that will be used by a service, rather than one of the built-in service accounts.

CHAPTER 12

User rights assignment policy	Function
Manage Auditing And Security Log	Users assigned this right can configure object access auditing options for resources such as files and AD DS objects. Users assigned this right can also view events in the security log and clear the security log. Because attackers are likely to clear the security log as a way of hiding their tracks, you should not assign this right to user accounts that would not normally be assigned local Administrator permissions on a computer.
Modify An Object Label	Users assigned this right can modify the integrity level of objects, including files, registry keys, or processes owned by other users.
Modify Firmware Environment Values	Determines which users can modify firmware environment variables. This policy is used primarily for modifying the boot configuration settings of Itanium-based computers.
Perform Volume Maintenance Tasks	Determines which accounts can perform maintenance tasks on a volume. Assigning this right is a security risk because it might allow access to data stored on the volume.
Profile Single Process	Determines which accounts can leverage performance-monitoring tools to monitor nonsystem processes.
Profile System Performance	Determines which accounts can leverage performance-monitoring tools to monitor system processes.
Remove Computer From Docking Station	When assigned, the user account can undock a portable computer from a docking station without signing in.
Replace A Process Level Token	When assigned, the account can call the *CreateProcessAsUser* API so that one service can trigger another.
Restore Files And Directories	Allows users assigned this right the ability to bypass permissions on files, directories, and the registry, so that they can overwrite these objects with restored data. This right represents a security risk because a user account assigned this right can overwrite registry settings and replace existing permissions.
Shut Down The System	Assigns the ability for a locally signed-in user to shut down the operating system.
Synchronize Directory Service Data	Assigns the ability to synchronize AD DS data.
Take Ownership Of Files Or Other Objects	When assigned, the account can take ownership of any securable object, including AD DS objects, files, folders, registry keys, processes, and threads. Represents a security risk because it allows an assigned user the ability to take control of any securable object.

CHAPTER 12

Service accounts

Service accounts allow services running on a computer to interact with the operating system as well as resources on the network. Windows Server uses three types of built-in service accounts, each of which is suitable for a specific set of circumstances. These accounts are as follows:

- The Local System (*NT AUTHORITY\SYSTEM*) account has privileges that are equivalent to those assigned to a user account that is a member of the local Administrators group on the computer. A service that uses this account can act by using the computer account's credentials when interacting with other resources on the network.

- The Local Service (*NT AUTHORITY\LocalService*) account has privileges that are equivalent to those assigned to a user account that is a member of the local Users group on the computer. A service that uses this account can access resources on the network without credentials. You use this account when a service doesn't need to interact with resources on the network and doesn't need local Administrator privileges on the computer on which it's running.

- The Network Service (*NT AUTHORITY\NetworkService*) account has privileges that are equivalent to those assigned to a user account that's a member of the local Users group on the computer. A service that uses this account accesses resources on the network by using the computer account's credentials.

In the past, when you've needed to create a custom service account, you've probably created a user account and then assigned it an appropriate set of permissions. The challenge with this type of account is password management. Many organizations configure custom service accounts with passwords that never expire.

Group Managed Service Accounts

A group Managed Service Account (gMSA) is a special type of account that has AD DS manage its password. The password of a gMSA is updated every 30 days. You don't need to know the password of a gMSA, even when configuring a service to use that password, because gMSA accounts provide you with a domain-based service account identity without all the hassle of service account password management.

You can use a gMSA only if the forest is running at the Windows Server 2012 functional level or higher. You also must have deployed the master root key for AD DS. You can deploy the master root key by running the following command using an account that is a member of the Enterprise Admins group:

```
Add-KdsRootKey -EffectiveTime ((get-date).addhours(-10))
```

You create the gMSA using the New-ADServiceAccount cmdlet. When creating the account, you specify a hostname as well as service principle names. These should be associated with the purpose for which you're creating the gMSA. For example, run this command to create a new gMSA named *SYD-SVC1* that's associated with the hostname *SYD-SVC1.adatum.com*:

```
New-ADServiceAccount SYD-SVC1 -DNSHOSTNAME SYD-SVC1.adatum.com
```

gMSAs are stored in the Managed Service Accounts container.

Once the gMSA is created, you need to configure permissions for specific computers to be able to install and use the account. The simplest way to do this is to create a security group and then use the `Set-ADServiceAccount` cmdlet to assign the group permissions to the account. You then add computers to the group. For example, to allow computers in the *SYD-SVRS* group to use the *SYD-SVC1* gMSA, run this command:

```
Set-ADServiceAccount -Identity SYD-SVC1 -PrincipalsAllowedToRetrieveManagedPassword
SYD-SVRS
```

Once you've added a computer to the group that you've given permission to retrieve the account, you can install the account on the computer using the `Install-ADServiceAccount` cmdlet. Once the account is installed, you can assign it to a service by setting the Log On settings for the service, as shown in Figure 12-1. You only need to specify the account name and can browse to the account. You don't need to specify the password setting because the password is managed by Active Directory.

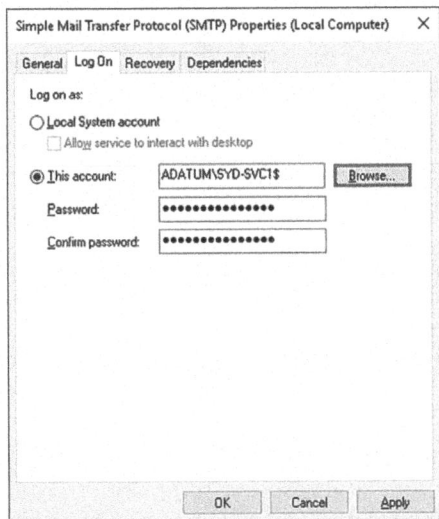

Figure 12-1   Group Managed Service Account

A virtual account is the computer local equivalent of a group Managed Service Account. You can create a virtual account by editing the properties of a service and setting the account name to *NT SERVICE\<ServiceName>*. As with a gMSA, you don't need to specify a password because this is managed automatically by the operating system.

> ## More Info
> ### Group Managed Service Accounts
> You can learn more about group Managed Service Accounts at *https://docs.micro-soft.com/en-us/windows-server/security/group-managed-service-accounts/group-managed-service-accounts-overview*.

Delegated Managed Service Accounts

Delegated Managed Service Accounts (dMSAs) are domain accounts tied to a single service on one host. Similar to gMSAs, they simplify password management because Active Directory automatically manages the account's password, and administrators can delegate specific rights for service use. dMSAs are typically used when a standalone service account with minimal privileges is required. dMSAs require Windows Server 2025 or later.

To enable dMSA usage on a computer, run the following command to update the registry:

```
$params = @{
Path = "HKLM:\SOFTWARE\Microsoft\Windows\CurrentVersion\Policies\System\Kerberos\
Parameters"
Name = "DelegatedMSAEnabled"
Value = 1
Type = "DWORD"
}
Set-ItemProperty @params
```

To create a dMSA, run the following code:

```
$params = @{
  Name = "YourDmsaName"
  DNSHostName = "YourHostName.yourdomain.com"
  CreateDelegatedServiceAccount = $true
  KerberosEncryptionType = "AES256"
  PrincipalsAllowedToRetrieveManagedPassword = "Machine$"
}
New-ADServiceAccount @params
# Set msDS-DelegatedMSAState to 3
$params = @{
  Identity  = "YourDmsaName"
  Replace   = @{ "msDS-DelegatedMSAState" = 3 }
}
Set-ADServiceAccount @params
```

In the target computer, install the dMSA using the `Install-ADServiceAccount` cmdlet. For example, to install the databaseservice dMSA, run the following command:

```
Install-ADServiceAccount -Identity databaseservice
```

Once the dMSA is installed, you can configure the dMSA to be used by the target service on the Log On tab of the service's properties.

Keep the following in mind when considering dMSA versus gMSA:

- dMSA allows you to replace a single-server legacy service account with a device-bound identity. This provides the strongest hardening because the secret stays on DC. dMSA provides per-device scoping but requires the computer to be running Windows Server 2025 or later.

- gMSA allows you to create one identity used by multiple hosts, which might be appropriate for web farms, app pools, and scheduled tasks. gMSA provide automatic password rotation. gMSA is appropriate for scale-out services and compatible with all supported versions of Windows Server.

Just Enough Administration

Just Enough Administration (JEA) allows you to implement Role-Based Access Control (RBAC) functionality through Windows PowerShell remoting. JEA allows you to specify which PowerShell cmdlets and functions can be used when connected to a specific endpoint. You can go further and specify which parameters within those cmdlets and functions are authorized; you can even specify which values can be used with those parameters.

For example, you could create a JEA endpoint where a user is able to run the `Restart-Service` command, but only where the `Name` parameter is set to DHCPServer. This would allow the user to restart the DHCPServer on the computer they connected to, but it would not restart any other service on the computer.

You can also configure a JEA endpoint to allow other command-line commands to be run, such as *whoami.exe*, though the drawback of this is that you don't have the same level of control when restricting how that command can be run.

JEA endpoints can leverage virtual accounts. This means that activities performed on the computer through the endpoint use a special temporary virtual account rather than the user's account. This temporary virtual account has local Administrator privileges but is constrained to only using the cmdlets, functions, parameters, and values defined by JEA. The benefits of this include the following:

- The user's credentials are not stored on the remote system. If the remote system is compromised, the user's credentials are not subject to credential theft and cannot be used to traverse the network to gain access to other hosts.

- The user account used to connect to the endpoint does not need to be privileged. The endpoint simply needs to be configured to allow connections from specified user accounts.

CHAPTER 12

- The virtual account is limited to the system on which it's hosted. The virtual account cannot be used to connect to remote systems. Attackers cannot use a compromised virtual account to access other protected servers.

- The virtual account has local administrator privileges but is limited to performing only the activities defined by JEA. You have the option of configuring the virtual account with the membership of a group other than the local administrators group to further reduce privileges.

JEA works on Windows Server 2016 and later and Windows 10 and later. It also functions on previous versions of Windows client and server as long as Windows Management 5.0 is installed. Virtual accounts are not available when using JEA on Windows 7 or Windows 2008 R2, and all activities are performed using the privileges assigned to the account connecting to the JEA endpoint.

Inside OUT

JEA drawbacks

The biggest drawback to JEA is the amount of time that it takes to configure manually. You'll need to customize each JEA endpoint, which requires that you understand exactly which cmdlets, functions, parameters, and values are required to perform specific tasks. This is somewhat easier today than it has been in the past given integration of AI tools such as GitHub Copilot into VS Code, and creating JEA artifacts using AI tools is increasingly common. The other drawback of JEA is that it relies upon administrative tasks being performed using the command line. While most Windows Server administrators are comfortable performing tasks using PowerShell, some may be reluctant to be placed in a position where they can use only PowerShell for specific tasks rather than falling back on the RSAT consoles. This may change with AI autocompletion being built in to future versions of command-line environments.

Role-capability files

A role-capability file is a special file that allows you to specify what tasks you can perform when connected to a JEA endpoint. You can do only tasks that are explicitly allowed in the role-capability file.

You can create a new blank role-capability file by using the New-PSRoleCapabilityFile cmdlet. Role-capability files use the .psrc extension. For example, run this command to create a new role capability file for a role that allows someone to manage a DNS server:

```
New-PSRoleCapabilityFile -Path .\DNSOps.psrc
```

Inside OUT

Authoring JEA

When creating JEA configurations, it usually makes sense to put them in their own folders. For example, create a DNSOps folder to store all the files related to configuring the DNSOps JEA configuration.

Once the .psrc file is created, you edit the role-capability file and add the cmdlets, functions, and external commands that are available when a user is connected to the endpoint. You can allow entire Windows PowerShell cmdlets or functions or list which parameters and parameter values can be used.

You can edit a role-capability file in VS Code or PowerShell ISE. Editing the file involves commenting out the appropriate sections and filling them in with the configuration items that you want to set.

Inside OUT

Cmdlets, functions, and aliases

Authoring role-capability files is one of those few times when you need to know whether something in PowerShell is a cmdlet or function. Mostly, people refer to commands in PowerShell as cmdlets, but some are actually functions and others are aliases. You need to know the appropriate type when configuring a role-capability file because if you put a function in as an allowed cmdlet, you won't get the expected result. You can figure out which designation is appropriate using the Get-Command cmdlet or by querying your favorite AI chatbot.

Table 12-2 describes the different options that you can configure in a role-capability file.

Table 12-2   Role-capability files

Capability	Description
ModulesToImport	JEA auto-loads standard modules, so you probably don't need to use this unless you need to import custom modules.
VisibleAliases	Specifies which aliases to make available in the JEA session. Even if an aliased cmdlet is available, the alias won't be available unless it's here.

Capability	Description
VisibleCmdlets	Lists which Windows PowerShell cmdlets are available in the session. You can extend this by allowing all parameters and parameter values to be used, or you can limit cmdlets to particular parameters and parameter values. For example, use the following syntax, if you want to allow the `Restart-Service` cmdlet to only be used to restart the DNS service: `VisibleCmdlets = @{ Name = 'Restart-Service'; Parameters = @{ Name='Name'; ValidateSet = 'DNS'}}`
VisibleFunctions	This field lists which Windows PowerShell functions are available in the session. You can choose to list functions, allowing all parameters and parameter values to be used, or you can limit functions to particular parameters and parameter values. For example, if you want to allow the Add-DNSServerResourceRecord, Get-DNS-ServerResourceRecord, and Remove-DNSServerResource functions to be used, you would use the following syntax: `VisibleFunctions = 'Add-DNSServerResourceRecord', 'Get-DNSServerResourceRecord', 'Remove-DNSServerResourceRecord'`
VisibleExternal-Commands	This field allows users who are connected to the session to run external commands. For example, you can use this field to allow access to `c:\windows\system32\whoami.exe` so that users connected to the JEA session can identify their security context by using the following syntax: `VisibleExternalCommands = 'C:\Windows\System32\whoami.exe'`
VisibleProviders	This field lists Windows PowerShell providers that are visible to the session.
ScriptsToProcess	This field allows you to configure Windows PowerShell scripts to run automatically when the session is started.
AliasDefinitions	This field allows you to define Windows PowerShell aliases for the JEA session.
FunctionDefinitions	This field allows you to define Windows PowerShell functions for the JEA session.
VariableDefinitions	This field allows you to define Windows PowerShell variables for the JEA session.
EnvironmentVariables	This field allows you to specify environment variables for the JEA session.
TypesToProcess	This field allows you to configure Windows PowerShell type files to load for the JEA session.
FormatsToProcess	This field allows you to configure Windows PowerShell formats to load for the JEA session.
AssembliesToLoad	This field allows you to specify which assemblies to load for the JEA session.

Session-configuration files

Session-configuration files determine which role capabilities are mapped to specific security groups. For example, if you want to allow only members of the *CONTOS\DNSOps* security group to connect to the JEA endpoint that is defined by the DNSOps role-capability file, you would configure this in the session configuration file.

You use the `New-PSSessionConfigurationFile` cmdlet to create a session configuration file. These files use the *.pssc* extension. For example, to create a new session configuration file for the DNSOps role, run the following command:

```
New-PSSessionConfigurationFile -Path .\DNSOps.pssc -Full
```

Session configuration files have elements described in Table 12-3:

Table 12-3   Session configuration files

Field	Explanation
SessionType	This field allows you to configure the session's default settings. If you set this to `RestrictedRemoteServer`, you can use the `Get-Command`, `Get-FormatData`, `Select-Object`, `Get-Help`, `Measure-Object`, `Exit-PSSession`, `Clear-Host`, and `Out-Default` cmdlets. The session execution policy is set to `RemoteSigned`. Example: `SessionType = 'RestrictedRemoteServer'`
RoleDefinitions	You use the `RoleDefinitions` entry to assign role capabilities to specific security groups. These groups do not need to have any privileges and can be standard security groups. Example: `RoleDefinitions =@{'CONTOSO\DNSOps' = @{RoleCapabilities='DNSOps'}}`
RunAsVirtual-Account	When enabled, this field allows JEA to use a privileged virtual account created just for the JEA session. This virtual account has local Administrators privileges on member servers and is a member of the Domain Admins group on a domain controller. Use this option to ensure that credentials are not cached on the server that hosts the endpoint. Remember that you can configure the virtual account to be a member of groups other than the local Administrators group.
Transcript-Directory	This field allows you to specify the location where JEA activity transcripts are stored.
RunAsVirtual-AccountGroups	If you don't want the virtual account to be a member of the local Administrators group (or Domain Admins on a domain controller), you can instead use this field to specify the groups in which the virtual account is a member.

JEA endpoints

A JEA endpoint is a Windows PowerShell endpoint that you configure so that only specific authenticated users can connect to it. When those users connect, they have access to only the Windows PowerShell cmdlets, parameters, and values defined by the appropriate session-configuration file that links security groups and role capabilities. When you use endpoints with virtual accounts, the activity that a user performs on the server that hosts the endpoint occurs using the virtual account. This means that no domain-based administrative credentials are stored on the server that hosts the endpoint.

A server can have multiple JEA endpoints, and each JEA endpoint can be used for a different administrative task. For example, you could have a DNSOps endpoint to perform DNS adminis- trative tasks and an IISOps endpoint to perform Internet Information Server–related administra- tive tasks. Users aren't required to have privileged accounts that are members of groups, such as the local Administrators group, to connect to an endpoint. Once connected, users have the privileges assigned to the virtual account configured in the session-configuration file.

Inside OUT

Non-privileged groups

JEA lets you provide IT Ops staff with administrative privileges on specific computers without adding them to traditional privileged groups, such as the Domain Admins or Enterprise Admins group.

You create JEA endpoints by using the `Register-PSSessionConfiguration` cmdlet. When using this cmdlet, you specify an endpoint name and a session-configuration file hosted on the local machine.

For example, to create the endpoint DNSOps using the *DNSOps.pssc* session-configuration file, enact the following command and then restart the WinRM service:

```
Register-PSSessionConfiguration -Name DNSOps -Path .\DNSOps.pssc
```

You can use the `Get-PSSessionConfigurationFile` to determine which endpoints are present on a computer. A user who wants to connect to a JEA session endpoint uses the `Enter-PSSession` cmdlet with the `ConfigurationName` parameter. For example, to connect to the DNSOps JEA end- point on server MEL-DNS1, you would use the command

```
Enter-PSSession -ComputerName MEL-DNS1 -ConfigurationName DNSOps
```

Once you've verified that JEA works, you'll need to lock down the default PowerShell end- point. By default, only members of the local Administrators group can connect to this default endpoint, and if you've implemented JEA properly, this group shouldn't need to have very many members anyway.

> ## More Info
>
> **Just Enough Administration**
>
> You can learn more about JEA at *https://aka.ms/JEA*.

Privileged Access Management

Privileged Access Management (PAM), also known as Just In Time (JIT) Administration, works on the concept that users can be granted permission for a finite amount of time rather than permanently. It uses temporary membership of a security group that has been delegated privileges, rather than permanent membership of a security group that has been delegated privileges, to accomplish this goal.

For example, a user named Rooslan requires that his password be reset and submits a ticket to the service desk to have Lynette perform this task. In a traditional environment, Lynette would use an account that is a member of a security group that has been delegated the reset-password privilege. In a PAM environment, Lynette requests the privilege to change Rooslan's user account password. The PAM process adds Lynette's user account temporarily to a group that has been delegated the reset password privilege on Rooslan's user account. Lynette then reset's Rooslan's user account password. After a certain period has elapsed, the PAM process removes Lynette's account from this group, removing the *reset-password* privilege for Rooslan's user account from Lynette's user account.

Privileges are assigned temporarily rather than permanently. Rather than assigning the IT Operations team privileged accounts, the IT Operations team members have standard accounts that are assigned privileges only when those privileges are required. PAM can be configured so that privileges are assigned when requested, assigned only after approval has been sought and granted, or assigned because of a mixture of these methods depending on which privilege is being requested. For example, requesting permission to reset the password of a nonprivileged user account might occur automatically, whereas permission to add a domain controller to the domain might require approval.

PAM benefits

When properly implemented, PAM can provide the following security improvements:

- You can configure your environment so that all accounts that the IT Operations team uses are standard user accounts. Privileges are only granted to these accounts after being requested and approved, and they're temporary. If a user account used by a member of the IT Operations team becomes compromised, the attacker gains no additional privi-leges beyond those assigned to a standard user account because any privileges that the account might hold are only ever assigned on a temporary basis.

- All requests for privileges are logged. In high-security environments, privilege use can be further tracked, with the activities of a user account granted temporary privileges written to a log file.

Once privileges are granted, a user needs to establish a new session by opening a new Windows PowerShell session or by signing out and signing in again to leverage the new group member-ships configured for their account.

PAM components

A PAM deployment consists of the following elements:

- **Administrative forest**   This is an ESAE forest in which you have deployed Microsoft Identity Manager (MIM) 2016. MIM 2016 remains supported until January 2029. Accounts from this forest are used to perform administrative tasks. This is also known as the Bastion forest.

- **A production forest**   This is the forest that hosts the resources used on a daily basis by the organization.

- **Shadow principals**   A shadow principal is a copy of an account or group that exists in the production or source forest. Shadow security groups that are used in PAM use a process called SID History mirroring. SID History mirroring allows the shadow security group in the administrative forest to have the security identifier of the security group in the production or source forest. When a user is added to a PAM role, MIM adds the user's shadow account in the administrative forest to the shadow group in the administrative forest. When a user logs in by using this account, the user's Kerberos token then includes a security identifier that matches the security identifier of the original group from the production forest. This functionally makes the user a member of the group that the shadow group is mirroring.

- **PAM Client**   This client includes a collection of Windows PowerShell cmdlets or a cus-tom solution that interacts with the PAM REST API to allow a PAM user to query and inter-act with the MIM PAM functionality. The PAM client is only required on computers where it's necessary to request access to a PAM role.

- **MIM Service**   The MIM server manages the privileged account management process, including adding and removing shadow principals from shadow groups when a PAM role is granted and when it expires.

- **MIM Portal**   The MIM Portal is a SharePoint site. It provides management and configu-ration functionality. For example, IT Operations users can sign in to this site to request privileges.

- **MIM Service Database**   The MIM service database can be hosted on SQL Server 2012 or later. This database holds configuration and identity information that the MIM Service uses.

- **PAM Component Service**   This manages the role-expiration process, removing the shadow account from the shadow group in the administrative forest.

- **PAM Monitoring Service**   This monitors the production forest and duplicates changes to the administrative forest or the MIM service.

- **PAM REST API**   This can be used to enable a custom client to interact with PAM.

PAM users and groups

You use the `New-PAMUser` cmdlet, which is available when you install MIM, to create a shadow user. When doing this, an existing PAM-created trust relationship between the ESAE forest and the production must exist. You must also specify the source domain and source account name. For example, to create a new shadow user based on the Lynette account in the *Adatum.com* domain, you would use the following command:

```
New-PAMUser -SourceDomain adatum.com -SourceAccountName Lynette
```

You use the `New-PAMGroup` cmdlet, available when you install MIM, to create a shadow group. When creating a shadow group, you need to specify the source group name, the source domain, and a source domain controller in the source domain. For example, to create a new shadow group for the *CorpAdmins* group in the *Adatum.com* domain by using the *mel-dc1.adatum.com* domain controller, issue the following command:

```
New-PAMGroup -SourceGroupName "CorpAdmins" -SourceDomain adatum.com -SourceDC mel-dc1.
adatum.com
```

PAM roles

A PAM role represents the privileged role to be requested. For example, you might configure a specific PAM role for performing password resets or another for configuring Active Directory Certificate Services. You can configure PAM role settings by viewing the properties of the PAM role in the MIM web interface. A PAM role consists of the following options:

- **Display Name**   This is the name of the PAM role.

- **PAM Privileges**   This is a list of security groups to which a user who is granted access to the role is temporarily added. This does not list the privileges actually assigned to this group. For example, if you delegate the Reset User Password privilege to the *CorpAdmins* group, this dialog box does not indicate that this privilege has been delegated. This dialog box also lists the name of the shadow principal, rather than the group in the original domain.

- **PAM Role TTL(sec)**   This is the maximum amount of time that the member can be granted this role. The default is 3,600 seconds (1 hour). You should configure the maximum lifetime for a Kerberos user ticket in line with the Time To Live (TTL) value to ensure that a user's ticket is updated to reflect the change in group membership after the PAM Role TTL expires.

- **MFA Enabled**   MIM's PAM functionality can be integrated with Azure Multifactor Authentication. When you enable this option, requests for a PAM role require two forms of authentication. This second form of authentication can include a text message or a telephone call to a registered number. When a text message is sent, the requesting user must enter the code sent to them. When a telephone call is made, the user must enter a PIN that they've previously configured.

- **Approval Required**   PAM roles can be configured so that PAM role membership is only granted if a PAM administrator approves the request. You configure PAM administrators by adding a user to the PAM Admins set. This can be done through the Sets section under Management Policy Rules in the MIM web console.

- **Availability Window Enabled**   When you configure an availability window for a role, the PAM role can be used only during certain hours. This provides an additional layer of security for a PAM role. For example, you might configure a role that allows modification to sensitive groups to be used only during business hours.

- **Description**   Use this option to provide a description of the PAM role.

Inside OUT

PAM and JEA

With JEA, you limit who can access a JEA endpoint on the basis of security group membership. With PAM, you add user accounts to security groups on a temporary rather than an ongoing basis. You can combine PAM with JEA to allow users to connect to JEA endpoints for a limited amount of time and to be able to do so only after they have explicitly requested access to a specific JEA endpoint.

More Info

Privileged Access Management

You can learn more about this subject at *https://learn.microsoft.com/microsoft-identity-manager/pam/privileged-identity-management-for-active-directory-domain-services*.

Windows Local Administrator Password Solution

Windows Local Administrator Password Solution (Windows LAPS) is a feature built in to Windows Server 2019 and later that enables the centralized management of local administrator passwords on domain-joined computers. Windows LAPS automatically manages the password of a specified local administrator account on domain-joined devices, backing it up to Active Directory for authorized retrieval. It also supports Directory Services Restore Mode (DSRM) account management on domain controllers. Once configured, LAPS rotates passwords per policy and stores those passwords in AD.

When Windows LAPS is enabled, you're able to manage local administrator passwords from Active Directory Users and Computers and PowerShell. Windows Local Administrator Password Solution is the replacement for Local Administrator Password Solution, which involved the download and installation of separate tools.

Windows LAPS has the following requirements:

- Requires a Windows Server 2016 domain functional level or higher for encrypted storage.

- Domain controllers must be running Windows Server 2019 or later.

- Windows LAPS–managed computers must be running Windows Server 2019 or later or Windows 10 or later.

- Prior to configuring Windows LAPS, ensure you take a backup of the Active Directory schema. You'll need schema modification privileges to deploy Windows LAPS.

Installing and configuring Windows LAPS

To install Windows LAPS, perform the following steps:

1. On a Windows Server domain controller or management server with the LAPS PowerShell module, run the following command to update the schema with the msLAPS-Password and msLAPS-EncryptedPassword attributes:

    ```
    Update-LapsADSchema -Verbose
    ```

2. You can verify that the schema has been updated by running this command:

    ```
    Get-ADObject -Identity "CN=msLAPS-Password,CN=Schema,CN=Configuration,DC=yourdomai
    n,DC=com"
    ```

3. Once the schema is prepared, configure each OU that hosts computer accounts so that the computers can update passwords by running the following command:

    ```
    Set-LapsADComputerSelfPermission -Identity "OU=YourOU,DC=yourdomain,DC=com"
    ```

4. Configure which groups have permission to access the stored passwords in Active Directory by running the following command:

```
Set-LapsADReadPasswordPermission -Identity "OU=YourOU,DC=yourdomain,DC=com"
-AllowedPrincipals "Domain\HelpDeskGroup"
```

5. Configure which groups have the ability to reset Windows LAPS–managed passwords using the following command:

```
Set-LapsADResetPasswordPermission -Identity "OU=YourOU,DC=yourdomain,DC=com"
-AllowedPrincipals "Domain\AdminGroup"
```

Windows LAPS group policy settings

Windows LAPS–related policies are located in the Computer Configuration\Policies\Administrative Templates\System\LAPS node of a group policy object on an up-to-date Windows Server 2019 or later domain controller. Table 12-4 lists Windows LAPS–related policies.

Table 12-4 Windows LAPS group policies

Policy Name	Description
BackupDirectory	Specifies password backup location (0: Disabled, 1: Entra ID, 2: AD)
AdministratorAccountName	Name of custom local admin account to manage (ignores built-in if set)
PasswordAgeDays	Max password age (1–365 days)
PasswordLength	Password length (8–64 characters).
PassphraseLength	Number of words in passphrase (3–10).
PasswordComplexity	Complexity level (1–4: Increasing characters, 5, improved readability, 6–8: Passphrases)
PostAuthenticationResetDelay	Delay after auth before actions (0–24 hours)
PostAuthenticationActions	Actions post-grace period (for example, reset, sign out, reboot)
ADPasswordEncryptionEnabled	Enables AD password encryption
ADPasswordEncryptionPrincipal	Group/user allowed to decrypt
ADEncryptedPasswordHistorySize	Number of historical encrypted passwords stored
ADBackupDSRMAccounts	Enables DSRM account backup on DCs
AutomaticAccountManagementEnabled	Auto-manages built-in admin (disables never-expire, and so on)

Working with passwords in Windows LAPS

You can retrieve passwords by using the LAPS tabs on computer objects. If this tab isn't visible, the schema has yet to be updated. You can retrieve passwords using the Get-LAPSADPassword cmdlet. For example, to retrieve the password from the computer named mel-fs1, run this command:

```
Get-LAPSADPassword -Identity mel-fs1 -AsPlainText
```

You can force rotation of the Windows LAPS password using the `Reset-LapsPassword` cmdlet.

Advanced auditing

There are two sets of audit policies in a Group Policy Object (GPO): traditional audit policies and advanced audit policies. The traditional audit policies are located in the *Computer Configuration\Policies\Windows Settings\Security Settings\Local Policies\Audit Policies* node. These are the audit policies that have been available with the Windows Server operating system since Windows 2000. The drawback of these policies is that they're general, and you can't be specific in the way you configure auditing. When you use these policies, you not only audit the events that you're interested in, but you also end up auditing many events that you don't need to know about.

The advanced audit policies enable you to be more specific in the types of activity you audit. The advanced audit policies are located under the *Computer Configuration\Policies\Windows Settings\Security Settings\Advanced Audit Policy Configuration* node.

There are 10 groups of audit policy settings and 61 individual audit policies available through Advanced Audit Policy Configuration. The audit policy groups contain the following settings:

- **Account Logon**   You can audit credential validation and Kerberos-specific operations.

- **Account Management**   You can audit account management operations, such as changes to computer accounts, user accounts, and group accounts.

- **Detailed Tracking**   You can audit encryption events, process creation, process termination, and RPC events.

- **DS Access**   You can audit Active Directory access and functionality.

- **Logon/Logoff**   You can audit logon, logoff, and other account activity events, including IPsec and Network Policy Server (NPS) events.

- **Object Access**   You can audit access to objects including files, folders, applications, and the registry.

- **Policy Change**   You can audit changes to audit policy.

- **Privilege Use**   You can audit the use of privileges.

- **System**   You can audit changes to the security subsystem.

- **Global Object Access Auditing**   You can configure expression-based audit policies for files and the registry.

Expression-based audit policies

Traditional object audit policies involve specifying a group and configuring the type of activities that trigger an event to be written to the security log. For example, you can specify that an audit event is written each time a member of the Managers group accesses a file in a specific folder.

Expression-based audit policies enable you to go further. These policies enable you to set conditions for when auditing might occur. For example, you might want to configure auditing so that tracking only occurs for members of the *Managers* group who have access to sensitive files when they access those files from computers that aren't part of the *Managers_Computers* group. This way, you don't bother tracking access when members of this group access sensitive files from within the office, but you do track all access to those sensitive files when members of this group are accessing them from an unusual location.

You can integrate expression-based audit policies with Dynamic Access Control (DAC) to create targeted audit policies that are based on user, computer, and resource claims. Instead of just adding claims based on user or device group membership, the claim can be based on document metadata, such as confidentiality settings and site location. You can configure expression-based audit policies at the file or folder level or apply them through Group Policy by using policies in the Global Object Access Auditing node of Advanced Audit Policy Configuration.

File and folder auditing

After you configure object access auditing either through traditional or advanced audit policies, you can configure auditing at the file and folder level. The simplest way to configure auditing is at the folder level because you can configure all folders and subfolders to inherit those auditing settings. If you change the auditing settings at the folder level, you can use the Replace All Child Object Auditing Entries option to apply the new auditing settings to the folder's child files and folders.

You can configure auditing for a specific file and folder through the Advanced button on the Security tab of the object's properties. You can configure basic success and failure auditing. You can also configure expression-based auditing so that a specific security group member's activity is audited only if other conditions, such as membership of other security groups, are also met.

The advantage of using Global Object Access Auditing is that when you configure it, you can use file classification to apply metadata to files and then automatically have auditing enabled for those files. For example, by using file classification and DAC, you can configure a Windows Server file server so that all files containing the phrase "code secret" are marked as Sensitive. You can then configure Global Object Access Auditing so that all attempts to access files marked as Sensitive are automatically audited. Instead of having an administrator track down all the files that are sensitive and configuring auditing on those files, the process is automatic. All that needs to happen to trigger the audit is that the phrase "code secret" is included in the file.

Using auditpol with auditing

`Auditpol.exe` is a command-line utility that you can use to configure and manage audit policy settings from an elevated command prompt. You can use `auditpol.exe` to perform the following tasks:

- View the current audit policy settings with the `/Get` subcommand

- Set audit policy settings with the `/Set` subcommand

- Display selectable policy elements with the `/List` subcommand

- Backup and restore audit policies using the `/Backup` and `/Restore` subcommands

- Delete all per-user audit policy settings and reset the system policy settings using the `/Clear` subcommand

- Remove all per-user audit policy settings and disable all system policy settings using the `/Remove` subcommand

For example, to enable success and failure auditing for the File System subcategory of Object Access, execute the following command:

```
Auditpol.exe /set /subcategory:"File System" /success:Enable /failure:Enable
```

To view the current audit policy settings for all audit policies, issue the following command:

```
Auditpol.exe /get /category:*
```

To view the current audit policy settings for a specific category, such as Object Access, issue the following command:

```
Auditpol.exe /get /category:"Object Access"
```

Windows Firewall with Advanced Security

Windows Firewall with Advanced Security (WFAS) is a bidirectional, host-level firewall. This means not only can you set it to protect a host from incoming traffic, but you can also have it block all or specific outgoing traffic. Generally, you can control outbound traffic only on very sensitive hosts. Controlling outbound traffic minimizes the chance of malware infecting the server that is phoning home. On sensitive hosts, you should allow outbound traffic on a per-application rule. For example, you should create a rule to allow a specific browser to communicate with the Internet rather than just allowing outbound traffic on port 80.

WFAS allows for the creation of rules based on program, port, or predefined rules. There are 45 predefined rules, which include categories such as Remote Desktop, Windows Firewall Remote Management, File and Printer Sharing, and Core Networking. One of the useful things about WFAS is that it generally enables the appropriate firewall rules when you enable a specific role,

role service, or feature. These default rules are appropriate most of the time, but you may want to edit the properties of these rules to make them more secure.

Firewall profiles

Firewall profiles allow you to treat traffic differently depending on the network to which the computer is connected. For example, the same server might be connected to the following:

- A remote site through a VPN connection that has the private profile applied

- A perimeter network by a network adapter, where the connection has the public profile applied

- To the organization's internal network through a second adapter that has the domain profile applied

The advantage of separate profiles is that each one allows you to have separate sets of firewall rules applied. You might allow Distributed File System (DFS) traffic on one profile, web traffic on another, and SMTP traffic on a third.

Profiles are independent of each other; the settings that you configure for one profile do not apply to other profiles. You can configure the following properties for each profile:

- **Firewall State**   You can set this to On (default) or Off.

- **Inbound Connections**   You can set this to Block (default), Block All, or Allow. The latter means firewall rules that allow connections are ignored.

- **Outbound Connections**   You can set this to Block or Allow (default).

- **Settings**   This allows you to configure whether notifications are displayed, whether unicast responses are transmitted to multicast or broadcast traffic, and whether to merge rules when rules apply both locally and through Group Policy.

- **Logging**   This allows you to specify logging settings.

Firewall logs are written to the %systemroot%\system32\LogFiles\Firewall\pfirewall. log file. The default settings don't log dropped packets or successful connections, which means that, unless you change the defaults, nothing is logged. Firewall logging is most useful when you've determined that a particular service is unavailable to the network because of the firewall.

You can turn on firewall logging on a per-profile basis by clicking the Customize button next to Logging on each profile's properties page. This displays the Customize Logging Settings dialog shown in Figure 12-2. You can then enable logging for dropped packets and successful connections. If you're having trouble with a newly installed service on a server, enable the logging of dropped packets to determine the properties of the packets dropped, so that you can create a firewall rule that allows your service to be accessed from the network.

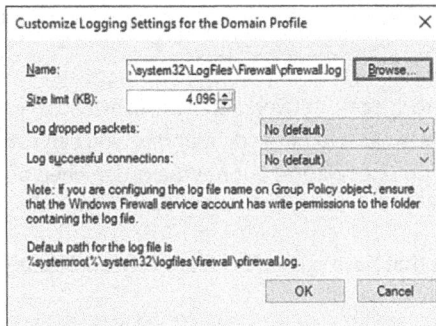

Figure 12-2   Custom logging settings

Inbound rules

Inbound rules are based on program, port, or one of 45 predefined categories, such as Branch-Cache Content Retrieval or Network Policy Server. You can also create custom rules that include a mixture of these, where you specify a program and a port as well as a rule scope. For example, you can use a custom rule to block all incoming traffic on port 80 to a particular application but not block port 80 traffic to other applications on the server. The basic aspects of creating a firewall rule involve specifying the following things:

- **A program or port**   When you specify a port, you must choose whether the rule applies to TCP or UDP traffic.

- **What action should be taken**   You can allow the connection, in which case, all traffic that matches the rule is allowed by the firewall. You can allow the connection if it's authenticated, in which case, traffic that meets the IPsec authentication requirements and the connection security rules is allowed, but traffic that isn't properly authenticated according to these conditions is dropped.

- **The network profiles in which the rule applies**   In general, rules should apply in all profiles, but there might be circumstances where you want to allow traffic from an interface connected to a domain network but block the same traffic if it comes from an interface connected to a public network.

After you have created the rule, you can then edit the rule's properties. Editing the rule's properties allows you to configure more advanced options than are present in the Rule Creation Wizard. By editing a rule's properties, you can

- Configure a rule to apply to a service rather than just a program.

- Limit the computers that can make authenticated connections. By default, if you configure the Allow Traffic If The Connection Is Authenticated option, any computer that can authenticate is able to successfully transmit traffic. By editing a firewall's rules, you can limit traffic to specific computers, rather than all authenticated computers. You can do the same with user accounts, limiting successful connections to specific users when authentication has successfully occurred.

- Edit the rule's scope, which is the local and remote IP address ranges to which the rule applies. You can also do this when you create a custom rule.

- Configure whether the rule applies to specific network interfaces, instead of just network profiles. For example, if your computer has two network adapters, you can configure a rule to apply so that it allows traffic on one adapter but not the other when both adapters have the same profile set.

- Configure whether to allow packets that have passed across a Network Address Translation (NAT) device.

Creating outbound rules

Default settings for Windows Firewall with Advanced Security don't block outbound traffic. In high-security environments, you should consider using outbound rules to block all but authorized outbound traffic.

The process for creating an outbound rule is almost identical to the process for creating an inbound rule. You specify the rule type on the New Outbound Rule Wizard, you specify whether the connection is blocked, allowed, or allowed only if authenticated, and you specify the network profiles in which the rule is active. By editing the properties of the rule after the rule is created, you can configure all of the advanced options configurable for inbound rules, such as rule scope, specific network interfaces, and to which computers or users the rule allows outbound connections.

Configuring IPsec

The IPsec Settings tab of Firewall Properties allows you to configure how IPsec is used when applied in connection security rules. On the tab itself, shown in Figure 12-3, you can configure whether you want to customize the IPsec defaults, exempt Internet Control Message Protocol (ICMP) traffic from IPsec, and whether you want to configure IPsec tunnel authorization.

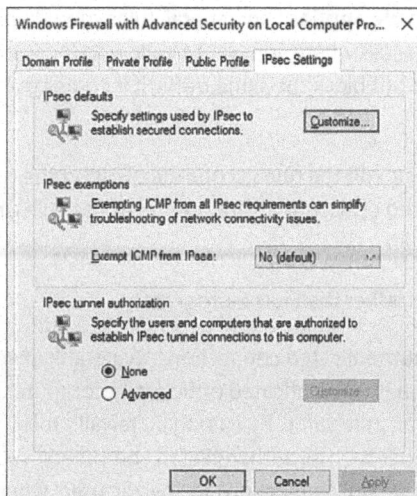

Figure 12-3   IPsec settings

Exempting ICMP traffic can be useful for diagnostic purposes because many administrators use the ping utility to diagnose whether a host has network connectivity. If connection security rules are enabled, the default IPsec settings mean that a successful IPsec negotiation must occur prior to an ICMP response being sent. If the IPsec negotiation is the problem, enabling ICMP response allows you to verify that there is network connectivity and that the problem just lies a bit further up the network stack.

If you click the Customize button next to the IPsec defaults, you can change the Key Exchange, Data Protection, and Authentication Method (see Figure 12-4). The default key exchange uses Diffie-Hellman Group 2 key exchange algorithm with a key lifetime of 480 minutes. You can modify these settings so that they use more secure methods, but this may reduce the ability to interact with some third-party devices.

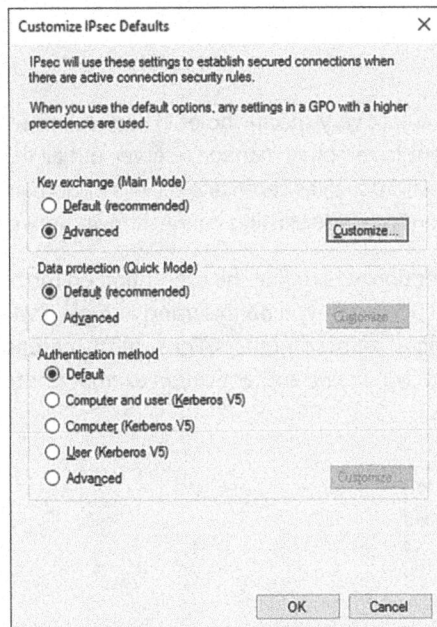

Figure 12-4 Customize IPsec defaults

The data protection settings allow you to configure the algorithms used for data integrity and encryption. Normally, there isn't much reason to change this; however, if you feel you need the strongest encryption possible to protect your organization's network traffic, you can use a different algorithm, such as AES-CBC with a 256-bit key length. In general, the stronger the encryption, the greater the resources needed to support that encryption. Although you can make the protection a lot stronger, the benefit of doing so might be only marginal given the value of the data being protected.

The default authentication method used for IPsec connections is Computer (Kerberos V5). This means that a domain controller must be present to verify the identity of each computer before an IPsec session can be established. You can also use Computer (NTLMv2), a computer certificate from this certification authority (CA), or a preshared key to authenticate IPsec connections. A preshared key is not a recommended method of authentication, but it might be necessary if there isn't a certificate services infrastructure and computers aren't members of a domain.

Connection security rules

Connection security rules are a more intelligent type of firewall rule than a simple port-based rule. An interesting adaption to firewalls has been an increase of traffic through ports traditionally used for common applications. Connection security rules are about trusting incoming connections based on the identity of the remote host, rather than the remote host's network address or the communication port it uses.

Authentication exemptions

Authentication exemptions allow you to create very specific holes in connection security rules. These are useful in the event that you want to remotely manage a server, but all the servers that would normally authenticate your connection, such as certificate servers or domain controllers, are unavailable. Authentication exemptions override existing connection security rules.

When you create an authentication exemption, you define the exemption on the basis of the source computer's IP address. As Figure 12-5 shows, you do this using a single IPv4 or IPv6 address, an IP address range, or a predefined set of computers. For security reasons, you should limit the number of IP addresses for which you create authentication exemptions to one or two specific privileged-access workstations.

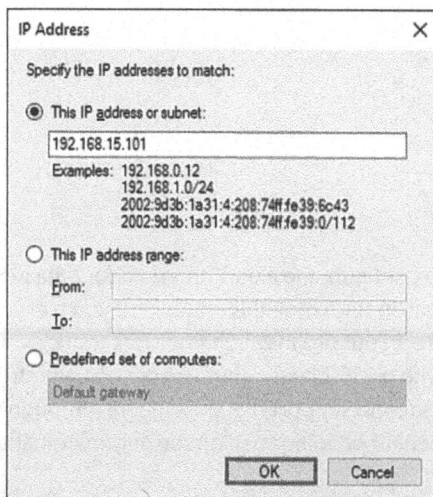

Figure 12-5   Authentication exemption

To create an authentication exemption, perform the following steps:

1. In Windows Firewall With Advanced Security, right-click the Connection Security Rules node and then click New Rule. This opens the New Connection Security Rule Wizard. Select Authentication Exemption.

2. In the Exempt Computers dialog, click Add.

3. In the IP Address dialog, enter the IP address, subnet, or IP address range of the computers that you want to exempt from connection security rules. You can also choose from a list of predefined addresses, including the Default Gateway, DHCP servers, the local subnet, or DNS servers.

4. Select the profile to which you want the rule to apply and specify a rule name.

Isolation rules

Isolation rules allow you to limit communication so that a server or computer communicates only with computers that have authenticated with it. Sometimes, these are called domain isolation policies because they limit hosts to only communicating with other servers that are members of the same Active Directory forest. When you configure an isolation rule, it applies to all traffic from all hosts; this is unlike tunnel or server-to-server rules, which apply to traffic to and from specific hosts.

To create an isolation rule, perform the following steps:

1. In Windows Firewall With Advanced Security, right-click the Connection Security Rules node and then click New Rule. This opens the New Connection Security Rule Wizard. Select Isolation and then click Next.

2. On the Requirements page, as shown in Figure 12-6, choose one of the following:

    -   Request Authentication For Inbound And Outbound Connections

    -   Require Authentication For Inbound Connections And Request Authentication For Outbound Connections

    -   Require Authentication For Inbound And Outbound Connections

3. Requiring authentication on both inbound and outbound connections is the strongest form of protection because it means that communication can be performed only with authenticated hosts.

CHAPTER 12

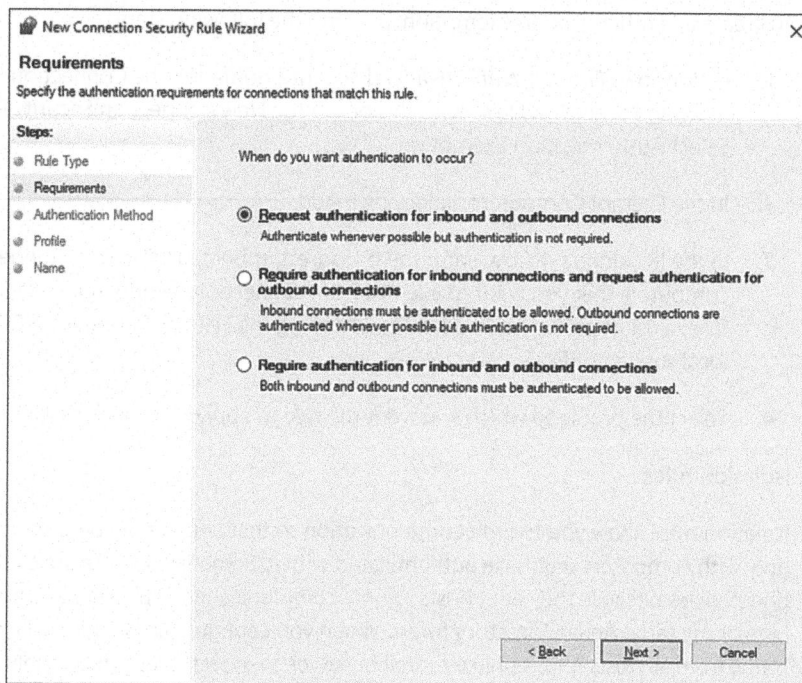

Figure 12-6   Connection security rule

4. Choose the authentication method. The default is to use the authentication method specified on the IPsec Settings tab of Firewall Properties. You can also choose between computer and/or user leveraging Kerberos version 5 for authentication, or you can configure advanced authentication options, which include certificate-based authentication. It's also possible, though not recommended, to use a preshared key for authentication, which is useful when you need to communicate with computers running third-party operating systems.

5. The final step in setting up a connection security rule is to configure the profiles in which the rule applies. Unless there is a good reason otherwise, you should apply connection security rules in all profiles.

Server-to-server rules

Server-to-server rules are used to authenticate communication between two groups of computers. This can be a rule authenticating and encrypting a single computer-to-computer connection, such as between a web server and a database server or between computers on two separate subnets. Server-to-server rules differ from isolation rules; isolation rules apply to communication from all hosts, whereas server-to-server rules apply to specific hosts.

To create a server-to-server rule, perform the following steps:

1. In Windows Firewall With Advanced Security, right-click the Connection Security Rules node and then click New Rule. This opens the New Connection Security Rule Wizard. Select the Server-To-Server rule.

2. In the Endpoints dialog page, enter the IP addresses of the computers that are at one end of the connection and the IP addresses of the computers that are at the other end of the connection. Figure 12-7 shows a rule defining one endpoint as the subnet 192.168.15.0/24, and the other endpoint as subnet 192.168.16.0/24.

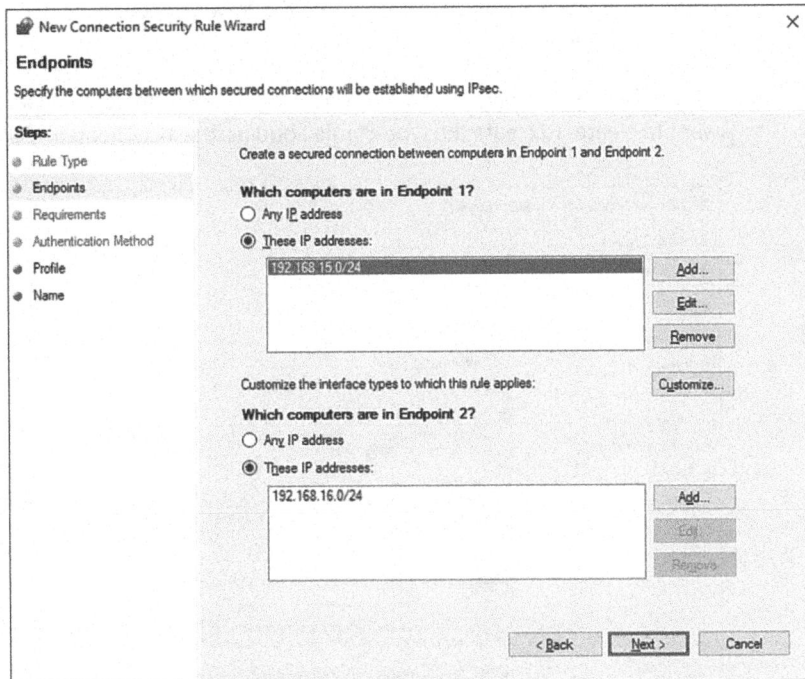

Figure 12-7   Connection security rule endpoints

3. On the Requirements page, specify how you want authentication to occur. If you want only this computer to communicate on the profile using encrypted and authenticated connections, select Require Authentication For Inbound And Outbound Connections.

4. Specify the authentication method. The default is to use a computer certificate issued by a designated CA. You can also specify computer-based Kerberos, NTLMv2, or a preshared key.

5. Specify the firewall profiles in which this connection security rule applies and add a name for the rule.

Tunnel rules

Tunnel rules allow client computers to communicate with computers on a secure network behind a remote gateway. For example, if you have a single server located at a branch office that you want to connect to an internal network at another office, using a tunnel rule, you specify the location of a host that functions as a gateway to that secure network. This allows you to create an IPsec tunnel through which secure communication can occur.

To create a tunnel rule, perform the following steps:

1. In Windows Firewall With Advanced Security, right-click the Connection Security Rules node and then click New Rule. This opens the New Connection Security Rule Wizard. Select Tunnel Rule.

2. On the Tunnel Type page, as shown in Figure 12-8, determine the type of tunnel that you want to create. To create the type of rule I outlined, select Client-To-Gateway.

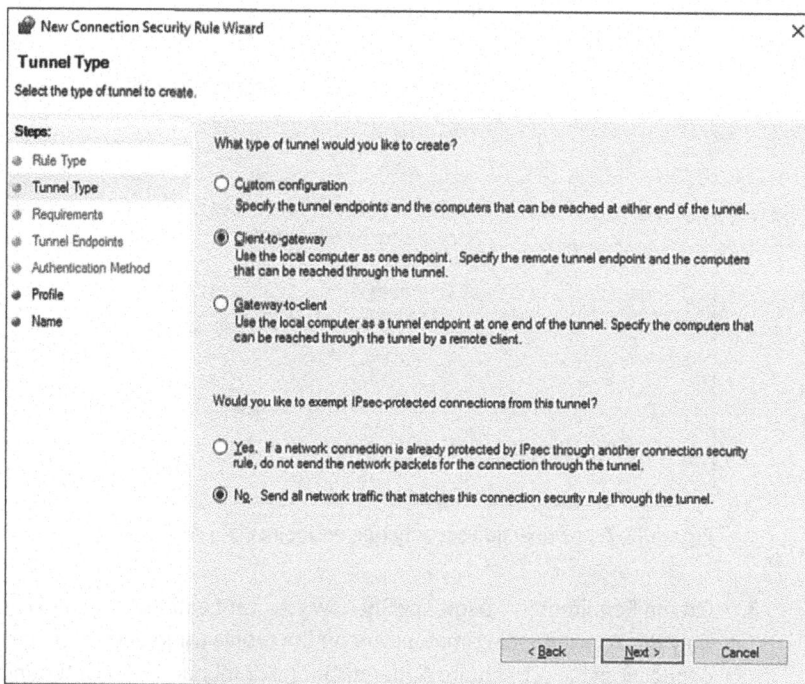

Figure 12-8   Tunnel Type

3. Choose whether you want to require authentication for inbound and outbound connections.

4. Specify the address of the computer that functions as the gateway to the secure network.

5. Specify the authentication method. The default is to use a computer certificate issued by a designated CA. You can also specify computer-based Kerberos, NTLMv2, or preshared key.

6. Specify the firewall profiles in which this connection security rule applies and add a name for the rule.

More Info

Windows Firewall with Advanced Security

You can learn more about deploying and managing Windows Firewall with Advanced Security, even though it deals with a previous version of Windows Server, at *https:// docs.microsoft.com/en-us/windows/security/threat-protection/windows-firewall/ windows-firewall-with-advanced-security*.

Shielded VMs

Shielded VMs are a special type of VM configuration that are protected against attacks against originating from the virtualization fabric. A virtualization fabric attack is one that comes from the infrastructure that hosts the virtual machine itself. Attacks that come from the virtualization infrastructure include the following:

- **Virtual machine export attacks**   Rather than compromise a running VM, an authorized administrator can simply use Hyper-V's built in export functionality to export a VM. Once exported, administrators can then examine the contents of the exported VM at their leisure without any evidence existing of their access. Anything that can be done by an authorized administrator can also be done by a nefarious third party who has gained access to the administrator's account or has local administrator access on a Hyper-V host. For example, someone with the appropriate privileges can export a virtualized domain controller, extract the *ntds.dit* Active Directory file, and then run an offline brute force analysis of that file to extract username and password data. They could then use that username and password data to gain administrative privileges and access that domain and its resources in a manner that seemed completely legitimate.

- **Virtual machine movement attacks**   Rather than exporting a VM, an attacker might attempt to move a shielded VM to an untrusted host. The intention in doing so would be to remove the protection associated with the VM. However, with shielded VMS, if the new host is not recognized as trusted based on an identifier related to the host's TPM, the shielded VM does not function and the contents of the VM remain protected.

Inside OUT

Exfiltrate all the things

In the past, you could ensure the physical security of a server by putting it in a locked cage in a highly secure datacenter that was also protected by security guards and might even be surrounded by a piranha-filled moat. Someone trying to steal the server had to be able to get past the piranhas, the security guard, and the locked cage. Today, the vast majority of servers are virtualized and are functionally just a bunch of very large files. Rather than getting past the piranhas, stealing a server is mostly a case of upload-ing the files that comprise the VM to a location you control somewhere on the Internet. Shielded VMs provide a way of protecting against this type of attack.

When you're thinking about shielded VMs, you separate the owner and operator of the VM—called the tenant—from the owner and operator of the virtualization fabric. (In most cases, this is you as the Hyper-V virtualization administrator.) Shielded VMs allow VM operators to run their workloads without the concern that anyone with local administrator privileges on the Hyper-V host server can access the data and applications stored on that VM.

Shielded VMs include the following security features and requirements:

- **Secure Boot must be present and enabled.**   This protects the boot environment of the VM from attacks that might modify the environment to introduce malware. This malware could be leveraged to gain access to the VM.

- **Virtual TPM must be present and enabled.**   Virtual TPMs function in a manner similar to hardware-based TPMs in that they provide a secure location for the storage of crypto-graphic keys and secrets.

- **VM must have BitLocker enabled.**   BitLocker protects the integrity of the boot envi-ronment, and it ensures that the VM's virtual hard disks are encrypted. If the virtual hard disk file was copied, it would be inaccessible unless the person attempting to access it had the necessary BitLocker recovery keys.

- **Only certain integration components are allowed.**   Tools such as PowerShell Direct and Data Exchange are blocked. Blocking these integration services components blocks a Hyper-V administrator from indirectly accessing data stored in the VM.

- **Virtual Machine Connection (console) cannot be enabled for the VM.**   Access must be through remote access methods enabled within the VM operating system, such as PowerShell remote sessions or Remote Desktop. The only way to access the content of the VM is where the VM operating system has granted access to that content.

- **Restricted keyboard and mouse access.** Human Interface Devices, such as keyboard and mice, are disabled for the VM and can't be used to interact with it. For example, this means that an administrator couldn't interrupt the VM's boot process or use another attack to inject code into the VM in the way they might do so when attacking a physically deployed computer.

- **COM/serial ports.** Access through other virtual ports to the VM is disabled. This blocks a nefarious administrator using out-of-band management tools to access the VM.

- **Debugger access.** A debugger cannot be attached to the VM process on a shielded VM.

Windows Server 2012 and later and Windows 10 and later support being run as Shielded VMs.

Shielded VMs can only be hosted on specially configured Windows Server 2016 and later Hyper-V servers that are part of a shielded fabric. Shielded VMs must use virtual hard disks in VHDX format that have the following properties:

- Configured as GPT disks.

- Must be basic rather than dynamic disks.

- Disk that hosts operating systems must be configured with at least two partitions. One partition stores the Windows operating system; the other stores the active partition, which includes the bootloader.

- Volumes on the disk must be formatted as NTFS.

While it's possible to convert an existing VM to a shielded VM, Microsoft recommends that shielded VMs be deployed from scratch from trusted installation media or digitally signed VM templates.

> ## More Info
> *Shielded VMs*
>
> You can learn more about shielded virtual machines at *https://learn.microsoft.com/windows-server/security/guarded-fabric-shielded-vm/guarded-fabric-configuration-scenarios-for-shielded-vms-overview.*

CHAPTER 12

Guarded fabric

Before you can deploy a shielded VM, you need to configure a guarded fabric on which to deploy the VM. A guarded fabric is a special cryptographically secure virtualization host environment. A guarded fabric is made up of one Host Guardian Service (HGS), usually a cluster of three nodes, a number of guarded virtualization hosts, and the shielded VMs that run on those hosts.

Host Guardian Service

The Host Guardian Service (HGS) is a Windows Server role that manages attestation and the Key Protection Service (KPS). The KPS stores and is responsible for securely releasing keys to shielded VMs. One of the keys that the KPS stores is the transport key. The transport key is used to encrypt a shielded VM's virtual TPM. Microsoft recommends that you deploy the HGS role on a physically secure physical server running the Server Core operating system.

Validating a Hyper-V host involves verifying both its identity and configuration. Once the attestation service verifies both its identity and configuration, the KPS provides the transport key to that host that is required to unlock and run shielded VMs on that host.

Configuring an HGS server involves the deployment of a dedicated single-domain AD DS forest. An HGS cluster comprises at least three nodes, and each HGS cluster node is a domain controller for the root domain of this dedicated AD DS forest. Deploying an HGS cluster is different from a traditional domain controller deployment, and you don't go through the traditional AD DS promotion process. Instead, you take a standalone server, install the HGS role on that server, and then run the `Initialize-HgsServer` PowerShell cmdlet.

Running the `Initialize-HgsServer` PowerShell cmdlet triggers the process of configuring the server as a domain controller for the newly created single-domain AD DS forest. The trusted Hyper-V hosts need to either be a member of the HGS forest or a member of a domain that has a one-way trust relationship with the forest. This second configuration must be even more secure because a compromised virtualization host won't be able to make any modifications to the HGS forest because the trust relationship goes only in the opposite direction.

TPM and admin-trusted attestation

Trusted attestation allows a shielded VM to verify that it is running on a virtualization host that participates in a guarded fabric. There are two methods that you can use to provide trusted attestation. The method that you provide depends on the hardware that you have available. Table 12-5 lists the different trusted attestation types.

CHAPTER 12

Table 12-5   Attestation types

Attestation type	Functionality and benefits
TPM-trusted	Provides strongest protection.
	Requires TPM 2.0 and UEFI 2.3.1 with secure boot.
	Guarded hosts are approved based on TPM ID, measured boot sequence, and code integrity policies.
	Each guarded fabric virtualization host's TPM must be registered with the guardian service. To do this, use the `Get-PlatformIdentifier` cmdlet to generate a special file containing the TPM endorsement key's public and private keys, and then use the `Add-HgsAttestationTpmHost` cmdlet in registering the TPM with the guardian service.
	It's necessary to generate a baseline code-integrity policy for each virtualization host hardware SKU. This policy allows validation of the integrity of the software and hardware environment of each guardian fabric virtualization host.
	The best practice is to use Hardware Security Module to store HSM-backed certificates, though this is not mandatory.
Host key attestation	Doesn't require TPM 2.0.
	Compatible with common server hardware.
	Guarded hosts are approved through possession of a cryptographic key.
	A guarded host forwards the request to the HGS using an encrypted REST API.
Admin-trusted	Deprecated from Windows Server 2019 onward.
	Doesn't require TPM 2.0.
	Compatible with common server hardware.
	Guarded hosts are approved by Host Guardian Service based on membership of specific AD DS security group.
	Guarded host forwards the request to the HGS using an encrypted REST API.
	Use the `Add-HgsAttestationHostGroup` cmdlet to authorize the specific security group's SID with the attestation service.
	Guarded fabric virtualization hosts need to have a one-way trust relationship to HGS domain.

CHAPTER 12

> ## More Info
>
> *Guarded fabric*
>
> You can learn more about guarded fabric at *https://learn.microsoft.com/windows-server/security/guarded-fabric-shielded-vm/guarded-fabric-and-shielded-vms.*

Encryption-supported VMs

An encryption-supported VM is a VM that can run in a semi-protected manner on a guarded fabric but doesn't have the stringent security requirements of a shielded VM. A virtualization administrator has a greater level of access to an encryption-supported VM. This makes the deployment less secure than a shielded VM. Encryption-supported VMs may be more appropriate for organizations where the VM administrator would normally have access to the VMs anyway, but for compliance reasons, VMs need to be run in a manner where the contents of virtual hard disks are encrypted.

Table 12-6 outlines how encryption-supported VMs differ from shielded VMs.

Table 12-6   Differences between encryption-supported and shielded VMs

Security setting	Encryption-Supported VM	Shielded VM
Secure Boot	Required but configurable	Required and enforced
vTPM	Required but configurable	Required and enforced
Encrypted VM state	Required but configurable	Required and enforced
Live migration traffic encryption	Required but configurable	Required and enforced
Integration components including PowerShell Direct	Configurable by fabric administrator with PowerShell Direct and Data Exchange allowed	Data Exchange and PowerShell Direct blocked
Virtual Machine Connection	Allowed	Disabled (can be enabled with Windows Server version 1803 and later)
Keyboard, mouse, HID devices	Allowed	Disabled
COM/Serial ports	Supported	Disabled
Attach debugger to VM process	Supported	Disabled

Shielding data file

The shielding data file (also called the provisioning data file or PDK file) is a special encrypted file that stores the following secrets:

- Administrator credentials.

- Answer file (`unattend.xml`).

- Security policy that determines whether VMs created using this shielded data file will be fully shielded VMs or encryption-supported VMs.

- An RDP certificate. This allows secure RDP communication with the VM.

- A volume signature catalog. This contains a list of trusted and signed template disk signatures from which a VM can be created. A shielded template disk is a template virtual hard disk that has a digital signature. This ensures that the template hard disk from which a new VM is deployed is trustworthy. During provisioning, the signature of the disk is computed and checked against a list of trusted and shielded template disk signatures stored in the catalog. If the signatures match, deployment continues. If the signatures do not match—indicating that the shielded template disk has been modified—the deployment fails.

- A Key Protector that specifies the guarded fabrics a shielded VM generated based on which this shielding data file is authorized to run.

Tenant keys protect this file and the tenant uploads the shielding data file to the secure fabric. Because tenant keys protect the file, the virtualization administrator doesn't have access to the contents of the shielding data file. This means that the virtualization administrators do not have access to the local administrator password used with virtual machines deployed on the fabrics that they manage.

The shielding data file ensures that any VMs are explicitly created with the parameters specified by the tenant. The virtualization administrator can't swap in their own template hard disks, answer files, or administrator passwords. Should a template hard disk be swapped out or modified by the virtualization administrator, it won't match the cryptographic signature of any authorized template hard disk listed in the shielding data file.

CHAPTER 12

Hardening Active Directory

Windows Server 2025 is Microsoft's most secure version of the Windows Server operating system, but you can configure the operating system to be far more secure than it is in a default deployment.

Hardening is the process of configuring security controls to improve security. The drawback of hardening a service such as Active Directory or Windows Server 2025 is that it reduces compatibility. Applying security controls is always a matter of balancing security with the requirements of the environment. For example, while you should disable older authentication protocols such as NTLM, doing so might block an older business-critical system in your environment from being able to authenticate against Active Directory.

Always perform hardening activities that are commensurate with your organization's risk profile. If you're managing the Active Directory environment for a federal government department, you have a substantially different risk profile than if you're managing the Active Directory environment for the local school district.

Active Directory controls the authentication, authorization, and the basic security configuration infrastructure of a Windows Server environment. You should make it as hard as possible for attackers to compromise your Active Directory infrastructure by enabling as many security controls as possible.

Implementing the advice in this chapter won't make your Active Directory deployment completely bulletproof, but it will make it substantially more challenging for even the most motivated of attackers to compromise.

Hardening domain controllers

Domain controllers are the vaults that host the "crown jewels" of any Windows Server network. Attackers who can compromise a domain controller can compromise the Active Directory instance hosted on that domain controller. This gives attackers the ability to grant themselves any Active Directory domain privilege they desire. You want to ensure that your organization's domain controllers are as secure as possible. Some obvious steps you can take to secure your organization's domain controllers include the following:

- **Only run the Server Core installation option**   The Server Core installation option of Windows Server has a smaller attack surface than the Server with Desktop Experience version of Windows Server.

- **Only host AD DS and DNS on domain controllers**   Generally, you should also avoid hosting workloads other than DNS on a computer configured as a domain controller as a further way of minimizing the attack surface. The more workloads a domain controller hosts, the more components there are for an attacker to attempt to exploit to gain control of that computer.

- **Run the most recent version of Windows Server**   Domain controllers should always run the most recent version of Windows Server. When a new version of Windows Server is released, the first thing you should do is deploy domain controllers running the new operating system and retire domain controllers running previous versions of Windows Server. Newer versions of Windows Server are inherently more secure than previous versions of Windows Server.

- **Ensure that the domain controller is deployed on a platform with TPM and virtualization-based security**   You want to enable UEFI Secure Boot and Dynamic Root of Trust for Measurement, and DMA protections to protect the domain controller against firmware-level attacks. Running Windows Server 2025 on a platform that supports virtualization-based security allows you to enable Credential Guard if it isn't enabled by default.

- **Enable BitLocker on all domain controller volumes**   Enabling BitLocker on all volumes protects the Active Directory database from offline attack in the event that an attacker gets access to the physical or virtual hard disk that hosts the AD Database file (NTDS.dit).

- **Stay up to date with monthly software updates**   You should ensure that you keep domain controllers patched with the most recent software updates. You should aggressively update domain controllers. Because you should not run workloads beyond Active Directory and DNS on a domain controller, you're unlikely to encounter compatibility problems with new software updates (though you should still test on one domain controller before rolling out to all of the others).

- **Enable Windows Defender Application Control**   Only authorized applications and processes should be able to run on an Active Directory domain controller. Application whitelisting is the process by which only authorized applications and processes can be run, and any application or process that is not explicitly authorized will be unable to run. The most effective method of applying application whitelisting is enabling Windows Defender Application Control (previously known as Device Guard). You'll learn more about Windows Defender Application Control in Chapter 14, "Security systems and services."

- **Block domain controllers from directly communicating with hosts on the Internet**   You should configure perimeter network firewalls so that domain controllers on internal networks can't directly communicate with hosts on the Internet. Software updates from domain controllers should be obtained from sources on the internal network, such as a WSUS server. Do not disable Windows Firewall on domain controllers.

- **Only accept administrative connections from authorized hosts**   Domain controllers should only accept RDP and remote PowerShell sessions from specific authorized hosts. These hosts should be privileged-access workstations or jump servers, which you learned about in Chapter 1, "Administration tools." Ensure that Windows Firewall is configured to block all but necessary incoming traffic.

- **Keep domain controllers in domain controllers OU**   Avoid moving domain controllers out of the default domain controllers OU because this can lead to unexpected configurations being assigned through group policy.

- **Ensure that Directory Services Restore Mode (DSRM) passwords are changed regularly**   This password allows out-of-band access to a domain controller. Passwords should be different for each domain controller; passwords should be updated every couple of months, and should be stored in a secure location, such as a safe. You can use Windows Local Administrator Password Solution (LAPS) in Windows Server 2025 to manage DSRM passwords. Windows LAPS was covered in Chapter 12, "Hardening Windows Server."

- **Disable the print spooler service**   Domain controllers should not function as print servers, and the print spooler service is an attack vector leveraged by more than 10 percent of Microsoft Security Response Center incidents related to Windows Server and Client.

- **Enable Hypervisor-Protected Code Integrity (HVCI)**   HVCI enforces Driver & DLL signature verification in kernel mode. This can prevent attackers from loading unsigned drivers or performing kernel exploits to bypass LSA protections.

- **Restrict physical access to domain controllers**   Ensure that you restrict physical access to domain controllers or virtualization hosts that host domain controller workloads. If using Hyper-V for virtualization, consider deploying domain controllers as shielded VMs or an equivalent technology. In environments where physical security is difficult to implement but a domain controller is necessary, deploy Read Only Domain Controllers.

Least-privilege

Least-privilege is the practice of assigning only the minimum required privileges to an account for the account to perform its assigned tasks. Put another way, accounts should not be assigned rights and privileges in excess of those required to perform the specific tasks for which the account is used.

The benefit of using least-privilege is that in the event that an attacker manages to compromise an account, that attacker is limited to acting with the privileges assigned to that account. Least-privilege also reduces the chance that damage might inadvertently be done to a system. For example, an account used for backup and recovery can't be used to add or remove software from the server if that account doesn't have permission to do anything beyond backup and recovery.

When it comes to assigning privileges, a very bad habit of many IT professionals is to simply add an account to the local Administrators group on the computer where the privilege is required. This is especially true with service accounts where proper procedure is to edit the local security group policies and assign very specific rights; however, many administrators take a quick shortcut and assign all necessary rights by adding the service account to the local Administrators group. This is one of the reasons that attackers go after service accounts, which often use a single, unchanging, and organization-wide password and that also are members of the local Administrator groups on which they're installed.

You should tightly limit the number of security principals that are members of the Domain Admins, Enterprise Admins, and Schema Admins groups. In highly secure environments, you might only use an account that has Domain Admin privileges in forest recovery scenarios, with everyday administrative accounts being specially crafted with limited delegated permissions. An environment is more secure when privileged accounts are tightly limited in scope and permissions and admins have to use different accounts to perform different tasks than an environment is when single accounts are loaded with permissions and are used as an administrator's daily driver.

Inside OUT

Day-to-day accounts

IT operations staff and developers in your organization should have separate accounts for performing day-to-day activities, such as reading email, browsing the Internet, and filling in TPS reports. The day-to-day accounts of IT operations staff and developers should not have local administrative privileges. Should a change in the configuration of IT staff workstations need to occur, a specific privileged account that exists to perform that task should be used. In highly secure and well-resourced organizations, privileged accounts can only be used on special privileged-access workstations (PAWs). These workstations are locked down using technologies such as Windows Defender Application Control and Credential Guard, which makes them especially resistant to malware, credential theft, and reuse attacks.

More Info

Least-privilege

You can learn more about least-privilege administrative models at *https://learn. microsoft.com/windows-server/identity/ad-ds/plan/security-best-practices/ implementing-least-privilege-administrative-models*.

Role-Based Access Control

Role-Based Access Control (RBAC) operationalizes the least-privilege principle. Instead of having all-powerful administrator accounts that can perform any task on any system, you instead parcel out administrative privileges that limit what an account can do and where an account can do it.

For example, rather than giving help desk support staff the ability to reset the passwords of any user in the domain, you instead delegate them the right to be able to reset only the passwords of user accounts in a specific organizational unit. This way, you allow the support staff to reset the passwords of a specific class of user account; for example, you could grant support staff the authority to reset passwords that are used by people in one department without giving them the ability to reset the passwords of domain administrator accounts.

You delegate privileges for organizational units in Active Directory using the Delegation Of Control Wizard, as shown in Figure 13-1.

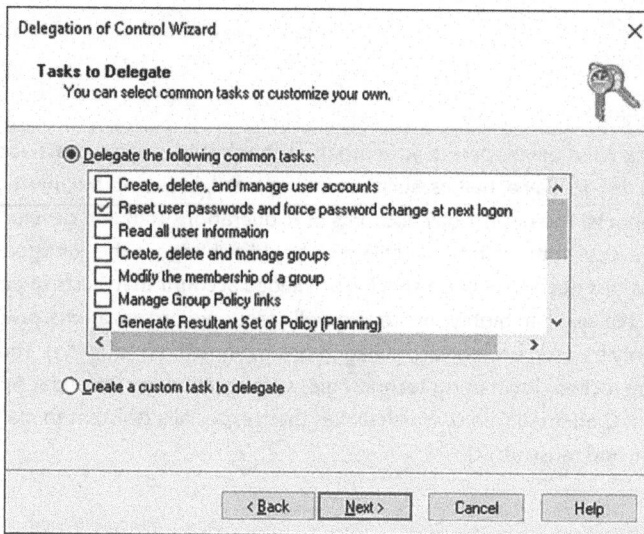

Figure 13-1   Delegating the reset password right

The Delegation Of Control Wizard allows you to delegate the following common tasks directly from the wizard:

- Create, delete, and manage user accounts

- Reset user passwords and force password change at next logon

- Read all user information

- Modify the membership of a group

- Join a computer to the domain

- Manage Group Policy links

- Generate Resultant Set of Policy (Planning)

- Generate Resultant Set of Policy (Logging)

- Create, delete, and manage inetOrgPerson accounts

- Reset inetOrgPerson passwords and force password change at next logon

- Read all inetOrgPerson information

inetOrgPerson is an LDAP object class that allows interoperability with other LDAP-compliant directory services. These objects are supported in Active Directory primarily to simplify migration to Active Directory from other LDAP directories.

You should delegate rights to security groups and not individual users and ensure that the security groups have meaningful names and descriptions that provide context about the rights delegated to the group. You should then tightly control and regularly audit the membership of those groups. Delegating to meaningfully named groups allows you to quickly determine which security principals have been delegated permissions.

If you choose the Custom Task To Delegate option in the Delegation Of Control Wizard, you can be more specific about which objects you delegate permission over rather than those included in the common tasks. There are approximately 150 different object types you can individually delegate control over using this wizard, so if the common tasks don't suit your needs, you should investigate those available by delegating a custom task.

You should document delegated rights and permissions and audit them on a regular basis. Security principals are often delegated rights, and then the delegation is forgotten. It's not unusual in many environments to see delegations that were performed to solve a problem some time ago still in effect.

Password policies

Account policies include both password policies and account lockout policies. You configure the domain password and lockout policies by configuring the default domain GPO. You can override the domain policies for specific security groups or user accounts using fine-grained password policies. You configure fine-grained password policies using the Active Directory Administrative Center console.

Default password policy settings include these:

- **Number Of Remembered Passwords**   Users cannot change their passwords to a password remembered by the system. By default, Active Directory remembers the previous 24 passwords that have been used by an account.

- **Maximum Password Age**   This is the maximum amount of time in days that a password can remain the same before it needs to be changed. The default value is 42 days. Many organizations have increased the number of days because advice from security analysts suggests that requiring frequent changes can reduce password security as users choose password patterns. Many organizations that use multifactor authentication may choose no expiration. If multifactor authentication isn't implemented, consider changing the value to 180 days, which forces two password changes a year rather than one every six weeks.

- **Minimum Password Age**   This is the minimum amount of time in days that a newly changed password must be kept. This policy prevents users from cycling through password changes to exceed the password history setting, so they can return to using the same password.

- **Minimum Password Length**   This is the minimum number of characters that are required for a password. The default in Windows Server 2025 is 8, raised from 7 in prior versions of Windows Server. Services such as Azure now require a minimum of 12 characters for administrator account passwords on IaaS virtual machines. Consider increasing password length and training users to use passphrases rather than passwords.

- **Password Complexity Requirement**   This setting determines whether passwords must include three of the four following characteristics: uppercase letters, lowercase letters, numbers, and symbols. This setting is enabled by default.

Lockout policy determines

- The period of time an account is locked out when a user enters a specific number of incorrect passwords in a specific amount of time. The default is that account is not locked out when incorrect passwords are entered. This means that an attacker or someone who is just forgetful can brute-force guess passwords without any lockout occurring.

- Number incorrect passwords that trigger a lockout over a specific period of time. When configuring this policy, you should allow users to make a reasonable number of guesses. If you don't, you'll end up flooding the service desk with password reset calls.

- The amount of time that must elapse before the account lockout counter is reset. A correctly entered password also resets the lockout counter.

- Monitor account lockout to determine if attacks are occurring or if the policy is too stringent. Investigate unusual activity related to accounts.

Account security options

There are additional security options that you should consider configuring for highly privileged accounts. These include configuring the following settings:

- **Logon Hours**   Use this setting to configure when users can use an account. AD DS does not authenticate someone attempting to sign in outside of these hours. By default, accounts are configured so that users can sign in at all times. Consider configuring privileged accounts so that users can use them only at specific times. This stops a user from signing in after hours, either specifically or with a compromised account, to get up to no good when they assume that no one is watching. Organizations that do need to use privileged accounts to perform after-hours maintenance tasks can create special accounts for those tasks, or they can temporarily modify an existing account.

- **Logon Workstations**   Use this setting to limit the computers to which a particular account can sign in. By default, users can use an account to sign in to any computer in the domain. Use this setting to ensure that users can use privileged accounts only on specific, specially configured administrative workstations or certain servers. Limiting which computers' users can use an account reduces the locations where that account can be used.

- **Password Never Expires**   You should use this setting reluctantly when configuring privileged accounts because it absolves the account from the domain password policy. You can use products such as Microsoft Identity Manager to assist with password management for privileged accounts.

- **Smart Card Is Required For Interactive Logon**   Use this setting to ensure that a smart card must be present for the account sign in to occur. In high-security environments, you should deploy smart cards and enable this option to ensure that only an authorized person who has both the smart card and the account credentials can use the privileged account.

- **Account Is Sensitive And Cannot Be Delegated**   Use this setting to ensure that trusted applications cannot forward the account credentials to other services or computers on the network. Enable this setting for highly privileged accounts.

- **This Account Supports Kerberos AES 256 Bit Encryption**   Use this setting to allow Kerberos AES 256-bit encryption. Where possible, you should configure this option for privileged accounts and have them use this form of Kerberos encryption over the AES 128-bit encryption option.

- **Account Expires**   Use this setting to configure an expiration date for an account. Configuring privileged accounts with expiration dates ensures that privileged accounts do not remain available to use beyond when they're required. Ensure that you track the expiration dates of important privileged accounts and also don't set them to all expire on the same day.

When you join a computer to a domain for the first time, it creates a computer account in the Computers container. If you want to create an account in a specific container, you'll need to pre-stage the computer account and place it in the appropriate OU. A prestaged computer account must have a name that matches that of the computer that is joining the domain.

Computer accounts can be made members of the domain security group. This group membership influences how the Local System and Network Service accounts on the computer function. This is because, by default, these services use the computer's credentials when interacting with resources on the network. This gives the computer account the rights and privileges assigned to any security group to which the computer is a member.

Computer accounts have automatically assigned passwords that are updated every 30 days. If a computer doesn't connect to a domain within 30 days, a new password is assigned the next time a connection is established. If you disable a computer account, the computer cannot connect to the domain, and domain users are unable to sign in to the computer until the account is reenabled.

CHAPTER 13

Resetting a computer account removes the relationship between the computer and the domain. To fix this, you'll need to either join the computer back to the domain or reestablish the broken trust relationship using the following PowerShell command, specifying the credentials of a member of the Domain Administrator group:

```
Test-ComputerSecureChannel -credential <domain>\<admin> -Repair
```

If you delete a computer account, it's necessary to rejoin the computer to the domain manually. When you delete a computer account, all information associated with the account is removed from Active Directory. You should only delete computer accounts once a computer has been decommissioned.

Protected accounts

The Protected Users group, shown in Figure 13-2, provides you with a method of protecting highly privileged user accounts from being compromised. It does this by blocking the use of less-secure security and authentication options.

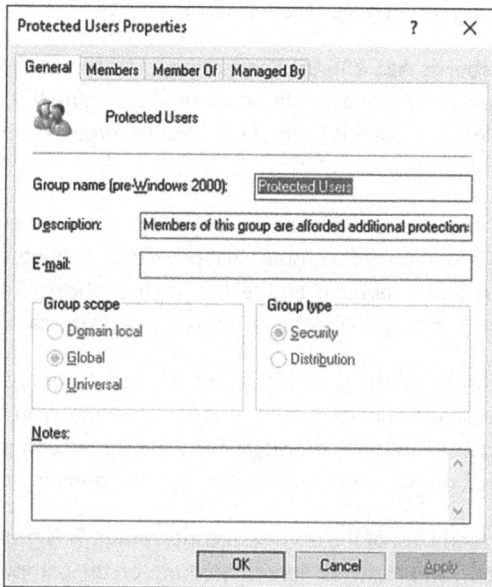

Figure 13-2   Protected Users Properties

Additionally, accounts that are members of this group cannot use the following security options:

- Default credential delegation (CredSSP)
- Windows Digest

- NTLM—NTOWF

- Kerberos long-term keys

- Sign-on offline

If the domain functional level is Windows Server 2012 R2 or higher, user accounts that are members of the Protected Users group cannot

- Use NT LAN Manager (NTLM) for authentication

- Use DES for Kerberos preauthentication

- Use RC4 cipher suites for Kerberos preauthentication

- Be delegated using constrained delegation

- Be delegated using unconstrained delegation

- Renew user tickets (TGTs) past the initial 240-minute lifetime

Only user accounts should be added to the Protected Users group. You should not add computer accounts or service accounts to this group. In secure environments, all privileged accounts should be members of this group, with exceptions occurring only when specific incompatibilities arise that cannot be resolved in another way.

> ## More Info
>
> **Protected Users security group**
>
> You can learn more about the Protected Users Security group at *https://learn.microsoft. com/en-us/windows-server/security/credentials-protection-and-management/ protected-users-security-group.*

Authentication policies silos

Authentication policy silos allow you to define relationships between the user, computer, and managed service accounts. A user, computer, and managed service account can only belong to a single authentication policy silo. This provides a more robust security method that goes beyond configuring log-in restrictions and restricting which accounts can access specific servers in your environment.

Accounts in an authentication policy silo are associated with a silo claim. You can use this silo claim to control access to claims-aware resources. For example, you can configure accounts so that only accounts that are associated with a specific silo claim can access particularly sensitive servers. This means only accounts that are associated with a Certificate Services silo claim can sign in to a computer that has the Active Directory Certificate Services role installed.

Authentication policies allow you to configure settings, such as the TGT lifetime and access-control conditions, which specify conditions that must be met before a user can sign in to a computer. For example, you might configure an authentication policy that specifies a TGT lifetime of 120 minutes and limit a user account so that users can only use it with specific devices, such as privileged-access workstations. You can only use authentication policies if you have configured the domain functional level at the Windows Server 2012 R2 or higher.

You configure authentication policies and authentication policy silos using Active Directory Administrative Center, as shown in Figure 13-3.

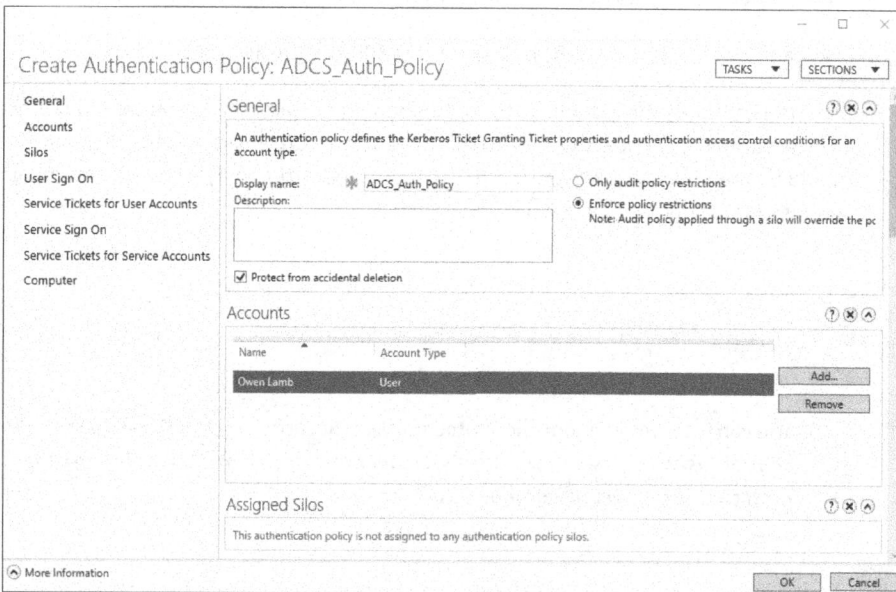

Figure 13-3   Authentication policies

More Info

Authentication policies and silos

You can learn more about authentication policies and silos at *https://learn.micro-soft.com/windows-server/security/credentials-protection-and-management/authentication-policies-and-authentication-policy-silos.*

Configure msDS-MachineAccountQuota

The default configuration of the msDS-MachineAccountQuota attribute in Active Directory allows any authenticated domain user to add up to 10 new computer accounts to the domain. This default configuration has been used in some attacks where an attacker has exploited this setting to create a new computer account and then use that computer account in a variety of attack chains.

Setting msDS-MachineAccountQuota to zero prevents standard domain users from creating computer accounts. You can do this by running the following command with Domain Admin privileges:

```
Set-ADDomain (Get-ADDomain).distinguishedname -Replace @
{"ms-ds-MachineAccountQuota"="0"}
```

When you run this command, only members of the Domain Administrators will be able to join computers to the domain by default. Should you want to allow nondomain admins to perform this function, you can create a special security group that has a limited membership and use the Delegation Of Control Wizard to assign that group the ability to perform domain join operations.

Constrained delegation

Delegation is a technique that enables a service to assume the identity of a client to access a second service on the client's behalf. This functionality is often used by multitier applications. For example, a user logs onto a front-end web server that needs to access a database on a back-end server where access to the database is mediated by the user's identity. Without delegation, the front-end service would either need to be granted direct access to the back-end resource or would have to manage the user's credentials for a second authentication.

When the Kerberos authentication protocol is configured for delegation, the initial service leverages the user's Kerberos authentication tickets to impersonate the user's identity when accessing the second service. There are three basic forms of delegation:

- **Unconstrained delegation**   A service is able to impersonate a user to access any other service in a domain. This traditional method is the least secure and should be avoided.

- **Kerberos constrained delegation**   Restricts this impersonation to a predefined set of target services.

- **Resource-based constrained delegation**   Rather than setting the delegation attributes on the delegating service, the configuration is placed on the target resource. This model allows the resource owner to specify which front-end services are permitted to delegate to it. Windows Server has supported resource-based constrained delegation since Windows Server 2012 R2.

Prior to configuring constrained delegation, you must register a Service Principal Name (SPN) for the back-end service that will be the target of the delegation. You can do this using the setspn command-line tool using the syntax `setspn -s ServicePrincipalName AccountName`. For example, to register a SharePoint web service running on a server named Tailwind-ShrPnt with a service account named svc-sharepoint, use this command:

```
setspn -S HTTP/Tailwind-ShrPnt svc-sharepoint
```

Configure Kerberos-constrained delegation

To configure Kerberos-constrained delegation, perform the following steps:

1. Open the Active Directory Users and Computers console and navigate to the delegating service account (which can be a user or computer account).

2. Right-click the account and select Properties.

3. In the Properties dialog, select the Delegation tab.

4. Choose the option Trust This User For Delegation To Specified Services Only. This enables Kerberos-constrained delegation for the account.

5. Select the Use Kerberos Only authentication protocol. This option enables Kerberos-constrained delegation. The service can only delegate on behalf of users who have already authenticated via Kerberos and presented a valid Kerberos ticket to the front-end service.

6. Click the Add button to specify the target service SPNs to which the account can delegate. In the dialog that appears, click Users or Computers, enter the name of the target server or service account, and select the corresponding registered SPN from the list.

Configure resource-based constrained delegation

You can configure resource-based constrained delegation only with PowerShell. To do this, identify the accounts of the users or computers for which you want to configure resource-based constrained delegation. For example, you want to configure resource-based constrained delegation from computer WEBSRV01 to SQLSRV02. To do this, run the following commands:

```
$webserver = Get-ADComputer -Identity WEBSRV01$
Set-ADComputer -Identity SQLSRV02 -PrincipalsAllowedToDelegateToAccount $webserver
```

Disable NTLM

NTLM is an older authentication protocol that is not as secure as Kerberos. You can disable NTLM by configuring the Network Security: Restrict NTLM: NTLM Authentication In This Domain policy in the default domain GPO and setting the policy to Disable, as shown in Figure

13-4. This policy can be found in the `Policies\Windows Settings\Security Settings\Local Policies\Security Options` node of the default domain GPO. Prior to disabling NTLM authentication, you should configure the Network Security: Restrict NTLM: Audit Incoming NTLM Traffic policy to determine if and where the NTLM protocol is still being used in your organization's environment.

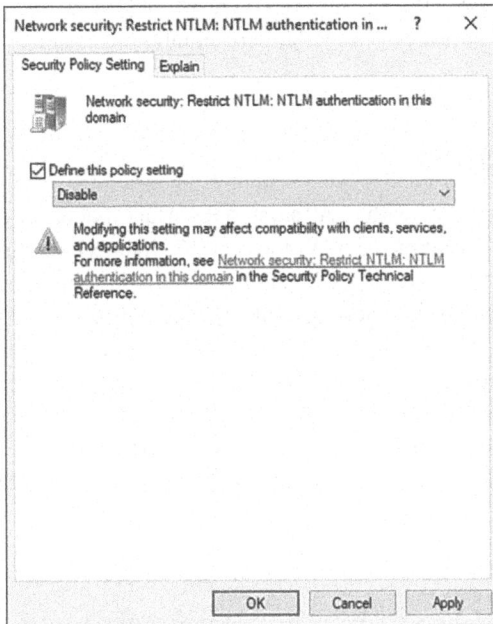

Figure 13-4   Disable NTLM

More Info

Disable NTLM

You can learn more about disabling NTLM at *https://learn.microsoft.com/en-us/previous-versions/windows/it-pro/windows-10/security/threat-protection/security-policy-settings/network-security-restrict-ntlm-ntlm-authentication-in-this-domain*.

Enforce LDAP signing

LDAP is the primary protocol used for communication in Active Directory environments. LDAP signing prevents unsecure LDAP communication. Without signing, unsigned network traffic is susceptible to man-in-the-middle attacks, where an intruder can capture packets between the client and server, modify them, and forward altered requests to the domain controller. When

LDAP signing is enforced, each LDAP request must include a digital signature that verifies the message hasn't been tampered with during transmission. LDAP signing has been available in Windows Server since Windows Server 2008.

You configure LDAP signing using the Domain Controller: LDAP Server Signing Requirements and Network Security: LDAP Client Signing Requirements policies, located in the `Computer Configuration\Windows Settings\Security Settings\Local Policies\Security options` node of a GPO. Setting both these policies to Require Signing will ensure that LDAP traffic is signed.

Enforce LDAP channel binding

LDAP channel binding works in conjunction with LDAP signing to ensure that only a single TLS session is used for specific LDAP communication. Without LDAP channel binding, it's possible for a sophisticated attacker to interrupt a TLS session used to transmit signed LDAP communication and then create a new session, signing manipulated malicious LDAP traffic. LDAP channel binding was introduced in March 2020, and updates have made it available for all supported versions of Windows Server. You configure LDAP channel binding using the Domain Controller: LDAP Server Channel Binding Token Requirements policy located in the `Computer Configuration\Windows Settings\Security Settings\Local Policies\Security options` node of a GPO. By setting this policy to always, channel binding will be enforced for LDAP communication.

LSASS as a protected process

When LSASS runs as a protected process, only trusted, signed code can load into it, mitigating many credential-dumping tools. Enabling LSA protection makes it more difficult for the Local Security Authority to be compromised. You can configure LSASS to run as a Protected process by configuring the Configure LSASS To Run As A Protected Process policy, located in the `Computer Configuration\Administrative Templates\System\Local Security Authority` node of a group policy. When enabling this policy, you can choose one of the following options:

- **Enabled With UEFI Lock**   LSASS runs protected, and the setting is stored in the UEFI variable.

- **Enabled without UEFI Lock**   LSASS runs protected without UEFI storage.

You can also configure protection on a domain controller by editing the registry:

1. Open the Registry Editor (`RegEdit.exe`) and navigate to the registry key that is located at `HKEY_LOCAL_MACHINE\SYSTEM\CurrentControlSet\Control\Lsa`.

2. Create (or set the value of) this registry key: "`RunAsPPL`"=`dword:00000001`.

3. Restart the computer.

> ## More Info
>
> *Local Security Authority Protection*
>
> You can learn more about configuring Local Security Authority protection at *https://learn.microsoft.com/windows-server/security/credentials-protection-and-management/configuring-additional-lsa-protection.*

Block server operators from scheduling tasks

Configuring the Domain Controller: Allow Server Operator To Schedule Tasks policy as disabled, as shown in Figure 13-5, will block someone who is signed in to a server using the AT command to configure scheduled jobs. By default, AT jobs run under the SYSTEM account, and attackers often exploit the AT command to elevate privileges. If you configure this policy, it will be necessary to specify account credentials when configuring a scheduled task.

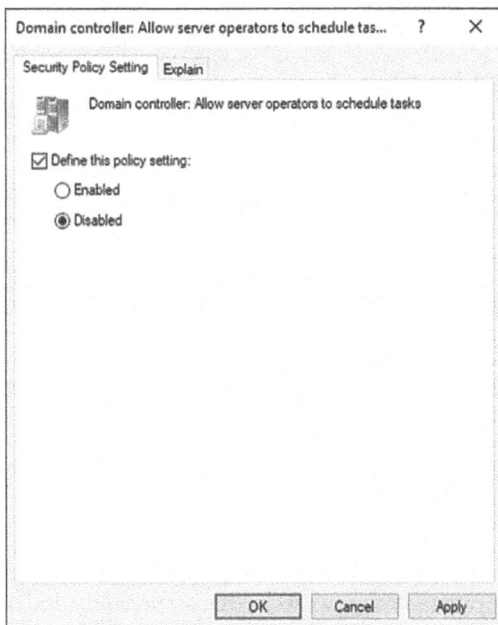

Figure 13-5   Block task scheduling using AT

KRBTGT account password

While you should definitely change the KRBTGT account password if your domain is compromised by an attacker or when someone who has had Domain Admin privileges leaves the organization, it's also good security hygiene to change the KRBTGT account password every six months. Changing the KRBTGT password involves an initial password change, waiting for rep-lication to occur, and then changing the password again. Many people wait 24 hours between the first and second changes. You must perform the password operation twice because of the way the password history of the KRBTGT account functions. Updating the KRBTGT password twice means that replication cannot occur using an older password. If you only do it once, and the domain has been compromised, an attacker might leverage the second stored password.

You can reset the KRBTGT account password by performing the following steps:

1. Open Active Directory Users And Computers.

2. In the View menu, click Advanced Features.

3. In the Users container of the domain, click the krbtgt user account, as shown in Figure 13-6.

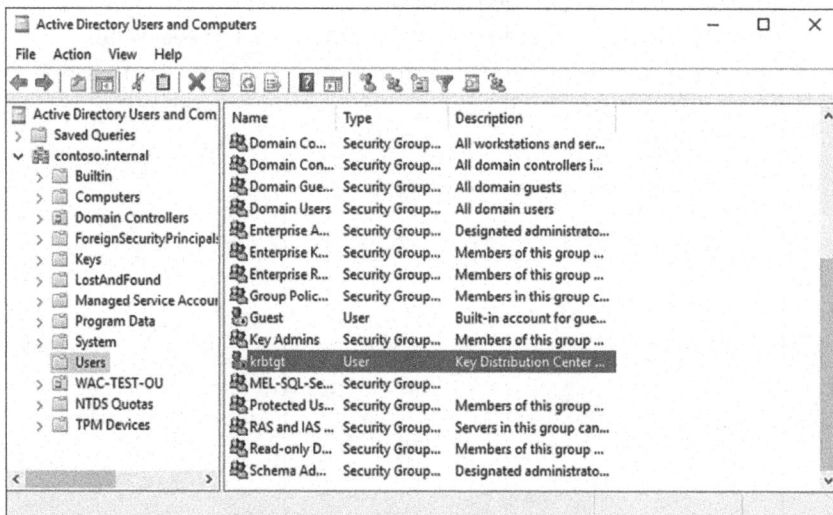

Figure 13-6   krbtgt account

4. From the Action menu, select Reset Password. You should then type in and confirm a new password. The password you enter in this dialog isn't important because Active Directory will trigger the creation of a separate strong password that's independent of the password you configure.

Enforce AES for Kerberos

Enforcing AES for Kerberos ensures that the RC4 cryptographic protocol isn't used. Microsoft has been recommending the deprecation of RC4 for Kerberos since the release of Windows Server 2012. You can enforce AES128 or AES256 for Kerberos, with AES256 being more cryptographically secure. You can enforce AES for Kerberos by configuring the Network

Security: Configure Encryption Types Allowed For Kerberos policy and setting it to AES256 as shown in Figure 13-7. This policy is located in the `Computer Configuration\Windows Settings\Security Settings\Local Policies\Security` options node of a GPO.

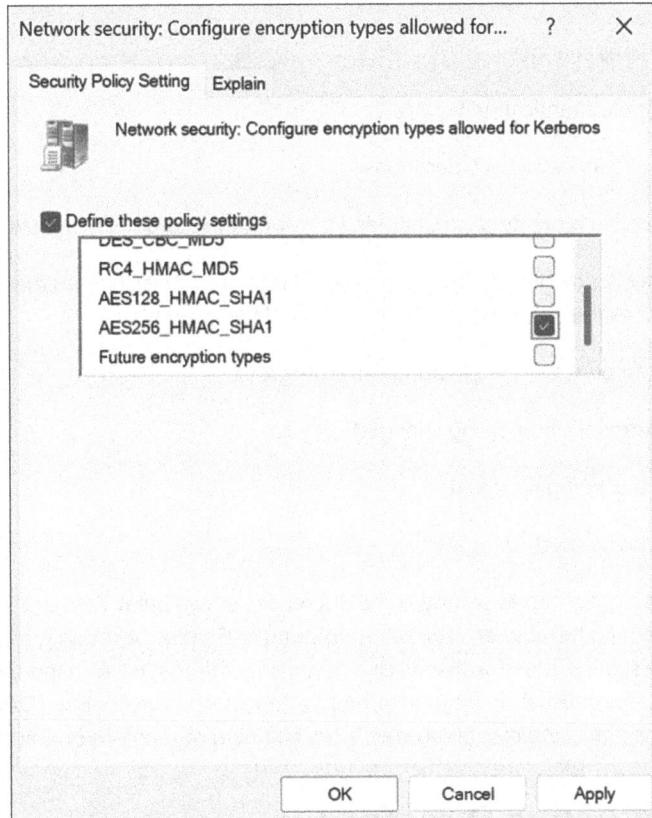

Figure 13-7   AES for Kerberos policy

Auditing, logging, and monitoring

Even with robust preventive controls, detecting suspicious activity quickly is vital. Ensure that you enable comprehensive auditing and monitoring on domain controllers. Turn on advanced auditing for

- Logon events
- Account logon events
- Account access

CHAPTER 13

- Object access

- Policy change

- Directory service access

- Directory services changes

- Audit Kerberos Authentication Service

- Audit Kerberos Service Ticket Operations

Audit logs are covered in more detail in Chapter 23, "Monitoring and maintenance."

Set up alerts for activities involving highly privileged roles or sensitive changes that are written to the event log. For example, configure alerts for the following events:

- When a user account is added to administrators group

- A domain controller's time being changed

- A replication link being modified

- DSRM mode being used

Although not often highlighted as security, time discrepancies can break Kerberos and also serve as an early warning because an attacker attempting a "Golden Ticket" may manipulate the Kerberos ticket timestamps. Monitor that all DCs have correct time sync. Also monitor Windows Firewall logs on DCs for unusual connection attempts. Repeated connection to LDAP or SMB from an unknown host may indicate an attacker port-scanning or trying to exploit.

Regular backup of Active Directory

Ensure you are regularly backing up Active Directory and practicing restoration procedures. You can't be sure that a backup is good until you try a recovery and many organizations that have had Active Directory compromised have found that their Active Directory backups are inadequate. Monitor your backup logs to ensure each Domain Controller's system state is successfully backed up on schedule and ensure that the backup data is stored in a secure offline manner.

Enhanced Security Administrative Environment forest

Enhanced Security Administrative Environment (ESAE) forests are an approach to Active Directory privileged access design in which you deploy a dedicated administrative Active Directory forest to host privileged accounts, privileged groups, and privileged access workstations for a production forest. In this design, the ESAE forest is configured with a one-way trust relationship with a production forest. A one-way trust relationship means that accounts from the ESAE forest can be used in the production forest; however, accounts in the production forest cannot be used in the ESAE forest.

Inside OUT

On premises approach

Some documentation on *learn.microsoft.com* suggests that you use Entra to replace ESAE forest going forward. Organizations that are wary of having a cloud dependency might be less than enthusiastic about this advice, which is why I've provide coverage of the more traditional approach. This architecture hasn't become invalidated and relies upon existing Active Directory forest trust functionality.

The production forest is the Active Directory forest in which an organization's day-to-day activities occur. You configure the production forest so that administrative tasks in the production forest can be performed only by using accounts that the ESAE forest hosts.

The ESAE forest design provides the following benefits:

- **Locked-down accounts**   A standard nonprivileged user account in the ESAE forest can be configured as a highly privileged user account in the production forest. For example, you make a standard user account in the ESAE forest a member of the Domain Admins group in a domain in the production forest. You can lock down the standard user account hosted in the ESAE forest so that it cannot sign in to hosts in the ESAE forest and can only be used to sign in to hosts in the production forest. Should the account be compromised, the attacker cannot use that account to perform administrative tasks in the ESAE forest.

- **Selective authentication**   ESAE forest design allows you to leverage a trust relationship's selective authentication feature. For example, you can configure sign-ins from the ESAE forest so that they can only occur on specific hosts in the production forest. One strategy is to configure selective authentication so that privileged accounts can only be used on privileged access workstations or jump servers in the production forest.

- **Simple way to improve security**   ESAE forest design provides substantive improvement in the security of existing production forests without requiring a complete rebuilding of the production environment. The ESAE forest approach has a small hardware/software footprint and only affects IT users. In this design, standard user accounts remain hosted in the production forest. Only privileged administrative accounts are hosted in the ESAE forest. As part of the transition to the ESAE forest model, you eventually remove almost all privileged accounts that are native to the production forest. Because they are hosted in a separate forest, privileged administrative accounts can be subject to more stringent security requirements than standard user accounts in the production forest.

Inside OUT

Failsafe admin account

With an ESAE forest design, you should remove almost all privileged accounts from the production forest as possible. You should leave a failsafe admin account in the production forest that allows you to fix things should everything go pear shaped, but this admin account should be given an insanely long and complex password that's stored securely in a safe that someone who is not a member of the IT operations staff has access to and should only be used as a last resort.

An ESAE forest design should have the following properties:

- Limit the function of the ESAE forest to hosting accounts of administrative users for the production forest.

- Do not deploy applications or additional resources in the ESAE forest. An exception to this is when you deploy technologies such as Microsoft Identity Manager, which is used to increase security when implementing Privileged Access Management.

- The ESAE forest should be a single-domain Active Directory forest. The ESAE forest only hosts a small number of accounts that need to have strict security policies applied.

- Only use one-way trusts. You should only configure a one-way trust where the production forest trusts the ESAE forest. This means that accounts from the ESAE forest can be used in the production forest but that accounts from the production forest cannot be used in the ESAE forest. Accounts used for administrative tasks in the production forest should be standard user accounts in the ESAE forest. If an account is compromised in the production forest, it cannot be used to elevate privileges in the ESAE forest.

Configure ESAE forest servers in the following ways:

- Validate installation media. Use the available checksums to validate that the media hasn't been modified.

- All servers should run the most recent version of the Windows Server operating system.

- Servers should be updated automatically with security updates.

- Security compliance manager baselines should be used as the starting point for server configuration.

- Servers should be configured with secure boot, BitLocker volume encryption, Credential Guard, and Device Guard.

- Servers should be configured to block access to USB storage.

- Servers should be on isolated networks. Inbound and outbound Internet connections should be blocked.

More Info

Securing privileged access

You can learn more about securing privileged access at *https://learn.microsoft.com/ security/privileged-access-workstations/privileged-access-access-model.*

Security systems and services

Windows Server 2025 includes a variety of new and existing technologies that you can use to secure the operating system. While implementing each of these technologies increases the security of your Windows Server 2025 deployment, it's important to understand implementing no single technology or set of technologies guarantees that your deployment can't be compromised by the most determined of attackers. By implementing each technology, you will make Windows Server just a bit more difficult to compromise, thereby increasing the security of your organization's Windows Server deployment.

Inside OUT

Assume breach

Assume breach is a security philosophy in which you design a security implementation around the hypothesis that an attacker already has compromised and has privileged access to at least some of your organization's protected resources. You should not rely upon the assumptions that hostile actors only exist outside the perimeter network and that critical protected systems have not already been compromised. You should design your organization's security to mitigate the risk of a privileged insider acting maliciously, either deliberately or because their credentials have been compromised by a nefarious, external third party. Don't assume that just because a host sits on a protected internal subnet that it won't be subject to malicious network intrusion attempts.

Security Compliance Toolkit

The Security Compliance Toolkit (SCT) is a collection of tools that allow you to manage security configuration baselines for Windows Server and other Microsoft products. The SCT includes the Policy Analyzer tool and the Local Group Policy Object (LGPO) tool.

SCT provides security baselines for

- Windows Server 2025

- Windows Server 2022

- Windows Server 2019

- Windows Server 2016

- Windows Server 2012 R2

- Windows 11

- Windows 10

- Microsoft Office

- Microsoft Edge

More Info

Security Compliance Toolkit

You can learn more about the Security Compliance Toolkit at *https://learn.micro-soft.com/windows/security/operating-system-security/device-management/windows-security-configuration-framework/security-compliance-toolkit-10.*

Policy Analyzer tool

The Policy Analyzer tool allows you to compare Group Policy Objects (GPOs). You can use the Policy Analyzer tool to perform the following tasks:

- Determine which existing GPO settings are redundant or are internally consistent

- Determine the differences between different versions or collections of group policies

- Compare GPO settings against a computer's local policy and registry settings

When downloading the SCT, you can also download security baseline GPOs. To perform an analysis of a system against a baseline, perform the following steps:

1. Open the Policy Analyzer and click Add to add downloaded baseline policies. You can specify a folder that contains multiple exported GPOs. When you do this, all exported GPOs under the selected folder path will be imported. After selecting which policies to import, click Import and save the selection of files as a policy rule.

2. You can then use the View/Compare button to compare policies and determine where they differ, as shown in Figure 14-1.

Policy Type	Policy Group or Registry Key	Policy Setting	Local policy	2019
Audit Policy	Account Logon	Credential Validation	Success	***CONFLICT***
Audit Policy	Account Logon	Kerberos Authentication Service	Success	Success and Failure
Audit Policy	Account Logon	Kerberos Service Ticket Operations	Success	Failure
Audit Policy	Account Logon	Other Account Logon Events	No Auditing	
Audit Policy	Account Management	Application Group Management	No Auditing	
Audit Policy	Account Management	Computer Account Management	Success	Success
Audit Policy	Account Management	Distribution Group Management	No Auditing	
Audit Policy	Account Management	Other Account Management Events	No Auditing	Success
Audit Policy	Account Management	Security Group Management	Success	Success
Audit Policy	Account Management	User Account Management	Success	Success and Failure
Audit Policy	Detailed Tracking	DPAPI Activity	No Auditing	
Audit Policy	Detailed Tracking	PNP Activity	No Auditing	Success
Audit Policy	Detailed Tracking	Process Creation	No Auditing	Success
Audit Policy	Detailed Tracking	Process Termination	No Auditing	
Audit Policy	Detailed Tracking	RPC Events	No Auditing	
Audit Policy	Detailed Tracking	Token Right Adjusted	No Auditing	
Audit Policy	DS Access	Detailed Directory Service Replica...	No Auditing	
Audit Policy	DS Access	Directory Service Access	Success	Failure
Audit Policy	DS Access	Directory Service Changes	No Auditing	Success

Policy Path:
  Advanced Audit Policy Configuration
  Audit Policy\Account Logon
  Kerberos Service Ticket Operations

  Kerberos Service Ticket Operations

  This policy setting allows you to audit events generated by Kerberos authentication ticket-granting ticket (TGT) requests submitted for user accounts.

  If you configure this policy setting, an audit event is generated after a Kerberos authentication TGT is requested for a user account. Success audits record successful requests and Failure audits record unsuccessful requests.
  If you do not configure this policy setting, no audit event is generated after a Kerberos authentication TGT is request for a user account.

  Volume: Low.

  Default on Client editions: No Auditing.

  Default on Server editions: Success.

Figure 14-1   Security Configuration Toolkit Policy Viewer

You can use the Policy Analyzer to export this report into a format that can be viewed in Excel.

The Policy Analyzer is a reporting tool, and you cannot use it to apply policies directly. To apply policies, you can manually update GPO policies within your environment incrementally until they match the secure baseline. Taking an incremental approach allows you to test whether there are any unexpected consequences by applying new policies.

CHAPTER 14

You should avoid simply importing the security baseline policies into Active Directory and applying them unless you want to spend the next few weeks or months figuring out exactly which new policy setting you applied caused problems with your organization's existing workloads.

Local Group Policy Object tool

The LGPO tool is a command-line utility that allows you to perform local group policy operations against domain-joined and nondomain-joined computers. You can use the LGPO tool to perform the following tasks:

- Import settings into a computer's local group policy store from GPO backups

- Import settings into a computer's local Group Policy store from component files including Registry Policy (`registry.pol`), security templates, and advanced auditing CSV files

- Export a computer's local policy settings to a GPO backup

- Enable the use of Group Policy client-side extensions when processing local policy

- Extract a Registry Policy (`registry.pol`) file into a readable text format that can then be edited and built into a new `registry.pol` file with different settings

Attack Surface Analyzer

The Attack Surface Analyzer is a tool that allows you to locate possible security vulnerabilities by tracking changes made to the following:

- File System

- User Accounts

- System Services

- Network Ports (listeners)

- System Certificate Stores

- Windows Registry

To use the Attack Surface Analyzer, you first scan a system to determine the baseline settings of the system. You then perform another scan after you install software or suspect an unauthorized change has been made. The Attack Surface Analyzer will generate a report detailing any modifications made between the baseline and subsequent scans.

Once you've downloaded the Attack Surface Analyzer's files from the project's GitHub page, you run the Attack Surface Analyzer by opening an elevated command prompt and running the following command, which launches a web server that you can connect to at the address *http://127.0.0.1:5000*, as shown in Figure 14-2:

```
Asa.exe gui
```

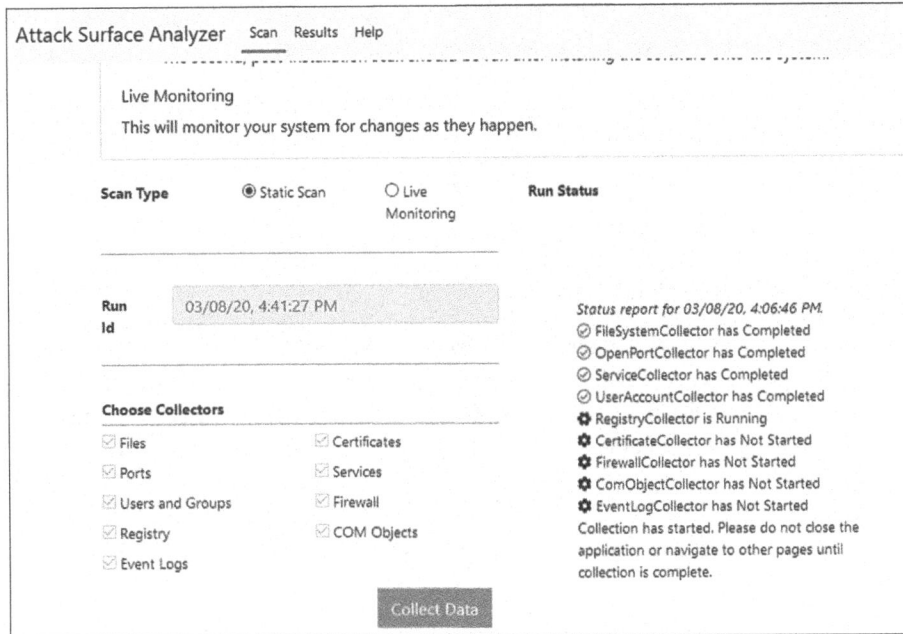

Figure 14-2   Attack Surface Analyzer

> ## More Info
>
> ### Attack Surface Analyzer
>
> You can learn more about the Attack Surface Analyzer at *https: https://github.com/ microsoft/attacksurfaceanalyzer.*

OSConfig

OSConfig is a security configuration and compliance management tool for Windows Server 2025 and later. OSConfig enables you to enforce security baselines, automate compliance, and prevent configuration drift on Windows Server 2025 computers. OSConfig is not supported on Windows Server 2022 or earlier versions of the Windows Server operating system.

OSConfig is available as a module from the PowerShell Gallery. You install it using the following command:

```
Install-Module -Name Microsoft.OSConfig -Scope AllUsers -Repository PSGallery -Force
```

If prompted to install or update the NuGet provider, type **Y** and press Enter.

You can verify that the module is installed with this command:

```
Get-Module -ListAvailable -Name Microsoft.OSConfig
```

You can ensure that you have an up-to-date version of the module and the baselines by running the following command:

```
Update-Module -Name Microsoft.OSConfig
```

To check which OSConfig cmdlets are available, run this:

```
Get-Command -Module Microsoft.OSConfig
```

OSConfig includes predefined security baselines tailored for different server roles: Domain Controller, Member Server, and Workgroup Member. These baselines enforce more than 300 security settings, such as TLS 1.2+, SMB 3.0+, and credential protections. You apply the security baseline by running the `Set-OSConfigDesiredConfiguration` cmdlet.

For example, to apply the Domain Controller baseline, run the command:

```
Set-OSConfigDesiredConfiguration -Scenario SecurityBaseline/WS2025/DomainController
-Default
```

To apply the Member Server baseline, run the command:

```
Set-OSConfigDesiredConfiguration -Scenario SecurityBaseline/WS2025/MemberServer -Default
```

To apply the Workgroup Member baseline, run the command:

```
Set-OSConfigDesiredConfiguration -Scenario SecurityBaseline/WS2025/WorkgroupMember
-Default
```

OSConfig also supports SecuredCore and Defender/Antivirus scenario security baselines.

You can view compliance from a PowerShell session or from the Security blade of Windows Admin Center as shown in Figure 14-3. To accomplish this using PowerShell for the Member Server baseline, run this command:

```
Get-OSConfigDesiredConfiguration -Scenario SecurityBaseline/WS2025/MemberServer | ft
Name, @{ Name = "Status"; Expression={$_.Compliance.Status} }, @{ Name = "Reason";
Expression={$_.Compliance.Reason} } -AutoSize -Wrap
```

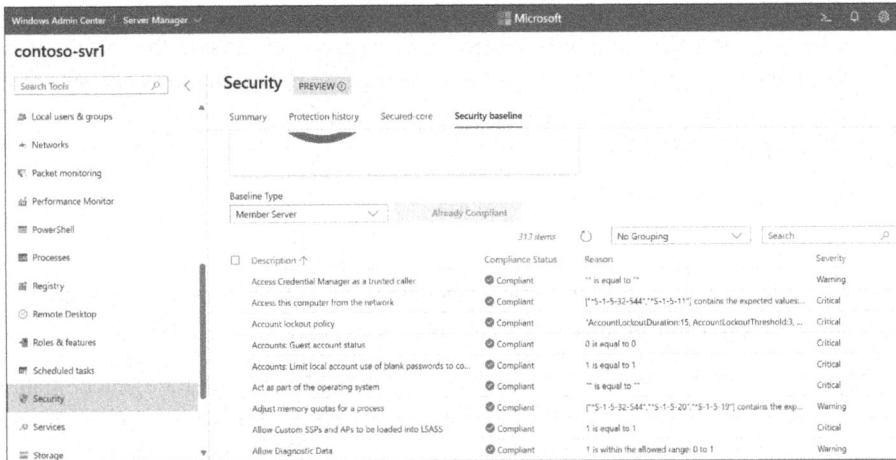

Figure 14-3   OSConfig

CHAPTER 14

The OSConfig drift control feature helps ensure that the system starts and remains in a known good security state. When you enable drift control, OSConfig automatically corrects any system changes that deviate from the desired state. OSConfig makes the correction through a refresh task. This task runs every four hours by default, which you can verify with the `Get-OSConfig-DriftControl` cmdlet. You enable drift control using the `Enable-OSConfigDriftControl` cmdlet. You can reset how often drift control runs using the `Set-OSConfigDriftControl` cmdlet. For example, to set it to 45 minutes, run this command:

```
Set-OSConfigDriftControl -RefreshPeriod 45
```

You disable OSConfig drift control using the `Disable-OSConfigDriftControl` cmdlet.

> **More Info**
>
> *OSConfig*
>
> **You can learn more about OSConfig *https://learn.microsoft.com/windows-server/security/osconfig/osconfig-overview*.**

Control Flow Guard

Control Flow Guard (CFG) is a security feature in Windows that implements a form of control-flow integrity. By placing tight restrictions on where an application can execute code, CFG makes it significantly harder for exploits to run malicious code on your server. CFG validates indirect calls in a program at runtime. When an application compiled with CFG starts, Windows creates a table of legitimate destinations for indirect calls. Every time the program attempts an indirect call, the operating system checks the target address against this safe list. If the target isn't in the list of valid locations, CFG raises an exception, and Windows immediately terminates the program to prevent the exploit from proceeding. Control Flow Guard is enabled by default on Windows Server 2025.

To configure CFG, perform the following steps:

1. On Windows Server 2025, open the Windows Security app. Under App & Browser Control, click Exploit Protection Settings under the Exploit Protection section. The system's Exploit Mitigation configuration panel opens.

2. Under the System Settings section, find Control Flow Guard (CFG). It's probably set to Use Default (On), which means CFG is enabled by default for all apps that don't have a custom setting. If it isn't set to Use Default (On), use the dropdown to change the setting, apply the changes, and restart the server.

You can also configure per-program settings in this same interface. Under Exploit Protection settings is a Program Settings section where you can add specific executables and override mitigations for them. For example, if one particular application needs CFG turned off for compatibility reasons, you could add that program here and set its CFG setting to Off.

To enable CFG system-wide via PowerShell: Open PowerShell as an administrator and run the following command:

```
Set-ProcessMitigation -System -Enable CFG
```

To disable CFG for specific applications, use `Set-ProcessMitigation` with the `Disable` flag. For example:

```
Set-ProcessMitigation -Name ExampleApp.exe -Disable CFG
```

Virtualization-based security

Virtualization-based security (VBS) allows Windows Server to use hardware virtualization to isolate and protect an area of computer memory from typical operating system processes. This "virtual secure mode" blocks malicious code from inserting itself into other high-integrity processes. VBS serves as an umbrella platform that enables multiple security features, including

- Credential Guard (protects authentication credentials)

- Memory integrity (HVCI)

- Secure Boot enforcement

You can enable VBS in the Windows Security app, as shown in Figure 14-4.

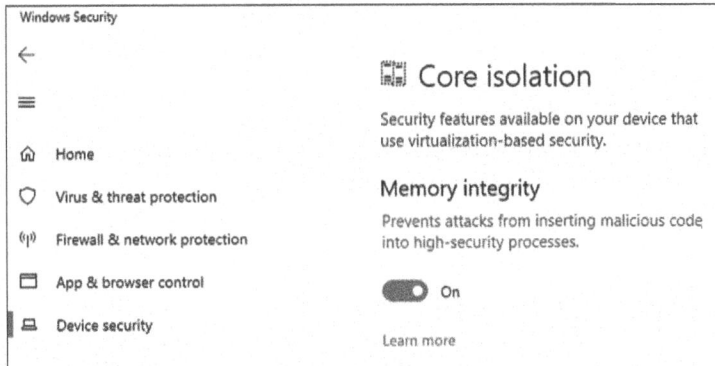

Figure 14-4   Enable VBS

CHAPTER 14

> ## More Info
> *Virtualization-based security*
>
> **You can learn more about virtualization-based security at** *https://learn.microsoft.com/
> en-us/windows-hardware/design/device-experiences/oem-vbs.*

Hypervisor-Protected Code Integrity

Hypervisor-Protected Code Integrity (HVCI), also known as Memory Integrity, is a specific security feature that runs within the VBS environment. You cannot have HVCI without VBS because HVCI requires the secure virtual environment that VBS provides. HVCI protects the Windows kernel by ensuring that only digitally signed and trusted code can execute in kernel mode.

HVCI includes the following functionality:

- **Code integrity enforcement**   Prevents unsigned or untrusted drivers from loading into system memory

- **Memory protection**   Ensures kernel memory pages are only made executable after passing code integrity checks

- **Code modification prevention**   Blocks executable code pages from being modified and prevents modified memory from becoming executable

More Info

Hypervisor-Protected Code Integrity

You can learn more about HVCI at *https://learn.microsoft.com/en-us/windows-hardware/drivers/bringup/device-guard-and-credential-guard*.

Windows Defender Application Control

Windows Defender Application Control (WDAC), known in previous versions of Windows Server as Device Guard and Configurable Code Integrity (CCI) policies, is a hardware- and software-based security system that restricts the execution of applications to those that are explicitly trusted. WDAC uses VBS to isolate a special service (the code integrity service) from the Windows kernel. Because the code integrity service is running as a trustlet in a special virtualized location, compromising the service is difficult, if not impossible, even if an attacker has complete control of the operating system. The WDAC name isn't present in all locations of the operating system, such as Group Policy, so occasionally you will still see references to Device Guard in items such as Group Policy.

WDAC includes the following features:

- **Virtual Secure Mode**   This is a special virtual container that isolates the LSASS.exe process from the operating system. Virtual Secure Mode is the underlying platform used by both Windows Defender Application Control for Code Integrity and Credential Guard for LSASS isolation.

- **Configurable Code Integrity**   This is the rules engine that, in conjunction with Virtual Secure Mode Protected Code Integrity, validates code that Windows Server attempts to enact.

- **Virtual Secure Mode Protected Code Integrity**   Uses two components to enforce Configurable Code Integrity policy:

    - User Mode Code Integrity manages whether user mode code can execute.

    - Kernel Mode Code Integrity manages whether kernel mode code can execute.

- **Platform and UEFI Secure Boot**   Ensures that the boot loader code and firmware are validated and prevents malware from modifying the boot environment.

To enable Virtual Secure Mode, perform the following steps:

1.   Enable Secure Boot and Trusted Platform Module (TPM).

2.   Enable Hyper-V.

3. Enable Isolated User Mode.

4. Configure the Turn On Virtualization Based Security Policy, located in the `Computer Configuration\Administrative Templates\System\Device Guard\` node.

5. Configure the BCD store to start Virtual Secure Mode. You do this by running the following command:

```
bcdedit /set vsmlaunchtype auto
```

By default, WDAC runs in Audit Mode. This allows you to tune a policy to ensure that the software that you want to run can run and won't be blocked. You have several options when it comes to controlling which software can run on a computer protected by Device Guard. These are as follows:

- Only allow software that is digitally signed by a trusted publisher to run on the server. If you're using internally written code, you can use your organization's code signing certificate to sign code digitally. You use the `New-CIPolicy` cmdlet to create an XML file with all relevant details about signed files on a system. Then you use the `ConvertFrom-CIPolicy` cmdlet to convert this XML file into a binary file that's placed in the `C:\Windows\System32\CodeIntegrity` folder and can be used by Device Guard to determine which software can run on the protected system.

- Use Package Inspector to create a catalog of all deployed and executed binary files for applications that you trust. You can use this when you need to deal with third-party applications that you trust but are not signed digitally. Package Inspector is included with the operating system and is located in the `C:\Windows\System32` directory. Package Inspector creates a catalog of hash files for each binary executable. Once the catalog file is created, you can digitally sign the catalog using `signtool.exe`, which is available in the Windows Software Development Kit (SDK) that you can download from Microsoft's website. Ensure that the signing certificate is added to the code integrity policy. WDAC blocks any software that is not in the signed catalog from running. You can use Group Policy and Configuration Manger to deploy code integrity policies and catalog files.

You can deploy WDAC on a test machine using the Device Guard and Credential Guard Readiness Tool. (The tool still uses the previous name for WDAC.) This tool assesses a computer's readiness to be configured for WDAC and allows you to perform a test deployment. Test deployments are important because you don't want to deploy WDAC and then find that business-critical software can no longer execute.

Once you've verified that a computer is ready for WDAC, you configure the Turn On Virtualization Based Security policy, located in the `Computer Configuration\Policies\Administrative Templates\System\Device Guard` section of a GPO and configure the policy so that the Virtualization Based Protection Of Code Integrity is set to either Enabled With UEFI Lock or Enabled Without Lock. The difference is that if you use the Enabled With UEFI Lock, as shown in Figure 14-5, the policy can only be disabled by signing in directly to the server.

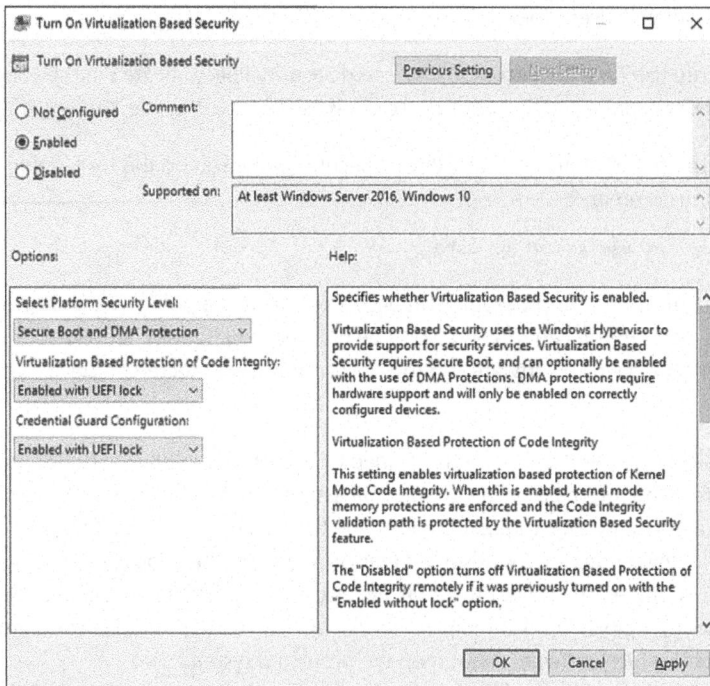

Figure 14-5   Turn On Virtualization Based Security

More Info

WDAC Deployment Guide

You can learn more about deploying WDAC at *https://learn.microsoft.com/en-us/ windows/security/application-security/application-control/app-control-for-business/ deployment/appcontrol-deployment-guide*.

Credential Guard

Credential Guard allows you to leverage virtualization-based security to isolate secrets, such as cached user credentials, in a special separate virtualized operating system. The special separate virtualized operating system is configured so that only specific processes and memory in the host operating system can access this secret data. The processes running in the separate virtualized operating system are termed *trustlets*.

Credential Guard is primarily a response to pass-the-hash or pass-the-ticket attacks. Should a host that has credential guard be compromised by an attacker, that attacker won't be able to successfully run a pass-the-hash attack tool to extract cached credentials and then use them to access other computers on the network.

Credential guard includes the following features and solutions:

- Stores derived domain credentials in a virtualized environment that's protected from the running operating system

- Can be managed by using Group Policy, Windows Management Instrumentation (WMI), or Windows PowerShell

Credential Guard does not allow

- Unconstrained Kerberos delegation

- NT LAN Manager version 1 (NTLMv1)

- Microsoft Challenge Handshake Authentication Protocol (MS-CHAPv2)

- Digest authentication

- Credential Security Support Provider (CredSSP)

- Kerberos DES encryption

You can use Credential Guard in conjunction with the Protected Users group in a layered approach to the protection of highly privileged accounts. The Protected Users group remains useful because your organization might not have computers that support Credential Guard. You can deploy Credential Guard only on computers that meet certain hardware requirements. Credential Guard is primarily useful for Privileged Access Workstations, but you should implement it eventually on any computer where IT operations personnel use privileged domain accounts.

Credential Guard has the following requirements:

- Windows Server 2016 or later or Windows 10 Enterprise or later

- UEFI firmware version 2.3.1 or higher

- Secure Boot

- Intel VT-x or AMD-V virtualization extensions

- Second Level Address Translation

- x64 processor architecture

- A VT-d or AMD-Vi IOMMU input/output memory management unit

CHAPTER 14

- TPM 2.0

- Secure firmware update process

- Firmware updated to support Secure MOR implementation

To enable Credential Guard on an appropriately configured computer, you need to configure the Turn On Virtualization Based Security policy, which is located in the `Computer Configuration\Administrative Templates\System\Device Guard` node of a GPO. This is the same policy that you also use to configure Windows Defender Application Control (previously known as Device Guard), which you learn about later in this chapter.

While configuring this policy, you must first set the policy to Enabled, and then you must set the platform security level to either Secure Boot or to Secure Boot and DMA Protection. Secure Boot with DMA Protection ensures that Credential Guard is used with Direct Memory Access protection.

Once this is done, you need to then set the Credential Guard Configuration option to Enabled With UEFI Lock or Enabled Without Lock. If you set the Enabled With UEFI Lock, Credential Guard cannot be remotely disabled and can only be disabled by having someone with local Administrator privileges sign on and disable Credential Guard configuration locally. The Enabled Without Lock option allows Credential Guard to be remotely disabled.

Credential Guard is enabled by default on Windows Server 2025 by default and is configured without UEFI lock. Promoting a computer to domain controller disables Credential Guard. Microsoft recommends against enabling Credential Guard on domain controllers because it may cause application compatibility issues with older administrative tools.

> ## More Info
> ### Credential Guard
>
> You can learn more about Credential Guard at *https://learn.microsoft.com/windows/security/identity-protection/credential-guard/*.

Controlled Folder Access

Controlled Folder Access is a security technology that allows you to protect specific folders on a Windows Server computer against malicious software. Controlled Folder Access is a useful tool for preventing ransomware from encrypting the folders that host file shares because you can use it to restrict which software can interact with specific paths on a computer running Windows Server. Controlled Folder Access allows trusted applications, such as those that are included with the operating system, to interact with protected folders. Only trusted apps, such as Microsoft-signed apps and those added to the allow list, can modify files in those protected locations.

Inside OUT

Protect file servers from ransomware

Controlled Folder Access can be used to protect file servers from ransomware. You should enable it on both file servers as well as any other computer that has access to the file share. You should also ensure that your file servers are regularly backed up to a safe location, such as an Azure Recovery Services Vault, so that you are able to recover data in the event that the ransomware is clever enough to get past other precautions you have put in place.

On computers running Windows Server with Desktop Experience, you can use the Virus & Threat Protection area of the Windows Security control panel to configure which folders are protected and which applications can interact with protected folders, as shown in Figure 14-6.

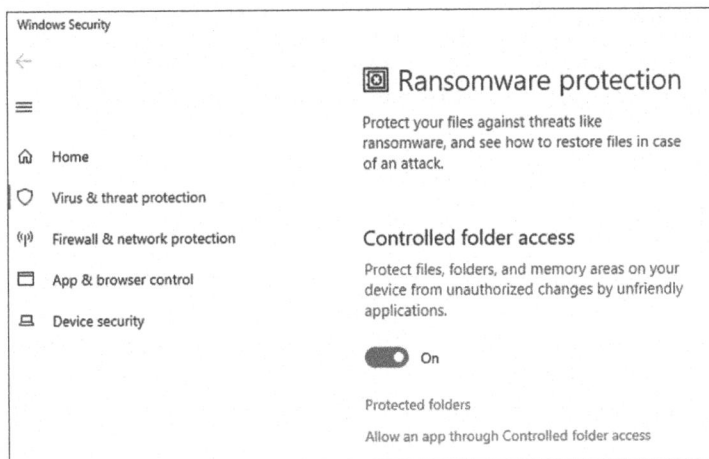

Figure 14-6   Controlled Folder Access

You can configure Controlled Folder Access from PowerShell using the `Set-MpPreference` cmdlet. To enable controlled folder access, run this command:

```
Set-MpPreference -EnableControlledFolderAccess Enabled
```

To disable Controlled Folder Access, run this command:

```
Set-MpPreference -EnableControlledFolderAccess Disabled
```

You can enable audit mode to test which applications would be blocked while not yet blocking them by running the command:

```
Set-MpPreference -EnableControlledFolderAccess AuditMode
```

To add a new location for Controlled Folder Access to monitor, run this command:

```
Add-MpPreference -ControlledFolderAccessProtectedFolders "E:\fileshare"
```

To remove a location from Controlled Folder Access monitoring, run this command:

```
Remove-MpPreference -ControlledFolderAccessProtectedFolders "E:\fileshare"
```

To allow an application to interact with a protected folder, run this command:

```
Add-MpPreference -ControlledFolderAccessAllowedApplications "c:\application\app.exe"
```

You can also use the `Remove-MpPreference` cmdlet to revoke an application's ability to interact with a protected location.

More Info

Controlled Folder Access

You can learn more about Controlled Folder Access at *https://learn.microsoft.com/en-us/ defender-endpoint/evaluate-controlled-folder-access.*

Exploit Protection

Exploit Protection allows you to configure extra security settings for Windows Server, such as Control Flow Guard (CFG) and Data Execution Prevention (DEP). In past versions of Windows Server, you would use the Enhanced Mitigation Experience Toolkit (EMET), a separate product that you download and install to perform this task. Figure 14-7 shows the Exploit Protection settings in the Windows Security Control Panel app.

Some Exploit Protection mitigation settings are configurable at the system level, and some are only configurable on a per-app basis. The settings that can be configured at both the system and app level are as follows:

- **Control Flow Guard**   Ensures control flow integrity for indirect calls

- **Data Execution Prevention**   Prevents code from being executed from data-only memory pages

- **Force Randomization For Images (Mandatory ASLR)**   Forces reallocation of memory images that haven't been compiled with the DYNAMICBASE option

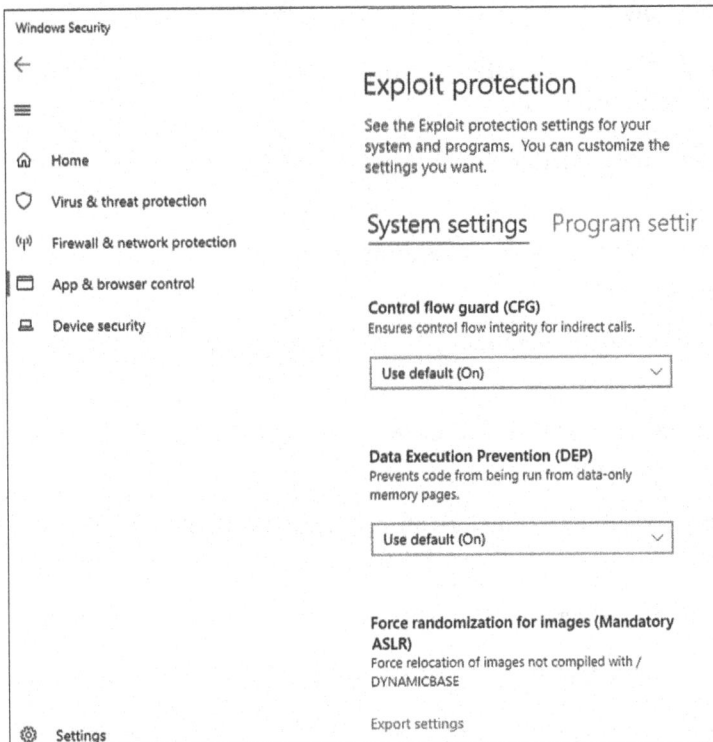

Figure 14-7   Exploit Protection

The settings that you can only configure at the application level are as follows:

- **Arbitrary Code Guard**   Prevent nonimage-backed executable code and code page modification

- **Block Low Integrity Images**   Block the loading of images marked with low integrity

- **Block Remote Images**   Block the loading of images from remote devices

- **Block Untrusted Fonts**   Block the loading of any GDI-based fonts not installed in the system Fonts directory

- **Code Integrity Guard**   Restrict the loading of images to those that have been digitally signed by Microsoft

- **Disable Extension Points**   Disable extensibility mechanisms that allow DLL injection into all processes

- **Disable Win32k System Calls**   Block programs from using the Win32K system call table

- **Do Not Allow Child Processes**   Prevent programs from spawning child processes

- **Export Address Filtering (EAF)**   Filter dangerous exported functions that are being resolved by malicious code

- **Import Address Filtering (IAF)**   Filter imported functions being resolved by malicious code

- **Randomize Memory Allocations (Bottom-Up ASLR)**   Randomize locations for virtual memory allocation

- **Simulate Execution (SimExec)**   Ensure that calls to sensitive functions are returned to legitimate callers

- **Validate API Invocation (CallerCheck)**   Ensure that sensitive APIs can only be invoked by legitimate callers

- **Validate Exception Chains (SEHOP)**   Ensures the integrity of an exception chain during dispatch

- **Validate Handle Usage**   Raises an exception on any invalid handle references

- **Validate Heap Integrity**   Terminates a program when heap corruption is detected

- **Validate Image Dependency Integrity**   Enforces code signing for Windows image dependency loading

- **Validate Stack Integrity (StackPivot)**   Ensures that the stack has not been redirected for sensitive functions

You configure exploit protection from PowerShell using the `Set-ProcessMitigation` cmdlet. For example, to enable Data Execution Prevention (DEP) at the system level, you would run the command:

```
Set-ProcessMitigation -System -Enable DEP
```

You can view which exploit protection settings are enabled by running the following command:

```
Get-ProcessMitigation -System
```

You can use the following command to export an Exploit Guard configuration:

```
Get-ProcessMitigation -RegistryConfigFilePath exportedconfig.xml
```

You can import an exported Exploit Guard configuration by using the following command:

```
Set-ProcessMitigation -PolicyFilePath exportedconfig.xml
```

> ## More Info
>
> *Exploit Protection*
>
> You can learn more about deploying Exploit Protection at *https://learn.microsoft.com/ en-us/defender-endpoint/enable-exploit-protection*.

Attack surface reduction rules

Attack surface reduction (ASR) rules in Microsoft Defender help reduce the attack surface of Windows Server by blocking or auditing risky behaviors such as launching child processes from Office, executing scripts via email, or abuse of credential theft techniques. In Windows Server 2025, ASR rules are managed through Microsoft Defender Antivirus and can be deployed with PowerShell or Group Policy.

You have to use GUIDs when working with ASR rules. Table 14-1 lists the available ASR rules.

Table 14-1   ASR rules and GUIDs

Rule #	Rule Name	GUID
1	Block executable content from email and webmail	be9ba2d9-53ea-4cdc-84e5-9b1eeee46550
2	Block Office applications from creating child processes	d4f940ab-401b-4efc-aadc-ad5f3c50688a
3	Block Office applications from injecting code into other processes	75668c1f-73b5-4cf0-bb93-3ecf-5cb7cc84
4	Block Office applications from creating executable content	3b576869-a4ec-4529-8536-b80a7769e899
5	Block JavaScript or VBScript from launching downloaded executable content	d3e037e1-3eb8-44c8-a917-57927947596d
6	Block execution of potentially obfuscated scripts	5beb7efe-fd9a-4556-801d-275e5ff-c04cc
7	Block credential stealing from LSASS	9e6c4e1f-7d60-472f-ba1a-a39ef669e4b2
8	Block process creations originating from PSExec and WMI commands	d1e49aac-8f56-4280-b9ba-993a6d77406c
9	Block untrusted and unsigned processes running from USB/removable drives	b2b3f03d-6a65-4f7b-a9c7-1c7ef74a9ba4
10	Block Office communication applications from creating child processes	26190899-1602-49e8-8b27-eb-1d0a1ce869

Rule #	Rule Name	GUID
11	Use advanced protection against ransomware	c1db55ab-c21a-4637-bb3f-a12568109d35
12	Block persistence through WMI event subscription	e6db77e5-3df2-4cf1-b95a-636979351e5b
13	Block Adobe Reader from creating child processes	7674ba52-37eb-4a4f-a9a1-f0f9a1619a2c
14	Block abuse of exploited vulnerable signed drivers	56a863a9-875e-4185-98a7-b882c64b5ce5
15	Block use of copied or modified LSASS credentials (variant of LSASS protection) *(same GUID as Rule 7)*	9e6c4e1f-7d60-472f-ba1a-a39ef669e4b2
16	Block executable files from running unless they meet a prevalence, age, or trusted list criterion	01443614-cd74-433a-b99e-2ecd-c07bfc25
17	Win32 API calls from Office macro	92e97fa1-2edf-4476-bdd6-9dd0b4dddc7b
18	Block use of copied or impersonated system tools	c0033c00-d16d-4114-a5a0-dc9b3a7d-2ceb
19	Block Webshell creation for Servers	a8f5898e-1dc8-49a9-9878-85004b8a61e6

Each rule can be set to enabled, disabled, not configured, warn, or audit using the `Enabled`, `Disabled`, `NotConfigured`, `Warn`, and `AuditMode` flags. For example, to configure Rule 8 on blocking PSExec lateral movement, you would run the command

```
Add-MpPreference -AttackSurfaceReductionRules_Ids d1e49aac-8f56-4280-b9ba-993a6d77406c
-AttackSurfaceReductionRules_Actions Enabled
```

`Audit` logs an event in the Microsoft-Windows-Windows Defender/Operational event log. `Warn` prompts the user with a notification when a rule would block an action but provides the ability for the user to bypass the rule. You can view existing ASR rule by running the following Power-Shell command:

```
Get-MpPreference | Select -ExpandProperty AttackSurfaceReductionRules_Ids
```

You can enable ASR rules by using the Attack Surface Reduction policy located in the `Computer Configuration\Administrative Templates\Windows Components\Microsoft Defender Antivirus\Microsoft Defender Exploit Guard` node of a GPO. You add rules by GUID and set the action using 0 for Disabled, 1 for Block, and 2 for Audit.

> ## More Info
> ### Exploit Protection
> You can learn more about deploying Exploit Protection at *https://learn.microsoft.com/ en-us/defender-endpoint/enable-exploit-protection.*

Windows Defender

Windows Server includes Windows Defender, the Microsoft antimalware solution. Windows Defender is enabled by default when you deploy Windows Server. To disable Windows Defender, you must remove it, either by using the Add Roles And Features Wizard or by using the following `Uninstall-WindowsFeature` command:

```
Uninstall-WindowsFeature -Name Windows-Server-Antimalware
```

You can use the following PowerShell cmdlets to manage Windows Defender on computers running the GUI or the Server Core version of Windows Server:

- `Add-MpPreference`   Modifies Windows Defender settings.

- `Get-MpComputerStatus`   View the status of antimalware software on the server.

- `Get-MpPreference`   View the Windows Defender preferences for scans and updates.

- `Get-MpThreat`   View the history of malware detected on the computer.

- `Get-MpThreatCatalog`   Get known threats from the definitions catalog. You can use this list to determine if a specific threat is known to Windows Defender.

- `Get-MpThreatDetection`   Lists active and past threats that Windows Defender has detected on the computer.

- `Remove-MpPreference`   Removes an exclusion or default action.

- `Remove-MPThreat`   Removes an active threat from the computer.

- `Set-MpPreference`   Allows you to configure scan and update preferences.

- `Start-MpScan`   Starts an antimalware scan on a server.

- `Start-MpWDOScan`   Triggers a Windows Defender offline scan.

- `Update-MpSignature`   Triggers an update for antimalware definitions.

> ## More Info
> *Windows Defender*
>
> You can learn more about Windows Defender at *https://learn.microsoft.com/windows-server/security/windows-defender/windows-defender-overview-windows-server.*

Microsoft Defender SmartScreen

Microsoft Defender SmartScreen, shown in Figure 14-8, provides you with a way of checking unrecognized files that have been downloaded to Windows Server against the properties of known malicious files that are stored in the Microsoft Graph security database. A good general security rule is to avoid downloading application files directly from the Internet and installing them on Windows Server; instead, you should download them to a separate location, test them, and then copy them remotely to Windows Server for installation.

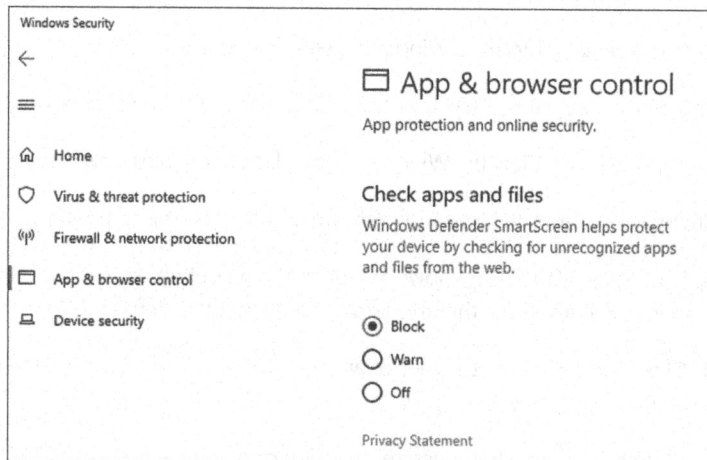

Figure 14-8   App & Browser Control

> ## More Info
> *Microsoft Defender Smart Screen*
>
> You can learn more about Microsoft Defender Smart Screen at *https://feedback.smartscreen.microsoft.com/smartscreenfaq.aspx.*

Entra ID Password Protection

Microsoft Entra ID Password Protection is a hybrid service that allows you to enforce strong password policies by blocking common weak passwords and their variants, both in the cloud and in on-premises Active Directory environments. Entra ID Password Protection uses a global banned password list that is updated and maintained by a Microsoft security team. It can be used in addition to your own custom banned password list to prevent users from setting common or compromised passwords.

When a user attempts to change or set a password on a domain controller (DC), the new password is evaluated against these banned lists. If the password contains too many weak elements, it will be deemed insecure. Depending on how you configure Entra ID Password Protection, the attempt will either be logged, if you have configured Audit mode, or blocked if you are enforcing password protection.

Entra ID Password Protection's on-premises deployment consists of three key components:

- **Entra ID Password Protection Proxy Service**   You install this service on one or more domain member servers. The proxy authenticates with and communicates with Microsoft Entra ID and downloads the latest banned password list, checking for updates to the list every hour. All communication between domain controllers and this proxy uses RPC over TCP within your network. Entra ID Password Protection does not require domain controllers to have line of sight to the internet.

- **Entra ID Password Protection DC Agent Service**   This service that runs on each writable domain controller in the environment. It operates in conjunction with a password filter to intercept password set/change events. The DC agent service uses the cached banned password policy that it retrieves via the proxy to evaluate passwords locally. It periodically synchronizes with the proxy to fetch updated password lists. These banned passwords use the domain's SYSVOL share for replication to other DCs. The agent monitors SYSVOL for changes, and if another DC has already updated the policy file, an agent can use that without resynchronizing with the proxy. This is useful in multisite architectures where you might only want the proxy deployed at one site and to allow SYSVOL replication to handle internal replication.

- **Entra ID Password Protection DC Agent Password Filter DLL**   A dynamic link library that is installed on each domain controller as part of the Entra ID Password Protection agent installation. This DLL is registered as a password filter on the DC. Whenever a user attempts to change or reset a password on that DC, Windows invokes this filter. The filter forwards the plaintext proposed password to the local DC agent service, which checks it against the banned password policy. If the password is found to contain disallowed terms, the filter will instruct Windows to reject the password change. If the password passes the check or if Entra ID Password Protection is configured in audit mode, the filter allows the operation to continue. A user whose new proposed password is rejected during a password change operation will see a message that explains "password does not meet requirements."

Entra ID Password Protection requirements

Entra ID Password Protection has the following requirements:

- Entra Tenant & Licenses: You have a Microsoft Entra ID tenant with enabled for the users in scope. Entra Password Protection is included with P1/P2 plans. Each user who will be protected should be licensed.

- Global Administrator or equivalent: You'll need an account with Global Administrator or equivalent permissions to perform initial registration of the password protection proxy with Entra. Subsequent proxy registration requires Security Administrator permissions. The account used to install agents on domain controllers requires Domain Admin and Enterprise Admin rights.

- Domain controllers running Windows Server 2012 R2 or later: Proxy service must also be running on Windows Server 2012 R2 or later. Given the importance of Active Directory, you should be running these servers on Windows Server 2025, but earlier versions are supported.

- The Active Directory domain must be using DFSR for SYSVOL replication rather than the deprecated FRS. If your domain still uses FRS, migrate to DFSR before deployment. Some organizations may have this because they have performed in-place upgrades without updating FRS. You can learn how to perform FRS to DFSR migration in Chapter 24, "Upgrade and migration."

- Servers that will host the proxy service need outbound connectivity to *login.microsoftonline.com, enterpriseregistration.windows.net,* and *autoupdate.msapproxy.net* using HTTPS.

- Configure the servers that host the proxy so that the computer accounts of all writable domain controllers have the Access This Computer From The Network right.

Entra ID Password Protection deployment

The first step in deploying Entra ID Password Protection is to deploy the proxy service. The proxy service can run on any domain member server in the forest. The proxy service should not be deployed on an RODC or writable domain controller. You can download the following files, still named Azure AD and not yet updated to Entra ID, by navigating to the Microsoft Download Center and searching for Entra ID Password Protection:

- `AzureADPasswordProtectionProxySetup.exe`

- `AzureADPasswordProtectionDCAgentSetup.msi`

The first file is for the proxy installation; the second file is to deploy the agent service on your domain controllers. Remember that you'll need to deploy the agent service on all writable domain controllers because you never know which one will be processing a password change. You can install each of these from the GUI or command line.

Verify that the proxy is installed correctly by running the command

```
Get-Service AzureADPasswordProtectionProxy | fl status
```

which should return that the service is running. Next, you need to register the proxy service with Entra. You do this by running the following command on the proxy server:

```
Register-AzureADPasswordProtectionProxy
```

You'll be prompted for your Entra credentials and then perform interactive device registration with Azure. The registration cmdlet performs a series of health checks to ensure that all necessary endpoints can be contacted. You will need to resolve any errors before proceeding. You can check the health of the connection using the command

```
Test-AzureADPasswordProtectionProxyHealth -TestAll
```

Once all errors are resolved, you need to register your on-premises forest. You can do this by running the following command on the proxy server using an account that is a member of the Enterprise Admins group in your on-premises environment:

```
Register-AzureADPasswordProtectionForest
```

When you run this command, you'll be prompted again for your Entra credentials. This command registers the on-premises forest with Entra and sets up a cryptographic object in Active Directory that is used as a connection point. You can verify that the forest is registered by rerunning this command:

```
Test-AzureADPasswordProtectionProxyHealth -TestAll
```

Once the forest has been successfully registered, you can install the domain controller agent on every writable domain controller. Running the MSI installer will require a domain controller boot. You can verify that deployment has occurred correctly by checking that the Azure AD Password Protection DC Agent service is running.

Once this is done, enable password protection in the Password Protection blade of the Entra ID section of the Azure portal. You do this by setting the Enable Password Protection On Windows Server Active Directory toggle to Yes. You also have the option of setting the password protection mode between Audit, which will only detect the use of bad passwords, or Enforced mode, which will block the use of bad passwords.

The Password Protection blade also enables you to manage your own custom banned password list. This custom list is useful if you want to block the use of passwords that are not on the current block list. For example, it's unlikely that some of the more unusual Australian town names are on the list, so you might manually add Wonthaggi, Tuggeranong, and Briagolong.

CHAPTER 14

Internet Information Services

Many organizations use Internet Information Services (IIS) to host both their public-facing website as well as internal intranet services. IIS also supports many different roles, from Outlook Web Access in Exchange Server deployments to SharePoint, Windows Server Update Services, and Certificate Services Web enrollment.

In this chapter, you learn about how to perform web server–administration tasks, from basic tasks, such as configuring new websites and virtual directories, to more advanced topics, such as configuring application pool recycling settings, setting FTP sessions to require TLS, and delegating administrative privileges.

Managing sites

You perform website management in IIS through the IIS Manager console. The key to understanding the IIS Manager console, shown in Figure 15-1, is the Details pane that allows you to configure items depending on the configuration node selected. You are presented with the Details pane when selecting a particular node in the Connections pane, such as the web server itself, the Applications Pool node, or individual websites. For example, if you open the Authentication node at the server level, it configures authentication options for the server. If you have a specific website selected, opening the same Authentication item configures authentication for only that website. If you want to configure an item that isn't present, you need to verify that the relevant role service is installed.

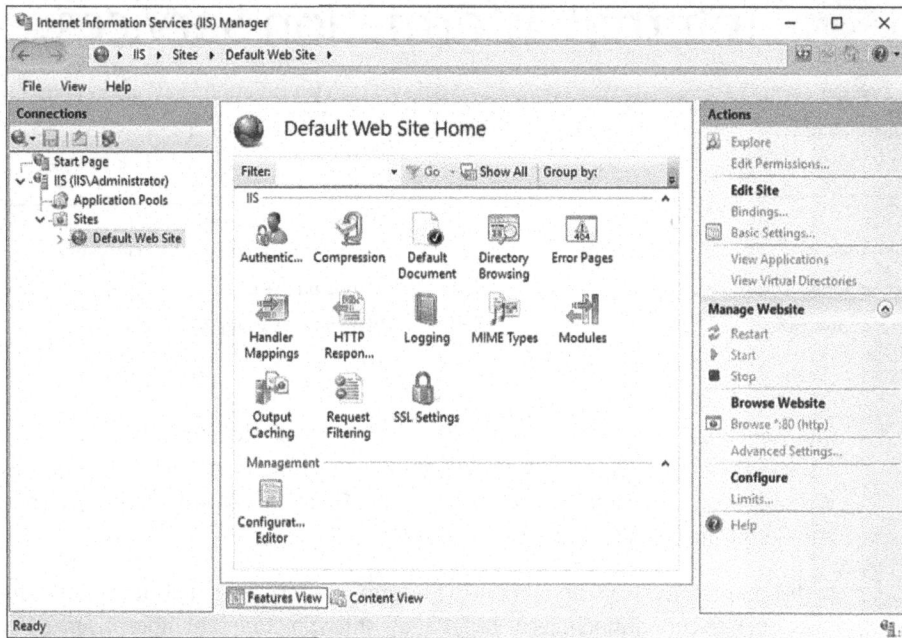

Figure 15-1 IIS Manager

Inside OUT

Missing items

Specific configuration items are only present within the IIS Manager when the appropriate role service is installed. IIS installs in a minimal configuration. If you can't find a specific option that you need to configure for a web application that you're hosting, check that the appropriate role service is installed.

Adding websites

The only practical limit for the number of websites that a server running IIS can host is hardware-related. Although you can probably run 10,000 different sites off the same computer or virtual machine, the hardware resources needed to support that number of sites in order to run in a fast and responsive manner are prohibitively expensive.

To run more than one site on IIS, the sites need to be different in one of the following ways:

- **Unique IP address** You can configure a different site for each IP address associated with the server. Although this isn't useful when you use one of the limited supply of IPv4 addresses, configuring different sites for each IP address associated with the server is useful when it comes to the more plentiful IPv6 addresses. You can use IP address differentiation to ensure that website traffic uses a specific network adapter.

- **Hostname**   If your server has only one IP address, you can still run multiple sites. You just need to ensure that each site uses a unique hostname. IIS parses the hostname in the HTTP request and directs the client to the appropriate site.

- **Port number**   You can also configure different sites that use the same IP address and hostname by assigning them different port addresses. The port address is a less popular way of differentiating websites; although it's an effective technique, most people have difficulty remembering to add a separate port address to a URL.

To add a website to an existing server, perform the following steps:

1. Open the IIS Manager console from the Tools menu of the Server Manager console.

2. Right-click the Server node, and then click Add Web Site.

3. On the Add Web Site dialog, shown in Figure 15-2, enter the following information:

   - **Site Name**   The name that represents the site on the server.

   - **Application Pool**   The application pool with which the site is associated. The default settings create a new application pool for each new site. You can click the Select button to select a different application pool.

   - **Physical Path**   This is where the website files are stored. You can configure site files to be stored on a remote network share. When you do this, you need to specify the authentication credentials used to connect to the network share or the file system. The default credentials use the web user's identity, so you'll need to configure authentication settings if you aren't using a specific account.

   - **Type**   Allows you to specify whether the site uses HTTP or HTTPS.

   - **IP Address**   Determines whether the site uses all unassigned IP addresses or a specific IP address assigned to the server.

   - **Port**   Determines whether the site uses the default port 80 or 443 for HTTPS sites.

   - **Host Name**   The hostname associated with the site.

   - **SSL Certificate**   Allows you to select the TLS certificate associated with the site. This option is only available if you select HTTPS at the time. Certificates can be imported if necessary.

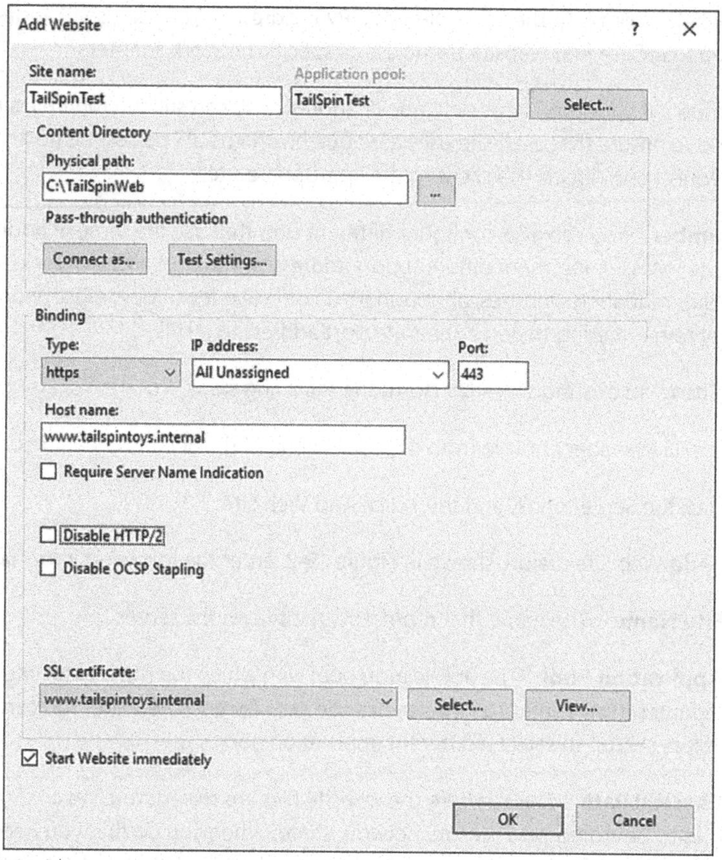

Figure 15-2   Add Website dialog

You can also create a new website with the New-IISSite cmdlet. For example, to create a new website on port 80 associated with the hostname *www.contoso.internal* in the c:\contoso folder, use this PowerShell command:

```
New-IISSite -Name "Contoso" -PhysicalPath C:\Contoso -BindingInformation "*:80:www.
contoso.internal"
```

Although you're more likely to use PowerShell to manage IIS on Windows Server, long-time IIS administrators often have scripts that call the appcmd.exe utility, which was available in several previous versions of Windows Server and is located in the c:\Windows\System32\inetsrv folder, to perform administrative tasks. For example, you can use appcmd.exe to create a new website on port 80 associated with the hostname *www.contoso.internal* and use the c:\contoso folder with the following command:

```
Appcmd.exe add site /name:contoso /physicalPath:c:\contoso /bindings:http/*:80:www.
contoso.internal
```

You can view a list of sites running on a server using the command:

```
Appcmd.exe list sites
```

Test certificates

You can create a self-signed TLS certificate from the IIS Manager console by selecting the Server Certificates item on the server instance home page and then selecting Create Self-Signed Certificate from the Action menu. In the Create Self-Signed Certificate dialog, provide a friendly name for the certificate, such as www.tailspintoys.internal, and select the certificate store for the certificate. The Personal store is appropriate if you have fewer than 30 certificates used on the IIS server. The Web Hosting store is appropriate if you have more than 30 certificates installed on the server. Some older roles and services that haven't been updated beyond basic maintenance for new versions of Windows Server only support the use of the Personal store.

You can create a self-signed TLS certificate using the New-SelfSignedCertificate cmdlet. For example, to create a self-signed certificate for the website *www.tailspintoys.internal* and to store that certificate in the Personal store, run this command:

```
New-SelfSignedCertificate -DNSName www.tailspintoys.internal -CertStoreLocation "cert:\
LocalMachine\My"
```

Virtual directories

You use virtual directories when you want to create a directory on the website that does not map to a corresponding folder in the existing website folder structure. For example, the site *www.fabrikam.com* might map to the c:\fabrikam folder on a computer running IIS. If you create the folder c:\fabrikam\products, people can access that folder by navigating to the URL *www.fabrikam.com/products*. Instead, if you put the Products folder on another volume, you can use a virtual directory to map the URL *www.fabrikam.com/products* to that alternate location.

To add a virtual directory using the IIS Manager console, perform the following steps:

1. Open the IIS Manager console and navigate to the site to which you want to add the virtual directory.

2. Right-click the site, and then click Add Virtual Directory.

3. In the Add Virtual Directory dialog, shown in Figure 15-3, enter the Alias for the virtual directory and the Physical Path to the virtual directory. If you're specifying a remote network share, you can configure which account is used to connect to that share.

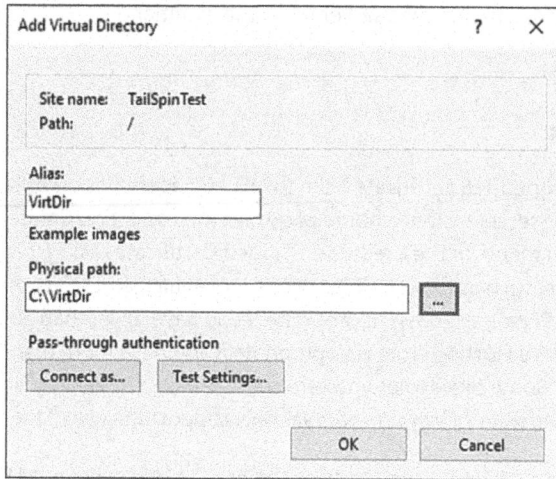

Figure 15-3   Add Virtual Directory dialog

Modifying site settings

After you create a website, you can change the settings of the site by viewing its Advanced Settings, as shown in Figure 15-4. This can be done by clicking the site in the IIS Manager console and clicking the Advanced Settings item in the Actions pane.

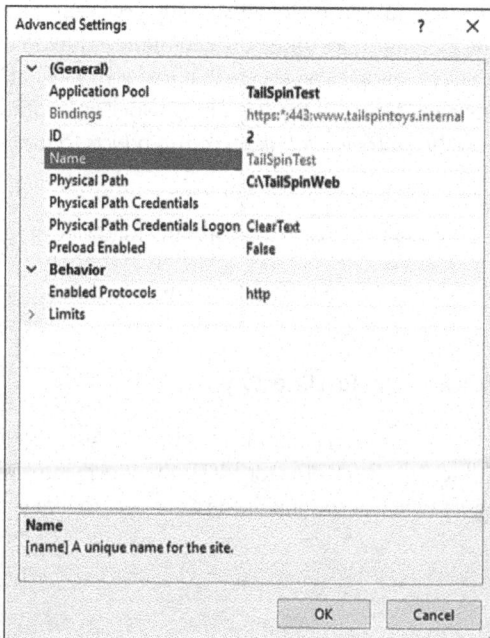

Figure 15-4   Advanced Settings

Adding web applications

A web application is a collection of content, either at a website's top level or in a separate folder under the website's top level. Applications can be collected in application pools. Application pools allow you to isolate one or more applications in a collection. When you create a website, it automatically creates a web application associated with that website. This web application has the same name as the website.

To create a web application, perform the following steps:

1. Open the IIS Manager console and navigate to the site for which you want to create a web application.

2. Right-click the site, and then click Add Application.

3. In the Add Application dialog, shown in Figure 15-5, enter the application's alias, choose which Application Pool the application is a member of, and specify the Physical Path to the application on the server.

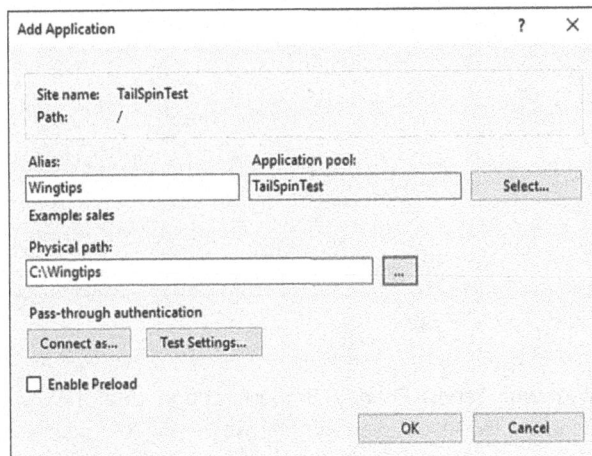

Figure 15-5   Add Application

Configuring TLS certificates

TLS certificates—often inaccurately referred to as "SSL certificates" because TLS is the successor protocol to SSL—allow clients to encrypt their session with the web server, minimizing the chance that communication between the client and the server can be intercepted; also, TLS certificates serve as an identity verification mechanism. You can configure TLS to be required at the server, site, web application, virtual directory, folder, and file levels.

CHAPTER 15

The first step you need to take prior to requiring TLS on a particular site is to request and then install a certificate. To do this, perform the following steps:

1. Open the IIS Manager console, select the Server node, and then double-click the Server Certificates item in the Details pane.

2. Click the Create Certificate Request item. In the Request Certificate dialog, shown in Figure 15-6, enter the name for the certificate and your organization's details and click Next.

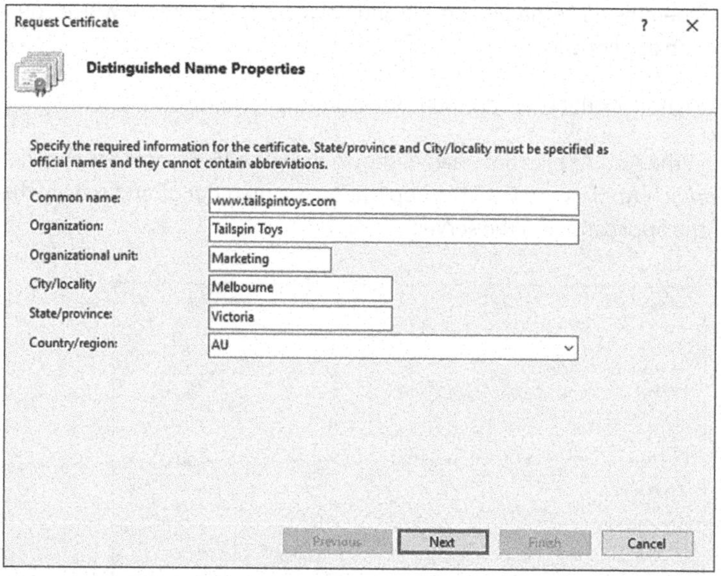

Request Certificate	? X

Distinguished Name Properties

Specify the required information for the certificate. State/province and City/locality must be specified as official names and they cannot contain abbreviations.

Common name:	www.tailspintoys.com
Organization:	Tailspin Toys
Organizational unit:	Marketing
City/locality:	Melbourne
State/province:	Victoria
Country/region:	AU

Previous | Next | Finish | Cancel

Figure 15-6   Request Certificate

3. On the Cryptographic Service Provider Properties page, enter the cryptographic service provider and the key length that you want to use for the TLS certificate, and then click Next.

4. Enter a name for the certificate request file. After the certificate request file is created, forward it to a CA.

5. After the certificate has been issued, open the Server Certificates item, and then click Complete Certificate Request.

6. On the Specify Certificate Authority Response page of the Complete Certificate Request Wizard, specify the location of the certificate issued by the CA and a friendly name with which to identify the certificate, and then click OK. This installs the certificate.

After the certificate is installed, you can configure the site, virtual directory, folder, or file to request or require HTTPS. To accomplish this goal, perform the following steps:

1. In IIS Manager, select the site on which you want to configure TLS.

2. Click Edit Bindings, and then click Add. In the Add Site Binding dialog, ensure that HTTPS is selected in the Type dropdown, and the TLS certificate that you installed is selected in the SSL Certificate dropdown, as shown in Figure 15-7.

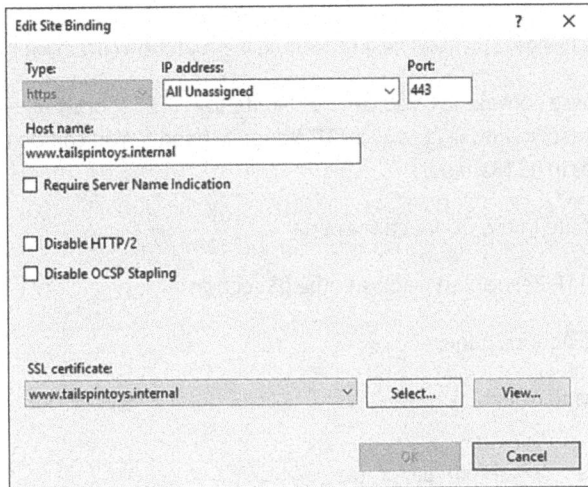

Figure 15-7   Edit Site Binding dialog

3. Select the site, virtual directory, folder, or file on which you want to enforce TLS settings.

4. Double-click the SSL Settings item in the Details pane. (This should be TLS settings, but SSL remains the commonly used term.)

5. On the SSL Settings page, ensure that Require SSL is selected, and then click Apply.

Enable TLS 1.3

To enable TLS 1.3 on IIS, you need to edit the registry. To do this, perform the following steps:

1. Open Registry Editor (regedit) and navigate to HKEY_LOCAL_MACHINE\SYSTEM\ CurrentControlSet\Control\SecurityProviders\SCHANNEL\Protocols.

2. Create a new key named **TLS 1.3**, then add subkeys **Client and Server** under it.

3. For both Client and Server subkeys, create a **DWORD** value named **Enabled** and set it to 1. Ensure DisabledByDefault is set to 0.

Enable HTTP/3 on IIS

HTTP/2 is supported natively in IIS on Windows Server 2016 and later and only needs a valid TLS certificate. HTTP/2 is not supported with Windows Authentication and Bandwidth Throttling.

HTTP/3 can be enabled on IIS in Windows Server 2022 and Windows Server 2025 as long as TLS 1.3 is enabled. To enable HTTP/3, run the following commands:

```
reg add "HKEY_LOCAL_MACHINE\SYSTEM\CurrentControlSet\services\HTTP\Parameters" /v
EnableHttp3 /t REG_DWORD /d 1 /f
Enable-TlsCipherSuite -Name TLS_CHACHA20_POLY1305_SHA256 -Position 0
Enable-NetFirewallRule -DisplayName "World Wide Web Services (QUIC Traffic-In)"
```

Once you have run these commands, you can bind a site to HTTPS (port 443) with a valid TLS certificate and add the following `alt-svc` HTTP response header. You can do this by performing the following steps in IIS Manager:

1. Select your website in the Connections pane.

2. Double-click HTTP Response Headers in the IIS section.

3. Click Add in the Actions pane.

4. Enter the following details:

    ```
    Name: alt-svc
    Value: h3=":443"; ma=86400; persist=1
    ```

H3=:443 sets HTTP/3 on port 443, ma=86400 sets the maximum age to 24 hours, and `persist=1` allows the client to maintain a cached alternative service.

Site authentication

Authentication methods determine how a user authenticates with a server or a website. You can configure authentication at the server level or at the site level. If there is a conflict between the authentication methods configured at the server and site levels, the site-level authentication settings have precedence. IIS supports the following authentication methods:

- **Active Directory Client Certificate**   This form of authentication works by checking client certificates. An internal certificate authority almost always issues these.

- **Anonymous Authentication**   This is the most typical form of authentication for a web server. Clients can access the web page without entering credentials.

- **ASP.NET Impersonation**   Use ASP.NET impersonation when it's necessary to execute an ASP.NET application under a different security context.

- **Basic Authentication**   Basic authentication works with all web browsers but has the drawback of transmitting unencrypted base64-encoded passwords across the network. If you use Basic Authentication, you should also configure the site to require an encrypted TLS connection.

- **Digest Authentication**   Digest authentication occurs against a Domain Controller and is used when you want to authenticate clients that may be accessing content through a proxy, something that can be problematic for clients if you configure a server to use Windows authentication.

- **Forms Authentication**   This method is used when you redirect users to a custom web page on which they enter their credentials. Once they've been authenticated, they are returned to the page that they were attempting to browse.

- **Windows Authentication**   Use this method for intranet sites when you want clients to authenticate using Kerberos or NTLM. It works best when client computers are members of the same forest as the computer hosting the web server role.

Inside OUT

Authentication methods

Authentication options are only available if you have installed them. If you can't find the method that you want to enable, ensure that you have installed it.

Remember that you need to disable Anonymous Authentication if you want to force clients to use a different authentication method. Web browsers always request content from a server anonymously the first time you attempt to access content. If Anonymous Authentication is enabled, other forms of authentication are ignored. To enable a specific form of authentication for a website, perform the following steps:

1. Open the IIS Manager console from the Administrative Tools menu.

2. Click the Web Server node. In the Content pane, scroll down, and then double-click the Authentication item.

3. In the list of available authentication technologies, shown in Figure 15-8, click the authentication technology that you want to enable, and then click Enable in the Actions pane.

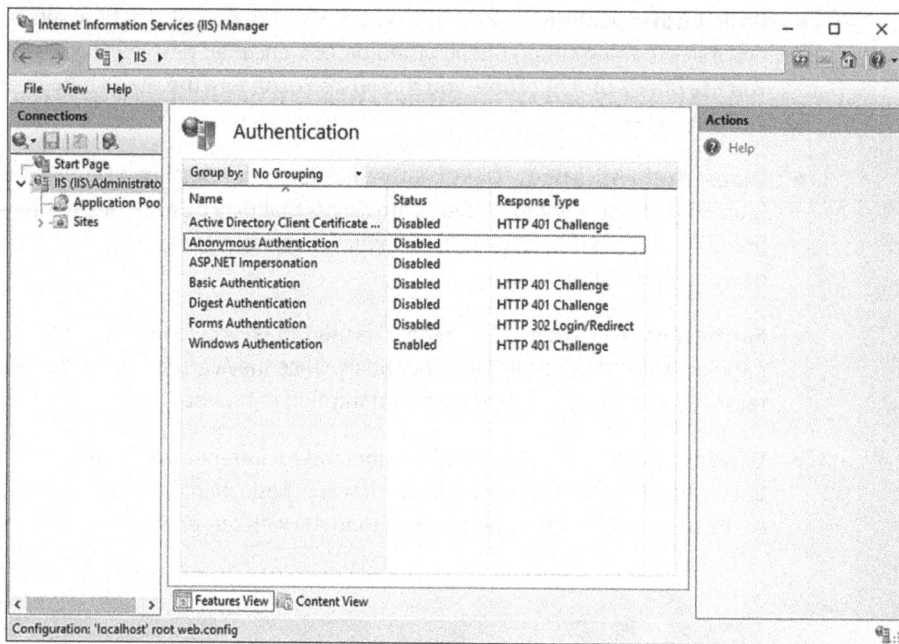

Figure 15-8   Configure Authentication

Modifying custom error response

Many sites customize their error responses so that users are provided with something more meaningful than a simple error message. Although the default error messages are perfectly serviceable, many organizations think they lack character and like to customize the most popular error messages, such as the 404 error message displayed by the web server when a page is not found.

To modify custom error message settings, perform the following steps:

1. Open the IIS Manager console and select the Server node.

2. Scroll down the Details pane and double-click the Error Pages item.

3. On the Error Pages pane, select the error code that you want to modify, and then click Edit.

4. In the Edit Custom Error Page dialog, shown in Figure 15-9, choose to forward clients to a static page based on file location, forward clients to a URL on the server, or forward clients to an absolute URL, which can be a page on another website.

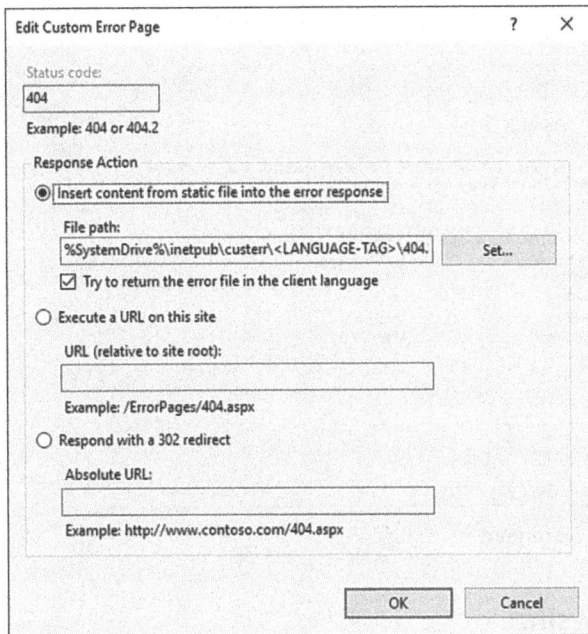

Figure 15-9   Edit Custom Error Page

Adding or disabling the default document

The default document is the document that loads when a client navigates to a web page but doesn't specify which page to load. The Default Documents role service is installed in a default installation of IIS, though this can be removed if you so choose. On servers running IIS, the following default documents are used:

- `default.htm`

- `default.asp`

- `index.htm`

- `index.html`

- `iisstart.htm`

- `default.aspx`

If more than one of these documents is present in the same folder, the document that is higher on the list overrides the documents that are lower on the list. You can add, reorder, or disable default documents using the IIS Manager console by double-clicking the Default Document item, either at the server or website level, as shown in Figure 15-10.

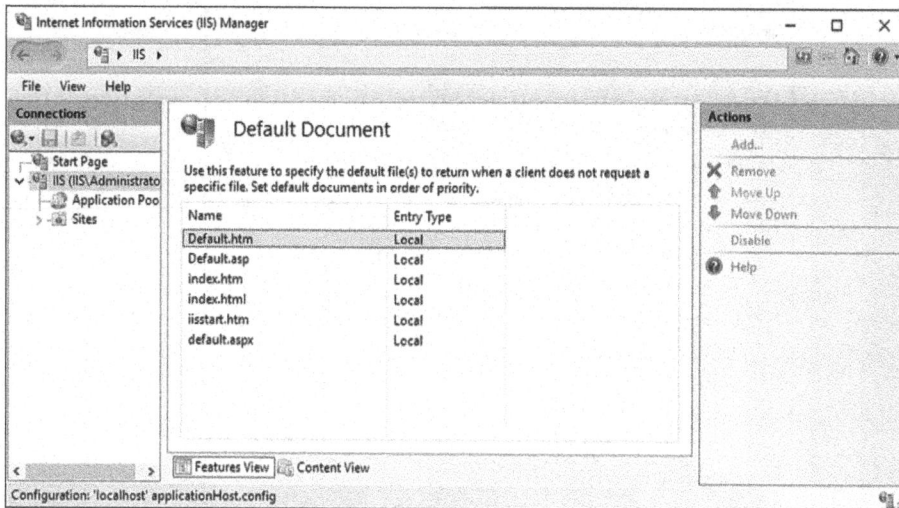

Figure 15-10   Default Document

Directory browsing

Directory browsing allows clients to view the files that are stored in a folder. Directory browsing works only if the default document is not present or has been disabled. To enable directory browsing, the Directory Browsing role service must be installed. To configure directory browsing, perform the following steps:

1. Open the IIS Manager console and select the site on which you want to enable directory browsing.

2. Scroll down in the Details pane and double-click the Directory Browsing item.

3. When Directory Browsing is shown in the Details pane, click Enable, and select the items that you want to allow to be displayed when the client is browsing. By default, the filename, time, size, extension, and date information are displayed.

IP address and domain name filtering

IP address and domain name restrictions allow you to block or allow access to a site based on a client's address. You can configure two types of rules: Allow Rules and Block Rules. When you configure an Allow Rule, only hosts that are on the Allow List can access your website. When you configure a Block Rule, hosts with an address on your Block List are blocked from accessing your site. You can configure Allow and Block rules at the server, site, application, virtual directory, folder, and file levels in IIS. You need to have the IP And Domain Restrictions role service installed to use IP address and domain name filtering.

To configure an IP address and domain name restriction, perform the following steps:

1. Open the IIS Manager console and select the site on which you want to implement an Allow List.

2. Double-click the IP Address And Domain Restrictions item.

3. If you want to configure an Allow List entry, click Add Allow Entry, and on the Add Allow Restriction Rule dialog, shown in Figure 15-11, enter the IP Address Range or Specific IP Address that you want to allow.

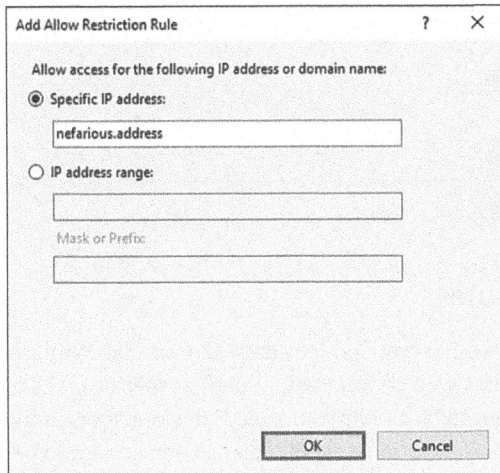

Figure 15-11   Add Allow Restriction Rule

4. If you want to configure a Deny entry, click Add Deny Entry, and on the Add Deny Restriction Rule dialog, enter the Specific IP Address range or IP Address Range that you want to block.

Dynamic IP restriction settings allow you to configure IIS to automatically block traffic based on suspicious request behavior, such as what can occur during a denial of service attack. As Figure 15-12 shows, you can choose to block traffic based on a maximum number of concurrent requests or a maximum number of requests over a specific period of time.

Dynamic IP Restriction Settings ? ✕

☑ Deny IP Address based on the number of concurrent requests

Maximum number of concurrent requests:

5

☑ Deny IP Address based on the number of requests over a period of time

Maximum number of requests:

20

Time Period (in milliseconds):

200

☐ Enable Logging Only Mode

OK   Cancel

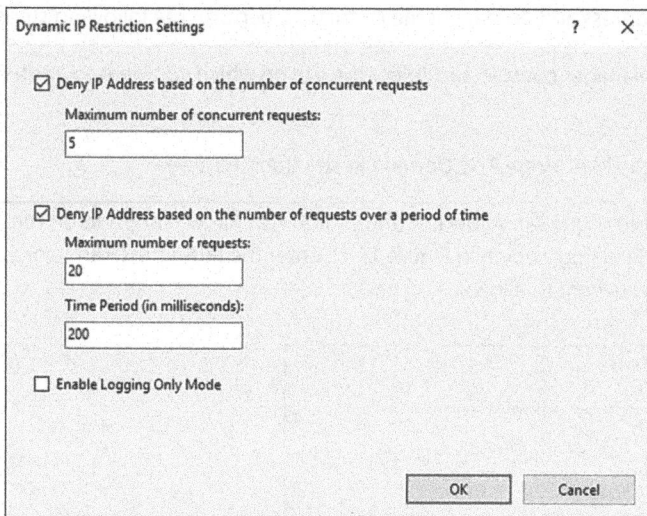

Figure 15-12   Dynamic IP Restriction Settings

URL authorization rules

URL authorization rules allow you to grant or deny access to specific computers, groups of computers, or domain access to sites, web applications, folders, or specific files. For example, you can use URL authorization rules to block everyone except the Managers group from accessing specific pages on the organization's intranet server. You can also configure URL authorization rules to apply only when the client attempts to use specific HTTP verbs, such as GET or POST. To use URL authorization rules, you need to ensure that the URL Authorization role service is installed on the server. There are two types of authorization rules: Allow Rules and Deny Rules.

To create an authorization rule, perform the following steps:

1. Open IIS Manager and navigate to the site, virtual directory, folder, or file on which you want to create the authorization rule.

2. Double-click the .NET Authorization Rules item in the Details pane.

3. Click Add Allow Rule or Add Deny Rule, depending on the type of authorization rule that you want to create.

4. On the Add Allow Authorization Rule or Add Deny Authorization Rule dialog, specify the users or groups for which you want to configure the rule and any specific HTTP verbs that you want to trigger the rule. Figure 15-13 shows the Add Allow Authorization Rule dialog.

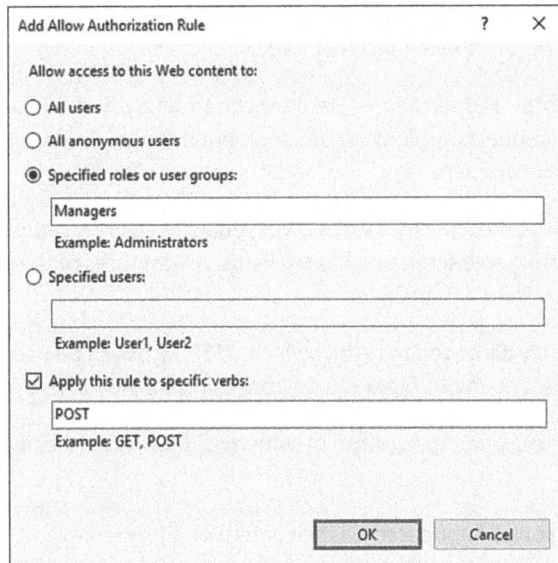

Figure 15-13   Add Allow Authorization Rule dialog

If you want to block access to everyone except a specific group of users, remove the default All Users Allow rule and replace it with the rule that grants specific access to the security principals in question.

Request filters

Request filters allow you to block clients from making certain types of requests of your web server. Request filters allow you to block a common form of attack against web applications—one where the attacker enters a specially formatted HTTP request in order to elicit an unplanned response from the web application. SQL injection attacks are one such kind of specially formatted HTTP request. There are several different types of request filters you can configure using the Request Filtering item. Request filters can be configured at the server, site, and file levels. To use request filtering, you need to ensure that you install the Request Filtering role service on the server.

You can configure the following types of request filters:

- **File Name Extensions**   This type of filter allows you to specify which type of files clients are not allowed to request from the web server on the basis of a file extension. The default request filtering settings block 43 different file extensions, and it's relatively easy to add additional extensions by clicking Deny File Name Extension on the File Name Extensions tab of the Request Filtering item.

- **Rules**   This allows you to configure specific rules that check the URL, query string, or both. If a match occurs, the request is blocked.

- **Hidden Segments**   Hidden Segments allow you to set a list of URL segments that will be blocked from requesting clients. A URL segment is the section of a URL path that lies between slash (/) characters.

- **URL**   They allow you to specify a set of URL sequences (such as *setup/config.xml*) that the Request Filtering role service blocks to clients. All instances of the URL sequence are blocked within the scope of the filter.

- **HTTP Verbs**   They allow you to restrict which HTTP verbs can be used in requests by clients. For example, you might block clients from using the PUT verb in requests.

- **Headers**   They allow you to specify a maximum URL size for a specific HTTP request header.

- **Query**   Allows you to filter based on the content of query strings.

You can modify the general request filtering settings, as shown in Figure 15-14, by clicking Edit Feature Settings in the Actions pane. Using this dialog, you can configure the following options:

- **Allow Unlisted File Name Extensions**   If this box is not checked, file extensions that are not explicitly allowed cannot be requested by clients.

- **Allow Unlisted Verbs**   If this box is not checked, HTTP verbs that are not explicitly allowed are blocked.

- **Allow High-Bit Characters**   If this box is not checked, unusual non-ASCII characters are blocked.

- **Allow Double Escaping**   If this box is not checked, URLs can contain double escape characters.

- **Maximum Allowed Content Length**   This text box specifies the maximum size of content that a request can process. Keep this figure small if you do not allow HTTP uploads to your site.

- **Maximum URL Length**   This allows you to restrict the maximum size of a URL request sent to your site.

- **Maximum Query String**   This allows you to restrict the maximum query string size in a URL request sent to your site.

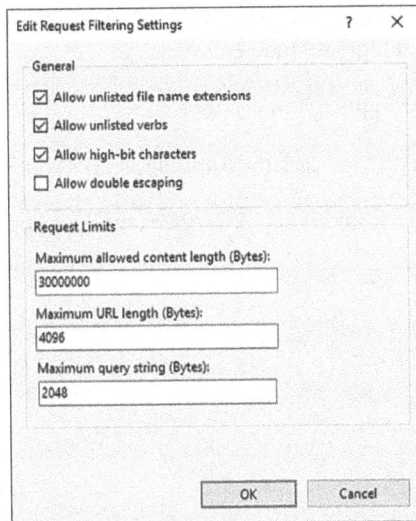

Figure 15-14   Edit Request Filtering Settings

Application pools

Application pools are collections of web applications that are served by a worker process or a group of worker processes. When you create a new website in IIS, IIS automatically creates an associated application pool. One of the ideas behind application pools is that by separating web applications into their own pools, the failure of one web application does not impact the functioning of other web applications. Application pools allow you to do the following:

- Collect sites and applications that use the same configuration settings.

- Improve security by allowing the use of a custom security account to run an application.

- Silo resources in such a way that one web application cannot address or influence resources in another web application.

Creating application pools

Although new application pools are created each time you create a new site, there are reasons why you want to configure a new application pool. Prior to creating a new application pool, you need to know what pipeline mode you want to use to process requests for managed code. Managed pipeline mode determines how IIS processes requests for managed code. The difference between the two managed pipeline modes is as follows:

- **Integrated**   This mode allows the request-processing pipelines of IIS and ASP.NET to process the request. Most web applications are likely to use this mode.

- **Classic**   This mode forwards requests for managed code through `aspnet_isapi.dll`. This is the same method used for processing requests on servers running older versions of

IIS. Use this mode if an older web application that you have migrated to IIS on Windows Server does not function well in integrated mode.

To create a new application pool, perform the following steps:

1.   Open the IIS Manager console, and then click the Application Pools node.

2.   Click Add Application Pool in the Actions menu. This opens the Add Application Pool dialog shown in Figure 15-15.

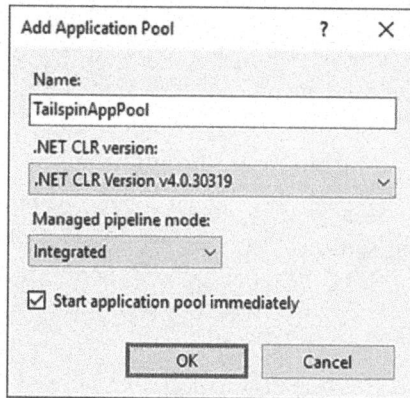

Figure 15-15   Add Application Pool

3.   In this dialog, provide a Name for the application pool, select the .NET CLR Version for the application pool, and choose the Managed Pipeline Mode.

Configuring application pool recycling settings

Not all developers write code that functions correctly over an extended period of time. If you find that a web application that you need to host on a computer running Windows Server starts to develop problems after it has run for a lengthy amount of time, you can deal with this by configuring the application pool recycling settings to recycle the processes related to the application on a regular basis. You configure application pool recycling settings on the Edit Application Pool Recycling Settings dialog shown in Figure 15-16. You can configure an application pool to be recycled when the following thresholds are met:

- By default, after a certain amount of time has elapsed, all application pools automatically recycle every 1,740 minutes.

- After an application pool has processed a certain number of requests.

- At specific times of the day.

- After an application pool exceeds a certain virtual memory threshold.

- After an application pool exceeds a specific private memory threshold.

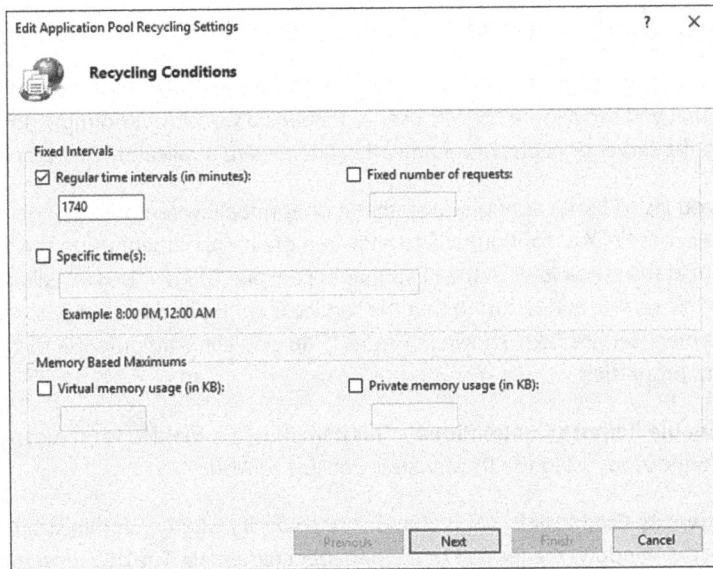

Figure 15-16   Application pool recycling settings

Through the Advanced Settings dialog, shown in Figure 15-17, you can configure basic settings such as the pipeline mode and recycling settings. You can also configure settings, including processor affinity, CPU limits, process orphaning, request limits, and rapid fail protection settings.

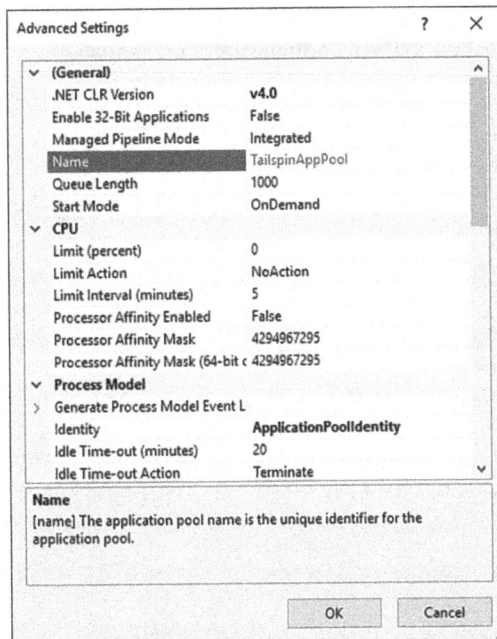

Figure 15-17   Application pool advanced settings

IIS users and delegation

IIS allows you to delegate the management of specific websites and web applications. This means that you can allow a specific user to manage a website without giving them logon privileges to the server or control over any other site or web application hosted by IIS.

When you install IIS, it's configured so that it does not allow remote management using the IIS Manager console. You configure IIS to allow remote management using the Management Service item at the server level in the IIS Manager console. This involves installing the Management Service role service and ensuring that the service is configured to start automatically. Using the Management Service item, shown in Figure 15-18, you can configure the following remote management properties:

- **Enable Remote Connections**   This item must be enabled for remote administration connections using the IIS Manager Console to work.

- **Identity Credentials**   This allows you to specify whether administrators can connect using Windows credentials or IIS Manager credentials. The default setting only allows Windows user accounts.

- **Connections**   This allows you to specify whether remote management connections can occur on any IP address interface or whether they are limited to a specific IP address interface. You can also specify which SSL certificate will be used to protect remote administration sessions.

- **IP Address Restrictions**   They allow you to specify which IP addresses or networks are allowed to successfully connect using the IIS Administrator credentials.

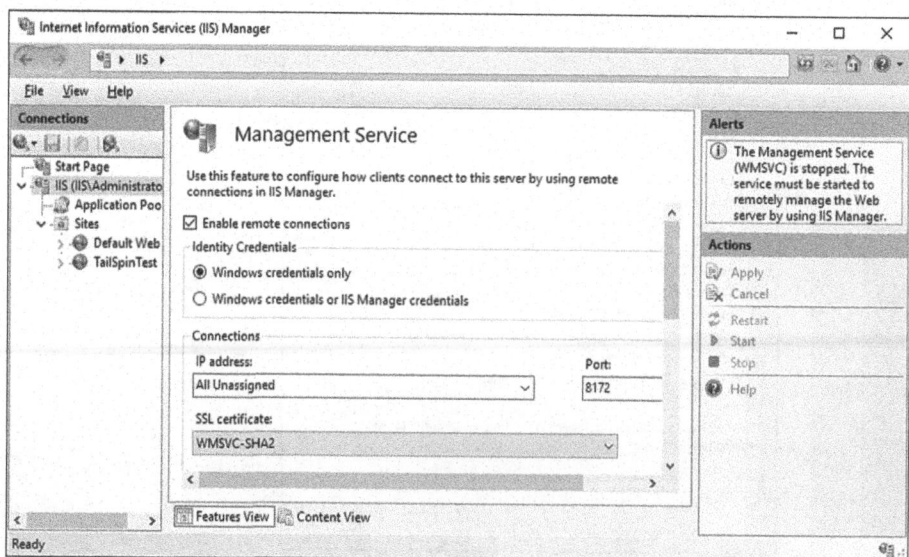

Figure 15-18   Management Service configuration

IIS user accounts

IIS allows you to create user accounts that exist only in IIS. These user accounts do not have any privileges outside IIS and cannot be used to log on locally to the server. This allows you to assign administrative permissions to users without having to create a corresponding machine local or domain user account.

To create an IIS Manager user, perform the following steps:

1. Open the IIS Manager console and double-click the IIS Manager Users item when the Server level is selected in the IIS Manager console.

2. Click Add User in the Actions pane. This opens the Add User dialog. Enter the username and password for the IIS user.

Delegating administrative permissions

After you have enabled remote management and, if you choose to create IIS users, configured the appropriate IIS user accounts, you can delegate management permissions on a site or web application through the IIS Manager Permissions item. You can check precisely which permissions users have been delegated by viewing the Feature Delegation item at the server level. You can also modify which configuration items are delegated using the Feature Delegation item.

To delegate administrative permissions over a site, perform the following steps:

1. Open the IIS Manager console and select the website for which you want to delegate administrative permissions.

2. Double-click the IIS Manager Permissions item in the Details pane.

3. In the Actions pane, click Allow User. On the Allow User dialog, select the Windows or IIS Manager User, and then click OK. Figure 15-19 shows user Rooslan's delegated permissions over the TailSpinTest site.

CHAPTER 15

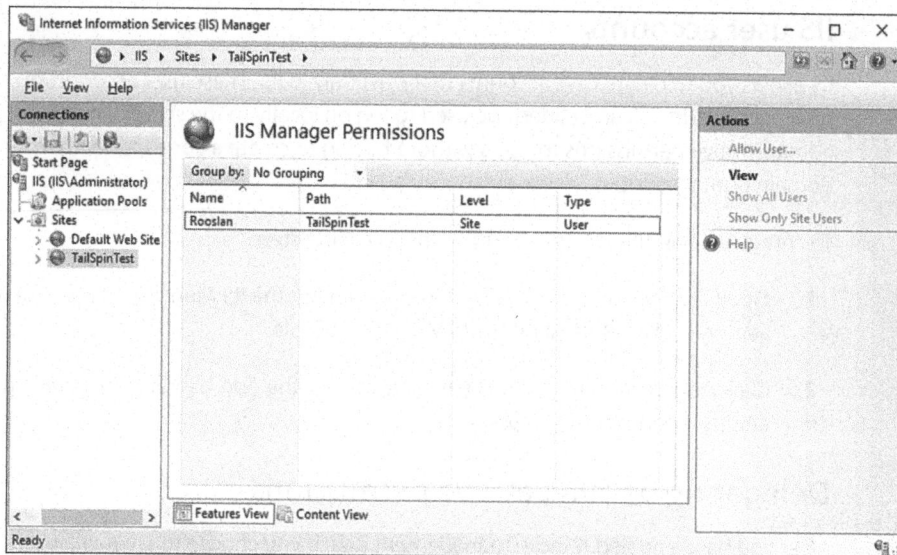

Figure 15-19   IIS Manager Permissions

IIS configuration backup and recovery

You can use AppCmd or PowerShell to back up an IIS server's configuration. To backup and restore using AppCmd, perform the following steps:

1. Open Command Prompt as Admin and navigate to the IIS directory: (%windir%\system32\inetsrv).

2. Run appcmd, specifying a unique backup name, such as

```
appcmd add backup "MyBackup_Feb-2025"
```

The backup files are stored in C:\Windows\System32\inetsrv\backup\MyBackup_Feb-2025. To restore them, ensure that the backed-up folder is present in C:\Windows\System32\inetsrv\backup on the target server and use the appcmd command to restore. For example, to restore the backup MyBackup_Feb-2025, run the command:

```
appcmd restore backup "MyBackup_Feb-2025" /stop:true
```

To back up and restore using PowerShell, use the Backup-Webconfiguration and Restore-WebConfiguration cmdlets. As with AppCmd, backups will be stored in the C:\Windows\System32\inetsrv\backup\ folder.

Managing FTP

Although FTP is a protocol that is almost as old as the Internet itself, and newer ways of transfer-ring files are becoming more popular, many organizations still use FTP as their primary method of uploading data to web servers such as IIS.

The FTP server in Windows Server supports TLS connections and is fully managed from the IIS Manager console.

From the IIS Management console, you can configure the following:

- **FTP Authentication**   This allows you to enable or disable Anonymous or Basic Authen-tication. The default settings have both forms of authentication disabled.

- **FTP Authorization**   It allows you to specify which users or groups are allowed to con-nect to the FTP server and whether they have read and write permissions when using FTP.

- **FTP Directory Browsing**   It allows you to specify whether MS-DOS or UNIX-style direc-tory listings are provided. It also allows you to specify whether the virtual directory, avail-able bytes, and four-digit years information are displayed.

- **FTP Firewall Support**   Allows you to configure the FTP server to accept passive connec-tions from a perimeter network firewall.

- **FTP IPv4 Address And Domain Name Restrictions**   This allows you to block or allow FTP clients based on IPv4 address or client domain name.

- **FTP Logging**   It allows you to configure the FTP logging settings, including how often log files are rotated.

- **FTP Messages**   It allows you to configure FTP banner settings. This is the informational text that is presented to new FTP sessions.

- **FTP Request Filtering**   Using this item, you can configure the following:

    - FTP to allow or block specific file name extensions from transfers

    - Block segments, such as sensitive folders, from being accessible in FTP

    - Block particular FTP URLs

    - Block specific FTP commands from being used during a session

- **FTP SSL Settings**   This allows you to specify which server certificate is used for TLS (though still called SSL) sessions. It also allows you to force the use of TLS as well as enforce 128-bit encryption on FTP SSL sessions.

- **FTP User Isolation**   It allows you to limit which folders an FTP user can navigate. You can configure a user to start in the FTP root directory or a specific username-related directory.

To add a new FTP site, perform the following steps:

1. Open the IIS Manager console, right-click the Sites node, and then click Add FTP Site.

2. On the Site Information page, enter a name for the site and the directory path that is used to host the site's files.

3. On the Binding And SSL Settings page shown in Figure 15-20, specify

   - Which IP addresses the FTP site listens on

   - Whether the FTP site uses a virtual host name

   - Whether the site starts automatically

   - Whether SSL/TLS is allowed or required

   - Which server certificate is used in conjunction with the FTP site

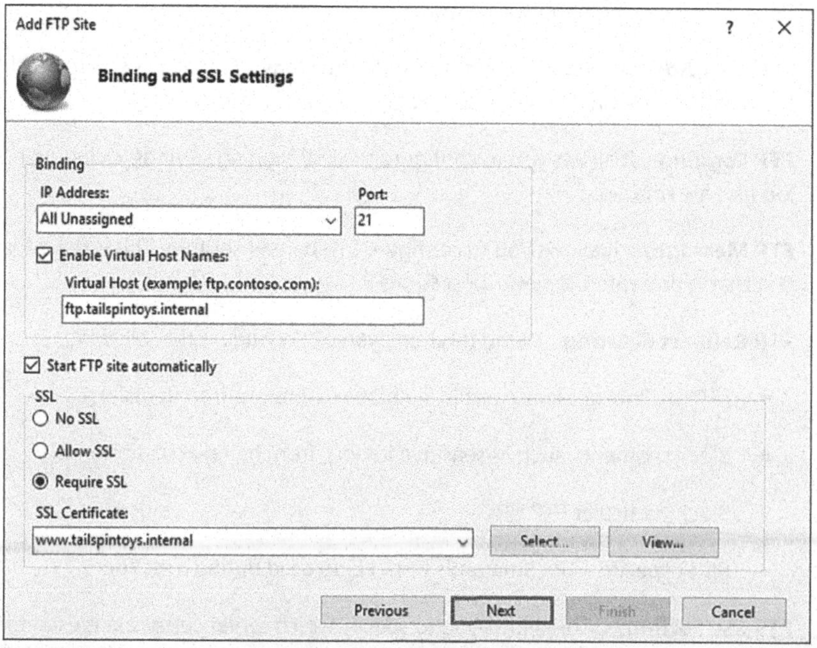

Figure 15-20   FTP site bindings and SSL settings

4. On the Authentication And Authorization Information page, specify whether you'll allow Anonymous and/or Basic Authentication. On the Authorization dropdown, specify whether you want to allow access for the following:

- All Users

- Anonymous Users

- Specified Roles Or User Groups

- Specified Users

5. If you choose to allow access only to specified roles or user groups, you need to specify which roles, users, or user groups you want to grant access.

Managing IIS using PowerShell

You can use cmdlets from two separate PowerShell modules to manage IIS and websites running on Windows Server. The IIS Administration PowerShell module contains a large number of cmdlets that you can use to manage IIS on Windows Server. These cmdlets are described in Table 15-1. The WebAdministration PowerShell module contains a large number of cmdlets that you can use to manage web and FTP sites running on Windows Server. These cmdlets are described in Table 15-2.

Table 15-1   IIS PowerShell cmdlets

Noun	Verbs	Function
IISAppPool	Get	View App Pool information
IISCentralCertProvider	Clear, Get, Set, Enable, Disable	Manage the IIS central certificate store
IISCentralCert-ProviderCredential	Set	Manage user account credentials for the IIS certificate store
IISCommitDelay	Stop, Start	Manage the delay of the commitment of changes
IISConfigAttribute	Remove	Remove the configuration attribute from the IIS configuration section or configuration element attribute
IISConfigAttributeValue	Set, Get	Manage the configuration attribute value for an IIS configuration section or configuration element attribute
IISConfigCollection	Get, Clear	Manage configuration element objects in an IIS configuration collection

Noun	Verbs	Function
IISConfig-CollectionElement	New, Remove, Get	Manage configuration element objects
IISConfigElement	Remove, Get	Manage configuration elements
IISConfigSection	Get	View the configuration section object
IISConfiguration	Export	Export IIS configuration
IISServerManager	Reset, Get	Manage IIS Server Manager
IISSharedConfig	Disable, Enable, Get	Manage IIS shared config
IISSite	Stop, Start, New, Get, Remove	Manage IIS Site

Table 15-2   Web Administration PowerShell cmdlets

Noun	Verbs	Function
WebAppDomain	Get	View application domains in which the IIS worker process is running
WebApplication	New, Convert, Remove, Get	Manage web applications in IIS websites
WebAppPool	Start, New, Restart, Remove, Stop	Manage application pools
WebAppPoolState	Get	View application pool states
WebBinding	New, Set, Remove, Get	Configure web bindings
WebCentralCertProvider	Clear, Get, Enable, Set, Disable	Manage configuration settings for the central certificate provider
WebCentralCertProvider-Credential	Set	Configure user account credentials for the central certificate provider
WebCommitDelay	Start, Stop	Manage the delay of the commitment of the changes
WebConfigFile	Get	View the file system path of the web.config file
WebConfiguration	Backup, Add, Select, Set, Restore, Clear, Get	Manage IIS configuration elements
WebConfigurationBackup	Get, Remove	Manage IIS configuration backups
WebConfiguration-Location	Remove, Get, Rename	Manage the location of configuration settings
WebConfigurationLock	Add, Get, Remove	Manage the lock status of the IIS configuration
WebConfiguration-Property	Set, Add, Remove, Get	Manage configuration properties

Noun	Verbs	Function
WebFilePath	Get	View the path to the location of a specific IIS module
WebFtpSite	New	Create a new FTP site
WebGlobalModule	Disable, New, Get, Remove, Enable, Set	Manage IIS global modules
WebHandler	Get, New, Remove, Set	Manage IIS request handlers
WebItem	Restart, Start, Stop	Manage application pools or websites
WebItemState	Get	View the state of the application pool or website
WebManagedModule	Get, Set, New, Remove	Manage IIS-managed modules
WebRequest	Get	View IIS requests currently being run
WebRequestTracing	Disable, Enable	Manage request tracing for a website
WebRequestTracing-Setting	Clear	Clears the request tracing configuration
WebRequestTracing-Settings	Clear	Clears request tracing configuration as well (not a duplicate)
Website	Start, Get, Stop, Remove, New	Manage websites
WebsiteState	Get	View the state of a website
WebURL	Get	View a website URL
WebVirtualDirectory	Remove, Get, New	Manage web virtual directories

A container is a portable isolated application execution environment. Containers allow developers to bundle an application and its dependencies in a single image. This image can easily be exported, imported, and deployed on different container hosts, from a developer's laptop computer, to Server Core on bare-metal hardware, and eventually to being hosted and run on Azure. Because an application's dependencies are bundled with the application within a container, IT operations can deploy a container as soon as it's handed off without worrying if an appropriate prerequisite software package has been installed or if a necessary setting has been configured. Because a container provides an isolated environment, a failure that occurs within one container only impacts that container and doesn't impact other containerized applications running on the container host.

Container concepts

Containers can be conceptually challenging. To understand how containers work, you first need to understand some of the terminology involving containers. While these concepts will be fleshed out more completely later in this chapter, you should understand the following terms at a high level:

- **Container image** A container image is a template from which a container is generated. There are two general types of container images, which are usually created for a workload: a base OS image and a specific image. The difference between these containers on Windows Server is as follows:

  - **Container base OS image** This is an image of the operating system upon which other container images are built. Four Windows OS container images are regularly published and updated by Microsoft. These images are available through an official public container registry:

    - ▼ **Windows Server Core** This is an image of the Windows Server operating system in the Server Core configuration. Containers don't run with a GUI, so Server with Desktop Experience is not available. This container image is suitable for traditional .NET Framework applications.

▼ **Nano Server**   This is a Windows Server image with all unnecessary elements stripped out. It's suitable for hosting .NET Core applications. The Nano Server image container image is what became of the Nano Server installation option that was available with the RTM version of Windows Server 2016. Because the image is stripped down to the essentials, it's far smaller than the Windows Server Core image and can be deployed and run more quickly.

▼ **Windows Server**   The Windows Server base image, introduced with Windows Server 2025, includes the full Windows API set and supports scenarios including UI frameworks and GPU acceleration for AI workloads. This is the largest Windows Server container image and only runs on Windows Server 2025 hosts.

▼ **Windows**   This is an image that provides the full Windows API set but doesn't include all the server roles and features that are available in the Server Core image. You should only use this option if the application you're trying to host has a dependency that isn't included in the Windows Server Core container image.

- **Container image**   A container image stores changes made to a running a container base OS image or another container image. For example, you can start a new container from a container base OS image, make modifications such as installing Java or a Windows feature, and then save those modifications as a new container image. The new container image only stores the changes you make; therefore, it's much smaller than the parent container base OS image. You can then create an additional container image that stores modifications made to the container image that has an installed Java and Windows feature. Each container image only stores the changes made to the image from which it was run.

- **Sandbox**   The sandbox is the environment in which you can make modifications to an existing container image before you commit the changes to create a new container image. If you don't commit those changes to a new image, those changes will be lost when the container is removed.

- **Image dependency**   A new container image has the container image from which it was created as a dependency. For example, if you create a container image named Web-Server-1.0 that has the IIS role installed from the Server Core base OS image, the Server Core base OS image is a dependency for the WebServer-1.0 image. This dependency is very specific, and you can't use an updated version of the Server Core base OS image as a replacement for the version that you used when creating the WebServer-1.0 image. You can then export this container image that only records the changes made to another container host. You can start the image as long as the dependency container OS base image is present on that container host. You can have multiple images in a dependency chain.

- **Container host** A container host is a computer that runs containers. A container host can be virtual, physical, or even a cloud-based Platform as a Service (PaaS) solution.

- **Container registries** Container registries are central storehouses of container images. While it's possible to transfer containers or copy them to file shares using tools like FTP, common practice is to use a container registry as a repository for container images. Public container registries, such as the one that hosts Microsoft's base OS images, also store previous versions of the container base OS images. This allows you to retrieve earlier versions of the container base OS image that other images may depend upon. Docker Hub is the primary public container registry used by Microsoft to publish images, though the container images themselves are hosted in the Microsoft Container Registry at *mcr.microsoft.com*. Container registries can be public or private. When working with your own organization's container images, you have the option of creating and maintaining a private container registry.

Inside OUT

Data and containers

Containers offer a nonpersistent, isolated application execution environment. An application should run in the container, but it shouldn't store application data in a container. Application data should be stored in a location that's separate from the container, such as in a back-end database server, Azure storage blob, or other persistent alternative. Containers are good at serving in stateless roles, such as load balanced front-end web servers; this is especially true because you can start new containers quickly to handle additional load as required.

Isolation modes

Windows Server supports two container isolation modes: process isolation mode and Hyper-V isolation mode. In previous versions of Microsoft's documentation, these isolation modes were occasionally called "Windows Server containers" and "Hyper-V containers." Windows client supports only Hyper-V isolation mode. Windows Server supports process isolation and Hyper-V isolation modes.

Process isolation

Process isolation mode provides a container with process and namespace isolation. Containers running in this isolation mode share a kernel with all other containers running on the container host. This is similar to the manner in which containers run on Linux container hosts. Process isolation is the default mode used when running a container. If you want to ensure that the container is being used, start the container using the `--isolation=process` option. Unlike previous versions of Windows Server, Windows Server 2025 hosts can now run down-level containers in process isolation. This means you can run Windows Server 2022 and Windows Server 2025 containers concurrently without having to use Hyper-V isolation.

Hyper-V isolation

A container running in Hyper-V isolation mode runs in a highly optimized virtual machine that also provides an isolated application execution environment. Hyper-V isolation mode containers neither share the kernel with the container host nor share the kernel with other containers on the same container host. You can only use Hyper-V isolation mode containers if you have enabled the Hyper-V role on the container host. If the container host is a Hyper-V virtual machine, you will need to enable nested virtualization. By default, a container uses the process isolation mode. You can start a container in Hyper-V isolation mode by using the `--isolation=hyperv` option.

For example, to create a Hyper-V container from the `microsoft/windowsservercore` image, issue this command:

```
docker run -it --isolation=hyperv mcr.microsoft.com/windows/servercore cmd.exe
```

> ## More Info
>
> *Container isolation*
>
> You can learn more about container isolation at *https://learn.microsoft.com/en-us/virtualization/windowscontainers/manage-containers/hyperv-container*.

Managing containers with Docker

Containers on Windows Server are managed using the Docker Engine. The advantage here is that the command syntax of Docker on Windows is almost identical to the command-line tools in Docker on Linux. While there is a community-maintained PowerShell module for managing containers on Windows Server available on GitHub, PowerShell is not the primary tool for Windows Server container management, and very few people use PowerShell to manage containers.

For Windows Server administrators unfamiliar with Docker syntax, the commands include extensive help support. Typing **docker** at the command prompt will provide an overview of the high-level Docker functionality. You can learn more about specific commands by using the `--help` command parameter. For example, the following command will provide information about the `docker image` command:

```
docker image --help
```

> ## More Info
>
> ### Docker Engine on Windows
>
> You can learn more about Docker Engine on Windows at *https://learn.microsoft.com/ en-us/virtualization/windowscontainers/manage-docker/configure-docker-daemon.*

Installing Docker

Docker is not included with the Windows Server installation media, and you don't install it as a role or feature. Instead, you need to install Docker using online tools. Although this is unusual for an important role on a Windows Server operating system, it does have the advantage of ensuring that you have the latest version of Docker.

To enable the containers feature, run the command, which will prompt a reboot:

```
Enable-WindowsOptionalFeature -Online -FeatureName Containers -All
```

Then download and run the following script from an elevated PowerShell prompt:

```
Invoke-WebRequest -UseBasicParsing "https://raw.githubusercontent.com/microsoft/Windows-
Containers/Main/helpful_tools/Install-DockerCE/install-docker-ce.ps1" -o install-
docker-ce.ps1
```

To install containerd as an alternative container runtime, run the following commands:

```
Invoke-WebRequest -UseBasicParsing "https://raw.githubusercontent.com/microsoft/Windows-
Containers/Main/helpful_tools/Install-ContainerdRuntime/install-containerd-runtime.ps1"
-OutFile install-containerd-runtime.ps1
.\install-containerd-runtime.ps1
```

You should only run one container engine on a host. The default provides the full Docker experience, including the familiar Docker CLI, image build capabilities, and tools like Docker Compose. The default is ideal if you want the easiest developer experience or need compatibility with the wealth of community tutorials and tooling that assume the Docker CLI.

Containerd is a lightweight, modular runtime that focuses solely on core container lifecycle management such as pulling images, handling snapshots, and starting or stopping containers. It does not ship with higher-level features like Docker Compose or image build tools, though wrappers such as nerdctl provide a Docker-like CLI interface. Containerd support is still evolving on Windows Server 2025 and is included here for completeness.

Daemon.json

If you want to change the default Docker Engine settings, such as whether to create a default NAT network, you need to create and configure the Docker Engine configuration file. This file doesn't exist by default. When it's present, the settings in the file override the Docker Engine's default settings.

You should create this file in the `c:\ProgramData\Docker\config` folder. Before editing the `Daemon.json` file, you'll need to stop the Docker service using the following command:

```
Stop-Service docker
```

You only need to add settings that you want to change to the configuration file. For example, if you only want to configure the Docker Engine to accept incoming connections on port 2701, you add the following lines to `daemon.json`:

```
{
    "hosts": ["tcp://0.0.0.0:2701"]
}
```

The Windows Docker Engine doesn't support all possible Docker configuration file options. The ones that you can configure are shown in the following example:

```
{
    "authorization-plugins": [],
    "dns": [],
    "dns-opts": [],
    "dns-search": [],
    "exec-opts": [],
    "storage-driver": "",
    "storage-opts": [],
    "labels": [],
    "log-driver": "",
    "mtu": 0,
    "pidfile": "",
    "cluster-store": "",
    "cluster-advertise": "",
    "debug": true,
    "hosts": [],
    "log-level": "",
    "tlsverify": true,
    "tlscacert": "",
    "tlscert": "",
    "tlskey": "",
    "group": "",
    "default-ulimits": {},
    "bridge": "",
    "fixed-cidr": "",
    "raw-logs": false,
    "registry-mirrors": [],
    "insecure-registries": [],
    "disable-legacy-registry": false
}
```

These options allow you to do the following when starting the Docker Engine:

- `authorization-plugins` Which authorization plugins the Docker Engine should load

- `dns` Which DNS server the containers should use for name resolution

- `dns-opts` Which DNS options to use

- `dns-search` Which DNS search domains to use

- `exec-opts` Which runtime execution options to use

- `storage-driver` Specify the storage driver

- `storage-opts` Specify the storage driver options

- `labels` Docker Engine labels

- `log-driver` Default driver for the container logs

- `mtu` Container network MTU

- `pidfile` Path to use for daemon PID file

- `group` Specify the local security group that has permissions to run Docker commands

- `cluster-store` Cluster store options

- `cluster-advertise` Cluster address to advertise

- `debug` Enable debug mode

- `hosts` Daemon sockets to connect to

- `log-level` Logging detail

- `Tlsverify` Use TLS and perform verification

- `tlscacert` Specify which certificate authorities to trust

- `tlscert` Location of the TLS certificate file

- `tlskey` Location of the TLS key file

- `group` UNIX socket group

- `default-ulimits` Default ulimits for containers

- `bridge` Attach containers to network bridge

- `fixed-cidr` IPv4 subnet for static IP address

- `raw-logs` Log format used

- `registry-mirrors` Preferred registry mirror

- `insecure-registries` Allow insecure registry communication

- `disable-legacy-registry` Block contacting legacy registries

Once you have made the necessary modifications to the daemon.json file, you should start the Docker service by running this PowerShell command:

```
Start-Service docker
```

Retrieving container OS image

You can retrieve the Server Core base OS container image by running the following command:

```
docker pull mcr.microsoft.com/windows/servercore:ltsc2025
```

You can retrieve the Nano Server base OS container image by running this command:

```
docker pull mcr.microsoft.com/windows/nanoserver:ltsc2025
```

The latest version of the Server Core image is updated frequently. Because of dependency issues when working with older containers, you might need an earlier version of the base OS image. To retrieve all versions of the WindowsServerCore image from the public registry, run this command:

```
docker pull -a mcr.microsoft.com/windows/servercore
```

Windows Server 2025 introduced a new base image with the name Windows Server. The Windows Server base image includes the full Windows API set and supports scenarios including UI frameworks and GPU acceleration for AI workloads. This is the largest Windows Server container image. To retrieve this image from the public registry, run this command:

```
docker pull -a mcr.microsoft.com/windows/server:ltsc2025
```

To retrieve all versions of the Nano Server image, run this command:

```
docker pull -a mcr.microsoft.com/windows/nanoserver
```

Container registries and images

Container registries are repositories for the distribution of container images. The main container registry that will be of interest to Windows Server administrators will be the DockerHub public repository. Microsoft posts container images on the DockerHub registry, including the base OS images, images that include evaluation editions of SQL Server, and technologies such as the latest builds of ASP.NET on containers and Azure CLI. You can view all Microsoft's published container images at *https://hub.docker.com/u/microsoft*.

From the DockerHub registry, you can retrieve the following Microsoft published container images:

- **Nanoserver**   This is the base image for the Nano Server container operating system.

  ```
  docker pull mcr.microsoft.com/windows/nanoserver:ltsc2025
  ```

- **Windows Server Core**   This is the base image for the Windows Server Core container operating system.

  ```
  docker pull mcr.microsoft.com/windows/servercore:ltsc2025
  ```

- **Windows Server**   This is the larger base image for the Windows Server operating system and includes the full Windows Server API set.

  ```
  docker pull mcr.microsoft.com/windows/server:ltsc2025
  ```

- **Windows IIS**   This includes the Internet Information Services on Windows Server Core container operating system.

  ```
  docker pull mcr.microsoft.com/windows/servercore/iis:windowsservercore-ltsc2025
  ```

- **Microsoft SQL Server**   This container image contains Microsoft SQL Server on Linux and will only run on Linux container hosts, rather than on Windows Server container hosts.

  ```
  docker pull mcr.microsoft.com/mssql/server:2025-latest
  ```

- **ASP.NET Core Runtime**   This includes ASP.NET Core on the Windows Server Core container operating system.

  ```
  docker pull mcr.microsoft.com/dotnet/aspnet:9.0-windowsservercore-ltsc2025
  ```

In cases where a multiple images exist, such as Windows Server Core and Nano Server, you can use the -a option with the Docker pull command to retrieve all images. This can be helpful if you don't know the image ID of the specific image that you want to retrieve.

When you pull an image from a registry, the action will also download any dependency images that are required. For example, if you pull an image that was built on a specific version of the Windows Server Core base image and you don't have that image on the container host, that image will also be downloaded from a container registry.

You can view a list of images that are installed on a Windows Server container host by using the following command:

```
docker image list
```

More Info

Official Microsoft container images

You can see which container images Microsoft has made available at *https://hub.docker.com/u/microsoft/*.

Managing containers

You use Docker to perform all container management tasks on computers running Windows Server. Windows Admin Center support is present but is limited.

Starting a container

You create a new container by specifying the container image from which you want to create the container. You can start a container and run an interactive session either by specifying cmd. exe or PowerShell.exe by using the -it option with docker run. Interactive sessions allow you to directly interact with the container through the command line from the moment the container starts. Detached mode starts a container, but it doesn't start an interactive session with that container.

For example, to start a container from the Microsoft/windowsservercore image and enter an interactive PowerShell session within that container once it's started, use this command:

```
docker run -it mcr.microsoft.com/windows/servercore:ltsc2025 powershell.exe
```

Also important is that, by default, containers use network address translation. This means that if you're running an application or service on the container that you want to expose to the net-work, you'll need to configure port mapping between the container host's network interface and the container. For example, if you had downloaded the Microsoft/iis container image and you wanted to start a container in detached mode, mapping port 8080 on the container host to port 80 on the container, you would run the following command:

```
docker run -d -p 8080:80 mcr.microsoft.com/windows/servercore/
iis:windowsservercore-ltsc2025
```

This is only the very basic sort of information you'd need to get started with a container, and you will learn more about container networking later in this chapter.

You can verify which containers are running using the docker ps command. The problem with the simple docker ps command option is that this will only show you the running contain-ers and won't show you any that are in a stopped state. You can see which containers are on a container host, including containers that aren't currently running, by using the docker ps -a command.

One thing that you'll notice about containers is that they appear to be assigned random names, such as *sarcastic_hedgehog*, *dyspeptic_hamster*, and *sententious_muppet*. Docker assigns ran-dom names rather than asking you for one because containers are a more ephemeral type of application host than a VM; because they are likely to only have a short lifespan, it isn't worth assigning any name that you'd need to remember to them. The reason for the structure of the random names is that they are easy to remember in the short term, which makes containers that you must interact with on a short-term basis easier to address than when using hexadecimal container IDs.

Earlier in the chapter, you learned that it was possible to start a container in detached mode. If you want to start an interactive session on a container that you started in detached mode, use the command `docker exec -i <containername> powershell.exe`. In some cases, it will be necessary to start a stopped container. You can start a stopped container using the `docker start <containername>` command.

Modifying a running container

Once you have a container running, you can enter the container and make the modifications that you want to make to ensure that the application the container hosts will run correctly. This might involve creating directories, using the `dism.exe` command to add roles, or using the `wget` PowerShell alias to download and install binaries such as Java. For example, the following code, when run from inside a container, downloads and installs an version of Java into a container based on the Server Core base OS container:

```
wget -Uri "https://download.oracle.com/java/25/latest/jdk-21_windows-x64_bin.exe"
-outfile javaInstall.exe
REG ADD HKLM\Software\Policies\Microsoft\Windows\Installer /v DisableRollback /t REG_
DWORD /d 1 /f | Out-Null
./javaInstall.exe /s INSTALLDIR=C:\Java REBOOT=Disable | Out-Null
```

Once you're finished modifying the container, you can type **Exit** to exit the container. A container must be in a shut-down state before you can capture it as a container image. You use the `docker stop <containername>` cmdlet to shut down a container.

Inside OUT

Containers and Chocolatey

Chocolatey offers another method of installing software on containers. You can spin up a new container, install Chocolatey, and then create a new image from that container. Each time you spin up a new container from that new image that includes Chocolatey, the process of installing additional software will be simpler. WinGet can only be used on container images that include the Desktop App Installer. This package isn't included with any Microsoft official images.

Creating a new image from a container

Once the container is in the desired state and shut down, you can capture the container to a new container image. You do this using the `docker commit <container_name> <new_image_name>` command. Once you have committed a container to a container image, you can remove

CHAPTER 16

the container using the docker rm command. For example, to remove the *elegant_spence* container, issue this command:

```
docker rm elegant_spence
```

Using Dockerfiles

Dockerfiles are text files that allow you to automate the process of creating new container images. You use a dockerfile with the docker build command to automate container creation, which is very useful when you need to create new container images from regularly updated base OS container images.

Dockerfiles have the elements shown in Table 16-1.

Table 16-1   Dockerfile element

Instruction	Description
FROM	Specifies the container image used in creating the new image creation. For example: FROM mcr.microsoft.com/windows/servercore:ltsc2025
RUN	Specifies commands to be run and captures them into the new container image. For example: RUN wget -Uri "http://javadl.sun.com/webapps/download/AutoDL?BundleId=107944" -outfile javaInstall.exe -UseBasicParsing RUN REG ADD HKLM\Software\Policies\Microsoft\Windows\Installer /v DisableRollback /t REG_DWORD /d 1 | Out-Null RUN ./javaInstall.exe /s INSTALLDIR=C:\Java REBOOT=Disable | Out-Null
COPY	Copies files and directories from the container host filesystem to the filesystem of the container. For Windows containers, the destination format must use forward slashes. For example: COPY example1.txt c:/temp/
ADD	Can be used to add files from a remote source, such as a URL. For example: ADD https://www.python.org/ftp/python/3.5.1/python-3.5.1.exe /temp/python-3.5.1.exe
WORKDIR	Specifies a working directory for the RUN and CMD instructions.
CMD	A command to be run when deploying an instance of the container image.

For example, the following Dockerfile will create a new container from the mcr.microsoft.com/windows/servercore:ltsc2025 image, create a directory named ExampleDirectory, and then install the iis-webserver feature.

```
FROM mcr.microsoft.com/windows/servercore:ltsc2025
RUN mkdir ExampleDirectory
RUN dism.exe /online /enable-feature /all /featurename:iis-webserver /NoRestart
```

To create a container image named example_image, change into the directory that hosts the Dockerfile (no extension) file and run the following command:

```
docker build -t example_image .
```

> ## More Info
> ### Dockerfile with Windows
> You can learn more about using `Dockerfile` with Windows at *https://learn.microsoft. com/virtualization/windowscontainers/manage-docker/manage-windows-dockerfile*.

Managing container images

To save a Docker image for transfer to another computer, use the `docker save` command. When you save a Docker image, you save it in `.tar` format. You can load a Docker image from a saved image using the `docker load` command. When you have multiple container images that have the same name, you can remove an image by using the image ID. You can determine the image ID by running the command `docker images`. You can't remove a container image until the last container created from that image either directly or indirectly has been deleted. You then remove the image by using the command `docker rmi` with the image ID. For example, remove the image with the *ID a896e5590871* using this command:

```
docker rmi a896e5590871
```

Service accounts for Windows containers

Although containers based on the Server Core and Nano Server operating systems have most of the same characteristics as a virtual machine or a bare-metal deployment of the Server Core or Nano Server versions of Windows Server, one thing that you can't do with containers is join them to a domain. This is because containers are supposed to be temporary rather than permanent, and domain-joining them would clog up Active Directory with unnecessary computer accounts.

While containers can't be domain joined, it's possible to use a group-managed service account (gMSA) to provide one or more containers with a domain identity similar to that used by a device that is realm joined. Performing this task requires downloading the Windows Server Container Tools and ensuring that the container host is a member of the domain that hosts the gMSA. When you perform this procedure, the container's LocalSystem and Network Service accounts use the gMSA. This gives the container the identity represented by the gMSA.

To configure gMSA association with a container, perform the following steps:

1. Ensure that the Windows Server container host is domain-joined.

2. Install the CredentialSpec PowerShell module with this command:

   ```
   Install-Module -Name CredentialSpec
   ```

CHAPTER 16

3. Add the container host to a specially created domain security group. This domain security group can have any name.

4. Create a gMSA and grant gMSA permission to the specially created domain security group of which the container host is a member.

5. Install the gMSA on the container host.

6. Use the `New-CredentialSpec` cmdlet on the container host to generate the gMSA credentials in a file in JSON format. This cmdlet is located in the `CredentialSpec` PowerShell module, which is available as a part of the Windows Server Container tools. For example, if you created a gMSA named *MelbourneAlpha*, you would run the following command:

```
New-CredentialSpec -Name MelbourneAlpha -AccountName MelbourneAlpha
```

7. You can verify that the credentials have been saved in JSON format by running the `Get-CredentialSpec` cmdlet. By default, credentials are stored in the `c:\ProgramData\Docker\CredentialSpecs\` folder.

8. Start the container using the option `--security-opt "credentialspec="` and specify the JSON file containing the credentials associated with the gMSA. For example, run the following command if the credentials are stored in the file `twt_webapp01.json`:

```
docker run --security-opt "credentialspec=file://twt_webapp01.json" --hostname
webapp01 -it mcr.microsoft.com/windows/servercore:ltsc2025 powershell
```

Once you've configured the container to indirectly use the gMSA for its Local System and Network Service accounts, you can provide the container with permissions to access domain resources by providing access to the gMSA. For example, if you want to provide the container with access to the contents of a file share hosted on a domain member, you can configure permissions so that the gMSA has access to the file share.

> **More Info**
>
> *Active Directory container service accounts*
>
> You can learn more about Active Directory container service accounts at *https://learn.microsoft.com/en-us/virtualization/windowscontainers/manage-containers/manage-serviceaccounts.*

Applying updates

One of the concepts that many IT operations personnel find challenging is that you don't update a container that is deployed in production. Instead, you create a fresh container from the original container image, update that container, and then save that updated container as a new container image. You then remove the container in production and deploy a new container to production that is based on the newly updated image.

For example, you have a container that hosts a web app deployed from a container image named WebApp1 that is deployed in production. The developers in your organization release an update to WebApp1 that involves changing some existing settings. Rather than modifying the container in production, you start another container from the WebApp1 image, modify the settings, and then create a new container image named WebApp2. You then deploy a new container into production from the WebApp2 container image and remove the original unupdated container.

While you can manually update your container base OS images by applying software updates, Microsoft releases updated versions of the container base images each time a new software update is released. Once a new container OS base image is released, you or your organization's developers should update existing images that are dependent on the container OS base image. Regularly updated container base OS images provide an excellent reason for eventually moving toward using Dockerfiles to automate the process of building containers. If you have a Dockerfile configured for each container image used in your organization, updating your container base OS images when a new container base OS image is released is a quick, painless, and automated process.

CHAPTER 16

Inside OUT

Keep old OS images

You'll need to keep your old container OS base images around until all the container images that are dependent on that old container OS base image have been replaced by newly updated container images.

Container networking

Each container has a virtual network adapter. This virtual network adapter connects to a virtual switch, through which inbound and outbound traffic is sent. Networking modes determine how network adapters function in terms of IP addressing—meaning whether they use NAT or are connected to the same network as the container host.

Windows containers support the following networking modes:

- **NAT** Each container is assigned an IP address from the private 172.16.0.0 /16 address range. When using NAT, you can configure port forwarding from the container host to the container endpoint. If you create a container without specifying a network, the container will use the default NAT network. The Docker service creates its own default NAT network. When the container host reboots, the NAT network will not be created until the Docker service has restarted. Any container that was attached to the existing NAT network and which is configured to persist after reboot (for example, because it uses the -restart always option) will reattach to the NAT network that is newly created when the Docker service restarts.

- **Transparent**   Each container endpoint connects to the physical network. The containers can have IP addresses assigned statically or through DHCP.

- **Overlay**   Use this mode when you have configured the Docker Engine to run in swarm mode. Overlay mode allows container endpoints to be connected across multiple container hosts.

- **L2 Bridge**   Container endpoints are on the same IP subnet used by the container host. IP addresses must be assigned statically. All containers on the container host have the same MAC address.

- **L2 Tunnel**   This mode is only used when you deploy containers in Azure.

You can list available networks using the following command:

```
docker network ls
```

To view which containers are connected to a specific network, run this command:

```
docker network inspect <network name>
```

You can create multiple container networks on a container host, but you need to keep in mind the following limitations:

- If you are creating multiple networks of the transparent or L2 bridge type, you need to ensure that each network has a separate network adapter.

- If you create multiple NAT networks on a container host, additional NAT networks prefixes will be partitioned from the container host's NAT network's address space. (By default, this is 172.16.0.0/16.) For example, these will be 172.16.1.0/24, 172.16.2.0/24, and so on.

NAT

Network Address Translation allows each container to be assigned an address in a private address space, while connecting to the container host's network uses the container host's IP address. The default NAT address range for containers is 172.16.0.0 /16. 172.16.0.0 /16 is the private range usually reserved for container workloads on networks. In the event that the container host's IP address is in the 172.16.0.0 /16 range, you will need to alter the NAT IP prefix. You can do this by performing the following steps:

1. Stop the Docker service.

2. Remove any existing NAT networks using the following command:

```
Get-ContainerNetwork | Remove-ContainerNetwork
```

3. Perform one of the following actions:

   - Edit the daemon.json file and configure the "fixed-cidr":"< IP Prefix > / Mask" option to the desired network address prefix.

   - Edit the daemon.json file and set the "bridge": "none" option and then use the docker network create -d command to create a network. For example, to create a network that uses the 192.168.15.0/24 range, the default gateway, 192.168.15.1 that, named CustomNat issues this command:

   ```
   Docker network create -d nat --subnet=192.168.15.0/24 --gateway=192.168.15.1
   CustomNat
   ```

4. Start the Docker service.

You can also allow connections to custom NAT networks when a container is run by allowing use of the --Network parameter and specifying the custom NAT network name. To do this, you need to have the "bridge: none" option specified in the daemon.json file. The command to run a container and join it to the CustomNat network created earlier is

```
docker run -it --network=CustomNat <ContainerImage> <cmd>
```

Port mappings allow ports on the container host to be mapped to ports on the container. For example, to map port 8080 on the container host to port 80 on a new container created from the windowsservercore image, and to run powershell.exe interactively on the container, create the container using the following command:

```
docker run -it -p 8080:80 mcr.microsoft.com/windows/servercore powershell.exe
```

Port mappings must be specified when the container is created or when it is in a stopped state. You can specify them using the -p parameter or the EXPOSE command in a Dockerfile when using the -P parameter. If you do not specify a port on the container host but you do specify one on the container itself, a random port will be assigned. For example, run this command:

```
docker run -itd -p 80 mcr.microsoft.com/windows/servercore/iis:windowsservercore-
ltsc2025 powershell.exe
```

A random port on the container host can be mapped through to port 80 on the container. You can determine which port is randomly assigned using the docker ps command. When you configure port mapping, firewall rules on the container host will be created automatically that will allow traffic through.

CHAPTER 16

Transparent

Transparent networks allow each container endpoint to connect to the same network as the container host. You can use the Transparent networking mode by creating a container network that has the driver name transparent. The driver name is specified with the -d option. You can do this with this command:

```
docker network create -d transparent TransparentNetworkName
```

If the container host is a virtual machine running on a Hyper-V host, and you want to use DHCP for IP address assignment, it's necessary to select the Enable MAC Address Spoofing option on the VM network adapter. The transparent network mode supports IPv6. If you're using the transparent network mode, you can use a DHCPv6 server to assign IPv6 addresses to containers.

If you want to manually assign IP addresses to containers, when you create the transparent network, you must specify the subnet and gateway parameters. These network properties need to match the network settings of the network to which the container host is connected.

For example, your container host is connected to a network that uses the 192.168.30.0/24 network and uses 192.168.30.1 as the default gateway. To create a transparent network that will allow static address assignment for containers on this network called TransNet, run this command:

```
docker network create -d transparent --subnet=192.168.30.0/24 --gateway=192.168.30.1
TransNet
```

Once the transparent network is created with the appropriate settings, you can specify an IP address for a container using the --ip option. For example, to start a new container from the windowsservercore image, enter the command prompt within the container. To assign it the IP address 192.168.30.101 on the TransNet network, run this command:

```
docker run -it –network=TransNet --ip 192.168.30.101 mcr.microsoft.com/windows/
servercore cmd.exe
```

As, when you use transparent network, containers are connected directly to the container host's network; you don't need to configure port mapping into the container.

Overlay

You can only use overlay networking mode if the Docker host is running in Swarm mode as a manager node. Each overlay network that you create on a swarm cluster has its own IP subnet defined by an IP address prefix in the private address space. You create an overlay network by specifying overlay as the driver. For example, you can create an overlay network for the subnet 192.168.50.0/24 with the name OverlayNet by running the following command from a swarm manager node:

```
docker network create --driver=overlay --subnet=192.168.50.0/24 OverlayNet
```

Layer 2 Bridge

Layer 2 Bridge (L2 Bridge) networks are similar to transparent networks in that they allow containers to have IP addresses on the same subnets as the container host. They differ in that IP addresses must be assigned statically. This is because all containers on the container host that use an L2 bridge network have the same MAC address.

When creating an L2 Bridge network, you must specify the network type as `l2bridge`. You must also specify subnet and default gateway settings that matches the subnet and default gateway settings of the container host. For example, to create a L2 Bridge network named `L2BridgeNet` for the IP address range 192.168.88.0/24 and with the default gateway address 192.168.88.1, use the following command:

```
docker network create -d l2bridge --subnet=192.168.88.0/24 --gateway=192.168.88.1
L2BridgeNet
```

> ## More Info
> ### Container networking
> You can learn more about networking of containers at *https://learn.microsoft.com/en-us/virtualization/windowscontainers/container-networking/architecture*.

Clustering and high availability

The primary high-availability technology available in Windows Server is failover clustering. Clustering allows you to ensure that your workloads remain available if server hardware or even a site fails. Windows Server also includes network load-balancing functionality, which allows you to scale out nonstateful workloads, such as web server front ends.

Failover clustering

Failover clustering is a stateful, high-availability solution that allows an application or service to remain available to clients if a host server fails. You can use failover clustering to provide high availability to applications such as SQL Server, as well as Scale-Out File Servers and virtual machines.

Failover clustering is supported in both the Standard and Datacenter editions of Windows Server. In some earlier versions of the Windows Server operating system, you only gained access to failover clustering if you used the Enterprise edition. Windows Server supports up to 64 nodes in a failover cluster.

Generally, all servers in a cluster should run either a similar hardware configuration or should have similarly provisioned virtual machines. You should also use the same edition and installation option. For example, you should aim to have cluster nodes that either run the full GUI or Server Core versions of Windows Server, but you should avoid having cluster nodes that have a mix of computers running Server Core and the full GUI version. Avoiding this mix ensures that you use a similar update routine. A similar update routine is more difficult to maintain when you use different versions of Windows Server.

You should use the Datacenter edition of Windows Server when building clusters that host Hyper-V virtual machines because the virtual machine–licensing scheme available with this edition provides the most VM licenses.

To be fully supported by Microsoft, cluster hardware should meet the Certified for Windows Server logo requirement. An easy way of accomplishing this is to purchase and deploy Azure Local (formerly named Azure Stack HCI), a prebuilt hyperconverged Windows Server installation available from select vendors. Even though it's called Azure Local (previously Azure Stack HCI) and sounds as though it's far more of a cloud-based solution, it's primarily just an optimized Windows Server deployment on a certified configuration with all the relevant clustering and "Software-Defined Datacenter" features lit up.

You can use serial-attached SCSI (SAS), iSCSI, Fibre Channel, or Fibre Channel over Ethernet (FcoE) to host shared storage for a Windows Server failover cluster. Failover clustering only supports IPv4- and IPv6-based protocols. You install failover clustering by installing the Failover Clustering feature and the Failover Clustering Remote Server Administration Tools (RSAT). RSAT allows you to manage other failover clusters in your environment.

Inside OUT

Highly available workloads

In the past, you likely clustered workloads such as Exchange and SQL to ensure that they were highly available. Today, both products come with technologies that allow you to have a highly available solution without deploying on a failover cluster. These technologies are Always On Availability Groups and Database Availability Groups. Today, you're more likely to deploy these workloads on virtual machines and to ensure that the virtual machine host is configured in a failover cluster than you are to directly make the workloads highly available by installing them on a failover cluster.

Cluster quorum modes

A cluster quorum mode determines how many nodes and witnesses must fail before the cluster is in a failed state. Nodes are servers that participate in the cluster. Witnesses can be stored on shared storage, on file shares, in Windows Server, and even on a USB drive attached to a network switch; shared storage is the preferred method. This recommendation might eventually change, however, as continuously available file shares are more widely adopted.

Inside OUT

No DFS Witness

For unknown reasons, some people use DFS shares as file share witnesses when setting up their failover clusters. To stop this type of shenanigan from occurring in the future, Microsoft has configured Windows Server 2019 and later failover clustering so that it explicitly blocks the use of DFS namespaces when configuring a file share witness.

Microsoft recommends you configure a cluster so that an odd number of total votes is spread across member nodes and the witness. This limits the chance of a tie during a quorum vote.

There are four cluster quorum modes:

- **Node Majority**   This cluster quorum mode is recommended for clusters that have an odd number of nodes. When this quorum type is set, the cluster retains quorum when the number of available nodes exceeds the number of failed nodes. For example, if a cluster has five nodes and three are available, the quorum is retained.

- **Node And Disk Majority**   This cluster quorum node is recommended when the cluster has an even number of nodes. A disk witness hosted on a shared storage disk, for example, iSCSI or Fibre Channel, that is accessible to cluster nodes has a vote when determining quorum, as do the quorum nodes. The cluster retains quorum as long as the majority of voting entities remain online. For example, if you have a four-node cluster and a witness disk, a combination of three of those entities needs to remain online for the cluster to retain a quorum. The cluster retains a quorum if three nodes are online or if two nodes and the witness disk are online.

- **Node And File Share Majority**   This configuration is similar to the Node And Disk Majority configuration, but the quorum is stored on a network share rather than on a shared-storage disk. It's suitable for similar configurations to Node And Disk Majority. This method is not as reliable as Node And Disk Majority because file shares generally do not have the redundancy features of shared storage.

- **No Majority: Disk Only**   This model can be used with clusters that have an odd number of nodes. It's only recommended for testing environments because the disk hosting the witness functions as a single point of failure. When you choose this model, as long as the disk hosting the witness and one node remain available, the cluster retains quorum. If the disk hosting the witness fails, the quorum is lost, even if all the other nodes are available.

When you create a cluster, the cluster quorum is automatically configured for you. You might want to alter the quorum mode, however, if you change the number of nodes in your cluster. For example, you might want to alter the quorum mode if you change from a four-node to a five-node cluster. When you change the cluster quorum configuration, the Failover Cluster Manager provides you with a recommended configuration, but you can choose to override that configuration if you want.

You can also perform advanced quorum configuration to specify what nodes can participate in the quorum vote, which you can set on the Select Voting Configuration page of the Configure Cluster Quorum Wizard. When you do this, only the selected nodes' votes are used to calculate the quorum. Also, it's possible that fewer nodes would need to fail to cause a cluster to fail than would otherwise be the case if all nodes participated in the quorum vote. This can be useful when configuring how multisite clusters calculate quorum when the connection between sites fails.

Cluster storage and cluster shared volumes

Almost all failover cluster scenarios require access to some form of shared storage. Windows Server failover clusters can use SAS, iSCSI, or Fibre Channel for Shared Storage. With the inclusion of the iSCSI Target software in Windows Server, iSCSI is one of the simplest and cheapest of these technologies to implement.

You should configure disks used for failover clustering as follows:

- Volumes should be formatted using NTFS or ReFS.

- Use Master Boot Record (MBR) or GUID Partition Table (GPT).

- Avoid allowing different clusters access to the same storage device. This can be accomplished through LUN masking or zoning.

- Any multipath solution must be based on Microsoft Multipath I/O (MPIO).

Cluster Shared Volumes (CSV) is a technology that was introduced in Windows Server 2008 R2 that allows multiple cluster nodes to have concurrent access to a single Logical Unit Number (LUN). Prior to Windows Server 2008 R2, only the active node had access to shared storage. CSV allows you to have virtual machines on the same LUN run on different cluster nodes. CSV also has the following benefits:

- Support for scale-out file servers

- Support for BitLocker volume encryption

- SMB 3.0 and later support

- Integration with Storage Spaces

- Online volume scan and repair

You can enable CSV only after you create a failover cluster and you have provided the storage that will be available to the CSV.

Windows Server 2025 clusters support using both Storage Spaces Direct (S2D) and Storage Area Networks. In this scenario, SAN disks must be completely separate from S2D disks and must not be used in the S2D storage pool. SAN volumes should be formatted using NTFS before being added to a CSV. S2D volumes should be formatted using ReFS before being added to a CSV.

Cluster networks

While you can create failover clusters with nodes that have a single network adapter, the best practice is to have separate networks and network adapters for the following:

- A connection for cluster nodes to shared storage

- A private network for internal cluster communication

- A public network that clients use to access services hosted on the cluster

In scenarios where high availability is critical, you might have multiple redundant networks connected through several separate switches. If you have a cluster where everything is connected through one piece of network hardware, you can almost guarantee that piece of network hardware is the first thing that fails.

You can either use IPv4 or IPv6 addresses that are dynamically or statically assigned, but you should not use a mix of dynamically and statically assigned IP addresses for nodes that are members of the same cluster. If you use a mixture of dynamically and statically assigned IP addresses, the Validate A Configuration Wizard generates an error.

Inside OUT

Default gateways

Even if the Cluster Validation Wizard only gives you warnings when you perform the test, you cannot create a failover cluster unless each node is configured with a default gateway. The default gateway doesn't have to be a host that exists, but if you're having trouble in your virtual machine lab with creating a failover cluster, go back and check whether you've configured a default gateway for each node.

MPIO

If there are multiple paths to physical storage on a server, you will need to enable multipath I/O (MPIO). Enabling MPIO aggregates multiple paths to a physical disk into a single logical path for data access. Enabling MPIO improves resiliency to failure. You should enable MPIO on all nodes that will participate in the cluster. You can enable MPIO with the following PowerShell command:

```
Install-WindowsFeature -ComputerName Node1 -Name MultiPath-IO
```

Cluster Aware Updating

Cluster Aware Updating (CAU) is a feature included with Windows Server that allows you to automate the process of applying software updates to failover clusters. Cluster Aware Updating integrates with Windows Update, Windows Server Update Services (WSUS), System Center

Configuration Manager, and other software update—management applications. CAU uses the following process:

1. Obtains the update files from the source location.

2. Puts the first node into maintenance mode.

3. Moves any cluster roles off the node to other nodes in the cluster.

4. Installs software updates.

5. Restarts the cluster node, if necessary.

6. Checks for additional updates. If updates are found, it performs Steps 4 through 6 until all updates are applied.

7. Brings the node out of maintenance mode.

8. Reacquires clustered roles that were moved to other nodes.

9. Puts the next node into maintenance mode and repeats the cycle starting at Step 3 until all nodes have been updated.

The main benefit of CAU is that it updates a process that previously had to be performed manually. You can configure CAU to automatically apply updates to cluster nodes when they are approved through WSUS or System Center Configuration Manager, or you can trigger CAU manually as needed.

You can configure the CAU options so that the updates are rolled back across the cluster if an update fails to install on a node after a specified number of attempts. You can also configure Advanced Options, such as requiring scripts to run before and after the update process has occurred and whether services hosted on the cluster require special shutdown or startup configurations.

Failover and preference settings

Cluster preference settings allow you to configure the preferred owner for a specific cluster role, and you can also configure different preferred owners for different cluster roles. Where possible, the role is hosted on the preferred owner. You can configure a list of preferred owners, so that if the most preferred owner isn't available, the next preferred owner hosts the role. You configure a role-preferred owner on the role's Properties dialog.

You configure whether the clustered role fails back to the preferred owner on the Failover tab of the cluster role's Properties dialog. When configuring failback, you need to

- Determine whether you want to prevent failback

- Determine whether you want to have failback occur automatically as soon as the preferred owner is in a healthy state

- Configure failback to occur within a certain number of hours of the preferred owner returning to a healthy state

Node quarantine settings allow you to configure a node so that it is unable to rejoin the cluster if the node fails a certain number of times within a certain period. Configuring node quarantine blocks workloads from being placed back on a quarantined node until the reason for the repeated failure can be dealt with by a server administrator.

A fault domain is a collection of hardware components that share a common point of failure. Windows Server allows you to configure fault domains at the site, rack, chassis, and node levels. You can use Storage Spaces and Storage Spaces Direct with fault domains to ensure that copies of data are kept in separate fault domains. For example, if you defined fault domains at the site level, you can configure storage spaces so that redundant data resides in separate sites rather than residing only on separate cluster nodes.

Multisite clusters

Failover clusters can span multiple sites. When configuring a cluster that spans two sites, you should consider the following:

- Ensure that there is an equal number of nodes in each site.

- Allow each node to have a vote.

- Enable dynamic quorum. Dynamic quorum allows the quorum to be recalculated when individual nodes leave the cluster one at a time. Dynamic quorum is enabled by default on Windows Server failover clusters.

- Use a file share witness. You should host the file share witness on a third site that has separate connectivity to the two sites that host the cluster nodes, as shown in Figure 17-1. When configured in this manner, the cluster retains quorum if one of the sites is lost. An alternative to a file share witness is a Cloud Witness.

CHAPTER 17

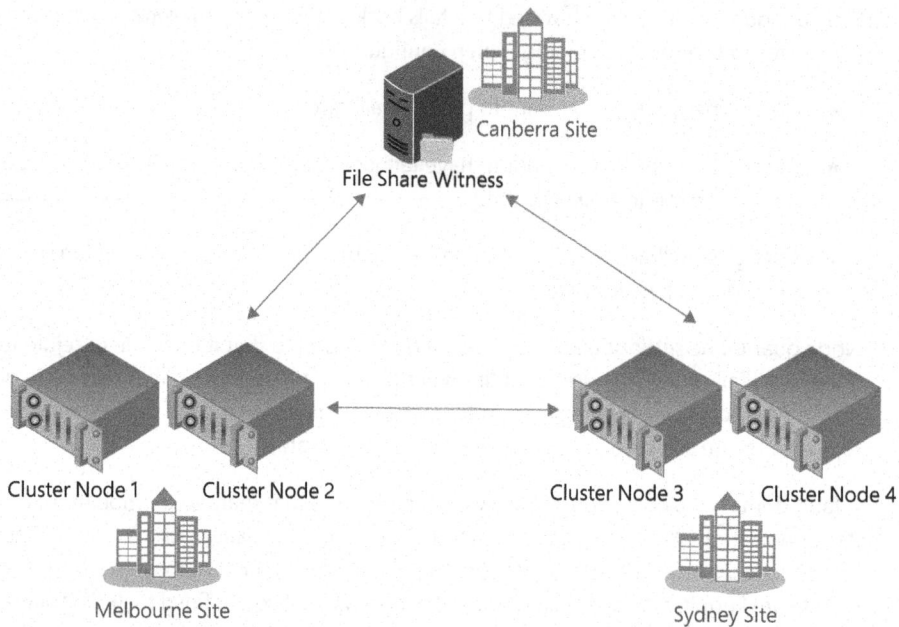

Figure 17-1   Multisite cluster

If you only have two sites and are unable to place a file share witness in an independent third site, you can manually edit the cluster configuration to reassign votes so that the cluster recalculates the quorum.

Manually reassigning votes is also useful to avoid split-brain scenarios. Split-brain scenarios occur when a failure occurs in a multisite cluster and when both sides of the cluster believe they have a quorum. Split-brain scenarios cause challenges when connectivity is restored and make it necessary to restart servers on one side of the multisite cluster to resolve the issue. You can manually reassign votes so that one side always retains a quorum if intersite connectivity is lost. For example, by setting the Melbourne site with two votes and the Sydney site with one vote, the Melbourne site always retains quorum if intersite connectivity is lost.

Stretch clusters

A stretch cluster is a multisite cluster that uses storage replica synchronous replication to maintain identical storage copies across sites. Stretch clusters must meet the normal failover cluster requirements as well as the requirements for storage replica synchronous replication. A storage replica in this configuration has the following requirements:

- The data and log disks must be initialized as GPT.

- The volumes must be formatted as NTFS or ReFS.

- The log volumes should use flash-based storage and high-performance resiliency settings. Microsoft recommends that the log storage be faster than the data storage.

- The log size defaults to 8 GB if unspecified. Your log volume must be at least 10 GB or larger based on log requirements and organizational needs.

- Each set of storage must allow the creation of at least two virtual disks, one for replicated data and one for logs.

- The replicated storage can't be located on the drive containing the Windows operating system folder.

- An average of 5 ms round-trip latency (or less) for synchronous replication.

The Datacenter edition of Windows Server is recommended.

> **More Info**
>
> *Stretch clusters*
>
> You can learn more about stretch clusters at *https://learn.microsoft.com/windows-server/storage/storage-replica/stretch-cluster-replicaiton-using-shared-strorage.*

Cloud Witness

Cloud Witness has the cluster witness role hosted in Azure rather than at a third site. Cloud Witness is suitable for multisite clusters. To configure a Cloud Witness, create a storage account in Azure, copy the storage access keys, note the endpoint URL links, and then use these links with the Configure Cluster Quorum Settings Wizard and specify a Cloud Witness, as shown in Figure 17-2.

> **More Info**
>
> *Cloud Witness*
>
> You can learn more about Cloud Witness at *https://learn.microsoft.com/windows-server/failover-clustering/deploy-cloud-witness.*

Cloud Witness can also be configured to use a managed identity rather than storage account keys.

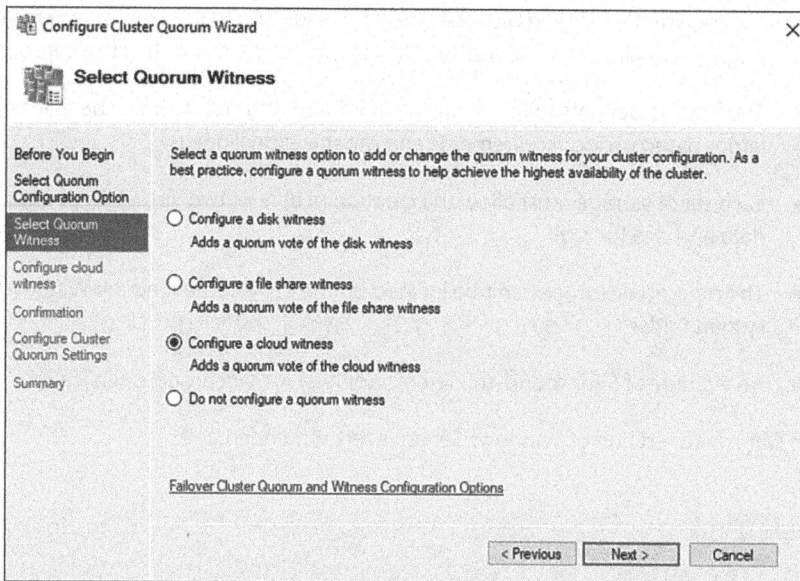

Figure 17-2   Configure Cloud Witness

Storage Spaces Direct Campus Clusters

Campus Clusters use Storage Spaces Direct rather than Storage Replica for cluster storage in high-bandwidth, low-latency environments. Campus Clusters topology allows organizations to configure rack fault domains in a failover cluster. Campus clusters use two-node or four-node topology, with one or two nodes per rack in the datacenter. With campus clusters, you can enable two-copy or four-copy volume configuration for improved resiliency. Each node hosts a copy of the data.

The four-copy volume scenario, with two nodes on each rack, offers "rack plus node" resiliency. This means you can lose an entire rack and a node in the other rack and still maintain full data availability.

S2D campus clusters have the following requirements:

- All drives must be SSD or NVMe drives. You should not use traditional magnetic storage for this cluster storage.

- 1 ms or lower latency between rack fault domains.

- RDMA network adapters are recommended but not required.

- Does not require a Layer 3 switch.

Virtual machine failover clustering

One of the most common uses for failover clusters is hosting virtual machines. By deploying a workload, such as SQL Server or Exchange on a highly available virtual machine, you can achieve high availability without the need for the application to be aware that it is now highly available. The virtual machine functions normally, provides services to clients on the network, and can switch between cluster nodes as necessary in the event that the individual cluster node hosting it requires maintenance or experiences some sort of failure. Building a Hyper-V failover cluster first involves creating a failover cluster and then adding the Hyper-V role to each node of the cluster.

Virtual machine storage

You should use cluster shared volumes to store virtual machines on a Hyper-V cluster because cluster shared volumes allow multiple cluster nodes to manage a single shared storage device. This allows you to put multiple virtual machines on the same shared storage device but have those virtual machines hosted by different nodes in the failover cluster. Cluster-shared volumes are mapped under the `C:\ClusterStorage` folder on cluster nodes.

When creating a new virtual machine on a failover cluster, first select which cluster node hosts the virtual machine.

When creating a highly available virtual machine, specify the cluster-shared volume path as the location to store the virtual machine. If you have an existing machine that you want to make highly available, you can move the virtual machine to this path. As an alternative, you also have the option to specify an SMB 3.0 file share as the storage location for the highly available virtual machine. Whether to select a cluster-shared volume or an SMB 3.0 file share depends on your organization's storage configuration.

After the virtual machine is created, you can control it by using the Failover Cluster Manager console. The Move option in the Actions pane allows you to select the cluster node to which you want to move the virtual machine.

In production environments, you should ensure that each Hyper-V host has an identical hardware configuration. However, in development environments, this is not always possible. If different processor types are used—for example, an Intel processor on one node and an AMD processor on another—you might have to perform a quick migration. Quick migration allows migration between nodes but disrupts client connectivity. You can allow migration between Hyper-V nodes with different processor types or versions by enabling the processor compatibility setting on the virtual machine.

VM load balancing

VM load balancing is a feature of Windows Server that identifies nodes in a Hyper-V cluster where CPU and memory resources are under pressure; VM load balancing redistributes workloads to other nodes that have lower CPU and/or memory utilization. By default, VM load balancing is enabled, and it automatically moves VMs to a new node after you add that node to an existing Windows Server Hyper-V cluster.

You can configure VM load balancing so that workload redistribution happens automatically when a specific threshold is reached, or you can configure load balancing to occur on a periodic basis. VMs are moved between Hyper-V cluster nodes using live migration without incurring downtime. You configure VM load balancing aggressiveness by using the following Windows PowerShell command:

```
(Get-Cluster).AutoBalancerLevel = <value>
```

The values listed in Table 17-1 determine automatic load balancer thresholds:

Table 17-1   Auto VM load balancer aggressiveness

AutoBalancerLevel	Aggressiveness	Action
1 (default)	Low	Move workloads when the node reaches 80 percent memory or processor utilization.
2	Medium	Move workloads when the node reaches 70 percent memory or processor utilization.
3	High	Move workloads when the node reaches 60 percent memory or processor utilization.

You configure how the balancer functions by using the following Windows PowerShell command:

```
(Get-Cluster).AutoBalancerMode = <value>
```

The values listed in Table 17-2 determine the automatic load balancer mode:

Table 17-2   Auto VM load balancer mode

AutoBalancerMODE	Aggressiveness
0	Disables VM load balancing
1	Load balances each time a new node joins the Hyper-V cluster
2 (default)	Load balances each time a new node joins the Hyper-V cluster and every 30 minutes

Rolling upgrades

Cluster OS Rolling Upgrade allows you to upgrade a cluster hosting Hyper-V or Scale-Out file server workloads without taking those workloads offline.

Upgrading a cluster involves either adding new nodes running a newer version of Windows Server, such as Windows Server 2025, to an existing cluster running an older version of Windows Server. Cluster rolling upgrades are different from taking a cluster node offline and performing an in-place upgrade and then rejoining the cluster node to the cluster.

The nodes that you can add to a cluster depend on the cluster's functional level. A cluster that only has nodes running Windows Server 2012 R2 is running at cluster functional level 8. Cluster functional level 8 supports nodes that run both Windows Server 2012 R2 and Windows Server 2016. You can also introduce cluster nodes that run either Windows Server 2012 or 2016 to the cluster as long as the cluster is still configured to use cluster functional level 8. It's even possible to roll back to Windows Server 2012 R2 when all nodes are running Windows Server 2016, as long as you haven't upgraded the cluster functional level from level 8.

A cluster running at functional level 9 supports nodes running Windows Server 2016 and Windows Server 2019. A cluster running at functional level 10 only supports nodes running Windows Server 2019. A cluster running at functional level 11 only supports nodes running Windows Server 2022. A cluster running at cluster functional level 12 only supports nodes running Windows Server 2025.

You should only upgrade the cluster functional level when you are absolutely certain that you don't want to roll back the cluster upgrade and that all nodes have been upgraded. You can determine which functional level a cluster is running at by running the following Windows PowerShell command:

```
Get-Cluster | Select ClusterFunctionalLevel
```

You can also use the Get-ClusterNodeSupportedVersion cmdlet on a computer running Windows Server to determine which nodes in the cluster are running at a specific functional level and cluster upgrade version.

You can upgrade the cluster functional level by using the Update-ClusterFunctionalLevel cmdlet.

Cluster OS Rolling Upgrade has the following conditions:

- You can only upgrade a Hyper-V cluster if the CPUs support Second-Level Addressing Table (SLAT). This is because Hyper-V is only supported on processors that support SLAT in Windows Server 2016 and later.

- When performing the rolling cluster upgrade, always use the most recent version of Windows Server to add nodes to the cluster.

- All cluster management tasks should be performed from the more recent operating system node than the previous version node.

CHAPTER 17

- Cluster rolling upgrade cannot be used to upgrade VM guest clusters that use a shared virtual hard disk as shared storage. VM guest clusters are clusters where each node is a virtual machine. A VM guest cluster that uses a shared virtual hard disk for shared storage cannot be upgraded, but a VM guest cluster that uses another form of shared storage, such as iSCSI, can be upgraded by using a rolling cluster upgrade.

- Before upgrading a node, drain the node of workloads and evict the node from the cluster. After you've upgraded the node's operating system, you can join it to the cluster again.

- Prior to commencing the Cluster OS Rolling Upgrade, ensure that all elements of the cluster and its workloads are backed up.

- You can't lower the cluster functional level after it has been raised.

- Cluster OS Rolling Upgrade only works when the original cluster is running Windows Server 2012 R2 or later. Cluster OS Rolling Upgrade does not work with Windows Server 2012, Windows Server 2008 R2, or Windows Server 2008.

More Info

Cluster OS Rolling Upgrade

You can learn more about rolling upgrades at *https://learn.microsoft.com/ windows-server/failover-clustering/cluster-operating-system-rolling-upgrade*.

Workgroup clusters

Workgroup clusters are a special type of cluster where cluster nodes are not members of an Active Directory domain. Workgroup clusters are also known as Active Directory Detached Clusters. The following workloads are supported for workgroup clusters:

- **SQL Server**   When deploying SQL Server on a workgroup cluster, it's recommended that you use SQL Server Authentication for databases and SQL Server Always On Availability Groups.

- **File Server**   A supported but not recommended configuration, as Kerberos will not be available as an authentication protocol for SMB traffic.

- **Hyper-V**   A supported but not recommended configuration. Hyper-V live migration is not supported, though it is possible to perform quick migration.

When creating a workgroup cluster, you first need to create a special account on all nodes that will participate in the cluster that has the following properties:

- The special account must have the same username and password on all cluster nodes.

- The special account must be added to the local Administrators group on each cluster node.

- The primary DNS suffix on each cluster node must be configured with the same value.

- When creating the cluster, ensure that the `AdministrativeAccessPoint` parameter when using the `New-Cluster` cmdlet is set to DNS. Ensure that the cluster name is present in the appropriate DNS zone, which depends on the primary DNS suffix, when running this command.

- You will need to run the following PowerShell command on each node to configure the `LocalAccountTokenFilterPolicy` registry setting to 1.

  ```
  new-itemproperty -path HKLM:\SOFTWARE\Microsoft\Windows\CurrentVersion\Policies\
  System -Name LocalAccountTokenFilterPolicy -Value 1
  ```

To create a workgroup cluster, use the `New-Cluster` cmdlet with the name parameter listing the cluster name, the node parameters listing the nodes that you want to join to the cluster, where the nodes have been configured according to the prerequisites, and the `administrativeaccesspoint` parameter configured for DNS. For example, to create a new workgroup cluster named `workgrpclst` with member nodes `node1` and `node2`, run the following command on one of the nodes:

```
New-Cluster -name workgrpclst -node node1,node2 -AdministrativeAccessPoint DNS
```

You can perform Hyper-V live migration on workgroup clusters if all the nodes are running Windows Server 2025.

Cluster sets

Cluster sets are a Windows Server 2019 and later technology that provides a method of grouping multiple failover clusters. When you implement cluster sets, you can combine smaller clusters into larger virtual clusters. These virtual clusters support virtual machine fluidity and a unified storage namespace, meaning that virtual machines can be moved between clusters in a cluster set as easily as they are moved between nodes in a traditional failover cluster. While virtual machines can be live-migrated between clusters, cluster sets do not allow virtual machines to fail over between clusters in a cluster set.

Only clusters running at the Windows Server 2019 cluster functional level 10.X or higher can participate in cluster sets. You cannot join clusters running Windows Server 2016 or Windows Server 2012 R2 to a cluster set. All clusters in a cluster set must be members of the same Active Directory forest.

CHAPTER 17

Cluster sets improve the failover cluster lifecycle. Rather than adding and removing nodes from a single cluster when the node hardware is to be retired, you can add a new cluster to the cluster set, migrate workloads across from the original cluster to the new cluster, and then retire that original cluster. Microsoft currently supports cluster sets for up to 64 cluster nodes, which is the same number of nodes supported in an individual failover cluster. That being said, there is no specific limit to the number of nodes that may exist within a cluster set, so going beyond 64 nodes in a cluster set is possible should you want to try it.

Cluster sets consist of a management cluster and member clusters. The management cluster is the cluster set that holds the management role for the cluster set and also hosts the unified storage namespace for the cluster set's Scale-Out File Server. The management cluster does not host workloads, such as virtual machines, and its role is to manage the relationship between other clusters in the cluster set and to host the storage namespace. The new role that the management cluster hosts is termed the "Cluster Set Master" (CS-Master). Member clusters hold the "Cluster Set Worker" (CS-Worker) role.

Cluster sets are deprecated in Windows Server 2025, meaning the feature is no longer in active development and will not receive further enhancements. However, cluster sets are still present and supported in Windows Server 2025. While you can continue to use cluster sets in Windows Server 2025, you should plan to transition away from them, as they may be removed in a future Windows Server release.

> ## More Info
> **Cluster sets**
>
> You can learn more about cluster sets at *https://learn.microsoft.com/windows-server/storage/storage-spaces/cluster-sets*.

Managing failover clustering with PowerShell

You can use cmdlets in the FailoverClusters module, as described in Table 17-3, to manage failover clusters on Windows Server.

Table 17-3   Failover cluster PowerShell cmdlets

Noun	Verbs	Function
Cluster	Get, Test, Stop, New, Start, Remove	Manage failover clusters
ClusterAccess	Block, Get, Remove, Grant	Manage permissions to control access to a failover cluster

Noun	Verbs	Function
ClusterAvailableDisk	Get	View disks that support failover clustering that are visible to all nodes but are not yet clustered disks
ClusterCheckpoint	Add, Remove, Get	Manage cryptographic keys or registry checkpoints for a cluster resource
ClusterDiagnosticInfo	Get	Get cluster diagnostic information
ClusterDisk	Add	Add a disk to a cluster
ClusterDiskReservation	Clear	Clears persistent reservations on a disk in a failover cluster
ClusterFaultDomain	Get, Set, Remove, New	Manage cluster fault domains
ClusterFaultDomainXML	Set, Get	Configure cluster fault domains using XML
ClusterFileServerRole	Add	Add the file server role to a cluster
ClusterFunctionalLevel	Update	Upgrade the cluster functional level
ClusterGenericApplicationRole	Add	Configure high availability for an application that was not originally designed to run in a failover cluster
ClusterGenericScriptRole	Add	Configure an application controlled by a script that runs in Windows Script Host on a failover cluster
ClusterGenericServiceRole	Add	Configure high availability for a service that was not originally designed to run in a failover cluster
ClusterGroup	Remove, Start, Stop, Add, Get, Move	Manage cluster roles and resource groups in a failover cluster
ClusterGroupFromSet	Remove	Remove a group from a cluster group set
ClusterGroupSet	Remove, Get, New, Set	Manage cluster group sets
ClusterGroupSetDependency	Add, Get, Remove	Manage cluster group set dependencies
ClusterGroupToSet	Add	Add a group to a cluster group set
ClusterIPResource	Update	Renew or release a DHCP lease for an IP address resource used by a failover cluster
ClusteriSCSITargetServerRole	Add	Create a highly available iSCSI Target server
ClusterLog	Get, Set	Manage cluster log settings
ClusterNameAccount	New	Create a cluster name account in Active Directory
ClusterNetwork	Get	View cluster network properties

Noun	Verbs	Function
ClusterNetworkInterface	Get	View cluster network interface properties
ClusterNetworkNameResource	Update	Register cluster resource names in DNS
ClusterNode	Get, Resume, Stop, Start, Remove, Add, Clear, Suspend	Manage specific cluster nodes
ClusterOwnerNode	Set, Get	Configure which nodes can own a resource
ClusterParameter	Set, Get	View and configure information about an object in a failover cluster
ClusterQuorum	Get, Set	Manage cluster quorum
ClusterResource	Remove, Move, Start, Suspend, Add, Get, Stop, Resume	Manage cluster resources
ClusterResourceDependency	Get, Set, Add, Remove	Manage cluster resource dependencies
ClusterResourceDependen-cyReport	Get	Generate a cluster resource dependency report
ClusterResourceFailure	Test	Test the failure of a cluster resource
ClusterResourceType	Add, Get, Remove	Manage cluster resource type
ClusterScaleOutFile-ServerRole	Add	Add a cluster Scale-Out File Server role
ClusterServerRole	Add	Add a cluster server role
ClusterSharedVolume	Get, Add, Remove, Move	Manage cluster shared volumes
ClusterSharedVolumeState	Get	View the state of cluster shared volumes
ClusterStorageSpacesDirect	Repair, Set, Disable, Enable, Get	Manage cluster storage spaces direct
ClusterStorageSpacesDi-rectDisk	Set	Configure cluster storage spaces for direct disks
ClusterVirtualMachineCon-figuration	Update	Update the configuration of a clustered virtual machine hosted on a failover cluster
ClusterVirtualMachineRole	Add, Move	Manage clustered virtual machine live migration
ClusterVMMonitoredItem	Add, Remove, Get	Manage clustered virtual machine–monitored items
ClusterVMMonitoredState	Reset	Reset the clustered virtual machine monitoring state

Network Load Balancing

Network Load Balancing (NLB) distributes traffic across multiple hosts in a balanced manner. NLB directs new traffic to cluster nodes under the least load. NLB works as a high-availability solution because it detects node failures and automatically redistributes traffic to available nodes. NLB is also scalable, which means that you can start with a two-node NLB cluster and keep adding nodes until you reach a maximum of 32 nodes. A node is a computer running the Windows Server operating system that participates in the NLB cluster. A computer can only be a member of one Windows NLB cluster.

NLB functions through the creation of a virtual IP and a virtual network adapter with an associated Media Access Control (MAC) address. Traffic to this address is distributed to the cluster nodes. In the default configuration, traffic is distributed to the least-utilized node. You can also configure NLB so that specific nodes are preferred and process more traffic than other nodes in the cluster.

NLB is a high-availability solution that is suitable for stateless applications. Imagine that you have a two-tier web application where you have four servers running IIS as the web tier and two servers running SQL Server as the database tier. In this scenario, you add Web Server 1, Web Server 2, Web Server 3, and Web Server 4 to an NLB cluster as web servers hosting stateless applications. To make the database servers highly available, you would configure a failover cluster or Always On Availability Group, but you wouldn't configure NLB because SQL Server is a stateful application.

NLB is failure-aware as long as the failure occurs on the node. For example, if you have a two-node NLB cluster that you use with a web application, and the network card fails on one of the nodes, NLB is aware of the failure and stops directing traffic to the node. If, instead of a network card failure, the web application fails, but everything else remains operational, NLB remains unaware of the failure and continues to direct requests to the node that hosts the failed web application. In a real-world environment, you'd set up more sophisticated monitoring that allows you to detect the failure of the application, not just the failure of the node. Some hardware-based NLB solutions are sophisticated enough to detect application failures rather than just host failures.

NLB is deprecated in Windows Server 2025. While NLB remains available and functional in Windows Server 2025, it will not receive further enhancements and may be removed in a future release. Existing implementations can continue to operate, but organizations should plan to transition to supported alternatives.

Network Load Balancing prerequisites

In terms of setup, NLB is straightforward and only requires you to install the feature. Although you can install the feature on a node, you must ensure that it meets some prerequisites before

CHAPTER 17

you can add it to a cluster. Before you add a host to an NLB cluster, you must ensure the following:

- All nodes in the NLB cluster must reside on the same subnet. While you can configure a subnet to span multiple geographic locations, the cluster is unlikely to converge successfully if the latency between nodes exceeds 250 milliseconds.

- All network adapters must either be configured as unicast or multicast. You can't use Windows NLB to create an NLB cluster that has a mixture of unicast and multicast addresses assigned to network adapters.

- If you choose to use the unicast cluster configuration mode, the network adapter needs to support changing its MAC address.

- The network adapter must be configured with a static IP address.

- Only TCP/IP is supported on the network adapter that is used for NLB. You cannot bind other protocols, such as IPX, Token Ring, or Banyan Vines, to the adapter.

There is no restriction on the number of network adapters in each host. You can have one host with three network adapters in a team and another host with five separate adapters participate in the same NLB cluster. You can run nodes on different editions of Windows Server, although considering that the only difference between the standard and Datacenter Edition is virtual machine licensing, you are unlikely to be running NLB on the Datacenter Edition. While it is possible to have working NLB clusters if you are running different versions of Windows Server, such as Windows Server 2012 R2, Windows Server 2016, and Windows Server 2019, you should upgrade all nodes as soon as possible to the same operating system. You should also attempt to ensure that nodes have similar hardware capacity or are running on similarly provisioned virtual machines so that a client doesn't get a radically different experience when connecting to different nodes.

NLB cluster operation modes

When configuring an NLB cluster, you can choose between one of three separate cluster-operation modes. The mode that you select depends on the configuration of the cluster nodes and the type of network switch to which the cluster nodes are connected. You can configure the cluster operation mode when creating the cluster. The operation modes are as follows:

- **Unicast Mode.** If you configure an NLB cluster to use the unicast cluster-operation mode, all nodes in the cluster will use the same unicast MAC address. Outbound traffic from node members uses a modified MAC address that is determined by the cluster host's priority settings. The drawback to using unicast mode with nodes that have a single adapter is that you can only perform management tasks from computers located on the same TCP/IP subnet as the cluster nodes. This restriction doesn't apply, however, when the cluster nodes have multiple network adapters that are not NIC team members. When you use unicast with multiple network adapters, one adapter is dedicated to cluster communication, and you can connect to any other adapters to perform management tasks. You can improve cluster operation by placing the adapters that you use for cluster communication and the adapters that you use for management tasks on separate VLANs.

- **Multicast Mode.**   This mode is suitable when each node only has one network adapter. When you configure multicast mode, each cluster host keeps its original network adapter's MAC address, but it is also assigned a multicast MAC address. All nodes in the cluster use the same multicast MAC address. You can only use multicast mode if your organization's switches and routers support it. Unless you've got bargain-basement network equipment, your current network hardware likely supports multicast mode for NLB.

- **IGMP Multicast.**   Internet Group Management Protocol (IGMP) multicast mode is an advanced form of multicast mode that reduces the chances of the network switch being flooded with traffic. It works by only forwarding traffic through the ports that are connected to hosts that participate in the NLB cluster, but it also requires a switch that supports this functionality.

Managing cluster hosts

You manage NLB clusters through the Network Load Balancing Manager console. The NLB console is available as part of the RSAT tools, meaning that you can manage one or more NLB clusters from a computer that is not a member of the cluster. You do, however, need to manage clusters by using an account that is a member of the local Administrators group on each cluster node. You can use this console to create and manage clusters and cluster nodes.

After the cluster is set up and functioning, most maintenance operations, such as applying software updates, are performed on cluster nodes. When performing maintenance tasks, you should perform the task on one node at a time so that the application the cluster provides to users continues to remain available. Prior to performing maintenance tasks on a node, you should first stop incoming connections and allow existing connections to complete naturally. When there are no connections to the node, you can then stop the node, apply the updates, and restart the node. You have the following options for managing cluster nodes:

- **Drainstop.**   Blocks new connections to the cluster node, but doesn't terminate existing connections. Use this prior to planned maintenance to evacuate the cluster of connections gracefully.

- **Stop.**   Stops the cluster node. All connections to the cluster node from clients are stopped. Use Stop after you use Drainstop so that you can then perform maintenance tasks, such as applying updates.

- **Start.**   Starts a cluster node that is in a stopped state.

CHAPTER 17

- **Suspend.** Pauses the cluster node until you issue the Resume command. Using Suspend does not shut down the cluster service, but it does terminate current connections as well as block new connections.

- **Resume.** Resumes a suspended cluster node.

Port rules

An NLB port rule allows you to configure how the NLB cluster responds to incoming traffic on a specific port and protocol, such as TCP port 80 (HTTP) or UDP port 69 (Trivial FTP). Each host in an NLB cluster must use the same port rules. While it is possible to configure port rules on a per-node basis, it's safer to configure them at the cluster level to ensure that they are consistent. The default port rule redirects traffic on any TCP or UDP port to each node in the cluster in a balanced way. If you want to create specific rules, delete the default rule.

Filtering and affinity

When you create a port rule, you also choose a filtering mode, which might require you to configure affinity. Filtering allows you to determine whether incoming traffic is handled by one, some, or all nodes in the NLB cluster. If you choose to allow multiple nodes to accept incoming traffic, you need to configure affinity. The affinity setting determines whether one node handles all subsequent requests from the same client or if subsequent requests from the same client are redistributed across other nodes. Affinity is often important with web applications, where a consistent session must exist between the client and one web server after the session is established. You can configure the following filtering modes:

- **Multiple Host.** This is the default filtering mode. This mode allows traffic to be directed to any node in the NLB cluster. You also need to specify one of the following affinity settings:

  - **Single.** When you configure this option, the incoming request is distributed to one of the cluster nodes. All subsequent traffic from the originating host is directed to that same node for the duration of the session. This is the default multiple host affinity. Don't confuse Multiple Host, Single Affinity with Single Host filtering.

  - **None.** Incoming traffic is distributed to the cluster node under the least load, even if there is an existing session. This means that multiple nodes may handle traffic from a single session.

  - **Network.** This option directs clients to cluster nodes based on the requesting client's network address.

- **Single Host.** A single node handles all traffic sent to the cluster on this port rule. In this case, no load balancing occurs. For example, if you have a four-node cluster, but you want node three to be the only one that handles traffic on TCP port 25, you would configure a port rule with the filtering mode set to Single Host.

- **Disable The Port Range.** When you configure this setting, the NLB cluster drops traffic sent to the cluster that matches the port rule.

Managing NLB with PowerShell

You can use the Windows PowerShell cmdlets listed in Table 17-4 to manage NLB clusters on Windows Server.

Table 17-4   NLB PowerShell cmdlets.

Noun	Verbs	Function
NlbClusterNode	Add, Get, Remove, Resume, Set, Start, Stop, Suspend	Configure and manage a cluster node.
NlbClusterNodeDip	Add, Get, Remove, Set	Configure the cluster node's dedicated management IP address.
NlbClusterPortRule	Add, Disable, Enable, Get, Remove, Set	Create and manage port rules.
NlbClusterVip	Add, Get, Remove, Set	Configure the cluster's virtual IP address.
NlbCluster	Get, New, Remove, Resume, Set, Start, Stop, Suspend	Configure and manage the cluster.
NlbClusterDriverInfo	Get	Provides information about the cluster driver.
NlbClusterNodeNetworkInterface	Get	Provides information about the node's network interface driver.
NlbClusterIpv6Address	New	Configure the cluster's IPv6 address.
NlbClusterPortRuleNodeHandling-Priority	Set	Manage priority on a per-port rule basis.
NlbClusterPortRuleNodeWeight	Set	Configure the node weight on a per-port rule basis.

CHAPTER 17

Active Directory Certificate Services

Active Directory Certificate Services is the infrastructure service that most administrators don't pay much attention to until they need to perform a task, such as generating certificates for an internal application or supporting a specific type of server deployment.

You can install Certificate Services on both Server Core and Server with a GUI system, with Server Core being the more secure option because of its reduced attack surface. Because Certificate Services is an important security role, you should consider deploying it on a computer separate from other roles. You should also limit access to the server hosting Certificate Services so that only those directly responsible for performing administration tasks have access.

CA types

Windows Server Certificate Authorities (CAs) come in four basic types: Enterprise root, Enterprise subordinate, standalone root, and standalone subordinate. The type that you deploy depends on your certificate needs. Unless you're performing a new deployment, the type of deployment also likely depends on the particular CA hierarchy that you want to use.

Before you can understand what type of CA you need to deploy, you need to understand how CA hierarchies work. The CA at the top of a hierarchy is known as the Root CA. A Root CA can have any number of subordinate CAs. Subordinate CAs can, in turn, function as the parent CAs of child CAs, which are also called subordinate CAs.

Each CA has a special certificate known as the CA certificate. The Root CA signs its own certificate. A subordinate CA has its CA certificate signed by a parent CA. For example:

- A Root CA named APEX_CA signs its own CA certificate.

- APEX_CA signs the CA certificate of a subordinate CA named CHILD_CA.

- CHILD_CA signs the CA certificate of a subordinate CA named GRANDCHILD_CA.

The way that certificate trust works is that if a client trusts the Root CA's CA certificate, it trusts all certificates issued by CAs that are directly or indirectly subordinate to that CA. For example, if a client trusts the ROOT_CA CA certificate, it automatically trusts the certificates issued by GRANDCHILD_CA.

You can use the PKIview console (pkiview.msc) to view your current organization's Certificate Services configuration. Figure 18-1 shows an enterprise PKI that has a root CA and a subordinate CA.

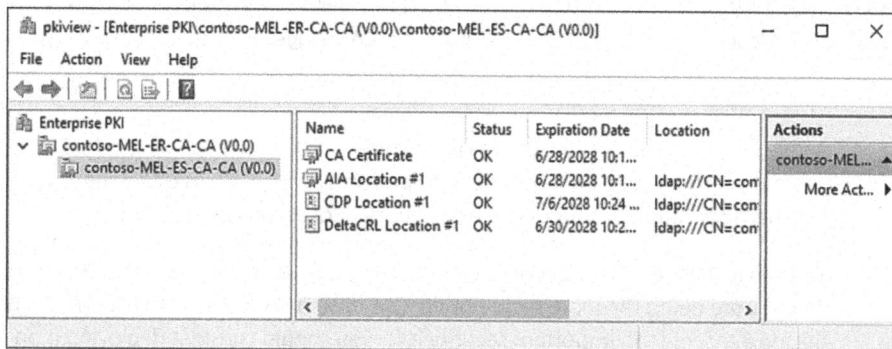

Figure 18-1   PKIview

Another concept that is important to understand in the context of CA hierarchies is certificate revocation. A parent CA can revoke a child CA's CA certificate. When this happens, all certificates issued by the child CA are also invalidated. For example, if the administrator of APEX_CA from the earlier example revoked the CA certificate of CHILD_CA, all the certificates issued by CHILD_CA would no longer function. This would include the CA certificate of GRANDCHILD_CA, which, in turn, would invalidate all the certificates issued by GRANDCHILD_CA. Needless to say, you only revoke the CA certificate of a subordinate CA in dire circumstances, such as when the child CA has been compromised by malware or hackers. If a child CA has been compromised, it might have issued certificates that you don't know about, and the most secure response is to revoke all certificates issued by the CA and to start over from scratch.

Some other things to keep in mind before we delve more into the types of CAs that you can configure with Windows Server are as follows:

- You can't convert a root CA to a subordinate CA.

- You can't convert a subordinate CA to function as a root CA; however, a subordinate CA can function as the parent CA of another subordinate CA.

- A subordinate CA's CA certificate cannot have a lifetime that extends beyond the current lifetime of the parent CA's certificate.

Inside OUT

Remember to renew CA certificates

Remember, a CA's server certificate needs to be renewed. A CA can't issue certificates that have a lifespan beyond that of its CA certificate. If a CA's certificate has expired, so have all the certificates issued by the CA.

Enterprise CA

An Enterprise CA is fully integrated with Active Directory. This has the following benefits:

- The Enterprise CA is automatically trusted by any computer that is a member of the same Active Directory forest.

- All certificates published by the CA are automatically trusted by members of the same forest.

- Certificate requests can be performed automatically and don't require the use of a request file.

- Certificate requests can be approved automatically, and certificates are automatically distributed and installed on domain clients.

- Certificate revocation information is published to Active Directory.

- Enterprise CAs can use certificate templates.

- Enterprise CAs can issue certificates to devices that have domain membership, and also can issue certificates to devices that are not members of an Active Directory domain.

- An Enterprise subordinate CA can have a standalone CA as a parent CA.

- A standalone subordinate CA can have an Enterprise CA as a parent CA.

One of the primary drawbacks of an Enterprise CA is that it always needs to be online. If an Enterprise CA goes offline, certificate services in the domain don't function properly. Temporary shutdowns due to maintenance are fine, but shutting down or having an enterprise CA offline for a couple of weeks is likely to lead to headaches. Enterprise CAs must also always be installed on computers that are members of an Active Directory domain.

Enterprise Root

An Enterprise Root CA is an enterprise CA that signs its own signing certificate. As mentioned earlier, an Enterprise Root CA can only be installed on a computer that is a domain member, and that computer should always be online. Because the Enterprise Root CA publishes certificate

CHAPTER 18

information to all domains in a forest, you need to configure it using an account that is a member of the Enterprise Admins group.

Inside OUT
Single CA deployments

Many smaller organizations, such as those with less than 300 users, have a single Enterprise Root CA as their only CA. While it's not the most secure way you can do things, a single Enterprise Root CA is a pragmatic solution for organizations that have basic certificate service requirements. The best practice is to use an Offline Root CA, which is discussed later in this chapter.

After you've installed the binary files for a CA, you are then able to configure it. You do this by running the AD CS Configuration Wizard. You can run this wizard using the signed-in user's credentials or by using separate credentials, which you specify on the Credentials page of the wizard shown in Figure 18-2. In the next few pages, we'll go through the process of installing an Enterprise Root CA. The process of installing an Enterprise Root CA is similar to the process of installing other CA types.

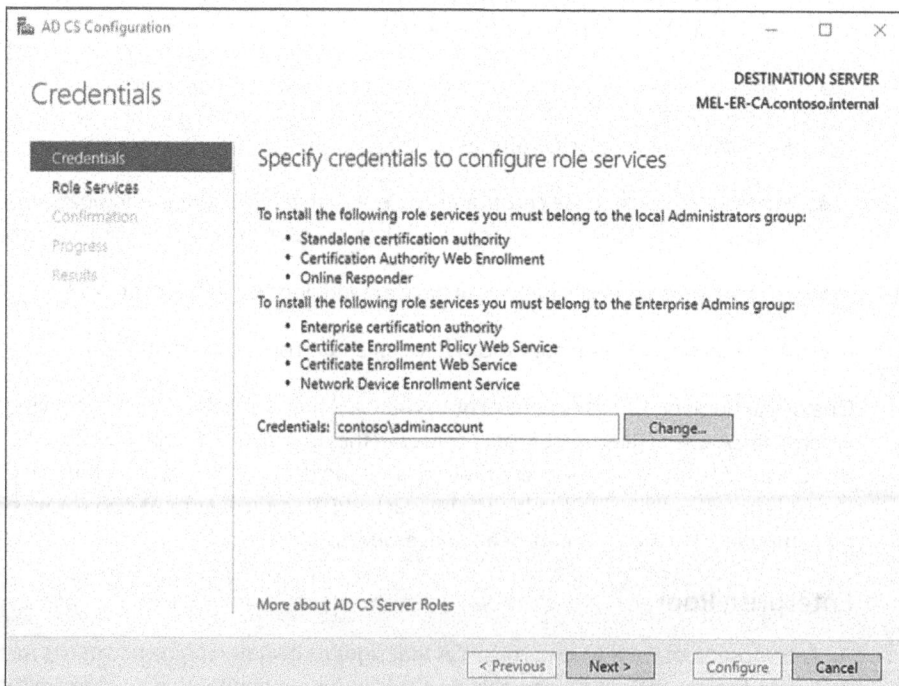

Figure 18-2   Configuration credentials

The next step in the wizard involves specifying which roles to configure. While it is possible to configure multiple roles at once, it's usually better to get the Certification Authority role functioning properly before adding and configuring additional role services, such as Certification Authority Web Enrollment. The other role services are discussed later in this chapter. Figure 18-3 shows the Certification Authority role selected.

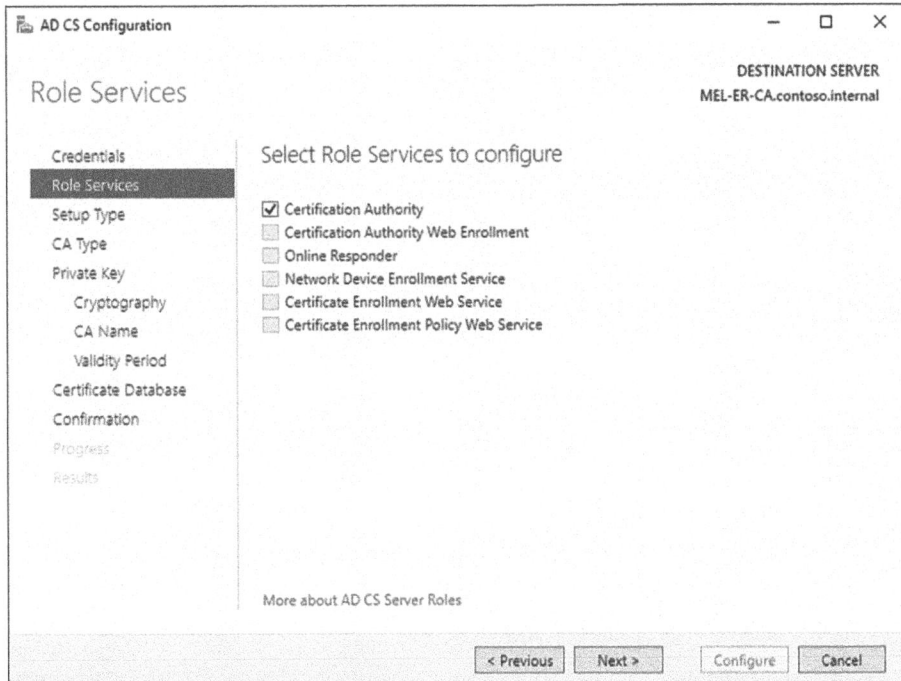

Figure 18-3   Certification Authority role

If the computer is a member of an AD DS domain, you get the option to install an Enterprise CA or a Standalone CA, as shown in Figure 18-4. If the computer is not a member of an AD DS domain, you can't select the Enterprise CA option. If you're sure that the computer is a member of the domain, but you can't select the Enterprise CA option, make sure that you are using an account that has Enterprise Admin privileges.

After you've chosen between Enterprise and Standalone CA, you need to choose between Root and Subordinate CA, as shown in Figure 18-5. Microsoft doesn't recommend having multiple enterprise root CAs in a forest , although it is possible to do so. Unless you're deploying a single CA, the recommendation is to have no enterprise root CAs and to use a combination of an offline standalone root CA and enterprise subordinate CAs because this provides the most secure deployment type.

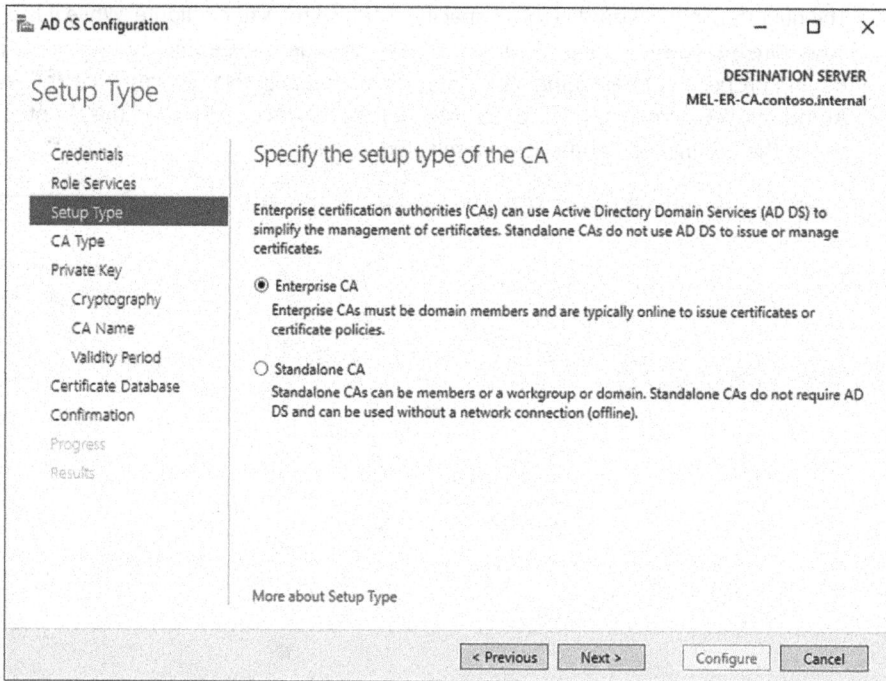

Figure 18-4   Enterprise CA

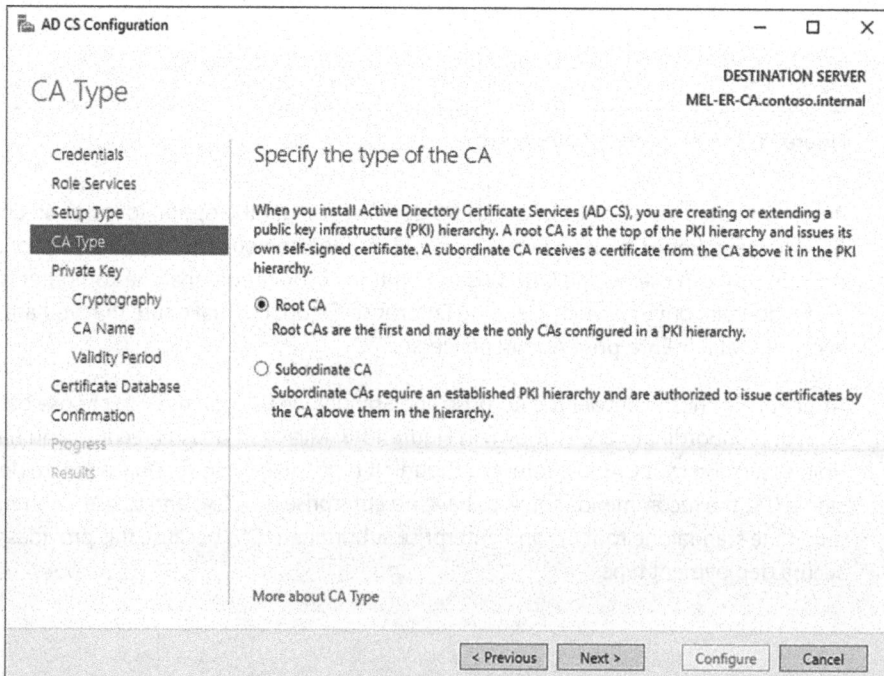

Figure 18-5   CA Type

On the Private Key page, shown in Figure 18-6, specify whether you want to create a new private key or use an existing private key. If you're deploying a new CA, create a new private key. If you're replacing a failed CA or migrating from an earlier version of Windows Server to a new Windows Server CA, use an existing private key. The trick with CA migration is to ensure that the destination server has the same name as the source server.

> ## More Info
>
> ### CA migration
>
> You can find out more about CA migration at *https://learn.microsoft.com/en-us/ troubleshoot/windows-server/certificates-and-public-key-infrastructure-pki/ move-certification-authority-to-another-server.*

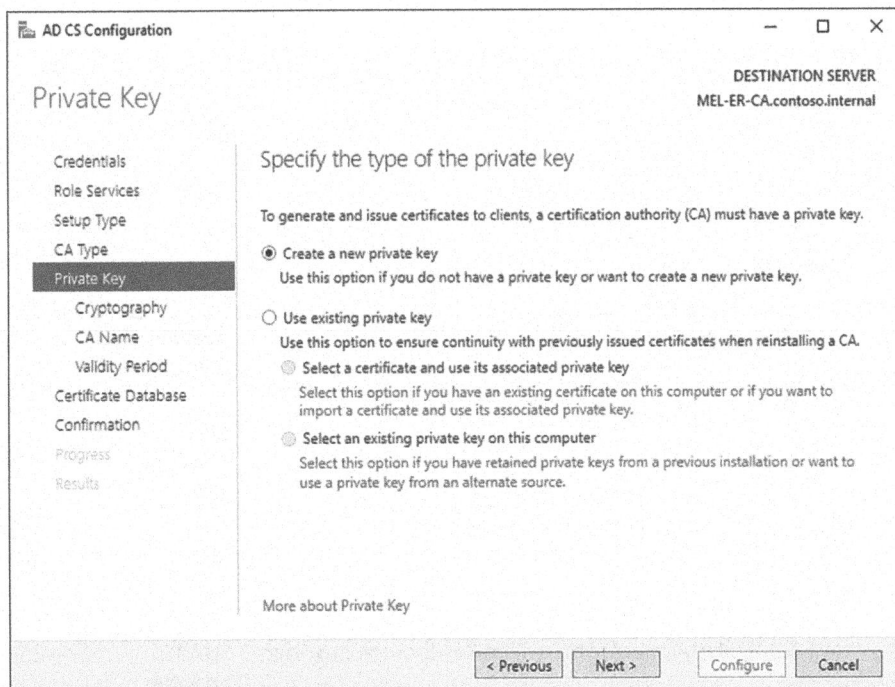

Figure 18-6   The Private Key page

If you choose to create a new private key, you need to specify the cryptographic options for that key. In most circumstances, the default options, shown in Figure 18-7, are fine. In some cases, however, you might want to configure stronger cryptographic options. The important thing to remember is that the more advanced and stronger the cryptography you use, the more you limit yourself as to which clients can interact with the key. Table 18-1 provides a list of available cryptographic options.

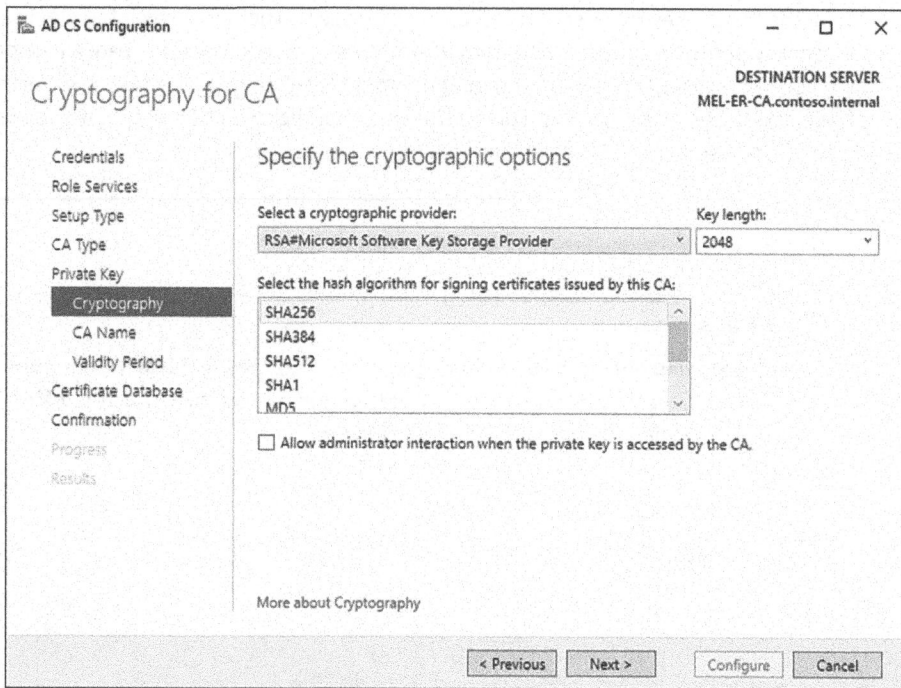

Figure 18-7 Cryptography For CA

Table 18-1 CA Private Key cryptography options

Cryptographic providers	Available hash algorithms	Available key lengths
Microsoft Base Smart Card Crypto Provider	SHA1 MD2 MD4 MD5	1,024 2,048 4,096
Microsoft Enhanced Cryptographic Provider v1.0	SHA1 MD2 MD4 MD5	512 1,024 2,048 4,096
ECDSA_P256#Microsoft Smart Card Key Storage Provider	SHA256 SHA384 SHA512 SHA1	256
ECDSA_P521#Microsoft Smart Card Key Storage Provider	SHA256 SHA384 SHA512 SHA1	521

Cryptographic providers	Available hash algorithms	Available key lengths
RSA#Microsoft Software Key Storage Provider (Default)	SHA256 SHA384 SHA512 SHA1 MD5 MD4 MD2	512 1,024 2,048 4,096
Microsoft Base Cryptographic Provider v1.0	SHA1 MD2 MD4 MD5	512 1,024 2,048 4,096
ECDSA_P521#Microsoft Software Key Storage Provider	SHA256 SHA384 SHA512 SHA1	521
ECDSA_P256#Microsoft Software Key Storage Provider	SHA256 SHA384 SHA512 SHA1	256
Microsoft Strong Cryptographic Provider	SHA1 MD2 MD4 MD5	512 1,024 2,048 4,096
ECDSA_P384#Microsoft Software Key Storage Provider	SHA256 SHA384 SHA512 SHA1	384
Microsoft Base DSS Cryptographic Provider	SHA1	512 1,024
RSA#Microsoft Smart Card Key Storage Provider	SHA256 SHA384 SHA512 SHA1 MD5 MD4 MD2	1,024 2,048 4,096
DSA#Microsoft Software Key Storage Provider	SHA1	512 1,024 2,048
ECDSA_P384#Microsoft Smart Card Key Storage Provider	SHA256 SHA384 SHA512 SHA1	384

CHAPTER 18

The CA name window, shown in Figure 18-8, is automatically populated based on the computer's identity information. This name is important because it's present on each certificate issued by the CA. The distinguished name suffix is automatically generated. Unless you're issuing certificates to outside third parties, the default names provided here are likely to suffice.

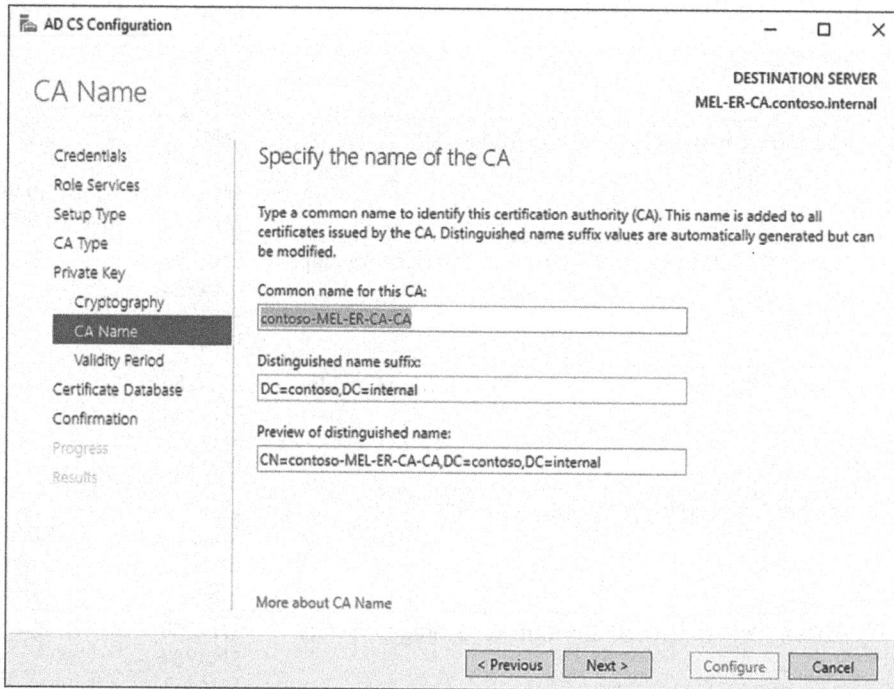

Figure 18-8   CA Name

On the Validity Period page, shown in Figure 18-9, specify the validity of the CA's certificate. When configuring this for a root CA, remember that no certificate issued by the CA or a subordinate CA can have a lifetime that exceeds the value of the CA's certificate. This is an important consideration when it comes to subordinate CAs. For example, let's say you're installing a subordinate CA, and you request a five-year CA certificate from a root CA. If the root CA issuing the subordinate CA certificate only has four years of validity left on its CA certificate, the expiration date of the subordinate CA certificate is four years, not five years.

The final configuration step for an Enterprise Root CA is the location of the certificate database and the database log, as shown in Figure 18-10. These locations are important primarily from the perspective of backing up and recovering the database. If you enable key archiving, which is covered later in this chapter, the private keys of certificates issued by the CA are also written to this database in encrypted form.

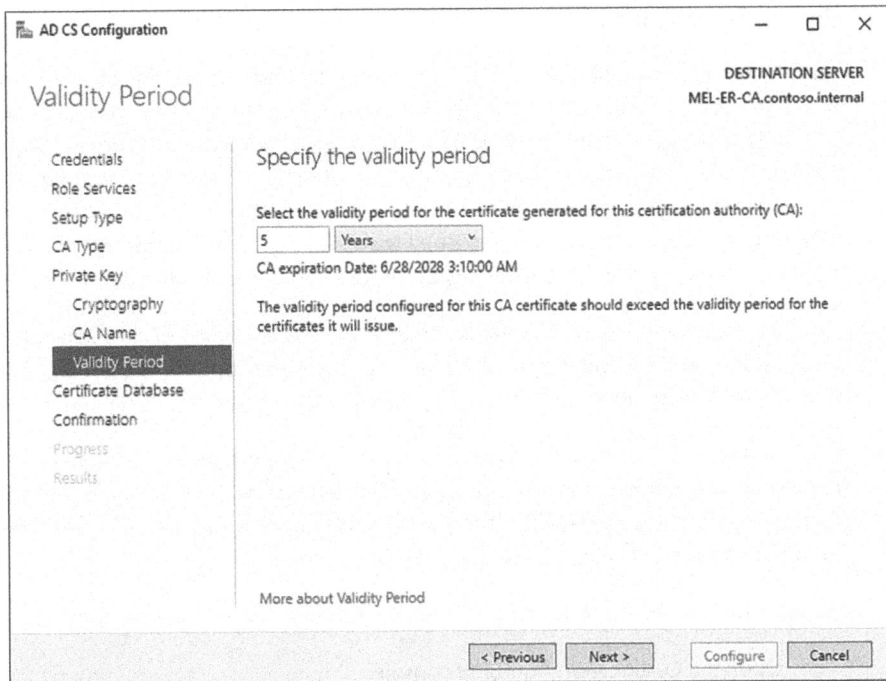

Figure 18-9   Validity Period

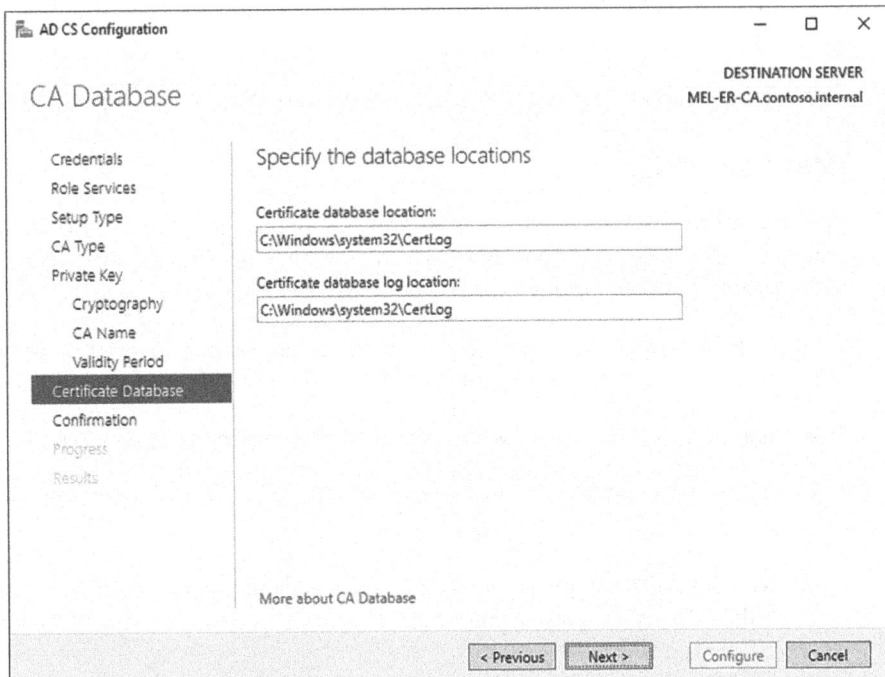

Figure 18-10   CA Database

Enterprise subordinate

An enterprise subordinate CA is a CA that is integrated into Active Directory but has another CA as the apex of the certificate trust chain. Similar to enterprise root CAs, enterprise subordinate CAs must remain online and must be members of an Active Directory domain. Domain membership means that computers that are members of the same forest as the enterprise subordinate automatically trust certificates issued by the CA. As is the case with enterprise root CAs, certificate revocation data is also published to Active Directory. Enterprise subordinate CAs can use certificate templates independently of where their CA certificate comes from.

You can acquire a signing certificate for an enterprise subordinate CA from an enterprise CA or from a standalone CA. Microsoft recommends using enterprise subordinate CAs with an offline root CA. You'll learn about offline root CAs later in this chapter.

If you're using a standalone CA, the installation wizard automatically generates a certificate request file and places it in the root directory on volume C when the wizard completes. You can then submit this file to the CA to generate the subordinate CA's certificate. Until you install the subordinate CA certificate, the CA is not operational.

To install the CA certificate issued by the parent CA, perform the following steps:

1. Open the Certification Authority console.

2. Select the CA. In the Action menu, click All Tasks and then click Install CA Certificate.

3. In the Install CA Certificate dialog, locate and open the certificate issued by the parent CA.

4. Ensure the CA is selected. In the Action menu, click All Tasks and then click Start Service.

Standalone CAs

Standalone CAs differ from enterprise CAs primarily in that enterprise CAs are highly integrated into Active Directory, and standalone CAs are not. Additional differences between standalone CAs and enterprise CAs include

- An enterprise CA must be installed on a domain member. You can install a standalone CA on a computer that isn't domain-joined or on a computer that is domain-joined.

- Standalone CA certificates are not automatically published to Active Directory.

- You can't use certificate templates with standalone CAs. The properties of the certificate are dependent on the certificate request.

- Standalone CAs cannot authenticate or use the identity of Active Directory users as part of the certificate request process, even when installed on computers that are members of the domain.

- By default, all certificate requests to a standalone CA must be approved before a certificate is issued. With an enterprise CA, you can configure whether a certificate is automatically approved by configuring template properties.

While you can use standalone CAs to issue certificates to domain clients, they aren't directly integrated into Active Directory in the way that an enterprise CA is. This means that domain members don't automatically trust certificates issued by a standalone CA and aren't automatically able to determine certificate revocation information by performing a query against Active Directory.

While you can deploy a standalone CA on a computer that's a domain member, standalone CAs are almost always deployed on computers that are not members of an Active Directory domain. Benefits of standalone CAs include

- Because the CA is not a member of the domain, it can be deployed on a perimeter network or in Azure.

- The CA can be shut down for extended periods.

- Members of Active Directory security groups, such as members of the Domain Admins group, don't have access to the CA if it's deployed on a computer that does not have domain membership.

You can configure a client to trust a CA by importing the CA's certificate into the client's Trusted Root Certification Authority store. To do this, perform the following steps:

1. Open the Certificates Snap-In of the Microsoft Management Console and set the snap-in to use the Computer Account, as shown in Figure 18-11.

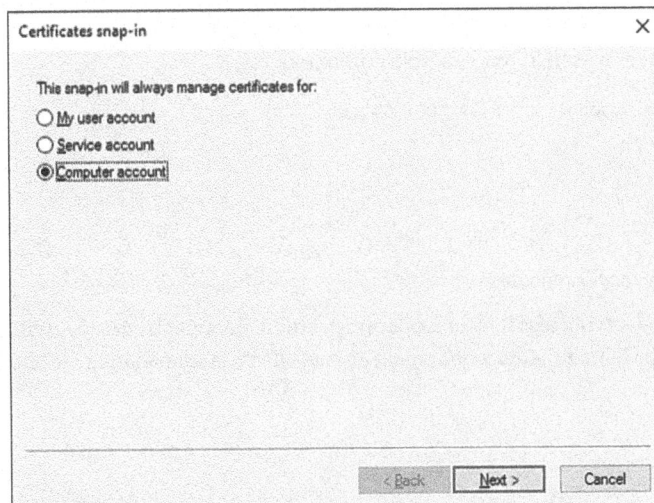

Figure 18-11   Selecting the Computer Account snap-in

2. Select the Certificates node under the Trusted Root Certification Authorities node, as shown in Figure 18-12. On the Action menu, click All Tasks and then click Import.

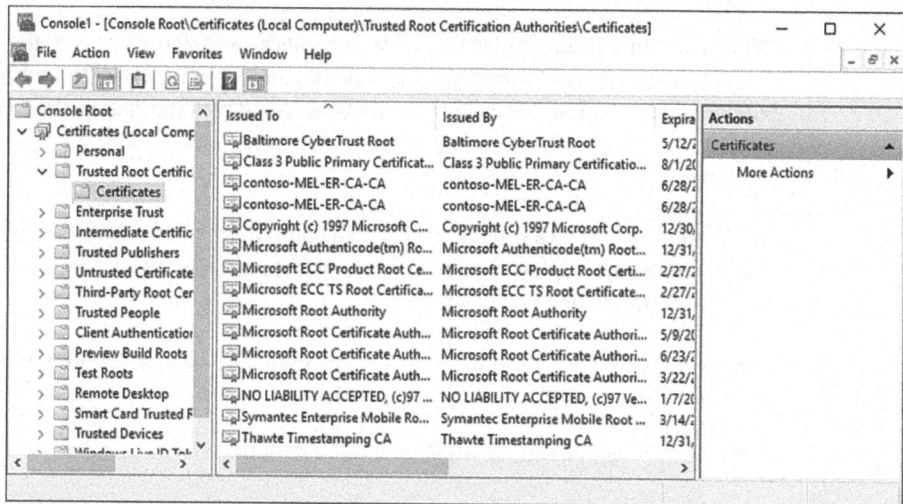

Figure 18-12 Trusted Root CAs

3. After you import the CA certificate, the client computer trusts all certificates issued by that CA. It also trusts all certificates issued by CAs that are subordinate to that CA in the trust chain.

If you want to have all clients in a domain trust the certificates issued by a standalone root CA, you can use the `certutil.exe` command to publish the root CA's certificate to Active Directory. To do this, you need to run the `certutil.exe` command. Do this using an account that has Domain Admin privileges and substitute the root CA certificate filename for the filename `SA_ROOT_CA.crt` used in this example command:

```
Certutil.exe -dspublish -f SA_ROOT-CA.crt
```

Inside OUT

Deploy root certificates

You can use Microsoft Intune or Configuration Manager to deploy root certificates to domain-joined clients, nondomain–joined clients, and managed mobile devices.

Standalone root

Standalone root CAs sign their own certificates, but they aren't directly integrated into AD DS. A standalone root CA can be offline, but this causes problems if an online certificate revocation list distribution point is not present. Standalone root CAs often have the Certification Authority Web Enrollment service installed as a method of allowing people to submit certificate requests to the CA. After a request is submitted to the CA, you can approve or deny the request using the Certification Authority console. If the request is in the form of a `.req` file, you can use the `certreq.exe` utility to manage the request. You'll learn more about managing certificate requests later in this chapter.

Standalone subordinate

A standalone subordinate CA can be the child CA of an Enterprise CA or a standalone CA. Standalone subordinates are often deployed on perimeter networks when it is necessary to issue certificates to people outside the organization. Don't use an Enterprise CA in this scenario because enterprise CAs can only be installed on domain–joined computers, and you should avoid deploying domain–joined computers on perimeter networks. As is the case with standalone root CAs, standalone subordinate CAs often have the Certification Authority Web Enrollment service installed as a method of allowing people to submit certificate requests to the CA and as a method of retrieving certificates after they are issued.

Offline root

An offline root CA is a CA that is secured by being turned off and is only brought online when specific tasks occur, such as revoking an existing signing certificate, issuing a new signing certificate, or publishing a new certificate revocation list (CRL). Because the CA is offline, it is much less likely to be compromised.

The trick with deploying an offline root CA is that you need to configure the Certificate Revocation List and Authority Information Access distribution points so they are hosted on a computer that remains online when the offline root CA is offline. You also need to export the CA certificate and place it in a location accessible to clients performing revocation checks. You should renew the CA certificate for the offline root CA after updating the CRL and Authority Information Access (AIA) information because it is included with the offline root CA certificate. You'll learn more about configuring CRLs and AIA distribution points later in this chapter.

> ## More Info
> *Offline root CAs*
> You can find out more about offline root CAs at *https://learn.microsoft.com/en-us/archive/technet-wiki/2900.offline-root-certification-authority-ca*.

CHAPTER 18

Certificate revocation lists

A certificate revocation list (CRL) is a list of certificates a CA has issued that are no longer considered valid. A delta CRL is a list of all certificates that have been revoked since the publication of the last CRL. By default, a CA publishes a new CRL every week, and a delta CRL is published every day. Both the CRL and the delta-CRL are stored on a CRL distribution point, also known as a CDP.

CRL distribution points

A CA can have multiple CDPs. CRL and CDP information is included with a certificate when the certificate is issued. Clients perform a check of certificate validity each time they encounter a new certificate and perform additional checks based on the CRL and delta-CRL publication intervals. Clients also check CDP locations in the order that they are configured on the CA.

You configure the CRL distribution point on the Extensions tab of the CA's properties, as shown in Figure 18-13. If you are publishing certificates that need to be used by people outside your organization, ensure that you have a CRL hosted in a publicly available location, such as on a web server on your perimeter network or in Microsoft Azure. Remember that any changes you make to CDP settings are only applied to certificates issued after the changes are made. If you make a change and then remove existing CDPs, clients encountering existing certificates can't perform revocation checks, and the certificates are deemed invalid.

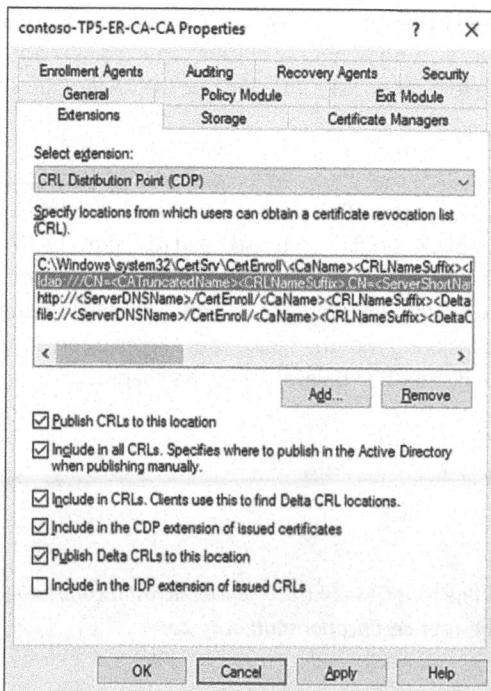

Figure 18-13   CRL DPs

Authority Information Access

The Authority Information Access (AIA) point settings specify where a client can retrieve the CA certificate of the CA that issued the certificate that the client has encountered. As with the CRL DP information, changes to the AIA information are only present in certificates issued subsequent to the change. This means that you need to keep existing AIA points in place until the currently issued certificates either expire or are renewed. You configure AIA extensions on the Extensions tab of the CA properties, as shown in Figure 18-14. The AIA extensions are visible when you set the Select Extension dropdown to Authority Information Access.

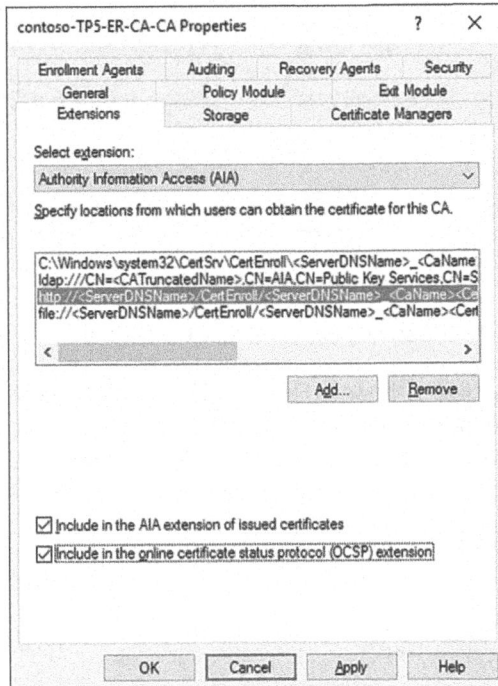

Figure 18-14   Selecting the Authority Information Access extension

Revoking a certificate

Revoking a certificate makes it invalid, and doing so also involves several steps. The first step is to revoke the certificate itself, something you do from the CA Management console. The second step is to update the CRL or delta CRL and then publish the updates to the appropriate location. Revoking a certificate requires that you know the identity of the certificate you are revoking.

To revoke a certificate, perform the following steps:

1. Locate the certificate in the list of issued certificates on the CA from which you issued the certificate. Certificate serial numbers are in hexadecimal but are listed sequentially in the console. Figure 18-15 shows a list of issued certificates.

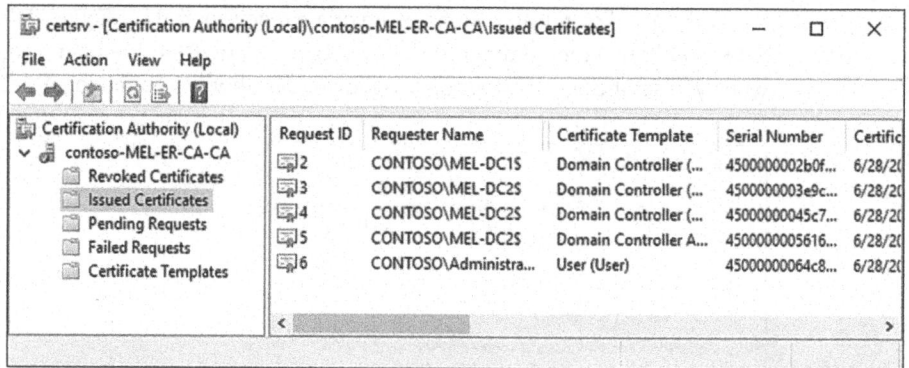

Figure 18-15   Issued certificates

2. On the Action menu, click All Tasks and then click Revoke Certificate.

3. In the Certificate Revocation dialog, shown in Figure 18-16, select the Reason Code for the certificate revocation when you want the certificate revocation to take place, with the default being immediately, and click Yes. You are asked to confirm the revocation. The revoked certificate is then listed in the Revoked Certificates node in the Certification Authority console.

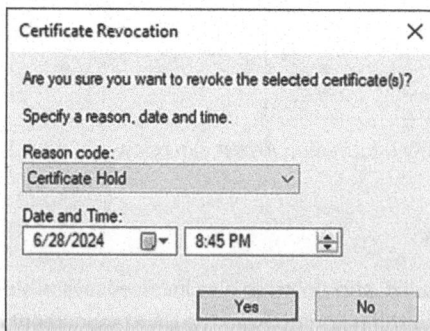

Figure 18-16   The Certificate Revocation dialog

When you revoke a certificate, you need to specify a Reason Code. The following Reason Codes are available:

- Unspecified

- Key Compromise

- CA Compromise

- Change Of Affiliation

- Superseded

- Cease Of Operation

- Certificate Hold

The Reason Code you specify is important if your organization is required to document why a specific certificate has been revoked. All Reason Codes except Certificate Hold are irreversible. If you choose the Certificate Hold reason, you can undo the certificate revocation at a later point in time. Depending on the reason for performing the revocation and its severity, such as finding a subordinate CA compromised by remote access Trojan malware, you might want to publish a CRL or delta CRL.

Publishing CRLs and delta CRLs

CRLs and delta CRLs are published automatically by CA. A new CRL is published by default once a week, and a new delta CRL is published once a day. You can configure the publication schedule using the Revoked Certificates Properties dialog, shown in Figure 18-17. To access the dialog, click the Revoked Certificates node of the Certification Authority console and then select Properties from the Action menu.

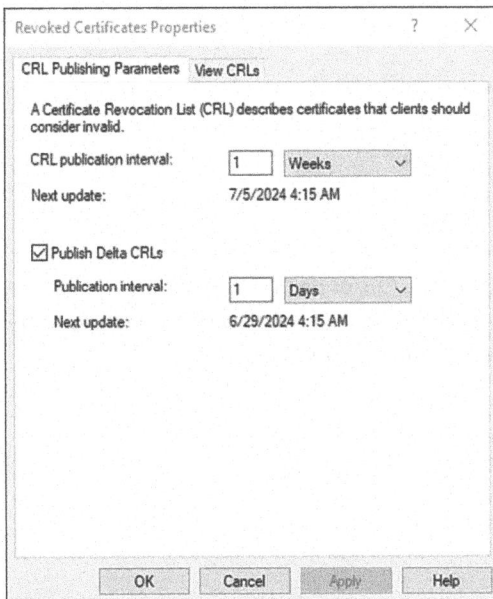

Figure 18-17   CRL Publishing Parameters

For most organizations, the default schedule is fine. If an organization issues certificates where revocation needs to propagate quickly, a shorter delta CRL publication interval would be more appropriate. This is because clients who have already accepted the certificate as valid have also learned about the CRL and delta CRL publication frequency. If you revoke a certificate, and you have a delta CRL publication frequency of once a week and a CRL publication frequency of once a month, it could take up to a week before all clients encountering that certificate recognize it as invalid.

You can view the last time a CRL was published on the View CRLs tab of the Revoked Certificates Properties dialog, shown in Figure 18-18.

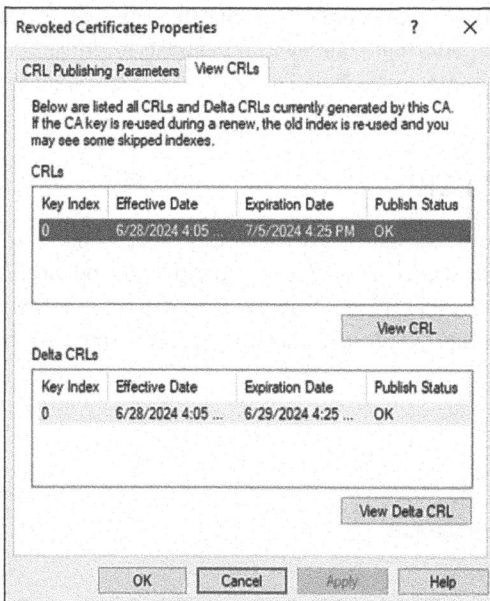

Figure 18-18   The View CRLs tab

You can manually trigger the publication of a CRL or delta CRL by right-clicking the Revoked Certificates node, clicking All Tasks, and then clicking Publish. Select whether you want to publish a New CRL or a Delta CRL Only, as shown in Figure 18-19.

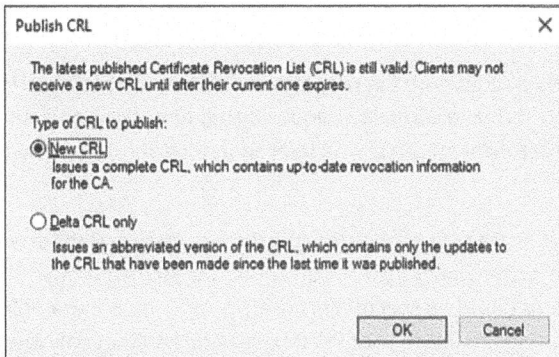

The following describes the Publish CRL dialog box shown in Figure 18-19.

Publish CRL

The latest published Certificate Revocation List (CRL) is still valid. Clients may not receive a new CRL until after their current one expires.

Type of CRL to publish:

- **New CRL**
  Issues a complete CRL, which contains up-to-date revocation information for the CA.

- **Delta CRL only**
  Issues an abbreviated version of the CRL, which contains only the updates to the CRL that have been made since the last time it was published.

Figure 18-19   Publish CRL

Certificate Services role services

The primary function of AD CS is the CA. In addition to the CA role, several ancillary roles can be used for certificate requests, enrollment, and to handle revocation traffic. These roles are as follows:

- **Certificate Enrollment Policy Web Service**   Allows computers that are not members of the domain to obtain certificate enrollment policy information.

- **Certificate Enrollment Web Service**   Enables users in the same forest as the CA to interact with the CA through a web browser to request certificates, renew certificates, and retrieve CRLs.

- **Certification Authority Web Enrollment**   This role service allows people to navigate to a webpage and perform a certificate request. This can be done either by filling out a web form with all the necessary details or by pasting the contents of a certificate request file into the form. When the certificate is issued, people can revisit this webpage to retrieve their issued certificate.

- **Network Device Enrollment Service**   The Network Device Enrollment Service is a special service that you can configure to allow network devices like routers, switches, firewalls, and hardware-based VPN gateways to obtain certificates from the CA.

- **Online Responder**   Online responders function in the same manner as CRL distribution points in that they provide a location where a client consuming a certificate can check whether a certificate is valid. The benefit of an online responder over a traditional CRL distribution point is that, instead of downloading the entire revocation list, the client queries the online responder with a specific certificate ID.

Certificate templates

Certificate Templates allow you to configure the properties of different types of certificates. While it is possible to manually format a certificate request using templates, an enterprise CA can automatically populate a certificate request with relevant information stored in Active Directory.

By default, Certificate Authorities are only configured to issue a subset of all the preconfigured certificate templates stored in Active Directory. You can configure each enterprise CA in your environment to issue certificates based on specific certificate templates. For example, as a security precaution, you might want to configure your PKI infrastructure so that only one CA can issue Data Recovery Agent certificates.

Deleting a template from the list of templates that can be issued in the Certification Authority console does not delete the certificate template from Active Directory. You can't remove any of the default certificate templates included with Windows Server from Active Directory using either the Certification Authority console or the Certificate Templates console. You can, however, remove custom certificate templates from Active Directory. Removing a certificate template just means that no new certificates can be issued from that template. It doesn't revoke certificates issued from the template that are already in circulation.

To configure a CA to issue a specific certificate template, perform the following steps:

1. Select the Certificate Templates node under the CA in the Certification Authority console, as shown in Figure 18-20. This shows you which certificate templates the CA is already configured to issue.

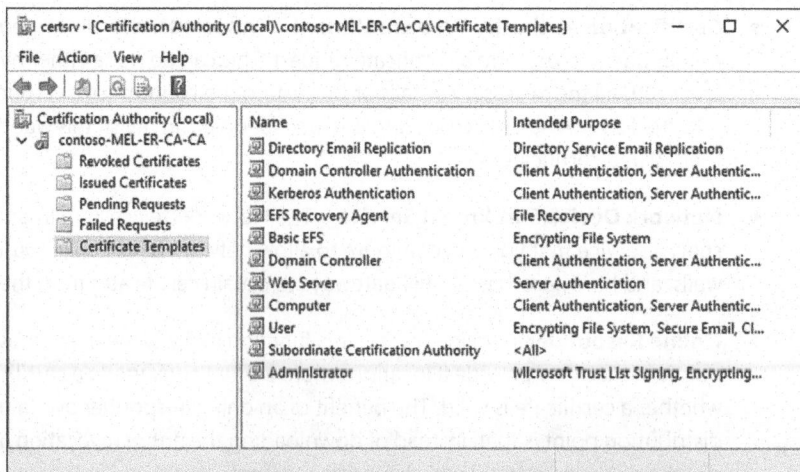

Figure 18-20   Certificate Templates in the Certification Authority console

2. If you want to have the CA issue certificates from a template not listed, you need to add the template. To do this, select the Certificate Templates node and click New from the Action menu. Next, click Certificate Template To Issue. This brings up the Enable Certificate Templates dialog, shown in Figure 18-21. Select the certificate template that you want to issue and then click OK.

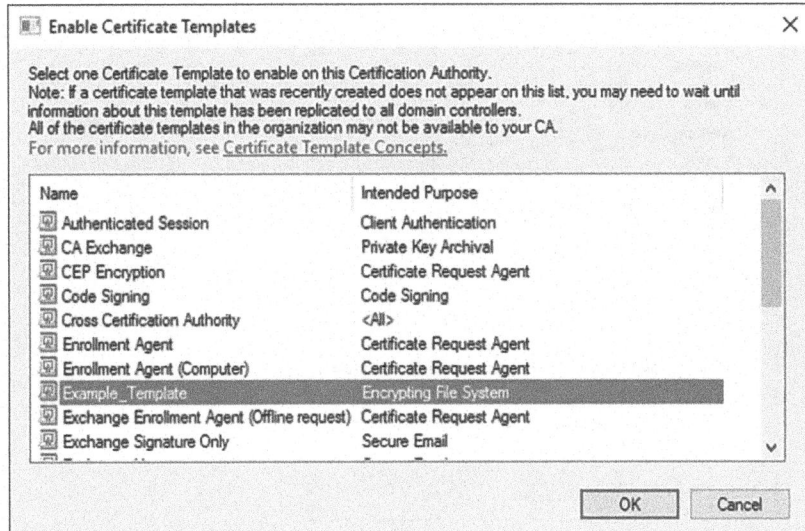

Figure 18-21   Enable Certificate Templates

Template properties

You manage certificate templates from the Certificate Templates console. Each certificate template has properties that you configure to determine how certificates are issued from the template function. The properties that are available in a template depend on the compatibility settings of the template. There are two compatibility settings, one for the CA and another for the certificate recipient. Figure 18-22 shows the CA setting configured for Windows Server 2016 and the certificate recipient set to Windows 10 / Windows Server 2016. Windows Server 2016 is the most recent version that can be configured on a CA running the Windows Server 2019 or later operating system, and there are no specific Windows Server 2019 or later settings or features. When you specify Windows Server 2016, this template can only be used with a Windows Server 2016 or later CA. Over the next few pages, you'll learn about some of the important areas of a certificate template's properties.

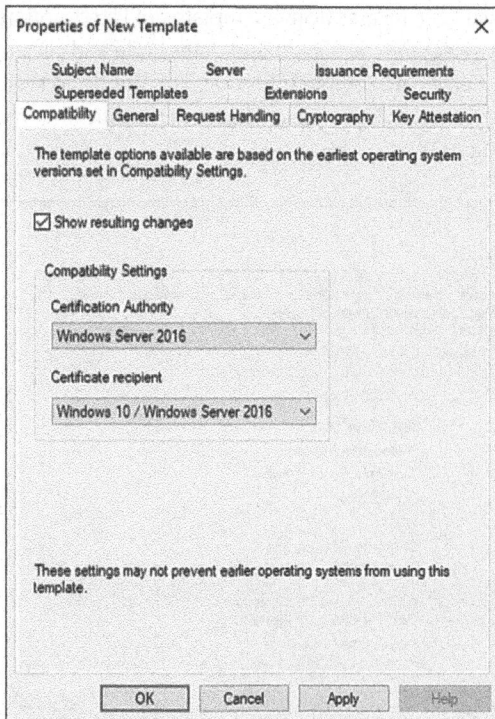

Figure 18-22   Compatibility tab

The General tab of a template, shown in Figure 18-23, allows you to configure both the Template Name and the Template Display Name. You also configure the certificate Validity Period and the Renewal Period in this tab. You can also choose whether the certificate is published in Active Directory. Publication to Active Directory is useful when other people in the organization might need to access a public certificate. If it's published in Active Directory, the public certificate doesn't have to be manually shared or retrieved. The private key is not published to Active Directory when the Publish Certificate in Active Directory option is enabled. In this example, Template Display Name is set to Example_Template. The Validity Period is set to 1 year, and the Renewal Period is set to 6 weeks. The template is configured to be published in Active Directory.

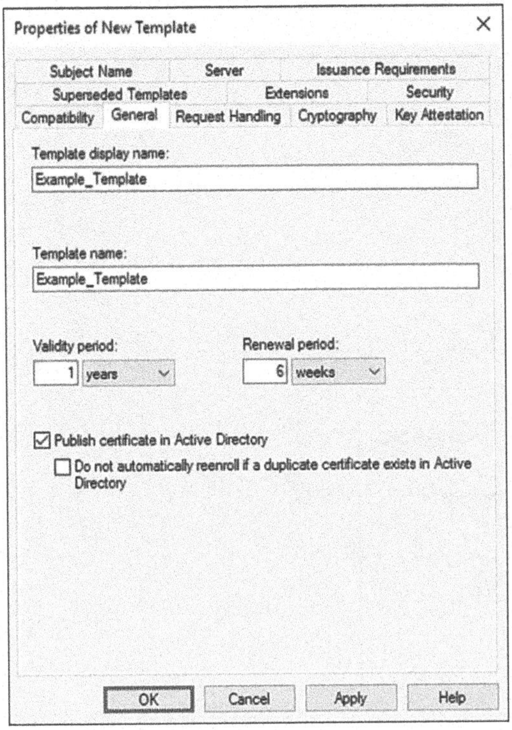

Figure 18-23 General tab

The Request Handling tab of the certificate template properties dialog, shown in Figure 18-24, allows you to specify the certificate's purpose, which can be one of the following:

- Encryption

- Signature

- Signature And Encryption

- Signature And Smartcard Logon

In Figure 18-24, the Purpose is set to Encryption. The Include Symmetric Algorithms Allowed By The Subject option is enabled. The Allow Private Key To Be Exported and the Enroll Subject Without Requiring Any User Input options are enabled. You can also use this tab to specify whether the subject's encryption private key is archived in the CA database, whether the private key can be exported, whether the user is prompted during enrollment, and when the private key is used.

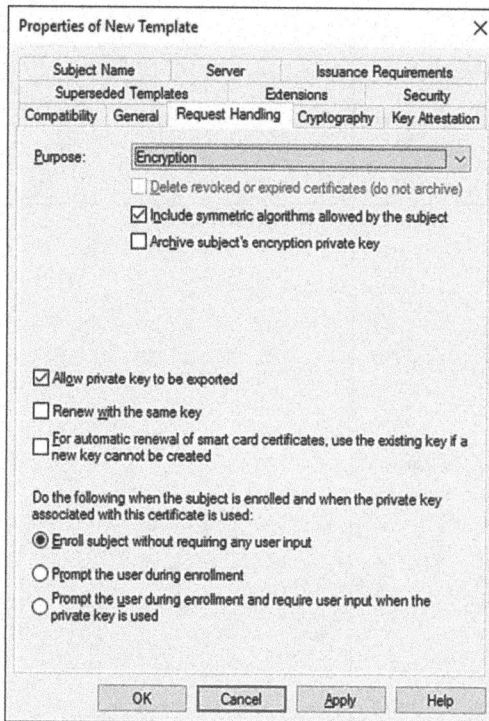

Figure 18-24   Request Handling tab

The Cryptography tab of a certificate's properties, shown in Figure 18-25, allows you to specify the cryptographic properties of the certificate issued from the template. This includes specifying a Minimum Key Size. You also use this tab to specify the properties of the cryptographic providers used for the certificate request. You do this to ensure that the certificate request meets a specific cryptographic benchmark. These settings are useful in environments that have very specific security requirements. In this example,

- Provider Category is set to Legacy Cryptographic Service Provider.

- Algorithm Name is set to Determined By CSP.

- Minimum Key Size is 2048.

- Microsoft Enhanced Cryptographic Provider v 1.0 is selected.

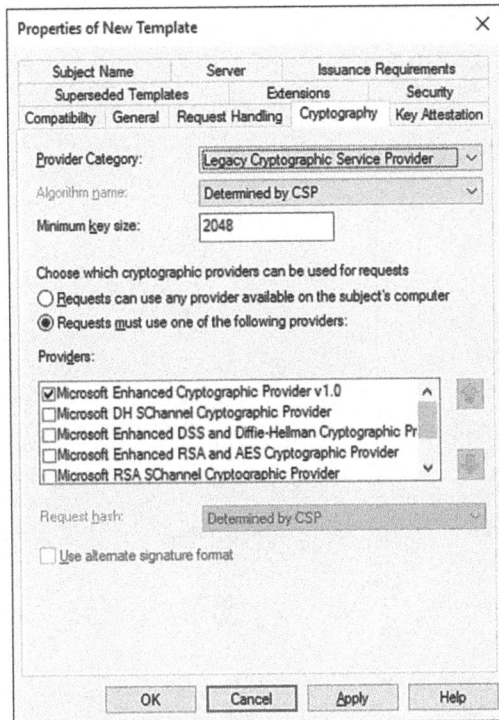

Figure 18-25   Cryptography tab

The Superseded Templates tab, shown in Figure 18-26, allows you to configure existing certificate templates that a newer template supersedes. For example, you might create a more advanced EFS certificate template that uses stronger cryptography and then specify the existing Basic EFS template as a template that the new template supersedes. When you configure autoenrollment correctly, a certificate from the new template automatically replaces the certificate from the superseded template.

The Security tab, shown in Figure 18-27, allows you to configure which users and groups have permission to enroll and autoenroll in the certificate. A user who has permission to enroll in the certificate can request the certificate. Autoenrollment means the certificate request is performed automatically. You configure autoenrollment through group policy. In Figure 18-27, the Admin Account is assigned the Read and Write (Allow) permissions. This process is described in more detail later in this chapter.

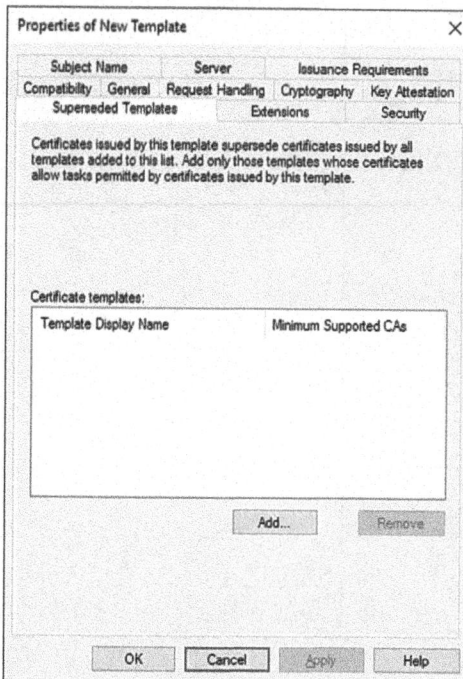

Figure 18-26   Superseded Templates tab

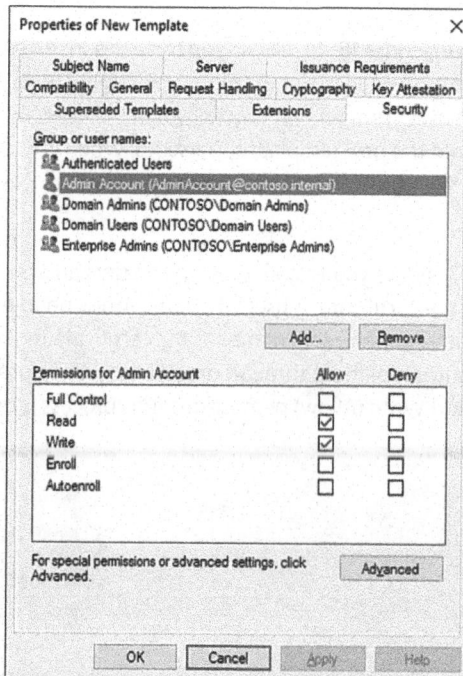

Figure 18-27   Security tab

You use the Issuance Requirements tab, shown in Figure 18-28, to specify whether requests against the template require certificate manager approval. You can also configure a certificate to require approval from more than one manager, which is useful for certificates issued from sensitive templates, such as the Key Recovery Agent template. In this example, the CA Certificate Manager Approval option is enabled. The This Number Of Authorized Signatures option is set to 1. The Policy Type Required In Signature option is set to Application Policy. The Application Policy is set to Any Purpose.

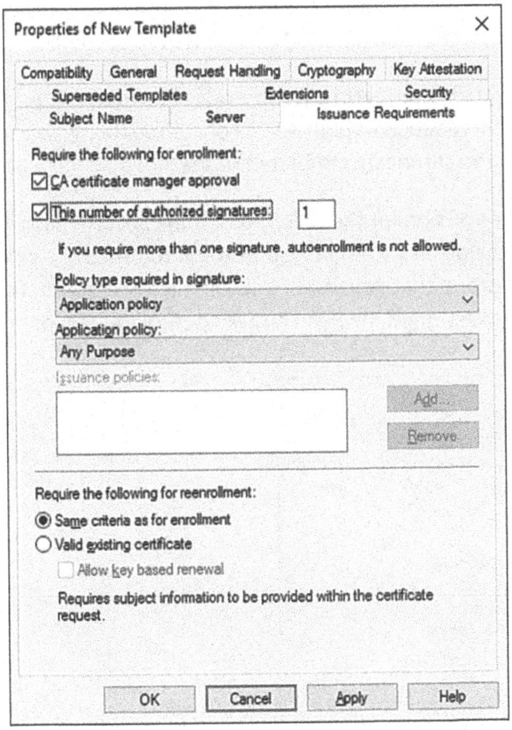

Figure 18-28 Issuance Requirements tab

Adding and editing templates

Windows Server 2019 and later include 34 built-in templates. While you can edit some of the default templates should you want to make modifications, the best practice is to create a duplicate of the default template and edit the duplicate. In the event that something goes wrong, you've still got the original. When your new certificate template is ready, you can add the new template to a CA and delete the old one from the CA. To create a duplicate template, right-click the template that you want to duplicate and click Duplicate Template. Templates are stored within Active Directory and automatically replicate to be available to any enterprise CA.

Certificate autoenrollment and renewal

An advantage of enterprise CAs is that they allow for automatic certificate enrollment and automatic certificate renewal. This means that certificates can be issued automatically to users, services, or devices without requiring them to perform any explicit action. Autoenrollment substantially reduces the amount of administrative effort required to deploy and update certificates.

To configure autoenrollment, you need to perform the following configuration steps for the certificate template associated with the certificate that you want to autoenroll:

- Ensure the certificate template for the certificate you want to allow autoenrollment for is configured for a Windows Server 2008 or higher level of compatibility. You configure this on the Compatibility tab of the certificate template's properties.

- Configure the Autoenroll permission for the certificate on the Security tab of the certificate template's Properties dialog, as shown in Figure 18-29. You should configure this permission for the security group that you want to automatically enroll. In this figure, the Authenticated Users group is assigned the Read and Autoenroll (Allow) permissions.

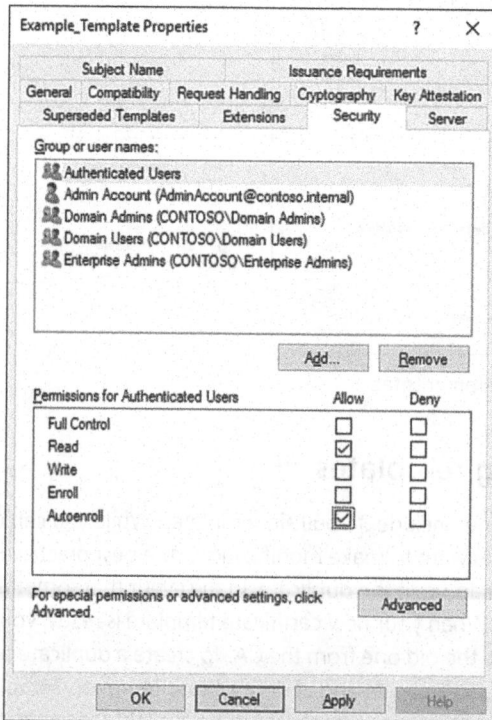

Figure 18-29   Security tab

The other half of configuring autoenrollment is configuring the Certificate Services Client policy in the Default Domain GPO. Depending on whether you want to configure autoenrollment for users or computers, this policy is found in one of the following nodes:

- `Policies\User Configuration\Windows Settings\Security Settings\Public Key Policies`

- `Policies\Computer Configuration\Windows Settings\Security Settings\Public Key Policies`

You can configure the following settings for this policy, as shown in Figure 18-30. In the figure, the Configuration Model, the Renew Expired Certificates, and the Update Certificates That Use Certificate Templates options are set to Enabled.

- **Configuration Model**   You can set this to Enabled, Disabled, or Not Configured. Setting this to Enabled allows certificate autoenrollment.

- **Renew Expired Certificates, Update Pending Certificates, And Remove Revoked Certificates**   When you configure this setting, certificates that are configured for autoenrollment are automatically renewed before they expire.

- **Update Certificates That Use Certificate Templates**   This policy triggers autoenrollment in certificates that use new templates configured to supersede certificates issued from an existing template. Supersede settings are configured within the new certificate's template. The new certificate also needs to be configured with an appropriate autoenrollment permission.

- **Expiration Notification**   When enabled, a user is prompted to trigger the reenrollment process. Notifications are triggered based on the remaining percentage of the certificate's lifetime.

CHAPTER 18

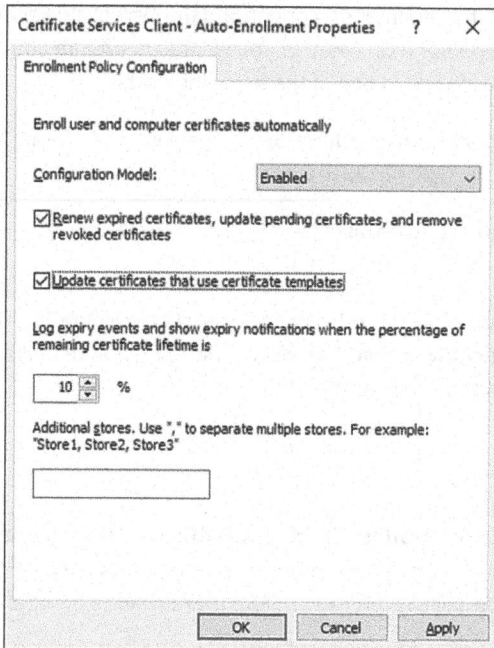

Figure 18-30 Enrollment Policy Configuration

CA management

You assign roles on a CA by assigning one of the following permissions, as shown in Figure 18-31. In the figure, the Enterprise Admins group has been assigned the Issue And Manage Certificates and Manage CA permissions.

- **Issue And Manage Certificates** You assign this permission when you want to allow someone to issue and revoke certificates.

- **Manage CA** You assign this permission when you want to allow someone to edit the properties of the CA. This includes the ability to assign CA permissions. You can't directly block someone to whom you have assigned the Manage CA permission from granting themselves the Issue And Manage Certificates permission. Only by configuring auditing and alerts are you able to restrict this action. By default, members of the Enterprise Admins, Domain Admins, and Local Administrators groups have the Manage CA permission on a computer that is a member of a domain.

- **Request Certificates**   You use this permission to control who can request certificates from the CA. Should you have a CA that you've configured to only issue certificates from especially sensitive templates, such as Key Recovery, you might choose to alter this setting.

- **Read**   You use this permission to allow someone to view CA information.

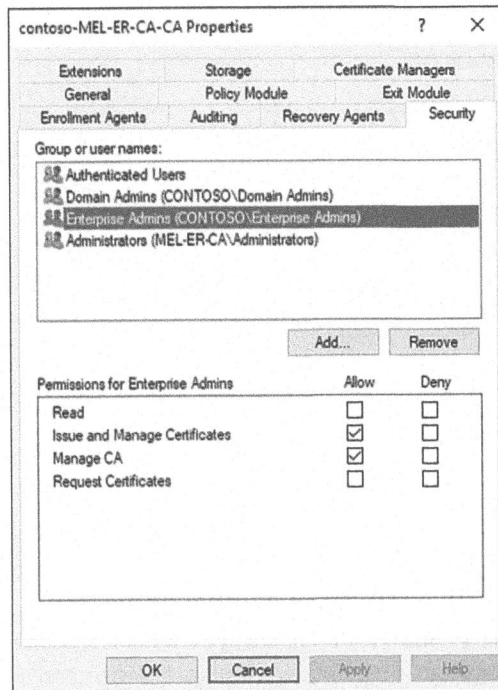

Figure 18-31   Security permissions

You can go further when configuring the ability to issue and manage certificates by configuring this ability based on certificate templates. To configure a security group so it can issue certificates based on a specific template, you first need to assign the group the Issue And Manage Certificates permission on the Security tab of the CA properties dialog. Then, on the Certificate Managers tab, you need to choose the Restrict Certificate Managers option. After you've done that, you edit the list of certificate templates for which each group can manage certificates. Figure 18-32 shows the local KRA_Cert_Managers group configured to manage certificates based on the Key Recovery Agent certificate template.

CHAPTER 18

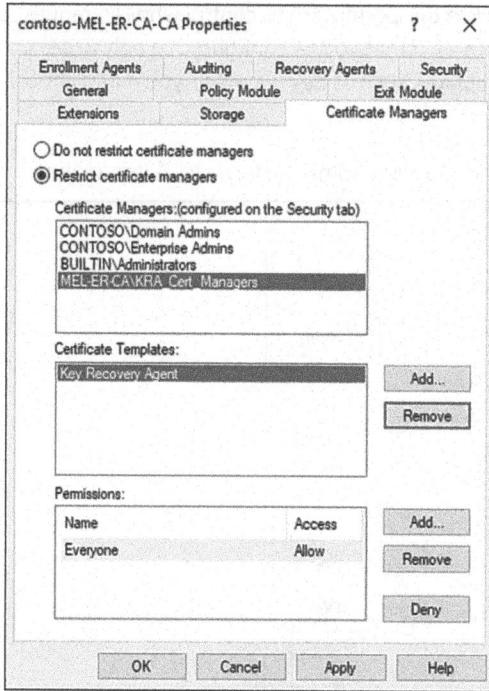

Figure 18-32   Certificate Managers

Handling certificate requests

By default, all certificates on a standalone CA require approval. An enterprise CA uses the properties configured in the CA template. To approve a certificate, navigate to the Pending Requests node of the Certification Authority console, select the Pending Requests node, select the certificate that you want to approve or deny, click All Tasks from the Action Menu, and then click either Issue or Deny.

You can alter whether an enterprise CA uses the template to determine whether approval is required—meaning all certificates require approval—by editing the properties of the CA. To do so, click the Properties button on the Policy Module tab. This opens the Properties dialog, as shown in Figure 18-33, where you can configure this setting. In the figure, Follow The Settings In The Certificate Template, If Applicable. Otherwise, the Automatically Issue The Certificate option is enabled. The other option, Set The Certificate Request Status To Pending, is not selected.

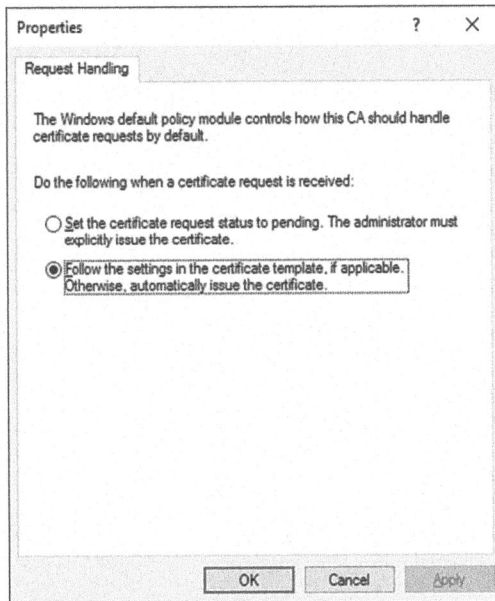

Figure 18-33 Request Handling

CA backup and recovery

You can back up and recover a CA, including the private key, CA certificate, CA database, and CA log from the Certification Authority console. To back up a CA, perform the following steps:

1. In the Certification Authority console, select the CA that you want to back up. On the Action menu, click All Tasks and click Back Up CA.

2. On the Welcome To The Certification Authority Backup page of the Certification Authority Backup Wizard, click Next.

3. On the Items To Backup page, choose from the following options, as shown in Figure 18-34. In the figure, the Private Key And CA Certificate and Certificate Database And Certificate Database Log settings are selected. Back Up To This Location is set to c:\cabackup\.

    - **Private Key And CA Certificate** Backs up the CA's private and public keys. Enables you to restore the CA on a different computer in the event that the CA fails.

    - **Certificate Database And Certificate Database Log** Enables you to recover the public keys of the certificates that the CA has issued. If key archiving is enabled, this option enables you to recover the private keys of these certificates.

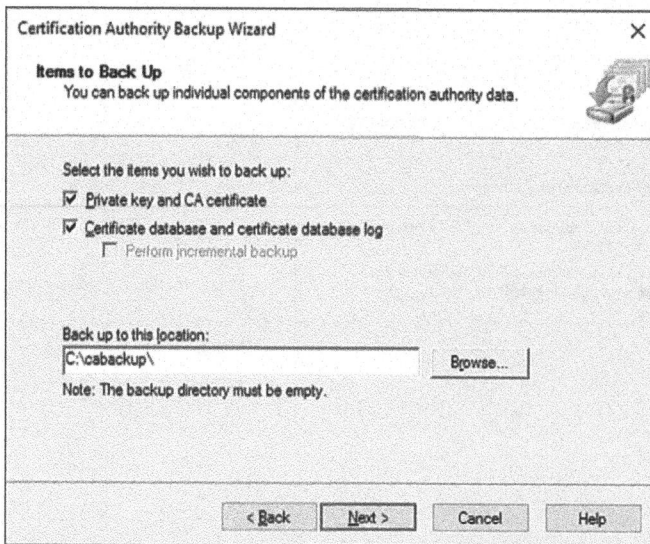

Figure 18-34   CA Backup Wizard

4.   Provide a password to encrypt the backup data.

To recover a backup, perform the following steps:

1.   In the Certification Authority console, right-click the CA, click All Tasks, and then click Restore CA.

2.   When you are warned about stopping Active Directory Certificate Services, click OK.

3.   On the Items To Restore page, shown in Figure 18-35, select the folder that holds the CA backup data and click Next. In this example, the Private Key And CA Certificate and Certificate Database And Certificate Database Log settings are selected. The Restore From This Location setting is set to c:\cabackup.

4.   Provide the password used to protect the backup data and then complete the wizard. When the restoration is complete, you are prompted to restart Active Directory Certificate Services.

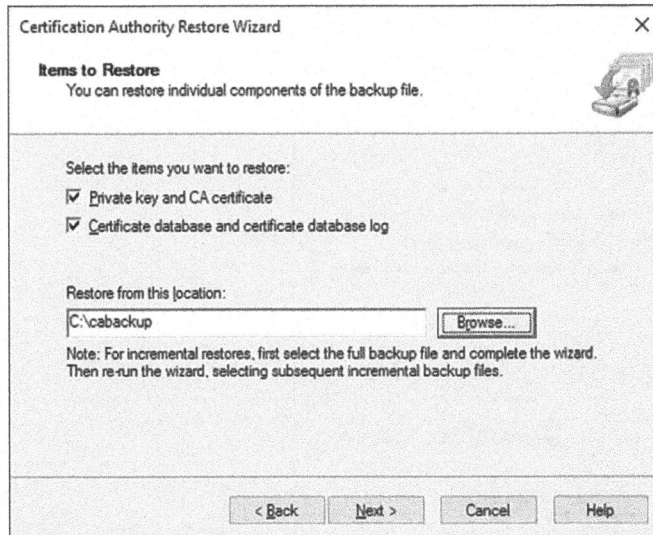

Figure 18-35   CA Restore

One thing that CA backup does not back up is the list of certificate templates that a specific enterprise CA has been configured to issue. If you have configured a CA to issue additional templates beyond the default templates, you need to configure a recovered CA to use the same templates. One method to keep track of which certificate templates a CA is configured to use is to use the `Get-CATemplate` PowerShell cmdlet. You can pipe the output of this cmdlet to a text file, which you can use as a record of which templates a specific CA has been configured to issue.

Key archiving and recovery

A key recovery agent allows an entity holding a properly configured key recovery agent certificate to recover a private key that has been archived in the AD CS database. To perform key recovery on a private certificate, the template from which the certificate is generated needs to be configured so that private keys are archived to the AD CS database. This is done on the Request Handling tab of the template's Properties, as shown in Figure 18-36. The Include Symmetric Algorithms Allowed By The Subject, Archive Subject's Encryption Private Key, and Allow Private Key To Be Exported options are enabled.

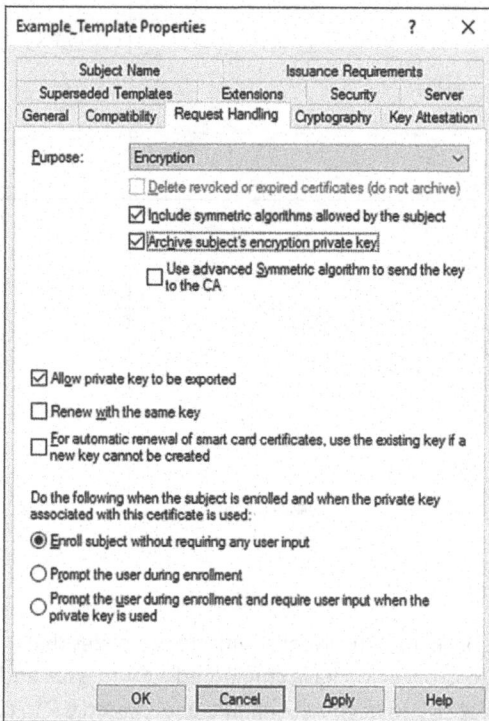

Figure 18-36 Archive private key

The CA also needs to be configured with one or more Recovery Agents. To configure a recovery agent, perform the following steps:

1. In production environments, create an account to be used by the recovery agent. While you can use the built-in administrator account, from a security perspective, you're much better off having a separate account for this role. In an ideal environment, the individual using this account is separate from the individuals who manage the CA. Requiring separate individuals ensures that private keys are only recovered in authorized circumstances. You want to avoid allowing just anyone to recover private keys without oversight, especially in scenarios that involve encryption.

2. Configure a CA to issue Key Recovery certificates. To do this, open the Certification Authority console, right-click Certificate Templates, click New, and then click Certificate Template To Issue. In the Enable Certificate Templates dialog, select Key Recovery Agent as shown in Figure 18-37, and click OK.

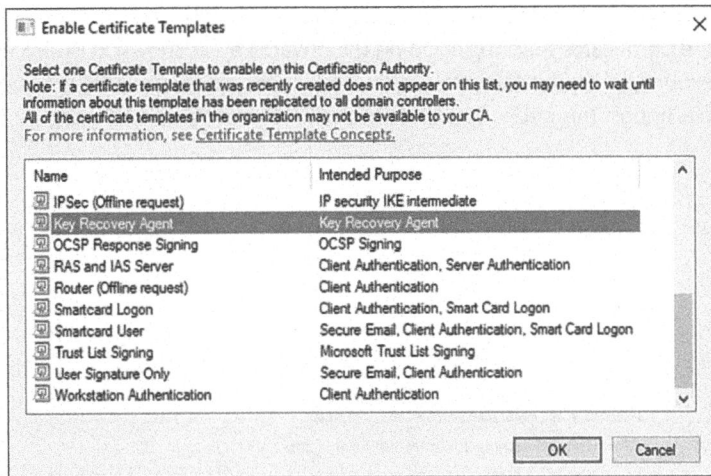

Figure 18-37   Certificate templates

3. Then the account you use for key recovery needs to request a certificate based on this template. This can be done using the Certificates snap-in of the Microsoft Management console, as shown in Figure 18-38.

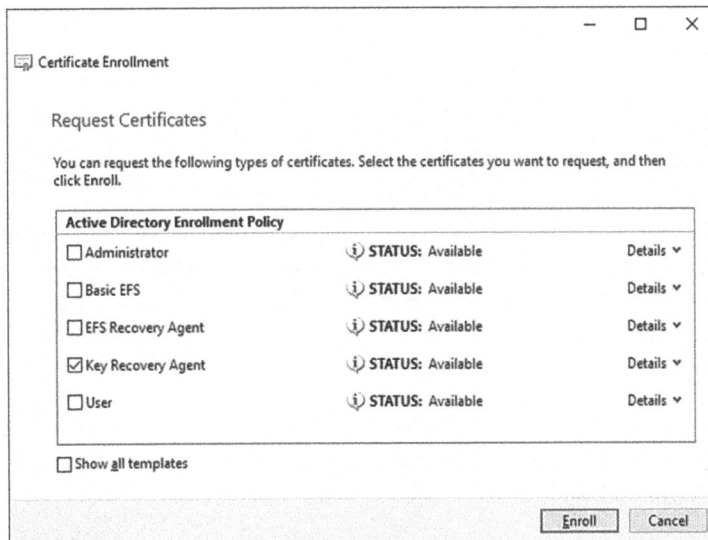

Figure 18-38   Certificate request

4. In the Certification Authority console, you need to approve the certificate request because the default template is configured to require approval, not to have the certificate issued automatically.

5. After the certificate is issued, export it from the Certificate Enrollment Requests node of the Certificates snap-in, including the private key, as shown in Figure 18-39. After you've exported the private key to a `.pfx` file, you should then export the public key to a `.cer` file. Import this public certificate to the CA to enable key recovery.

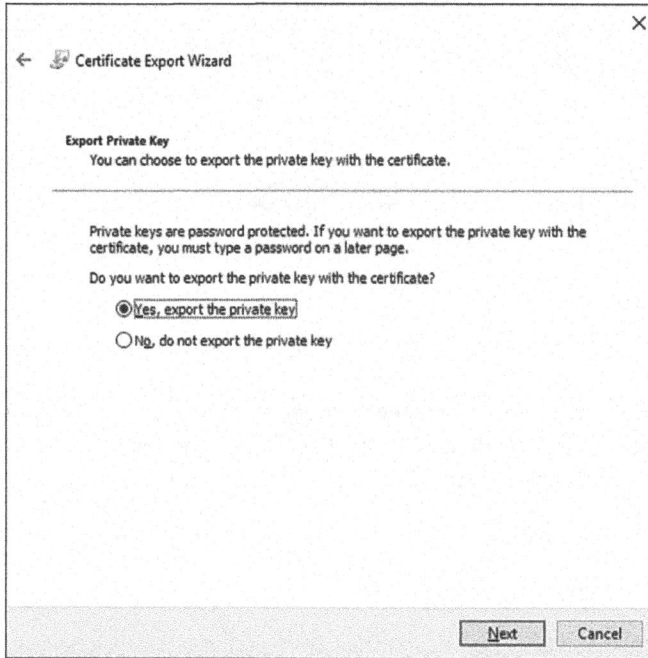

Figure 18-39   Export private key

6. To configure the CA to archive private keys, on the Recovery Agents tab, select Archive the key, click Add, and on the Key Recovery Agent Selection dialog, shown in Figure 18-40, click the certificate; then click OK. Note in Figure 18-40 that the name of the user account is `KeyRecovery`. If your key recovery account has a different name, it's listed in this dialog.

7. You need to restart the CA before the changes take place. When you've restarted the CA, the key recovery agent certificate is listed as Valid on the Recovery Agents tab, as shown in Figure 18-41.

CHAPTER 18

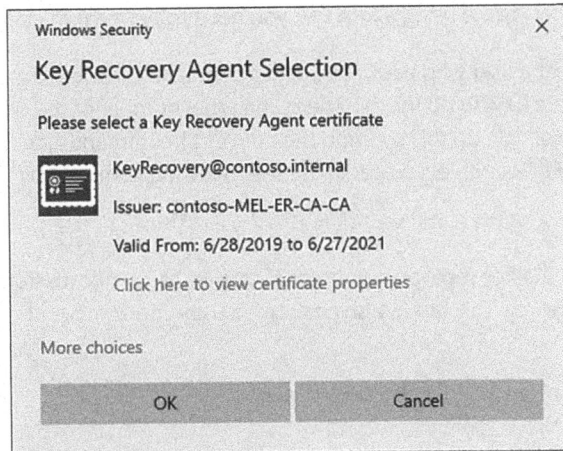

Figure 18-40   KRA selection

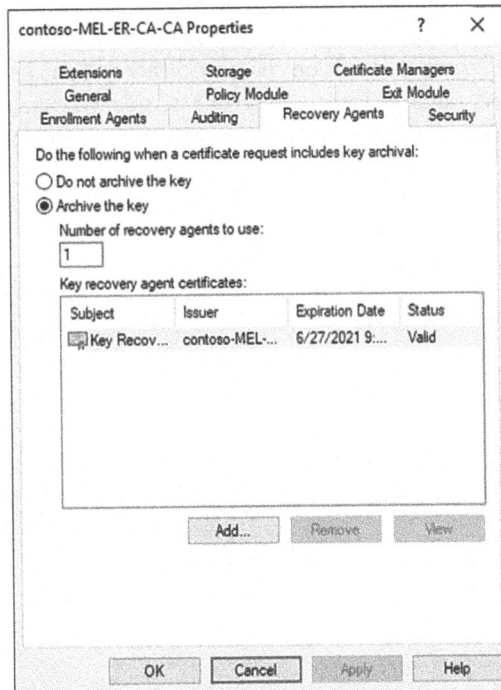

Figure 18-41   Recovery Agents

To recover an archived certificate using a KRA key, you need to perform the following steps:

1.   The first step is that a user who has CA Manager permissions needs to extract a blob that contains the private key. To do this, you need the serial number of the certificate that you want to recover. You do this by using the `certutil` command-line utility with the `-getkey` option. For example, you could use the following command:

```
Certutil -getkey <certificate_serial_number> outputblob
```

2.   The user who has the key recovery agent certificate in the certificate store then needs to recover the private key. This task is also performed using the `certutil` command-line utility.

```
Certutil -recoverkey outputblob recoveredkey.pfx
```

CAPolicy.inf

The `CAPolicy.inf` file, located in the `%systemroot%` (usually `C:\Windows`) folder, allows you to customize CA settings. This file is not mandatory and is not present by default, but it does allow you to provide a collection of settings to configure the CA automatically. You would use this primarily when providing certificates used outside your organization. If you have an internal CA that is only being used by organizational clients, and no one outside the organization consumes the certificates, you likely don't have to worry about using a `CAPolicy.inf` file.

The file is a text file. For example, the following `CAPolicy.inf` file could be used for a root CA:

```
[Version]
Signature= "$Windows NT$"
[Certsrv_Server]
RenewalKeyLength=4096
RenewalValidityPeriod=Years
RenewalValidityPeriodUnits=10
LoadDefaultTemplates=0
```

An enterprise CA could use the following `CAPolicy.inf` file:

```
[Version]
Signature= "$Windows NT$"
[PolicyStatementExtension]
Policies = LegalPolicy, LimitedUsePolicy
[LegalPolicy]
OID = 1.1.1.1.1.1.1.1
URL = "http://www.contoso.com/Policy/LegalPolicy.asp"
URL = "ftp://ftp.contoso.com/Policy/LegalPolicy.txt"
[LimitedUsePolicy]
OID = 2.2.2.2.2.2.2.2
URL = "http://www.contoso.com/Policy/LimitedUsePolicy.asp"
URL = "ftp://ftp.contoso.com/Policy/LimitedUsePolicy.txt"
LoadDefaultTemplates=0
```

The OIDs listed in the preceding code are just for examples. In a real `CAPolicy.inf` file, you would use OIDs that you obtained from the ISO Name Registration Authority.

> ## More Info
>
> *CAPolicy.inf*
>
> You can find out more about the syntax of `CAPolicy.inf` files at *https://learn.microsoft. com/en-us/windows-server/networking/core-network-guide/cncg/server-certs/ prepare-the-capolicy-inf-file.*

Managing Certificate Services using PowerShell

There are a number of PowerShell cmdlets that you can use to install and configure Certificate Services. These cmdlets are included in the `ADCSAdministration` and `ADCSDeployment` modules and are listed in Tables 18-2 Table 18-3.

Table 18-2   ADCSAdministration PowerShell Module cmdlets

Cmdlet	Function
`Add-CAAuthorityInformationAccess`	Add a uniform resource identifier (URI) for the Authority Information Access (AIA) or Online Responder OCSP address for a CA.
`Add-CACrlDistributionPoint`	Add a CRL distribution point to all subsequently issued certificates.
`Add-CATemplate`	Add a certificate template stored in Active Directory to the CA so that the CA can issue certificates from that template.
`Backup-CARoleService`	Backs up both the CA database and the CA private key.
`Confirm-CAAttestation-IdentityKeyInfo`	Checks whether a CA trusts the attestation identity key for specific secure hardware.
`Confirm-CAEndorsementKeyInfo`	Checks whether a CA trusts specific secure hardware for key attestation.
`Get-CAAuthorityInformationAccess`	View the AIA and OCSP URI information configured for the CA.
`Get-CACrlDistributionPoint`	View the CRL distribution point information configured for the CA.
`Get-CATemplate`	View the list of templates that the CA is configured to issue. This is not the entire list of templates stored within AD DS.
`Remove-CAAuthorityInformation-Access`	Remove a URI for the AIA or Online Responder OCSP address for a CA.

Cmdlet	Function
Remove-CACrlDistributionPoint	Remove a CRL distribution point. This applies only to all subsequently issued certificates. Existing certificates still retain distribution point information that was valid at the time the certificate was issued.
Remove-CATemplate	Removes a certificate template from a CA.
Restore-CARoleService	Restore a CA database and private key from an existing backup.

Table 18-3   ADCSDeployment PowerShell Module

Cmdlet	Function
Install-AdcsCertificationAuthority	Configures a CA. This cmdlet does not install the binaries, which need to be added separately using the Install-WindowsFeature cmdlet.
Install-AdcsEnrollmentPolicyWebService	Configures the Enrollment Policy Web Service on a computer where the binaries are already present.
Install-AdcsEnrollmentWebService	Configures the Enrollment Web Service on a computer where the binaries are already present. It can also be used to add additional instances of the service on the computer.
Install-AdcsNetworkDeviceEnrollment-Service	Configure the Network Device Enrollment Service on a computer where the binaries are already present.
Install-AdcsOnlineResponder	Configures the Online Responder role service on a computer where the binaries are already present.
Install-AdcsWebEnrollment	Configures the Web Enrollment role service on a computer where the binaries are already present.
Uninstall-AdcsCertificationAuthority	Removes the CA role service and deletes associated configuration information.
Uninstall-AdcsEnrollmentPolicy-WebService	Removes the Certificate Enrollment Policy Web Service.
Uninstall-AdcsEnrollmentWebService	Removes the Certificate Enrollment Web Service or specific instances of the service if more than one is present.
Uninstall-AdcsNetworkDeviceEnrollment-Service	Removes the Network Device Enrollment service from a computer it has been deployed on.

Cmdlet	Function
Uninstall-AdcsOnlineResponder	Removes the Online Responder service from a computer it has been deployed on.
Uninstall-AdcsWebEnrollment	Removes the Web Enrollment role service from a computer on which it has been deployed.

Managing Certificate Services using Certutil.exe and Certreq.exe

Not all Certificate Services functionality is available through PowerShell in Windows Server. There are still several tasks that you need to use the certutil.exe and certreq.exe command-line tools to perform.

Certutil.exe

Certutil.exe allows you to manipulate local certificates as well as to configure and manage Certificate Services. Some certutil.exe functionality is present in available PowerShell cmdlets. Over time, all functionality that is present in certutil.exe will likely be available through PowerShell.

Important certutil.exe options are listed in Table 18-4.

Table 18-4   Certutil.exe options

Option	Function
-deny	Use this to deny a pending certificate request.
-resubmit	Resubmit a pending certificate request.
-revoke	Revoke a certificate.
-CRL	Publish a new CRL.
-renewCert	Renew the CA certificate.
-backup	Back up the AD CS.
-backupDB	Back up the AD CS database.
-backupKey	Back up the CA certificate and private key.
-restore	Restore AD CS from a backup.
-restoreDB	Restore the AD CS database from a backup.
-restoreKey	Restore the CA certificate and private key from a backup.
-dsPublish	Publish a certificate or CRL to AD.
-ADTemplate	List templates stored in AD.
-TemplateCAs	List CAs configured to issue a template.

CHAPTER 18

More Info

Certutil.exe

You can find out more about the `certutil.exe` command at *https://learn.microsoft. com/en-us/windows-server/administration/windows-commands/certutil.*

Certreq.exe

You can use `Certreq.exe` to import a certificate request file and submit it to a CA. If the user running `certreq.exe` has the appropriate permissions on the CA, they can save the issued certificate. Important `certreq.exe` options are listed in Table 18-5.

Table 18-5 Certreq.exe options

Option	Function
-Submit	Submits a request to a CA
-Retrieve	Retrieves a response from a CA
-Enroll	Enrolls for a new certificate or renews a certificate
-Accept	Accepts and installs a certificate request response

More Info

Certreq.exe

You can find out more about the `certreq.exe` command at *https://learn.microsoft. com/en-us/windows-server/administration/windows-commands/certreq_1.*

Active Directory Federation Services

Active Directory Federation Services (AD FS) is Microsoft's identity federation solution. Identity federation allows identification, authorization, and authentication to occur across organizational boundaries. When a federated trust is established, users can use their local credentials to access resources hosted by another organization. When configured properly, federation also enables users to access resources hosted in the cloud. Although it's possible to configure full-forest or domain-trust relationships when users in one organization need to use their credentials to access resources in another organization, these trust relationships are often more comprehensive than is necessary. AD FS makes it possible to configure highly restricted access to information and resources between partner organizations while still allowing each partner to authenticate using its own credentials.

AD FS components

AD FS deployments in Windows Server consist of two components:

- **Federation Server**   The computer that hosts the federation server role manages requests involving identity claims. There must be at least one federation server in an Active Directory forest when deploying AD FS.

- **Web Application Proxy**   When you want to provide AD FS functionality to clients on untrusted networks, such as on the Internet, you deploy the computer that functions as a web application proxy on a perimeter network. This server relays connections to the Federation Server on the internal network, and this role can also be installed on a standalone computer. In Windows Server 2012 and earlier versions of AD FS, this role was known as the Federation Proxy.

Claims, claim rules, and attribute stores

AD FS provides claims-based authentication. Claims-based authentication works on the basis of a claim about the user, such as "allow access to this web application if this user is a full-time employee of the partner organization." AD FS uses the following when building tokens that contain claim data:

- **Claim**   Claims are descriptions made about an object based on the object's attributes. For example, a user account name, employee type, or security group membership can constitute a claim. Claims are also used with Dynamic Access Control, which is covered in Chapter 20, "Active Directory Rights Management Services."

- **Claim rules**   Claim rules determine how a federation server processes a claim. You can have a simple rule, such as treating a user's email address as a valid claim. Claim rules can also be more complex, where an attribute, such as a job title from one organization, is translated into a security group membership in the partner organization.

- **Attribute store**   An attribute store holds the values used in claims. AD FS generally uses Active Directory as an attribute store. For example, a lookup of a user's Managed By attribute returns a value that lists the user account assigned as that user's manager.

Figure 19-1 shows how to create a claim rule where Active Directory functions as the attribute store and the Employee-Type attribute is mapped to an outgoing claim.

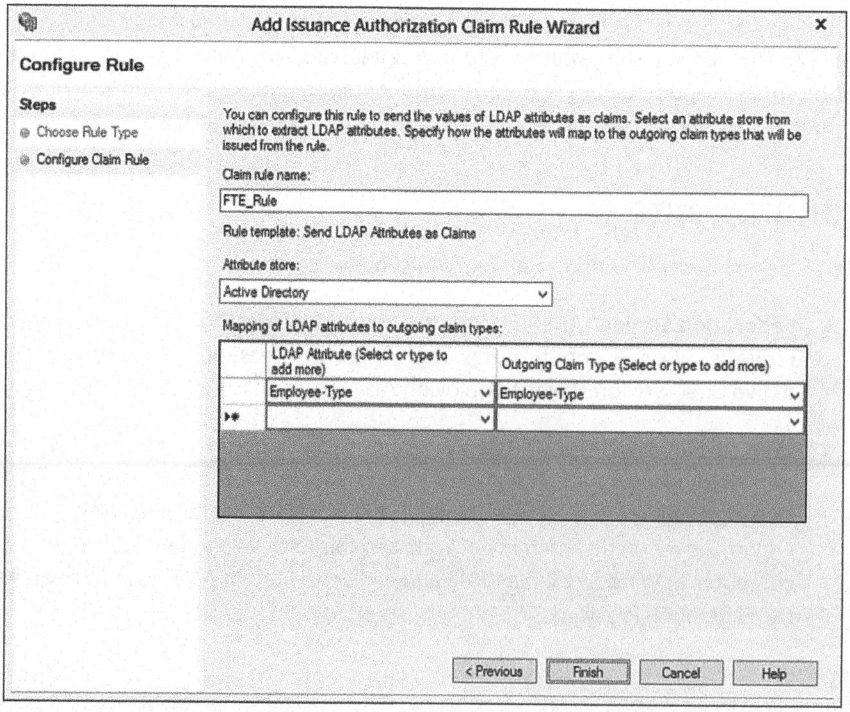

Figure 19-1   Claim Rule Name

Claims provider

A claims provider is a federation server that provides users with claims. These claims are stored within digitally encrypted and signed tokens. When a user needs a token, the claims provider server contacts the Active Directory deployment in its native forest to determine whether the user has authenticated. If the user is properly authenticated against the local Active Directory deployment, the claims provider then builds a user claim by using attributes located within Active Directory and other attribute stores. The attributes that are added to the claim are dependent on the attributes required by the partner.

Relying party

The relying party server is a member of the Active Directory forest that hosts the resources that the user in the partner organization wants to access. The relying party server accepts and validates the claims contained in the token issued by the claims provider. The relying party server then issues a new token that the resource uses to determine what access to grant the user from the partner organization.

Inside Out

Nonexclusive roles

A single AD FS server can function as both a claims provider server and a relying party server. This enables users in each partner organization to access resources in the other organization through a federation trust.

Relying party trust

You configure the relying party trust on the AD FS server that functions as the claims provider server. Although this might initially seem counterintuitive, it makes sense when you consider it as a statement: "A relying party trust means that a claims provider trusts a specific relying party." Figure 19-2 shows the Add Relying Party Trust Wizard, where the address of the relying party server to be trusted is ad1-dc.wingtiptoys.internal.

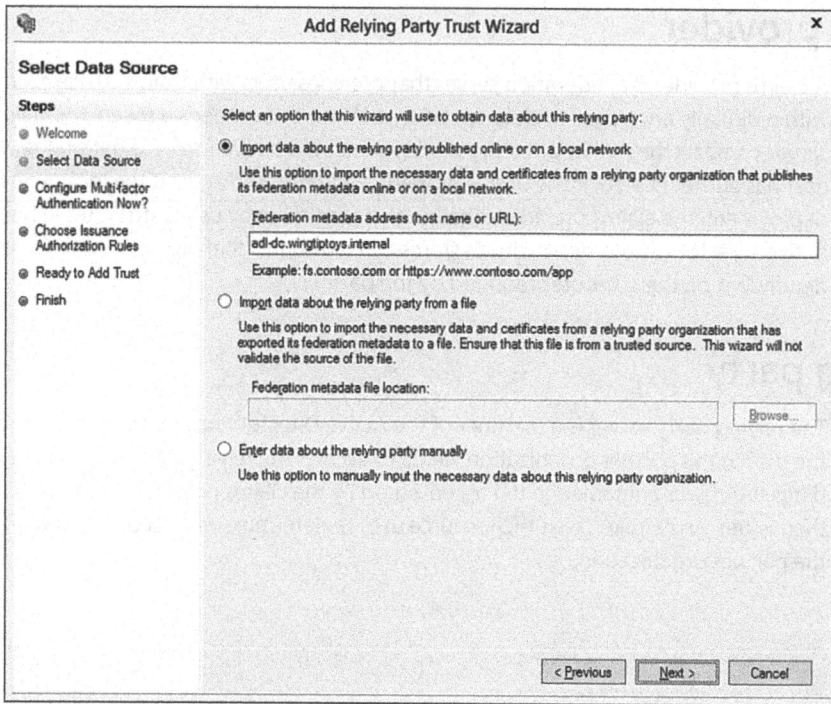

Figure 19-2   Relying party information

Claims provider trust

You configure the claims provider trust on the Federation Server that functions as the relying party. This also seems counterintuitive until you consider the claims provider trust as a statement: "A claims provider trust means that a relying party trusts a specific claims provider." Figure 19-3 shows how to set up a claims provider trust where the address of the claims provider to be trusted is cbr-dc.contoso.com.

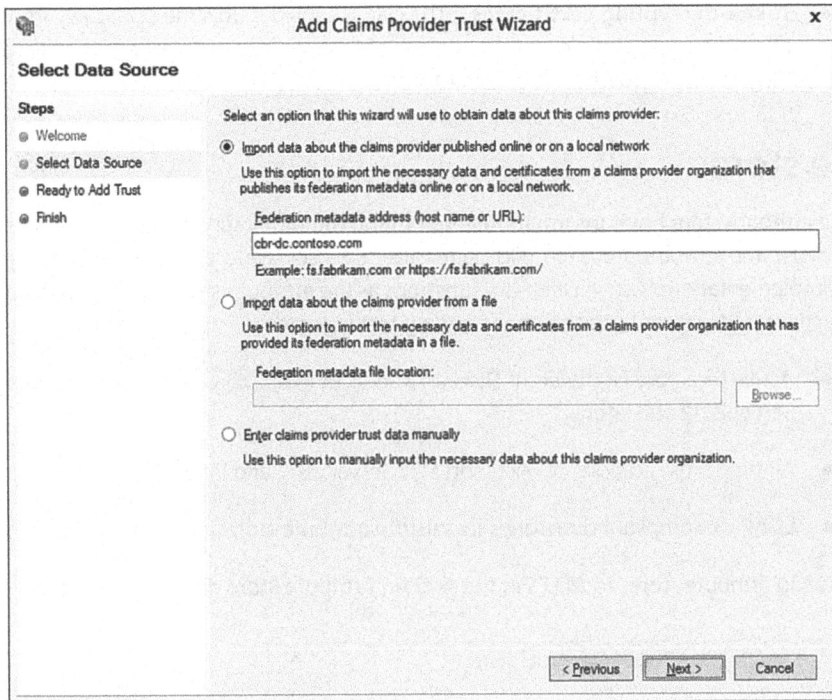

Figure 19-3   Claims Provider Trust

Configuring certificate relationship

You need to configure partners so that the certificates issued by the opposite partner are trusted. You can accomplish this by using a trusted third-party CA or by configuring CA trusts between partners. To configure a CA trust, you need to import the CA certificate of the partner organization's CA into the Trusted Root CA store. You can do this directly on the AD FS server, or you can configure Group Policy so that all computers within the policy's scope trust the partner organization's CA.

You can use a certificate issued from the computer certificate template, which is available through an Active Directory Certificate Services enterprise CA, to secure the federation server endpoint. When using a trusted third-party CA, you can also use a typical Transport Layer Security (TLS) certificate.

AD FS uses the following certificates:

- **Token-signing certificates**   The federation server uses the token-signing certificate to sign all the tokens that it issues. The server that functions as the claims provider uses the token-signing certificate to verify its identity. The relying party uses the token-signing certificate when verifying that a trusted federation partner issued the token.

- **Token-decrypting certificates**   The claims provider uses the public key from this certificate to encrypt the user token. When the relying party server receives the token, it uses the private key to decrypt the user token.

Attribute stores

The attribute store holds information about users. The AD FS server uses the information contained in the attribute store to build claims after the user is authenticated. In the majority of AD FS implementations, Active Directory functions as the attribute store. You can configure additional attribute stores based on the following technologies:

- Active Directory Lightweight Directory Services (AD LDS) on computers running Windows Server 2012 and later

- All supported editions of Microsoft SQL Server 2012 and later

- LDAP v3-compliant directories (as custom attribute stores)

You add attribute stores to AD FS in the Add An Attribute Store dialog, as shown in Figure 19-4.

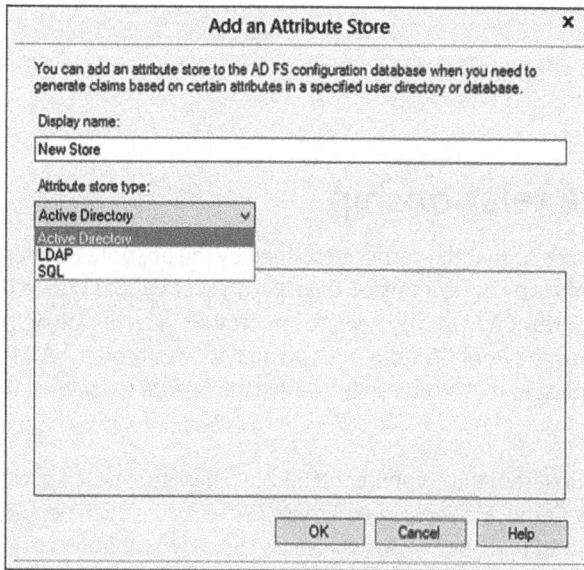

Figure 19-4   Add An Attribute Store

Claim rules

Claim rules determine how AD FS servers send and consume claims. AD FS supports two different types of claim rules: relying party trust claim rules and claims provider trust claim rules.

Relying party trust claim rules

Relying party trust claim rules determine how the claims about a user are forwarded to the rely-ing party. You can configure these rules by editing the relying party trust's claim rules on the AD FS server that functions as the claims provider. There are three types of relying party trust claim rules:

- **Issuance transform rules**   Determine how claims are sent to the relying party.

- **Issuance authorization rules**   Determine which users have access to the relying party. An issuance authorization claim rule is shown in Figure 19-5.

- **Delegation authorization rules**   Determine if users can act on behalf of other users when accessing the relying party.

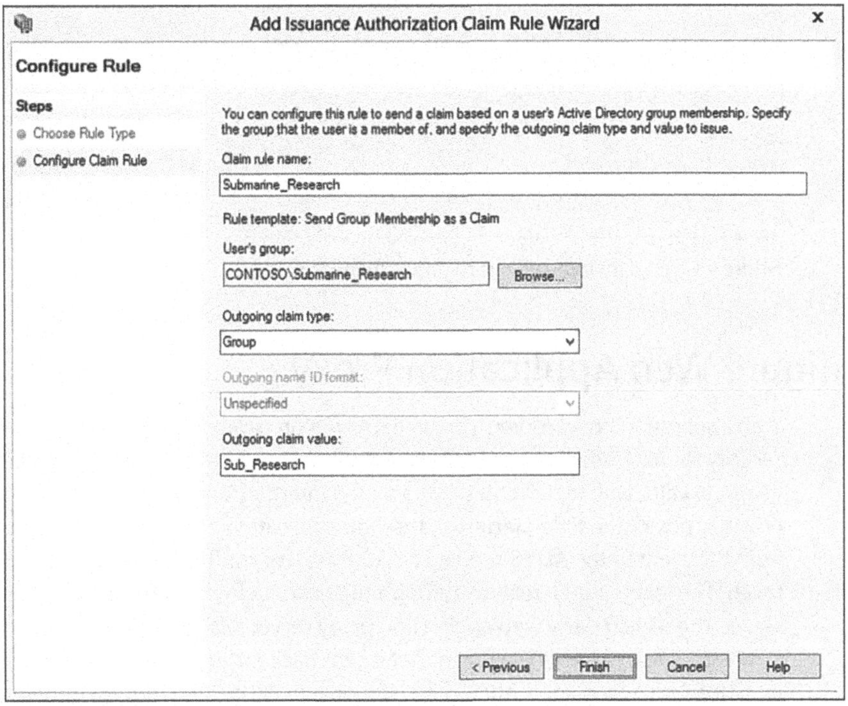

Figure 19-5   Choose a rule type

Claims provider trust claim rules

Claims provider trust rules determine how the relying party filters incoming claims. You can configure these rules by editing the claims provider trust's claim rules. All claims provider trust claim rules are acceptance transform rules. Figure 19-6 shows an incoming claim type related to group membership.

CHAPTER 19

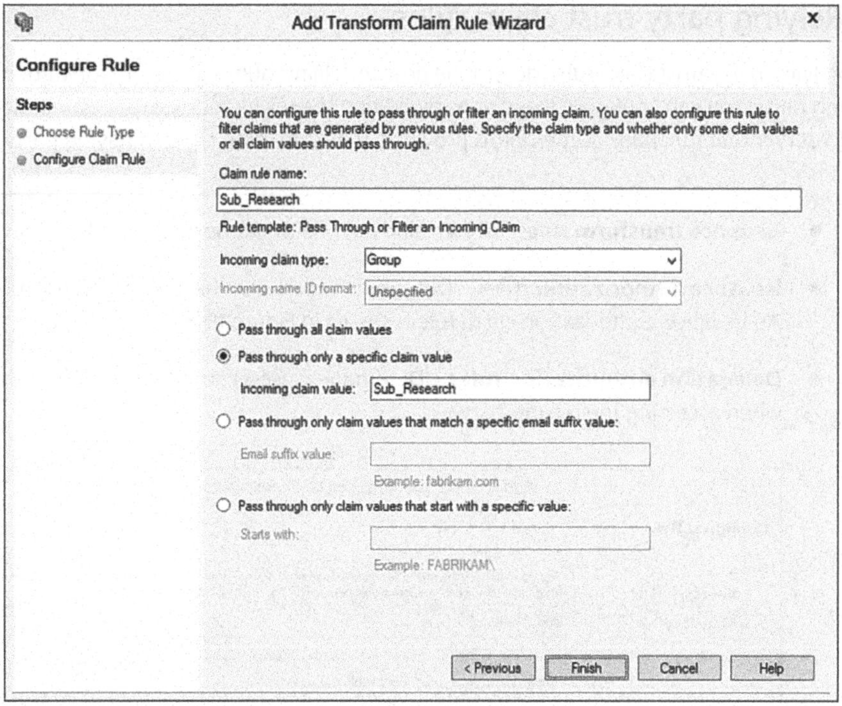

Figure 19-6 Claim type related to group membership

Configure Web Application Proxy

Web application proxy servers can be deployed on perimeter networks as a way to increase security for AD FS deployments. Clients communicate with the AD FS proxy server, which then communicates with federation servers on the internal network. For example, on the claims provider side of the federated trust, the web application proxy forwards authentication data from the client to the AD FS server. The AD FS server confirms the authentication and issues the token. The token is then relayed through the proxy to the relying party web application proxy server. The relying party web application proxy server relays the token to the relying party AD FS server, which issues a new token that is sent back through the proxy to the original client. At no point does a web application proxy server actually create claims or generate tokens. All communication between a web application proxy server and a federation server occurs using the HTTPS protocol.

In Windows Server 2012 and earlier versions of AD FS, the web application proxy server role was performed by an AD FS proxy server. A web application proxy server in Windows Server 2016 and later differs from the AD FS proxy role service available in Windows Server 2012 because it has the following features:

- It is deployed as a Remote Access role service.

- It provides secure remote access to web-based applications hosted on the internal network.

- It functions as a reverse proxy for web-based applications.

- It can be used to publish access to Work Folders.

When deploying a web application proxy server, you need to ensure that the following certificates are present in the server's certificate store:

- A certificate that includes the federation service name. If the web application proxy server must support Workplace Join, the certificate must also support the following subject alternative names:

  - `<federation servicename>.<domain name>`

  - `Enterpriseregistration.<domainname>`

- A wildcard certificate, a subject alternative name certificate, or individual certificates to cover each web application that is accessible through the web application proxy.

- A copy of the certificate that external servers use if you are supporting client certificate preauthentication.

The server hosting the web application proxy role must also trust the certificate authority that issues these certificates. After deploying the web application proxy role service, run the Web Application Proxy Configuration Wizard. Running the wizard involves specifying the federation service name and the credentials of an account that has AD FS administrative privileges, as shown in Figure 19-7.

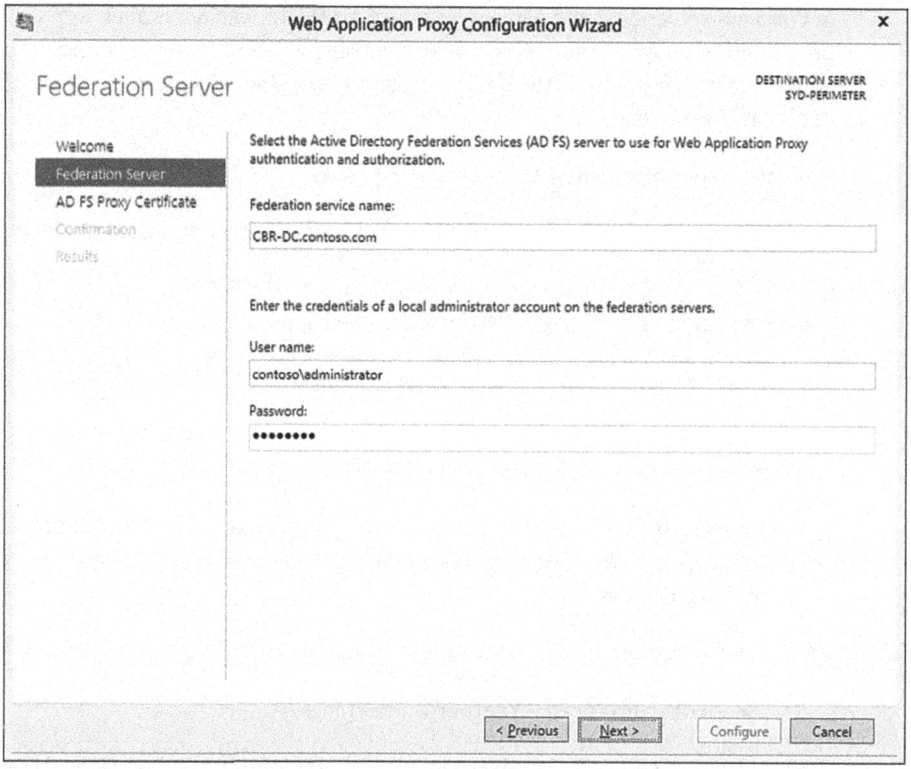

Figure 19-7 Web Application Proxy Configuration

You also need to specify the certificate that the AD FS proxy component of the web application proxy uses, as shown in Figure 19-8. You need to have access to the certificate's private key as well as the public key when configuring the web application proxy's AD FS proxy component.

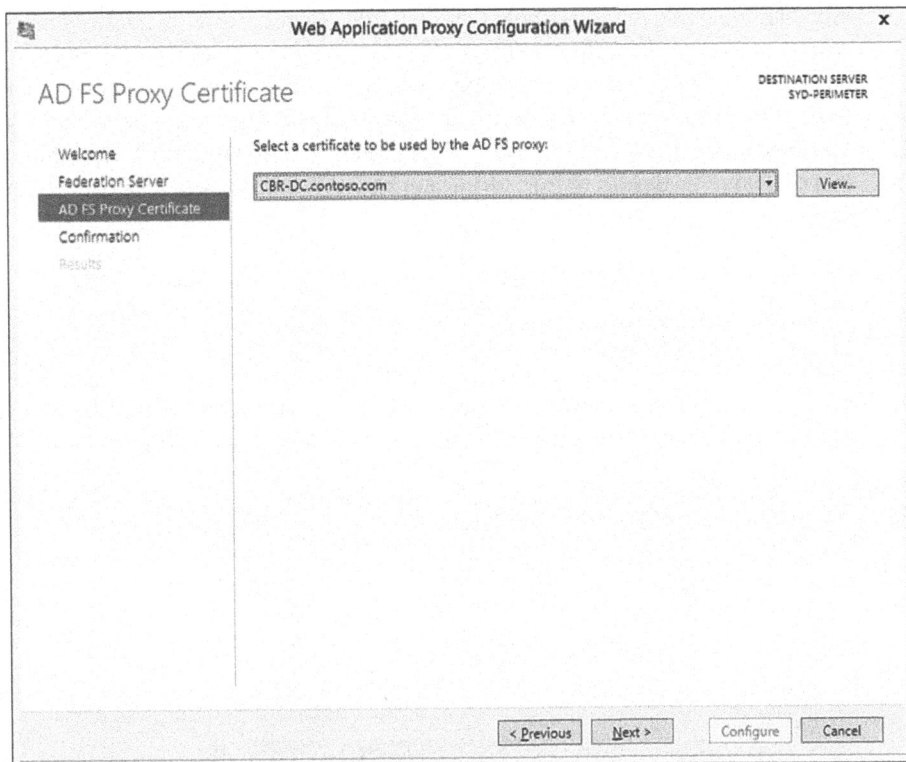

Figure 19-8   AD FS Proxy Certificate

Workplace Join

Workplace Join is a feature available in Windows Server 2012 R2 and later that you can use to allow non-domain-joined devices and computers to access domain resources and claims-enabled applications securely. When a non-domain-joined device or computer performs a Workplace Join, a special object representing the device is created in AD DS. The object stores attributes that describe the device that you can use when configuring access rules.

Workplace Join requires the following components:

- Windows 10 or later, Android 7 or later, or iOS 7 or later devices

- Claims-aware application

- AD FS deployment on an internal network

- Web application proxy deployed on the perimeter network

- Device registration service

Workplace Join also supports single sign-on (SSO). When a user authenticates to access one claims-aware application, that authentication carries over to other claims-aware applications hosted by the organization as well. When supporting Workplace Join, consider acquiring certificates from trusted third-party CAs because the majority of the devices performing Workplace Join are managed by their owners rather than centrally by the IT department, which means that getting those devices to trust certificates from an internal CA requires extra administrative effort.

Enable Workplace Join by running the following Windows PowerShell cmdlets:

```
Initialize-ADFSDeviceRegistration
Enable-ADFSDeviceRegistration
```

After you've enabled Workplace join, you can enable device authentication by editing the Global Authentication Policy through the AD FS console, as shown in Figure 19-9.

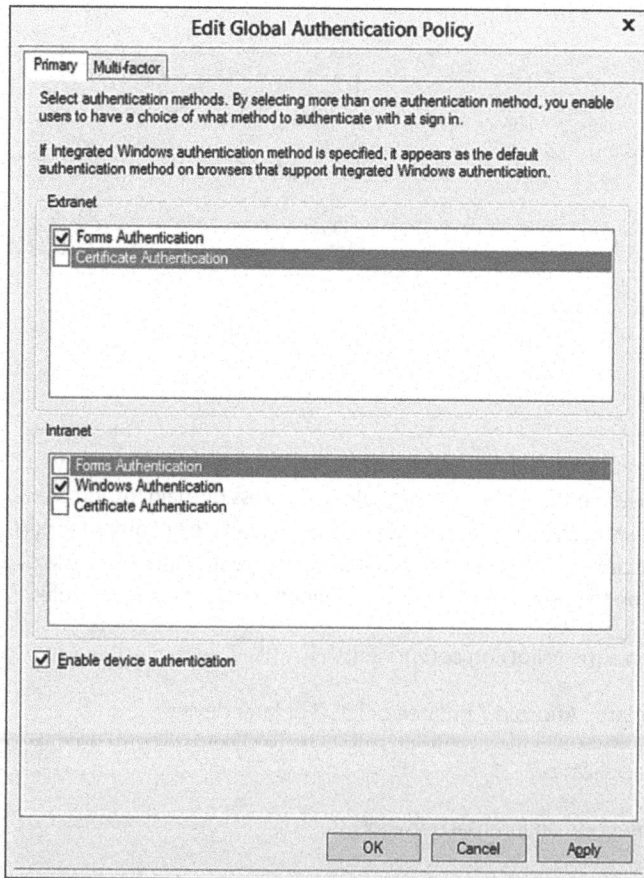

Figure 19-9   Enabling device authentication

Users authenticate by using their UPNs. When configuring Workplace Join, ensure that you configure your organization's external DNS zone with a record that maps *enterpriseregistration. upndomainname.com* (where *upndomainname.com* is the UPN suffix) to the Web Application Proxy server's IP address or the AD FS server that you've configured to support Workplace Join.

Multifactor authentication

AD FS supports multifactor authentication. When you implement multifactor authentication, more than one form of authentication is required. For example, a username, password, and a code from an authenticator application running on a mobile device might be required. You can either configure multifactor authentication in AD FS globally, as shown in Figure 19-10, or on a per-relying party trust basis.

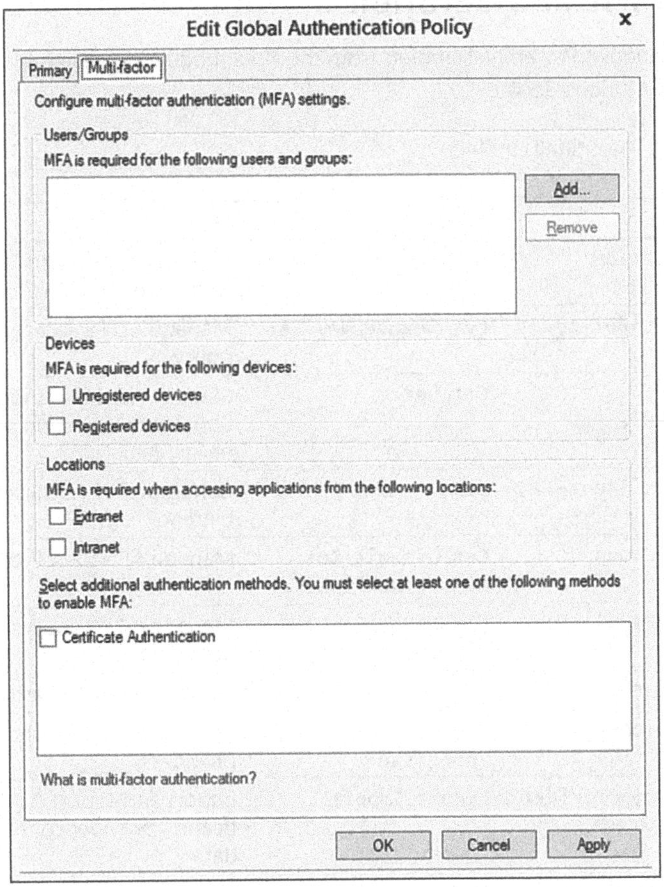

Figure 19-10   Multifactor authentication

You can configure multifactor authentication by using a third-party vendor's product, or you can integrate Microsoft's Azure multifactor authentication service. Azure multifactor authentication allows the following authentication methods:

- **Telephone call**   An automated telephone call is made to the user's registered telephone number. The user enters the data provided in the call when authenticating.

- **Text message**   A text message is sent to the user's registered mobile telephone. The user enters the data provided in the text message when authenticating.

- **Mobile app**   The user installs a mobile authentication app on their mobile device that generates a periodically changing code. The user enters this code when authenticating.

Managing AD FS with PowerShell

You can use the Windows PowerShell cmdlets from the ADFS module, listed in Table 19-1, to manage AD FS on Windows Server.

Table 19-1   AD FS PowerShell cmdlets

Noun	Verbs	Function
ADDeviceRegistration	Initialize	Initializes the Device Registration service config in the forest
AdfsAccessControlPolicy	Get, Remove, New, Set	Manage AD FS access control policy
AdfsAdditional-AuthenticationRule	Get, Set	Manage rules that trigger additional authentication providers to be invoked
AdfsAlternateTlsClient-Binding	Set	Configure TLS certificate client binding
AdfsApplicationGroup	Get, Disable, Set, Remove, New, Enable	Manage AD FS application groups
AdfsApplicationPermission	Grant, Set, Get, Remove	Manage AD FS application permissions
AdfsAttributeStore	Set, Add, Get, Remove	Manage the AD FS attribute store
AdfsAuthenticationProvider	Register, Get, Unregister	Configure AD FS authentication providers
AdfsAuthenticationProvider-ConfigurationData	Export, Import	Import and export AD FS authentication provider configuration data
AdfsAuthenticationProvider-WebContent	Get, Remove, Set	Configure the authentication provider for web content

CHAPTER 19

Noun	Verbs	Function
AdfsAzureMfaConfigured	Get	Get the Azure multifactor authentication configuration
AdfsAzureMfaTenant	Set	Configure an existing Azure multifactor authentication tenant
AdfsAzureMfaTenant-Certificate	New	Configure a new AD FS Azure multifactor authentication tenant certificate
AdfsCertificate	Get, Update, Remove, Set, Add	Configure an AD FS certificate
AdfsCertificateAuthority	Disable, Get, Set	Configure an AD FS certificate authority
AdfsCertSharingContainer	Set	Configure an AD FS certificate-sharing container
AdfsClaimDescription	Remove, Add, Get, Set	Manage claim descriptions
AdfsClaimRuleSet	New	Create a new AD FS claim rule set
AdfsClaimsProviderTrust	Set, Get, Update, Disable, Enable, Remove, Add	Configure an AD FS claims provider trust
AdfsClaimsProviderTrusts-Group	Remove, Get, Add	Configure an AD FS claims provider trusts group
AdfsClient	Remove, Set, Disable, Add, Get, Enable	Configure an AD FS client
AdfsContactPerson	New	Configure a new AD FS contact person
AdfsDeploymentSQLScript	Export	Export an SQL script for AD FS deployment
AdfsDeviceRegistration	Enable, Set, Disable, Get	Configure AD FS device registration
AdfsDeviceRegistration-UpnSuffix	Get, Set, Remove, Add	Configure an AD FS device registration UPN suffix
AdfsEndpoint	Disable, Set, Get, Enable	Manage an AD FS endpoint
AdfsFarm	Install	Install an AD FS farm
AdfsFarmBehaviorLevel	Restore	Restore a farm behavior level to a previous level
AdfsFarmBehaviorLevelRaise	Test, Invoke	Test or perform a farm behavior level raise
AdfsFarmBehaviorLevelRestore	Test	Check whether the prerequisites have been met to restore the existing AD FS farm behavior level

CHAPTER 19

Noun	Verbs	Function
AdfsFarmInformation	Set, Get	View and configure information about the AD FS farm
AdfsFarmInstallation	Test	Performs checks to test whether you can install a new federation server farm
AdfsFarmJoin	Test	Performs checks required before you run the Add-AdfsFarmNode cmdlet to add a computer to a farm
AdfsFarmNode	Remove, Add	Manage AD FS farm nodes
AdfsGlobalAuthentication-Policy	Set, Get	Configure AD FS global authentication policy
AdfsGlobalWebContent	Get, Set, Remove	Configure AD FS global web content
AdfsLdapAttributeToClaim-Mapping	New	Configure AD FS attribute claim mapping
AdfsLdapServerConnection	New	Create a connection to an LDAP server for AD FS
AdfsLocalClaimsProviderTrust	Get, Enable, Disable, Add, Set, Remove	Configure AD FS Local Claims Provider Trust
AdfsNativeClientApplication	Remove, Get, Add, Set	Configure the AD FS client application
AdfsNonClaimsAwareRelying-PartyTrust	Set, Enable, Disable, Add, Remove, Get	Configure a non-claims-aware relying party trust
AdfsOrganization	New	Create a new AD FS organization
AdfsProperties	Set, Get	Configure AD FS properties
AdfsProxyTrust	Revoke	Remove the proxy trust
AdfsRegistrationHosts	Get, Set	Configure AD FS registration hosts
AdfsRelyingPartyTrust	Set, Add, Enable, Update, Disable, Get, Remove	Configure relying party trusts
AdfsRelyingPartyTrustsGroup	Remove, Add, Get	Configure the relying party trust group
AdfsRelyingPartyWebContent	Set, Remove, Get	Manage web content for the relying party
AdfsRelyingPartyWebTheme	Get, Set, Remove	Configure the web theme for the relying party
AdfsSamlEndpoint	New	Create a new AD FS SAML endpoint
AdfsScopeDescription	Add, Remove, Set, Get	Manage the AD FS scope description
AdfsServerApplication	Remove, Set, Get, Add	Manage AD FS server applications

Noun	Verbs	Function
AdfsSslCertificate	Set, Get	Configure AD FS TLS certificates
AdfsSyncProperties	Set, Get	Manage AD FS sync properties
AdfsTrustedFederationPartner	Get, Remove, Add, Set	Manage AD FS trusted federation partners
AdfsWebApiApplication	Get, Remove, Set, Add	Manage AD FS web API applications
AdfsWebApplicationProxy-RelyingPartyTrust	Add, Set, Disable, Get, Remove, Enable	Manage the relying party trust for the web application proxy
AdfsWebConfig	Get, Set	Configure AD FS web customization configuration settings
AdfsWebContent	Import, Export	Import and export properties of all web content objects
AdfsWebTheme	New, Get, Export, Set, Remove	Manage AD FS web themes

Managing Web Application Proxy with PowerShell

You can use the Windows PowerShell cmdlets from the WebApplicationProxy module, listed in Table 19-2, to manage AD FS on Windows Server.

Table 19-2 Web Application Proxy PowerShell cmdlets

Noun	Verbs	Function
WebApplicationProxy	Install	Install the Web Application Proxy role
WebApplicationProxy-Application	Remove, Set, Add, Get	Configure Web Application Proxy applications
WebApplicationProxyAvailable-ADFSRelyingParty	Get	View the Web Application Proxy available in the AD FS relying party configuration information
WebApplicationProxy-Configuration	Get, Set	View and configure Web Application Proxy configuration information
WebApplicationProxyDevice-Registration	Update	Configure AD FS SSL endpoint listeners that correspond to UPN suffixes
WebApplicationProxyHealth	Get	View the health status of the Web Application Proxy
WebApplicationProxySsl-Certificate	Get, Set	Configure the AD FS TLS certificate for the federation server proxy component of the web application proxy

Active Directory Rights Management Services

Active Directory Rights Management Services (AD RMS) provides a way of securing content through encryption and through rules that are applied to the operating system and applications on what actions the user can perform with that content. Dynamic Access Control (DAC) provides a way to dynamically assign access permissions to content based on the content's properties and information about the user and device that are attempting to access the content. If correctly implemented, both technologies can minimize the chance of information that should stay within organizational boundaries finding its way outside of those boundaries.

The DAC and AD RMS features for Windows Server haven't seen development for several editions of Windows Server. It's unlikely that these roles and features will be developed further, as Microsoft's strategy is to gently shepherd customers toward similar cloud services that require a monthly subscription fee. Although they're not under active development, DAC and AD RMS are unlikely to be removed from Windows Server anytime soon, and the versions in Server 2025 will be supported through the late 2030s. As with several other features of the Windows Server operating system, the core necessary functionality is present to accomplish your goals, but the tooling to implement that functionality in production environments isn't as good as it could be.

Increasingly, it's possible to create your own management tools for these services with the assistance of Generative AI. This has led some organizations that are reluctant to pay for cloud services that require a monthly subscription to functionality equivalent to that provided by DAC and AD RMS to build their own interface on top of these robust Windows Server technologies already present in the operating system.

Dynamic Access Control

If you've worked with NTFS permissions for a while, you're most likely aware that they are rarely properly implemented. At first glance, the system seems logical. You create a collection of groups that represent ways of describing a user or computer's place in the organization. You then use those groups to apply permissions to restrict access to files and folders. This is great in theory, but it requires that security groups are kept up to date and that the permissions themselves are accurately configured. In many organizations, the process of ensuring group membership is erratic and piecemeal, with users only being added to groups after they lodge service desk tickets.

Dynamic Access Control (DAC) allows you to configure security using the properties of a user account or a computer account and the properties of the file. For example, you can configure DAC so that only people who have Don Funk as a manager are able to open files that contain the word *Cake*. You can do this by setting up classification rules and claims so that every file is checked to see if it contains the word *Cake*, and if it does, a custom attribute is configured to reflect that status. Another rule can be configured to set permissions on the file so that anyone whose Active Directory user account has the Managed By attribute set to Don Funk has access to open the file. Access is still mediated by NTFS permissions, but those NTFS permissions are configured based on the properties of the file and the accessing user, not using the traditional method of right-clicking the file or parent folder and setting them manually.

DAC has the following requirements:

- **Windows Server 2012 R2 and later with the File Server Resource Manager (FSRM) role service are required.** Both a minimum of Windows Server 2022 R2 and the File Server Resource Manager (FSRM) role service must be installed on the file servers that host files protected through DAC.

- **Windows 8 or later computers are required to support device claims.** Windows 10 will have reached the end of support the year this book is published (though it will be possible to purchase extended support agreements). Unless you have hidden Windows 7 systems you don't know about, you're likely fine here.

- **A Windows Server 2012 or higher domain functional level is required.** Given you're reading this book sometime after mid-2025, you should be at least on Windows Server 2016 functional level and be pushing to move to the Windows Server 2025 domain functional level because you should always run domain controllers with the latest version of Windows Server.

Configuring Group Policy to support DAC

Configuring Active Directory to support DAC requires that you configure a Group Policy that applies to all domain controllers in the domain. You can do this in a policy that applies to the domain or just to domain controllers. To enable support for DAC, enable the KDC Support For Claims, Compound Authentication And Kerberos Armoring policy. You can find this policy in the `Computer Configuration\Policies\Administrative Templates\System\KDC` node.

Configuring user and device claims

Before you can configure access rules, you need to configure claims. Claims are bits of information about users and computers and are usually derived from Active Directory attributes. You can edit Active Directory attributes by using Active Directory Administrative Center as well as by using other tools. DAC supports the following types of claims:

- **User claim**   This is information about the user and can be based on a user account's attributes, such as EmployeeType. You can also use claims related to group membership.

- **Device claim**   This is information about the computer from which the user is accessing the file. For example, you could edit the computer account's Location attribute and set it to Secure. This allows you to configure DAC so a user can access a file from a computer that has the Location attribute set to Secure, but cannot access the same file from another computer that does not have the Location attribute set to Secure.

You create claims in Active Directory Administrative Center by navigating to the Claim Types section under the Dynamic Access Control section. When creating a claim type, select an existing Active Directory attribute as the basis for the claim. In Figure 20-1, you can see that the Department attribute forms the basis of a claim type. When you configure a claim, select whether the claim relates to Users or Computers. You can also specify suggested values to associate with the claim. In the case of a claim related to the Department attribute, this might be a list of departments within your organization.

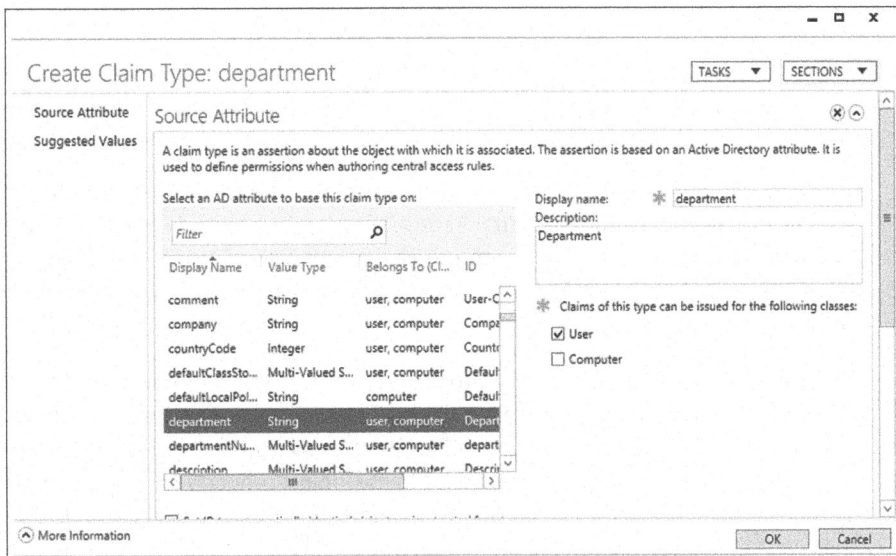

Figure 20-1   Create Claim Type: Department

Configuring resource properties

Resource properties determine the resource attributes that you can use when configuring central access rules. Windows Server ships with a collection of default resource properties, but you can also add extra resource properties based on available attributes. Figure 20-2 shows a custom resource property named Project and two value options, Hovercraft or Submarine. Resource Properties can be assigned to files either manually or automatically by configuring File Server Resource Manager File Classification Rules.

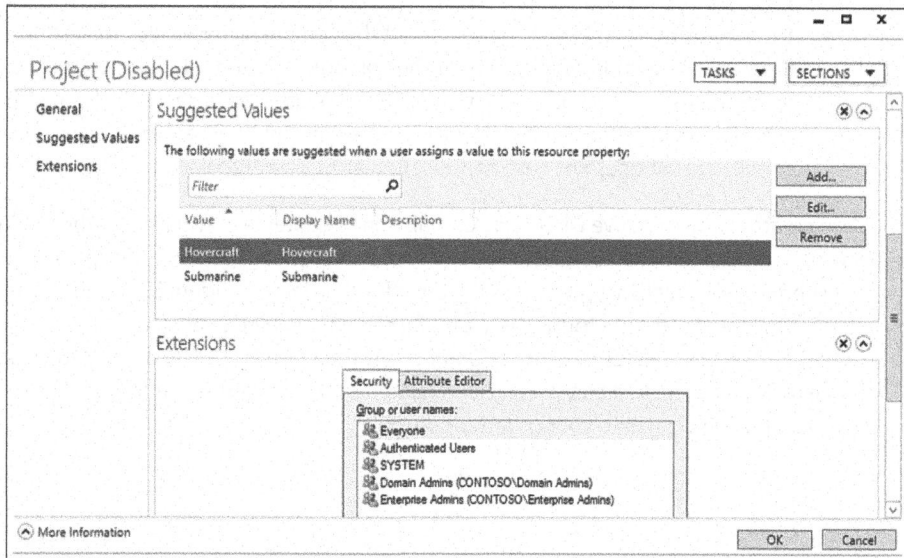

Figure 20-2   Hovercraft project

The Global Resource Property List, shown in Figure 20-3, is a list of all resource properties that you can use when configuring Central Access Rules. You can add and remove these properties as necessary. When you publish a property list through Active Directory, you can then assign these properties to files and folders either manually or automatically using File Server Resource Manager.

You use File Server Resource Manager to apply properties to files through File Classification Rules. You can configure a classification rule to look for a particular string of text in a file and then assign a particular property to that file based on the string. The example in Figure 20-4 shows that the Submarine value is assigned to the Project property for files that meet the classification requirements, the classification requirements in this case being any file that contains the text string submarine.

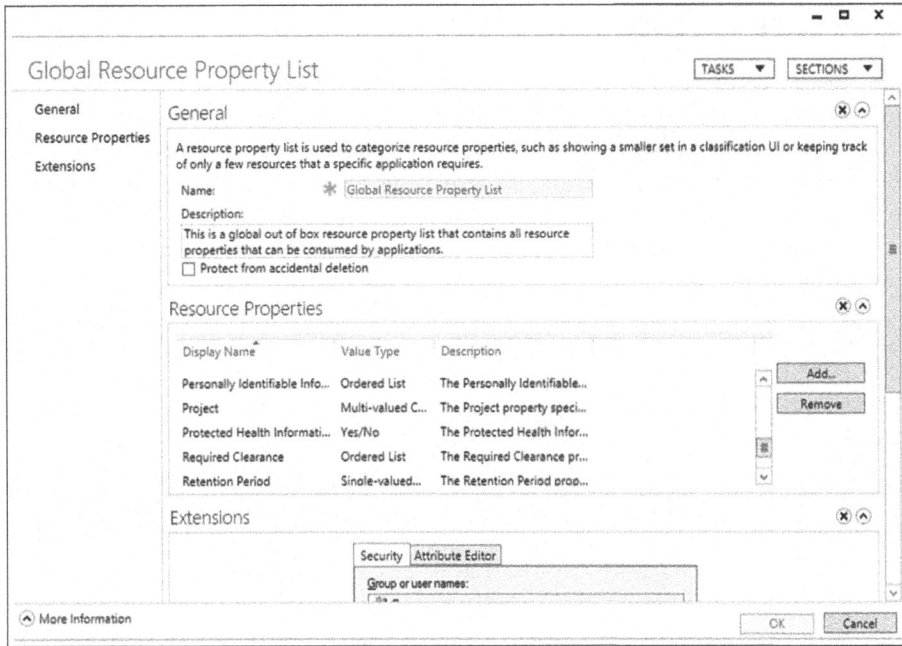

Figure 20-3   Global Resource Property List

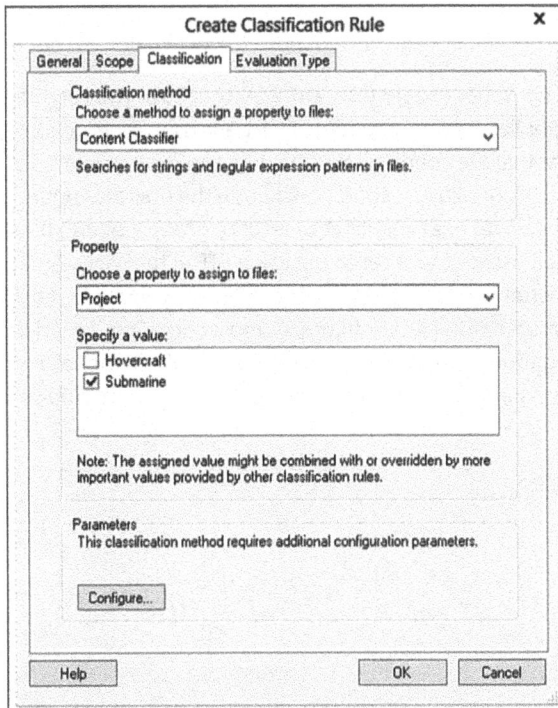

Figure 20-4   Create Classification Rule dialog

Central access rules

Central access rules include a set of permissions and the conditions under which those permissions are applied. For example, in Figure 20-5, the rule applying the permissions spelled out in the permissions entry is applied to the file or folder if the file or folder has the Project resource property set to Hovercraft. You can have multiple conditions in a central access rule. You can, for example, require that the Project resource property be set to Hovercraft and the Confidentiality resource property be set to High for the permissions configured in the permissions entry to be applied.

CHAPTER 20

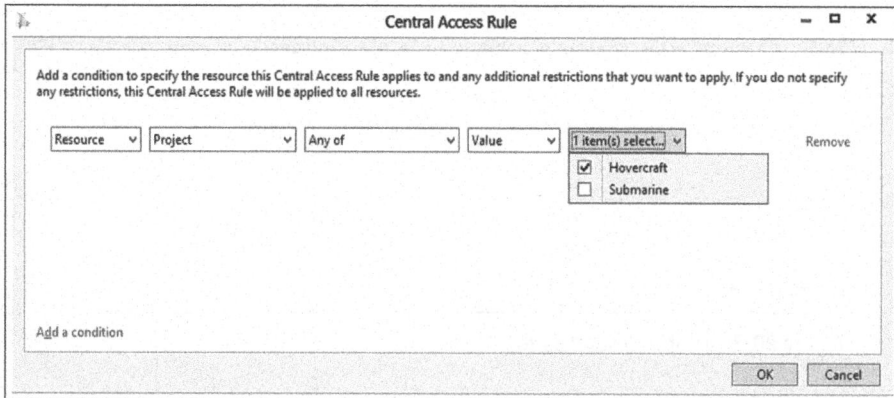

Figure 20-5 Central Access Rule

After you configure the conditions that trigger the Central Access Rule, you can then specify the set of permissions that is applied. Unlike standard NTFS permissions, permission entries allow you to apply permissions that are conditional upon user and device claims. For example, the permissions entry shown in Figure 20-6 is conditional upon the user attempting access to not only be a member of the Hovercraft_Project security group, but also have the EmployeeType attribute in their user account set to the value FTE. If the user's EmployeeType attribute isn't set to FTE, the permissions assigned through the user's Hovercraft_Project group membership are not granted. You can configure multiple conditions based on user and device claims when configuring a permissions entry. For example, in the case of sensitive documents, you might also require that the computer account have an attribute set to indicate that it's a secure computer.

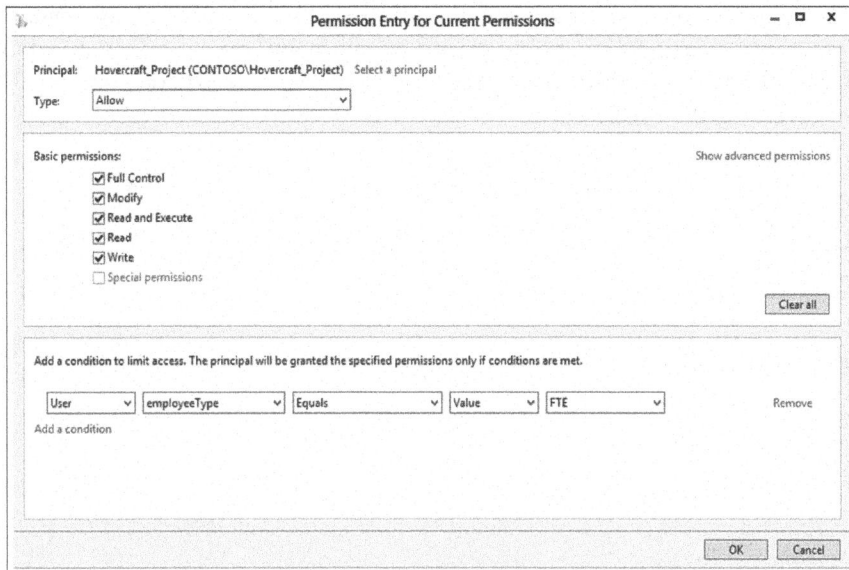

Figure 20-6 Permission Entry for Current Permissions

Central access policies

A central access policy is a collection of central access rules. For example, the Contoso Policy Central Access Policy, shown in Figure 20-7, publishes two central access rules: Research_Projects and Secret_Projects. Only file servers that are within the scope of the central access policy apply the rules that are contained within the policy.

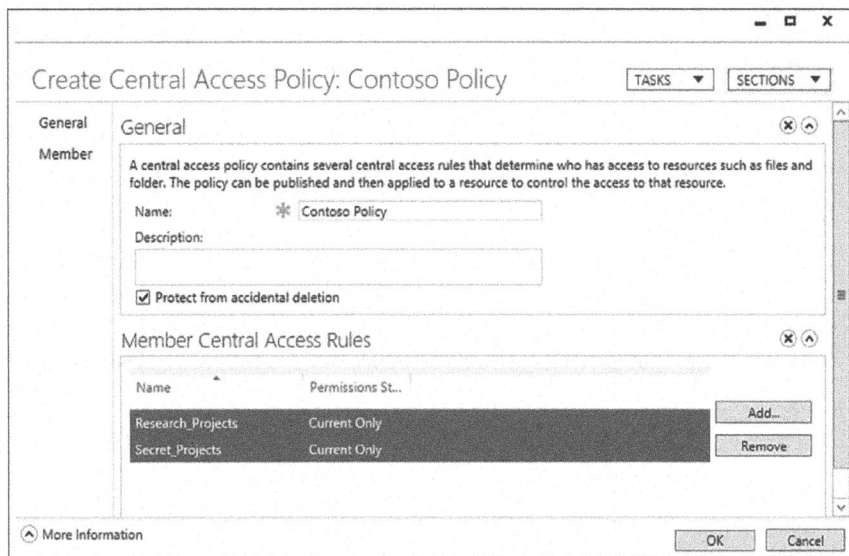

Figure 20-7 Create Central Access Policy: Contoso Policy

You distribute central access policies through Group Policy. You do this by configuring the Manage Central Access Policies policy, which is located in the `Computer Configuration\Policies\Windows Settings\Security Settings\File System` node. This policy is shown in Figure 20-8.

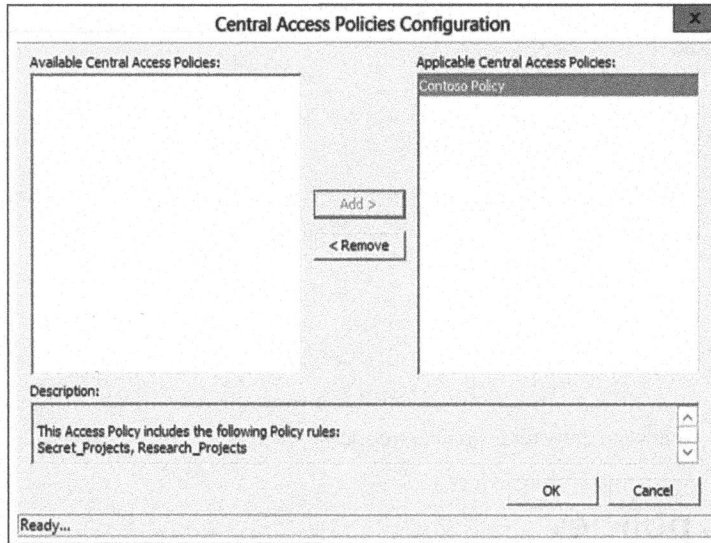

Figure 20-8   Central Access Policies Configuration

Staging

Staging allows you to configure a set of proposed, rather than applied, permissions. You use auditing to determine the results of these staged permissions before implementing them. You must enable auditing through Group Policy to determine the results of staged permissions. The policy you need to enable is the Audit Central Access Policy Staging Properties policy, which is located in the `Computer Configuration\Policies\Windows Settings\Security Settings\Advanced Audit Policy Configuration\Audit Policies\Object Access` node of a Group Policy Object (GPO).

You configure staged permissions in the Proposed area of a Central Access Rule by selecting the Enable Permission Staging Configuration option, as shown in Figure 20-9. You can verify the functionality of the proposed permissions by checking the Security event log. To do this, sign in to the file server that hosts the files and search for events with event ID 4818.

CHAPTER 20

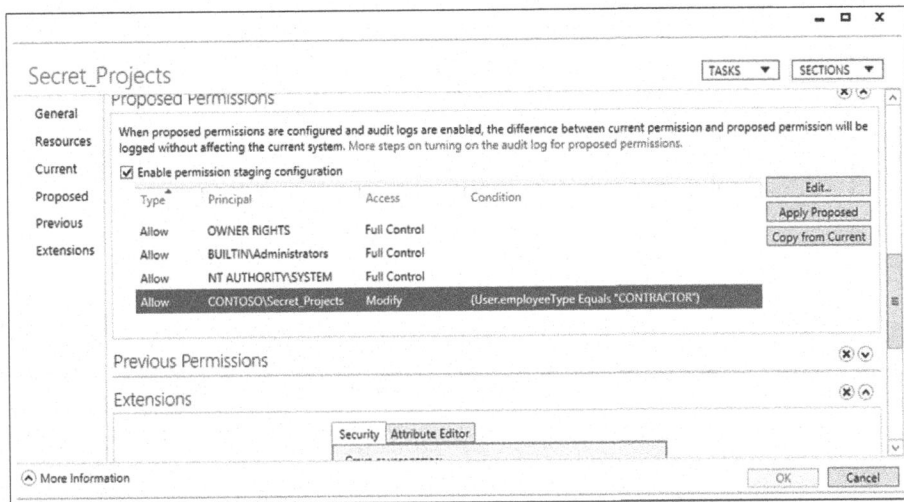

Figure 20-9 Proposed permissions

Access Denied Assistance

Access Denied Assistance is a feature available to Windows clients that provides an informational dialog explaining to users that they're unable to access a file because they don't have appropriate permissions. It's also possible to configure Access Denied Assistance so that an email can be forwarded to the support desk if the help desk's assistance is needed to untangle permissions and allow the user to access a file.

You configure the Access Denied Assistance by configuring the Customize Message For Access Denied Errors policy, as shown in Figure 20-10. This policy is located in the `Computer Configuration\Policies\Administrative Templates\System\Access-Denied Assistance` node of a GPO.

CHAPTER 20

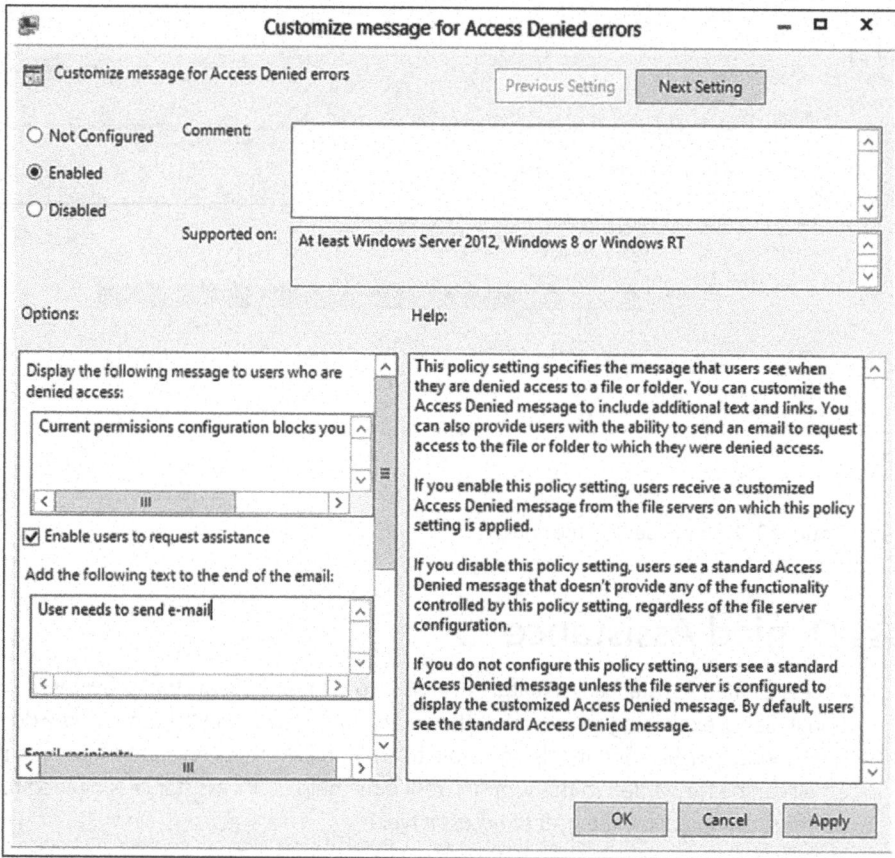

Figure 20-10   Customize Message For Access Denied Errors

Installing AD RMS

AD RMS uses the term "cluster" to describe an AD RMS deployment, even though it has nothing to do with failover clustering or network load balancing. When you deploy AD RMS, you first deploy a root cluster. An AD RMS root cluster is responsible for managing all the AD RMS licensing and certificate traffic for the forest in which it is installed. You should only have one AD RMS root cluster per forest. Organizations that have multiple forests should deploy multiple AD RMS root clusters. After you have deployed a root cluster, you can configure additional licensing-only clusters. Licensing only clusters distribute licenses that clients use to consume and publish content.

Installing AD RMS involves performing the following steps:

1. **Specifying the database that AD RMS uses to store configuration information.**
    You can use a Microsoft SQL Server instance to perform this role or deploy the
    Windows Internal Database. You should only use Microsoft SQL Server in large AD RMS
    deployments. AD RMS can use any supported version of SQL Server.

2. **Specifying a service account.** This account needs to be a domain account, and best practice is to use a specially configured group-managed service account for this role. Using a group-managed service account ensures that the account password is managed by Active Directory and does not need to be manually updated on a periodic basis by an administrator.

3. **Choose a cryptographic mode.** Mode 2 uses RSA 2048-bit keys and SHA-256 hashes. Mode 1 uses RSA 1024-bit keys and SHA-1 hashes. Mode 2 is more secure than mode 1 and is, therefore, the recommended choice.

4. **Specify Cluster Key Storage.** This determines where the cluster key is stored. The default is to have the key stored within AD RMS, although you can also use a cryptographic service provider (CSP) if one is available. When you use a CSP, you must perform manual key distribution when adding additional AD RMS servers.

5. **Specify a cluster key password.** This password is used to encrypt the cluster key. You need to provide this password when joining additional AD RMS servers to the cluster and when recovering an AD RMS cluster from backup.

6. **Input the cluster address.** This is a website address in FQDN format that is usually hosted on the AD RMS server. Best practice is to configure an SSL certificate with the FQDN of the AD RMS server. Although it's possible to specify a non-SSL-protected address, doing so removes the ability to use AD RMS with identity federation. The cluster address and port cannot be altered after you deploy AD RMS.

7. **Specify a Licensor certificate name.** This is the name used with the licensor certificate and should represent the certificate's functionality.

8. **Determine whether to register the service connection point (SCP) in Active Directory.** The SCP allows domain members to locate the AD RMS cluster automatically. A user account must be a member of the Enterprise Admins security group to register an SCP. SCP registration can occur after AD RMS is deployed if the account used to deploy AD RMS is not a member of this security group.

AD RMS certificates and licenses

AD RMS uses four specific types of certificates. These certificates have the following functions:

- **Server licensor certificate (SLC)**   This certificate is created when you install the AD RMS role on the first server in the AD RMS cluster. This certificate is valid for 7,150 days and is used to issue the following certificates and licenses:

  - SLCs to additional servers that join the cluster

  - Rights account certificates

- Client licensor certificates

- Publishing licenses

- Use licenses

- Rights policy templates

- **AD RMS machine certificate**   This certificate identifies a trusted device. The machine certificate public encrypts Rights Account Certificate private keys, and the machine certificate private key decrypts Rights Account Certificates.

- **Rights account certificate (RAC)**   This certificate identifies a user. AD RMS can only issue RACs to AD DS users whose user accounts are configured with an email address. By default, an RAC has a validity of 365 days. Temporary RACs are issued when a user accesses content from a device that is not a member of a trusted forest and has a validity of 15 minutes.

- **Client licensor certificate**   This certificate allows AD RMS–protected content to be published to computers that cannot connect directly to the AD RMS cluster. These certificates are tied to a user's RAC. Other computer users are unable to publish AD RMS–protected documents until a new connection to the AD RMS cluster is established from the computer.

In addition to the four certificate types, AD RMS uses two license types:

- **Publishing license**   A publishing license determines the rights that apply to AD RMS content. This license contains the content key, URL, and digital signature of the AD RMS server.

- **End-user license**   The end-user license allows a user to access AD RMS–protected content. An end-user license is issued per user, per document. End-user licenses are cached by default, although it's possible to disable caching, so that an end-user license must be obtained each time the user attempts to access protected content.

AD RMS templates

Rights Policy Templates allow you to apply rights policies to documents. When an author creates a document or sends an email message, the author can apply a template to that document. It's also possible to use File Server Resource Manager to automatically apply templates to documents based on the properties of those documents, such as the document having a particular resource property or containing a specific text string.

Rights Policy Templates are created by using the AD RMS Management Console. When creating a template, you can enable the following rights on a per-user group or per-user basis, with any right not granted unavailable to the user:

- **Full Control** The user has full control over the AD RMS–protected content.

- **View** Gives the user the ability to view the AD RMS–protected content.

- **Edit** Allows the user to modify the AD RMS–protected content.

- **Save** Allows the user to save the AD RMS–protected content.

- **Export (Save as)** Allows the user to use the save as function with the AD RMS–protected content.

- **Print** Allows the user to print the AD RMS–protected content.

- **Forward** Used with Microsoft Exchange, allows the user to forward a protected message.

- **Reply** Used with Microsoft Exchange, allows the user to reply to a protected message.

- **Reply All** Used with Microsoft Exchange, allows the recipient of a protected message to use the Reply All function.

- **Extract** Allows a user to copy data from the AD RMS–protected content.

- **Allow Macros** Allows the user to use macros with the AD RMS–protected content.

- **View Rights** Allows the user to view rights assigned to the AD RMS–protected content.

- **Edit Rights** Allows the user to modify rights assigned to the AD RMS–protected content.

Figure 20-11 shows the rights assigned to the `submarine_project@contoso.com` group. You can assign different rights to multiple groups. If a user is a member of more than one group, the rights are cumulative.

When configuring an AD RMS Template, you can configure content expiration settings. Content expiration settings allow you to have content expire either on a certain date or after a certain number of days. The example in Figure 20-12 shows content expiration configured to expire 14 days after content publication. An additional setting allows you to configure the Use License Expiration, which allows you to configure how often a user must connect to the AD RMS cluster to obtain a new license to access the content.

CHAPTER 20

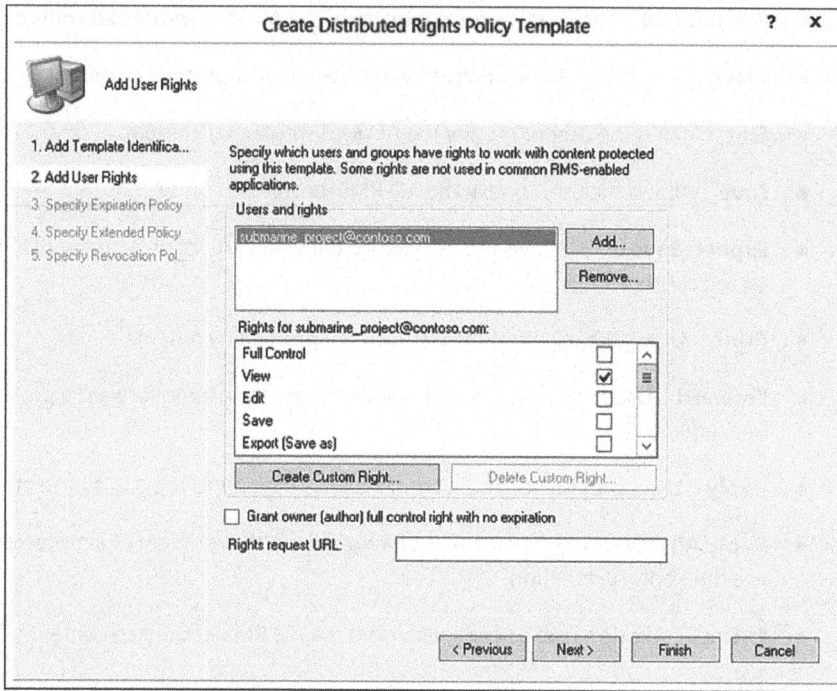

Figure 20-11   Create Distributed Rights Policy Template

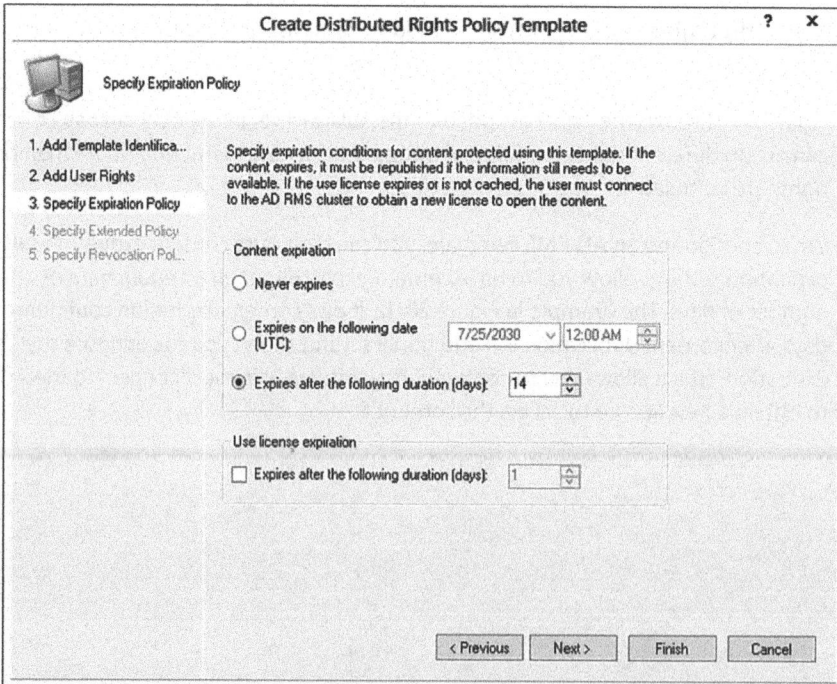

Figure 20-12   Create Distributed Rights Policy Template

The Extended Policy settings, as shown in Figure 20-13, allow you to configure whether AD RMS content can be viewed using a browser add-on and whether a new license must be obtained each time content is consumed.

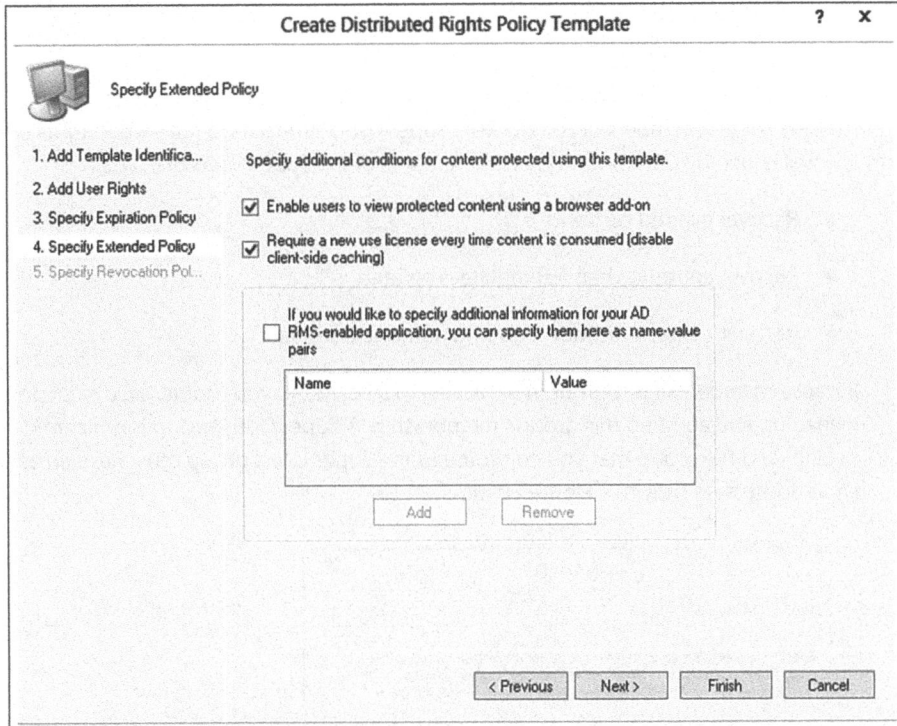

Figure 20-13   Configure browser and content settings

Inside Out

FSRM to apply templates

FSRM can classify files according to content, location, or other metadata, and then use these classifications to apply RMS rights policy templates. This method is the simplest way to automate the template application.

AD RMS Administrators and Super Users

There are three separate local groups on an AD RMS server that you can add users to when you want to assign them privileges within AD RMS:

- **AD RMS Enterprise Administrators**   Members of this group can perform any task within AD RMS, including enabling the AD RMS Super Users group.

- **AD RMS Template Administrators**   Users who are members of this group can configure and manage AD RMS templates.

- **AD RMS Auditors**   Users who are members of this group are not able to make modifications to AD RMS server settings and templates, but can view the properties of the server and templates.

The AD RMS Super Users group is a special group that you can configure and enable on the AD RMS server. Members of the AD RMS Super Users group have full owner rights over all use licenses issued by the AD RMS cluster. Members of the Super Users group can

- Recover expired content

- Recover content when a template is deleted

- Recover content without requiring author credentials

Because members of this group have access to all content, you should have strict policies about managing and auditing this group's membership. A Super Users group is not configured by default, and the group that you configure as the Super Users group must have an associated email address, as shown in Figure 20-14.

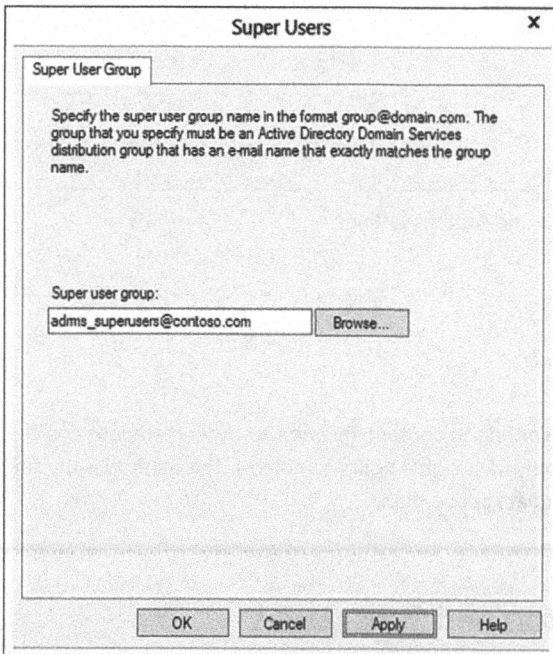

Figure 20-14   Super User Group

Trusted User Domains and Trusted Publishing Domains

Trusted User Domains (TUDs) allow you to configure an AD RMS cluster to manage requests for CLCs for users that have been issued RACs from a different AD RMS cluster. For example, if an organization has two separate Active Directory forests, and each forest has its own AD RMS deployment, you'd configure Trusted User Domains so that clients from one forest can issue CLCs to clients with RACs issued from the other forest. TUDs can be one-way or bidirectional. When configuring TUDs, you must export the TUD from the partner before importing the TUD locally.

Trusted Publishing Domains (TPDs) allow the AD RMS cluster in one forest to issue end-user licenses to content published with licenses issued from an AD RMS cluster in another forest. You must export the TPD file and have it imported by the partner AD RMS cluster before the AD RMS cluster in the partner forest can issue end-user licenses to local AD RMS clients.

Exclusion policies

Exclusion policies allow you to deny specific entities the ability to interact with AD RMS. You can configure exclusions on the basis of application, user, and lockbox version. Exclusion works in the following ways:

- **User Exclusion**   You can exclude a user based on email address or based on the public key assigned to the user's RAC. Use email-based exclusions for users in the forest and public key-based exclusions for external users.

- **Lockbox Exclusion**   Lockbox exclusion allows you to exclude specific client operating systems. Each version of the Windows operating system has a specific lockbox identity. If you want to block clients running Windows 7 from interacting with AD RMS, configure an exclusion where the minimum lockbox version to the version available is Windows 8.

- **Application Exclusion**   This allows you to exclude specific applications from interacting with AD RMS. You must specify the application file name, the minimum version, and the maximum version.

When you configure an exclusion, the exclusion only applies to new certificate or licensing requests. Licenses and certificates that were issued during the exclusion period still exclude the application, user, or lockbox version. If you remove an exclusion, the removal only applies to new licenses or certificates.

Apply AD RMS templates automatically

You can use File Server Resource Manager to apply AD RMS templates to files automatically. You do this by performing the following general steps:

1. Create a new file management task with an appropriate name related to the template.

2. On the Scope tab, set the scope of the task to the folders that host the files to which you want to apply the AD RMS template.

3. On the Condition tab, specify the condition that allows the rule to recognize the files that you want to apply the AD RMS template to. For example, you can create a rule that is triggered if the file contains the text "SECRET."

4. On the Action tab of the Create File Management Task dialog, shown in Figure 20-15, specify RMS Encryption as the action type and the AD RMS template that you want to apply to the file.

5. On the Schedule tab, configure how often the file management task should run and whether it should classify only new files or periodically attempt to reclassify existing files.

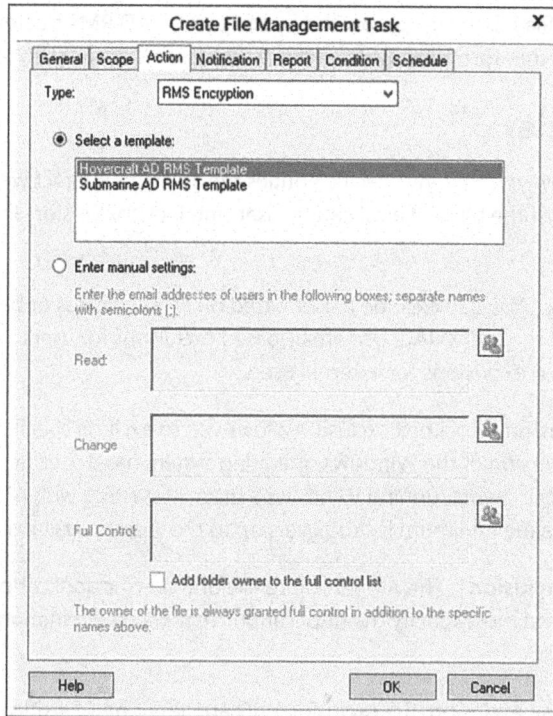

Figure 20-15   Create File Management Task

Managing AD RMS with Windows PowerShell

AD RMS PowerShell cmdlets are available in the ADRMS and ADRMSADMIN Windows PowerShell modules. The functionality of these cmdlets is described in Table 14-1.

Table 14-1 AD RMS PowerShell cmdlets.

Noun	Verbs	Function
ADRMS	Install, Uninstall, Update	Install, remove, and update AD RMS after the binaries have been installed on the target server
RmsCertChain	Get	Generates a report detailing information on the certificate chain of a specific user request on the AD RMS server
RmsCertInfo	Get	Generates a report about a specific certificate used in a user request for the AD RMS cluster
RmsChildCert	Get	Returns all child certificates from a parent certificate used in a user request to an AD RMS cluster
RmsCluster	Update	Updates the RMS cluster information
RmsCryptoMode2	Initialize	Configure an RMS cluster to transition to cryptographic mode 2
RmsEncryptedIL	Get	Determine the use-license information from an issuance license associated with a user request
RmsMfgEnrollment	Install, Update, Uninstall	Configure Microsoft Federation Gateway service enrollment
RmsMfgSupport	Install, Uninstall	Install or remove a Microsoft Federation Gateway configuration
RmsReportDefinition-Language	Export	Export AD RMS report definition files
RmsRequestInfo	Get	Generate a report on a specific user request
RmsSvcAccount	Set, Get	Configure the RMS service account
RmsSystemHealthReport	Get	View the RMS system health
RmsTPD	Export, Import	Import and export trusted publishing domain information
RmsTUD	Import, Export	Import and export a trusted user domain
RmsUserRequestReport	Get	View information about an RMS user request

CHAPTER 20

Routing and remote access

Today, we expect to be able to access work resources whether we're in the office, in an airline lounge, in a coffee shop, or at home on the couch. Remote access technologies allow authorized users to make a connection from their laptops and tablet computers to resources on their organization's internal network from any location on the public Internet.

In this chapter, you learn about Windows Server remote access technologies and how you can leverage those technologies to enable remote access to your organization's internal network. You learn how each technology is appropriate for a specific use case and why you might want to use several technologies to support all of the clients in your organization.

Remote Desktop Gateway

Remote Desktop (RD) Gateway allows users to make a connection from a host on the Internet to a host on the local area network using the Remote Desktop Connection (RDC) Client software. Remote Desktop Client software is included in all currently supported versions of Windows and is also available for Mac OS X computers, as well as iOS and Android devices. Although RD Gateway is typically used to connect to Remote Desktop Session Host servers or VDI virtual machines, you can also configure it to connect to desktop workstations. This allows a user to use an RD Gateway server to connect to their work PC from their laptop computer without having to connect through a VPN.

RD Gateway servers, like any other remote access servers, need to be placed on perimeter networks and need to have at least one public IP address. Connections to RD Gateway servers occur by using the Remote Desktop Protocol (RDP) over the HTTPS protocol. When configuring the external firewall, network administrators need to allow access on port 443 from hosts on the Internet to the RD Gateway server. Connections from the RD Gateway server to RDP hosts on the internal network occur on port 3389.

RD Gateway servers don't need to be members of an Active Directory domain, but it is substantially more difficult to configure the RD Resource Authorization Policy (RAP) to limit connections to specific hosts without such membership. You can accomplish something similar through firewall rules by restricting access through network addresses. However, the drawback to domain membership is the risk involved in placing a domain-joined computer on a perimeter network and configuring the internal firewall to support the configuration.

RD Gateway connection and resource policies

RD Gateway connection and resource policies allow you to specify under what conditions users are able to connect to an RD Gateway server. RD Connection Authorization Policies (CAPs) can be stored on the RD Gateway server or in a Central RD CAP Store. Some of the benefits of using a Central CAP Store are that the same CAPs can apply to multiple RD Gateway servers without having to reproduce them on each server, and that they can also be centrally updated as needed. However, if your organization only has a single RD Gateway server, there is no need to use a central RD CAP Store.

On an RD Gateway server that is not a member of a domain, you might have to create a separate local user group with local user accounts to allow users to authenticate against the RD Gateway server prior to authenticating against the session target.

To create an RD Gateway CAP, perform the following general steps:

1. In the RD Gateway Manager console, right-click Connection Authorization Policies, click Create New Policy, and then click Custom.

2. On the New RD CAP dialog, enter a policy name on the General tab.

3. On the Requirements tab, select Password or, if your organization supports it, Smart Card. Next, click Add Group to specify the User Group to which you want to grant access to RD servers through the RD Gateway server. You should create a separate security group for users you want to grant access to, which makes granting and revoking access just a matter of removing the user's account from this group.

4. On the Device Redirection tab, choose whether you want to enable device redirection for all client devices or disable it for specific types, such as volumes, clipboards, and plug-and-play devices. You also can restrict connections to only clients that enforce RD Gateway device redirection policies. You might do this if you want to block access to clients running non-Microsoft operating systems.

5. On the Timeouts tab, you can enable an idle timeout, which disconnects users who aren't interacting with their session, and a session timeout, which limits all sessions, including active sessions. Click OK to finish creating the policy.

After you have configured an RD CAP, you need to configure an RD Resource Authorization Policy (RAP). An incoming connection must meet the conditions specified in one RD CAP and one RD RAP before it can be successfully established. To create an RD RAP, perform the following steps:

1. In the RD Gateway Manager console, right-click Resource Authorization Policies, click Create New Policy, and then click Custom.

2. On the New RD RAP page, enter the policy name.

3. On the User Groups page, click Add to add the user groups that the policy applies to.

4. On the Network Resource page, choose between the following options:

   - Select An Active Directory Domain Services Group
   - Select An Existing RD Gateway-Managed Group
   - Allow Users To Connect To Any Network Resource

5. On the Allowed Ports page, choose to restrict connections from the RD Gateway server to port 3389, which is the default, to another specific port, or through any port. Unless the RD servers use alternate ports, the default is appropriate.

Configuring server settings

RD Gateway servers need a TLS certificate to encrypt and authenticate the RDP over an HTTPS connection. As is always the case with TLS certificates, obtaining a certificate from a trusted, third-party certification authority (CA) may cost money and time (At the time of writing, the most popular CA provides TLS certificates free of charge), but this investment means that any client can use the RD Gateway without problems. Using an internal certificate is cheaper because it isn't necessary to purchase a certificate, but it does require you to configure RD Gateway clients to trust the issuing authority. Given the organizational cost to support the distribution of an internal or self-signed certificate, it's usually just easier to obtain a certificate from a trusted, third-party CA.

Configuring clients to use RD Gateway

You can configure clients to use an RD Gateway server either by manually configuring the server's address by editing the advanced properties of Remote Desktop Connection, as shown in Figure 21-1, or by configuring the server's address through Group Policy.

Figure 21-1   RD Gateway Server Settings

Three RD Gateway-related Group Policy items can be configured to simplify the process of ensuring that clients connect to the correct server. These policy items are located in the `User Configuration\Policies\Administrative Templates\Windows Components\Remote Desktop Services\RD Gateway` node of a standard GPO. These policies can be used to configure the following:

- **Set RD Gateway Authentication Method**   This policy allows you to force a user to use a particular authentication method, but it also allows you to set a default authentication method that the user can override. The options are as follows:

  - Ask For Credentials; Use NTLM Protocol

  - Ask For Credentials; Use Basic Protocol

  - Use Locally Logged-In Credentials

  - Use Smart Card

  - Negotiate Protocol

- **Enable Connection Through RD Gateway**   When this policy is enabled, the client attempts to connect through the configured RD Gateway server if it's unable to establish a connection to the specified target of the RD Connection. Set this policy and the RD Gateway Address Policy to ensure that domain clients connect through RD Gateway when they aren't connected to the internal network.

- **Set RD Gateway Server Address**   This policy allows you to configure the RD Gateway server address, either on the basis of an IP address or a fully qualified domain name (FQDN). This policy should be set in conjunction with the Enable Connection Through RD Gateway policy to ensure that remote domain clients transparently connect through the RD Gateway server without having to configure anything themselves.

Virtual private networks

Windows Server supports four separate virtual private network (VPN) technologies: PPTP, L2TP/IPsec, SSTP, and IKEv2. By default, PPTP and L2TP/IPsec are disabled in Windows Server 2025 but can be manually enabled if required. If you're performing an in-place upgrade to Windows Server 2025 of an existing remote access server which is configured to allow PPTP and L2TP/IPsec connections, those protocols will be enabled after the upgrade completes.

Inside OUT

VPN certificates

If you're using VPN protocols that rely on certificates generated by an internal enterprise CA, ensure that a Certificate Revocation List (CRL) Distribution Point (CDP) or Online Responder is accessible to clients on the Internet. Remember that clients need to be able to check the revocation status of certificates, which is difficult if the CDP is only accessible to clients on the internal network. You can deploy a CRL DP on the perimeter network or host it in the cloud, which is more common today.

IKEv2 Always On VPN protocol

The IPsec Tunnel Mode with Internet Key Exchange version 2 (IKEv2) VPN protocol was introduced with the release of Windows 7 and Windows Server 2008 R2. Starting with Windows 10 and Windows Server 2016, Microsoft introduced Always On VPN, a new VPN platform that can use IKEv2/IPsec among other protocols, but also includes broader capabilities beyond the protocol itself. The main benefit of Always On VPN is its capability to allow automatic reconnection without requiring reauthentication when the connection is disrupted. Automatic reconnection can occur even if the client's connection address changes and reconnection is possible for up to eight hours. For example, imagine that a user is connected to the internal network using an Always On connection through a laptop computer's cellular modem and then boards an airplane and connects to the airplane's WiFi. Under an Always On scenario, the connection is automatically reestablished without requiring the user to manually reauthenticate, even though the connection method, from cellular network to airplane WiFi, has changed. Connections only have to be reestablished when a user puts the computer into hibernation mode.

Always On/IKEv2 has the following features:

- Supports IPv6

- Enables VPN reconnect

- Supports EAP and computer certificates for client authentication

- Does not support PAP or CHAP

- Only supports MS-CHAPv2 with EAP

- Supports data origin authentication, data integrity, replay protection, and data confidentiality

- Uses UDP port 500

To configure Always On VPN server running Windows Server, you need to do the following:

1. Deploy an enterprise CA.

2. Create a new certificate template based on the IPsec template. You need to modify the application policies of this template to ensure that it supports the IP security IKE intermediate policy and Server Authentication certificate.

3. Install a certificate generated from this template on the VPN server.

4. Ensure that at least one Certificate Revocation List Distribution Point is accessible to clients on the Internet. You can place this CRL DP on the perimeter network or host it in the cloud.

5. Ensure that all clients trust the enterprise CA that issued the VPN server's certificate.

Windows clients running the Windows 8 operating system or later attempt to establish an Always On VPN session before they try SSTP or L2TP/IPsec. If those options are unsuccessful, the client falls back to PPTP.

More Info

Always On VPN

You can find out more about Always On VPN at *https://learn.microsoft.com/ Windows-server/remote/remote-access/tutorial-aovpn-deploy-setup.*

SSTP VPN protocol

Some locations block the ports that some VPN protocols use. The advantage of the SSTP VPN protocol is that it allows computers that might not normally be able to establish a remote access connection to do so through TCP port 443, which is usually used for TLS connections to websites. While it doesn't have the performance of other protocols, SSTP almost always works, even if it has to traverse NAT, firewalls, and proxy servers. However, SSTP doesn't work if there is a web proxy in place that requires manual authentication. For example, if you're in a hotel and you have to sign on to the WiFi network through a browser, you need to perform this action before you attempt to establish an SSTP connection.

SSTP has the following requirements:

- You need to install a TLS certificate on the VPN server.

- All clients need to trust the CA that issued the TLS certificate.

- You need to configure the TLS certificate with a name that matches the FQDN that maps to an IP address associated with the external network interface of the VPN server.

- The Certificate Revocation List Distribution Point of the CA that issued the TLS certificate needs to be accessible to clients on the Internet.

L2TP/IPsec protocols

Layer Two Tunneling Protocol with IPsec (L2TP/IPsec) is a VPN protocol that has been used with Windows Server operating systems and clients since the release of Windows 2000. It works with almost every Windows and third-party operating system. L2TP/IPsec is disabled by default in Windows Server 2025 but can be manually enabled if required.

When configuring L2TP/IPsec, you need to ensure that you have configured a CA that is able to automatically issue certificates to connecting clients. As is the case with other VPN protocols, the CA needs to be trusted by the client and the CDP must be accessible to clients making connections from the Internet. You would primarily deploy L2TP/IPsec as a way of providing secure access to clients that are not able to leverage the simpler-to-implement Secure Socket Tunneling Protocol (SSTP) VPN protocol. Although L2TP/IPsec usually requires you to deploy digital certificates, it's possible, with a special configuration, to get L2TP/IPsec to work with preshared keys.

PPTP VPN protocol

PPTP is the oldest VPN protocol available in Windows Server and is also the least secure. This protocol is disabled by default in Windows Server 2025. It's most often used when organizations need to support clients running unsupported operating systems, such as Windows XP, or in situations where it isn't possible to deploy the certificate infrastructure required to implement

L2TP/IPsec. PPTP connections provide data confidentiality but do not provide data integrity or data origin protection. This means that captured data can't be read, but you also can't be sure that the transmitted data was the same data sent by the client.

Inside OUT

PPTP

PPTP requires no additional configuration beyond setting up the VPN server and ensuring that port 1723 is open for clients from the Internet. Just remember, PPTP has been around for a long time and isn't a secure VPN protocol.

VPN authentication

Although Windows Server supports many protocols that have been in use for some time, these protocols are often less secure than more recently developed protocols. Windows Server supports the following protocols, listed from most to least secure:

- **Extensible Authentication Protocol-Transport Level Security (EAP-TLS)**   Use this protocol with Smart Cards or digital certificates. You can only use this protocol if you are using RADIUS authentication or if the remote access server performing authentication is domain-joined.

- **PEAP (Protected EAP)**   Encapsulates EAP inside a TLS tunnel. Supports inner methods like MS-CHAPv2 or EAP-TLS. More compatible with client devices than raw EAP-TLS.

- **EAP-MS-CHAPv2**   Common inner method for PEAP. Vulnerable like MS-CHAPv2, but protected by TLS tunnel.

- **Microsoft Challenge Handshake Authentication Protocol version 2 (MS-CHAPv2)**   Provides mutual authentication, which means that not only is the user authenticated, but the service that the user is connecting to is also authenticated. Allows for the encryption of the authentication process and the session.

- **Challenge Handshake Authentication Protocol (CHAP)**   Authentication data is encrypted through MD5 hashing. The data is not encrypted.

- **Password Authentication Protocol (PAP)**   This protocol does not encrypt authentication data, meaning that if the authentication is captured, credentials can be recorded.

Deploying a VPN server

To configure a Windows Server computer that has one network card connected to the perimeter network, which is accessible to clients on the Internet, and a second network card that is connected to the internal network to support VPNs, perform the following general steps:

1. Ensure that the prospective VPN server is connected to the Active Directory domain and log in with an account that is a Domain Admins group member.

2. Open an elevated PowerShell prompt and enter the following commands:

    ```
    Install-WindowsFeature -IncludeAllSubfeature RemoteAccess
    ```

3. Open the Routing And Remote Access console, right-click the server name, and click Configure And Enable Routing and Remote Access. This opens the Routing And Remote Access Server Setup Wizard. Click Next.

4. On the Configuration page, select Remote Access (Dial-Up Or VPN) and then click Next.

5. On the Remote Access page, select VPN and then click Next.

6. On the VPN Connection page, select the network connection that is connected to the Internet and then click Next.

7. On the IP Address Assignment page, choose between assigning IP addresses automatically from an existing scope or from a specified range of addresses.

8. On the Manage Multiple Remote Access Servers page, select No, Use Routing And Remote Access To Authenticate Connection Requests, click Next, and then click Finish.

Disable VPN protocols

By default, Windows Server supports SSTP and IKEv2 remote access connections. If you want to limit incoming connections to a specific protocol or disable an existing protocol, you need to edit the port properties related to that protocol. If you don't disable a specific protocol, clients might use that protocol to connect to the VPN server. To configure which VPN protocols are available, perform the following general steps:

1. Open the Routing and Remote Access console, right-click the Ports node under the VPN server, and then click Properties.

2. On the Ports Properties dialog, select the VPN protocol for which you want to limit connections, and then click Configure.

3. On the Configure Device dialog, set the Maximum Ports to 1 and ensure that the Remote Access Connections (Inbound Only) item is not selected. Click OK.

Enable VPN protocols

To enable a disabled VPN protocol, such as L2TP/IPsec, perform the following general steps:

1. Open the Routing and Remote Access console, right-click the Ports node under the VPN server, and then click Properties.

2.   On the Ports Properties dialog, select the VPN protocol for which you want to allow connections, and then click Configure.

3.   On the Configure Device dialog, set the Maximum Ports to 128 (or a number you choose) and ensure that the Remote Access Connections (Inbound Only) item is selected. Click OK.

Granting Access to a VPN server

If you only have a small number of users, you can grant access to those users on an individual basis by editing their user account properties in Active Directory Users And Computers. To grant access to an individual user, choose Allow access under Network Access Permission on the Dial-In tab of the user's Account Properties.

The default setting for network access for access to a Windows Server VPN server is for it to be controlled through a Network Policy Server (NPS) network policy. To be granted access, a user must meet the conditions of a connection request policy and a network policy. A connection request policy includes type of access, time of access, and which authentication protocols are available. A network policy can be as simple as specifying that a particular user group has access.

When you install a VPN server, a default connection request policy called Microsoft Routing And Remote Access Service Policy is created. You can view the policy's properties under the `Policies\Connection Request Policies` node of the Network Policy Server console on the VPN server. To configure this policy, perform the following steps:

1.   Open the Network Policy Server console on the VPN server.

2.   Expand the `Policies\Connection Request Policies` node. Right-click Microsoft Routing And Remote Access Service Policy and then click Properties.

3.   On the Conditions tab, verify that the day and time restrictions match those that you want to enforce for the remote access policy. You can also use this tab to add conditions to the policy. Clients must meet all specified conditions, so keep in mind that the more conditions you add, the fewer clients the policy applies to. Conditions that you can add include the following:

 - **User Name**   Specifies a specific HCAP username.

 - **Access Client IPv4 Address**   Specifies the RADIUS client IPv4 address.

 - **Access Client IPv6 Address**   Specifies the RADIUS client IPv6 address.

 - **Framed Protocol**   Specifies the protocol used for framing incoming packets, such as Point-to-Point Protocol (PPP) or Serial Line Internet Protocol (SLIP).

- **Service Type**   Limits clients to a specific service, such as Point-to-Point protocols.

- **Tunnel Type**   Restricts clients to a specific tunnel type, such as PPTP, L2TP, and SSTP.

- **Day and Time Restrictions**   Specifies when connections can be active.

- **Calling Station ID**   Specifies the Network Access Server telephone number.

- **Client Friendly Name**   Specifies the RADIUS client name.

- **Client IPv4 Address**   Specifies the RADIUS client IPv4 address.

- **Client IPv6 Address**   Specifies the RADIUS client IPv6 address.

- **Client Vendor**   Specifies the RADIUS client vendor.

- **Called Station ID**   Specifies the NAS identification string or telephone number.

- **NAS Identifier**   Specifies the NAS identification string.

- **NAS IPv4 Address**   Specifies the IPv4 address of NAS.

- **NAS IPv6 Address**   Specifies the IPv6 address of NAS.

- **NAS Port Type**   Specifies the RADIUS client access type, such as ISDN, VPN, IEEE 802.11 wireless, etc.

4. Settings are a set of categories that are required. You can select from the following:

   - **Authentication Methods**   This setting enables you to specify which protocols clients can use to connect to the VPN server. The VPN server attempts to use the most secure protocol first and then, in order of most to least secure, attempts less secure protocols until it reaches the least secure protocol supported by the policy.

   - **Authentication**   This setting determines whether the VPN server performs authentication or whether authentication credentials are passed to another server.

   - **Accounting**   This setting enables you to record authentication information to a log file or SQL server database. Recording this information gives you a record of which people have gained access through VPN connections.

   - **Attribute, RADIUS Attributes Standard & Vendor Specific**   These settings are only necessary if you're placing the VPN server into an existing RADIUS infrastructure.

Inside OUT
Default conditions and settings

In most situations, the default conditions and settings are likely to be adequate. Most administrators are just worried about ensuring that clients have remote access and are less concerned about whether a client is coming from a particular IPv6 address. Many of the available conditions are really only appropriate for site-to-site links rather than client VPN links. Because most organizations use dedicated hardware devices for site-to-site VPN links, this topic is not covered in this book.

After you ensure that the details of the connection request policies meet your needs, you can configure a network policy. Network policies are useful when you want to give remote access to a large number of users but do not want to configure access on a per-account basis. To create a new network policy that allows this access, perform the following general steps:

1. Open the Network Policy Server console. Right-click the Policies\Network Policies node and then click New. The Specify Network Policy Name And Connection Type dialog opens.

2. Enter a name for the policy, set the Type of Network Access Server dropdown to Remote Access Server (VPN-Dial Up), and then click Next.

3. On the Conditions page, click Add | Add Conditions. The conditions that you can add are as follows:

   - **Windows Groups**   Limits access to user or computer groups

   - **Machine Groups**   Limits access to members of the specified computer group

   - **User Groups**   Limits access to members of the specified user group

   - **Day And Time Restrictions**   Restricts when the policy can be used for access

   - **Access Client IPv4 Address**   Specifies the network address of the client

   - **Access Client IPv6 Address**   Specifies the network address of the client

   - **Authentication Type**   Defines acceptable authentication protocols

   - **Allowed EAP Types**   Defines allowed EAP authentication protocols

   - **Framed Protocol**   Specifies the protocol used for framing incoming packets, such as Point-to-Point Protocol (PPP) or Serial Line Internet Protocol (SLIP)

- **Service Type**   Limits clients to a specific service, such as Point-to-Point protocols

- **Tunnel Type**   Restricts clients to a specific tunnel type, such as PPTP, L2TP, and SSTP

- **Calling Station ID**   Specifies the Network Access Server telephone number

- **Client Friendly Name**   Specifies the RADIUS client name

- **Client IPv4 Address**   Specifies the RADIUS client IPv4 address

- **Client IPv6 Address**   Specifies the RADIUS client IPv6 address

- **Client Vendor**   Specifies the RADIUS client vendor

- **MS-RAS Vendor**   Specifies the Network Access Server (NAS) vendor

- **Called Station ID**   Specifies the NAS identification string or telephone number

- **NAS Identifier**   Specifies the NAS identification string

- **NAS IPv4 Address**   Specifies the IPv4 address of NAS

- **NAS IPv6 Address**   Specifies the IPv6 address of NAS

- **NAS Port Type**   Specifies RADIUS client access type, such as ISDN, VPN, IEEE 802.11 wireless, and so on

After you have configured the network policy, it should be possible to establish a VPN connection.

LAN routing

You can configure Windows Server to function as a network router in the same way that you configure traditional hardware devices to perform this role. LAN routing is often used with virtual machines to connect private or internal virtual machine networks with an external network. To perform the LAN routing function, Windows Server must have two or more network adapters. Windows Server supports using Key Routing Information Protocol v2 (RIP) for route discovery. You can also use the Routing And Remote Access console to configure static routes.

To configure Windows Server to function as a router, perform the following steps:

1. From the Tools menu of Server Manager, click Routing And Remote Access.

2. In the Routing And Remote Access console, click the server you want to configure. In the Action menu, click Configure And Enable Routing And Remote Access.

3. On the Welcome page of the Routing And Remote Access Server Setup Wizard, click Next.

4. On the Configuration page, select Custom Configuration and click Next.

5. On the Custom Configuration page, select LAN Routing and click Next.

6. Click Finish. In the Routing And Remote Access dialog, click Start Service.

If you want to enable IPv6 routing, perform the following additional steps:

1. In the Routing And Remote Access console, right-click the server and click Properties.

2. On the General tab of the server properties dialog, select IPv6 Router to enable the server to also route IPv6 traffic.

Network Address Translation (NAT)

Network Address Translation (NAT) enables you to share an Internet connection with computers on an internal network. In a typical NAT configuration, the NAT server has two network interfaces, where one network interface is connected to the Internet and the second network interface connects to a network with a private IP address range. Computers on the private IP address range can then establish communication with computers on the Internet. It is also possible to configure port forwarding so all traffic that is sent to a particular port on the NAT server's public interface is directed to a specific IP address/port combination on a host on the private IP address range.

To configure a computer running the Windows Server operating system with two network adapters to function as a NAT device, ensure one adapter has connectivity to the Internet and perform the following steps:

1. Open the Routing And Remote Access console from the Tools menu in Server Manager.

2. Select the server you want to configure. On the Action menu, click Configure And Enable Routing And Remote Access.

3. On the Welcome To The Routing And Remote Access Server Setup Wizard, click Next.

4. On the Configuration page, select Network Address Translation (NAT) and click Next.

5. On the NAT Internet Connection page, select the network interface that connects to the Internet and click Next.

6. Click Finish to close the Routing And Remote Access Server Setup Wizard.

You can configure NAT properties by right-clicking the NAT node in the Routing And Remote Access console and by clicking Properties. Using the properties dialog, you can configure address assignments for hosts on the private network, as shown in Figure 21-2. You can use the Name Resolution tab to determine how name resolution works on the private network. It enables clients to communicate using single names or FQDNs rather than IP addresses.

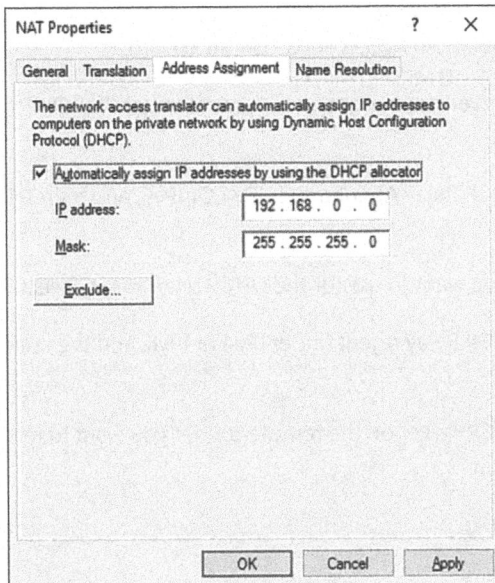

Figure 21-2   NAT address assignment

DHCP Relay Agent

The DHCP relay agent allows you to relay DHCP requests from a logical network or VLAN without a DHCP server to a subnet that does. Windows Server supports the deployment of a DHCP relay agent as part of the Routing and Remote Access role. When configuring the DHCP relay agent component of Routing and Remote Access, you specify the IP address of the DHCP server that is used to provision IP addresses. Because configuring Routing and Remote Access to support a DHCP relay agent is more complicated than deploying a new DHCP server, some organizations simply opt to deploy a new DHCP server and manage the relevant scopes through IPAM. Alternatively, most organizations configure routers to forward DHCP requests, and in those environments, it isn't necessary to configure a DHCP relay agent.

To configure Windows Server with the RRAS role to function as a DHCP Relay Agent on a computer that has the remote access role installed, perform the following steps:

1. Open the Routing and Remote Access console, right-click the server, and then select Configure And Enable Routing and Remote Access to open the Routing And Remote Access Server Setup Wizard.

2. In the Welcome to the Routing and Remote Access Server Setup Wizard, select Next.

3. Under Configuration, select LAN Routing, and then select Next.

4. In Custom Configuration, select VPN Access, and then select Next to open the Completing The Routing And Remote Access Server Setup Wizard.

5. In the left pane, expand the server name, right-click General under IPv4 Or IPv6, and select New Routing Protocol.

6. In the left pane, right-click DHCP Relay Agent under IPv4 Or IPv6, and then select New Interface.

7. Select the network interface you want to use for the DHCP relay agent. Select OK.

8. In the left pane, right-click DHCP Relay Agent under IPv4 or IPv6, and then select Properties.

9. Enter the IP address of the DHCP server on the remote subnet you want to relay DHCP requests to, and then select Add.

10. Select OK to save your settings.

DirectAccess

DirectAccess is an always-on remote access solution, which means that if a client computer is configured with DirectAccess and connects to the Internet, a persistent connection is established between that computer and the organization's internal network. One big advantage of DirectAccess is that it does not require users to directly authenticate. The client computer determines that it is connected to the Internet by attempting to connect to a website that is only accessible from the internal network. If the client determines that it is on a network other than the internal network, it automatically initiates a connection to the internal network.

When determining its network connection status, the client first attempts to determine whether it's connected to a native IPv6 network. If the client has been assigned a public IPv6 address, it can make a direct connection to the organization's internal DirectAccess servers. If the client determines that it isn't connected to a native IPv6 network, it attempts to create an IPv6 over IPv4 tunnel using the 6to4 and then Teredo technologies. If connections cannot be established using these technologies, it attempts to use IP-HTTPS, which is similar to the SSTP protocol discussed earlier, except that it encapsulates IPv6 traffic within the HTTPS protocol.

When a connection is established, authentication occurs using computer certificates. These computer certificates must be preinstalled on the client, but the benefit of this requirement is that user intervention is not required. Authentication occurs automatically, and the connection occurs seamlessly.

Another big advantage of DirectAccess is that it supports remote client management through a feature named Manage Out. Manage Out enables remote management functionality for

DirectAccess clients, allowing administrative tasks, including tasks that in the past could only be performed on computers on a local area network, to be performed on clients.

The primary drawback of DirectAccess is that it requires a domain-joined computer that runs one of the following operating systems:

- Windows 7 Enterprise Edition

- Windows 7 Ultimate Edition

- Windows 8 Enterprise Edition

- Windows 8.1 Enterprise Edition

- Windows 10 Enterprise Edition

- Windows 11 Enterprise Edition

DirectAccess clients are configured through GPOs. The configuration GPO is automatically cre-ated through the DirectAccess setup process. This GPO is filtered, so it only applies to the secu-rity group that you've designated to host the DirectAccess clients.

Unlike the version of DirectAccess that shipped with Windows Server 2008 R2, DirectAccess in Windows Server 2012 and later does not require two consecutive public IPv4 addresses, nor is it necessary to have an Active Directory Certificate Services server deployed on the internal network.

DirectAccess topologies

DirectAccess supports multiple deployment topologies. You don't have to deploy the DirectAc-cess server with a network adapter directly connected to the Internet. Instead, you can integrate the DirectAccess server with your organization's existing edge topology. During your DirectAc-cess server deployment, the Remote Access Server Wizard asks you which of the topologies reflects your server configuration. The differences between them are as follows:

- **Edge**   This is the traditional DirectAccess deployment method. The computer hosting the server has two network adapters. The first network adapter is connected directly to the Internet and has been assigned one or more public IPv4 addresses. The second net-work adapter connects directly to the internal trusted network.

- **Behind An Edge Device (With Two Network Adapters)**   In this type of deployment, the DirectAccess server is located behind a dedicated edge firewall. This configuration includes two network adapters. One of the network adapters on the DirectAccess server is connected to the perimeter network behind the edge firewall. The second network adapter connects directly to the internal trusted network.

CHAPTER 21

- **Behind An Edge Device (With A Single Network Adapter)**   In this type of deployment, the DirectAccess server has a single network adapter connected to the internal network. The edge firewall passes traffic to the DirectAccess server.

DirectAccess server

The DirectAccess server is a domain-joined computer running Windows Server 2012 or later that accepts connections from DirectAccess clients on untrusted networks, such as the Internet, and provides access to resources on trusted networks. The DirectAccess server performs the following roles:

- Authenticates DirectAccess clients connecting from untrusted networks

- Functions as an IPsec tunnel mode endpoint for DirectAccess traffic from untrusted networks

Before you can configure a computer running Windows Server 2012 or later to function as a DirectAccess server, you must ensure that it meets the following requirements:

- The server must be a member of an Active Directory domain.

- If the server is connected directly to the Internet, it must have two network adapters: one that has a public IP address and one that is connected to the trusted internal network.

- The DirectAccess server can be deployed behind a NAT device, which limits DirectAccess to use IP over HTTPS (IP-HTTPS).

- A server connected to the Internet only requires a single public IPv4 address. However, Two-Factor Authentication, using either a Smart Card or a One-Time Password (OTP), requires two consecutive public IPv4 addresses.

- The DirectAccess server can also host a VPN server. This functionality was not present in the Windows Server 2008 R2 version of DirectAccess.

- You can configure DirectAccess in a network load-balanced configuration of up to eight nodes.

- The TLS certificate installed on the DirectAccess server must contain an FQDN that resolves through DNS servers on the Internet to the public IP address assigned to the DirectAccess server or to the gateway through which the DirectAccess server is published.

- The TLS certificate installed on the DirectAccess server must have a Certificate Revocation List (CRL) distribution point that is accessible to clients on the Internet.

Inside OUT

DirectAccess TLS certificate

You should strongly consider obtaining the TLS certificate for your organization's DirectAccess server from a public CA. If you obtain the certificate this way, you don't have to worry about publishing the CRL from your internal certificate services deployment to a location that is accessible to the Internet. Using a trusted third-party CA ensures that the CRL is available to clients on the Internet.

A DirectAccess implementation also relies on the following infrastructure being present:

- **Active Directory domain controller**   DirectAccess clients and servers must be members of an Active Directory domain. By necessity, when you deploy a domain controller, you also deploy a DNS server. Active Directory, due to its basic nature, also makes Group Policy available.

- **Group Policy**   When you configure DirectAccess, the setup wizard creates a set of Group Policy Objects (GPOs) that are configured with the settings you choose in the wizard. They apply to DirectAccess clients, DirectAccess servers, and servers that you use to manage DirectAccess.

Prepare DNS servers by removing the ISATAP name from the global query block list. You must take this step on all DNS servers that are hosted on computers running Windows Server operating systems. To complete this step, remove ISATAP from the `GlobalQueryBlockList` value on the `Computer\HKEY_LOCAL_MACHINE\SYSTEM\CurrentControlSet\Services\DNS\Parameters` hive of the registry, so that it contains only the `wpad` entry, as shown in Figure 21-3. After making this configuration change, you must restart the DNS server.

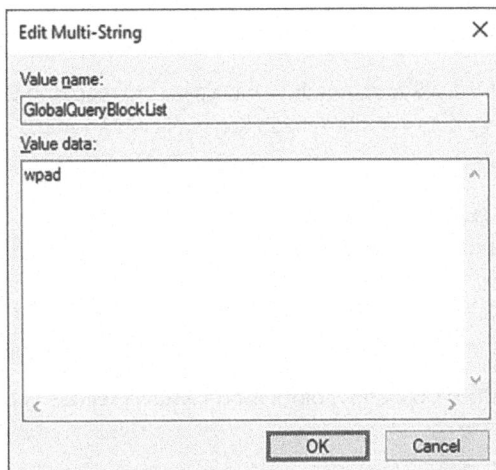

Figure 21-3   GlobalQueryBlockList registry entry

As an alternative to editing the registry, you can also remove ISATAP from the DNS global query block list by issuing the following command on each DNS server and restarting the DNS Server service:

```
Dnscmd /config /globalqueryblocklist wpad
```

Network Location Server

The Network Location Server (NLS) is a specially configured server that enables clients to determine whether they are on a trusted network or an untrusted network. The NLS server's only function is to respond to specially crafted HTTPS requests. When the client determines that it has a connection to any network, it sends this specially crafted HTTPS request. If there is a response to this request, the client determines that it is on a trusted network and disables the DirectAccess components. If there is no response to this request, the client assumes that it is connected to an untrusted network and initiates a DirectAccess connection.

DirectAccess clients are informed of the NLS's location through Group Policy. You don't have to configure these policies manually because they're created automatically when you use the DirectAccess Setup Wizard. Any server that hosts a website and has an SSL certificate installed can function as the NLS. You should ensure that the NLS is highly available because if this server fails, it causes all clients that are configured for DirectAccess on the trusted network to assume that they are on an untrusted network.

Configuring DirectAccess

After you understand the infrastructure requirements, configuring DirectAccess is straightforward. To configure DirectAccess, perform the following steps:

1. Create a security group in Active Directory and add all of the computer accounts for computers that are DirectAccess clients. This security group can have any name, but a name such as DirectAccess_Clients makes it easy to remember why you created it.

2. Ensure that you configure DNS with the following information:

   - The externally resolvable DNS zone needs to have a record mapping the FQDN of the DirectAccess server's external interface to the public IPv4 address of the DirectAccess server.

   - If you use a certificate issued by your organization's CA, ensure that a DNS record exists for the CRL location.

   - The internal DNS zone needs a record mapping the name of the NLS to an IP address.

   - Remove ISATAP from the global query block list on all DNS servers in the organization.

3. If you use your organization's CA, you must configure an appropriate certificate template, as well as deploy a CRL distribution point in a location that can be accessed by clients on the Internet. The certificate template can be a duplicate of the Web Server Certificate Template. You can use this certificate for both the NLS's TLS certificate and the IP-HTTPS certificate for the DirectAccess server. If you don't use your organization's CA to issue certificates, you can use certificates from a public CA for the NLS and the DirectAccess server.

4. Configure firewall rules for all hosts on the trusted network that should be accessible to DirectAccess clients so that they enable inbound and outbound ICMPv6 echo requests. You can configure these rules in a GPO that applies to hosts that DirectAccess clients can access. The rules should have the following properties:

- **Rule Type** Custom

- **Protocol Type** ICMPv6

- **Specific ICMP Types** Echo Request

5. Install the Remote Access role on the computer that functions as the DirectAccess server.

6. Open the Remote Access console and then choose between running the Getting Started Wizard and the Remote Access Setup Wizard. The Getting Started Wizard enables administrators to quickly deploy DirectAccess by requiring only a minimal amount of information. The Remote Access Setup Wizard requires more detailed responses but enables administrators to customize their deployment. The rest of this procedure deals with the Remote Access Setup Wizard.

7. The Configure Remote Access page of the Configure Remote Access Wizard enables you to choose between deploying DirectAccess and VPN, deploying DirectAccess only, or deploying VPN only.

8. If you select Deploy DirectAccess Only, you are provided with the Remote Access Setup diagram. This diagram involves a series of steps that enable you to configure the DirectAccess server, clients, and infrastructure. There are four steps:

- Step 1: Remote Clients

- Step 2: Remote Access Server

- Step 3: Infrastructure Servers

- Step 4: Application Servers

CHAPTER 21

Step 1: Remote Clients

The Step 1: Remote Clients section of Remote Access Setup enables you to configure which computers function as DirectAccess clients. When you click the Configure button in the Step 1 area, a three-page wizard appears that enables you to configure the following settings:

1. Choose Deploy Full DirectAccess For Client Access And Remote Management or Deploy DirectAccess For Remote Management Only. If you choose the first option, the people using DirectAccess clients can access internal network resources when they have an active Internet connection. If you choose the second option, you can perform management tasks on the computer when it's connected to the Internet, but the user can't access internal resources.

2. Select which security groups containing computer accounts you want to enable for DirectAccess. On this page, you can choose Enable DirectAccess For Mobile Computers Only and Use Force Tunneling. When you enable force tunneling, computers designated as DirectAccess clients connect through the remote access server when they connect to both the Internet and the internal trusted network.

3. On the Network Connectivity Assistant (NCA) page, you can configure connectivity information for clients, such as providing the DirectAccess connection name, the helpdesk's email address, and whether DirectAccess clients use local name resolution.

Step 2: Remote Access Server

The Step 2: Remote Access Server section of the Remote Access Setup diagram has a three-page wizard that enables you to do the following:

1. Configure the network topology and specify the public name or IPv4 address that clients use to connect to DirectAccess. The topology options are Edge, Behind Edge (Two Network Adapters), and Behind Edge (Single Network Adapter), which were discussed in the DirectAccess topology section of this chapter.

2. On the Network Adapters page, verify the network adapter configuration. You can also choose which certificate to use to authenticate IP-HTTPS connections. The certificate you choose should be a typical SSL certificate that uses an FQDN that clients use for connections. You can choose to use a self-signed certificate, although this is not recommended except on test deployments.

3. On the authentication page, choose whether you want to use Active Directory or two-factor authentication. You can also configure authentication to use computer certificates, but when you do this, you must specify the CA that the computer certificates must be issued from.

Step 3: Infrastructure Servers

After you have configured the remote access clients and the remote access server, the next step is to configure the infrastructure servers. The Infrastructure Server Setup Wizard takes you through the following steps:

1. On the first page, specify the location of the NLS by using the server's URL, and if you are specifying a separate server, remember to use HTTPS rather than HTTP in the address. You also have the option to configure the DirectAccess server as the remote access server and use a self-signed certificate; however, self-signed certificates are more appropriate for tests rather than production deployments.

2. The DNS page enables you to specify the DNS suffixes that should be used with the name resolution and the address of the internal DNS server. On this page, you can also configure how clients should use the DNS server of their local Internet connection by choosing one of the following options:

   - Use the DNS server of the local connection if the name isn't resolvable using the DNS server on the trusted network.

   - Use the DNS server of the local connection if the name isn't resolvable using the DNS server on the trusted network or if the DNS server on the trusted network cannot be contacted.

   - Use the DNS server of the local connection if any DNS error occurs.

3. The DNS Suffix Search List enables you to configure any DNS suffixes that the client should use for any unqualified names. The default settings add the domain name suffix.

4. The Management Servers page enables you to configure the servers used for DirectAccess client management. You can also configure NAP remediation servers if you are using NAP with DirectAccess.

Step 4: Application Servers

Step 4 of the Remote Access Management Console setup enables you to configure the addresses of application servers that require end-to-end authentication when interacting with DirectAccess clients. Unlike the other steps, this step involves configuring only one dialog, where you specify the security group containing the computer accounts that you want to require end-to-end authentication and encryption for. You can also use this dialog to limit DirectAccess clients so they can only connect to servers in the listed groups and can't connect to other servers on the trusted network. Use this option in environments with stringent security requirements.

Managing Remote Access using PowerShell

The Remote Access PowerShell module contains a large number of cmdlets that you can use to manage all aspects of Routing and Remote Access on Windows Server. These cmdlets are described in Table 21-1.

Table 21-1   Remote Access PowerShell cmdlets

Noun	Verbs	Function
BgpCustomRoute	Add, Remove, Get	View and manage BGP (Border Gateway Protocol) route information
BgpPeer	Get, Remove, Set, Start, Add, Stop	View and manage BGP peer configuration
BgpRouteAggregate	Get, Set, Add, Remove	View and manage aggregate BGP routes
BgpRouteFlapDampening	Clear, Enable, Get, Set, Disable	Manage the configuration of a BGP route-dampening engine
BgpRouteInformation	Get	View BGP route information
BgpRouter	Get, Add, Remove, Set	Manage configuration information for BGP routers
BgpRoutingPolicy	Set, Add, Remove, Get	Manage BGP routing policies
BgpRoutingPolicyForPeer	Set, Remove, Add	Manage BGP peer routing policies
BgpStatistics	Get	Retrieves the BGP peering-related message and route advertisement statistics
DAAppServer	Remove, Get, Add	Manage DirectAccess application server security groups
DAAppServerConnection	Set	Configures the properties of the connection to application servers and the IPsec security traffic protection policies for the connection
DAClient	Get, Set, Remove, Add	Manage the client security groups used for DirectAccess client configuration
DAClientDnsConfiguration	Get, Remove, Set, Add	Manage Name Resolution Policy Table (NRPT) entries and local name resolution properties
DAEntryPoint	Add, Get, Set, Remove	Manage DirectAccess entry-point settings

Noun	Verbs	Function
DAEntryPointDC	Set, Get	Configure DirectAccess entry point domain controller settings
DAMgmtServer	Update, Add, Remove, Get	Manage DirectAccess management servers
DAMultiSite	Disable, Enable, Get, Set	Manage global settings applied to all DirectAccess entry points in a multisite deployment
DANetworkLocationServer	Get, Set	Manage DirectAccess NLS settings
DAOtpAuthentication	Disable, Set, Enable, Get	Manage DirectAccess one-time password settings
DAServer	Get, Set	Manage DirectAccess Server Settings
RemoteAccess	Get, Install, Uninstall, Set	Manage DirectAccess and VPN configuration
RemoteAccessAccounting	Get, Set	Configure remote access accounting
RemoteAccessConfiguration	Get, Set	Manage remote access configuration
RemoteAccessConnection-Statistics	Get	View information about DirectAccess and VPN connections
RemoteAccessConnection-StatisticsSummary	Get	View summary information about DirectAccess and VPN connections
RemoteAccessHealth	Get	View the current health of a RemoteAccess (RA) deployment
RemoteAccessInboxAccounting-Store	Set, Clear	Manage the inbox of the remote access accounting store
RemoteAccessIpFilter	Add, Remove, Set, Get	Manage remote access IP filters
RemoteAccessLoadBalancer	Get, Set	Manage remote access load balancer settings
RemoteAccessLoadBalancerNode	Remove, Add	Add and remove remote access load balancer nodes
RemoteAccessRadius	Add, Get, Set	Manage RADIUS servers
RemoteAccessRoutingDomain	Get, Set, Disable, Enable	Manage remote access routing domains

CHAPTER 21

Noun	Verbs	Function
RemoteAccessUserActivity	Get	Displays the resources accessed over the active DirectAccess and VPN connections and the resources accessed over historical DirectAccess and VPN connections
RoutingProtocolPreference	Set, Get	Manage routing protocol preferences
VpnAuthProtocol	Set, Get	Manage VPN server authentication parameters
VpnAuthType	Set	Configure VPN server authentication types
VpnIPAddressAssignment	Set	Manage the VPN server IPv4 address assignment
VpnIPAddressRange	Remove, Add	Manage the VPN server address range
VpnS2Sinterface	Set, Add, Connect, Remove, Disconnect, Get	Manage site-to-site VPN interfaces
VpnS2SInterfaceStatistics	Clear, Get	View site-to-site VPN interface statistics
VpnServerConfiguration	Get, Set	Manage the VPN server configuration
VpnSstpProxyRule	Add, Get, New, Set, Remove	Manage Tenant ID to gateway mappings
VpnTrafficSelector	New	Creates a VPN Traffic selector object that configures the IKE traffic selector
VpnUser	Disconnect	Disconnects a VPN connection originated by a specific user or originating from a specific client computer

CHAPTER 21

Remote Desktop Services

Remote Desktop Services (RDS) allows an application to run on one computer with the graphical output of that computer displayed on another computer. The benefits of RDS include allowing relatively resource-poor clients to run resource-intensive applications remotely, or to run applications that are unable to run on one operating system to be accessed by users of another operating system.

There are several ways that you can leverage RDS in Windows Server 2025. The first is using Remote Desktop Session Host. In this form of RDS, people connect to remote desktop sessions that run on a server in a special isolated environment. In versions of Windows Server prior to Windows Server 2008 R2, Remote Desktop Session Host was called Terminal Services. The other primary way to leverage RDS in Windows Server 2025 is through Remote Desktop Virtualization Host. In this form of RDS, users connect to virtual machines to use their desktop environment to run their applications. Remote Desktop Virtualization Host is a form of Virtual Desktop Infrastructure or VDI.

Deployment

Remote Desktop Services deployment differs from other role and feature deployments. With all other roles and features, you select the Role-Based Or Feature-Based Installation option when running the Add Roles And Features Wizard. With Remote Desktop Services, you instead select the Remote Desktop Services installation option, as shown in Figure 22-1.

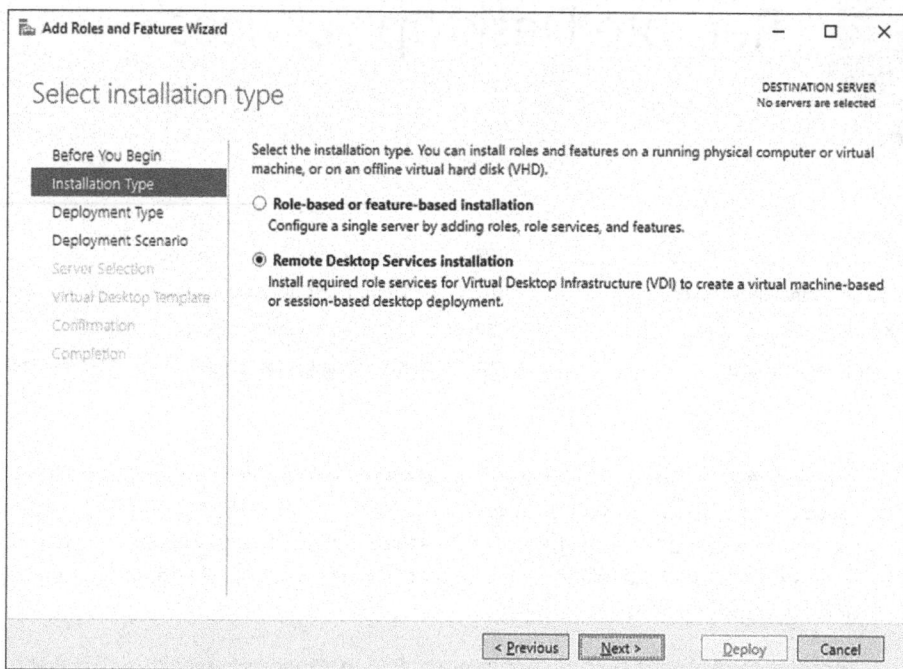

Figure 22-1   Installation type options

Once you've selected Remote Desktop Services installation, the next page in the wizard allows you to choose between the following options:

- **Standard deployment**   Choose this when you are deploying Remote Desktop Services across multiple servers.

- **Quick Start**   Use this option if you are deploying a single Remote Desktop Services server.

Another option is to use multipoint services, which is a Feature on Demand. Use the MultiPoint services option if you are creating a multipoint server deployment. Multipoint server allows you to run multiple client terminals with multiple keyboards, monitors, and mice directly connected to a single multipoint server. Multipoint services are used in classroom and lab environments.

When you choose the Standard deployment or Quick Start options, you then get to select the deployment scenario, as shown in Figure 22-2.

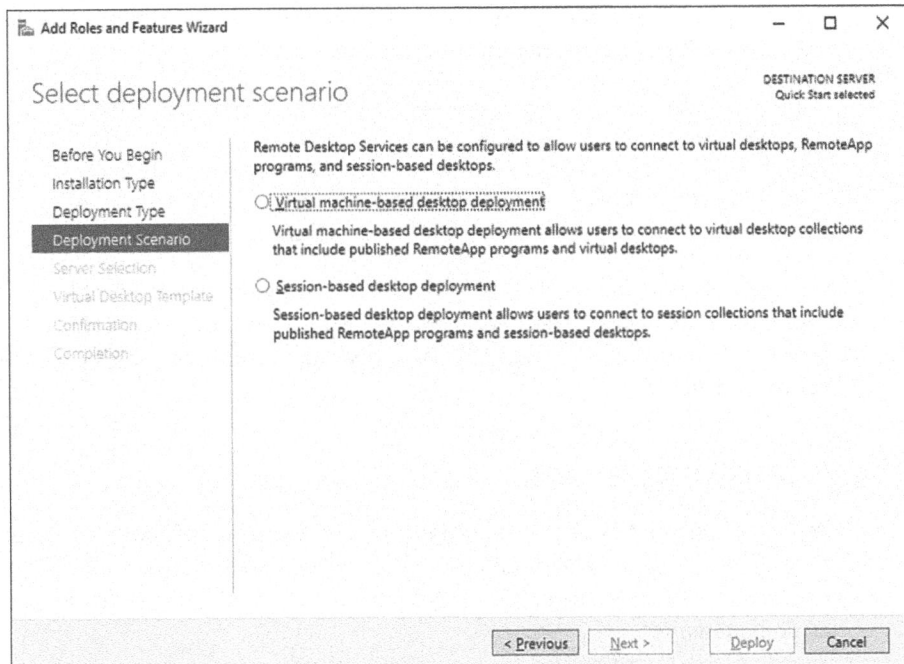

Figure 22-2   Deployment scenario

Session-based deployments are generally less resource-intensive than virtualization-host deployments because they don't require that the session host server host full virtual machines for each session. Virtualization host deployments are more likely to provide better application compatibility because some applications don't support being deployed in a Session host-based environment.

Depending on your selection, completing the wizard involves selecting the server on which the deployment will occur, selecting a virtualization template for a virtualization host deployment, installing the roles, and then rebooting the server to complete the installation.

Remote Desktop Connection broker

When initiating a connection, either through Remote Desktop Connection client software or RD Web Access interface, users connect to a session on a Remote Desktop Session Host server or a VDI virtual machine on a Remote Desktop Virtualization Host server through the Remote Desktop Connection Broker. The Remote Desktop Connection Broker role service provides the following functionality:

- Connects incoming remote desktop clients to the appropriate RD session host or virtualization host server.

- Reconnects disconnected remote desktop clients to the appropriate RD session host session or RD virtualization host virtual machine.

- Load balances incoming remote desktop client connections according to session collection settings.

- Allows organizations to scale out the RD session host or RD virtualization host deployment by adding RD session host or RD virtualization host servers.

In previous versions of Remote Desktop and Terminal Services, it was possible to directly connect to the session host server. In Windows Server 2012, Windows Server 2012 R2, Windows Server 2016, and Windows Server 2025, all connections are mediated by the Remote Desktop Connection Broker.

Deployment properties

Deployment properties allow you to configure settings for both RD Session Host and RD Virtualization Host servers. Available through the Collections node of the Remote Desktop Services section of the Server Manager console, you can use Deployment Properties to configure the following settings:

- **RD Gateway**   This allows you to specify RD Gateway settings for your deployment. This includes whether the RD Gateway server is automatically determined, whether one is assigned, or whether to block the use of an RD Gateway server and the sign-in method when using an RD Gateway server.

- **RD Licensing**   It allows you to configure the licensing mode and licensing servers. You can configure multiple RD license servers and the order in which they will be queried to obtain a license for a Remote Desktop Services client.

- **RD Web Access**   The address of the RD Web Access server. Clients can use this to connect to RemoteApp and Remote Desktop sessions using a browser instead of through the Remote Desktop Connection client.

- **Certificates**   Shown in Figure 22-3, use this section to configure certificates for the Remote Desktop Services deployment.

- **Active Directory**   This is for RD Virtualization Host servers and allows you to configure the domain and organizational unit that computer accounts for VDI virtual machines will be added to once they are joined to the AD DS domain.

- **Export Location**   The location where the virtual desktop template is copied to once selected for use when generating further RD virtualization host virtual machines.

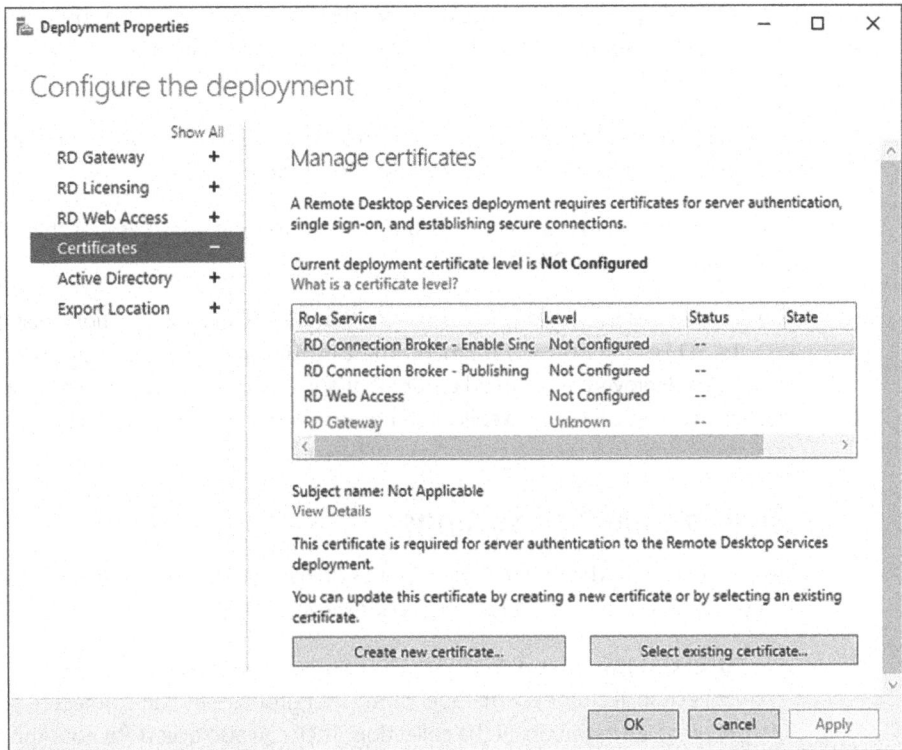

Figure 22-3   Certificates

Remote Desktop Session Host

Remote Desktop (RD) Session Host provides a full desktop environment to a user. Users connect to the RD Session Host server from a thin client, such as a Windows Thin PC or the Remote Desktop Connection client, which ships with Windows operating systems. An RD Session Host provides a full screen or window that reproduces a Windows desktop, including the taskbar, Start menu, and desktop icons.

The benefits of using RD Session Host include

- You can deploy an application to many users by installing it on a small number of RD Session Host servers. Users can run applications on RD Session Host servers that might be incompatible with their operating systems.

- Application updates are simplified. You update an application on the RD Session Host server rather than having to push the patch down to individual operating systems.

- It allows you to grant access to a standardized corporate desktop experience for users who have chosen to use their own computer at work in BYOD (Bring Your Own Device) scenarios.

- It allows you to grant access, through a VPN, to a standardized corporate desktop for users at remote locations or for those who telecommute.

- It allows you to grant access to applications for operating systems that do not support RD Web Access or RD RemoteApp.

The drawback to RD Session Host servers is that they require applications that are compatible with the RD Session Host environment. These applications must be installed after the session host role is deployed. You should ensure that applications are installed on all servers that are available to a specific session collection because you won't know which RD session host server a user connecting to a session collection will be connected to.

Session collection settings

Session collections determine the properties of RD Session Host servers. You can configure the following RD Session Host settings on a per-session collection basis:

- **User Groups**   This determines which user groups are associated with a specific session collection. If a user is a member of the user group, they can connect to session host servers that are members of the collection. They can also access RemoteApp applications published to the collection.

- **Sessions**   Shown in Figure 22-4, these settings determine the amount of time after which a session that is disconnected is automatically ended. The default value is Never. You can configure the value to be as short as one minute. You can also configure active session limits, how long before an idle session is disconnected, and then determine what happens when a disconnection occurs. Should the session be automatically terminated, or should reconnection be allowed? You can also use the settings contained in this area to configure whether to use temporary folders and whether those folders are deleted when the session ends.

- **Security settings**   They allow you to configure whether Remote Desktop Connections require RDP Security or TLS security. Encryption options include Low, Client Compatible, High, and FIPS Compliant. You should generally select High unless you're required to use FIPS Compliant. The drawback of doing so is that some older third-party remote desktop clients may not support this level of encryption.

- **Load balancing**   This section allows you to configure the load balancing settings for a session collection, including the relative weight the server is assigned when multiple session host servers are available to the session collection and the limit to the number of sessions each session host server can host.

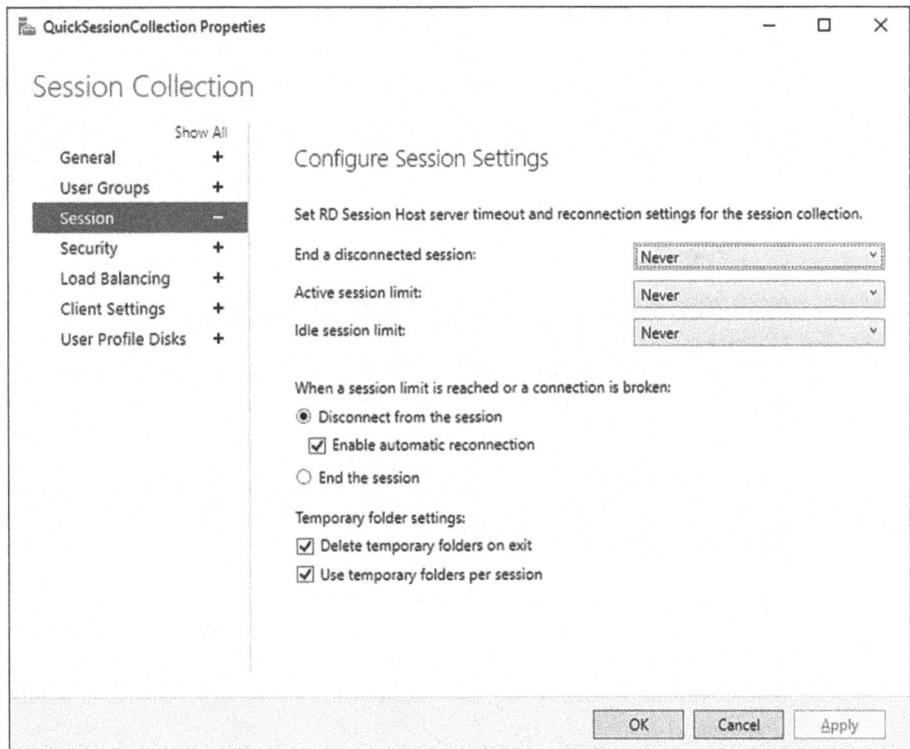

Figure 22-4   Session settings

- **Client settings**   The Client Settings section allows you to configure which redirection options to enable. You can configure redirection for the following:

  - Audio and video playback

  - Audio recording

  - Smart cards

  - Plug and play devices

  - Drives

  - Clipboard

  - Printers, including using the default client printing device and the Remote Desktop Easy Print driver

  - Monitor redirection

- **User profile disks**   User profile disks allow users to store settings and folders in a central location. This is useful to allow users to persist data and settings across different session host settings on multiple servers. You can choose the following user profile disk settings:

  - User profile disk location

  - Maximum size

  - Store all user settings and data on the profile disk, with specified folders excluded

  - Store only certain folders on the user profile disk

You can also use Session Collection settings to configure which remote app programs will be available to the Session Collection. You can also add and remove session host servers from the session collection. These servers should already have the RD Session Host role installed prior to performing this task.

Personal session desktops

Personal session desktops are a feature of Windows Server that allows you to create a special type of Session Collection where each user has access to their own personal session host, where they enjoy administrative rights. Personal session desktops can be useful for developers who might need administrative rights without giving them those rights over a remote desktop session host server.

RemoteApp

Rather than open a full session, including a desktop, Start menu, and a taskbar, RemoteApp allows a user to run one or more applications directly. The application runs in such a way that it appears as if it's executing on the local computer. When a client invokes multiple applications from the same host server, the server transmits the applications to the client using the same session.

RemoteApp includes the following benefits:

- Any application that can be run on the RD Session Host server can be run as a Remote-App application.

- You can associate RemoteApp applications with local file extensions. This means that the RemoteApp application starts when the user attempts to open an associated document.

- Users are often unaware that an application is running remotely.

- RemoteApp applications can be used with RD Gateway, allowing access to clients on remote networks such as the Internet.

You publish a RemoteApp program to a Session Collection once you've installed it on an RD Session Host server through the session collection area of the Server Manager console.

Group Policy configuration

The `Computer Configuration\Policies\Administrative Templates\Windows Compo-nents\Remote Desktop Services\Remote Desktop Session Host` server node of Group Policy contains several policies that you can use to configure Session Host servers. Many settings can only be configured through Group Policy and PowerShell, which are not available in the Remote Desktop Services area of the Server Manager Console. The coverage here is brief, as there are a vast number of policies, and you've already learned about the functionality that most of them implement.

- **Application Compatibility**   Through the Application Compatibility node, you can access

  - Turn Off Windows Installer RDS Compatibility

  - Turn On Remote Desktop IP Virtualization

  - Select The Network Adapter To Be Used For Remote Desktop IP Virtualization

  - Do Not Use Remote Desktop Session Host Server IP Address When Virtual IP Address Is Not Available

- **Connections**   Through the Connections node, you can access the following policies:

  - Automatic Reconnection

  - Allow Users To Connect Remotely Using Remote Desktop Services

  - Deny Logoff Of An Administrator Logged In To The Console Session

  - Configure Keep-Alive Connection Interval

  - Limit Number Of Connections

  - Suspend User Sign-In To Complete App Registration

  - Set Rules For Remote Control Of Remote Desktop Services User Sessions

  - Select RDP Transport Protocols

  - Select Network Detection On The Server

  - Restrict Remote Desktop Services Users To A Single Remote Desktop Services Session

  - Allow Remote Start Of Unlisted Programs

  - Turn Off Fair Share CPU Scheduling

CHAPTER 22

- **Device and Resource Redirection**   Through the Device and Resource Redirection node, you can configure the following policies:

  - Allow Audio And Video Playback Redirection

  - Allow Audio Recording Redirection

  - Limit Audio Playback Quality

  - Do Not Allow Clipboard Redirection

  - Do Not Allow COM Port Redirection

  - Do Not Allow Drive Redirection

  - Do Not Allow LPT Port Redirection

  - Do Not Allow Supported Plug And Play Device Redirection

  - Do Not Allow Smart Card Device Redirection

  - Do Not Allow Video Capture Redirection

  - Allow Time Zone Redirection

- **Licensing**   You can access the Licensing node to configure the following policies:

  - Use The Specified Remote Desktop License Servers

  - Hide Notifications About RD Licensing Problems That Affect The RD Session Host Server

  - Set The Remote Desktop Services Licensing Mode

- **Printer Redirection**   Through the Printer Redirection node, you can configure the following policies:

  - Do Not Set Default Client Printer To Be Default Printer In A Session

  - Do Not Allow Client Printer Redirection

  - Use Remote Desktop Easy Print Printer Driver First

  - Specify RD Session Host Server Fallback Printer Driver Behavior

  - Redirect Only The Default Client Printer

- **Profiles**   You can find the following policies in the Profiles node:

    - Limit The Size Of The Entire Roaming User Profile Cache

    - Set Remote Desktop Services User Home Directory

    - Use Mandatory Profiles On The RD Session Host Server

    - Set Path For Remote Desktop Services Roaming User Profile

- **RD Connection Broker**   You can find the following policies in the RD Connection Broker node:

    - Join RD Connection Broker

    - Configure RD Connection Broker Farm Name

    - Use IP Address Redirection

    - Configure RD Connection Broker Server Name

    - Use RD Connection Broker Load Balancing

- **Remote Session Environment**   You can use the Remote Session Environment node to locate the following policies:

    - Limit Maximum Color Depth

    - Enforce Removal Of Remote Desktop Wallpaper

    - Use The Hardware Default Graphics Adapter For All Remote Desktop Services Sessions

    - Use WDDM Graphics Display Driver For Remote Desktop Connections

    - Limit Maximum Display Resolution

    - Limit Number Of Monitors

    - Remove Disconnect Option From Shut Down Dialog

    - Remove Windows Security Item From Start Menu

    - Use Advanced RemoteFX graphics For RemoteApp

    - Prioritize H.264/AVC 444 Graphics Mode For Remote Desktop Connections

    - Configure H.264/AVC hardware Encoding for Remote Desktop Connections

CHAPTER 22

- Configure Compression For RemoteFX Data

- Configure Image Quality For RemoteFX Adaptive Graphics

- Enable RemoteFX Encoding For RemoteFX Clients Designed For Windows Server 2008 R2 SP1

- Configure RemoteFX Adaptive Graphics

- Start A Program On Connection

- Always Show Desktop On Connection

- Allow Desktop Composition For Remote Desktop Sessions

- Do Not Allow Font Smoothing

- **RemoteFX for Windows Server 2008 R2** This node contains the following policies:

  - Configure Remote FX

  - Optimize Visual Experience When Using RemoteFX

  - Optimize Visual Experience For Remote Desktop Service Sessions

- **Security** The Security node contains the following policies:

  - Server Authentication Certificate Template

  - Set Client Connection Encryption Level

  - Always Prompt For Password Upon Connection

  - Require Secure RPC Communication

  - Require Use Of Specific Security Layer for Remote (RDP) Connections

  - Do Not Allow Local Administrators To Customize Permissions

  - Require User Authentication For Remote Connections By Using Network Level Authentication

- **Session Time Limits** You can find the following policies in the Session Time Limits Node:

  - Set Time Limit For Disconnected Sessions

  - Set Time Limit For Active But Idle Remote Desktop Services Sessions

  - Set Time Limit For Active Remote Desktop Services Sessions

- ■ End Session When Time Limits Are Reached

- ■ Set Time Limit For Logoff Of RemoteApp Sessions

- ● **Temporary Folders**   The Temporary Folders node contains the following policies:

  - ■ Do Not Delete Temp Folder Upon Exit

  - ■ Do Not Use Temporary Folders Per Session

Inside OUT
Useful policies

The most useful policy groups are in the Connections and Session Time Limits nodes. These contain policies that control how many clients are connected to each RD Session Host server and how long they remain connected, affecting the RD Session Host server's capacity.

Remote Desktop Virtualization Host

The Remote Desktop Virtualization Host allows you to configure Remote Desktop technologies to support Virtual Desktop Infrastructure (VDI). You can use RD Virtualization Host to allow clients to connect using Remote Desktop to personal virtual machines running on Hyper-V hosts. You can configure RD Virtualization Host to assign users to a specific unique virtual machine, or you can configure RD Virtualization Host to direct users to a pool of shared virtual machines. The RD Virtualization Host role service needs to be installed on a computer that hosts the Hyper-V role and the client virtual machines.

This type of virtualization takes substantially more resources than RD Session Host sessions but also allows greater customization of the user experience. Virtual machines can be treated just like desktop machines, with users using a thin client to access the RD Virtualization Host virtual machines. RD Virtualization Host integrates with RD Session Broker to ensure that users are redirected to their existing virtual machine in the event that their session is disconnected.

RD Virtualization Host computers have the following requirements:

- ● Must be available remotely via Windows PowerShell.

- ● Must be domain-joined.

- ● Must be running Hyper-V.

CHAPTER 22

- Server must support hardware-assisted virtualization. This means that you cannot run an RD Virtualization Host server within Hyper-V nested virtualization. Nested virtualization is supported by Windows Server 2016 and later.

- Server must have a network adapter that supports the creation of a Hyper-V virtual switch.

- RD Connection Broker server must have the right to join virtual desktops to the AD DS domain.

- If performing a quick start deployment, a prepared virtual desktop template, as shown in Figure 22-5.

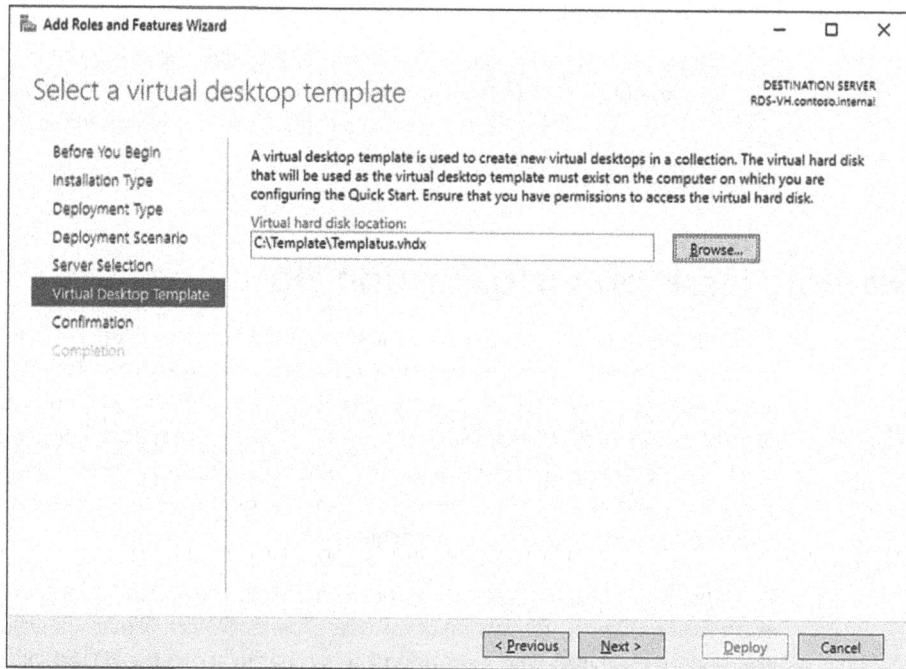

Figure 22-5   Specify template for RD Virtualization Host server

Virtual machine preparation

To prepare a virtual machine for use as a template in an RD Virtualization Host deployment, you should perform the following tasks:

- Deploy the virtual machine and install all of the applications that will be available to users of the RD virtualization host VMs. Perform this deployment on one of the Hyper-V servers that will function as an RD virtualization host. You can build this virtual machine on another computer and then import it on the RD virtualization host. You should configure this virtual machine as a Generation 2 VM because this will give you the greatest flexibility in terms of virtual machine configuration.

- Once the applications are installed, sysprep the virtual machine, generalize and set it to boot using the Out Of Box Experience setting. Once sysprepped, the virtual machine will be shut down.

Virtual desktop collections

Virtual desktop collections function in a manner similar to a session collection. You configure who can connect and select the resources they have access to on a per-collection basis. When creating the virtual desktop collection, you need to provide the following information:

- **Collection Name**   Name of the virtual desktop collection.

- **Collection Type**   This can be a pooled virtual desktop collection or a personal virtual desktop collection.

- **Virtual Desktop Template**   The prepared template virtual machine.

- **Virtual Desktop Settings**   You can specify a Sysprep answer file or provide unattended installation settings. This information is used to join the virtual machine to the domain. This requires that the computer account of the host computer has permission to perform the AD DS domain join.

- **Unattended Settings**   Provide the time zone, AD DS domain, and organizational unit used in the domain join operation.

- **Users And User Groups**   This setting allows you to specify which users and groups have access to the collection (see Figure 22-6). It also allows you to configure the number of virtual desktops to be created in the collection, and the name prefix and suffix for the computer accounts of RDS VDI virtual machines.

- **Virtual Desktop Allocation**   Allows you to specify the allocation of VDI virtual machines in the collection to RD virtualization host servers. For example, you can have 10 virtual machines on one host server and 20 on another.

- **Virtual Desktop Storage**   Allows you to configure the type of storage used for the virtual desktops.

- **User Profile Disks**   Allows you to configure and enable user profile disk settings and the location.

CHAPTER 22

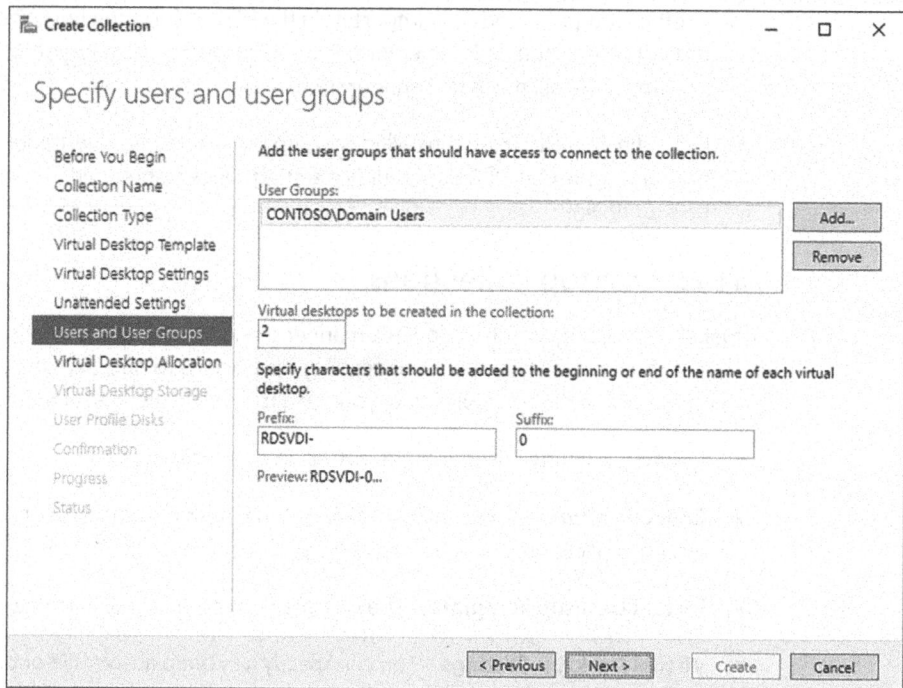

Figure 22-6   RDS VDI User and user group settings

Once the virtual desktop collection is created, you can also configure client settings for the collection. This determines whether functionality such as audio and video playback, audio recording, smart cards, plug-and-play devices, drives, the clipboard, and printers is redirected from the Remote Desktop client to the RD virtual machine.

Pooled virtual desktops

Pooled virtual desktops are collections of identically configured virtual machines that users connecting a Remote Desktop virtualization host through a remote desktop connection broker are assigned. A user will be connected to the first available pooled virtual desktop on the first sign-in and only redirected to the same pooled virtual desktop in the event their connection is disrupted and they haven't signed off. If they sign off and reconnect, they may be assigned to a new virtual desktop within the pool. Pooled virtual desktops do not retain session information. When a user signs off from a pooled virtual desktop, the virtual machine reverts to its original pre-sign-in state.

Personal virtual desktops

You use personal virtual desktops when you want to assign users persistent VDI virtual machines. This means that users can make customizations and store data on the virtual machines that persist across sessions. The virtual machines are associated with the user, and they're automatically connected to that virtual machine when they initiate a session through the Remote Desktop connection broker. Personal virtual desktops retain session information across connections and are not reverted to their original pre-sign-in state when the session ends.

DDA and RemoteFX

Discrete Device Assignment (DDA) and RemoteFX allow virtual machines in a VDI deployment to leverage the graphical processing power of compatible graphics cards. This, in turn, allows workloads that need to leverage substantive graphical processing power, such as those used in Computer-Aided Design (CAD). RemoteFX has been deprecated since Windows Server 2019 in favor of Discrete Device Assignment (DDA). Chapter 6, "Hyper-V," includes more information on DDA. Graphics cards used for DDA must be installed on the Remote Desktop Virtualization Host, and special graphics adapter drivers will need to be configured for each virtual machine that takes advantage of DDA.

Remote Desktop Web Access

You can use Remote Desktop (RD) Web Access to allow clients to connect to an RD Session Host or Virtualization Host session through a web page link rather than through Remote Desktop Connection client software or by running a RemoteApp application. To use RD Web Access, clients need to run a supported version of the Windows Client or Windows Server operating system. You can also use Remote Desktop Web Access to publish applications directly to the Start menu of computers running Windows client operating systems.

Remote Desktop licensing

Each client or user that accesses a Remote Desktop server, either through an RD Session Host session, a RemoteApp application, or an RD Web Access application, needs to have a license. This special type of license is not included with the licenses you get when you purchase Windows Server or a Windows client operating system such as Windows 11. This license is called a Remote Desktop Services Client Access License (RDS CAL). You install RDS CALs on an RD license server. When a user, computer, or thin client initiates a session to a Remote Desktop Services server, the server performs a check to verify that a valid license has been issued or is available.

You configure licensing settings for a Remote Desktop server through Deployment Properties, as shown in Figure 22-7.

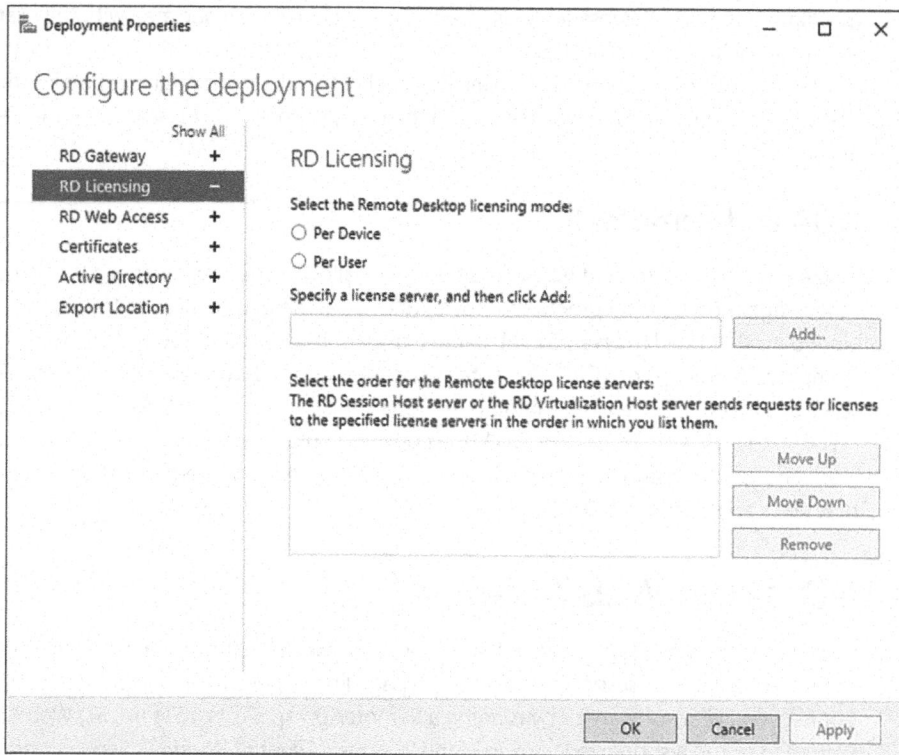

Figure 22-7   RD Licensing settings

Installing RDS CALs

You can install several types of licenses on an RD license server. The different license types are as follows:

- **RDS Per User CAL**   An RDS Per User CAL gives a specific user account the ability to access any RD Session Host server in an organization from any computer or device. This type of CAL is a good idea when you have the same person accessing Remote Desktop from different devices.

- **RDS Per Device CAL**   The RDS Per Device CAL licenses a specific device, such as a normal computer or thin client, with the ability to connect to an RD Session Host server. RDS Per Device CALs are reset automatically by the RD license server after a random period between 52 and 89 days. This means that if a computer or thin client is decommissioned, the license assigned to it is reclaimed automatically and can be used again. If you are decommissioning a large number of computers, you can revoke 20% of the RDS Per Device CALs.

- **RDS External Connector**   Use this license type to allow people who are external to your organization to access a single Remote Desktop Server. A separate RDS External Connector license must be purchased for each remote desktop server accessible to external users.

- **Service Providers License Agreement**   This is a special type of license agreement for service providers. It's useful when providing Remote Desktop Services to multiple organizations.

You can mix and match RDS Per User CALs and RDS Per Device CALS as necessary. When using Remote Desktop Virtualization Hosts, you also need to purchase a Virtual Enterprise Centralized Desktop licensing agreement for the VDI operating system. You can use the Manage RDS CALs Wizard in the RD Licensing Manager console to

- Migrate RDS CALs to different RD Licensing Servers

- Rebuild the RD Licensing Server database

Inside OUT

Licensing is complicated

Unless you're certain about the licensing, ensure that you check in with a Microsoft licensing specialist about your licensing configuration.

Activating a license server

You must activate an RD license server before it's able to issue CALs. The activation process is reasonably similar to the one that you need to go through when you perform product activation for a Windows operating system or for an application such as Microsoft Office. The method you use depends on whether the RD license server has an Internet connection. If the server has an Internet connection, you can perform automatic activation. If the server does not have a direct Internet connection, you can perform an activation using a telephone, or you can navigate to a website on an Internet-connected computer or mobile device and perform activation by filling out a form and entering the activation code on the RD license server.

Managing Remote Desktop Services using PowerShell

The Remote Desktop PowerShell module contains a large number of cmdlets that you can use to manage all aspects of Remote Desktop Services on Windows Server. These cmdlets are described in Table 16-1.

Table 22-1   Remote Access PowerShell cmdlets

Noun	Verbs	Function
RDActiveManagementServer	Set	Configure an active RD Connection Broker server
RDAvailableApp	Get	View applications that can be published from a collection
RDCertificate	Get, New, Set	Manage Remote Desktop Services certificate configuration
RDClientAccessName	Set	Manage the DNS name that clients use to connect to the RDS deployment
RDConnectionBrokerHigh-Availability	Get, Set	Configure the connection broker's high availability
RDDatabaseConnectionString	Remove, Set	Configure RD database connection strings
RDDeploymentGatewayConfiguration	Get, Set	Manage the RD deployment gateway configuration
RDFileTypeAssociation	Get, Set	Manage RD file type associations
RDLicenseConfiguration	Get, Set	Configure RD licensing
RDPersonalSessionDesktop-Assignment	Export, Get, Import, Remove, Set	Manage the association between a personal session and a user
RDPersonalVirtualDesktop-Assignment	Export, Get, Import, Remove, Set	Manage the association between a virtual desktop and a user
RDPersonalVirtualDesktopPatch-Schedule	Get, New, Remove, Set	Configure personal virtual desktop patch schedule
RDRemoteApp	Get, New, Remove, Set	Manage RD RemoteApp
RDRemoteDesktop	Get, Set	Publish a remote desktop to a collection
RDServer	Add, Get, Remove	Manage server membership of a Remote Desktop deployment
RDSessionCollection	Get, New, Remove	Manage RD session collections
RDSessionCollectionConfiguration	Get, Set	Manage RD session collection configurations
RDSessionDeployment	New	Create a new RD session deployment

Noun	Verbs	Function
`RDSessionHost`	Add, Get, Remove, Set	Manage RD Session Host session collection server membership
`RDUser`	`Disconnect`	Disconnect a connected RD user
`RDUserLogoff`	`Invoke`	Sign off a connected RD user
`RDUserSession`	`Get`	View RD user session information
`RDUserMessage`	`Send`	Send a message to an RD user
`RDVirtualDesktop`	`Get, Move`	Manage RD virtual desktops
`RDVirtualDesktopADMachine-AccountReuse`	`Disable, Enable, Test`	Manage whether the RD Connection Broker server reuses existing AD computer accounts for pooled virtual desktops created using a template in a managed collection
`RDVirtualDesktopCollection`	Add, Get, New, Remove, Set, Update	Manage virtual desktop membership of virtual desktop collections
`RDVirtualDesktopFromCollection`	Remove	Remove a virtual desktop from a collection
`RDVirtualDesktopCollection-Configuration`	Get	View virtual desktop collection configuration
`RDVirtualDesktopCollectionJob`	Stop	End a virtual desktop collection job
`RDVirtualDesktopCollectionJob-Status`	Get	View virtual desktop connection job status
`RDVirtualDesktopConcurrency`	Get, Set	Manage virtual desktop concurrency
`RDVirtualDesktopDeployment`	New	Create a new virtual desktop deployment
`RDVirtualDesktopIdleCount`	Get, Set	Manage virtual desktop idle settings
`RDVirtualDesktopTemplateExport-Path`	Get, Set	Configure virtual desktop template paths
`RDWorkspace`	Get, Set	Manage workspace name settings for Remote Desktop deployment
`RDOUAccess`	`Grant, Test`	Configures OU access for the RD Connection Broker server

CHAPTER 22

Just like any other form of precision equipment, servers need to be monitored and maintained over their operational lifespans to ensure that they continue to function as well as they possibly can. Monitoring and maintenance not only involves regularly checking performance and event logs but also ensuring that servers and the data that those servers host are backed up in such a way that all important data and settings can be recovered in the event of a catastrophic failure. In this chapter, you learn how to monitor Windows Server performance, manage event logs, configure advanced auditing, and use the built-in backup and recovery tools.

Data collector sets

Data collector sets enable you to gather performance data, system configuration information, and statistics into a single file. You can use Performance Monitor or other third-party tools to analyze this information to determine how well a server is functioning against an assigned workload.

You can configure data collector sets to include the following:

- **Performance counter data** The data collector set not only includes specific performance counters but also the data generated by those counters.

- **Event trace data** Enables you to track events and system activities. Event trace data can be useful when you need to troubleshoot misbehaving applications or services.

- **System configuration information** Enables you to track the state of registry keys and record any modifications made to those keys.

Windows Server includes the following built-in data collector sets:

- **Active Directory diagnostics** Available if you have installed the computer as a domain controller and provides data on Active Directory health and reliability.

- **System diagnostics** Enables you to troubleshoot problems with hardware, drivers, and STOP errors.

- **System performance** Enables you to diagnose problems with sluggish system performance. You can determine which processes, services, or hardware components might be causing performance bottlenecks.

To create a data collector set, perform the following steps:

1. Open Performance Monitor from the Tools menu of the Server Manager console.

2. Expand Data Collector Sets.

3. Click User Defined. On the Action menu, click New and then click Data Collector Set.

4. You're given the option to create the data collector set from a template, which enables you to choose from an existing data collector set or create a data collector set manually. If you choose to create a data collector set manually, you have the option to create a data log, which can include a performance counter, event trace data, and system configuration information or create a performance counter alert.

5. If you select Create Data Logs and select Performance Counter, next choose which performance counters to add to the data collector set. You also specify how often Windows should collect data from the performance counters.

6. If you choose to include event trace data, you need to enable event trace providers. A large number of event trace providers are available with Windows Server. You use event trace providers when troubleshooting a specific problem. For example, the Microsoft Windows-AppLocker event trace provider helps you diagnose and troubleshoot issues related to AppLocker.

7. If you choose to monitor system configuration information, you can select registry keys to monitor. Selecting a parent key enables you to monitor all registry changes that occur under that key while the data collector set is running.

8. Specify where you want data collected by the data collector set to be stored. The default location is the %systemdrive%\PerfLogs\Admin folder. If you intend to run the data collector set for an extended period of time, you should store the data on a volume that is separate from the one hosting the operating system because this ensures that you don't fill up your system drive by mistake.

9. Specify the account under which the data collector set runs. The default is Local System, but you can configure the data collector set to use any account that you have the credentials for.

You can schedule when a data collector set runs by configuring the Schedule tab of a data collector set's properties.

Alerts

Performance counter alerts enable you to configure a task to run when a performance counter, such as available disk space or memory, falls under or exceeds a specific value. To configure a performance counter alert, you create a new data collector set, choose the Create Manually option, and select the Performance Counter Alert option.

You add the performance counter, threshold value, and whether the alert should be triggered if the value exceeds or falls below the set value. When you create an alert by default, it only adds an event to the event log when it's triggered. This is useful if you have tools that allow you to extract this information from the event log and use the information as a way of tracking when alerts occur. You can also configure an alert to run a scheduled task when it's triggered. You can do this by editing the properties of the alert and by specifying the name of the scheduled task on the Task tab.

CHAPTER 23

Event Viewer

Event Viewer enables you to access recorded event information. Windows Server not only offers the application, security, setup, and system logs, but it also contains separate application and service logs. These logs are designed to provide information on a per role or per application basis, rather than having all application and role service-related events funneled into the application log. When searching for events related to a specific role service, feature, or application, check to see whether that role service, feature, or application has its own application log.

Event log filters

Filters and event logs enable you to view only those events that have specific characteristics. Filters only apply to the current Event Viewer session. If you constantly use a specific filter or set of filters to manage event logs, you should instead create a custom view. Filters only apply to a single event log. You can create log filters based on the following properties:

- **Logged** Enables you to specify the time range for the filter.

- **Event Level** Enables you to specify event levels. You can choose the following options: Critical, Warning, Verbose, Error, and Information.

- **Event Sources** Enables you to choose the source of the event.

- **Event IDs** Enables you to filter based on event ID. You can also exclude specific event IDs.

- **Keywords** Enables you to specify keywords based on the contents of events.

- **User** Enables you to limit events based on user.

- **Computer** Enables you to limit events based on the computer.

To create a filter, perform the following steps:

1. Open Event Viewer and select the log that you want to filter.

2. Determine the properties of the event that you want to filter.

3. On the Actions pane, click Filter Current Log.

4. In the Filter Current Log dialog, specify the filter properties.

Event log views

Event log views enable you to create customized views of events across any event log stored on a server, including events in the forwarded event log. Rather than looking through each event log for specific items of interest, you can create event log views that target only those specific items. For example, if there are certain events that you always want to look for, create a view and use the view rather than comb through the event logs another way. By default, Event Viewer includes a custom view named Administrative Events. This view displays critical, warning, and error events from a variety of important event logs such as the application, security, and system logs.

Views differ from filters in the following ways:

- **Persistent** You can use a view across multiple Event Viewer sessions. If you configure a filter on a log, it isn't available the next time you open the Event Viewer.

- **Include multiple logs** A custom view can display events from separate logs. Filters are limited to displaying events from one log.

- **Exportable** You can import and export event log views between computers.

The process for creating an event log view is similar to the process for creating a filter. The primary difference is that you can select events from multiple logs and you give the event log view a name and choose a place to save it. To create an event log view, perform the following steps:

1. Open Event Viewer.

2. Click the Custom Views node and then click Create Custom View from the Actions menu.

3. In the Create Custom View dialog, select the properties of the view, including

   - When the events are logged

   - The event level

   - Which event log to draw events from

   - Event source

   - Task category

   - Keywords

   - User

   - Computer

4. In the Save Filter To Custom View dialog, enter a name for the custom view and a location to save the view in. Click OK.

5. Verify that the new view is listed as its own separate node in the Event Viewer.

You can export a custom event log view by selecting the event log view and clicking Export Custom View. Exported views can be imported on other computers running Windows Server.

Event subscriptions

Event log forwarding enables you to centralize the collection and management of events from multiple computers. Rather than having to examine each computer's event log by remotely connecting to that computer, event log forwarding enables you to do one of the following:

- **Configure a central computer to collect specific events from source computers**   Use this option in environments where you need to consolidate events from only a small number of computers.

- **Configure source computers to forward specific events to a collector computer**   Use this option when you have a large number of computers that you want to consolidate events from. You configure this method by using Group Policy.

Event log forwarding enables you to configure the specific events that are forwarded to the central computer. This enables the computer to forward important events. However, it isn't necessary to forward all events from the source computer. If you discover something from the forwarded traffic that warrants further investigation, you can log on to the original source computer and view all the events from that computer in a normal manner.

Event log forwarding uses Windows Remote Management (WinRM) and the Windows Event Collector (wecsvc). You need to enable these services on computers that function as event forwarders and event collectors. You configure WinRM by using the `winrm quickconfig` command, and you configure wecsvc by using the `wecutil qc` command. If you want to configure subscriptions from the security event log, you need to add the computer account of the collector computer to the local Administrators group on the source computer.

To configure a collector-initiated event subscription, configure WinRM and Windows Event Collector on the source and collector computers. In the Event Viewer, configure the Subscription Properties dialog with the following information:

- **Subscription Name** The name of the subscription.

- **Destination Log** The log where collected events are stored.

- **Subscription Type And Source Computers: Collector Initiated** Use the Select Computers dialog to add the computers that the collector retrieves events from. The collector must be a member of the local Administrators group or the Event Log Readers group on each source computer, depending on whether access to the security log is required.

- **Events To Collect** Create a custom view to specify which events are retrieved from each of the source computers.

If you want to instead configure a source computer-initiated subscription, you need to configure the following Group Policies on the computers that act as the event forwarders:

- **Configure Forwarder Resource Usage** This policy determines the maximum event forwarding rate in events per second. If this policy is not configured, events are transmitted as soon as they are recorded.

- **Configure Target Subscription Manager** This policy enables you to set the location of the collector computer.

Both of these policies are located in the `Computer Configuration\Policies\ Administrative Templates\Windows Components\Event Forwarding` node. When configuring the subscription, you must also specify the computer groups that hold the computer accounts of the computers that are forwarding events to the collector.

Event-driven tasks

Event Viewer enables you to attach tasks to specific events. A drawback to the process of creating event-driven tasks is that you need to have an example of the event that triggers the task already present in the event log. Events are triggered based on an event having the same log, source, and event ID.

To attach a task to a specific event, perform the following steps:

1. Open Event Viewer. Locate and select the event that you want to base the new task on.

2. On the Event Viewer Actions pane, click Attach Task To This Event. The Create Basic Task Wizard opens.

3. On the Create A Basic Task page, review the name of the task that you want to create. By default, the task is named after the event. Click Next.

4. On the When An Event Is Logged page, review the information about the event. This lists the log that the event originates from, the source of the event, and the event ID. Click Next.

5. On the Action page, you can choose the task to perform. The Send An E-Mail and Display A Message tasks are deprecated, and you receive an error if you try to create a task using these actions. Click Next

6. On the Start A Program page, specify the program or script that should be automatically triggered as well as additional arguments.

7. After you create the task, you can modify the task to specify the security context under which the task executes. By default, event tasks only run when the user is signed on, but you can also choose to configure the task to run whether the user is signed on or not.

Network monitoring

Network monitoring enables you to track how a computer interacts with the network. Through network monitoring, you can determine which services and applications are using specific network interfaces, which services are listening on specific ports, and the volume of traffic that exists. There are two primary tools that you can use to perform network monitoring on computers running Windows Server:

- Resource Monitor

- Packet Monitoring

Resource Monitor

Resource Monitor enables you to monitor how a computer running the Windows Server operating system uses CPU, memory, disk, and network resources. Resource Monitor provides real-time information. You can't use Resource Monitor to perform a traffic capture and review activity that occurred in the past, but you can use Resource Monitor to view activity that is currently occurring.

CHAPTER 23

Resource Monitor provides the following information that is relevant to network monitoring:

- **Processes With Network Activity** This view lists processes by name and ID and provides information on bytes sent per second, bytes received per second, and total bytes per second.

- **Network Activity** Lists network activity on a per-process basis but also lists the destination address, sent bits per second, received bits per second, and total bits per second.

- **TCP Connection** Provides information on connections based on local address, port, and remote address and port.

- **Listening Ports** Lists the ports and addresses that services and applications are listening on. This option also provides information about the firewall status for these roles and services.

Packet Monitor

Packet Monitor is a utility that is built in to Windows Server that allows you to

- Capture live network traffic directly in the OS (kernel-level)

- Monitor dropped packets and filtering rules

- Export data for analysis in Wireshark

- Run interactively or in the background

You can use Packet Monitor to troubleshoot connectivity issues, assess firewall or NAT configuration, and diagnose network traffic issues. You can use Packet Monitor from the command line using the pktmon.exe command or through an extension to Windows Admin Center. The basic process of using Packet Monitor involves

1. Configuring filters

2. Capturing packets

3. Analyzing captured traffic

To create a filter, you can use the pktmon filter add command. You can add filters for MAC address, VLAN ID, Layer 2 protocol, transport protocol, IP address, source or port number, cluster heartbeat, and encapsulation. For example, to create a filter for ping traffic from host 10.10.10.10, you would run this command:

```
pktmon filter add PingTraffic -I 10.10.10.10 -t ICMP
```

To capture packets, use the `pktmon start` command. You can use options to enable packet counters only or specify how many bytes to log from each packet, designate which components to capture packets on, and designate which packet monitor events are logged. You can also specify a provider name, keywords, and logging level. When capturing packets, you should specify a name to capture the packets to, the maximum file size for the log, and whether you want to use circular, multifile, memory, or real-time logging. If you don't specify a log file name, captures will be written to the file `pktmon.etl`. The following command starts a capture based on the configured filter:

```
pktmon start --capture
```

To analyze packets, convert to a format that is more easily readable. For example, to convert a capture named `capture.etl` to text format, use this command:

```
pktmon format capture.etl -o packets.txt
```

To convert a file named `capture.etl` to wireshark format, use this command:

```
pktmon format capture.etl -o capture.pcapng
```

You can perform these tasks using the Windows Admin Center Packet Monitoring extension, including performing analysis in the Windows Admin Center interface. You can also use the Windows Admin Center interface to convert packet captures to pcapng format for analysis in WireShark.

Azure Monitor

Azure Monitor allows you to centrally collect performance counter and event log data for storage and analysis in Azure. You can use the automation functionality to perform tasks on the local server when specific events or thresholds are met. While not nearly as fully featured as a System Center Operations Manager deployment, Azure Monitor allows you to leverage the analytics capabilities of Azure at a scale that's not possible with an on-premises monitoring solution.

To install Azure Monitor on a computer running Windows Server, connect to the server using Azure Arc and perform the following steps:

1. Install the Azure Monitor agent by running the following command:

   ```
   azcmagent extension add --name AzureMonitorWindowsAgent
   ```

2. In Azure CLI, create a data collection rule. The following code creates a data collection rule named WinSrv-EventLogs-DCR for a log analytics workspace in the Australia East Datacenter named AzureUpdateLAW:

   ```
   # Variables
   RESOURCE_GROUP="law-rg"
   LOCATION="australiaeast"
   ```

```
DCR_NAME="WinSrv-EventLogs-DCR"
WORKSPACE="AzureUpdateLAW"

# Get the workspace resource ID
WORKSPACE_ID=$(az monitor log-analytics workspace show \
  --resource-group $RESOURCE_GROUP \
  --workspace-name $WORKSPACE \
  --query id -o tsv)

# Create the DCR with event logs as a data source
az monitor data-collection rule create \
  --resource-group $RESOURCE_GROUP \
  --location $LOCATION \
  --name $DCR_NAME \
  --data-flows "[{'streams':['Microsoft-Event'], 'destinations':['la'] }]" \
  --destinations "[{'name':'la','workspaceResourceId':'$WORKSPACE_ID'}]" \
  --data-sources "[{'name':'eventlog','streams':['Microsoft-Event'], 'eventLo
gs':[{'xPathQueries':['Security!*[System[(Level=1 or Level=2 or Level=3)]]]',
'name':'Security'}, {'xPathQueries':['System!*[System[(Level=1 or Level=2 or
Level=3)]]]', 'name':'System'}, {'xPathQueries':['Application!*[System[(Level=1 or
Level=2 or Level=3)]]]', 'name':'Application'}]}]"
```

3. Next, assign the data collection role to the Arc-enabled Windows Server machine. In this
    case, the Windows Server computer is listed in Azure Arc as MEL-WS2026.

```
# Variables
RESOURCE_GROUP="law-rg"
LOCATION="australiaeast"
DCR_NAME="WinSrv-EventLogs-DCR"
WORKSPACE="AzureUpdateLAW"
# Get the Arc machine ID
ARC_MACHINE_ID=$(az resource show \
  --resource-group $RESOURCE_GROUP \
  --name MEL-WS2026 \
  --resource-type "Microsoft.HybridCompute/machines" \
  --query id -o tsv)

# Associate DCR
az monitor data-collection rule association create \
  --name ${DCR_NAME}-assoc \
  --rule-id $(az monitor data-collection rule show \
      --resource-group $RESOURCE_GROUP \
      --name $DCR_NAME \
      --query id -o tsv) \
  --resource $ARC_MACHINE_ID
```

4. Once the connection is configured, you can review analytics information in the
    appropriate log analytics workspace in the Azure portal as shown in Figure 23-1.

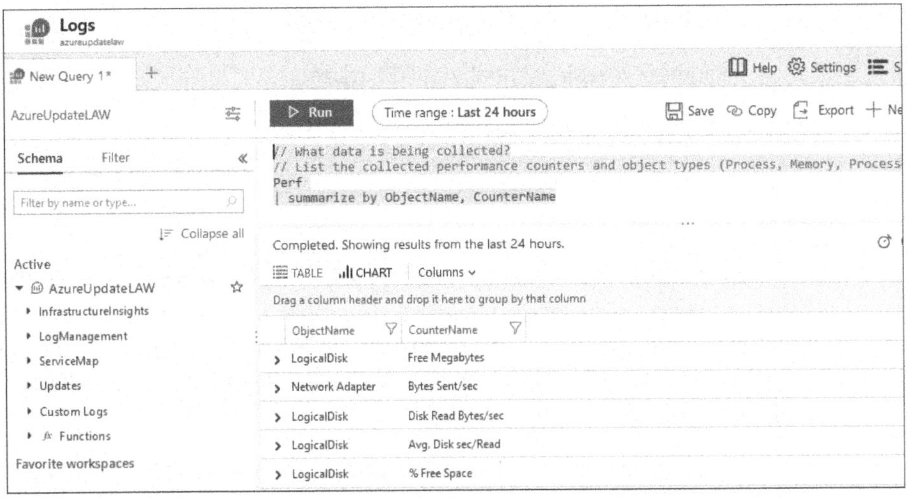

Figure 23-1   Log Analytics workspace

More Info

Azure Monitor

You can learn more about Azure Monitor at *https://learn.microsoft.com/azure/azure-monitor/fundamentals/overview.*

Windows Server Backup

Windows Server Backup is the default backup application included with Windows Server. Windows Server Backup is a basic backup solution, and it only enables you to back up to disk or network share. Tasks for long-term retention, like export to tape, require a more sophisticated solution, such as System Center Data Protection Manager. Windows Server Backup has a minimal level of reporting functionality and has no native functionality that makes it possible to send alerts to an administrator through email if a backup fails.

Windows Server Backup enables you to back up and recover the following:

- Full server (all volumes)

- Specific volumes

- Specific folders

- System State data

- Individual Hyper-V hosted virtual machines

- Volumes exceeding 2 terabytes (TB) in size

- Volumes with 4 kilobyte (K) sector size

- Cluster Shared Volumes

Although you can connect from the Windows Server Backup console to other computers to manage Windows Server Backup remotely, you can only use an instance of Windows Server Backup to back up the local computer. For example, whereas you can back up network shared folders that the computer is able to access, such as a mapped network drive, you can't configure Windows Server Backup on one computer to do a full volume or System State backup of another computer.

You can configure exclusions for backup jobs run on Windows Server Backup. Exclusions are specific file types that you want to exempt from the backup process. You can configure exclusions based on file type, or you can choose to exclude the contents of entire folders and their subfolders. For example, you can configure an exclusion that stops files with the `.tmp` extension in the `c:\shared-docs` folder and its subfolders from being written to backup.

Users who are local Administrators or members of the Backup Operators group can use Windows Server Backup to back up the entire computer, volumes, files or folders, and the System State. You can grant other security principals this right by editing the Back Up Files And Directories Group Policy item. Windows Server Backup does not encrypt backups by default, which means that the data stored in those backups might be read if the backup media falls into the wrong hands. When you're backing up data, you can configure access control so that only users with specific credentials can access the backup, but this still does not encrypt the backup.

Inside OUT

Backup security

The security of backups is important. Anyone who has access to backed up data can restore it to a separate location where they have complete access to that data. The security of backed up data is just as important as the security of the servers being backed up.

Backup locations

Windows Server Backup enables you to back up to any locally attached disk, a volume, the storage area network (SAN), or any network folder. When configuring a scheduled backup, you should specify a destination volume or disk that is empty. If the disk is local or connected to the SAN, Windows Server Backup performs a full back up at least once every 14 days and incremental backups on subsequent backups. Incremental backups in Windows Server use block-level backups rather than file-level backups, meaning that the incremental backups are much smaller. Rather than backing up all the files that have changed since the last backup, only the data blocks that have changed on the hard disk are backed up. For example, if you change one image in a 25-megabyte (MB) PowerPoint file after it is backed up, only the data blocks associated with that image are backed up next time, not the whole 25-MB file.

Inside OUT

Backup location

Although you can write backup data to a different volume on the same disk, you should back up data to a different disk so that if your disk fails, you don't lose both the data being protected and the backup itself.

There is an exception to the rule about how data is written during scheduled automatic full and incremental backups. This exception occurs when the backup data is written to a network folder. When you back up to a network folder, as opposed to a SAN-connected disk, which appears as local to Windows Server, each backup is a full backup and the previous full backup that was stored on the network share is erased. Because only one backup at a time can be stored on a network share, if you choose to back up to this location, you can't recover data from any backup other than the most recently performed one.

You can modify the performance of full system and full volume backups by using the Optimize Backup Performance dialog, and you can increase backup performance by using the Faster Backup Performance option. The drawback of selecting this option is that it reduces disk performance on the disks that host the volumes you're backing up.

Backing up data

You can back up data using a variety of methods with Windows Server Backup. You can configure a scheduled backup, which means a backup occurs on a scheduled basis. You can also perform a one-off backup. When you perform a one-off backup, you can either use the existing scheduled backup settings, or you can configure a separate set of settings for one-off backups. For example, you can configure Windows Server Backup to perform a full server backup twice a day to a locally attached disk. You can connect at any time and perform a one-off backup where you select only specific files and folders and have them written to a location on the network.

CHAPTER 23

Role- and application-specific backups

Most Windows Server roles and features store data in locations that are backed up when you perform a System State backup. System State data is automatically backed up when you perform a full server backup or select it for backup. Depending on the roles and features installed on the computer running Windows Server, the System State can contain the following data:

- Registry

- Local users and groups

- COM+ Class Registration database

- Boot files

- Active Directory Certificate Services (AD CS) database

- Active Directory database (`Ntds.dit`)

- SYSVOL directory

- Cluster service information

- System files under Windows Resource Protection

- Internet Information Services (IIS) settings

Some applications also register themselves with Windows Server Backup. This means that when you perform a full server backup, you can recover data that is only relevant to the application without having to perform a full system restore. Support for application registration depends on the application. You can't select a specific application for back up using Windows Server Backup, but you can restore applications that have registered themselves with Windows Server Backup as long as you've previously performed a full server backup.

Restore from backups

Windows Server Backup enables you to restore data that has been backed up on the local computer, or data that was backed up on another computer using Windows Server Backup that is accessible to the local computer. You can use Windows Server Backup to do the following:

- You can use Windows Server Backup to restore files and folders as well as applications.

- You can use Windows Server Backup to restore the System State data. After the System State data is restored, you need to restart the computer.

- You can use Windows Server Backup to restore any volume except the one that hosts the operating system. If you want to restore the volume that hosts the operating system, you need to boot into the Windows Recovery Environment.

- You can use the Windows Recovery Environment to perform a full server restore, also known as a bare metal recovery. When you do this, all existing data and volumes on the server are overwritten with the backed-up data.

If multiple backups of the data you want to restore exist, you need to select which version to restore. If you're unsure which date holds the data you want to restore, you should restore to multiple alternative locations and then perform the comparison. This process saves you from restoring, figuring out you've restored the wrong data, performing another restore, and then figuring out that restore isn't right either.

Windows Server Backup writes backups to .vhdx files, the same type of file that is used with Hyper-V and when creating disks for Internet Small Computer System Interface (iSCSI) targets and disks in storage pools. Windows Server also allows you to mount the contents of a virtual hard disk (VHD), which allows you to examine those contents without having to perform a full restoration using Windows Server Backup.

Restore to an alternative location

When you are performing data restoration, you can choose to restore data to the original location or to an alternative location. It's not uncommon when restoring data to the original location for backup administrators to unintentionally overwrite good, live data with older, restored data. If you restore to an alternative location, it's possible to compare the restored data against the current data. It's also important when restoring data that you retain permissions associated with data.

If you choose to restore to the original location, you can configure Windows Server Backup to perform one of the following tasks:

- Automatically create copies if an original exists

- Overwrite existing versions

- Do not recover any item that exists in the recovery destination

Azure Backup

The Microsoft Azure Recovery Services (MARS) Agent allows you to back up data directly to a Microsoft Azure backup recovery services vault service. You install the MARS agent client on the Internet-connected computer server that you want to back up, and the backup data is stored in an Azure Recovery Vault. The MARS agent functions as an offsite data storage and recovery service and can be used in conjunction with Windows Server Backup. If a site is lost, you can still recover this important data from Azure.

CHAPTER 23

You can run both the Windows Server Backup and Azure Backup Agent services in parallel. This approach enables you to perform local backups and backups to Azure on the same server. You can then do frequent full-server backups locally, with infrequent critical data backups to Azure. When you employ this strategy, you mostly restore data from your local backups. It's only when something goes drastically wrong that you need to restore data from Azure.

The key to understanding what data to back up to Azure is looking at what types of information your organization might lose if a site has some type of disaster. You can always reinstall operating systems and applications from media that you can easily obtain again. The data stored on your servers however, such as documents and settings, is something that you can't generate from installation media. By storing data in the cloud, you can recover it in the event of a disaster after you've rebuilt your server infrastructure.

Preparing Azure Backup

The entire process of configuring and managing Azure Backup can be performed from Windows Admin Center. This includes the creation of a Recovery Services Vault that's used to store backup data in Azure.

To configure Azure Backup with Windows Admin Center, perform the following steps:

1. When you're connected to the server you want to configure with Azure Backup, click Backup in Windows Admin Center.

2. With Backup selected, click Set Up Azure Backup.

3. If you aren't already signed in to an account with Azure administrator permissions, you'll be required to sign in to Azure.

4. By default, an Azure datacenter and recovery services vault will be selected for creation. You also have the option of creating your own recovery services vault, and you can specify a Resource Group and datacenter Location.

5. By default, you can back up System State data and selected folders and files to be protected. By default, backups will occur weekly and be retained for four weeks. You can alter what is protected using the Azure Backup Utility that will be installed on your server.

6. You will be prompted to provide an encryption passphrase. You will need to ensure that you keep a record of this passphrase somewhere other than a text file on the desktop of the server because without the passphrase, you won't be able to perform restore operations. Microsoft can't perform a restoration for you if you lose the passphrase because they are never provided with a copy and just store the backup data encrypted with the passphrase. The passphrase must be a minimum of 16 characters long, and you can save it to an external location, such as a USB storage device.

7. Once you click OK, the infrastructure in Azure will be created for you, and the selected backup schedule will be enacted.

Backing up data to Azure Backup Agent

Modifying an Azure Backup Schedule and selections is very similar to the Schedule Backup Wizard in Windows Server Backup. After the Azure Backup Agent is installed by Windows Admin Center, you can run the tool to do the following:

- **Select which items to back up**   Item selection is file and folder based. Although you can select a volume to back up, you don't use Azure Backup to perform full volume recovery in the same way you would use Windows Server Backup. When selecting items to back up, you can configure exclusions for file types, folders, or folder trees.

- **Select a backup schedule**   This option determines how often a synchronization occurs. You can configure Azure Backup to synchronize up to three times per day. You can also configure bandwidth throttling. Throttling enables you to limit the utilization of bandwidth and ensures that your organization's Internet connection isn't choked with backup traffic replicating to the recovery vault on Azure during business hours.

- **Configure backup retention**   The retention setting, which you configure on the Specify Retention Setting page, determines how long backup data is stored in Azure before it's deleted. You can configure retention for Windows Server Backup when creating a policy in Windows PowerShell.

Restore from Azure Backup

Azure Backup enables you to restore files and folders that are stored in your Azure Recovery Services Vault. You can't perform a full server recovery, System State recovery, or volume recovery using Azure Backup directly; you can only restore files and folders. Of course, if you've backed up all the files and folders on a volume, you can either restore them individually or all at one time or use the MARS agent to restore. Azure Backup also enables you to restore data from another server that you've backed up to Azure. Recovering data using Azure Backup involves performing the following steps:

1. Select the server that you want to recover data from.

2. Select whether you want to browse or search for files to recover.

3. Select the volume that hosts the data you want to recover and the specific backup date and time that you want to recover data from.

4. Select the items that you want to recover. You can recover files, folders, and folder trees.

5. Select Recovery Options, including whether to restore to the original location or an alternative location, or you want to create copies or overwrite original files. You can also use this page of the wizard to choose whether to restore the original permissions.

To remove all backup data from a recovery vault using Azure Backup, you'll need to go into the Azure Console and generate a security PIN. The PIN is valid only for a short period of time.

More Info

Azure Backup

You can learn more about Azure Backup at *https://learn.microsoft.com/azure/backup/backup-overview.*

Vssadmin

Volume Shadow Copy Services (VSS) is a technology that provides a snapshot of data on a volume as it existed at a specific point in time. VSS enables you to make a consistent backup of a file that is in use, such as a mailbox database or SQL Server database. Prior to the introduction of VSS, you might have needed to take such a database offline to ensure that the database's backup was consistent. Consistency issues arise when it takes so long to back up a large file or system that the configuration of the system or the contents of the file change during the backup. Windows Server Backup, Azure Backup Agent, and other backup products, such as Data Protection Manager, use VSS to ensure that the data backed up is consistent and represents the state of the backed up data as it was at the point when the backup started without having to take in-use files offline.

Vssadmin is a command-line utility that enables you to manage volume shadow copy snapshots. You can use VSS admin to perform the following tasks:

- Configure the location of shadow copy storage.

- Create a shadow copy.

- Delete a shadow copy.

- Delete shadow copy storage.

- View existing shadow copies.

- View existing shadow copy storage.

- View volumes that are configured with shadow copies.

- View subscribed shadow copy writers and providers (special software that creates and manages shadow copies).

- Resize shadow copy storage.

You can also view shadow copy status on a per-volume basis through the Previous Versions tab. When used with file shares, the VSS snapshots exposed through the Previous Versions function-ality enable users to recover previous versions of files and folders without having to restore from backup. To do this, right-click the parent folder or volume and click Restore Previous Versions. You can then select previous versions of files that correspond to existing VSS snapshots.

Although Vssadmin allows you to create and manage VSS snapshots, you can't use Vssadmin to configure a schedule to automatically create VSS snapshots. You can configure a schedule to create VSS snapshots on a per-volume basis by right-clicking a volume and by clicking Config-ure Shadow Copies. After you enable shadow copies, you can configure a schedule in the Set-tings dialog. By default, when you enable Shadow Copies, a shadow copy is created at 07:00 and noon every weekday, but you can modify the schedule so that copies are created more often. When doing this, remember that after the initial allocated space used to store shadow copies is consumed, older shadow copies are removed to make space to store new versions. The amount of space needed to store shadow copies and the retention period depends on the properties of the data stored on the volume.

Windows Server Update Services

You can install Windows Server Update Services (WSUS) as a role on Windows Server in both the Server Core and GUI configurations. Although WSUS does include Windows PowerShell support, not all WSUS functionality has been replicated in Windows PowerShell, and you'll likely need to manage a WSUS server deployed on Server Core using the RSAT tools.

When you install WSUS, you can choose between using a local Windows Internal Database (WID) or a SQL Server instance. The advantage of using a SQL Server instance is that it's easier to back up, and you can run more complex reports. The majority of WSUS deployments use the built-in WID database. When you install WSUS on Windows Server, all prerequisite components are also installed.

Inside OUT
Deprecated, but not forgotten

WSUS has been announced as a deprecated feature. This means that new features won't be added, and, at some point, it will be taken out of the Windows Server operating system. For now, it's still supported. As you will be aware of by now, many features that have been dep-recated remain in the Windows Server operating system. That means they will be functional for the support lifespan of the operating system. I wouldn't be surprised if WSUS is still something you can deploy on new versions of Windows Server released in the 2030s.

Products, security classifications, and languages

During setup, you're asked to choose which update you want to download based on product name, security classification, and languages. Although you can choose to download updates for all product categories for all classifications in all languages, you'll minimize the amount of configuration required later if you download updates only for products used on your organizational network.

When WSUS synchronizes, it may update the list of available product names to reflect newly released software. If your organization deploys a new product or retires an old product, or if you simply want to alter which updates are synchronized, you can modify which products are updated using the Products And Classifications dialog, available through Options in the Update Services console.

Autonomous and replica modes

A single WSUS server can support approximately 25,000 clients. Large organizations often have multiple WSUS servers because it's better to have a local WSUS server at each large site rather than having clients pull updates and approvals across wide area network (WAN) links. Instead of administrators performing the same approvals on each WSUS server in the organization, you can configure a WSUS server as a replica of another server. When you configure a WSUS server as a replica, the downstream server copies all update approvals, settings, computers, and groups from its parent. You can configure the Update Source settings, as well as specify information that enables WSUS to use a proxy server, through the Update Source And Proxy Server item in Options in the Update Services console.

Update files

One of the benefits of deploying WSUS is that clients on the local network download their updates from the WSUS server rather than downloading updates from the Microsoft Update servers on the Internet. You can configure update storage location settings using the Update Files And Languages item in the Options area of the Update Services console. You can configure the following options:

- **Store Update Files Locally On This Server**   When you choose this option, you can choose whether to download files only after they have been approved; download express installation files, which install quicker on clients; or download files from Microsoft Update. With the last option, you can configure a server as a replica server but have update files downloaded from Microsoft Update rather than the upstream replica server.

- **Don't Store Update Files Locally; Computers Install From Microsoft Update**   When you configure this option, clients use WSUS for update approvals but retrieve the updates from the Microsoft Update servers on the Internet. This option is most appropriate when you're providing update approvals to clients located outside of the organizational network.

WSUS security roles

In large organizations, you're more likely to separate the roles of server administrator and update administrator. When you install WSUS, two local security groups are created. By adding users to these groups, you grant users the permission to perform the tasks assigned with these roles. The roles are as follows:

- **WSUS Administrators**   Users who are added to the local WSUS Administrators group can perform any WSUS administration task. These tasks include approving updates, managing computer groups, configuring automatic approval rules, and modifying the WSUS server's update source.

- **WSUS Reporters**   Users who are members of this role can run reports on the WSUS server. These reports detail the update compliance status on the basis of update and computer. For example, a user who is a member of this group can run a WSUS report and determine which computers are missing a specific critical update.

WSUS groups

You can use WSUS groups to organize computers for the purpose of deploying updates. For example, you might have a WSUS group for servers in Sydney and another WSUS group for servers in Melbourne. A computer can be a member of multiple WSUS groups, and WSUS groups can exist in parent-child relationships. For example, the Australia WSUS group might have both the Melbourne and Sydney WSUS groups as members. Updates approved for the Australia group are automatically approved for members of the Melbourne and Sydney groups unless overridden.

You can assign computers to WSUS groups manually or through Group Policy. Computers can be assigned to WSUS groups through Group Policy only if the computer groups already exist on the WSUS server. To assign a computer manually, the computer must have already reported to the WSUS server. Computers that have reported to the WSUS server but have not been assigned to a group are members of the Unassigned Computers group.

An administrator must create WSUS groups. To create a WSUS group, perform the following steps:

1. Open the Update Services console.

2. Click the group you want to have as the parent group. The Computers/All Computers group is the parent group for all groups.

3. From the Action menu, click Add Computer Group.

4. Specify the computer group name and click Add.

CHAPTER 23

WSUS policies

You can configure most WSUS client options through Group Policy. Many of these policies are related to the experience that users of client operating systems have when updates are installed and are not directly applicable to updating server operating systems. Windows Update policies are located in the `Computer Configuration\Policies\Administrative Templates\Windows Components\Windows Update` node of a standard GPO, as shown in Figure 23-2.

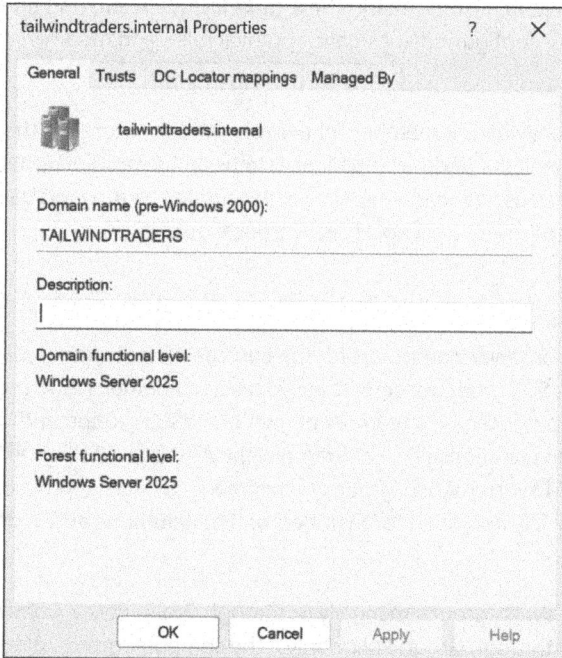

Figure 23-2   Update policies

The most important policies from the perspective of the server administrator are as follows:

- **Configure Automatic Updates**   You can enable automatic updating, specify a day for update installations, and specify a time for update installation to occur. It's usually not a good idea to have this one policy apply to all servers in your organization. Having all servers install and reboot at the same time can cause substantial disruptions.

- **Specify Intranet Microsoft Update Service Location**   You can specify the location of the WSUS server and the statistics server. (The statistics server receives information on successful update installation and is usually the same as the WSUS server.)

- **Automatic Update Detection Frequency**   Determines how often the computer checks for updates.

- **Enable Client-Side Targeting**   Use this policy to specify which WSUS groups computers should be a member of. If the names do not match, those computers end up in the Unassigned Computers group.

Deploying updates

When you deploy updates, you decide whether to deploy the update, to which computer groups you deploy the update, and what deadline should apply to the deployment. You can deploy an update multiple times to different groups, so you can deploy an update to a test group and then, if no issues arise with the update, deploy the update more generally. Prior to deploying updates, you should perform a synchronization, which ensures that the WSUS server is to be up to date before choosing whether to deploy updates.

To deploy an update, perform the following steps:

1. Open the Update Services console and select the Updates\All Updates node. You can also select a child node, such as Critical Updates, if you want to view only available critical updates.

2. Set the Approval setting to Unapproved, set the Status to Any, and click Refresh. All unapproved updates are then listed.

3. Click one or more updates and then click Approve in the Actions pane.

4. In the Approve Updates dialog, select which computer groups the update is approved for. You can choose between the following settings:

    - **Approved For Install**   Approves the update

    - **Approved For Removal**   Removes a previously deployed update

    - **Not Approved**   Does not approve the update

    - **Keep Existing Approvals**   Inherits the approval from the parent group

    - **Deadline**   Specifies an update deployment deadline

Automatic approval rules

Automatic approval rules enable specifically categorized updates to be automatically approved. For example, you might choose to automatically approve critical updates for the Sydney-Development-Servers WSUS group.

To configure an automatic approval rule, perform the following steps:

1. Open the Update Services console. You can do this from the Tools menu of Server Manager or by right-clicking the server in a Server group and clicking Windows Server Update Services.

2. In the Update Services console, click Options and then click Automatic Approvals.

3. In the Automatic Approvals dialog, click New Rule.

4. In the Add Rule dialog, choose the following rule options:

   - **When An Update Is In A Specific Classification**   You can choose that the rule applies when an update matches a specific classification or number of classifications. Update classifications include Critical Updates, Definition Updates, Drivers, Feature Packs, Security Updates, Service Packs, Tools, Update Rollups, and Updates. Microsoft includes classifications for each software update when it publishes the update.

   - **When An Update Is For A Specific Product**   You can specify products, either by category, such as Exchange, or by specific product, such as Exchange Server 2019.

   - **Approve The Update For A Specific Computer Group**   The update can be approved for selected computer groups.

   - **Set An Approval Deadline**   Sets an installation deadline for the update based on the time and date the update was first approved.

Inside OUT

Canary users

Automatic approval rules aren't suitable for production servers hosting important workloads because it's possible that an update will be installed without being properly tested. Automatic approval rules are suitable for test groups. You should populate your test group with users who are more likely to offer feedback if something goes wrong. Just as a canary in a coal mine was used by miners to detect dangerous gas, "canary users" are likely to raise an alarm when a software update causes problems that indicate it shouldn't be deployed in a production environment. Users who complain are much more valuable as deployment targets for update testing than users who ignore problems and do not provide feedback.

> ## More Info
> ### WSUS
>
> You can learn more about WSUS at *https://learn.microsoft.com/en-us/win-dows-server/administration/windows-server-update-services/get-started/windows-server-update-services-wsus.*

Azure Update Manager

Azure Update Manager allows you to automate the deployment of updates to computers running both the Windows and Linux operating systems. You can configure Azure Arc–enabled on-premises Windows Servers to use Azure Update Manager by using Windows Admin Center. To manage an on-premises Windows Server with Azure Update Manager, you Azure Arc–enable the machine so it appears as a resource in Azure. Azure Arc is covered in more detail by Chapter 9, "Azure Arc and hybrid services."

Once a computer is Azure Arc enabled, navigate to Azure Update Manager in the Azure portal. Click Enable Now or Check For Updates on the machine's Update page to trigger an update scan. This will deploy a lightweight Azure Update Manager agent extension on the Arc-enabled machine, which communicates with Windows Update on that computer via the Arc agent.

Once the assessment completes, the Azure Update Manager dashboard will display the machine's update compliance status. You can use this to determine which pending updates are available for that server. You can then deploy updates to that server by choosing Install Updates Immediately. This triggers the extension to download and apply all selected updates.

Azure Update Manager uses Maintenance Configurations to define recurring patch schedules through which you run automated update deployment. To do this, create a schedule in which you specify start time, frequency, and duration of the update window. For example, you might create a schedule to run every second Sunday at 2:00 a.m. and specify a four-hour window for a collection of servers. Azure Update Manager will then automatically install updates during that four-hour window on the selected computers.

When creating the schedule, you can include or exclude specific updates by classification or KB ID/package. For example, you could have the schedule install only updates classified as Security and Critical updates. You can also configure the reboot settings within the schedule, choosing to never reboot, always reboot, or reboot if required.

Azure Update Manager provides integrated dashboards to track update compliance across your hybrid environment. The Update Manager Overview shows summary statistics for computers that are compliant and missing critical updates. You can view the update status of individual machines to determine which ones might have been missed in a scheduled update run.

CHAPTER 23

> ## More Info
>
> *Azure Update Manager*
>
> You can learn more about Azure Update Manager at *https://learn.microsoft.com/ azure/ update-manager/*.

Monitoring- and maintenance-related PowerShell cmdlets

There are a variety of PowerShell cmdlets that you can use for monitoring and maintenance tasks. These cmdlets are described in Table 23-1.

Table 23-1   Cmdlets used for event logs and Windows Server Backup

Noun	Verbs	Function
EventLog	Clear, Get, Limit, New, Remove, Show, Write	Manage Windows Event logs, including viewing events, creating events, and clearing logs
WinEvent	Get, New	View and create events from traditional event logs, as well as files generated by Event Tracing for Windows
WBApplicationRecovery	Start	Start application recovery
WBBackup	Start, Resume	Start or resume an existing backup
WBBackupSet	Get, Remove	Manage backups
WBBackupTarget	Get, Remove, Add, New	Manage backup targets
WBBackupVolumeBrowsePath	Get	View backup volumes
WBBareMetalRecovery	Remove, Get, Add	Configure bare metal recovery
WBCatalog	Restore, Remove	Manage Windows Server Backup catalog
WBDisk	Get	View disks online on the local computer
WBFileSpec	Get, New, Remove, Add	Manage items to include or exclude from a backup
WBHyperVRecovery	Start	Start Hyper-V VM recovery
WBJob	Stop, Get	Manage Windows Backup jobs
WBPerformanceConfiguration	Set, Get	Configure performance options
WBPolicy	Get, Remove, Set, New	Configure Windows Backup policies
WBSchedule	Set, Get	Configure Windows Backup schedule

Noun	Verbs	Function
WBSummary	Get	View backup summary information
WBSystemState	Add, Get, Remove	Manage backup of system state data
WBVirtualMachine	Add, Remove, Get	Manage the backup of virtual machines
WBVolume	Add, Remove, Get	Configure Windows Backup volumes
WBVolumeRecovery	Resume, Start	Manage volume recovery
WBVssBackupOption	Get, Set	Configure VSS backup options

WSUS-related PowerShell cmdlets

There are a variety of PowerShell cmdlets that you can use for WSUS tasks. These cmdlets are described in Table 23-2.

Table 23-2   Cmdlets used for Windows Server Update Services

Noun	Verbs	Function
WsusClassification	Set, Get	Managed which update classifications are synchronized
WsusComputer	Add, Get	Manage computers registered with the WSUS server
WsusDynamicCategory	Add, Remove, Get, Set	Manage WSUS dynamic categories
WsusProduct	Set, Get	Manage which products WSUS will synchronize updates for
WsusServer	Get	View the properties of a WSUS server
WsusServerCleanup	Invoke	Cleans up obsolete computer and updates registered with the WSUS server
WsusServerSynchroniza-tion	Set	Configures WSUS server synchronization with Microsoft Update or upstream server
WsusUpdate	Get, Approve, Deny	Manage specific updates

CHAPTER 24

Upgrade and migration

In most cases, organizations that are deploying a new version of Windows Server such as Windows Server 2025 will be deploying the operating system into an existing Windows Server environment. While new workloads will be hosted on new servers, most organizations adopting the new version of Windows Server will be interested in upgrading or migrating existing workloads to the operating system.

In this chapter, you'll learn about upgrading or migrating several core Windows Server roles and features from previous supported versions of the Windows Server operating system to Windows Server 2025.

Supported upgrade and migration paths

A general rule about supported upgrade and migration paths is that you need to ensure that the product that you're upgrading from is still within Microsoft's extended support window and that you've applied all released service packs and software updates to the workload before attempting migration or upgrade. The difference between migration and upgrade is as follows:

- **Migration** More common than an upgrade, a migration involves moving roles and data from an existing server running a supported version of Windows Server to a freshly deployed server running Windows Server 2025. Migration is Microsoft's preferred option and fits better with the "treat servers as cattle not and not as pets" philosophy of systems administration. This philosophy dictates that installation and configuration be as automated as possible, so instead of painstakingly crafting the configuration of an individual server, administrators can apply complex configurations quickly so that server upgrade or replacement is considered an uncomplicated routine operation rather than one that requires painstaking attention to arcane and not entirely understood processes.

- **Upgrade** Sometimes called an in-place upgrade, this usually involves running the Windows Server 2025 setup routine from within an existing Windows Server deployment. Windows Server 2025 differs from earlier versions of Windows Server in that you can perform a direct upgrade of an activated version of Windows Server 2012 R2 or later directly to Windows Server 2025. This includes upgrading Active Directory domain controllers and Hyper-V servers. With Windows Server 2022 and earlier, you could only perform in-place upgrades from the prior two releases. It's also possible to perform an in-place upgrade to Windows Server 2025 even if the server you're upgrading doesn't have a TPM 2.0 chip, though this will limit what security features you can enable.

Inside OUT

End of support

Windows Server versions enjoy approximately 10 years of security update support after release. Windows Server 2025, released in late 2024, reaches its end of support on October 10, 2034. In addition to the 10 years of security updates, Microsoft also makes extended security updates available for approximately three years, but you can only access them for a fee. This fee also increases each year as an incentive for organizations to upgrade to a supported version of Windows Server.

When you perform an in-place upgrade, all the applications, data, roles, and features that were present on the source server remain available on the upgraded server. While the applications, data, roles, and features will remain present, that doesn't mean that they will all be functional. Prior to attempting an in-place upgrade, you should check whether applications that are hosted on the source operating system are compatible with the new version of Windows Server. Unless you've enabled some of the new security features on the most recent versions of Windows Server, any workload that runs on Windows Server 2012 R2 or later is likely to be compatible.

You can upgrade from the Standard Edition to the Standard or Datacenter Edition. You can only upgrade a computer running the Datacenter Edition of Windows Server to the Datacenter Edition.

Upgrading roles and features

Upgrades are constrained by the following additional limitations:

- Upgrades from one language to another are not supported. For example, you can't upgrade a French edition of Windows Server 2012 R2 to a German edition of Windows Server 2025.

- You cannot upgrade a Server Core installation to a Server with a Desktop installation.

- You cannot upgrade a Server with a Desktop installation to a Server Core installation.

- You cannot upgrade from a licensed version of a Windows Server operating system to an evaluation edition. Microsoft recommends that you only install evaluation editions as clean installations.

- You can't perform an in-place upgrade of an evaluation version of Windows Server 2012 R2 or Windows Server 2016 to Windows Server 2025.

Converting the evaluation version to a licensed version

Although it's far from best practice, many organizations that deploy the 180-day evaluation version of Windows Server as part of a project prototype find, several months later, that the prototype has morphed into a critical component in the organization's workflow. Rather than reinstall Windows Server and migrate the prototype deployment to a properly licensed, long-term production platform, it's instead possible to convert an evaluation version of Windows Server to a properly licensed version by performing the following steps:

1. From an elevated command prompt, run the slmgr.vbs /dlv command to display the current computer's licensing information, as shown in Figure 24-1.

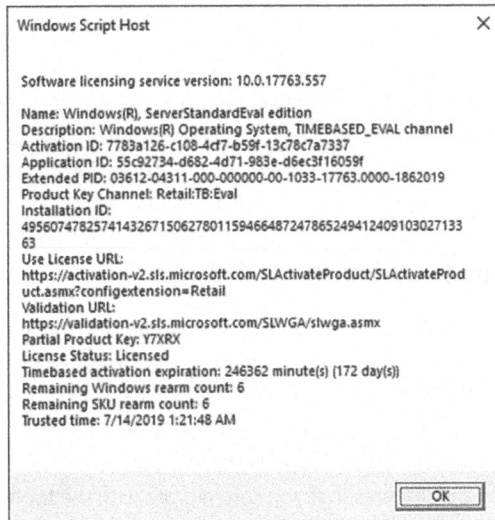

Figure 24-1   Software licensing information

2. Determine the current edition by running the DISM /online /Get-CurrentEdition command. This will display the edition ID, such as ServerStandard or ServerStandardCore. You will need this edition ID for the next step.

3. Once you've determined the edition, run the DISM /online /Set-Edition:<editionID> /ProductKey:XXXXX-XXXXX-XXXXX-XXXXX-XXXXX / AcceptEula command.

> ## Inside OUT
> ### Evaluation domain controllers
>
> You can't switch a computer that's running as a domain controller on an evaluation version of Windows Server to a retail version of the operating system. If you have a domain controller running on an evaluation version that you want to convert, Microsoft recommends that you install an additional Windows Server domain controller running a non-evaluation and licensed version of Windows Server into the domain. Then, you should transfer FSMO roles, remove AD DS from the server running the evaluation version, perform the switch to the full activated version, and then reinstall AD DS.

Upgrading editions

You can also use DISM to upgrade from one edition of Windows Server to another. For example, if you want to upgrade from the Standard Edition of Windows Server to the Datacenter Edition, specify the ServerDatacenter or ServerDatacenterCore product edition and enter the appropriate product key using the `DISM /online /Set-Edition:<editionID> /ProductKey:<productkey>` command.

You can use `slmgr.vbs` to switch between a retail license and a volume license. To do this from an elevated prompt, use the `slmgr.vbs /ipk <key>` command, where <key> is the volume license key. If you're trying to convert an evaluation version of Windows Server to a volume-licensed version, you must switch to a retail version, as described earlier.

Windows Server Migration Tools

The Windows Server Migration Tools (WSMT) is a Windows Server feature that you can use to migrate a specific set of server roles, features, shared folders, operating system settings, and data from a source computer running the Windows Server 2008 R2 or later operating system. The WSMT hasn't been updated for several editions of Windows Server, with the most recent version being for Windows Server 2016, but these tools are still included with the operating system as of Windows Server 2025. As most of the roles and features that you can migrate with the tools also haven't been updated much since Windows Server 2016, the WSMT offers a good first option for moving the following roles and features from an older version of Windows Server to a more recent one:

- Active Directory Certificate Services
- Active Directory Federation Services
- Active Directory Rights Management Services
- File and storage services
- Hyper-V

- Network Policy Server

- Remote Desktop Services

- Windows Server Update Services

- Cluster Roles

- DHCP Server

- Web Server (IIS)

Inside OUT

Storage Migration Services

While WSMT supports migration of file servers, Storage Migration Services provides a more comprehensive way of migrating file servers. You'll learn more about Storage Migration Services later in the chapter.

The WSMT supports

- Migration from physically deployed operating systems to virtually deployed operating systems.

- Server Core and Server with a GUI installation option on Windows Server 2008 R2 and later.

- WSMT can only be used if the source and destination operating systems are using the same UI language. The system UI language is the one used when setting up the operating system.

Inside OUT

Where possible, Server Core

The Server Core installation option is the Windows Server default. When migrating to Windows Server, strongly consider shifting as many workloads to hosts running the Server Core installation option rather than the Desktop Experience installation option. Unless you are in an environment with a small number of servers, it's likely that you already use remote consoles and PowerShell to manage servers (and rarely, RDP) to the server desktop. You won't be able to do it with all servers, especially those running applications that require desktop components, but you will be able to do it with a good number of servers, such as those hosting boring roles, such as functioning as file servers, DHCP servers, DNS servers, and domain controllers. With the ongoing improvements

> in Windows Admin Center, a Server Core first-deployment strategy makes more sense.
> Though having said all that, every time I ask audiences at an event if anyone is running
> Server Core in their environments, only a fraction of the audience puts up their hands.
> The recommendation is to use Server Core. However, in practice, even though it's been
> available for almost two decades, it's rarely done.

The WSMT has the following requirements:

- Must be deployed using an account that has local administrator privileges on the source and destination server.

- The source server must have at least 23 MB of free space to store the WSMT deployment folder.

- The source server must have the .NET Framework 3.51 installed.

- You should always use the version of the WSMT provided with the most recent version of Windows Server.

Installing the WSMT

You can install the WSMT on the destination server using the `Install-WindowsFeature Migration` PowerShell command or by installing the role using the Add Roles And Features Wizard. When you do this, the WSMT is deployed in the `%WinDir%\System32\ServerMigrationTools` folder on the destination server.

Once you've installed the WSMT, you need to configure a deployment folder from which you will deploy the appropriate version of the WSMT. Rather than deploy a generic version of the tools, deploy a version tailored for the source operating system. For example, to create a set of tools for a source computer running Windows Server 2016, issue this command:

```
Smigdeploy.exe /package /architecture amd64 /os WS16 /path <path to share>
```

As the WSMT hasn't been updated since Windows Server 2016, that's the most recent version of the tools that you can configure.

You can either copy the contents of the deployment folder to the source computer or run the tools remotely over a network connection by running `smigdeploy.exe` from an elevated command prompt. If you're running the tools on a computer that is configured with the Server Core installation option, open an elevated PowerShell session and run the following command to add the WSMT cmdlets:

```
Add-PSSnapin Microsoft.Windows.ServerManager.Migration
```

Active Directory

Active Directory Domain Controllers are the workload that Microsoft always recommends you run on the latest version of Windows Server. This is because the latest version of Windows Server is always the most secure, and you always want your identity infrastructure to be running the most secure version of Windows Server.

Microsoft's recommended strategy for upgrading domain controllers in a domain or forest to the latest version of Windows Server is to

- Add member servers running the most recent version of Windows Server to a domain

- Promote those member servers to domain controllers

- Transfer FSMO roles across to the domain controllers running the most recent version of Windows Server from the domain controllers running previous versions of the Windows Server operating system

- Demoting those domain controllers running the older version of the operating system

In some circumstances, you might need to perform an upgrade of a domain controller rather than using the recommended strategy. For example, in an environment where you have a Windows Server 2012 R2 domain controller that you want to perform an in-place upgrade to Windows Server 2025, prior to attempting the upgrade, you'll need to manually run adprep / forestprep and adprep /domainprep from the \support\adprep folder from the Windows Server installation media.

You should upgrade the domain controllers in the forest root domain and then upgrade the domain controllers in any child domains. Once you've upgraded all the domain controllers in your organization, you can then raise the domain functional level of each domain in the forest to Windows Server using the Active Directory Domains And Trust console. Windows Server 2025 introduced the Windows Server 2025 domain and forest functional level, as shown in Figure 24-2. The highest you could raise the functional level if you had Windows Server 2016, Windows Server 2019, or a domain where all domain controllers were running Windows Server 2022 domain controllers is the Windows Server 2016 domain and forest functional level.

If all of the domain controllers in the forest are running the Windows Server 2025 operating system, you can upgrade all the forest functional levels and all domain functional levels at the same time.

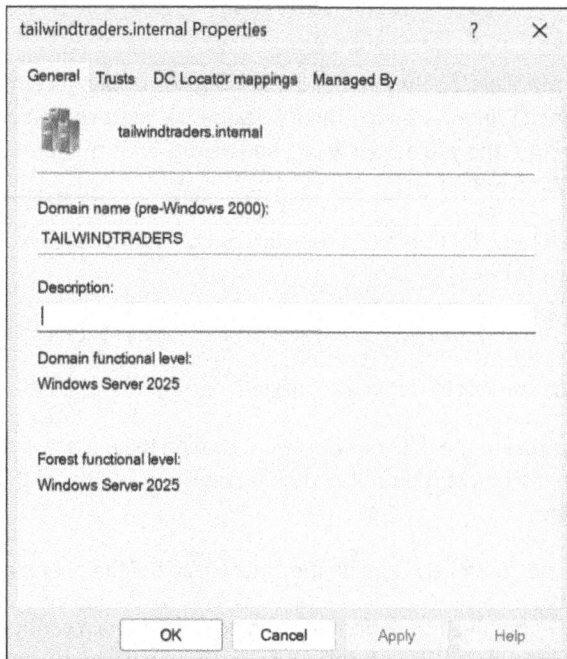

Figure 24-2   Domain and forest functional level

More Info

Upgrading domain controllers

You can learn more about upgrading domain controllers at *https://learn.microsoft.com/ windows-server/identity/ad-ds/deploy/upgrade-domain-controllers*.

FRS to DFSR migration

Depending on the age of your organization's Active Directory deployment—especially if a domain once functioned at the Windows Server 2003 functional level—and how diligently Active Directory upgrades were performed, SYSVOL replication may be configured to use the older inefficient File Replication Service, rather than the more efficient Distributed File System.

You can check whether SYSVOL replication is configured to use FRS or DFS using the dfsrmig. exe utility with the /globalstate parameter. If the output state of the command shows Eliminated, as in Figure 24-3, then SYSVOL already uses DFS for replication.

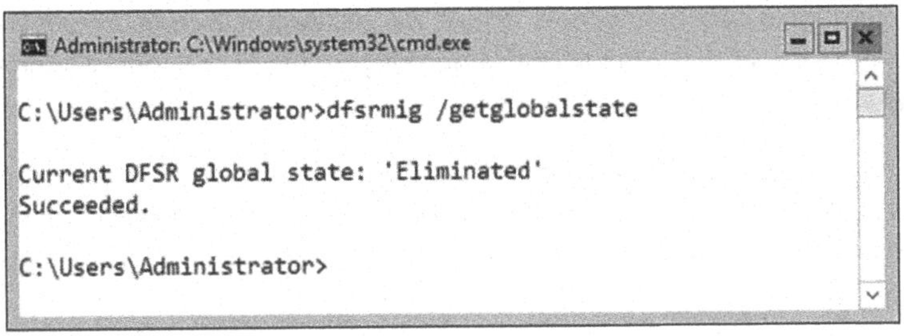

Figure 24-3 SYSVOL migration state

If the output of dfsrmig.exe instead shows that migration has yet to be initialized, you should update the SYSVOL replication. You should only use FSR for SYSVOL replication if your organization still has domain controllers running the Windows Server 2003 or Windows Server 2003 R2 operating systems. Because Windows Server 2003 and Windows Server 2003 R2 have not been supported for some time, you shouldn't be running domain controllers with these operating systems.

To upgrade SYSVOL replication to DFS from FRS, perform the following steps:

1. Sign in to a domain controller with credentials that are a member of the Domain Admin or Enterprise Admin groups.

2. Start PowerShell and then run the dfsrmig /setglobalstate 1 command. Depending on the number of domain controllers in the domain, it can take more than an hour to reach the prepared state. You can verify that the prepared state has been reached by running the dfsrmig /getmigrationstate command. When preparation is completed, the utility will report that the global state is Prepared.

3. Next, set the DFSR state to Redirected. You do this using the dfsrmig / setglobalstate 2 command. You use dfsrmig /getmigration to verify that the DFSR state is set to Redirected.

4. Once the DFSR state is set to Redirected, run the dfsrmig /setglobalstate 3 command. This will finalize the transition of SYSVOL to the Eliminated state, and DFS will be used for replication instead of FRS.

Migrating to a new forest

Many organizations have had their current Active Directory environment for more than a decade. The older an Active Directory environment is, the more likely it is to have an inefficient domain and OU structure, derelict user and computer accounts, unutilized sites, and forgotten group policy objects and groups. Just as Microsoft recommends performing fresh installations rather than in-place upgrades for individual computers, it may make more sense to migrate to a new forest than it does to remain with an existing Active Directory forest. This is especially true if an organization is considering moving toward a secure administrative model where the privileged accounts in a production forest are unprivileged standard accounts in the secure administrative forest.

The Active Directory Migration Tool (ADMT) is a special tool that you can use to migrate Active Directory objects to and from any Active Directory environment, from moving accounts within a forest to migrating accounts to a new Active Directory forest. Like other migration tools, it's been some time since it's been updated, but it serves as a good first option for this type of migration.

You can use ADMT to perform an interforest restructure or an intraforest restructure. An intraforest restructure allows you to modify your current domain and forest structure to reduce complexity. An interforest restructure involves creating a brand-new, simplified forest structure using Active Directory objects from your existing forest.

Table 24-1 lists the differences between each restructure type.

Table 24-1   Migration differences

Consideration	Interforest restructure	Intraforest restructure
Object preservation	Objects, such as accounts, will be cloned. The original object remains in the source forest.	User and group objects are migrated and are no longer present in the source location. Computer and managed service account objects are copied and remain in the source location.
SID history maintenance	SID history maintenance is optional.	SID history is mandatory for user, group, and computer accounts. It isn't required for managed service accounts.
Password retention	Password retention is optional.	Passwords are always retained.
Profile migration	Local profiles can be migrated using ADMT.	Local profiles are automatically migrated, and the GUID account is preserved.

The Active Directory Migration Tool requires that you have access to a SQL Server instance. This can be a full SQL Server deployment or a local SQL Server Express instance. In the official documentation, ADMT requires SQL Server 2008 R2, but there is anecdotal evidence that you can use SQL Server Express 2022 without encountering any issues. Unlike SQL Server 2003, most workloads that ran on SQL Server 2008 R2 will probably work on the more recent versions of SQL Server. The ADMT includes the wizards shown in Figure 24-4:

- **User Account Migration Wizard**   Allows you to perform an intraforest or interforest migration of user account objects.

- **Group Account Migration Wizard**   Allows you to perform an intraforest or interforest migration of group account objects, including group membership information.

- **Computer Migration Wizard**   Allows you to perform an intraforest or interforest migration of computer account objects.

- **Security Translation Wizard**   Wizard that allows you to transfer security permissions during object migration.

- **Reporting Wizard**   Generate the following reports:

  - **Migrated Users, Groups And Managed Service Accounts Report**   Summarizes the result of the migration of user, group, and managed service accounts.

  - **Expired Computers Report**   Shows a list of computers that have expired computer account passwords.

  - **Account References Report**   Shows a list of accounts that have been assigned permissions for resources on a specific computer.

  - **Name Conflicts Report**   Shows a list of user accounts and groups that are present in both the source and target domains.

- **Service Account Migration Wizard**   Allows you to perform intraforest or interforest service account migration.

- **Managed Service Account Migration Wizard**   Allows you to perform an intraforest or interforest managed service account migration.

- **Password Migration Wizard**   Allows you to perform intraforest or interforest password migration.

CHAPTER 24

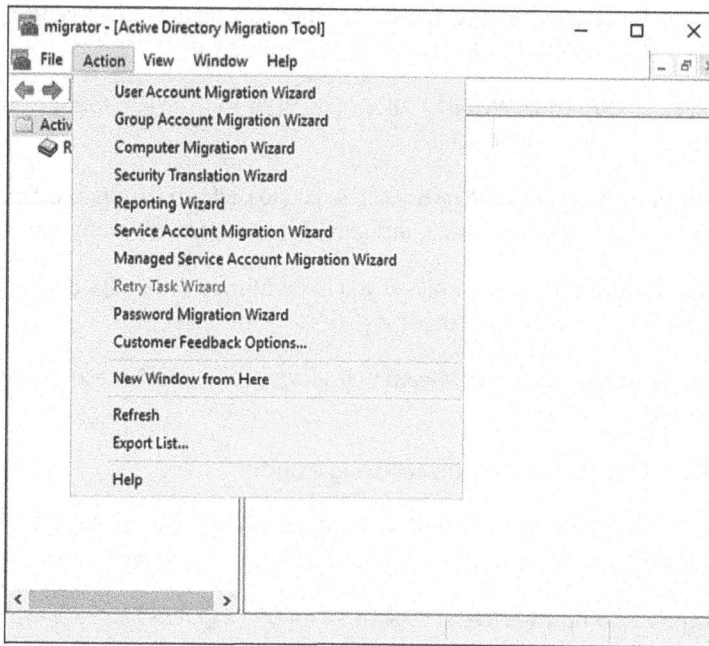

Figure 24-4   Active Directory Migration Tool

More Info

Active Directory Migration Tool

You can learn more about the Active Directory Migration Tool at *https://learn.microsoft.com/en-us/training/modules/active-directory-domain-services-migration/.*

Active Directory Certificate Services

You can use WSMT to migrate an AD CS deployment from one server to another. The WSMT method works best when you're migrating a standalone root or subordinate CA. Prior to performing AD CS migration, you need to be aware of the following:

- It will be necessary to either turn off the source CA or stop the source server's certificate services.

- The destination CA must have the same name as the source CA. The CA name is separate from the computer name.

- While the computer name of the destination CA does not need to match that of the source CA, the destination CA name must not be identical to the name assigned to the destination computer. For example, ContosoRootCA is the name of the source CA that is hosted on a computer named MEL-CA. When migrated, the destination CA will be called ContosoRootCA and might be hosted on a computer named MEL-NEW-CA. The destination computer just cannot be named ContosoRootCA.

- During migration, the CA will be unable to issue certificates or publish CRLs.

- To ensure that revocation status checking can occur, ensure that a CRL is published prior to migration that will remain valid to a point in time after the expected completion of the migration.

- Ensure that at least one of the CRL distribution points specified for existing certificates remains available during migration. Enterprise CAs publish to Active Directory, but standalone CAs may only publish to the local server. If the CRL distribution point is unavailable, clients will be unable to perform revocation checks.

- The Authority Information Access (AIA) and CRL distribution point extensions of previously issued certificates may reference the name of the source CA. This is the default setting and will only be different if you explicitly changed it.

- If migrating an enterprise CA or standalone CA on a computer that is a member of a domain, the account used to perform the migration must be a member of the Enterprise Admins or Domain Admins group.

Inside OUT

AD CS upgrades

You can directly upgrade a computer running Windows Server 2012 R2 or later that hosts the AD CS role to Windows Server 2025. It's substantially easier to do it this way if you have a complex configuration that includes an enterprise CA, CA web enrollment, online responders, network device enrollment, and the certificate enrollment web services— all on the same host. When it comes to AD CS—especially AD-integrated CAs—servers are definitely far more in the category of "pets" rather than "cattle."

CA migration can be carried out in three general phases:

- Preparation

- Migration

- Verification and post-migration tasks

CHAPTER 24

Preparation

To prepare the source server, perform the following steps:

1. Export the CA templates list. This is the list of templates that the CA is configured to issue. The master list of templates is stored within Active Directory. You can export this list from the Certificate Services console by right-clicking the Certificate Templates node and selecting Export. You can also do this using the command `certutil.exe -catemplates > catemplates.txt`.

2. Make a note of the CA's Cryptographic Service Provider (CSP) and which signature algorithm is used. This is visible on the CA's Properties dialog, as shown in Figure 24-5. You can also do this using the command `certutil.exe -getreg ca\csp\* > csp.txt`.

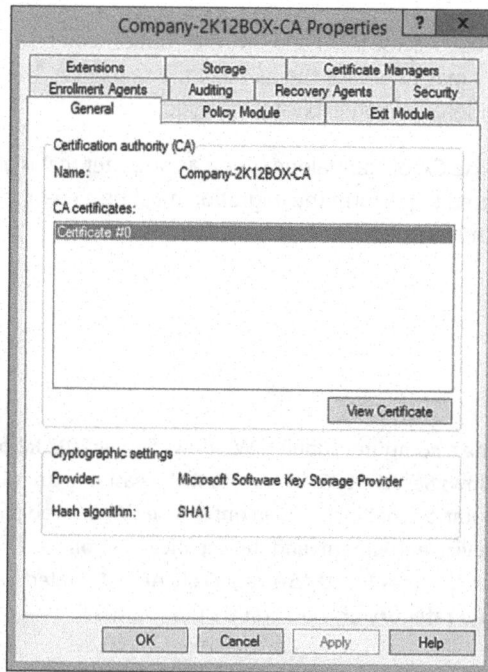

Figure 24-5   CSP and signature algorithm

3. Back up the source server CA, including the private key, CA certificate, Certificate Database, and Certificate Database Log. You can do this using the Certification Authority Backup Wizard, as shown in Figure 24-6. Copy the contents of the backup folder to a location that will be accessible to the destination server.

4. Stop the Certificate Services service. You can do this using the Services console or by using the `Stop-Service certsvc` Windows PowerShell command. This will block the current certificate server from issuing additional certificates.

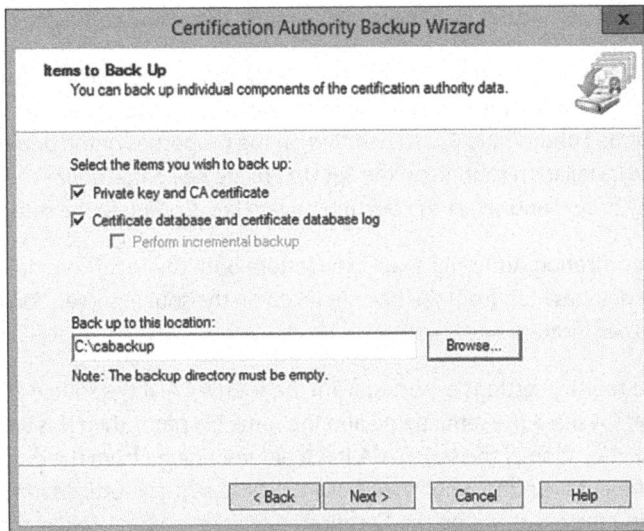

Figure 24-6   CA Backup Wizard

5. Back up the registry settings of the CA using the following command, and place it in a location that is accessible to the destination server:

```
reg export HKLM\SYSTEM\CurrentControlSet\Services\CertSvc\Configuration <output
file>.reg
```

6. If the source CA uses a custom CAPolicy.inf file, you should copy this file to a location that is accessible to the destination server.

Migration

Once you have performed the necessary preparation steps, you should perform the following steps to complete the migration of the CA:

1. Once you have backed up the source CA and its registry settings, remove the CA role service from the source server. This is important because removing the role service from the server will also clean up data stored in Active Directory associated with the CA. If you don't perform this cleanup, you will encounter problems when introducing the migrated CA that shares the original CA's name. Removing the role service from the CA does not delete the CA database, private key, or CA certificate. This means that if the migration fails, you will be able to restore the CA by reinstalling the Certificate Services role on the server.

2. Microsoft also recommends manually removing the source server from the domain prior to deploying the destination server. This is especially important if the source and destination servers share the same computer name.

3. Change the name of the destination server to match the name of the source server.

4. Join the destination server to the domain.

5. Import the CA certificates into the local computer's Personal certificate store.

6. Once the computer is domain-joined, add the CA role service to the destination server. Ensure that you install the server in the same manner, such as installing an Enterprise Root or Standalone Subordinate CA, depending on the properties of the original source CA. During the installation routine on the Set Up Private Key page, utilize the Use Existing Private Key option and select the existing private key. Complete the setup wizard.

7. Use the Certification Authority snap-in to restore both the certificate database and the certificate database log from the backup taken on the source server. You will need to restart the certificate services server.

8. Import the registry settings exported from the source CA. If the source CA and the destination CA share the same name and the same file paths then this can be done without modification. If the source CA has a different name from the destination CA or uses different file paths, you'll need to alter these registry settings manually. Prior to importing the registry, stop the Certificate Services service. Use the command `reg import backup.reg` to import the registry file. Restart the certificate service.

9. Import the list of CA templates that are issued from the CA using the command `certutil -setcatemplates`, and then provide a list of templates that you backed up from the source server in comma-separated format.

Verification and post-migration tasks

To verify that the CA has migrated successfully, verify that you can successfully request and enroll a new certificate. You should also verify that you can successfully publish a CRL. Performing these tasks is covered in Chapter 18, "Active Directory Certificate Services."

DNS

Migrating DNS is easiest when the DNS zones are Active Directory integrated. In that scenario, you add member servers running the most recent version of Windows Server to an existing domain, promote those servers to domain controllers, and make sure that you add the DNS role. Any existing AD integrated zones that are configured to replicate to other domain controllers in the domain will replicate to the newly promoted domain controller. Remember to add custom partitions if you have AD-integrated zones that only replicate to specific domain controllers.

The trick to migrating primary zones from one DNS server to another is first to configure the destination server to host a secondary zone of the primary zone. Once the zone has replicated to the intended destination server, convert the zone from a secondary zone to function as a primary zone. You can do this by performing the following steps:

1. On the General tab of the secondary zone Properties, click Change (see Figure 24-7).

2. In the Change Zone Type dialog, shown in Figure 24-8, select Primary Zone and then click OK.

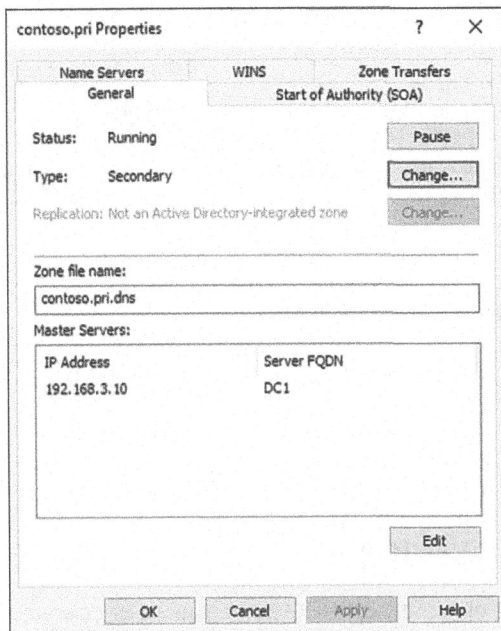

Figure 24-7 Zone General Properties tab

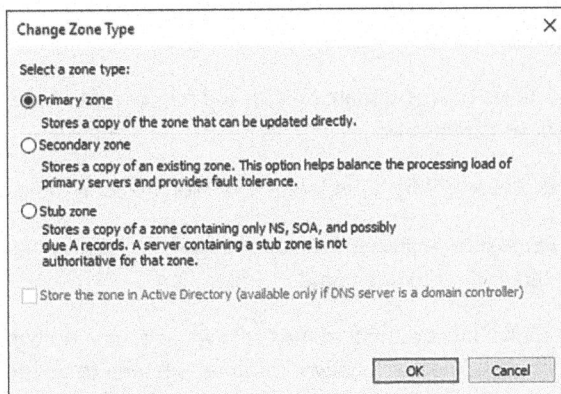

Figure 24-8 Change Zone Type

DHCP

You can use the WSMT to migrate a DHCP server, scopes, and settings from computers running Windows Server 2008 and later to the most recent version of Windows Server. WSMT DHCP migration functions for both the Server Core and Server with GUI installation options.

To perform a migration of a DHCP server using WSMT, you need access to accounts with the following permissions:

- Permission to authorize the DHCP server in Active Directory

- Membership of the local Administrator group on the computers that are both the source and destination DHCP servers

- Permission to write data to the WSMT migration store location

DHCP migration follows the following general steps:

- Preparation

- Migration

- Verification and post-migration tasks

Preparing to migrate DHCP

Before you start the process of migrating a DHCP server and its associated scopes and settings to a more recent version of Windows Server, you'll need to perform several preparation steps.

- Determine which current DHCP servers you want to migrate and which servers running a new version of Windows Server will host the migrated DHCP server roles, associated scopes, and settings.

- Ensure that all critical updates, update rollups, and service packs have been installed on the source and destination servers.

- Deploy the Windows Server Migration Tools (WSMT) on the source and destination servers.

- Install the DHCP role service on the destination server. This service must be present on the destination server prior to beginning the migration.

- Ensure that the source and destination servers have the same number of network adapters. Determine which subnet each network adapter is bound to on the source server and ensure that the destination server has network adapters bound to the same subnets. This will ensure that the migrated DHCP server can service the same subnets as the source DHCP server.

- Determine the IP address strategy for the destination server. DHCP servers should use static IP addresses on network interfaces that are used by the DHCP server service to manage DHCP traffic. Options include

  - **Assigning the destination server different static IP addresses that are on the same subnets as the static IP addresses assigned to network interfaces on the source server**   Doing this will allow you to perform the migration with both the source and destination server online.

- **Assign the destination server the same IP addresses that are used as the network interfaces on the source server**   While this is possible, it will mean that the source and destination server cannot be online at the same time without causing IP address conflicts, or it would require extensive preparation of network virtualization. Because existing clients will be able to renew their IP address information after migration from a destination server with a new IP address on the same subnet, you should only keep the same IP addresses on the source and destination server if there are substantive reasons for doing so.

- If the source server does not use the default path for the DHCP server database, such as having the database stored on a separate volume, the destination server will need to have a volume configuration that matches that of the source server. For example, if the DHCP database is stored on volume H: of the source server, the destination server will need a properly formatted volume H: for migration to be successful.

- Ensure that the migration store location is accessible to both the source and destination servers.

- Ensure that both the source and destination servers have network access to the AD DS environment.

- Perform a backup of the DHCP server from the DHCP console, rather than the Windows Server Backup, as shown in Figure 24-9. You can do this by right-clicking the DHCP server node, selecting Backup, and specifying a location for the backup.

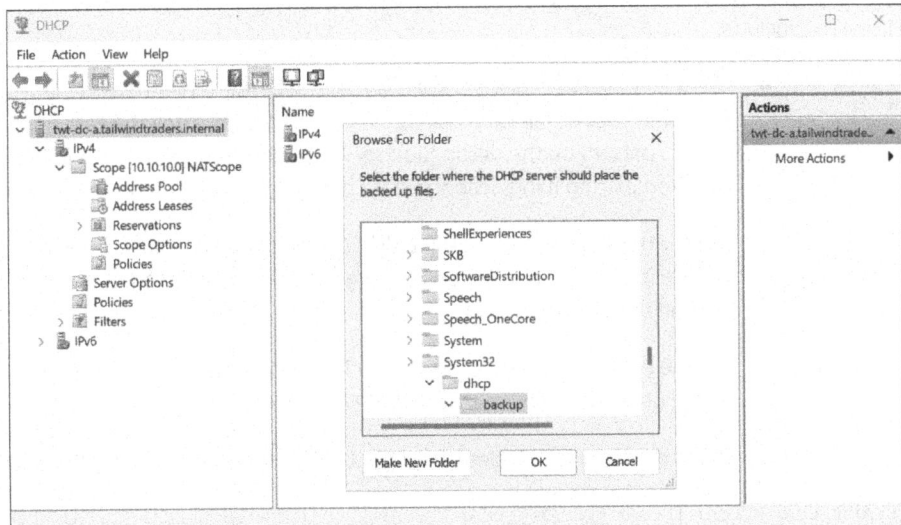

Figure 24-9   Backup DHCP database

- Once the backup is complete, stop the DHCP service on the source and the destination server, either by using the Services console or by running the `Stop-Service DHCPserver` Windows PowerShell cmdlet.

Migration

Once the source and destination servers are prepared, the next step is to open the Windows Server Migration Tools PowerShell session. You perform the migration using the `Export-SmigServerSetting` PowerShell cmdlet. Specific parameters of the `Export-SmigServerSetting` cmdlet that are relevant to DHCP server migration include

- Use the `FeatureID DHCP` to specify that the DHCP server role is what you want to migrate.

- Use the `Users` parameter if the DHCP administrators group includes local user accounts. Use the `Group` parameter to migrate all members of the DHCP administrators group that don't include a local user but do include domain users and groups.

- You can use the `IPConfig` parameter if you want to export the IP address configuration of the source server to the destination server.

- Use the `Path` parameter to specify the location of the `svrmig.mig` file. If you don't specify a network location, you'll need to manually transfer this file to a location that is accessible to the destination server.

Considerations for using the `Import-SmigServerSetting` cmdlet on the destination server include:

- Use the `FeatureID DHCP` to specify that the DHCP server role is what you are importing. While the `Import-SmigServerSetting` cmdlet will install the DHCP server role if it is not already present on the destination server, Microsoft recommends installing the service and then placing it in a stopped state before importing data using the WSMT.

- Use the `Users` parameter if the DHCP Administrators group on the destination server will include local users. Use the `Group` parameter if the DHCP administrators group contains domain users and groups.

- Use the Path parameter to specify the location of the `svrmig.mig` file. This file can be stored on an accessible network share or stored locally.

- Once migration is complete, start the DHCP server service using the `Start-Service DHCPServer` cmdlet.

- If you haven't done so already, you'll need to authorize the DHCP server in Active Directory before it will function.

Verification and post-migration tasks

Once the migration has occurred, ensure that the DHCP server service on the source server remains in a stopped state, as well as on a client release, and then renew an IP address to verify that the DHCP server service on the destination server is functioning properly. You should also manually check that the scopes and settings that were present on the source server are also present on the destination server. Once you have verified that the migration has completed successfully, remove the DHCP server service from the source computer.

File and storage servers

You can use both the WSMT and Storage Migration Services to migrate file servers to a new version of Windows Server. Storage Migration Service is a newer tool, and you should attempt migration using this tool first and fall back to WSMT only if you encounter a scenario that Storage Migration Service does not support.

Migrate file servers using Storage Migration Service

Storage Migration Service is a service included in Windows Server 2019 and later that leverages Windows Admin Center to allow you to inventory the settings and data of a source file server, transfer the files and settings to a destination server, and then configure the destination server with the settings and identity that were present on the source server. The advantage of Storage Migration Service over WSMT is that it can:

- Inventory multiple servers and the data they store

- Quickly transfer files, file shares, and security settings from source servers

- Apply the identity of the source server to the destination server, including name and IP address settings, so that users and applications do not have to alter their existing behavior and configuration

While copying files and their permissions has always been something that most administrators could generally figure out how to do fairly quickly, it was often a bit more challenging to copy the settings of the shared folders that hosted those files. Storage Migration Service allows you to migrate all the flags, settings, and security settings of SMB file shares. The flags that Storage Migration Service migrates include

- Share State

- Availability Type

- Share Type

- Folder Enumeration Mode (aka Access-Based Enumeration or ABE)

- Caching Mode

- Leasing Mode

- SMB Instance

- CA Timeout

- Concurrent User Limit

- Continuously Available

- Description

- Encrypt Data

- Identity Remoting

- Infrastructure

- Name

- Path

- Scoped

- Scope Name

- Security Descriptor

- Shadow Copy

- Special

- Temporary

There are some limitations to what you can transfer using Storage Migration Service. These include not allowing you to migrate the following folders and files:

- Windows

- Program Files

- Program Files (x86)

- Program Data

- Users

- $Recycle.bin

- Recycler

- Recycled

- System Volume Information

- $UpgDrv$

- $SysReset

- $Windows.~BT

- $Windows.~LS

- Windows.old

- boot

- Recovery

- Documents and Settings

- pagefile.sys

- hiberfil.sys

- swapfile.sys

- winpepge.sys

- config.sys

- bootsect.bak

- bootmgr

- bootnxt

- Any file or folder on the source server that conflicts with folders assigned the exclusion designation on the destination server.

You can't use Storage Migration Service to migrate file servers that are members of separate domains. You also can't use Storage Migration Service to migrate file servers between workgroups.

Deploy Storage Migration Service

Storage Migration Service Orchestrator servers manage the migration process. It's important to note—especially if you are building your own test lab—that you can't deploy the Storage Migration Service Orchestrator from a host installed using an Evaluation version of Windows Server. To install the Orchestrator service on a computer, open the Windows Admin Center and click Storage Migration Service. Note that Storage Migration Service will not be present if you're connected to an evaluation version of Windows Server.

Storage Migration Service requires that the following rules be enabled within Windows Firewall:

- File and Printer Sharing (SMB-In)

- Netlogon Service (NP-In)

- Windows Management Instrumentation (DCOM-In)

- Windows Management Instrumentation (WMI-In)

If you're using a third-party firewall product, ensure that you open TCP ports 135, 445, and 1025-65535. The service ports are TCP 28940 for the Orchestrator and TCP 28941 for the Proxy.

To perform a migration, you need access to the credentials of accounts with the following permissions:

- Administrator permission on the source and destination computers

- Administrator permissions on the computer that hosts the Storage Migration Service Orchestrator role

Inside OUT

Local users, local groups, Samba, and failover clusters

You can also use Storage Migration Services to migrate file shares from source servers that use Samba versions 3.6.x and later on RedHat, CentOS, Debian, Ubuntu, and SUSE Linux Enterprise Server (SLES). Storage Migration Services will also allow you to migrate local users and groups from a source server to a destination server.

Inventory source servers

When migrating file shares from one server to another, you should

- Inventory the source servers to discover what shares are present

- Determine what files and folders are present

- Identity information related to the source server

To do this, perform the following steps:

1. With Storage Migration Services selected in Windows Admin Center, click New Job. Provide a name for the job and then click OK.

2. On the next page of the Inventory Wizard, provide the credentials of an account with administrative privileges. This page also allows you to choose whether to migrate the contents of administrative shares.

3. Click Add to start the Add A Device Wizard. In this wizard, provide the hostname for the server that hosts the files that you want to migrate. You can use the Add button to add multiple source servers on this page.

4. When you're finished adding source servers, click Start Scan. Storage Migration Services will generate an inventory of the listed servers.

5. After the inventory completes, you can click the server and view the server shares, configuration, network adapters, and volumes.

6. Once you have reviewed the information generated by the inventory scans, click Next to begin the data copy process.

Copy data

The data copy process copies data from the source to the destination server. Although this process is sometimes termed the "transfer process," it's important to note that the data is only copied. It isn't actually moved from one server to another. This means that if something goes wrong, you still have the original source server in its premigration condition.

To begin the copy process, perform the following steps:

1. Ensure that the firewall rules listed earlier are configured on the destination server.

2. Provide the credentials of an account that has administrative rights on the destination server.

3. Provide the address of the destination device. You can do this using an IP address or the FQDN (fully qualified domain name). Click Scan Device, and the destination server will be inventoried. If the scan doesn't work, verify that the firewall rules are configured correctly.

4. On the Adjust Transfer Settings page, set the checksum settings for transmitted files, the maximum duration of the transfer job, how many retries to attempt for files that fail to transfer properly, and the delay between transfers.

5. On the Validate Source And Destination Devices page, click Validate and review any warnings.

6. On the Start The Transfer page, click Start The Transfer.

7. When the transfer completes, you can check the error log to determine which, if any, files and settings failed to transfer.

Cutover to new servers

The cutover phase is an optional phase that allows you to configure the destination server to assume the name and identity of the source server. This is one of the coolest parts of this technology because it means that you can have Storage Migration Service create a Windows Server 2025 clone of a Windows Server 2003 server, with the Windows Server 2025 server assuming the network identity of the server it's replacing; this means users and applications aren't aware that any change has occurred. To perform the cutover, perform the following steps:

1. On the Enter Credentials page, provide administrative credentials for the source and destination devices.

2. On the page with the source server name, specify how you want network identity information transferred from the source to the destination server. You can also configure the source computer to be assigned a random name during the cutover process, or you can have it choose a new name to ensure that there are no conflicts once the destination server assumes the source server's identity.

3. After validating settings and providing any credentials required to update the Active Directory information for the computers that are being managed, you can perform one final validation.

4. You then begin the cutover by clicking Start Cutover. When the cutover completes, click Finish.

> ## More Info
>
> ### Storage Migration Service
>
> You can learn more about Storage Migration Service at *https://learn.microsoft.com/ windows-server/storage/storage-migration-service/overview*.

Migrate file and storage servers using WSMT

While you should use Storage Migration Service to migrate file servers to Windows Server 2019 and later, should you really want to, you can use the WSMT to migrate the following file and storage services information from a computer running Windows Server 2008 and later:

- Server identity information

- Local users and groups

- Data and shared folders

- Shadow copies of Shared Folders

- Data Deduplication

- DFS Namespaces

- DFS Replication

- File Server Resource Manager (FSRM)

- Group Policy Settings related to SMB

- Group Policy settings for Offline Files

- iSCSI Software Target settings

- Network File System (NFS) shares

- Remote Volume Shadow Copy Service

The following migration scenarios are supported for file and storage services:

- The file server is a member of a domain.

- The file server is a member of a workgroup.

- File server data and shares are located on an external storage location, such as a SAN or on direct-attached storage, as long as either storage medium preserves data permissions and file share permissions.

It's important to note that file migration using the WSMT is aimed at moving data sets smaller than 100GB, because only one file at a time is copied over an HTTPS connection. When moving larger data sets, Microsoft recommends using the `robocopy.exe` utility included with Windows Server.

Migration permissions

Depending on the type of migration that you want to perform, a variety of permissions are necessary. If you're going to migrate data and shared folders, you must use an account that has local administrator permissions on the destination server.

Migration of DFS can be performed if an account is a member of the Domain Admins group. Alternatively, if there is more than one namespace server, the account used doesn't have to be a member of the Domain Admins group as long as it has permission to administer all namespaces on the source server and is a member of the local Administrators group on the source and destination server.

Users who trigger migration of DFS replicas must either be members of the Domain Admins group or must have been delegated permission to the appropriate replication groups and replication members. If the user account is used to perform this action, it must be a member of the local Administrators group on the source and destination servers.

Preparing to migrate

To prepare to migrate the file and storage services role and data from a source server to a destination server, perform the following steps:

- Ensure that the source and destination server have their time correctly set. If the clocks on the source and destination servers are out of synchronization, the migration will fail.

- Ensure that the same File Services role services are present on both the source server and the destination server.

- Ensure that Windows Server Migration Tools are deployed on both the source server and the destination server.

- Configure a firewall rule to allow traffic on TCP and UDP ports 7000 between the source server and the destination server on both the source and destination servers. TCP and UDP port 7000 are used by the Send-SmigServerData and Receive-SmigServerData cmdlets when establishing data migration connections. TCP and UDP ports 7001 and 7002 are also used if the migration occurs across subnets.

- Ensure that the destination path has sufficient disk space to migrate data. If you have a configured NTFS quota or folder management, ensure that the quota limit allows the migration of data.

- If migrating File Server Resource Manager data and settings, ensure that the destination server has the same volume configuration as the source server.

- While file and folder permissions are preserved during migration, remember that migrated files and folders inherit permissions from their parent folders. You should ensure that parent folders on the destination server have permissions that match those on the source server.

- If you're performing a DFS migration, ensure that the DFS Namespaces role service is installed and configured on the destination server. The DFS Namespace service must be running prior to commencing migration.

- If you're migrating DFS namespaces, back up the source server using a system state or full server backup. If the DFS namespaces are integrated into AD DS, it will be necessary to back up the system state on a domain controller to ensure that the AD DS configuration information for DFS namespaces is backed up.

- Ensure that the Server service on the destination computer is set to use the Automatic startup type.

- You can back up the configuration information of a domain-based DFS namespace using the following command:

  `dfsutil.exe root export <\\<DomainName>\NameSpace> <BackupFileName>`

Migrating file and storage services

Once you have completed the migration preparation steps, use the `Export-SmigServerSetting` cmdlet to capture the following settings on the source server so that you can import them on the destination server using the `Import-SmigServerSetting` cmdlet:

- SMB (Server Message Block) settings
- Offline Files settings
- DFS Namespaces configuration
- File Server Resource Manager settings
- Shadow Copies of Shared Folders

Running the cmdlet will generate the migration `svrmig.mig` file, which you'll need to then transfer to and import on the destination server. If you want to migrate local users and groups from the source server to the destination server, use the User All and Group parameters with the `Export-SmigServerSetting` cmdlet. Remember to specify the same parameters with the `Import-SmigServerSetting` cmdlet on the destination server.

Once settings have been transferred from the source server to the destination server, use the `Send-SmigServerData` and the `Receive-SmigServerData` cmdlets to transfer data between the source and destination servers.

CHAPTER 24

For example, to send files from the `e:\fileshare` folder on the source computer to the `f:\`
`fileshare` folder on a destination computer named MEL-FS-2K16, use the following command:

```
Send-SmigServerData -ComputerName MEL-FS-2K16 -SourcePath e:\fileshare -DestinationPath
f:\fileshare -Recurse -Include All -Force
```

You must start the `Receive-SmigServerData` cmdlet in an elevated session on the destination
server within five minutes of it being executed on the source server. Data transfer between the
source and the destination server is encrypted.

Troubleshooting

This chapter provides general guidelines for solving problems beyond the simple "Is it plugged into the network?" or "Did you switch it on and off again?" Today, with generative AI tools like M365 Copilot, ChatGPT, Claude, Grok, and Gemini, troubleshooting can be simpler than it used to be. However, just because an AI tool provides a result that looks like a solution to your problem, it doesn't mean you should implement the steps it suggests in your production environment.

Troubleshooting methodology

There are a couple of tricks to troubleshooting problems. The first is to realize that you'll be far more effective at troubleshooting if you approach the problem systematically rather than trying random solutions.

The next is that, jokes aside, there is far more to IT troubleshooting than typing some problem characteristics into (this being a Microsoft Press book) M365 Copilot or Bing and diligently applying any solution that turns up.

Some problems with using a search engine or AI chatbot approach include the following:

- Unless you understand all the symptoms, it's possible that the proposed solutions aren't relevant to the problem you're troubleshooting.

- Posts to public threads and AI prompts often provide an incomplete description of problem symptoms. This is often because the person asking for help in the post hasn't developed a full understanding of the nature of the problem they're trying to solve by posting a request for help. Generative AI is trained on publicly available information on the Internet. As you know, not everything on the Internet is factually correct. A chatbot may suggest a solution that seems superficially similar to the problem you've encountered but which might be entirely unrelated.

- Even when other posters in the same thread respond that the solution worked for them, you can't be certain that they had the same problem as you or that they implemented the solutions proposed in responses to the post correctly.

This doesn't mean that you can't find the solution to a complex problem by consulting online forums or the output of your favorite chatbot; it's just that you should treat solutions offered to other people's problems with an appropriate degree of skepticism. Solutions posted on the Internet might work or they might not, but finding out through experimentation on your production environment probably isn't the best way to display your technical aptitude.

Inside OUT

Thinking, fast and slow

Nobel prize winner Daniel Kahneman discusses how we arrive at conclusions in his best-selling book *Thinking, Fast and Slow*. Where this book is illuminating for people troubleshooting problems in information technology is its ideas around intuitive and reasoned decision-making. Kahneman suggests that our first response when tasked with solving a problem is to rely upon intuitive thinking. The problem with intuitive thinking is that it almost always involves jumping to conclusions with only minimal justification or evidence. As Kahneman explains, intuitive thinking is often no better than a random guess. Sometimes, we justify this guesswork by assuming that our own long prior experience in IT troubleshooting other problems must have given us superhuman intuition about the causes of technological problems. A good troubleshooting strategy involves reducing the amount of guesswork and intuitive thinking and emphasizing deductive reasoning. Good troubleshooters know to distrust their first assumptions about a complex problem and to spend some time investigating the problem further before becoming certain as to the cause and the resolution.

Redeployment

When I got started in IT, I'd often spend hours, if not days, troubleshooting a problem with a server or desktop computer because each computer had a unique configuration, which meant deploying from scratch would take substantially longer. Not only would it be necessary to reinstall the operating system, but it would be necessary to locate the correct drivers, something that was a lot more challenging in the early days of the web when many hardware vendors weren't online, let alone providing websites with easy-to-locate driver downloads. With early versions of Windows, it was often necessary to keep a "library" of disks containing drivers to support each hardware configuration. The process of installing server applications was often similarly fraught. Vendor documentation was scarce, and other than the occasional helpful newsgroup post, there wasn't much help available online when it came to troubleshooting. Getting a server up and running in the 1990s could be such an involved process that you would take the time to troubleshoot whatever problem you had as much as possible and only redeploy the workload when all other avenues were exhausted.

With Windows Server, the vast majority of drivers utilized by the operating system are included or are easily accessible on vendor websites. It's relatively straightforward to back up and reinstall applications, and the web provides a cornucopia of documentation and advice on trouble-shooting existing workloads.

If a workload with a known configuration has worked in the past and is still experiencing errors now, one of the options that you have at your disposal is to redeploy rather than spend time troubleshooting. With tools such as desired-state configuration, it's quite likely that you can redeploy in less time than it takes you to diagnose, research, and solve the problem you face.

The trick with all this is that you need to have workload configuration and deployment highly automated. Building out that configuration automation will take a substantial amount of time, and you will need to ensure that the configuration automation is updated each time you update the configuration of the workload in question. The argument for this approach is easy to make if you have a large number of servers that have similar configurations. In scenarios where you are only dealing with a small number of servers and where each workload is unique, you may end up spending more time automating configuration than you ever would deploying servers.

You'll also need to ensure that data is decoupled properly from the workload. A long-term aspirational goal of any server administrator should be to automate the configuration of any workload that they manage, so that they can redeploy it quickly in another VM or on another physical chassis should something catastrophic happen with the original workload. It's likely that you're far from that goal at the moment in your own environment, but as you get closer to it, you'll find that redeployment as a troubleshooting step becomes a viable first response strategy to complex problems. Admittedly, if it works, redeployment doesn't answer the tricky question of what might have caused the problem in the first place. However, if it does work, you can ponder the question of what actually happened as an existential problem, rather than as a practical one.

In some cases, redeploying the workload from what is believed to be a good configuration will not solve the issue. In that scenario, you'll need to perform a deeper investigation as to what is causing the problem.

Symptoms and diagnosis

Before you can solve a problem, you need to understand the nature of the problem. The first step in understanding the nature of a complex problem is to understand the symptoms of that problem.

The easiest symptoms to document are the ones that caused you to notice the problem in the first place. The thing that's important to realize is that there are likely to be other symptoms present that you might not have noticed. It's understanding all these symptoms and their relationship with one another that will allow you to diagnose the cause and resolution of the problem. It might be that the first thing you notice about a problem is only tangential to that problem. By investigating further, you discover that far more problematic things are occurring than the thing that drew your attention to the problem in the first place.

Inside OUT

More than one cause

Anyone who has diagnosed a complex problem knows that a single set of symptoms may have separate root causes. That's one reason why you might need to try multiple resolutions when troubleshooting. Generally, though, the more evidence you can collect about problem symptoms, the better idea you can have about diagnosing the problem.

A diagnostic hypothesis is a hypothesis as to what might be causing the problem. It's what you suspect may be causing the problem before you have verification that what you suspect is causing the problem is *actually* causing the problem.

Rather than latching on to the first diagnostic hypothesis that occurs to you, try to list other things that might also be causing the problem. When thinking up other things, you're likely to gain more of an understanding about how you should be investigating the problem. You'll be looking at the problem more broadly, rather than focusing on the symptoms that first came to your attention.

You want to get as much evidence as possible about what's causing the problem before you try to solve it. As every experienced IT person knows, applying the wrong solution to a problem can often make the problem worse. By having as much information about the problem as possible, you reduce the chance that you'll apply an incorrect solution when attempting to solve the problem.

Dependencies

There's an old IT pro joke that "it's always DNS." The foundation of this joke is that almost everything in IT is dependent on DNS, so if an apparently unrelated system, workload, or service isn't functioning, the cause of that malfunction may actually be that DNS isn't working. So, even though it's a bit of a joke, before troubleshooting any complex problem, it probably doesn't hurt to fire up a console and run `nslookup`.

On a more serious note, systems, workloads, and services rarely stand alone, and they almost always depend on other things. As another part of your troubleshooting and diagnostic process, determine the dependency chain of the issue that you're troubleshooting. Working out the dependency chain will give you more items against which to test your hypothesis. It may also allow you to discover more symptoms of the problem than you were initially aware of.

For example, if a Windows service has failed and won't start, determine what the service is dependent on. You can determine what Windows service depends on, and what is dependent on that service, by looking on the Dependencies tab of the service's Properties, as shown in Figure 25-1.

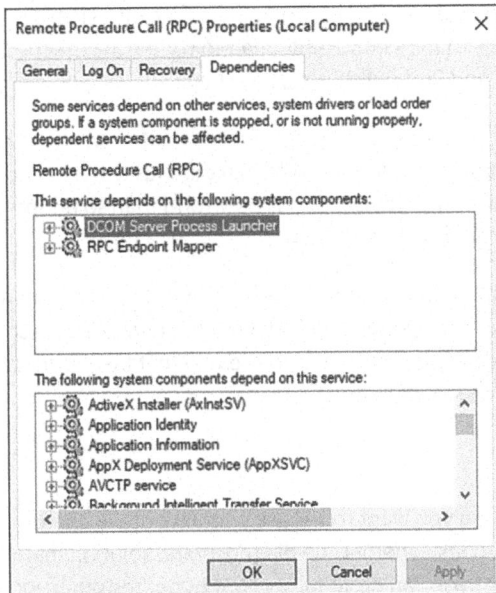

Figure 25-1   Service dependencies

Ranking hypothetical solutions

A solution is hypothetical until it works. While simple problems often have obvious solutions, complex problems are likely to have a variety of apparent solutions, and you generally won't know which is the appropriate solution until you've applied it and found that it works. Before you apply a hypothetical solution in an attempt to solve a problem, you should rank the hypothetical solutions. Consider the following factors when ranking the order in which you should apply hypothetical solutions:

- Rank hypothetical solutions that are simple to implement and involve minimally changing the existing configuration higher than solutions that involve substantial changes to the existing configuration. This is because if the hypothetical solution turns out to be incorrect, you'll need to roll back the configuration changes before trying the next hypothetical solution. This is easier to do if the changes are less complicated than it is to do with a complex set of configuration changes. If a solution doesn't work, you need to go back to where you started rather than continuing to make further configuration changes when a solution you tried didn't work.

- Rank hypothetical solutions for which you have more evidence higher than solutions where there isn't as much evidence. As mentioned earlier, try to figure out what other evidence you should see if your hypothesis about what is causing the problem is correct rather than just focusing on the symptoms that brought the problem to your attention in the first place. Try to think of ways to disprove a diagnostic hypothesis without taking invasive action. It's better to discard an incorrect solution before implementing it because you find evidence that indicates that it's impossible than to try the incorrect solution in your production environment and find out that it doesn't work.

- Rank hypothetical low-impact solutions above high-impact solutions. Always keep in the back of your mind that applying a solution could make things worse, so prioritize the solutions that will cause fewer problems if things go wrong than solutions that might require you to stay at work longer if it goes wrong.

- Rank hypothetical solutions that require a shorter amount of time to implement above solutions that take much longer to implement. When you don't know which solution is going to solve your problem, you're better off trying the one that takes a couple of minutes over the one that takes a couple of hours.

Applying solutions

Once you've determined which solution you want to try, ask your favorite AI chatbot what noninvasive methods you could use to test whether the diagnosis and solution might work. The AI chatbot might suggest a simple test you can do to falsify your hypothesis that you haven't thought of.

It's important that when you apply a hypothetical solution and it doesn't resolve the problem, you find a way to revert to the configuration that existed prior to attempting the hypothetical solution. If you're diagnosing problems with a workload in a virtual machine, you should use snapshots or checkpoints to roll back to the "last known-bad" configuration, which is much better than building a "completely undocumented and worse" configuration.

You want to avoid trying a number of different hypothetical solutions that don't pan out and involve you making a large number of undocumented configuration changes to your production servers. When you continually modify the configuration of one server in an attempt to resolve one problem, you might end up causing a host of other problems.

Before applying any solution, ensure that you have a rollback strategy that will allow you to return to the current configuration. Put another way, always ensure that you have an escape route for when your meticulously crafted plans go wrong.

The other thing you should do before applying any solution is to have developed a set of criteria to determine what constitutes a resolution of the problem that you're trying to troubleshoot. You need to know what the problem resolution will look like. You should also test whether any of the characteristics of what you've decided constitute the resolution are present before you apply the resolution. If you don't do this, it's entirely possible that part of your benchmark for declaring the problem solved may have been met before you attempted the solution. This can lead you to believe that you've solved a problem when the problem is still present. Alternatively, finding that one of your benchmarks for declaring the problem is solved prior to implementing a solution might provide further evidence that you don't fully understand all the characteristics of the problem.

Using Windows Debugger

The Windows Debugger (WinDbg) allows you to diagnose and resolve system issues on Windows Server, including post-mortem crash dump analysis and live debugging of running systems. WinDbg is invaluable for understanding stop errors such as the traditional blue-screen crashes, performance bottlenecks, driver failures, and other complex issues. You can install WinDbg through WinGet by using the command:

```
WinGet install Microsoft.windbg
```

After installing WinDbg, you should install symbols files. Symbols provide WinDbg with function names, variable names, and other debug info. Microsoft publishes public symbols for Windows binaries. Configure the symbol path so WinDbg can download the correct symbol (.pdb) files. In WinDbg's UI, go to File, Settings, Debugging Settings, and select Symbol File Path; then enter the Microsoft Symbol Server path. To have the symbols cached in C:\Symbols and retrieved from the Microsoft website, enter this:

```
srv*C:\Symbols*https://msdl.microsoft.com/download/symbols
```

Crash dump analysis

When a Windows Server crashes with a stop error, also known colloquially as a Blue Screen of Death (BSOD), it creates a memory dump file that captures the state of the system at the crash moment. Analyzing this crash dump with WinDbg may pinpoint the cause of the crash.

By default, Windows Server writes minidumps (small dumps) to C:\Windows\Minidump\ or a full kernel dump to C:\Windows\Memory.dmp depending on system settings

If you don't see dump files, you may need to configure Startup and Recovery settings in Windows to enable crash dumps. You can do this via System Properties, choosing Startup and Recovery and ensuring Write Debugging Information is set to at least a kernel or small memory dump. You can accomplish this with the following PowerShell command:

```
Set-ItemProperty -Path 'HKLM:\System\CurrentControlSet\Control\CrashControl' -Name 'CrashDumpEnabled' -Value 1
```

The possible values for CrashDumpEnabled are listed in Table 25-1.

Table 25-1   Crash dump options

Value	Dump Type	Description
0	None	Disables dump file
1	Complete memory dump	Writes the content of all physical memory to the dump file
2	Kernel memory dump	Dumps kernel memory but not user memory
3	Small memory dump (64 GB)	Minimal information including the STOP error code and which drivers were loaded
7	Automatic memory dump	Default, which balances size and info. Similar to kernel dump

Common dump files are located in the following locations by default:

- **Small memory dump**, `%SystemRoot%\Minidump\Mini####.dmp`   This dump is about 256 KB and contains basic info.

- **Kernel memory dump**, `%SystemRoot%\Memory.dmp`   This dump captures kernel-mode memory at the time of the crash.

- **Complete memory dump**, `%SystemRoot%\Memory.dmp`   You can configure this dump to capture entire contents of RAM at the time of the error, which means it can be very large on some systems.

To analyze a crash dump, launch WinDbg and open the crash dump file. You can do this by selecting Open Crash Dump from the File menu. You then select either the main dump file or the mini dump file. All dump files have the `.dmp` extension. WinDbg will load the dump and break in, showing a command prompt like 0:kd> (for kernel dump) or 0:000> (for user-mode dump).

At the command prompt, type **!analyze -v** and press Enter. The `!analyze` command will process the dump and output a summary of what it finds. The `-v` flag provides additional detail. The report includes the following fields:

- **BugCheck code and parameters**   This identifies the type of crash. You can look up the code in Microsoft's Bug Check reference if needed or use generative AI to query for an explanation.

- **MODULE_NAME and IMAGE_NAME**   Indicates the component that likely caused the crash. For instance, you might see something like MODULE_NAME: mydriver and IMAGE_NAME: mydriver.sys, meaning a driver named mydriver.sys is implicated. If a Windows component is listed (for example, ntoskrnl.exe or win32kfull.sys), it could be a core OS issue or still possibly triggered by a third-party driver.

- **FAILURE_BUCKET_ID or DEFAULT_BUCKET_ID**   This is an identifier for the crash type.

- **Stack trace**   WinDbg will often show a stack of function calls leading up to the crash point.

A newer technique is to copy the output of the `!analyze` command and paste it into a chatbot such as M365 Copilot, ChatGPT, Claude, or Grok and ask for an explanation and analysis.

Additional commands beyond `!analyze` include these:

- **Stack Trace (k)**   Use the k command (kp for parameters, kv for verbose) to see the call stack at the time of crash. This often shows the chain of function calls leading to the error. For example, after a driver crash, k might show the driver's function at the top, with functions from Windows below it. This can confirm the context of failure.

- **Loaded Modules (lm)**   Use `lm` to list modules to determine if a suspect driver or module is loaded and note its properties. You can use `lmvm` *<module>*, which displays detailed info about a specific module: its base address, version number, timestamp, path, and so on. This information is useful for identifying the exact version of a driver. For instance, `lmvm mydriver` shows whether `mydriver.sys` is signed, its file path, and build date, which helps determine if it's outdated or mismatched.

Analyze performance problems

WinDbg can also analyze performance problems like application hangs, high CPU usage, or memory leaks. To do this, obtain a snapshot (dump) of the misbehaving process (or the whole system) during the problem and then use WinDbg to determine what is occurring.

To diagnose a high-CPU process or a process that's leaking memory, you can manually create a dump using Task Manager. To do this, locate the process in Task Manager, right-click it, and choose Create Dump File. The dump will be written, and Task Manager will show the file path. Dump files are usually stored with their name with the path `%Temp%\ProcessName.dmp`. You can also use the Sysinternals ProcDump tool to perform this task. Once you have the dump file, load it in WinDbg using the same method as you used to load crash dumps. The following WinDbg commands are useful for analyzing performance problems:

- `!runaway`   Which threads are utilizing the CPU

- `!analyze -hang`   Allows you to analyze deadlocks or waits in the dump file

- `!locks`   Allows you to locate critical section locks held by threads

- `!thread`   Display thread wait reasons

- `!address`   Summarizes address space usage

- `!memusage`   Show memory usage

Using Driver Verifier to diagnose suspect drivers

Driver Verifier is a built-in Windows tool that stresses drivers to catch problematic behavior. If you suspect a driver is causing problems, but you aren't able to find conclusive evidence by analyzing normal crash dumps, you can enable Driver Verifier to monitor one or more drivers. Driver Verifier will induce a STOP error (BSOD) immediately when it detects problematic driver behavior, including memory leaks and IRQL violations. This should give a more direct crash dump that indicates the offending driver. To enable Driver Verifier, perform the following steps:

1. Open an elevated command prompt and run the command `verifier.exe`. This launches the Driver Verifier GUI.

2. In Driver Verifier, choose Create Custom Settings or Create Standard Settings.

3. Select the drivers you want to verify. You can choose Select Driver Names From A List and then pick the specific driver. You can also choose Unsigned Drivers or All Drivers Except Microsoft. The drawback of tracking too many drivers is that it can make the system very slow or unstable.

4. Once you've done this, restart the server.

If the suspect driver does something problematic, such as writing to a memory address it shouldn't, Driver Verifier will bugcheck the system at the offending call, with a special error code. The crash dump from that will clearly implicate the driver and the type of violation. You then use WinDbg on that crash dump, and it will likely report that driverxyz.sys caused a violation. You then remediate the driver by obtaining an update.

You can disable Driver Verifier by running the command `verifier /reset` from an elevated command prompt.

Windows Memory Diagnostic

Windows Memory Diagnostic allows you to perform extensive tests on the integrity of your computer's RAM. Performing a memory test involves restarting the computer in a special mode in which the memory diagnostic is performed. While the computer is performing the memory diagnostic, you'll be unable to use it. You can trigger Windows Memory Diagnostic by searching for it from the Start menu or by running the `mdsched.exe` command. Windows Memory Diagnostic can detect the following problems with a computer's memory:

- Timing issues

- Adjacent bit interference

- Pattern sensitivity

- Stuck bits

- Memory addressing errors

You can choose to perform a basic, standard, or extended test. You can also choose to toggle the cache on or off during the test process. The Standard test is selected by default. This option is sufficient for most memory troubleshooting scenarios. The Extended test performs additional tests but takes significantly longer to complete. You should choose the Extended option if you suspect memory errors and they haven't been found by the Standard set of tests.

To view the results of the memory diagnostic test, open Event Viewer after the computer completes the tests and restarts; in the System log, look for events that have MemoryDiagnostics-Results as the event source.

CHAPTER 25

Hosting large language models on Windows Server

Large language models (LLMs) function as the back end for modern AI chatbots. While you can subscribe to LLMs from various vendors like OpenAI, Anthropic, Google, and x.AI for a monthly fee or run LLMs in an environment like Azure Foundry with a monthly subscription, there's a large and healthy ecosystem of freely available open-source LLM models that can be run locally on an appropriately spec'ed machine. The free LLM models aren't as competent as the cutting edge models, but it isn't unusual for the free open models to achieve the same benchmark scores on problem-solving and reasoning within 12 to 18 months.

Computer hardware always gets more powerful over time, and today's expensive server system might be functionally as powerful as a good desktop PC in five years' time. As computer hardware becomes more powerful and free LLMs more competent, it's not unreasonable to expect that many organizations will run an increasing percentage of their AI workloads on local hardware rather than in the cloud. Running AI locally in your datacenter or server room neatly bypasses a lot of concerns that many organizations have with chatting about sensitive business information with AI chatbots hosted in the cloud. Simply provision a server with sufficient RAM, CPU, and GPU resources and point people in your organization to their own local AI chatbot rather than dealing with the complexity of per-seat AI licensing.

In this chapter, I briefly discuss two local LLM server products that you can run on Windows Server. The first is Ollama, an open-source engine that allows you to download and run a variety of free LLMs. The second is Microsoft's own Azure Foundry Local, a product that's in preview at the time of writing but aims to be a local AI solution that plugs directly into your Microsoft-based identity and software ecosystem.

Ollama on Windows Server

Ollama is an open-source project that allows you to run large language models locally. It has a command-line interface if you want to interact with it directly. Because it's open source, which is fine if you're so inclined, but most people want to interact with AI chatbots using a web interface. There's a wide catalog of LLMs available for Ollama, including Microsoft's phi and Meta's Llama. Some of these have performance that's comparable to recent generations of the flagship models. They aren't cutting edge, but they also come without a subscription fee.

CHAPTER 26

Inside OUT

The future is not evenly distributed

This chapter is a lot more speculative than the rest of those in the book. My reason for including it is that I've encountered a lot of IT professionals who haven't considered running AI locally because their perception was that running AI required inordinate amounts of compute. Whereas training AI requires extraordinary resources, running a trained LLM simply requires RAM, CPU, and GPU resources. There are small models like Microsoft's Phi series and versions of Meta's Llama that run well on consumer hardware and can perform most of the tasks that people are paying one of the big AI services for. If you take nothing else away from this chapter, realize you can run AI workloads locally for your organization without having to send even a packet of confidential business information over the perimeter network firewall.

Ollama has cross-platform support for Linux, macOS, and Windows. Ollama comes with its own GUI, but you can also enable it to be accessed over the network. The Open WebUI project, separate from Ollama, allows you to interact with an Ollama instance through a web browser in the same way that you might interact with the more well-known LLMs.

To install Ollama, run the following command from an elevated command prompt:

```
winget install Ollama.Ollama
```

Once Ollama is installed, you can open the GUI app from the Start menu. Here you can access settings as shown in Figure 26-1. Use the settings to make the Ollama endpoint available to other hosts on the network.

More Info

Ollama

You can learn more about Ollama at *https://ollama.com/*.

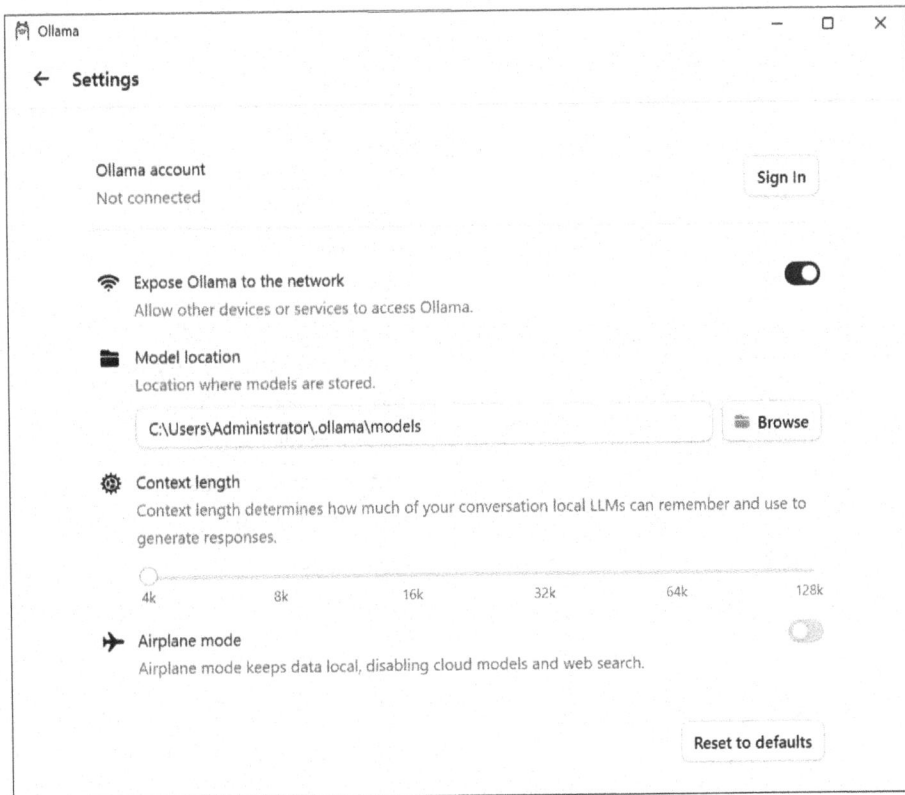

Figure 26-1 Exposing Ollama to the network

Using Ollama from the command line

You use Ollama form the command line with the ollama command. For example, to download the Microsoft Phi-3 model from the Ollama model registry, run the command:

```
ollama pull phi3
```

You can view the models that are available in the Ollama registry by navigating to *https://ollama.com/library*. At the time of writing, there is no method of listing models available in the library from the Ollama command line. Ollama includes the commands shown in Table 26-1.

Table 26-1   Ollama command-line options

Command	Function
ollama serve	Start Ollama
ollama create	Create a model
ollama show	Show information about a model
ollama run	Run a model
ollama stop	Stop a running model
ollama pull	Pull a model from a registry
ollama push	Push a model to a registry
ollama signin	Sign in to ollama.com
ollama signout	Sign out of ollama.com
ollama list	List downloaded models
ollama ps	List running models
ollama cp	Copy a model
ollama rm	Remove a downloaded model
ollama help	Provides details on a specific command

To run the model interactively from the command line, use the `ollama run` command. For example, to get Ollama to explain how to use Ollama remotely from another host on the network using the Phi model, run this command:

```
ollama run phi3 "Explain how to use ollama remotely from another host on the network"
```

Integrating Ollama into VS Code

You can configure Ollama to function in a manner similar to GitHub Copilot, except that instead of using an LLM running in the cloud, you use an LLM running on a Windows Server host in your datacenter. To use VS Code with a local Ollama instance, you need to run Ollama in server mode, and you need to install a VS Code extension that allows you to connect VS Code to Ollama. Two popular VS Code extensions at the time that enable this functionality are Ollama Copilot and Local LLM Copilot. You can install these through the extensions functionality of VS Code. In the extension's settings, you need to configure Ollama as the provider and specify the endpoint. If you're running Ollama locally, this will be *http://localhost:11434*, unless you've manually changed it using the `OLLAMA_HOST` environment variable.

Using Open WebUI with Ollama

Open WebUI is a project separate from Ollama that provides a web front end that is similar to those used by commercial LLM chatbots. Open WebUI So the aim is to create a web server that you can deploy on your local area network that people in your organization can interact with like they would any other intranet site.

To install Open WebUI on Windows Server, first navigate to *https://github.com/BrainDriveAI/ OpenWebUI_CondaInstaller/releases* and download the file `OpenWebUIInstaller.exe` to C:\Temp.

Once you've downloaded this installer, you need to set up the environment in which to run it because of the complex Python dependencies to run Open WebUI on Windows Server.

```
winget install -e --id Anaconda.Miniconda3 --scope machine

$env:Path = 'C:\ProgramData\miniconda3;' + $env:Path
$env:Path = 'C:\ProgramData\miniconda3\Scripts;' + $env:Path
$env:Path = 'C:\ProgramData\miniconda3\Library\bin;' + $env:Path

conda.exe tos accept --override-channels --channel https://repo.anaconda.com/pkgs/main
conda.exe tos accept --override-channels --channel https://repo.anaconda.com/pkgs/r
conda.exe tos accept --override-channels --channel https://repo.anaconda.com/pkgs/msys2

C:\Temp\OpenWebUIInstaller.exe
```

When you run this executable from the prepared command line, you'll be presented with the AY System Installer. Choose Install to install Open WebUI. After running into challenges with Python environment dependencies, I found this the most reliable way to get Open WebUI working on Windows Server without resorting to using WSL or a Linux Container. Once Open WebUI is installed, click Start Open WebUI. Once Open WebUI has started, as shown on the dialog in Figure 26-2, you can access the Open WebUI web service

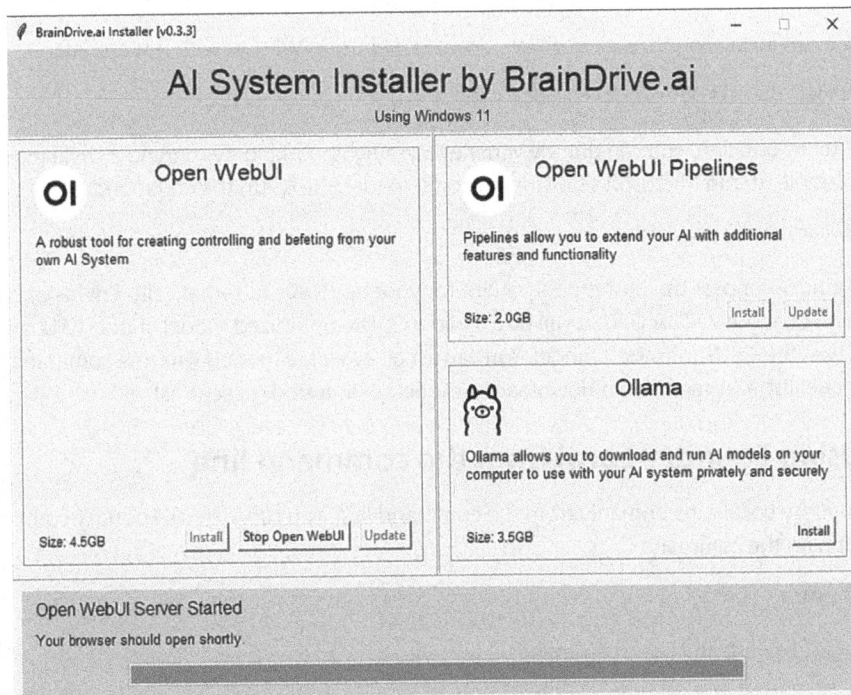

Figure 26-2   Open WebUI installer

You can make Open WebUI available to other hosts on the network by changing the URL to *http://servername:8080* and creating a firewall rule to allow TCP and UDP traffic on port 8080. You can use Task Scheduler to automatically start Ollama and Open WebUI so that it will be available across server reboots.

Azure Foundry Local on Windows Server

Azure AI Foundry Local is Microsoft's on-device AI inference solution. At the time of writing, Foundry Local is in public preview. Similar to Ollama, it allows you to run LLMs entirely on your own hardware. Foundry Local on Windows Server has the following requirements:

- **Operating system**   Windows Server 2025 (also runs on Windows 11).

- **Hardware**   Minimum 8 GB RAM and 3 GB free disk; recommended 16 GB RAM and 15 GB disk.

- **Network**   Internet connectivity for initial model downloads. Foundry can run fully offline once the model is downloaded.

- **Optional accelerators**   NVIDIA GPU (RTX 2000 series or newer), AMD GPU (6000+), Intel integrated GPU, or Qualcomm Snapdragon X Elite NPU. Foundry automatically uses available accelerators for best performance (for example, DirectML on GPUs).

- **Permissions**   Administrator privileges on the server for installation.

You can install Foundry Local on Windows Server using WinGet with this command:

```
winget install Microsoft.FoundryLocal
```

After installation, you can quickly verify everything is working by running a small model. For example, to run Microsoft's tiny instructional model Phi-4, run the command

```
foundry model run phi-4
```

Foundry chooses the best model variant for your hardware automatically. For instance, if your server has an NVIDIA GPU, it will download a CUDA-optimized model. If only CPU is available, it uses the CPU-optimized model. You can list all available models with the command foundry model list. You can list and downloaded models with foundry cache list.

Using Foundry Local from the command line

Foundry Local runs primarily from the command line. You can view all Foundry commands by running the command

```
Foundary --help
```

Table 26-2 lists the basic commands.

Table 26-2   Foundry local commands

Command	Functionality
`foundry model --help`	View the command options of a Foundry model.
`foundry model list`	List available models. This lists all available models online. This is an advantage over Ollama where you have to navigate to a web page to view available models.
`foundry model run <model>`	Run a model and make it available in interactive chat mode. If the model hasn't already been downloaded, this will also download the model.
`foundry model info <model>`	Displays model information.
`foundry model download <model>`	Downloads a model.
`foundry model load <model>`	Loads a model into the service.
`foundry model unload <model>`	Unloads a model from the service.
`foundry service start`	Starts the Foundry Local service.
`foundry service stop`	Stops the Foundry Local service.
`foundry service ps`	Lists all models.
`foundry cache list`	Lists all models in the local cache.
`foundry cache remove <model>`	Deletes a model from the local cache.
`foundry cache location`	Displays the cache directory.

Foundry Local provides an interactive mode when you run a model. Launching the model starts a command-line chat interface. You can type **/?** to list available help options or enter your query at the prompt, as shown in Figure 26-3.

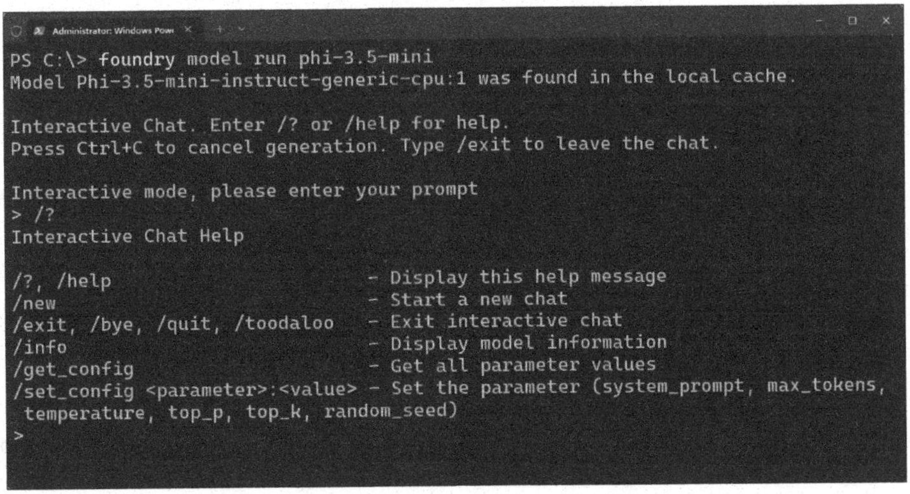

```
PS C:\> foundry model run phi-3.5-mini
Model Phi-3.5-mini-instruct-generic-cpu:1 was found in the local cache.

Interactive Chat. Enter /? or /help for help.
Press Ctrl+C to cancel generation. Type /exit to leave the chat.

Interactive mode, please enter your prompt
> /?
Interactive Chat Help

/?, /help                          - Display this help message
/new                               - Start a new chat
/exit, /bye, /quit, /toodaloo      - Exit interactive chat
/info                              - Display model information
/get_config                        - Get all parameter values
/set_config <parameter>:<value>    - Set the parameter (system_prompt, max_tokens,
  temperature, top_p, top_k, random_seed)
>
```

Figure 26-3   Running Foundry Local from the command line

Configuring Foundry Local as a service

If you want to configure Windows Server with Foundry Local as a centralized AI server, you need to ensure that Foundry Local runs persistently in the background and is accessible via a network API. Foundry Local includes a built-in OpenAI-compatible REST service that enables this. By default, running any model automatically starts the local inference service. You can also explicitly start the back-end service via the CLI. For example, the commands `foundry service start` and `foundry model load <model-name>` launch the service without interactive prompts. When active, the service opens a REST endpoint on a dynamically assigned port on localhost. You can check the status and find the port by running this command:

```
foundry service status
```

This will show the service's process ID and the listening endpoint URL, including the port. Important to note is that the port changes each time the Foundry Local service is instantiated. One way to deal with this is to write a script that pins a stable port and assigns it to the dynamic port in a script.

The Foundry Local REST service implements the same API schema as OpenAI's GPT endpoints. This means client applications can treat your Foundry server like an OpenAI endpoint, pointing their API base URL to your server and using an API key if required. By default, no authentication is required for local use because the service does not enforce an API key unless you configure one.

> ## More Info
> ### Azure Foundry Local
> You can learn more about Azure Foundry Local at *https://learn.microsoft.com/azure/ai-foundry/foundry-local/what-is-foundry-local*.

Use Open WebUI with Foundry Local

You can use Open WebUI to interact with a Foundry Local instance. To do this, install the Open WebUI package using the instructions outlined earlier in this chapter on a Windows Server computer that has Foundry Local Installed. Once Open WebUI is installed, you need to perform two steps. The first is to enable direct connections by doing the following:

1. In the Admin panel in the Profile menu, shown in Figure 26-4, choose Settings and then select Connections.

2. On the Connections page, shown in Figure 26-5, toggle the Direct Connections option to on.

3. This allows connections to customize OpenAI-compatible API endpoints such as the one provided by Azure Foundry Local. Save this configuration.

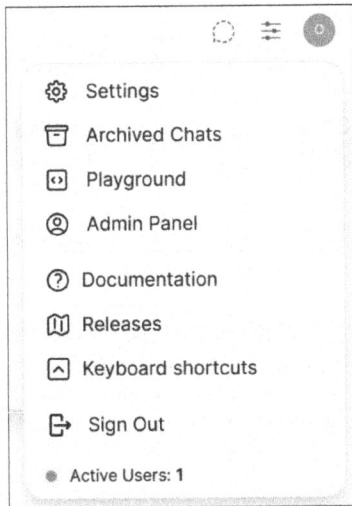

Figure 26-4   Open WebUI Admin menu

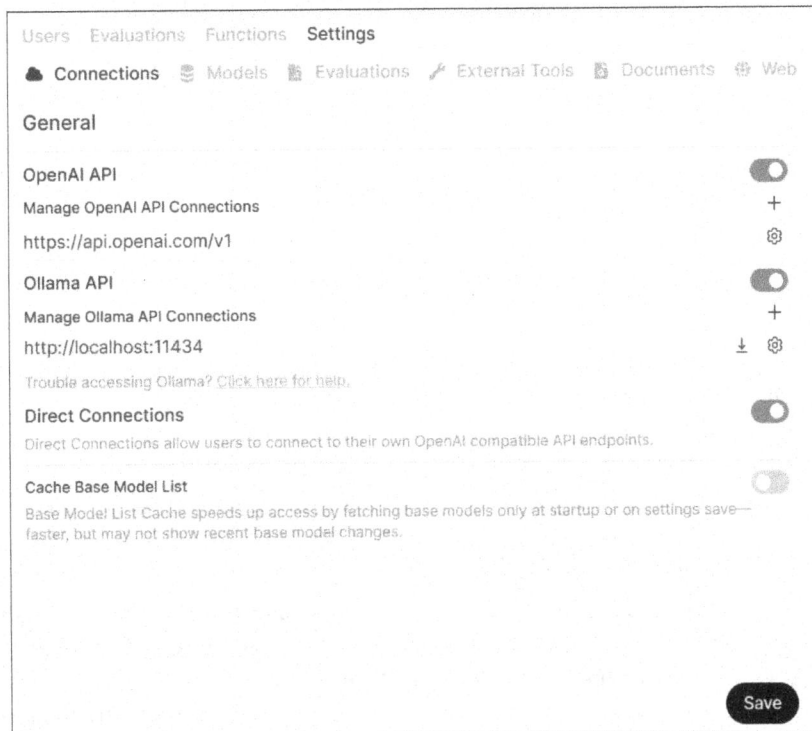

Figure 26-5   Toggle direct connections

4. In the Profile menu, select Settings.

5. Select Settings in the profile menu.

6.   Select Connections in the navigation menu.

7.   Select + by Manage Direct Connections.

8.   For the URL, enter **http://localhost:PORT/v1** where PORT is the Foundry Local endpoint port (use the CLI command `foundry service status` to find it).

9.   For the Auth, select None.

10. Select Save.

This allows remote connections to be made to the Open WebUI web app running on Windows Server and interaction to occur with loaded LLMs as shown in Figure 26-6.

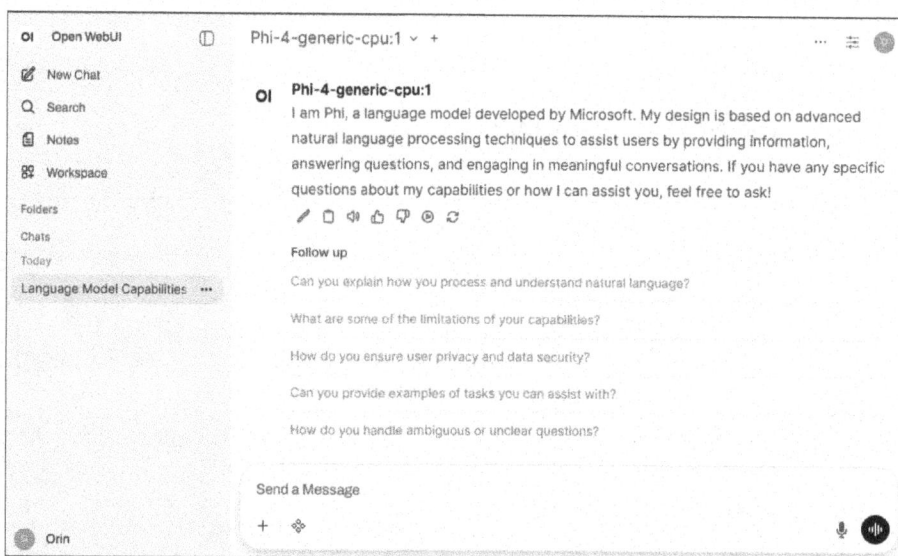

Figure 26-6   Open WebUI connected to a Foundry Local instance

Inside OUT

Ollama versus Foundry Local

Ollama and Foundry Local essentially do the same thing, and both can be installed and run on Windows Server. If I was to speculate, I would suggest that Foundry Local is more likely to end up with integrations into the Microsoft identity ecosystem, such as being able to use Active Directory user accounts, than Ollama is. The advantage of both services is that they allow you to chat with LLMs that are instantiated on your side of the perimeter network, and you don't have the compliance concerns that might exist in using an AI model hosted in an external cloud provider.

Index

Hear about it first.

Since 1984, Microsoft Press has helped IT professionals, developers, and home office users advance their technical skills and knowledge with books and learning resources.

Sign up today to deliver exclusive offers directly to your inbox.

- New products and announcements
- Free sample chapters
- Special promotions and discounts
- ... and more!

MicrosoftPressStore.com/newsletters

Ⓟ Pearson

Plug into learning at

MicrosoftPressStore.com

The Microsoft Press Store by Pearson offers:

- Free U.S. shipping

- Buy an eBook, get multiple formats – PDF and EPUB – to use on your computer, tablet, and mobile devices

- Print & eBook Best Value Packs

- eBook Deal of the Week – Save up to 60% on featured title

- Newsletter – Be the first to hear about new releases, announcements, special offers, and more

- Register your book – Find companion files, errata, and product updates, plus receive a special coupon* to save on your next purchase

Discounts are applied to the list price of a product. Some products are not eligible to receive additional discounts, so your discount code may not be applied to all items in your cart. Discount codes cannot be applied to products that are already discounted, such as eBook Deal of the Week, eBooks that are part of a book + eBook pack, and products with special discounts applied as part of a promotional offering. Only one coupon can be used per order.

Ⓟ Pearson